MW00354797

CALIFORNIA
REAL ESTATE LAW

William H. Pivar and Robert J. Bruss

This publication is designed to provide accurate and authoritative information in regard to the subject matter covered. It is sold with the understanding that the publisher is not engaged in rendering legal, accounting, or other professional advice. If legal advice or other expert assistance is required, the services of a competent professional should be sought.

President: Dr. Andrew Temte
Chief Learning Officer: Dr. Tim Smaby
Vice President, Real Estate Education: Asha Alsobrooks
Development Editor: Julia Marti

CALIFORNIA REAL ESTATE LAW EIGHTH EDITION
©2012 Kaplan, Inc.
Published by DF Institute, Inc., d/b/a Dearborn Real Estate Education
332 Front St. S., Suite 501
La Crosse, WI 54601

Printed in the United States of America
Second revision, August 2013
ISBN: 978-1-4277-3823-3 / 1-4277-3823-8
PPN: 1523-0208

CONTENTS

Introduction   viii

About the Authors   xvi

Acknowledgments   xvii

CHAPTER 1   Sources of Law and the Judicial System   1

Key Terms   1
Definition of Law   1
Influences on Our Legal System   2
Constitutional And Statutory Law   3
Court Structure   12
Lawsuit Procedure   15
Judicial Remedies   16
Equitable Remedies   17
Alternative Dispute Resolution (ADR)   18
Summary   19
Discussion Topics   19
Discussion Cases   21
Chapter Quiz   24

CHAPTER 2   Law of Agency   29

Key Terms   29
Agents and Agency Defined   29
Types of Agents   30
How Agencies Are Created   31
Proof of Agency   38
Authority of Agents   38
Fiduciary Duties of an Agent   40
Liability of Agents   46
Liability of Principals   46
Breach of Agency   48
Termination of Agency   48
Summary   50
Discussion Cases   51
Chapter Quiz   54

CHAPTER 3   Duties and Responsibilities of Licensees   59

Key Terms   59
Law and Ethics   59
Salesperson Status   60
Agent's Duties to the Principal   62
Agent's Duties to Buyers   67
Duties to Other Brokers   81

Fees to Nonlicensees   83
Duty of Buyers   84
Summary   85
Discussion Cases   86
Chapter Quiz   90

CHAPTER 4   Regulation Of Licensees   95

Key Terms   95
The Department of Real Estate   95
Activities Requiring a License   96
When Licensing Is Not Required   98
License Requirements   99
License Renewals   101
Late Renewals   102
Grounds for Disciplinary Action   102
Mortgage Brokers   105
Real Property Syndicates   110
Mineral, Oil, and Gas Brokers   110
Table Funding   111
Federal Secure and Fair Enforcement For Mortgage Licensing Act of 2008 (Safe Act)   111
Escrow Agent   111
Mobile Home Sales   112
Advance Fee Rental Agents   114
Business Opportunity Brokers   115
Appraisers   118
Fair Housing   118
Summary   133
Discussion Cases   134
Chapter Quiz   139

CHAPTER 5   Law of Contracts   145

Key Terms   145
Types of Contracts   145
Essentials of a Valid Contract   147
Void and Voidable Contracts   157
Options to Contract   158
Interpretation of Contracts   160
Discharge of Contracts   161
Contractual Remedies   164
Assignment of Contract   169
Statute of Frauds   169
Statute of Limitations   172
Laches   173
Seals   173
Judgments   173
Summary   174
Discussion Cases   176
Chapter Quiz   179

CHAPTER 6   Real Estate Contracts   183

Key Terms   183

Listings   183
Options   196
Broker's Forms   199
Real Estate Purchase Contract   200
Leases   216
Broker-Salesperson Agreement   216
Retention of Records   216
Disclosures   216
Summary   218
Discussion Cases   226
Chapter Quiz   230

CHAPTER 7   Property, Estates, and Recordings   235

Key Terms   235
Origin of California Land Ownership   235
Property   236
Degree of Ownership   241
Recording of Real Property Interests   246
Summary   251
Discussion Cases   252
Chapter Quiz   254

CHAPTER 8   Ownership of Real Property   259

Key Terms   259
Ownership in Severalty   260
Tenancy in Common   260
Joint Tenancy   261
Community Property   265
Tenancy in Partnership   270
Real Estate Investment Trusts   275
Corporations   276
Unincorporated Associations   277
Multiple Housing Developments   278
Owner Liability   281
Summary   286
Discussion Cases   288
Chapter Quiz   292

CHAPTER 9   Acquisitions and Conveyances   297

Key Terms   297
Voluntary Transfers of Real Property   297
Involuntary Transfers of Real Property   306
Transfers of Real Property upon Death   313
Summary   318
Discussion Cases   320
Chapter Quiz   322

CHAPTER 10   Real Property Security Devices   327

Key Terms   327
Promissory Notes   328
Mortgages and Trust Deeds   335
Loan Types, Conditions, and Regulations   350
Consumer Protection Acts   355

Summary   360
Discussion Cases   362
Chapter Quiz   365

CHAPTER 11   Involuntary Liens and Homesteads   369

Key Terms   369
Involuntary Liens   369
Declaration of Homestead   382
Summary   386
Discussion Cases   387
Chapter Quiz   389

CHAPTER 12   Adjacent Property Rights   393

Key Terms   393
Boundary Disputes   393
Encroachment   395
Nuisance   397
Water Rights   399
Support   400
Easements   401
License   409
Summary   409
Discussion Cases   411
Chapter Quiz   414

CHAPTER 13   Land Use Controls   419

Key Terms   419
Zoning   419
Covenants, Conditions, And Restrictions   427
Regulation of Subdivisions   431
Environmental Law   436
Builder and Developer Liability   441
Summary   442
Discussion Cases   444
Chapter Quiz   449

CHAPTER 14   Escrow and Title Insurance   453

Key Terms   453
Escrows   453
Title Insurance   463
Summary   469
Discussion Cases   471
Chapter Quiz   474

CHAPTER 15   Landlord-Tenant Law   479

Key Terms   479
Types of Tenancies   479
The Lease   481
Assignments and Subleases   485
Termination of Leases   487
Rights and Responsibilities of Landlords   488
Rights and Responsibilities of Tenants   496
The Eviction Process   498

Mobile Home Tenancies   502
Condominium Conversions   504
Rent Control   505
Summary   507
Discussion Cases   509
Chapter Quiz   514

Discussion Case Analyses   519

Glossary The Language of Real Estate Law   569

Index of Cases (Cross-Indexed Plaintiff-Defendant)   586

Subject Index of Cases   600

Index   610

INTRODUCTION

■ ABOUT THE TEXT

California Real Estate Law is an introduction to the vast body of law that governs real estate transactions in California. It will not, however, qualify you to give legal advice, which would be the unauthorized practice of law. Rather, it will help you to recognize situations in which legal counsel should be sought and to help you understand rights and obligations under the law. Only by understanding these rights and obligations can you professionally serve and protect the interests of your clients, as well as the public.

Perhaps the most useful of the pedagogical features in this text are the many *Case Studies* and *Discussion Cases* presented throughout. Case Studies are the author's synopses of actual cases, including the facts, the courts' decisions, and some of the reasons for their decisions. These learning aids directly relate to the topics they appear with, illustrating key principles of the discussion.

End-of-chapter Discussion Cases also summarize actual court cases and are relevant to the preceding chapter. However, instead of presenting their final decisions, they pose a question to the reader, prompting individual consideration or classroom discussion.

Each of the 15 chapters of this text opens with a list of *key terms*, alerting readers to important vocabulary words that will be discussed in that chapter.

These terms appear in boldface the first time they are introduced in the chapter discussions, and they are then briefly defined in a *Glossary* that appears at the end of the book.

Every chapter also ends with a *Chapter Quiz*, consisting of multiple-choice questions similar in form, content, and difficulty level to questions found on the California Real Estate Brokers' Examination.

Legal citations are included for both the Case Studies and the Discussion Questions. You might wish to look up cases at one of your county's law libraries. Law libraries that are open to the public generally are located in the buildings housing superior courts. Many of the cases cited can also be found on the Internet.

■ THE EIGHTH EDITION

This is the Eighth Edition of *California Real Estate Law*, first published in 1987. In each new edition, we have updated the text with new relevant cases and updates to the discussions spurred by developments in the real estate field and by changes in our laws. We also carefully incorporated the input of many instructors and students concerning ways in which we could better meet their needs.

WEB LINK @

From time to time, we will add *brand-new* Case Studies related to this Eighth Edition of *California Real Estate Law* at *www.dearborn.com*. These will be divided by text chapter topic for easier reference. Be sure to check the site periodically not only as you complete your course but throughout your professional career. These ever-changing case studies will help you to stay sharp and to keep up-to-date on recent court decisions affecting California's real estate law.

On the following pages, we also offer guidance on using various search engines to access the massive database that is the Internet. We also list several useful Web sites you can use to further broaden your legal research capabilities.

■ LEGAL CITATIONS

A legal citation has three parts: volume, particular set of books, and page. The letter C. stands for *California Reports*, which are cases from the California Supreme Court. The letters C.A. refer to *California Appellate Reports* from the California appellate courts. Most of the citations listed are from these two sets of law books.

Because of the sheer number of volumes, books have gone into new series, so *2d* means *second series*. A citation 19 C.A.3d 468 would mean *Volume 19* of the *3rd Series* of *California Appellate Reports*, and the case cited would be on page 468.

Besides separate state reporters of appellate and supreme court cases, there are regional reporter series covering state supreme court and appellate court cases from a number of states. Examples are the *Atlantic Reporter*, shown by the letter A, and the *Pacific Reporter*, shown by P. California cases are also in the *Pacific Reporter*.

Federal district court cases are reported in *The Federal Supplement* series and are shown as *F. Supp.* Federal appellate court cases are reported in the *Federal Reporter*, shown as *F.*, or *Second Series*, shown as *F.2d.*

U.S. Supreme Court cases are found in *United States Reports*, indicated by *U.S.*, or *Lawyers Edition Second Series*, shown as *L.Ed.2d*, or *Supreme Court Reporter*, shown as *S. Ct.*

WEB LINK @

The majority of statutes relating to activities in real estate are contained in one inexpensive volume entitled *Real Estate Law*, which is published by the California Department of Real Estate and available through many college bookstores or directly from the Department of Real Estate. You can also access this book without charge on the following website: *www.dre.ca.gov*.

Laws are not static. Besides annual changes in the statutes that create new law, court decisions can change duties and responsibilities under existing statutes. The changing nature of laws requires a real estate agent to keep current with these changes through professional papers and magazines, seminars, and continuing education. It is hoped that this book will be just one step in your continuing program of professional training.

■ INTERNET RESOURCES

The Internet can be an important tool for the real estate professional. It has applications toward all aspects of real estate, including the law, and its usefulness can be expected to increase significantly in the future.

Search engines are Internet sites that enable a computer user to find information by typing a word or combination of words. They search what is currently 23 billion pages. The growth of the database has resulted in searches that cover just a fraction of the available data.

Assume you wanted information about a tenant's right to claim constructive eviction in order to be released from lease obligations. Using a search engine such as *hotbot.com*, if you searched *California real estate law* you would find thousands of references, too many to make a meaningful search. If you used *California real estate law/landlord/tenant*, you would reduce the number of sites to several hundred. Defining your interest by using *California real estate law/constructive eviction* would reduce your search to a manageable number of matches. Use of additional search engines would give you a number of additional sites. Some additional search engines are Northernlight, Excite, Snap, Altavista, Infoseek, Microsoft, Google, Yahoo, and Dialer.

The following Internet sites will help you meet your legal research needs:

www.boe.ca.gov
Board of Equalization site for sales tax registrations.

www.callaw.com
A daily briefing on California law and California courts.

www.calrealestatelaw.com
This site, which has an annual fee of $24.95, provides online legal update service including case summaries, laws, current issues, etc.

www.car.org
California Association of REALTORS® website, real estate legal news, proposed laws, CAR opinions, a legal strategic defense link and lots more.

www.ceres.ca.gov
This information site developed by the California Resource Agency includes a database containing California environmental law and links to federal law.

www.courtinfo.ca.gov
Information about the California court system.

www.courtinfo.ca.gov/opinions
California Supreme Court and appellate court listings.

www.dfeh.ca.gov
California Department of Fair Employment and Housing website.

www.dir.ca.gov
California Department of Industrial Relations.

www.donotcall.gov
National Do Not Call Register.

www.dre.ca.gov
California real estate salesperson and broker license status, how to get a real estate license, and lots of other valuable material.

www.epa.gov
The Environmental Protection Agency site provides information on programs and laws.

www.fairhousing.com
The site of the National Fair Housing Advocate offers information on housing discrimination issues.

www.fanniemae.com
This site of the Federal National Mortgage Association includes information on FNMA-owned properties, FNMA services, and FNMA mortgage-backed securities.

www.fastsearch.com/law
The Web's premier law and legal research page. Court decisions, state laws, newspapers, law school libraries—this site is great!

www.fcc.gov/cgb/donotcall
FCC Do Not Call registry.

www.fedstats.gov
Access is provided to statistics prepared by various federal agencies.

www.fema.gov
This site provides information on FEMA programs including National Flood Insurance.

www.findlaw.com
Lots of links to cases, statutes, lawyers, law schools, subjects, directories, U.S. Supreme Court opinions since 1893, and endless resources. One of the best Web sites. Also, *www.findlaw.com/cacases* is devoted to California cases.

www.firsttuesday.us/downloads.cfm
California real estate forms available online.

www.freddiemac.com
This is the site of the Federal Home Loan Mortgage Corporation. It includes information on mortgage-backed securities and services.

www.ftb.ca.gov/forms/index.htm
California state income tax forms back to 1994.

www.ftc.gov
FTC Trade Commission primary website. The FTC enforces the Sherman Anti-trust Act.

www.ftc.gov/spam
FTC regulations regarding e-mail solicitations.

www.ginniemae.gov
Site of the Government National Mortgage Association, it includes information on mortgage-backed securities and GNMA services.

www.gksoft.com/govt/en/
Through this database you can link to any U.S. government agency.

www.housingandurbandevelopment.info
Information on HUD programs and initiatives.

www.hud.gov
This site offers information on HUD programs.

www.hud.gov/fairhousing
HUD office of fair housing and equal opportunity.

www.hud.gov/offices/hsg/mfh/hc/mfhc.cfm
HUD Multifamily housing clearinghouse

www.inman.com
Most complete source of up-to-the-minute real estate news. This site is linked to *www.bobbruss.com*, which includes a featured weekly real estate article.

www.ired.com
Directory of 25,000 real estate websites. *International Real Estate Digest.* Click on *Law and Legal.* This real estate directory offers links to bulletin boards on a wide range of subjects.

www.irs.ustreas.gov/prod/forms_pubs/inidex.html
Federal income tax forms back to 1992.

www.justanswer.com
Allows you to ask real estate law questions to lawyers for online answers.

www.law.cornell.edu/topics
Lots of information on federal and state mortgage law and court decisions.

www.lawforum.net
This site can help you locate law firms in your area with real estate specialties.

www.lawnewsnetwork.com
Up-to-date legal news from the *National Law Journal.*

www.legalzoom.com
Do-it-yourself legal forms.

www.leginfo.ca.gov
This State of California website includes an index of all of California's statutory law. Search by key word.

www.leginfo.ca.gov/const.html
The California Constitution Web site.

www.martindale.com
Directory of lawyers, a who's who in American law. Click on *lawyers.com* to locate a nearby real estate attorney.

www.meganslaw.ca.gov
Provides access to names, addresses, and zip codes of registered sex offenders.

www.nolo.com
Great self-help law center, even lawyer jokes. Click on the legal encyclopedia for great real estate law information.

www.nsc.org
The National Safety Council site offers information on environmental hazards (lead poisoning).

www.orea.ca.gov
Office of Real Estate Appraisers. Licensing, certification, and regulation of appraisers.

www.realtimes.com
Real estate consumer and industry news presented in a lively format. Late developments on legal aspects from a consumer view.

www.realtor.com
Lots of information for real estate agents, homebuyers, and sellers, legal questions and answers, and much more. One of the most complete real estate websites.

www.realtor.org
National Association of REALTORS® website.

www.relibrary.com
Click the legal and professional page. Lots of forms, articles, case histories, and legal journals in the legal library.

www.ss.ca.gov
Secretary of State site for information on the Uniform Commercial Code, tax liens, limited partnerships, limited liability company, and corporate records.

www.trueforms.com
California-Professional Publishing's Real Estate forms in plain language.

www.va.gov
The informational site on VA programs.

www.westlaw.com
More than 10,000 databases of statutes, cases, and public records; some material is free, other is fee-based.

www.weblocator.com/attorney/ca/law/c22.html
A research site offering a menu of topics.

Note: While the Internet is an extremely valuable tool for obtaining information, do not confuse information with legal advice. For the applicability of information to specific situations, consider obtaining the services of an attorney.

Members of the California Association of REALTORS® (CAR) can obtain advice from CAR's legal staff by calling 213-739-8282 (Monday through Friday 9:00 am to 6:00 pm).

CAR members can be provided late-breaking legal information by e-mail through *REALEGAL*™, a broadcast e-mail service.

ABOUT THE AUTHORS

■ WILLIAM H. PIVAR

From 1971 to 1994, William Pivar served as Real Estate Coordinator and Professor of Business Education at College of the Desert, Palm Desert, California, where he is now a professor emeritus. Prior to choosing an academic career, he practiced as a private, corporate, and government attorney specializing in real property.

Pivar is author of more than 30 textbooks and numerous articles. He holds a bachelor's degree and a law degree from the University of Wisconsin. He was the recipient of the California Real Estate Education Association's Norman Woest Award for California's Outstanding College Real Estate Teacher in 1994.

His other publications include *Real Estate Ethics, Real Estate Exam Guide, Classified Secrets, Power Real Estate Listing, Power Real Estate Selling, Power Real Estate Negotiation, Power Real Estate Letters,* and *California Real Estate Practice,* all published by Real Estate Education Company®.

■ ROBERT J. BRUSS

Robert Bruss played a key role in making this book user friendly. He set criteria for case selections based on applicability to the business needs of real estate professionals as well as subject matter that would interest the reader and enhance retention.

Robert Bruss died in 2007 and his keen intellect and encyclopedic knowledge of California real estate law are sorely missed. However, his legacy will continue in the direction he provided to enhance learning and professionalism in real estate education.

For more than 33 years, Robert Bruss wrote the weekly syndicated "Real Estate Mailbag" question-and-answer newspaper column, the "Real Estate Notebook" feature on real estate trends, "Real Estate Law and You" articles about new court decisions affecting real estate, and "Real Estate Book Review" features. Inman Real Estate News Service distributed these features to several hundred newspapers nationwide each week.

Bruss also published two monthly real estate newsletters, *The Robert Bruss California Real Estate Law Newsletter* and *The Robert Bruss National Real Estate Newsletter.*

The California newsletters are now being published by the Robert J. Bruss Revocable Trust (Harold Justman, Esq. is Editor). He was the author of the books *The Smart Investor's Guide to Real Estate* and *The California Foreclosure Book: How to Earn Big Profits in California Foreclosure and Distress Properties*.

Originally from Minneapolis, Bruss graduated from Northwestern University School of Business in Evanston, Illinois. He received his Juris Doctor degree from the University of California's Hastings College of the Law in San Francisco. He was a California real estate attorney and licensed real estate broker, as well as a lifetime member of the National Association of Real Estate Editors. Bruss taught Real Estate Law at the College of San Mateo as well as real estate courses for the University of Southern California's College of Continuing Education.

Robert Bruss was the 1997 recipient of the Norman Woest award for outstanding real estate educator of the year.

ACKNOWLEDGMENTS

The author wishes to acknowledge the many attorneys, educators, and other professionals who have responded to our user survey, as well as the following reviewers who contributed so much thought and effort to this Eighth Edition:

Roger Lawson Smith, City College of San Francisco

We would also like to recognize those who helped with past editions of *California Real Estate Law*.

Michael Botello, El Camino College

Jill A. Carter, West Los Angeles College

David J. Deka, JD, Dearborn/Anthony Schools

Ed Estes, Jr., Palomar College

Michael C. Glazer, Ivy Tech State College

Bruce Gold, Orange Coast College

Ignacio Gonzalez, Mendocino Community College

Abigail Hatch, Allied Business Schools, Inc.

Gerald Haight, Modesto Junior College

Paul Hammann, First American Title Company, Santa Ana

Ben Hernandez, Jr., Allied Schools

Steven Johnson, Old Republic Title Company, Redwood City

Don Kalal, California Broker's Institute

Robert R. Keeling, Sacramento City College

Alan R. Klofkorn, Irvine Valley College

Meldy Langager, Diablo Valley College

James Lawson, The Real Estate School, Woodland

William A. McGrath, JD, Sacramento City College

James F. Miller, Esq., University of Southern California

Jay Mumford, Chabot College

Michael A. Olden, Diablo Valley College

Robert J. Pacheco, Crofton Hills College

Marc B. Robinson, Hartmann & Robinson LLP, Stockton

John Smylie, Palomar Community College

Kartik Subramaniam, ADHI Schools, LLC

Bobra G. Tahan, Dearborn/Anthony Schools

Jesse Votaw, San Jose City College

Jason K. Wolins, Humphreys College

Joe Wood, Evergreen Valley College

Dat Yen, Glendale College, Los Angeles City College

Frank Zotter, Jr., Chief Deputy County Counsel, County of Mendocino

1

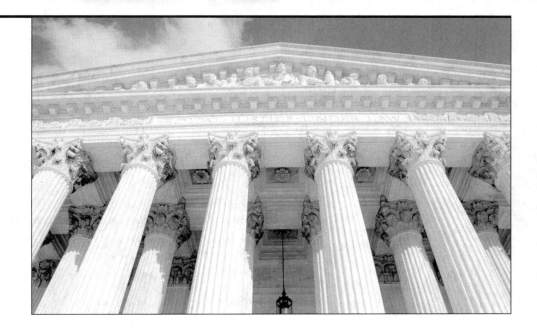

SOURCES OF LAW AND THE JUDICIAL SYSTEM

■ **KEY TERMS**

administrative agency
Administrative
   Procedure Act
arbitration
civil law
common law
compensatory damages
constitutional law
declaratory relief action

Department of Real
   Estate
exemplary damages
foreclosure
injunction
liquidated damages
jurisdiction
mediation
nominal damages

quiet title
reformation
regulatory law
rescission
specific performance
stare decisis
statutory law
venue

■ **DEFINITION OF LAW**

Law is the body of principles governing our conduct that can be enforced through our judicial system. Laws serve various purposes, such as protecting the health, safety, morals, and general welfare of the citizens; protecting the state; protecting property; and achieving equity or justice. Every civilization has realized the necessity for laws because without the guidance of laws, there would be chaos.

The law is not static. It reflects the views of our society, and as our views change, so do our laws. Because law is in a constant state of evolution, it is not always possible to predict the outcome of a dispute. A slight difference in facts can affect the outcome, as can current trends in opinion and even the philosophy of the court where a case is being heard. Courts will often differ regarding interpretations of the law and rights under the law.

■ INFLUENCES ON OUR LEGAL SYSTEM

English Influence

Most of the basic precepts of our real estate law as well as our legal vocabulary have evolved from English common law. Establishment of a centralized court system at the time of the Norman Conquest (AD 1066) made precedent, or previous decisions, the basis for judging disputes. This reliance on previous decisions is known as **stare decisis**. Thereafter, a body of judge-made law developed. While judges already had been able to differentiate among situations, reliance on previous decisions gave the legal system stability because laws were now more likely to be changed by slight degree than by radical departure from the past. The precepts developed by the courts became known as the **common law**.

The rigid system imposed on the courts by previous decisions often, however, resulted in injustice. In addition, the courts of common law had to wait until a wrong had been committed to make a decision. People would petition the king for special relief, which at times would be granted. This led to the establishment of a second court system, known as *courts of equity* (i.e., chancellory court) that could offer remedies based on what was just and equitable rather than solely on the decisions of the past.

Because of the large number of court decisions, attorneys seldom have a problem finding precedent for conflicting views. State courts rely most heavily on the most recent decisions of higher courts within their own state system. They also consider court decisions from other states, especially sister states (states with similar laws), as well as cases decided through the federal court system. Previous decisions of particular courts, and even particular justices, can influence decisions.

Case decisions might differ among California or federal courts. Conflicts of law can exist until they are clarified by a higher court. For example, a U.S. Supreme Court decision would clarify conflicts between two U.S. courts of appeals decisions. Federal district courts place the greatest emphasis on appellate decisions of their own appellate circuit (the court of appeals that would rule on any appeal from that court). Similarly, California superior courts place the greatest emphasis on appellate decisions of their own appellate court.

Often, the decisions of an individual state's courts exhibit a particular trend that characterizes that court system over the years. California courts have been leaders in favoring consumer rights. Throughout this book, the case studies indicate our courts' contribution to expanding consumer protection.

Roman Influence

In the United States, we follow the Roman system of civil law. **Civil law** refers to laws enacted by legislative bodies and codified as statutes. English common law served as a basis for much of our statutory law. Our courts interpret the laws. We have merged the functions of the English common-law courts and the courts of equity into a single system in which judges may follow previous decisions but are not bound to them and have both legal and equitable remedies at their disposal.

Case law really serves to define and, at times, modify our statutes. It aids in defining the law under specific fact situations.

Spanish Influence

The Treaty of Guadalupe Hidalgo (1848) ended the Mexican-American War, resulting in California becoming part of the United States. Under this treaty the United States agreed to recognize the property rights of Mexican citizens. This agreement represented more than just recognizing title to property, however. It also made California a community property state. Mexico had adopted from Spain the concept of community property, in which property acquired during marriage is owned equally by husband and wife. (See Chapter 8 for details on community property rights.)

■ CONSTITUTIONAL AND STATUTORY LAW

All levels of government (federal, state, and local) enact legislation affecting real property. Law set forth in federal or state constitutions, or **constitutional law**, is distinguished from law based on enacted statutes, or **statutory law**.

Figure 1.1 illustrates the sources of California real estate law.

FIGURE 1.1
Sources of California Real Estate Law

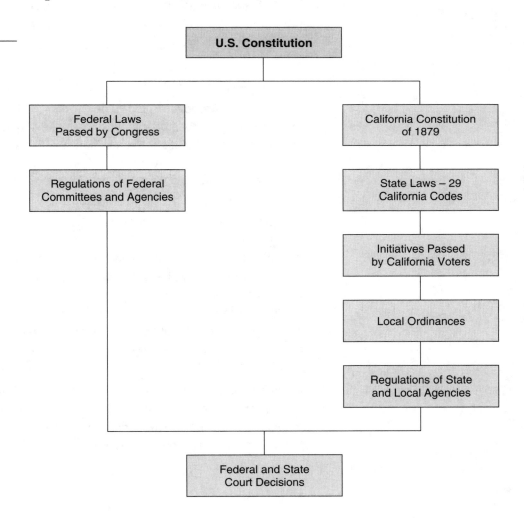

Federal U.S. Constitution.   The original 13 states granted power to our federal government through the U.S. Constitution. The states reserved to themselves all powers not granted to the federal government. The Constitution is the supreme law of the land, and all legislation enacted at any level must conform to it.

Parts of the Constitution of particular importance to real estate law include the following amendments.

First Amendment (Rights of Free Speech)   This amendment protects the right to place For Sale signs on property, as well as to advertise real estate.

Case Study

The case of *Greater Baltimore Board of REALTORS® v. Baltimore County* (1990) 752 F. Supp. 193 involved a county statute barring real estate agents from door-to-door or telephone solicitations for listings. The county claimed the law was necessary to stop blockbusting. The court held that the First Amendment of the U.S. Constitution protects commercial speech from un-warranted governmental regulation. Although the purpose of the law was allegedly to prevent blockbusting, the prohibition was too broad to serve its intended purpose and was therefore an unconstitutional prohibition of commercial free speech.

Case Study

The case of *Pruneyard Shopping Center v. Robins* (1980) 447 U.S. 74 involved high school students who were seeking support for opposition to a United Nations resolution against Zionism. The plaintiffs set up a card table in the corner of a courtyard at a shopping center in Campbell, California. The activity violated policies of the shopping center and the plaintiffs were required to leave.

The California Supreme Court held that the speech and petition provisions of the California State Constitution protect speech and petitioning reasonably exercised, even in privately owned shopping centers. The court noted that shopping centers have supplanted the town square as a meeting place where free speech can be exercised. The California court held that where rights of individual property owners conflict with the interests of society, individual interests must be subordinated, although, reasonable rules could be imposed by the shopping center. *Robins v. Pruneyard Shopping Center* (1979) 23 C.3d 899.

On appeal to the U.S. Supreme Court, the court held that Pruneyard's regulations violated the students' free speech. California's Constitution protected "speech and petitioning, reasonably exercised in shopping centers even when the shopping centers are privately owned."

Case Study

In the case of *Maldonado v. Kemptor* (2006) 422 Fed Supp 2nd 1169, the plaintiff, Maldonado had a double sided billboard on top of a commercial building he owned. The California Outdoor Advertising Act (COAA) regulates billboards and prohibits all billboard advertising along a landscaped freeway unless the billboards advertise goods and services available on the property.

Maldonado was cited in 1993 and 1996 for violating COAA by having advertisements displayed for a shopping center, a Holiday Inn, and Skyway Cellular. After a trial, Maldonado was enjoined from any advertising on his billboard without CalTrans permission. Maldonado then posted "Available for onsite use 650-366-2979" on his billboard. The trial court found Maldonado in contempt. The court even instituted contempt proceedings for a Habitat for Humanity billboard that Maldonado displayed.

Maldonado challenged the constitutionality of COAA because the act stills noncommercial speech, including political advertising rendering COAA in violation of the First Amendment.

The Court agreed with Maldonado "As COAA applies to noncommercial speech, as matter of law, the act impermissibly favors commercial over noncommercial billboards where it permits on-premises commercial billboards." COAA therefore violated the First Amendment and that part of the act is unconstitutional and invalid.

Note: This was a case of poor draftsmanship. The law could have prohibited commercial advertising except for goods and services available on the property. By banning all advertising other than the on-site commercial exception, they clearly were in violation of the First Amendment.

Case Study

In the case of *Bank of Stockton v. Church of Soldiers of the Cross of Christ* (1996) 44 C.A.4th 1623, the bank obtained an injunction against the Church of Soldiers of the Cross of Christ from soliciting donations from bank customers at the bank entrance on bank property.

The Court of Appeal ruled that church members could not solicit on the property because it was a modest retail business and not a public place required to allow free speech. The court held that the bank did not have to show interference with its operation to prohibit free speech on the property. The court held that the First Amendment would apply to public forums, such as large supermarkets and shopping centers.

Case Study

The case of *Van v. Target Corp.* (2007) 155 C.A. 4th 1375 was an action for injunctive relief to prevent stores from barring voter-signature gathering at entrances to stores in shopping centers; the trial court held in favor of the stores. While the First Amendment protects gatherings in common areas of shopping centers, it does not protect gatherings in store entrances that are not public walkways.

The Court of Appeal affirmed that store entrances were designed for customers to come and go and not for gathering political signatures.

Note: This case limits the *Pruneyard* case as to areas that are considered a public forum.

Fourth Amendment (Security from Unwarranted Search and Seizure)   This amendment protects private property from unreasonable searches and seizures. Search warrants will be issued only on the basis of probable cause.

Fifth Amendment (Rights of Accused)   This amendment states that an accused shall not "be deprived of life, liberty, or property, without due process of law." Before property can be taken away from its owner, that person must be given their day in court.

The Fifth Amendment also prohibits the taking of private property for public use without just compensation and in effect gives the government the power to condemn private property for public use upon payment of just compensation (called the *power of eminent domain*). The Fourteenth Amendment makes the Fifth Amendment applicable to the states.

Case Study

In the U.S. Supreme Court decision of *Kelo v. City of New London* (Connecticut) (2005) 125 S. Ct. 2655, Susette Kelo and 15 other property owners in the Fort Trumbull neighborhood sued the city, claiming the area is not blighted or run-down and taking their properties by eminent domain would violate the "public use" requirement of the Fifth Amendment because the land would then be turned over to a private developer for construction of a hotel, offices, and shopping area. The city council approved the redevelopment plan that would create over 1,000 jobs, increase tax and other revenues, and revitalize the economically distressed city of 24,000. The New London Superior Court granted Kelo and her neighbors a permanent restraining order injunction prohibiting taking of the properties. On appeal, the Connecticut Supreme Court reversed, ruling the city's takings were valid because they were for a "public use" and in the "public interest" and because title would be turned over to a developer to be selected and the resulting economic development benefits are a valid public use.

Kelo and her neighbors appealed to the U.S. Supreme Court on the Constitutional issue that the eminent domain condemnation was not for "public use" but would primarily benefit the developer and other private owners. In a close 5-to-4 vote, the U.S. Supreme Court affirmed, upholding the proposed takings of private property, ruling the eminent domain condemnation qualifies as a "public use" under the "takings clause" of the Fifth Amendment because the economic development of the area is for a "public purpose." The Court emphasized promoting economic development is a traditional and long-accepted function of government and there was no evidence the property would be turned over to particular private entities. In her dissent, Justice Sandra Day O'Connor wrote, "The specter of condemnation hangs over all property. Nothing is to prevent the State from replacing any Motel 6 with a Ritz-Carlton, any home with a shopping mall, or any farm with a factory."

Note: California's eminent domain condemnation statute requires a finding of "blight" before a property can be taken for redevelopment.

Tenth Amendment (Powers Reserved for States)   This amendment allows the states all powers not delegated to the federal government or prohibited to the states. The states are empowered to enact legislation under this amendment. (The U.S. Constitution determines when the states do not have authority.)

Thirteenth Amendment (Abolishment of Slavery)   This amendment has been held to be the basis for the Civil Rights Act of 1968.

Fourteenth Amendment (Equal Protection)   This amendment makes the Fifth Amendment applicable to the states. It also provided the basis for our antidiscrimination laws.

Treaties. Federal treaties with other governments and with Native American tribes have effected both the ownership of real property and the rights to use property. For example, treaties that gave Indian tribes special sovereignty over reservation lands have exempted the lands from local land-use control. As previously noted, the Treaty of Guadalupe Hidalgo recognized the property rights of Mexican citizens in the United States. This agreement had a particularly strong impact in California and is the basis of our community property laws.

Federal Statutes

A number of federal statutes directly affect real property transactions. Federal statutes are diverse, ranging from antidiscrimination measures to consumer and debtor protection. Examples of federal legislation include

- Federal Housing Act, 12 U.S. Code §1701 et seq.;
- Real Estate Settlement Procedures Act, 12 U.S. Code §2601 et seq.;
- Truth-in-Lending Act, 15 U.S. Code §1601 et seq.;
- Equal Credit Opportunity Act, 15 U.S. Code §1691 et seq.;
- Fair Credit Reporting Act, 15 U.S. Code §1681 et seq.;
- Federal Bankruptcy Act, 11 U.S. Code;
- Civil Rights Act of 1968, 18 U.S. Code §241 et seq.;
- Civil Rights Act of 1866, C.31, 14 Stat. 27;
- Interstate Land Sales Full Disclosure Act, 15 U.S. Code §1701 et seq.;
- Financial Institutions Reform, Recovery and Enforcement Act of 1989 (FIRREA) 18 U.S. Code §1014;
- Foreign Investment in Real Property Tax Act (FIRPTA), I.R.C. 13455 et seq.; and
- Can Spam Act, 151 U.S. Code 7701 et seq.

Federal Administrative Agencies. An **administrative agency** makes rules and regulations to implement our federal laws. While these rules and regulations are not law, they have the force and effect of law. Rules and regulations of administrative agencies are referred to as *regulatory law*. The Department of Housing and Urban Development (HUD) is responsible for enforcing civil rights laws, the Interstate Land Sales Act, and numerous other federal laws. The Federal Trade Commission (FTC) enforces the Truth-in-Lending Act. The Federal Housing Administration (FHA) is involved with real estate loans and subsidized housing. The Environmental Protection Agency (EPA) makes rules and regulations protecting our environment.

Administrative agencies have the power to prohibit action and to impose fines for violations. Each agency conducts its investigation, prosecution, and decision making in administrative hearings. Unlike the courts, the agency is not bound by legal principles of evidence and can even make decisions prior to a hearing.

The right to an attorney supplied by the government or to a jury trial does not apply to proceedings before an administrative agency. Decisions of administrative agencies can be appealed to the courts, provided all administrative appeals have been exhausted. Courts will overturn administrative agency decisions only if they are found to be arbitrary or capricious.

California Constitution.   While the California State Constitution is the supreme law of California, it is subordinate to the U.S. Constitution. In the event of any conflict, the federal Constitution takes precedence. The California Constitution can be found on the Internet at *www.leginfo.ca.gov/const.html.*

WEB LINK @

California Statutes.   The Civil Code contains the fundamental principles of California real estate law, including ownership rights. Additional statutes related to real estate are scattered throughout California's various legal codes, including the Business and Professions Code, Code of Civil Procedure, Corporations Code, Financial Code, Government Code, Labor Code, Penal Code, and Public Resources Code. California codes can be accessed on the Internet at *www.leginfo. ca.gov/calaw.html.*

Real estate licensing is covered in Sections 1000 through 10581 of the Business and Professions Code. The regulation of real estate licensees is covered in Sections 11000 through 11030 of the Business and Professions Code. The primary purpose of these statutes is to protect the public by regulating those engaged in the real estate business.

California has incorporated English common law in the Civil Code: "The common law of England, so far as it is not repugnant to or inconsistent with the Constitution of the United States, or the constitution or laws of this state, is the rule of decision in all the courts of this state." (Civil Code Section 22.2) In 1939, the California Supreme Court held that where the codes and other statutes are silent, the common law will govern (*In re Patterson's Estate*, 34 C.A.2d 305).

Uniform Codes.   Because of a need for conformity in the statutes of various states, the National Conference of Commissioners on Uniform State Laws drafted recommended statutes for adoption by the states. The Uniform Commercial Code is one of those statutes. Areas covered by the Uniform Commercial Code of particular interest to real estate licensees include the definition of personal property, security interests in personal property, what constitutes a fixture, negotiable instruments, and laws governing commercial property, the Bulk Sales Act, and the Statute of Frauds for personal property. There is, however, no uniform code for real property laws that vary significantly among the states.

WEB LINK @

The California Secretary of State Website *www.ss.ca.gov* provides information on The Uniform Commercial Code.

State Administrative Agencies. The Office of Real Estate Appraisers in the Business, Transportation, and Housing Agency regulates the licensing and certification of California appraisers. The Department of Corporations regulates California real estate syndicates, franchise sales, and independent escrow agents. The Department of Health is concerned with safety and health standards, including water quality and waste disposal. Other state agencies also have regulations that affect the real estate business and transactions in real property. When adopting regulations, administrative agencies must follow the procedures set forth in the California Administrative Procedure Act, which include public hearings. To be upheld by the court, administrative regulations must be reasonably necessary to carry out statutes and must not conflict with or exceed the scope of statutes. Individuals have the right to petition the Department of Real Estate to adopt or repeal a regulation. Courts will generally overrule an administrative regulation only if it was enacted without authority, proper procedures were not followed, or the regulation is arbitrary, capricious, or otherwise unreasonable.

Department of Real Estate The **Department of Real Estate**, which is also included in the Business, Transportation, and Housing Agency, is the primary state agency to administer California real estate law. The primary purpose of California real estate law is the protection of the public in real estate and mortgage transactions. To carry out this purpose, the real estate commissioner has adopted regulations that are enforceable as the exercise of the police power of the state to promote health, safety, morals, and general welfare of citizens. The department was created by legislative act in 1917 and provided the first law in the United States for the licensing and regulation of real estate agents. These laws became a model for legislation in many other states.

Discipline Procedures The real estate commissioner, appointed by the governor, is the chief executive officer of the department. The commissioner determines administrative policy and enforces the provisions of the real estate law in a manner that provides maximum protection for the purchasers of real property and those persons dealing with real estate licensees.

The real estate commissioner can issue regulations to aid in the administration and enforcement of the law. These regulations, formally known as the *Regulations of the Real Estate Commissioner*, are set forth in Title 10 of the California Code of Regulations starting with Section 2705 and have the force and effect of the law.

The **Administrative Procedure Act** authorizes the commissioner to hold formal hearings to determine issues involving a licensee, license applicant, or subdivider. After a hearing, the commissioner may suspend, revoke, or deny a license or halt sales in a subdivision. A corporation may be disciplined for the action of a corporate broker who was acting on behalf of the corporation.

Actions of the real estate commissioner can be appealed to the courts. The California Supreme Court has held that power to regulate cannot be the arbitrary power to grant or refuse a license. In *Riley v. Chambers* (1919) 181 C. 589, the supreme court held: "While the right to engage in a lawful and useful occupation cannot be taken away under the guise of regulation, such an occupation may be subjected to regulation in the public interest even though such regulation involves in some degree a limitation upon the exercise of the right regulated."

Case Study

The case of *Donaldson v. California Department of Real Estate* (2006) 134 C.A. 4th 948 involved a real estate salesman, Donaldson who was found guilty of unlawful intercourse with a minor (his wife's 16-year old sister). The Real Estate Commissioner filed a disciplinary accusation that he had committed crimes involving moral turpitude. She alleged the crimes were substantially related under Section 2910, Title 10 California Code of Regulations to the qualifications, functions or duties of a real estate licensee. The Commissioner failed to adopt the Administrative Law Judge proposal decision for a restricted license and revoked Donaldson's license. She wrote that the convictions "were for crimes involving moral turpitude that are substantially related to the qualifications, functions, or duties of a real estate licensee." The Superior Court denied Donaldson's petition for administrative mandamus (a request that the Superior Court review and reverse the final decision of an administrative agency).

The Court of Appeal reversed ruling the license revocation was not authorized because the conviction was not substantially related to his professional conduct. "A determination that a licensee's conviction justifies discipline can not rest on the moral responsibility of the underlying conduct, but requires a reasoned determination that the conduct was in fact substantially related to the licensee's fitness to engage in the profession."

Note: A 2008 amendment to the Business and Professions Code eliminated the need to show moral turpitude.

The real estate commissioner does not have the authority to settle commission disputes. These matters are determined through a court of law; through the state labor commissioner, Department of Industrial Relations (for employer-employee disputes); or by arbitration if agreed to by the parties.

City and County Ordinances.   Under their police power, cities and counties can enact legislation concerning the use of real property to protect health, safety, morals, and general welfare. Such measures include local building codes, health ordinances, police and fire ordinances, and zoning.

City and County Administrative Agencies. Local agencies also make decisions that affect real property. By law, every city and county is charged with the development of a general plan. Local planning agencies not only develop planning, but also hear and decide on requests for rezoning. Community redevelopment agencies carry out redevelopment at a local level.

■ COURT STRUCTURE

Federal Courts

Because much of our real estate law is based on appellate judicial decisions, it is important to have a basic knowledge of our federal and state court systems. (See Figure 1.2.) The appellate process provides judicial guidance in the form of interpretation and clarification to ensure uniformity in the application of our laws.

FIGURE 1.2
State and Federal Court Systems

California Courts

Supreme Court
Has jurisdiction over all other California courts.

Courts of Appeals
Primarily hear appeals from superior court.
Limited original jurisdiction.

Superior Courts	**Appellate Division**
Original jurisdiction in civil and criminal cases.	Hear appeals from small claims courts.
Handle most real estate matters and probate.	

Superior Court – Limited Jurisdiction
Original jurisdiction for civil matters under $25,000.

Small Claims Courts
Matters of $7,500 or less for individuals. $5,000 limit for businesses.
No attorneys allowed.
Plaintiff cannot appeal (defendant can).

Federal Courts

U.S. Supreme Court
At its discretion, it hears appeals from the federal court of appeals, as well as from state supreme courts if a federal issue is involved.

Courts of Appeals
They are appellate courts only.

District Courts
Original jurisdiction in matters relating to federal law.
They also accept diversity of citizenship cases involving more than $75,000.*

* Note that there are several U.S. courts of limited jurisdiction, such as tax court, court of claims, customs court, and bankruptcy court.

District Courts.   District courts are courts of original jurisdiction. Of the 98 federal district courts, 4 of them are in California (Northern, Southern, Eastern, and Central districts). Besides hearing matters relating to federal law, they accept cases in which plaintiff and defendant are residents of different states (diversity of citizenship) if the case involves a claim of more than $75,000.

Court of Appeals.   These courts are limited to hearing appeals from federal district courts. The United States has 13 appeal courts. California is in the Ninth Circuit. (See Figure 1.3.)

FIGURE 1.3

The Thirteen Federal Judicial Circuit Courts

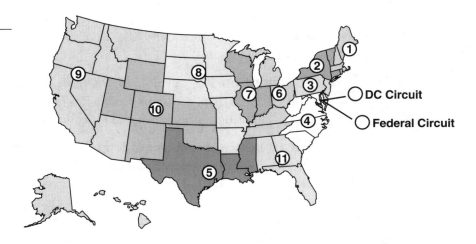

U.S. Supreme Court.   The U.S. Supreme Court is the highest court in the land. The nine justices are appointed by the president with approval of the U.S. Senate and serve for life. The U.S. Supreme Court can hear appeals from the highest state court if a federal statute, treaty, or constitutional issue is involved. It also hears appeals from the federal courts of appeals.

The Supreme Court is able to hear only a small percentage of the appeals brought to it. Therefore it tries to choose cases involving important issues. If the Supreme Court refuses to hear an appeal, the lower court decision stands.

The Supreme Court has the power of judicial review of the legislative branch. This power is, however, not set forth in the U.S. Constitution.

Case Study
In *Marbury v. Madison* (1803) 1 Cranch 137, the Supreme Court indicated the legislative branch must take notice of the Constitution. The court declared that an act of Congress that is repugnant to the Constitution of the United States cannot become a law, and it is the province of the judiciary to declare when a law is in conflict with the Constitution.

Special Courts. A number of special federal courts, including the tax court, court of military appeals, customs court, and court of claims, have very limited jurisdiction.

California Courts

Small Claims Courts. The small claims court is a branch of the superior court. A small claims court commissioner, temporary judge, or judge may preside. Cases are limited to matters involving $7,500 or less. They originally were intended to be consumer courts; but today, they are often used by creditors against consumers. Small claims courts follow a relatively informal procedure, with the parties pleading and defending their own cases; attorney representation is not allowed. A plaintiff (party bringing the action) who loses a case may not appeal, but a defendant (party being sued) who loses may appeal the decision to the superior court, Appellate Division.

Superior Courts. As of July 1998, judges in each county were allowed to vote if they wanted their county to combine its municipal and superior courts. By 2001, every California county had opted for court unification.

What were formerly municipal courts became limited jurisdiction superior courts that handle civil matters under $25,000 as well as minor criminal matters (misdemeanors). General jurisdiction superior courts have original jurisdiction in civil cases in excess of $25,000—felonies, probate, marriage dissolution, mortgage foreclosures, quiet title actions (actions to clear real estate titles), and most real estate disputes. Civil cases involving less than $25,000 are known as limited civil cases, including unlawful detainer evictions. Every California county has a superior court.

Superior Court, Appellate Division. Each superior court has an appellate division. It can adjudicate small claims court appeals brought by defendants (plaintiffs who lose in small claims court have no right of appeal). The appellate division also hears appeals of unlawful detainer evictions and limited civil cases involving less than $25,000.

California Courts of Appeal. These courts have very limited original jurisdiction and hear primarily appeals from the superior courts. There are six courts of appeal in California: Fresno, Los Angeles, San Diego, San Francisco, San Jose, and Sacramento. Each court of appeal consists of several panels, each composed of a presiding justice plus two associate justices.

California Supreme Court. While in some states Supreme Court justices are elected, in California they are appointed by the governor and approved by the state senate. The court consists of a chief justice and six associate justices, the California Supreme Court has discretionary appellate jurisdiction over all other California courts. If the California Supreme Court declines to accept a case, then the decision of the lesser court stands. The supreme court can decertify decisions of a court of appeal, which means that while a decision stands, it cannot be cited as a precedent for future decisions.

WEB LINK @

Additional information about California's court system can be researched at *www. courtinfo.ca.gov.*

■ LAWSUIT PROCEDURE

This book uses the case study method as a primary teaching tool. Because most real estate cases are civil matters adjudicated between the parties, rather than criminal matters (where the defendant is charged by the state with a criminal offense), understanding lawsuit procedure will enhance your understanding of the cases to be studied.

A civil lawsuit begins when a plaintiff files a complaint in court. The complaint describes the claim and requests relief. A copy of the complaint, as well as a summons to respond, is then served on the defendant.

Venue is the proper court location for a lawsuit to be tried. In most real estate cases, the proper venue is the county where the real estate is located. However, the plaintiff and/or defendant may petition the court for a change of venue to a more convenient location, such as the county where the real estate contract was signed. The **jurisdiction** of a court is the authority of the court to adjudicate the type of case and make a decision affecting the parties involved.

The defendant then has the option of

- answering the complaint, denying or admitting the allegations;

- filing a complaint of his or her own (a countersuit) against the plaintiff or against a third party, making the third party part of the action; or

- requesting dismissal based on, among other reasons, lack of jurisdiction; res judicata (a prior judgment on the issue between the parties); the facts, if true, not stating a cause of action (demurrer); the statute of limitations (the plaintiff waited too long to begin action); or the party bringing the action has no standing to sue.

During the pretrial period, a discovery process might take place (there is no discovery in small claims cases). During discovery, parties will subpoena witnesses to provide sworn testimony and may also use written interrogatories (questions presented in writing). Parties are also allowed access to records.

Most cases are settled prior to trial. If the lawsuit goes to trial, the trial begins with opening statements by the plaintiff and defendant. The plaintiff then brings forth witnesses. The plaintiff's examination of witnesses is called a *direct examination.* After the plaintiff's examination, the defendant has the right to examine the witness (called a *cross-examination*). The plaintiff may then question the witness—redirect examination—and the defendant then has an opportunity to re-cross-examine.

Next, the defendant has the right to produce witnesses, and the examination process is repeated. Finally, the parties make their closing statements.

If there is a jury, the court will direct questions of fact to the jury. For example: "Did the plaintiff give the defendant a $2,000 cash deposit?" "What is the amount of monetary damages sustained by the plaintiff?" The judge, not the jury, determines questions of law. Unless appealed, the decision of the court trial is binding on the parties.

■ JUDICIAL REMEDIES

The English common-law remedies, or legal remedies, were primarily monetary damages. Remedies developed by the chancellory courts were known as *equitable remedies*. The equity courts did not generally award monetary damages; their remedies were based on conscience, or what was right. As previously stated, U.S. courts are not limited to legal remedies and can award equitable remedies to right a wrong.

Monetary Remedies (Damages)

Compensatory Damages.   **Compensatory damages** are money damages to cover the loss for the injury sustained. The court also can assess a party with court costs when provided for by contract or by statute. Attorney fees also may be recoverable.

For example, if a seller forged a termite inspection report that indicated no infestation or damage and, after the sale, the purchaser discovered serious infestation and damage, a court might award the buyer actual costs to correct the problem (compensatory damages) plus exemplary damages.

Exemplary Damages.   **Exemplary** (or punitive) **damages** go beyond actual compensation for an injury. They are awarded to punish the wrongdoer for an action that was aggravated by its willful nature, malice, fraud, or wanton and wicked conduct.

For example, if a seller breached a contract to sell a house for $150,000 so as to sell the house to another buyer for $200,000, the court might award exemplary damages, in addition to the compensatory damages, for this wrongful and willful breach of contract.

Liquidated Damages.   Parties can agree what the damage will be in the event a party breaches a contract. Courts will enforce these damages as long as they are reasonable estimates of the damages that will result. If they are excessive, they would be considered a penalty and would not be enforced. As an example, a construction contract might have damages for each day of delay in the completion of performance.

Nominal Damages.   **Nominal damages** are monetary damages in a token sum such as $1. They are awarded to show a defendant was in the wrong but no substantial damage to person, property, or reputation occurred. An example would be a trespass where a person crossed the land of another without permission or right but caused no damage.

■ EQUITABLE REMEDIES

Remedies of Conscience

These are the remedies available when judicial remedies are inadequate and equity or conscience demands them.

Specific Performance. The court can force a person to perform as agreed. **Specific performance** is an equitable remedy usually awarded where money damages are inadequate. Because every parcel of real property is considered unique, specific performance is a proper remedy for breach of a real property sales agreement. While the remedy of specific performance is readily available to purchasers, courts rarely force buyers to buy because money damages are ascertainable. A seller who consequently sells to another buyer for less money usually will receive damages amounting to the difference in the sales prices. (For an exception, see *BD Inns v. Pooley*, cited in Chapter 5, where the buyer was forced to complete the sale.)

Specific performance is not available for personal services. That is, the court will not require one person to work for another, because that would violate the Thirteenth Amendment to the U.S. Constitution.

Specific performance will not be granted if the court does not deem the consideration adequate.

Rescission. **Rescission** is the mutual release of the parties to a contract. The contract is set aside, and the consideration that was given is returned. This equitable remedy would be used when promises were made because of a mutual mistake, when the contract became impossible to perform, or when the performance of the contract, while legal when the contract was made, became illegal because of a change in the law.

Reformation. Through **reformation**, a court rewrites a contract to read as it was intended to be read by the parties rather than as stated. For example, a court would likely reform a lease that described the wrong premises when it was clear from the evidence which premises were intended to be leased.

Injunction. Using an **injunction** as an equitable remedy, courts will order a party to cease and desist from an activity, such as a trespass or a nuisance.

Foreclosure. **Foreclosure** is an *action in rem*, an action against property, rather than an *action in personam*, which is an action directed against a specific person, such as an action for damages. A foreclosure action seeks to terminate a person's interest in property. Foreclosure actions would be brought by lienholders such as a lender or a holder of a mechanic's lien. Foreclosure is discussed in detail in Chapter 10.

Quiet Title.   Quiet title is a legal action to determine the ownership or rights in real property. It can be used to wipe out claims against a property to provide an owner with a marketable title, as well as to clear any cloud on a title (such as a misspelled name on a deed).

Declaratory Relief Action.   Under common law, a party had to wait until rights had been violated to obtain a legal interpretation of the rights involved. Now, however, a unique equitable remedy is available. Called a **declaratory relief action**, it can be brought to have the court determine rights *before* an invasion of rights has occurred. The purpose is to avoid a violation of law or contract. Courts will not consider hypothetical questions, there must be a real interest in the matter, as well as uncertainty. As an example, a party could ask for a declaratory judgment as to the legality and enforceability of a restrictive covenant that prohibits the party from engaging in a particular business on a property. A declaratory relief action may be used in conjunction with the demand for other relief, such as an injunction.

Criminal Versus Civil Wrongs

Criminal wrongs involve crimes against the state for which the state provides penalties that include fines and/or imprisonment. Civil law involves wrongs committed against individuals for which damages are appropriate. A single act could involve both criminal and civil wrongs. As an example, an act of fraud, such as selling property that the seller does not own, could be criminal and subject the wrongdoer to criminal penalties and also entitle the victim to civil damages.

■ ALTERNATIVE DISPUTE RESOLUTION (ADR)

In addition to judicial remedies, nonjudicial remedies of arbitration and mediation are available to disputing parties.

Arbitration

Arbitration is a process for final resolution of disputes. Many contracts call for mandatory arbitration, and the courts generally will enforce these agreements. The contracts usually provide for the choosing of the arbitrator and may state that the rules of the American Arbitration Association apply. In some cases, the courts can order nonbinding arbitration. Also, parties can agree to voluntary private arbitration, in which the arbitrator serves much as a judge in hearing a case but is not bound by the legal rules of evidence or normal court formalities.

The principal benefits of arbitration are that it is faster and less expensive than court action. Matters that could take years before they are heard in court might be decided in days at a small fraction of the cost that would have been incurred in a trial. Because of these benefits, arbitration has been gaining interest as a logical way to resolve disputes. However, parties agreeing to arbitrate disputes give up their legal rights to a jury trial, and the right to appeal the arbitrator's decision, even if it is contrary to established law. After the arbitrator makes a written decision, it can be presented to the local superior court for confirmation as a judgment of that court. At the court confirmation hearing, the judge cannot change the arbitrator's decision.

Mediation

Mediation is a process in which a neutral third party (mediator) works with the parties in a dispute to help them reach a satisfactory solution. The mediator suggests solutions and alternatives and might confer with the parties separately as well as together. Unlike an arbitrator, the mediator has no decision powers. The mediation process is not binding on the parties.

■ SUMMARY

We are governed by a system of laws enacted by our representatives that are enforceable through our legal system. Our laws range from the U.S. Constitution, which is the supreme law of the land, to local ordinances. The basic precepts of much of our real estate law, as well as a great deal of our legal vocabulary, come from English common law. The common law, however, was judge-made law rather than the statutory law that governs our conduct. The common law was built up over generations by legal precedent.

In addition to law courts, England also developed separate courts of equity. Courts in the United States combine the equity functions of the English equity courts with those of the common-law courts.

We have parallel federal and state court systems that provide for appeals from trial court decisions. The appellate systems provide greater uniformity in our courts.

To effectuate justice, our court system has a wide variety of remedies available to it. These include the remedies available to the English common-law courts as well as the courts of equity. An injured party can request a remedy that best meets his or her specific needs.

Alternative dispute resolution includes arbitration and mediation.

■ DISCUSSION TOPICS

The maxims of jurisprudence (fundamental principles of law) were developed in English common law. California has enacted these maxims into its Civil Code. Rather than being inflexible rules, they are aids to the just application of statutory law. The maxims do not nullify specific statutes.

The majority of the maxims are included below, along with the Civil Code citation. Consider the meaning and purpose of each of the following maxims as it relates to real property law:

Civ. Code §3510   When the reason of a rule ceases, so should the rule itself.

Civ. Code §3511   Where the reason is the same, the rule should be the same.

Civ. Code §3512   One must not change his or her purpose to the injury of another.

Civ. Code §3513	Anyone may waive the advantage of a law intended solely for his or her benefit, but a law established for a public reason cannot be contradicted.
Civ. Code §3514	One must use his or her own rights so as not to infringe on the rights of others.
Civ. Code §3515	One who consents to an act is not wronged by it.
Civ. Code §3516	Acquiescence in error takes away the right of objecting to it.
Civ. Code §3517	No one can take advantage of his or her own wrong.
Civ. Code §3518	One who has fraudulently dispossessed himself of a thing may be treated as if he still had possession.
Civ. Code §3519	One who can and does not forbid what is done on his or her behalf is deemed to have bidden it.
Civ. Code §3520	No one should suffer by the acts of another.
Civ. Code §3521	One who takes the benefit must bear the burden.
Civ. Code §3522	One who grants a thing is presumed to grant also whatever is essential to its use.
Civ. Code §3523	For every wrong there is a remedy.
Civ. Code §3524	Between those who are equally in the right or equally in the wrong, the law does not interpose.
Civ. Code §3525	Between rights otherwise equal, the earliest is preferred.
Civ. Code §3526	No person is responsible for what no person can control.
Civ. Code §3527	The law helps the vigilant before those who sleep on their rights.
Civ. Code §3528	The law respects form less than substance.
Civ. Code §3529	That which ought to have been done is to be regarded as done, in favor of the one to whom, and against the one from whom, performance is due.
Civ. Code §3530	What does not appear to exist is to be regarded as if it did not exist.
Civ. Code §3531	The law never requires impossibilities.
Civ. Code §3532	The law neither does nor requires idle acts.
Civ. Code §3533	The law disregards trifles.

Civ. Code §3534	Particular expressions qualify those that are general.
Civ. Code §3535	Contemporaneous exposition is in general the best.
Civ. Code §3536	The greater contains the less.
Civ. Code §3537	Superfluity does not vitiate.
Civ. Code §3538	That is certain which can be made certain.
Civ. Code §3539	Time does not confirm a void act.
Civ. Code §3540	The incident follows the principal and not the principal the incident.
Civ. Code §3541	An interpretation that gives effect is preferred to one that makes void.
Civ. Code §3542	Interpretation must be reasonable.
Civ. Code §3543	Where one of two innocent persons must suffer by the act of a third, the person by whose negligence it happened must be the sufferer.
Civ. Code §3545	Private transactions are fair and regular.
Civ. Code §3546	Things happen according to the ordinary course of nature and the ordinary habits of life.
Civ. Code §3547	A thing continues to exist as long as is usual with things of that nature.
Civ. Code §3548	The law has been obeyed.

WEB LINK @

Note: All of the California codes can be accessed on the Internet through *www. leginfo.ca.gov.*

■ DISCUSSION CASES

1.   A homebuyer who was not satisfied with the workmanship in her new home posted signs saying, "I bought a $200,000 fixer-upper," "My house leaks and no one gives a damn," and "We moved to Paradise Hills but we live in hell." At various times, up to 20 other homeowners posted similar signs. The developer sued, alleging that the statements were made with intent to injure the developer's sales activity. The developer did not allege that the statements made were false. **Was the homeowner acting within her rights?**

Paradise Hills Associates v. Procel (1991) 235 C.A.3d 1528

2. A man was prohibited from distributing religious tracts in the parking lot of a shopping center. **Were his constitutional rights violated?**

Savage v. Trammell Crow Co., Inc. (1990) 223 C.A.3d 1562

3. Antiabortion activists protested in the parking lot of a medical center. They handed out material and prayed aloud. An agent of the landlord sought injunctive relief to prohibit the activities of the protestors. **Should it be granted?**

Allred v. Harris (1993) 14 C.A.4th 1386

4. Golden Gateway Center includes a retail center plus 1,254 residential rental units. Building management prohibits door-to-door solicitations and leafleting within the buildings. The center sought to enjoin the tenant association from distributing newsletters. The association cross-complained for injunctive and declaratory relief. The San Francisco Superior Court ruled in favor of the tenant association. The building owner appealed. **Should the superior court ruling be upheld?**

Golden Gateway Center v. Golden Gateway Tenants Association (1999) 73 C.A.4th 908

5. A city ordinance prohibited homeowners from displaying signs on their property except resident identification, for sale, and warning signs. The city refused to permit a homeowner to place a sign on her front lawn opposing the Persian Gulf War. **Is the restriction on signs justified?**

City of Ladue v. Gilleo (1994) 114 S. Ct. 2038

6. **When there is a binding arbitration agreement and the arbitrator has clearly made an erroneous decision, will the courts set it aside?**

Moore v. First Bank of San Luis Obispo (1998) 68 C.A.4th 768

7. A city passed an ordinance requiring landlords to evict all occupants of a rental unit when the chief of police suspects that a tenant is engaged in or permits illegal drug activity, gang-related crimes or a drug-related nuisance in or near the property. **Will the courts enforce this ordinance?**

Cook v. City of Buena Park (2005) 126 C.A.4th 1

8. A police officer posed as a prospective buyer in order to obtain access to a home. Based on the officer's observations, a search warrant was obtained and the owner was arrested and sentenced on a methamphetamine charge. **Was the officer's use of a ruse to gain entry a violation of the owner's Fourth Amendment protection against unwarranted search and seizure?**

People v. Lucatero (2008) 166 C.A. 4th 1110

9.   A union picketed a store in a shopping mall. The mall sought to stop the picketing because it was detrimental to business in other stores. **Was the picketing proper?**

Fashion Valley Mall L.L.C. v. National Labor Relations Board (2007) 42 C.A. 4th 850

■ CHAPTER QUIZ

1. Most of California real estate law originally came from

   a. Spanish law.

   b. Mexican law.

   c. English common law.

   d. the commissioner's regulations.

2. Reliance on previous decisions is best described as

   a. common law.   b. stare decisis.

   c. equity.   d. civil law.

3. Our system of statutes in California could best be described as

   a. civil law.   b. stare decisis.

   c. equity.   d. constitutional law.

4. The Equal Credit Opportunity Act is best described as

   a. stare decisis.   b. common law.

   c. civil law.   d. constitutional law.

5. The power of eminent domain is based on which amendment to the U.S. Constitution?

   a. The First Amendment   b. The Thirteenth Amendment

   c. The Fifth Amendment   d. The Fourteenth Amendment

6. Which constitutional amendment allows a homeowner to place a For Sale sign on his or her home?

   a. The First Amendment

   b. The Fifth Amendment

   c. The Fourteenth Amendment

   d. The Twenty-Sixth Amendment

7. Laws governing ownership rights are set forth in

   a. state statutes.   b. local ordinances.

   c. federal statutes.   d. the English common law.

8. The regulation of real estate licensees is covered in the

    a. Administrative Code.

    b. Corporation Code.

    c. Civil Code.

    d. Business and Professions Code

9. There is no uniform code for

    a. personal property.   b. commercial paper.

    c. real property.   d. all the items above.

10. The commissioner's regulations are

    a. considered to have the force and effect of law.

    b. known as the real estate law.

    c. included in the Business and Professions Code.

    d. none of the above.

11. In adopting regulations, an administrative agency must provide for

    a. alternative remedies.   b. arbitration of disputes.

    c. a public hearing.   d. all the above.

12. The real estate commissioner conducts hearings in accordance with the

    a. Administrative Procedure Act.

    b. Business and Professions Code.

    c. Labor Code.

    d. Public Resources Code.

13. Decisions of the Department of Real Estate

    a. are binding and final.

    b. may be appealed to the courts.

    c. must be made unanimously by the commission.

    d. must be concurred with by a majority of the commission.

14. Damages awarded by a court in excess of actual damages suffered by a plaintiff are known as

    a. liquidated damages.   b. nominal damages.

    c. exemplary damages.   d. compensatory damages.

15. The California court that has original jurisdiction for a claim of $100,000 would be the:

    a. California Supreme Court.
    b. superior court.
    c. small claims court.
    d. court of appeal.

16. Most real estate disputes are adjudicated in

    a. federal courts.
    b. superior courts.
    c. court of appeal.
    d. the supreme court.

17. Most lawsuits involving real estate matters can be described as

    a. criminal proceedings.
    b. administrative agency actions.
    c. common-law actions.
    d. civil actions.

18. Which statement about lawsuits is NOT correct?

    a. The defendant commences the action with a complaint.
    b. A direct examination of a witness is followed by a cross-examination.
    c. Most lawsuits are settled before trial.
    d. If there is a jury, the jury determines questions of fact.

19. Money awarded to an injured person for damages received is called

    a. exemplary damages.
    b. compensatory damages.
    c. nominal damages.
    d. specific performance.

20. Equitable remedies include all below EXCEPT

    a. monetary damages.
    b. reformation.
    c. rescission.
    d. specific performance.

21. The remedy in which a person is ordered to cease and desist from an activity is known as

    a. reformation.
    b. specific performance.
    c. injunction.
    d. none of the above.

22. A legal action to determine ownership rights in real property would be

    a. an injunction.
    b. reformation.
    c. a declaratory relief action.
    d. a quiet title action.

23. Which is *NOT* an advantage of voluntary arbitration?

    a. Savings in money

    b. Right to appeal

    c. Savings in time

    d. None of the above

24. The process whereby a third person works to resolve a problem but cannot impose a decision on the parties is known as

    a. arbitration.

    b. mediation.

    c. declaratory relief.

    d. quiet title.

25. Mediation could be described as

    a. empowering a third person to make a decision for you.

    b. a judicial process.

    c. both a and b.

    d. neither a nor b.

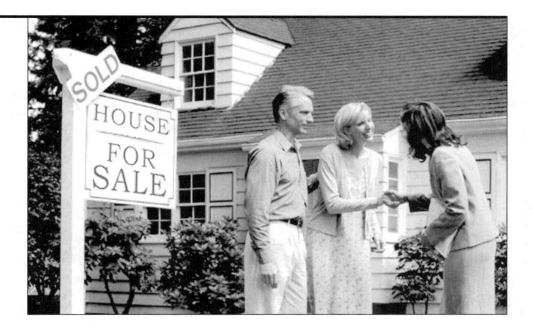

CHAPTER TWO

LAW OF AGENCY

■ KEY TERMS

agency	estoppel	power of attorney
agency coupled with an interest	express agency	principal
	express authority	ratification
agent	fiduciary duty	respondeat superior
attorney-in-fact	general agent	secret agent
customary authority	implied agency	special agent
dual agency	implied authority	tort
equal dignities rule	ostensible agency	vicarious liability

■ AGENTS AND AGENCY DEFINED

Section 2295 of the California Civil Code states, "An **agent** is one who acts for or represents another, called the **principal,** in dealings with third persons. Such representation is called an **agency.**" Therefore, an agent is one who acts for or represents another.

Because an agent represents a principal, payment to the agent is generally considered payment to the principal. In the same manner, notifying the agent of a fact is the same as notifying the principal. The legal relationship of an agency requires free consent of both the agent and the principal. Courts will not force an agency relationship on parties against their will, nor will they generally require the continuance of an agency if either party wants to end it. Therefore, the principal or the agent can generally end an agency relationship at any time. A party who does so, however, might be liable for damages if terminating the agency breaks a contractual promise. (As an example, while a principal could arbitrarily cancel a listing contract and end the agency, the principal would be liable to the agent for damages in accordance with provision of the listing contract.)

Those who can't perform an act themselves can legally appoint someone to act as their agent to perform the act.

Civil Code Section 2296 states, "Any person having the capacity to contract may appoint an agent and any person may be an agent." A person who wishes to appoint an agent must have both the legal and mental capacity to do so. Legal capacity involves age and/or legal restrictions on contracting, while mental capacity is defined by state of mind. (Legal and mental capacity are covered in detail in Chapter 5.) Principals who lack the capacity to perform an act or become contractually bound cannot appoint an agent to perform the act or to contractually bind them. If an act must be in writing, the appointment of someone to perform the act must be in writing.

■ TYPES OF AGENTS

General Agent

A **general agent** has the authority to perform all necessary acts for the principal within a specified area. For example, a court-appointed conservator of an individual who is unable to manage their affairs is a general agent for managing the conservatee's finances, arranging the conservatee's care, and making other important decisions, such as signing real estate contracts.

Special Agent

While a general agent has broad powers to act for the principal, a **special agent** is limited to those acts specifically set forth in the agency agreement. For example, a real estate licensee is normally a special agent of an owner with authority to locate a buyer for a property or a property for a buyer. (The real estate agent normally has no power to sell the owner's property, buy property for the buyer, or contractually bind the owner.)

Power of Attorney

A **power of attorney** is a written agreement whereby a principal appoints an agent, known as an **attorney-in-fact,** to act in their place. An attorney-in-fact should not be confused with an attorney-at-law. Powers of attorney are normally given for specific purposes, such as to sign a deed when the owner is not available; this is an example of a specific power of attorney. A general power of attorney conveys broad powers to the attorney-in-fact to operate in the place of the principal and to contractually bind the principal within the specified area of the agency. The power of attorney document should be in recordable form, including acknowledgment of the principal's signature by a notary public, so it can be recorded allowing the attorney-in-fact to sign recordable documents on behalf of the principal. However, when the principal dies, the power of attorney is automatically terminated. The statutory power of attorney form is found in Civil Code Section 2450.

Because a principal can sell property owned by the principal without possessing a real estate license and an attorney-in-fact can act in the shoes of the principal, an attorney-in-fact need not possess a real estate license. The exemption from licensing applies only to particular or isolated transactions and may not be used as a substitute for a broker's license.

■ HOW AGENCIES ARE CREATED

Express Agency

An **express agency** is an agency created by a specific agreement, either written or oral. Most agencies are express agencies. Listings are the written agency agreements used to authorize an agent to procure buyers or lessees or to locate property for purchase or lease or to locate property for a buyer or lessee.

Agency agreements that must be in writing are covered in Chapters 5 and 6.

Implied Agency

Most agencies are express agencies created by a written or oral agreement. An **implied agency** is not the result of a stated agreement but is created by the actions of the parties that indicate reasonable intent to form an agency. As an example, an owner who tells a broker, "Find me a tenant" is implying that there should be an agency relationship. Agents should be aware that promises to serve the best interests of another could be construed as an agreement to act in an agency capacity even if the promise is gratuitous.

> ### Case Study
> In the case of *Smith v. Home Loan Funding* (2011) 192 C.A. 4th 1331, a homeowner approached a Home Loan Funding loan officer to obtain a home equity line of credit. The loan officer indicated he would shop around and get her the best loan. The loan officer then convinced the homeowner that it was in her best interests to refinance with a new first loan from Home Funding.
>
> The homeowner discovered that she was qualified for a better interest rate from another lender.
>
> In a suit for damages, the trial judge ruled that the loan officer was acting as a mortgage broker as well as a lender and breached his fiduciary duty. The lender was held liable for the discounted difference between the mortgage payments the borrower would make for 30 years and the payments the borrower was qualified for, a difference of $72,187.17.
>
> The Court of Appeal affirmed, stating that an oral promise to shop for the best loan created an oral brokerage agreement and the lender was liable for breach of fiduciary duty.

Ostensible Agency

California Civil Code Section 2298 states, "An agency is either actual or ostensible." If one person causes others to believe that another person is their agent when that is not true, the courts can declare the principal bound due to the existence of an apparent or **ostensible agency.** Section 2300 of the Civil Code states, "An agency is ostensible when the principal intentionally, or by want of ordinary care, causes a third person to believe another to be his agent who is not really employed by him." For example, assume a real estate agent took a prospective tenant to a property owner's place of business and asked the owner of the property for the key to show the property. Assume the owner complied in the presence of the prospective tenant. A court may declare that the owner's actions (or inaction) resulted in the prospective tenant's reasonably believing that an agency existed. The owner could therefore be liable to the tenant for actions of the ostensible agent.

Agency of Estoppel

When an ostensible agency is created and a third person reasonably acts to that person's detriment based on the belief of the existence of the agency, the person who allowed the ostensible agency to exist would be estopped (barred) from denying the existence of the agency. For example, assume an out-of-town owner informed a broker that the owner's cousin had the authority to give a listing on the owner's property. The broker, acting on this assertion, listed and then procured a buyer for the owner's property. The owner would be estopped from denying the existence of the agency because his other words led the broker to act to the broker's detriment. The agency created what is called an *agency by estoppel*. The doctrine of **estoppel** is one of equity to achieve justice. (See *Phillippe v. Shapell Indus. Inc.*, Chapter 5.)

Agency by Ratification

By accepting the benefits of an agreement made by an unauthorized agent or by an agent who has exceeded their authority, a principal can form an agency by **ratification.**

If a principal had the authority to permit the unauthorized act at the time it was performed, the principal has the authority to ratify or approve the act after it was done. A principal cannot ratify part of an indivisible agreement; the entire agreement must be ratified.

After knowing of the unauthorized act, the principal can ratify the act by words or actions that indicate the intent to be bound by said act. The principal can also ratify through silence or the failure to repudiate an unauthorized act after receiving knowledge of it. For example, an owner who accepts the rents under a lease entered into by an unauthorized agent could be ratifying all of the provisions of the lease.

A principal can void prior ratification if the ratification were made with imperfect knowledge of the material facts of the transaction (Civil Code Section 2314). Assume that in ratifying a tenancy, the owner believed the unauthorized agent had entered into a month-to-month tenancy. Upon discovering the tenancy was actually for 20 years, the owner could rescind the ratification.

> ## Case Study
>
> In the case of *Behniwal v. Mix* (2005) 133 C.A.4th 1027, a real estate agent allegedly, without authority, signed the sellers' names to a counter offer, which was accepted by the Behniwals. Subsequently, the owners signed the transfer disclosure statement, database disclosure form regarding registered sex offenders, a natural hazards disclosure statement, agent's disclosure, seller's affidavit of nonforeign status, as well as water heater and smoke detector compliance statements. Subsequently, Mr. Mix was taken to a hospital and sent a handwritten note to cancel escrow because of health reasons. This action was brought by the Behniwals for specific performance (actions were also commenced by both parties against the agent and her broker).
>
> The trial court ruled that because the owners never signed the counter offer addendum, no contract was formed.
>
> The Court of Appeal reversed ruling that the sellers ratified the unauthorized signatures by providing required disclosures.

Dual Agency

A **dual agency** exists when an agent represents two principals who are negotiating with each other and have conflicting interests. Any conduct that reasonably leads a buyer to believe that a seller's agent is representing both buyer and seller might create a dual agency.

Because agents often serve as confidants and advisers to purchasers, purchasers easily could be led to believe that the agent is representing them. To avoid the possibility of a court determination that a dual agency exists, a broker must make certain that buyers fully understand that the broker might not be their representative.

While some purchase agreements state that the broker is the representative of the seller, not the buyer, this probably would not be enough to avoid a determination of dual agency if the agent's conduct has led a buyer to believe they were being represented.

Agency Disclosure

Because of misunderstandings by buyers and sellers as to whom the agent represents and what the agency duties are, California now requires the agent to provide a written agency disclosure to the parties for the sale, purchase, exchange, or lease of one to four residential units and mobile homes (Civil Code Section 2375). The listing agent can elect to be either a seller's agent or a dual agent representing both seller and buyer. Because the listing agent has specific duties to the seller, the listing agent cannot elect to be solely a buyer's agent. The selling agent who locates a buyer, however, can elect to be a seller's agent, a buyer's agent, or a dual agent, (See Figure 2.1). The listing would set forth the agency contemplated, and the purchase form would include agency confirmation.

The California Association of Realtors® (CAR) Form AD indicates the agency duties. Figure 2.2 explains the agent's responsibility as seller's agent, buyer's agent, or dual agent representing both seller and buyer. There are three steps in agency disclosure.

1. Disclose—written explanation of the types of agency relationships that are possible

2. Elect—a decision about the type of agency relationship for the transaction

3. Confirm—written signed confirmation of agency (usually part of a purchase agreement)

Case Study

In the case of *Huijers v. De Marrais* (1993) 11 C.A.4th 676, a real estate agent failed to provide the owner with a copy of the residential agency disclosure form at the time the listing was taken. The Court of Appeal ruled that the listing agent's failure to provide the discloser (as required by Civil Code Section 2373, etc.) at the time of listing relieved the sellers of any duty to pay a sales commission.

Case Study

The case of *Brown v. FSR Brokerage, Inc.* (1998) 62 C.A.4th 766, involved a situation where an agent from Fred Sands Realty listed Brown's home for $2,695,000. The seller's agent orally informed Brown that he was Brown's exclusive agent. The agent told Brown that unless the price was reduced to $2.4 million, he would lose a prospective buyer. (During the negotiation process, the agent had told the seller how much the buyer was willing to offer and also told the buyer how little the seller was willing to accept, but eventually advised the seller not to accept less than a full-price offer.) While no written offer was presented to Brown, the agent said it was time to go to escrow. Brown signed, but failed to read the agency confirmation stating that the agent was a dual agent.

The superior court ruled that the agency had been properly confirmed. The Court of Appeal reversed, holding that a dual agency must be disclosed as soon as practical. The agency was represented as being a seller's agent, and the agent misrepresented whom he was representing until the confirmation. The court also pointed out that the agent breached duties by revealing to each party the position of the other party.

FIGURE 2.1

Agency Election

<u>Listing Agent</u>	<u>Selling Agent</u>
Seller's Agent	Seller's Agent
Dual Agent	Buyer's Agent
	Dual Agent

Some states allow a broker to take a transaction broker or facilitator position. The broker is not considered an agent but rather a third-party middleman with no advocacy or fiduciary duties to either buyer or seller. However, the broker does have duties of confidentiality as to information received from either party, as well as duties of fair and honest dealing and to meet the needs of the parties.

While compensation is an indication of an agency relationship, an agent need not receive consideration for an agency relationship to exist.

In the case of *McPhetridge v. Smith* (1929) 101 C.A.122, the court held: "A gratuitous agent upon entering into the performance of the agency is, in common with all other agents, bound to exercise the utmost good faith in dealing with his principal." Doing someone a favor could result in liability if a licensee breaches an agency duty. The fact that the buyer does not directly pay the broker does not mean that the broker is not the buyer's agent.

A broker who acts for more than one party to a transaction without the knowledge and consent of all parties involved would be subject to disciplinary action. An undisclosed dual agency also would be grounds for rescission of the contract as well as forfeiture of rights to compensation.

Note: While California law allows dual agencies, some states prohibit a real estate agent from representing both buyer and seller. This is based on the belief that there is a conflict of interest in giving one agent duties to both parties to a transaction. Besides buyer and seller separate agency, some states have allowed a designated agency whereby one agent in a brokerage office represents the buyer, and another agent in the same office represents the seller. This creates a possible conflict of interest because both agents are under the supervision of a single broker. Designated agencies are not authorized in California.

FIGURE 2.2
Agency Disclosure Form

DISCLOSURE REGARDING
REAL ESTATE AGENCY RELATIONSHIP
(As required by the Civil Code - Confirmation Separate)

THIS FORM FOR USE
IN CALIFORNIA ONLY

Real Estate Forms
Since 1966

When you enter into a discussion with a real estate agent regarding a real estate transaction, you should from the outset understand what type of agency relationship or representation you wish to have with the agent in the transaction.

SELLER'S AGENT

A Seller's agent under a listing agreement with the Seller acts as the agent for the Seller only. A Seller's agent or a subagent of that agent has the following affirmative obligations:

To the Seller:
   A fiduciary duty of utmost care, integrity, honesty, and loyalty in dealings with the Seller.

To the Buyer and the Seller:
   (a) Diligent exercise of reasonable skill and care in performance of the agent's duties.
   (b) A duty of honest and fair dealing and good faith.
   (c) A duty to disclose all facts known to the agent materially affecting the value or desirability of the property that are not known to, or within the diligent attention and observation of, the parties.

An agent is not obligated to reveal to either party any confidential information obtained from the other party that does not involve the affirmative duties set forth above.

BUYER'S AGENT

A selling agent can, with a Buyer's consent, agree to act as agent for the Buyer only. In these situations, the agent is not the Seller's agent, even if by agreement the agent may receive compensation for services rendered, either in full or in part from the Seller. An agent acting only for a Buyer has the following affirmative obligations:

To the Buyer:
   A fiduciary duty of utmost care, integrity, honesty, and loyalty in dealings with the Buyer.

To the Buyer and the Seller:
   (a) Diligent exercise of reasonable skill and care in performance of the agent's duties.
   (b) A duty of honest and fair dealing and good faith.
   (c) A duty to disclose all facts known to the agent materially affecting the value or desirability of the property that are not known to, or within the diligent attention and observation of, the parties. An agent is not obligated to reveal to either party any confidential information obtained from the other party that does not involve the affirmative duties set forth above.

AGENT REPRESENTING BOTH SELLER AND BUYER

A real estate agent, either acting directly or through one or more associate licensees, can legally be the agent of both the Seller and the Buyer in a transaction, but only with the knowledge and consent of both the Seller and the Buyer.

In a dual agency situation, the agent has the following affirmative obligations to both the Seller and the Buyer:
   (a) A fiduciary duty of utmost care, integrity, honesty and loyalty in the dealings with either Seller or the Buyer.
   (b) Other duties to the Seller and the Buyer as stated above in their respective sections.

In representing both Seller and Buyer, the agent may not, without the express permission of the respective party, disclose to the other party that the Seller will accept a price less than the listing price or that the Buyer will pay a price greater than the price offered.

The above duties of the agent in a real estate transaction do not relieve a Seller or Buyer from the responsibility to protect his or her own interests. You should carefully read all agreements to assure that they adequately express your understanding of the transaction. A real estate agent is a person qualified to advise about real estate. If legal or tax advice is desired, consult a competent professional.

Throughout your real property transaction you may receive more than one disclosure form, depending upon the number of agents assisting in the transaction. The law requires each agent with whom you have more than a casual relationship to present you with this disclosure form. You should read its contents each time it is presented to you, considering the relationship between you and the real estate agent in your specific transaction.

This disclosure form includes the provisions of Sections 2079.13 to 2079.24, inclusive, of the Civil Code set forth on the reverse hereof, or on an attached page. **Read it carefully.**

I/We have read this disclosure and acknowledge receipt of a copy of this disclosure and a copy of Civil Code Sections 2079.13 to 2079.24 attached hereto.

Buyer/Seller _____   Date _____

Buyer/Seller _____   Date _____

Buyer/Seller _____   Date _____

Buyer/Seller _____   Date _____

Agent _____
                (Print Name of Agent/Broker)

By _____   Date _____
            (Associate Licensee Signature)

Source: Professional Publishing

FIGURE 2.2

Agency Disclosure Form, Continued

CHAPTER 2 OF TITLE 9 OF PART 4 OF DIVISION 3 OF THE CIVIL CODE

Article 2.5. Agency Relationships in Residential Real Property Transactions

§2079.13. As used in Sections 2079.14 to 2079.24, inclusive, the following terms have the following meanings:

(a) "Agent" means a person acting under provisions of Title 9 (commencing with Section 2295) in a real property transaction, and includes a person who is licensed as a real estate broker under Chapter 3 (commencing with Section 10130) of Part I of Division 4 of the Business and Professions Code, and under whose license a listing is executed or an offer to purchase is obtained.

(b) "Associate licensee" means a person who is licensed as a real estate broker or salesperson under Chapter 3 (commencing with Section 10130) of Part I of Division 4 of the Business and Professions Code and who is either licensed under a broker or has entered into a written contract with a broker to act as the broker's agent in connection with acts requiring a real estate license and to function under the broker's supervision in the capacity of an associate licensee.

The agent in the real property transaction bears responsibility for his or her associate licensees who perform as agents of the agent. When an associate licensee owes a duty to any principal, or to any buyer or seller who is not a principal, in a real property transaction, that duty is equivalent to the duty owed to that party by the broker for whom the associate licensee functions.

(c) "Buyer" means a transferee in a real property transaction, and includes a person who executes an offer to purchase real property from a seller through an agent, or who seeks the services of an agent in more than a casual, transitory, or preliminary manner, with the object of entering into a real property transaction. "Buyer" includes vendee or lessee.

(d) "Dual agent" means an agent acting, either directly or through an associate licensee, as agent for both the seller and the buyer in a real property transaction.

(e) "Listing agreement" means a contract between an owner of real property and an agent, by which the agent has been authorized to sell the real property or to find or obtain a buyer.

(f) "Listing agent" means a person who has obtained a listing of real property to act as an agent for compensation.

(g) "Listing price" is the amount expressed in dollars specified in the listing for which the seller is willing to sell the real property through the listing agent.

(h) "Offering price" is the amount expressed in dollars specified in an offer to purchase for which the buyer is willing to buy the real property.

(i) "Offer to purchase" means a written contract executed by a buyer acting through a selling agent which becomes the contract for the sale of the real property upon acceptance by the seller.

(j) "Real property" means any estate specified by subdivision (1) or (2) of Section 761 in property which constitutes or is improved with one to four dwelling units, any leasehold in this type of property exceeding one year's duration, and mobile homes, when offered for sale or sold through an agent pursuant to the authority contained in Section 10131.6 of the Business and Professions Code.

(k) "Real property transaction" means a transaction for the sale of real property in which an agent is employed by one or more of the principals to act in that transaction, and includes a listing or an offer to purchase.

(l) "sell," "sale," or "sold" refers to a transaction for the transfer of real property from the seller to the buyer, and includes exchanges of real property between the seller and buyer, transactions for the creation of a real property sales contract within the meaning of Section 2985, and transactions for the creation of a leasehold exceeding one year's duration.

(m) "Seller" means the transferor in a real property transaction, and includes an owner who lists real property with an agent, whether or not a transfer results, or who receives an offer to purchase real property of which he or she is the owner from an agent on behalf of another. "Seller" includes both a vendor and a lessor.

(n) "Selling agent" means a listing agent who acts alone, or an agent who acts in cooperation with a listing agent, and who sells or finds and obtains a buyer for the real property, or an agent who locates property for a buyer or who finds a buyer for a property for which no listing exists and presents an offer to purchase to the seller.

(o) "subagent" means a person to whom an agent delegates agency powers as provided in Article 5 (commencing with Section 2349) of Chapter 1 of Title 9. However, "subagent" does not include an associate licensee who is acting under the supervision of an agent in a real property transaction.

§ 2079.14. Listing agents and selling agents shall provide the seller and buyer in a real property transaction with **a copy** of the disclosure form specified in Section 2079.16, and, except as provided in subdivision (c), shall obtain a signed acknowledgment of receipt from that seller or buyer, except as provided in this section or Section 2079.15, as follows:

(a) The listing agent, if any, shall provide the disclosure form to the seller prior to entering into the listing agreement.

(b) The selling agent shall provide the disclosure form to the seller as soon as practicable prior to presenting the seller with an offer to purchase, unless the selling agent previously provided the seller with a copy of the disclosure form pursuant to subdivision (a).

(c) Where the selling agent does not deal on a face-to-face basis with the seller, the disclosure form prepared by the selling agent may be furnished to the seller (and acknowledgment of receipt obtained for the selling agent from the seller) by the listing agent, or the selling agent may deliver the disclosure form by certified mail addressed to the seller at his or her last known address, in which case no signed acknowledgment of receipt is required.

(d) The selling agent shall provide the disclosure form to the buyer as soon as practicable prior to execution of the buyer's offer to purchase, except that if the offer to purchase is not prepared by the selling agent, the selling agent shall present the disclosure form to the buyer not later than the next business day after the selling agent receives the offer to purchase from the buyer.

§ 2079.15. In any circumstance in which the seller or buyer refuses to sign an acknowledgment of receipt pursuant to Section 2079.14, the agent, or an associate licensee acting for an agent, shall set forth, sign, and date a written declaration of the facts of the refusal.

§ 2079.17. (a) As soon as practicable, the selling agent shall disclose to the buyer and seller whether the selling agent is acting in the real property transaction exclusively as the buyer's agent, exclusively as the seller's agent, or as a dual agent representing both the buyer and the seller. This relationship shall be confirmed in the contract to purchase and sell real property or in a separate writing executed or acknowledged by the seller, the buyer, and the selling agent prior to or coincident with execution of that contract by the buyer and the seller, respectively.

(b) As soon as practicable, the listing agent shall disclose to the seller whether the listing agent is acting in the real property trans- action exclusively as the seller's agent, or as a dual agent representing both the buyer and seller. This relationship shall be confirmed in the contract to purchase and sell real property or in a separate writing executed or acknowledged by the seller and the listing agent prior to or coincident with the execution of that contract by the seller.

(c) The confirmation required by subdivisions (a) and (b) shall be in the following form:

_____ is the agent of (check one):   _____ is the agent of (check one):,
            (Name of Listing Agent)   (Name of Selling Agent if not the same as the Listing Agent)

❑ the seller exclusively; or   ❑ the buyer exclusively; or
❑ both the buyer and seller.   ❑ the seller exclusively; or
                                                                     ❑ both the buyer and seller.

(d) The disclosures and confirmation required by this section shall be in addition to the disclosure required by Section 2079.14.

§ 2079.18. No selling agent in a real property transaction may act as an agent for the buyer only, when the selling agent is also acting as the listing agent in the transaction.

§ 2079.19. The payment of compensation or the obligation to pay compensation to an agent by the seller or buyer is not necessarily determinative of a particular agency relationship between an agent and the seller or buyer. A listing agent and a selling agent may agree to share any compensation or commission paid, or any right to any compensation or commission for which an obligation arises as the result of a real estate transaction, and the terms of any such agreement shall not necessarily be determinative of a particular relationship.

§ 2079.20. Nothing in this article prevents an agent from selecting, as a condition of the agent's employment, a specific form of agency relationship not specifically prohibited by this article if the requirements of Section 2079.14 and Section 2079.17 are complied with.

§ 2079.21. A dual agent shall not disclose to the buyer that the seller is willing to sell the property at a price less than the listing price, without the express written consent of the seller. A dual agent shall not disclose to the seller that the buyer is willing to pay a price greater than the offering price, without the express written consent of the buyer.

This section does not alter in any way the duty or responsibility of a dual agent to any principal with respect to confidential information other than price.

§ 2079.22. Nothing in this article precludes a listing agent from also being a selling agent, and the combination of these functions in one agent does not, of itself, make that agent a dual agent.

§ 2079.23. A contract between the principal and agent may be modified or altered to change the agency relationship at any time before the performance of the act which is the object of the agency with the written consent of the parties to the agency relationship.

§ 2079.24. Nothing in this article shall be construed to either diminish the duty of disclosure owed buyers and sellers by agents and their associate licensees, subagents, and employees or to relieve agents and their associate licensees, subagents, and employees from liability for their conduct in connection with acts governed by this article or for any breach of a fiduciary duty or a duty of disclosure.

FORM 110.42 CAL (**04/2007**)

Form generated by: **True Forms**™   www.TrueForms.com   800-499-9612

Source: Professional Publishing

■ PROOF OF AGENCY

The burden of proving the existence of an agency relationship is on the person who seeks to benefit by the existence of the agency. Persons seeking such benefit might include an agent seeking compensation from a principal or a principal who wishes to prove that a person was in fact their agent to establish the existence of agency duties. A third person might wish to prove that the person they contracted with was actually an agent so as to hold a principal liable. As an example, rather than bring a lawsuit against a defendant with little money and no insurance, an injured party might assert that the person who caused the injury was an agent. In this way, the injured party might be able to sue a principal who has money and/or insurance.

Case Study
L. Byron Culver & Assoc. v. Jaoudi Industrial & Trading Corporation (1991) 1 C.A.4d 300 involved a broker who had been locating suitable property for Del Rayo for several years. The broker obtained Del Rayo's permission to initiate negotiations to acquire property owned by Jaoudi. A salesperson for the broker then obtained a one-time listing for the property that provided for a 3 percent sales commission. The salesperson then brought in an offer from Del Rayo for $1,750,000. Jaoudi inquired if the broker Culver and Del Rayo were associated in any way. The salesperson denied any association. Jaoudi later instructed the escrow not to pay Culver any commission. The Court of Appeal, in affirming a superior court decision denying compensation, stated, "An agent has a fiduciary duty to his principal to disclose all information in the agent's possession relevant to the subject matter of the agency," and in a real estate agency, the penalty for failure to disclose a dual agency at the time of the transaction is forfeiture of the real estate sales commission. The Court of Appeal noted that the fact that the agent acted fairly and honorably to both principals did not affect the forfeiture of commission. Jaoudi believed the agent was acting solely as his agent, but the inevitable conclusion is that Culver represented both the buyer and the seller.

■ AUTHORITY OF AGENTS

Express Authority

Agents have the stated authority given to them in the agency agreement (either oral or written). This is known as **express authority**.

A person cannot orally authorize an agent to perform an act that is required to be in writing. According to the **equal dignities rule,** if the statute of frauds requires the act to be in writing, the agency agreements, such as listings and sales contracts, must be in writing to be legally enforceable. (The statute of frauds is covered in Chapter 5.)

Civil Code Section 1624 states that no contract for the sale of real property can be enforced unless signed by the person against whom enforcement is sought. Therefore, a document signed by a real estate agent "as per phone conversation" would be unenforceable.

Implied Authority

Agents also have **implied authority** to perform the acts reasonably necessary to accomplish the purpose of the agency. For example, a managing agent with the power to enter into commercial leases has the implied authority to engage an attorney to draft a lease.

Customary Authority

Customary authority is authority implied by the agent's position. A person dealing with an agent could assume that the agent has the authority customary for such an agency. A general manager of a real estate office would have the customary authority to order stationery and place advertisements.

Secret limitations on the agent's authority that are not known by persons dealing with the agent do not limit the agent's customary authority. Assume a real estate agent was the rental and management agent for a commercial building. The agency agreement required all leases for more than 18 months to be signed by the owner. If a tenant received a lease for two years signed by the agent without any knowledge of the limitations on the agent's authority, the tenant could rely on the customary authority of such an agent. (Of course, the agent could be liable to the owner for exceeding authority.)

A third person should not rely on an agent's claim to have greater than customary authority. If, for example, a leasing agent indicates she has authority to give the prospective tenant an option to purchase the property as part of the lease, the prospective tenant has a duty to ascertain whether the agent actually has this authority.

In the normal real estate brokerage situation, the real estate listing agent has express authority (set forth in a listing) to seek buyers for the property of a principal. The broker usually has no express or implied authority to obligate the principal contractually.

Delegation of Agent's Authority

Unless expressly authorized by the principal, an agent has no authority to delegate agency duties, with the exception of

- purely mechanical acts, such as erecting signs, maintaining buildings, and making repairs;
- acts the agent cannot lawfully perform, such as functions requiring an attorney; and
- acts that commonly are delegated, such as the closing function (delegated to an escrow firm).

Unless a listing authorizes an agent to work with other agents, a broker does not have the authority to cooperate with other agents or to disseminate listing information through a multiple-listing service.

■ FIDUCIARY DUTIES OF AN AGENT

Fiduciary Duty

An agent has a duty of trust and must protect the principal's interests. Under this **fiduciary duty**, the agent must act in a manner that is consistent with the best interests of the principal. The agent may not obtain any advantage over the principal by misrepresentation, duress, or adverse pressure.

For an example of a breach of fiduciary duty case, see *Mitchell v. Gould* (1928) 90 C.A. 647, where the principal wanted a short-term lease, but the broker got the tenant to offer a long-term lease. The broker lost his commission.

The agent must account for all funds received or disbursed on behalf of the principal. Making a secret profit would be a breach of the agent's fiduciary duty. The agent's only benefits must be those agreed to by the principal.

A dual agency in which the agent is employed by written contract with a seller to sell a property and is also undertaking to assist the buyer to purchase that property presents a peculiar and touchy question of duty. An agent may not act for more than one party in a transaction without the knowledge or consent of all the parties thereto [Business and Professions Code Section 10176(d)]. The consent should be in writing. In a dual agency situation, the agent has an affirmative obligation to both the seller and the buyer as follows:

- ■ A fiduciary duty of utmost care, integrity, and loyalty in any dealings with either the buyer or the seller

- ■ A duty to exercise diligent, reasonable skill and care in the performance of the agent's duties

- ■ A duty of honesty, fair dealings, and good faith

- ■ A duty to disclose all facts that the agent knows or should know to affect the value or desirability of the property

Case Study

The case of *Warren v. Merrill* (2006) 143 C.A.4th 96 involved a buyer, Warren, who wished to buy a condo but did not have the income or downpayment necessary to buy the unit he wanted. Merrill, the real estate broker, who refers to herself as "The Condo Queen," agreed to lend Warren her commission ($27,000) so he could have 20 percent down. To show proper income, Merrill suggested her daughter, Charmaine, be a co-borrower and filled out the loan application showing her daughter earned $7,500 per month although she earned far less as a waitress. Before closing, Merrill obtained Warren's signature on an amendment where title would vest in Charmaine's name alone. Charmaine never signed a promised quit claim deed to Warren. Warren entered the Betty Ford center for substance abuse and fell behind on payments. Merrill made the payments to prevent foreclosure. When Warren left the Betty Ford Center he found himself locked out of the condo, which was now rented to tenants.

Warren sued Merrill for breach of fiduciary duty and fraud and sought quiet title, as well as damages. The Superior Court quieted title in Warren, imposed a constructive trust on the condo, and awarded Warren $15,000 noneconomic damages plus $50,000 punitive damages. Merrill appealed.

The Court of Appeal affirmed, ruling the evidence supported the finding that Merrill breached her fiduciary duty to the buyer by fraudulently procuring title to the property in her daughter's name with no intent to deliver a quit claim deed to Warren. The court also ruled that the unclean hands doctrine did not apply as the parties were not equally at fault. The court also ruled that the statute of frauds did not apply because Warren sought equitable remedies rather than legal remedies.

Note: The trial court was shocked by Merrill's testimony and her lack of concern about defrauding the lender. She was cautioned by the judge regarding her Fifth Amendment Rights not to incriminate herself, but she proceeded with her testimony. The trial judge stated, "From the beginning of the transaction, she did not intend to perform her promises of placing his name on title."

Figure 2.3 Summarizes the elements of an agent's fiduciary duty.

FIGURE 2.3
Fiduciary Duty of an Agent

Full Disclosure	Accounting
Due Care	Integrity
Loyalty	Obedience
Honesty	

Full Disclosure

Notice to an agent is considered to be notice to the principal. Therefore, the agent has a duty to inform the principal of any facts that would be likely to influence the principal in making a decision. Unless expressly instructed by the owner not to present such an offer, or unless the offer is patently frivolous, every offer received, whether oral or written, must be communicated promptly to the principal. For example, offers must be presented even if received after the principal has accepted an offer and is contractually bound. The principal may wish to breach the existing contract, suffer the damages, and accept the new offer. The best rule for agents is to present all offers to the seller and let the seller decide to accept, reject, or counteroffer.

Case Study

The case of *Roberts v. Lomanto* (2003) 112 C.A.4th 1553 involved the sale of a shopping center. Owner Roberts hired real estate agent Lomanto as exclusive leasing and sales agent. They agreed on a 2 percent sales commission for the sale of the property. When the shopping center didn't sell, Lomanto made a purchase offer of the $11 million asking price. She told Roberts the shopping center was not worth more than that. Relying on that representation, Roberts signed a sales contract with her. Before escrow closed, Lomanto requested permission to assign her purchase contract to Pan Pacific. Lomanto again told Roberts the property was only worth $11 million.

Upon close of escrow, Roberts paid Lomanto her sales commission of $110,000. Roberts later read in the newspaper that Pan Pacific had paid $12.2 million for the shopping center. Roberts sued Lomanto for fraud, breach of fiduciary duty, constructive fraud, negligent representation, and breach of contract. The superior court granted summary judgment for broker Lomanto. Roberts appealed.

The Court of Appeal reversed, ruling Lomanto's purchase contract did not terminate her real estate agency fiduciary duties to Roberts, or her duty of full disclosure of material facts including her $1.2 million secret profit. The appellate court ruled Roberts was entitled to $1.2 million in damages, plus exemplary damages and restoration of the sales commission.

Note: Unless the principal knows of and consents to an agent's retention of profit, profit belongs to the principal rather than the agent. It is hard to understand why the superior court gave summary judgment for Lomanto.

Full disclosure extends to warning the principal about any dangers or financial problems to be considered, as well as to accurately conveying information about value. Negligence of an agent alone is not enough to make the agent liable; there must be damages.

Case Study

The case of *Strebel v. Brenlar* (2006) 135 C.A. 4th 740 involved a buyer of a Sonoma house through a Frank Howard Allan real estate agent who was acting as a dual agent.

Strebel was selling his San Bruno home contingent upon the purchase of the Sonoma home. He contacted his agent for the Sonoma home prior to closing his sale and was told the Sonoma purchase was on track. Unknown to Strebel, there were IRS tax liens against the Sonoma home that exceeded its sale price. The dual agent was aware of these liens, which precluded the sale completion. The plaintiff was unable to find another home to purchase and was priced out of the Sonoma County market by rising prices. Strebel sued the broker for unfair business practices, fraud, negligence and breach of fiduciary duty. The trial court found that the agent had intentionally concealed material facts with the intent to defraud Strebel. Strebel was awarded $300,0000 economic damages plus $50,000 noneconomic emotional distress damages.

The Court of Appeals affirmed the economic damages, but reduced the amount to $202,273 because an appraisal expert failed to substantiate the balance. The economic damages related to the loss of appreciation of the San Bruno home which would not have been sold had Strebel known that the Sonoma property could not be purchased. The court reversed as to $50,000 emotional damages.

Note: Agent who breaches fiduciary duty can be liable for lost appreciation in a former home.

Due Care

An agent must exercise reasonable or due care in carrying out the duties of the agency. Real estate agents' duties are based on their having the higher knowledge and skills required of a real estate licensee.

> ### Case Study
> The case of *Furla v. Jon Douglas Co.* (1998) 65 C.A.4th 1069 involved a list-ing broker who had stated that a house was approximately 5,500 square feet, but qualified it with "information deemed reliable but not guaranteed." The list-ing agent had received this information from the owner's daughter who said it came from the architectural plans. During negotiations with the seller and the buyer's agent, Furla, the buyer said, "OK! Fifty-five hundred square feet. I'll pay $170 a square foot." The offer was accepted.
>
> When the buyer later decided to sell, an agent told him "a knowledgeable REALTOR® would easily recognize that the residence is substantially less than 5,500 square feet." Furla hired an appraiser who said it was 4,615 square feet. Another appraiser measured it at 4,437 square feet. Furla then sued the listing agent for negligent misrepresentation. While the superior court granted summary judgment for the listing broker, the Court of Appeal reversed hold-ing that there are genuine issues of material fact regarding whether the listing agent had the reasonable basis to report the house as 5,500 square feet and if the buyer relied on this representation. The Court of Appeal emphasized that the square-feet estimate was not merely inaccurate; it was "grossly inac-curate," by more than 20 percent. The court remanded the issues to a jury.
>
> *Note:* The selling broker was not sued, probably because the purchase con-tract strongly recommended that the buyer obtain independent inspections. It also stated that the buyer's agent, Fred Sands Realty, made no representa-tions as to the size of the structure.

Loyalty

The agent cannot, without permission, disclose to third parties any confidential facts about the principal or agency that would not be in the principal's best inter-ests. This duty continues even after the agency has terminated.

A dual agent cannot disclose to one principal information received in confidence from the other principal, such as that the seller will accept less or the buyer will pay more.

Honesty

The agent must not only fully disclose all material facts to the principal but must do so in a fair and honest manner so as not to prejudice the judgment of the prin-cipal. The agency duty of fairness and honesty extends to all persons with whom the agent is dealing.

Accounting

The agent has a duty to account for all funds received or disbursed and must remit funds due the principal in a prompt manner.

Integrity

An agent's moral conduct in dealings must be beyond reproach. The agent should strive to eliminate even the appearance of conflict of interest. Others should be able to rely on the agent's word.

An agent cannot compete with the principal. For example, a buyer's agent may not submit their own higher offer when submitting an offer from the buyer.

> **Case Study**
>
> The case of *Field v. Century 21 Klowden-Forness Realty* (1998) 63 C.A.4th 18 involved buyers who sued their buyer agent for negligent representation. The agent failed to recommend inspection of the septic system for code compliance, did not advise buyers to check for a room addition building permit, and did not advise buyers to obvious physical defects. The agent also failed to check the preliminary title report to determine the scope of the easement revealed by the seller's Transfer Disclosure Statement. The easement gave the Otay Water District the right to flood part of the property. The superior court held that the agent breached her fiduciary duty to the buyers.
>
> The Court of Appeal affirmed and pointed out that the broker's fiduciary duty to clients requires the highest good faith.
>
> The court differentiated between the statutory duty that is a nonfiduciary duty mandated after *Easton v. Strassburger* (1984) 152 C.A.3d 90 and the common-law fiduciary duty of an agent that demands the highest good faith and undivided service and loyalty. The court indicated this duty may encompass the duty to research, investigate, and counsel.
>
> The court's decision was that the case was not barred by the two-year statute of limitations. The three-year statute of limitations (from date of discovery of the breach) applies to the breach of fiduciary duties.

Obedience

An agent has a duty to obey the lawful instructions of the principal (illegal instructions, such as not to show a home to a member of a minority group, must not be followed). An agent who fails to obey lawful instructions or exceeds the authority granted could be held liable for resulting damages.

Agent's Duty to Third Persons

An agent has a duty of honest and fair dealings with others. The principal and agent could be held liable for the agent's misrepresentation, fraud, or failure to disclose to a third party detrimental information that the agent knew or should have known.

Many agents arrange loans for buyers. If an agent is to receive a fee for arranging a loan, this fact must be conveyed to the buyer who must understand that they can make loan arrangements without use of the agent's services.

Once an agent takes on the responsibility of obtaining a loan for a buyer, the agent is put in an agency position even though the broker was the sole agent of the seller for the purpose of the sale. The agent then has a duty to obtain the loan that best meets the needs of the buyer, not the loan that provides the greatest financial remuneration for the agent. In fact, the broker could be liable to a borrower if the broker by negligence or design recommended a loan to a borrower that was clearly not in the borrower's best interest.

■ LIABILITY OF AGENTS

Agents are personally liable for their torts and crimes even when committed at the direction of the principal. A **tort** is a civil wrong or violation of a duty. Civil wrongs that are torts include libel, slander, trespass, assault, negligent injury to others, etc. Some torts, such as assault or trespass, can also be crimes. The principal also could be liable.

An agent who does not disclose to third parties that they are acting in an agency capacity can be held personally liable by the third party, even when the principal has directed the agent to maintain secrecy. A principal might, for example, direct an agent or agents not to reveal the agency when the purpose of the agency is to buy up parcels needed for a development (assemblage).

A third party who suffers injury because of a breach of contract can seek recovery from either the agent or the principal, but not both. The **secret agent** would, of course, have the right to be reimbursed by the principal for losses suffered if the agent was acting properly within the scope of the agency.

Section 2336 of the Civil Code provides that, "One who deals with an agent without knowing or having reason to believe that the agent acts as such in the transaction, may set off against any claim of the principal arising out of the same, all claims which he might have set off against the agent before notice of the agency."

A person who claims to be an agent without having authority would be liable for their acts. Section 2342 of the Civil Code states, "One who assumes to act as an agent thereby warrants to all who deal with him in that capacity that he has the authority which he assumes."

Agents who violate their agency duties can be held liable to their principal for resulting damages.

While an agent normally must obey the instructions of the principal, at times, such as emergencies, obeying those instructions would not be in the best interests of the principal. For example, it could be in the principal's best interests for a managing agent to exceed limitations on expenditures to protect a property from flood damage when the agent is unable to contact the principal. Civil Code Section 2320 provides for this type of situation: "An agent has power to disobey instructions in dealing with the subject of the agency, in cases where it is clearly for the interest of his principal that he should do so, and there is no time to communicate with the principal."

■ LIABILITY OF PRINCIPALS

The doctrine of **respondeat superior** is that a master is liable for the actions of servants or employees. The principle also applies to agencies. **Vicarious liability** is created not by an act of the principal but because the agent was acting for the principal. The principal is therefore liable for the acts or omissions of a real estate agent acting within the scope of the real estate agency. This liability extends to subagents and includes liability for negligence and misrepresentation. The principal bears the risk of loss of the buyer's deposit caused by the negligence or fraud of the agent.

Case Study

A basement apartment was advertised as "ideal for two men." A woman was refused the rental, and the unit was rented to two men. A jury determined that the property manager had discriminated against the woman because of her gender. The jury failed to award damages against the owner, who had directed the manager in writing not to discriminate.

The 4th U.S. Circuit Court of Appeal, however, held the owner liable. It was pointed out that an owner cannot shirk a duty to pay taxes or meet safety standards simply because the owner gave someone else responsibility. The duty to comply with the law rests on the owner. *Walker v. Crigler* (1992) 976 F.2d 900.

The principal can be held liable for the misrepresentation of the agent even when the misrepresentation is made without the principal's knowledge. Unless the agent's actions are directed by the principal, however, the principal will not be held criminally liable for crimes of the agent, though the principal could be civilly liable for damages.

For an example of an agent fraud case, see *Ach v. Finkelstein* (1968) 264 C.A.2d 667.

The principal is not liable to third parties who know or should know from the agent's actions that the agent is exceeding the agent's authority. Where the agent's actions are clearly inconsistent with the best interests of the principal, third parties should realize that the agent is exceeding the authority granted.

If an agent exceeded authority in appointing a subagent, then the subagent would be the agent of the broker and not of the principal. In such a case, the principal would not be liable for actions of the subagent (Civil Code 2350).

If the agent suffers a personal loss because they followed the instructions of the principal, the principal will be obligated to the agent for that loss.

The principal has a duty to deal in good faith with their agent. The principal is liable to the agent for compensation as agreed to by their agency.

The principal could be liable for acts of an agent after termination of the agency if third parties dealing with the agent do not know of the termination and the former agent continues to act as if a valid agency continues. Of course, the former agent would be liable to the principal for damages suffered by their wrongful actions.

■ BREACH OF AGENCY

Either the principal or the agent might breach the agency. If the principal wrongfully terminates the agency agreement, the agent is entitled to damages. Listing contracts customarily provide for a full commission should the principal wrongfully terminate. The agent generally cannot, however, force the owner to continue the agency because an agency requires the consent of the parties.

Because the agent's interest is the commission, the agent cannot force the owner to accept an offer in conformance with the listing (specific performance). However, if an owner rejects a purchase offer that meets the exact terms of the listing, the agent is entitled to a full sales commission.

Exceeding the authority granted, breaching agency duties, and wrongfully renouncing the agency are examples of agents' breaches. Should the agent breach the agency, the agent is liable in damages to the principal. The agent also could be liable for punitive damages for breach of duty if the courts determine that the act was of such a willful and outrageous nature that the agent should be punished.

■ TERMINATION OF AGENCY

An agency agreement may be ended in a number of ways:

1. *Expiration of its term.* An agency automatically ends with the expiration of its stated term.

2. *Extinction of the subject matter.* The destruction of the property automatically terminates a listing or management agency agreement in the absence of any agreement to the contrary. In other words, impossibility terminates the agency. For example, if an agent were employed to find a tenant for a property, the destruction of that property would terminate the agency.

3. *Death.* Because an agency is a personal relationship, death of either the principal or the agent terminates the agency. If either the principal or the agent is a corporation, the death of corporate officers would not terminate the agency because a corporation is considered a separate legal entity.

4. *Renunciation.* Because an agency requires consent of the parties, either the principal or the agent can renounce the agency. As stated earlier, if a party wrongfully breaches the agency, that party could be liable for damages.

5. *Incapacity of agent or principal.* If the agent is no longer capable of acting as an agent, or the principal becomes mentally incapacitated, the agency terminates. An agent who loses their license would be incapable of performance, so the agency would terminate.

6. *Agreement of the parties.* The principal and the agent can mutually agree to terminate their agency.

7. *Full performance.* Satisfactory completion of the object of the agency terminates the agency.

8. *Bankruptcy.* The trustee in a bankruptcy can terminate an agency or allow it to continue. If the bankruptcy of an agent impairs the agent's ability to perform, the principal can terminate the agency.

Agency Coupled with an Interest

In an **agency coupled with an interest**, the agent has an interest in the subject matter of the agency. That is, the agency is created to benefit the agent or a third party. For example, an agent might advance a principal money to stop a foreclosure under an agreement to obtain a listing. The agent then has an interest in the property.

Section 2356 of the Civil Code states that an agency coupled with an interest cannot be terminated by death or incapacity of the principal or by the unilateral act of the principal.

> ### Case Study
> In the case of *Pacific Landmark Hotel, Ltd. v. Marriott Hotels, Inc.* (1993) 19 C.A.4th 615, the owner of a San Diego hotel had signed a 50-year management contract with Marriott Hotels, Inc., for a management fee plus 30 percent of the cash flow. At the time of the agreement, Marriott subsidiary corporations made trust deed loans of $23 million to the hotel. The owner filed a lawsuit against Marriott Hotels, Inc., and various subsidiaries, seeking damages for breach of contract, as well as for cancellation of the management contract. Marriott refused to give up management, claiming an agency coupled with an interest. The San Diego Superior Court denied a preliminary injunction terminating the agency because the agency was coupled with an interest.
>
> The Court of Appeal reversed and ruled as a matter of law that the loans were made by other Marriott corporations, so Marriott Hotels, Inc., had no interest. Therefore, the agency could be terminated. (Each corporation was a separate legal entity.)

■ SUMMARY

An agency relationship is a legal relationship whereby a principal (which in real estate is an owner or prospective buyer) appoints an agent (the broker) to act on their behalf.

Agents can be given broad powers or limited powers. In real estate, the agent customarily has the limited power to obtain a buyer.

Agencies can be created in several ways. While most agencies are formed by express agreements, an agency can be implied by the actions of the parties or created by estoppel or ratification. In real estate, the agency is created by the listing or management agreement.

To prevent misunderstandings about whether the agent is the buyer's agent, the seller's agent, or a dual agent, California requires that an agent provide written disclosure to buyers and sellers for the sale, purchase, or exchange of one to four residential units or mobile homes, and for leases that exceed one year.

The agent has duties based on the good faith and trust required in an agency relationship. These duties include

- fiduciary responsibility—the agent has a duty of trust and must act in the best interests of their principal;

- full disclosure—the agent must disclose to the principal all facts that would be likely to influence the principal's decisions;

- due care—an agent not only must use reasonable care in carrying out the agency but also must use the special knowledge and skills that the agent possesses;

- accounting—an agent must account for all funds received and/or expended;

- loyalty—an agent's primary duty is to the principal. The agent cannot act in a self-serving manner to the detriment of the principal or in any manner not in the principal's best interests; and

- obedience—an agent has a duty to obey the legal instructions of their principal.

The duties of agents go beyond obligations to the principal. The agent has a duty of honest, good-faith dealings with all parties. An agent who breaches duties can be held personally liable.

The principal is liable for acts of the agent within the scope of the agency. The principal has the duty of good-faith dealing with the agent.

Besides the express authority given to the agent by the principal, the agent has implied power to do those acts that are reasonably necessary to carry out the purpose of the agency.

Agencies can be terminated by expiration of the term, destruction of the subject property, death, renunciation by or agreement of the parties, incapacity of the agent or principal, or bankruptcy.

■ DISCUSSION CASES

1. A property was listed for sale at $100,000. An offer for $90,000 was accepted, but the sale failed because the prospective buyer could not obtain financing. A real estate agent later informed a prospect that the property could be purchased for less than its listed price. **What, if any, are the problems in this scenario?**

2. A broker helped the seller determine the list price for a net listing. The broker subsequently sold the property to his daughter and son-in-law without informing the seller of his relationship with the buyers. Should the fact that it was a net listing and the seller got what they wanted affect the agency duty? **In this case, what were the duties of the broker?**

   Sierra Pacific Industries v. Carter (1980) 104 C.A.3d 579

3. A broker represented to the owner that an offer of $300 per acre was a fair price. The broker knew that a very similar tract of land had been sold for $400 per acre but failed to inform the seller of this sale. **What has the broker done wrong, and what would be the appropriate remedy?**

   Moore v. Turner (1952) 137 WV 299, 71 S.E.2d 342

4. A mortgage broker failed to inform the principal that the mortgage broker was going to receive a fee from the lender. In fact, the mortgage broker affirmatively denied he would receive any lender compensation. The mortgage broker did, however, receive such a fee. **Discuss the wrongs and remedy.**

   Spraltin v. Hawn (1967) 156 S.E.2d 402

5. Several brokers were engaged in a property exchange. It became apparent that to provide cash for the commissions, a property that an owner wanted $100,000 for would have to be sold for a higher price. A buyer was induced to pay $115,000 for the property. She was told that the price was firm. After the close of escrow, she learned that the owner had wanted only $100,000 for the property. **What are the buyer's rights?**

   Crogan v. Metz (1956) 47 C.2d 398

6. The plaintiff agreed to list property at $15,900 based on the defendant broker's advice. Both the owner and the broker knew that the property eventually would be condemned for a highway. Prior to actually listing the property, the broker opened an escrow with his name as the buyer. After listing the property, the broker told the owner he was advertising it, but no effort actually was made to do so. The broker indicated to the owner that he had a purported buyer at less than list price. Eventually, a transaction was closed at a price of $13,000. The broker did not reveal that the buyer was a friend who was applying for a salesperson's license under the broker. The offer accepted provided for title to be in the name of the purchaser or a party to be named later. The owner signed a deed in blank. The broker inserted the names of his wife and himself. Revenue stamps were affixed to indicate a sales price of $40,000, which the broker later claimed he had paid. The broker wanted $100,000 from the state for the property. **What are the problem areas that would concern the parties in a lawsuit?**

Smith v. Zak (1971) 20 C.A.3d 785

7. A purchaser declined to complete the 10 percent deposit as required and indicated willingness to forfeit the deposit that had been made. The owners were told that the broker would be participating in the purchase. Not disclosed were the facts that the original purchaser had declined to complete the deposit and that the balance was to be paid by the broker. The broker also failed to inform the owner that his participation amounted to a seven-eighths interest. **Was the broker's disclosure adequate?**

Bate v. Marsteler (1959) 175 C.A.2d 573

8. The defendants listed a residential property for sale. They received an offer less than the list price and persuaded the plaintiffs to accept it. They informed the plaintiffs that the purchaser intended to live in the property, although they knew the purchasers were investors who intended to resell it. After the sale the defendants obtained a listing on the property and resold it at a profit. **Have the defendants breached an agency duty?**

Jorgensen v. Beach 'N' Bay Realty Inc. (1981) 125 C.A.3d 155

9. The plaintiff sellers accepted a promissory note secured by a first trust deed on property other than what was being sold. The sellers' agent represented to the plaintiffs that the security was adequate and the maker was financially responsible. The encumbered property was actually inadequate security for the note, and the maker was in shaky financial condition. The trust deed for $12,000 was created by the defendant by conveying the property on August 15 (day of sale) to the Fullmers. On August 15, the Fullmers then reconveyed the property to Schmidt. It appears these conveyances had the sole purpose of creating paper to be used for the purchase. **In what ways did the agent breach his duties?**

Banville v. Schmidt (1974) 37 C.A.3d 92

10. A real estate agent used the key in a multiple-listing lockbox to show a home. While the listing indicated the house was occupied, the agent discovered it to be unfurnished except for some stereos and television sets in cabinets and closets. The agent contacted the police, who searched the house. In addition to stolen property, they discovered drugs. **Was the agent's action proper?**

People v. Jaquez (1984) 163 C.A.3d 918

11. An appraisal by a professional appraiser showed a property value of $610,000 for a home. While the appraisal indicated the appraiser had studied the property, he had not done so. The appraisal had been prepared by an employee of the appraiser. The appraisal misstated the number of bedrooms, baths, skylights, and fireplaces, as well as the total square footage. It also failed to point out that construction work was still in progress. Based on the appraisal, the plaintiff made a $200,000 loan secured by a second trust deed on the property. When the borrower defaulted, the lender sued the appraiser. **Is the appraiser liable?**

Foggy v. Ralph F. Clark & Assoc. Inc. (1987) 192 C.A.3d 1204

12. A licensed real estate salesperson, working as a loan agent, submitted a loan package to his real estate broker. The broker rejected it. Nevertheless, the salesperson submitted the package to a mortgage lender. The borrower had never authorized the loan, and her signature was forged on the application. The true value of the property was only $480,000, but the $600,000 loan application showed an $800,000 purchase price. The loan was funded. The broker was sued for loss suffered by the mortgage lender based on respondeat superior, negligent supervision, and equitable indemnity. The broker argued that when the salesperson committed the fraudulent acts, he was not acting within the scope of his agency. **Do you agree?**

Inter Mountain Mortgage, Inc. v. Salimen (2000) 78 C.A.4th 1434

13. In a lease transaction where both lessor (developer) and lessee were represented by agents, it was alleged that after the lease was entered into for a building to be built to tenant's specifications, the tenant's agent became aware of financial problems of the tenant. **Did the tenant's agent have a disclosure duty to the developer?**

Blickman Turkus L.P. v. MF Downtown Sunnyvale, L.L.C. (2008) 162 C.A. 4th 858

■ CHAPTER QUIZ

1. A legal agency requires that

   a. the agent have the capacity to contract.

   b. consideration flow from the principal to the agent.

   c. all of the agency duties be stated in writing.

   d. the parties consent to the agency.

2. An agency relationship could be created by all of the following *EXCEPT*

   a. court order.   b. verbal agreement.

   c. implication.   d. ratification.

3. The relationship that exists between a broker and an owner under a listing is most likely a(n)

   a. employer-employee relationship.

   b. special agency.

   c. universal agency.

   d. general agency.

4. An agency created by a principal who intentionally, or by want of ordinary care, causes a third person to believe another to be his or her agent who is not really employed by him or her would be a(n)

   a. express agency.   b. power of attorney.

   c. ostensible agency.   d. special agency.

5. You made a statement that induced a person to act in reliance on that statement. The legal principle that now prevents you from asserting facts that are contrary to your previous declaration is known as

   a. estoppel.   b. ratification.

   c. respondeat superior.   d. laches.

6. Broker Thomas, who was not your agent, told prospective tenants that he was your agent to lease your property. Thomas leased your property, and you accepted the rent from the tenant. You *CANNOT* now deny the agency because of

   a. ratification.

   b. interest coupled with the agency.

   c. waiver.

   d. estoppel.

7. An undisclosed agent breached a contract with a third party. Which of the following is a true statement as to liability for the breach?

   a. The agent could be held personally liable.

   b. The principal could be held liable.

   c. The agent and principal would be jointly liable.

   d. Both a and b are correct.

8. A selling agent can represent

   a. the buyer only.

   b. both buyer and seller.

   c. the seller only.

   d. any of the above.

9. A real estate agency disclosure form is NOT required to be given to the buyer and seller of a(n)

   a. single-family home.

   b. condominium apartment unit.

   c. triplex.

   d. office building.

10. An agent failed to give an owner a copy of the agency disclosure form at the time the residential listing was taken. The most likely consequence for the agent will be

    a. a fine and/or prison.

    b. inability to collect a commission should a sale be made.

    c. automatic revocation of the agent's license.

    d. no action because disclosure is required only upon sale.

11. Which is NOT a requirement of an agency relationship?

    a. Compensation to the agent

    b. Contractual capacity of principal

    c. Loyalty of agent to principal

    d. Full disclosure by agent to principal

12. The equal dignities rule concerns

    a. discriminating practices.

    b. the requirement that certain agency agreements be in writing.

    c. ratification of unauthorized acts.

    d. the implied authority of an agent standing in the shoes of the principal.

13. Which statement is correct as to agencies?

    a. To be valid, an agency requires consideration.

    b. An agent who exceeds his or her authority will always be personally liable.

    c. All agency duties must be expressly agreed to.

    d. Some agency duties are implied.

14. A seller's agent, in selling a home, *MUST*

    a. get compensated by the seller.

    b. disclose the agency representation to both buyer and seller.

    c. do both a and b.

    d. do neither a nor b.

15. A fiduciary relationship exists between

    a. a broker and his or her principal.

    b. a seller and buyer.

    c. both a and b.

    d. neither a nor b.

16. A seller's listing agent is required to

    a. reveal confidential information received from the other party.

    b. disclose to a buyer all material facts known affecting value.

    c. accomplish both a and b.

    d. accomplish neither a nor b.

17. A dual agent *MUST*

    a. tell the buyer that the seller will accept less.

    b. tell the seller that the buyer will pay more.

    c. require compensation from both buyer and seller.

    d. do none of the above.

18. Agents could be held personally liable if they

    a. claimed to be acting as a principal.

    b. made false representations upon the direction of their principal.

    c. exceeded their authority.

    d. did any of the above.

19. An agent exceeds a secret limitation in the agency agreement while dealing with a third party. Which statement would be correct?

    a. The agent could be personally liable to the principal.

    b. The third party could hold the principal liable for the agent's action.

    c. Both a and b are correct.

    d. Both a and b are not correct.

20. Which is *TRUE* about real estate agents' liability?

    a. An agent will always be liable for disobeying a principal's instructions.

    b. An agent will not be liable for a tort committed at the direction of the principal.

    c. The principal will never be liable for acts of the agent after termination of the agency.

    d. An agent can be held liable for a tort committed by the agent during the agency.

21. When an agent commits a tort while carrying out agency duties, the

    a. principal has no liability for the tort.

    b. principal would not be liable if the principal told the agent not to commit any torts.

    c. agent is exonerated from liability for the tort because the act was committed in an agency capacity.

    d. agent would be personally liable for the tort.

22. When broker Clyde died, he had 36 exclusive listings. The executor of his estate, who was also a broker, wanted to continue the business until it could be sold. The executor *MUST*

    a. notify the owners that he or she has taken over the duties of broker Clyde.

    b. obtain Department of Real Estate approval for the substitution.

    c. renegotiate all listings.

    d. record his or her authority.

23. All these events would terminate an agency *EXCEPT*

    a. the death of a corporate officer of the agent's principal.

    b. agreement of the parties.

    c. renunciation by the principal.

    d. extinction of the subject matter.

24. An agency for a stated period of time would be terminated prior to the expiration date by all these *EXCEPT*

    a. termination by the principal without cause.

    b. termination by the agent.

    c. refusal of the principal to accept an offer.

    d. destruction of the subject matter of the agency.

25. A principal *CANNOT* unilaterally terminate an agency when

    a. the agency is a written agreement.

    b. the agency is coupled with an interest.

    c. the principal has received benefits from the agency.

    d. consideration is due the agent.

CHAPTER THREE

DUTIES AND RESPONSIBILITIES OF LICENSEES

■ KEY TERMS

"as is"	independent contractor	puffing
blind ad	latent defects	rent skimming
Cartwright Act	market allocation	respondeat superior
caveat emptor	Megan's Law	secret profit
Easton v. Strassburger	misrepresentation	Sherman Antitrust Act
employee	Natural Hazards	subagents
ethics	Disclosure Statement	subordination clauses
finder's fee	net listing	tie-in agreements
franchise	option listing	Transfer Disclosure
fraud	patent defects	Statement
group boycotting	price fixing	

■ LAW AND ETHICS

Ethics is not the same as legality. What is legal could still be unethical, and in some instances, conduct that passes the test of being ethical could be regarded as being illegal.

Laws are enacted to set what was considered at the time to be the minimum standards of acceptable human behavior. **Ethics** go far beyond the law and determine not if an action is legal, but whether it is right or just.

Real estate licensees no longer simply can rely on the letter of the law in determining whether behavior is legal. They also must ask themselves if it is ethical. The time-tested method to determine if an action is ethical is to apply the golden rule. If you would not wish to be treated in a particular manner, you know it is not ethical.

Ethics often precedes the law. Actions that formerly were legal but unethical are now often illegal as well. Court decisions have been applying the precepts of ethics to activities in real estate and determining that legal duties exist where no duties formerly were recognized. Licensees who pursue an unethical course of action run the risk of having a court determine that they have breached a duty and are liable for the resulting damages, even though such action had been considered legal in the past.

For a full understanding of the duties of licensees, the relationship among licensees must be examined.

■ SALESPERSON STATUS

Employee Versus Independent Contractor

The sales agent working for a broker is often regarded by members of the public as an **employee** of the broker. Every real estate broker must have a written contract with a salesperson or broker associates.

Most sales agents contract as independent contractors working in a brokerage under a broker's supervision. The broker, not the sales agent, is really the principal's agent. The sales agent is the broker's agent authorized to obtain listings, negotiate sales contracts, and provide other real estate services to the brokerage clients.

An **independent contractor** is one who is engaged to perform a duty but is not under the direct control of the principal. An independent contractor is accountable only for results. Control is the determining factor when considering employee versus independent contractor status. An independent contractor is reimbursed for results and is not subject to control and direction regarding how those results are achieved.

Most real estate brokers use contracts that specify the salesperson is an independent contractor rather than an employee. They take this measure to avoid withholding income taxes and contributing to Social Security. The Internal Revenue Service will treat the real estate salesperson as an independent contractor if the following three criteria are met:

1. The salesperson is licensed as a real estate agent.

2. Reimbursement is based solely on sales, not on hours worked.

3. There is a written contract that specifies the salesperson shall be treated as an independent contractor for tax purposes.

The IRS treatment of a real estate salesperson as an independent contractor applies only to income tax withholding and Social Security contributions. It does not alter the employer-employee relationship for other purposes.

Brokers will often use independent contractors in an attempt to avoid liability for acts of agents or employees. Despite independent contractor agreements, real estate salespersons are considered employees as to liability for torts (wrongful acts), which were discussed in Chapter 2. The broker is liable for the torts of his or her employees within the scope of their employment. Likewise, independent contractor agreements do not appear to protect brokers from injury claims by salespersons under workers' compensation. Brokers are specifically exempt from unemployment compensation insurance requirements. Brokers, therefore, should obtain workers' compensation coverage.

Labor code Section 2802(a) requires that an employer indemnify his or her employee for all necessary expenditures or losses incurred by the employee in direct consequence of the discharge of his or her duties or in obeying the lawful instructions of the employer. Because the agent is an employee of the broker for real estate purposes, the labor code provisions apply.

Case Study

The case of *Barry v. Raskov* (1991) 232 C.A.3d 447 involved an investor who was induced to put $55,000 into a $175,000 second mortgage on a property subject to a first trust deed of $100,000. The broker's appraiser indicated a property value of $400,000. The loan broker earned a $30,000 commission on the transaction. After default, another appraisal set the value of the property at $98,000.

The court held Raskov (the loan broker) liable for the torts of the appraiser. The court held that the fact that the appraiser may have been an independent contractor did not protect Raskov as Section 10232.5 of the Business and Professions Code requires the broker to give potential lenders a statement of the estimated fair value of the property. This duty cannot be delegated.

Note: The court refused to award punitive damages because it did not feel the evidence of fraud was clear and convincing.

Grubb & Ellis Company v. Spengler (1983) 143 C.A.3d 890 indicates that real estate salespersons are not entitled to minimum wages or unemployment compensation.

Section 10177(h) of the Business and Professions Code requires that brokers supervise their salespeople. Exercise of supervision precludes an independent contractor relationship. Therefore, a salesperson is an employee of his or her broker regardless of what the contract with the broker claims the relationship to be [*Payne v. White House Properties Inc.* (1980) 112 C.A.3d 465].

Formerly, the broker had a duty to review contracts prepared by salespersons within five days. This has been replaced by a "reasonable supervision policy."

WEB LINK @

A salesperson who has a commission dispute with his or her broker could, as an employee, take the dispute to the state labor commissioner in the Department of Industrial Relations. (*www.dir.ca.gov*)

While a salesperson can be compensated only by his or her own broker, a salesperson can be compensated directly from an escrow company if the broker issues specific instructions on a case-by-case basis for such direct payment.

Because a broker can be held liable for the torts of his or her salespeople within the scope of employment (the doctrine of **respondeat superior**), the broker should ascertain that all salespersons carry and maintain adequate automobile insurance coverage. In addition, brokers should strongly consider maintaining a high-limit general liability policy as well as an errors and omissions policy (malpractice) that covers the broker and all employees for negligence but not for intentional acts, such as misrepresentation. Salespeople may obtain their own errors and emissions policy if not covered by their broker.

Due to their potential liability, many brokers astutely check references and past employers of prospective salespeople. A salesperson who places his or her own interests above honesty to all parties could mean financial ruin for his or her broker.

Franchisees

A **franchise** is a right to operate under a common name and marketing plan. Many large real estate firms are franchises.

Franchisees ordinarily are independent contractors, and the franchisor is not liable for the wrongful acts of the franchisee. If, however, the actions of the franchisor and franchisee are such that third parties could assume that the franchisee is an agent, the franchisor could be held liable for the acts of the franchisee. The franchisor should, therefore, make certain that advertising clearly reveals that the franchisee is an independent operator.

■ AGENT'S DUTIES TO THE PRINCIPAL

An agent's primary responsibility is to the principal, ordinarily the owner of property listed for sale or lease (although the principal could be the buyer alone or both buyer and seller under a dual agency).

In listing property, the agent has a duty to ascertain the value of the property. An agent could be held liable for suggesting a sales price that was too low and could not be justified by acceptable appraisal methods. Even if the owners suggest a sales price, the agent, as a real estate specialist, has a duty to provide the owner with a supported opinion of value. An agent could not knowingly arrange a sale of the principal's property at an amount significantly less than market value and escape liability with the defense that the owner set the price and did not ask the agent what the property was worth.

An agent must protect his or her principal. Sharp operators often seek to trade property of dubious value or to get sellers to accept offers that are not what they appear to be and are not in the sellers' best interests. The owner must be warned about offers with **subordination clauses**. Subordination clauses allow later loans to take priority over seller financing and endanger the seller's security in the property. They allow the purchaser to wipe out the seller's security interest by placing priority liens against the property. The owner also must be warned about exchanges involving trust deeds on other properties and about any transaction in which the purchaser will end up receiving cash.

Another fraudulent activity is **rent skimming**, where a purchaser takes possession with little if any down payment, but promising the seller to be "cashed out" in a short period of time. Usually, the false promise involves the close of a nonexistent escrow. The buyer then rents the property, keeping rent receipts and making no payments. The definition of rent skimming has now been expanded to include collecting rents and deposits for property not owned or controlled by the landlord (protection for tenants) (Civil Code Section 890).

In general, the agent must caution the seller about any transaction in which the seller's interests are in any way endangered.

The agent must protect the principal from the fraud of others. In exchange situations the broker should make no representation about value that has not been appraised adequately, and the agent should provide the basis for the appraisal. The agent should suggest that expert help be obtained for situations beyond the agent's ability.

> **Case Study**
> In the case of *Schoenberg v. Romike Properties* (1967) 251 C.A.2d 154, a real estate agent induced the plaintiffs to part with valuable property in exchange for worthless security. The defendants told the owner that the buyer's security was better than taking security on the property sold. The agent failed to inform the owner that no investigation of the value of the security taken was made and that the agent had no knowledge of its true value. The agent had accepted an appraisal made for the owner that set value at ten times the real value. The court held that the plaintiffs had a right to rely on the defendants' statements and had no duty to make an independent investigation. The defendants' actions were held to be, at the very least, culpable negligence, and the buyer's fraud was held not to excuse that negligence.

The agent has a duty to reveal all pertinent information. For example, in a transaction where the seller is financing the buyer, the fact that the buyer borrowed the down payment could be pertinent. The agent should not make statements about the creditworthiness of the buyer unless such statements can be supported by fact. As protection from later owner claims of credit misrepresentation, the agent should arrange for a credit report on the purchaser to be obtained.

An agent must disclose all offers, including oral offers. The agent must keep the principal informed on all matters likely to influence decision making. Included would be offers received after an offer has been accepted, right up to the close of escrow. However, acceptance of a second offer after a first offer has already been accepted and should be conditioned on the seller's release from the first offer. Such a second offer is called a *backup offer*.

If acceptance of an offer is not in the principal's best interests, the agent must be careful not to encourage its acceptance. An agent could be liable for abusive pressure on a principal. Present case law does not indicate that an agent has an affirmative duty to recommend rejection of offers the agent believes to be unreasonable. However, because of the fiduciary relationship between the agent and the principal, a future decision about this duty is conceivable.

The agent cannot make a **secret profit**. The agent works for the principal and is entitled only to the compensation agreed on. The fact that the principal received a good price and was treated fairly is immaterial. The principal is entitled to any secret profit the agent receives. As an example, if the agent were in fact the purchaser through secret control of a corporation that purchased the property, the agent would have to give up the profit made on the subsequent resale. In addition, the agent would have to return any commission received because the agent breached his or her fiduciary duty.

If a buyer intends to relist the property or another property with the agent, the agent has a duty to reveal the fact that the owner's acceptance of an offer would put the agent in a position of being able to earn another commission.

The agent has a duty of confidentiality. The seller's agent could be held liable for revealing to a purchaser without the owner's authorization information that weakens the principal's bargaining ability. The agent's duty of confidentiality continues even after the expiration of the agency. An agent who later uses confidential information obtained through the agency relationship to the detriment of the former principal is breaching his or her fiduciary duty.

An agent could be liable for negligence in drafting an agreement and should consider this potential liability before attempting to draft any agreement or make major modifications to a printed contract. Obtaining professional legal assistance should be considered. An agent must avoid the unauthorized practice of law. An agent's duty does not extend to giving tax advice to buyers and sellers.

> ### Case Study
> The case of *Carleton v. Tortosa* (1993) 14 C.A.4th 745 concerned an experienced investor, Carleton, who listed property for sale. Carleton asked the agent how many days he had to reinvest the sale proceeds. The agent told the owner to "ask your tax person." Carleton was unable to reach his accountant, but the accountant's assistant told Carleton that he had 45 days. After the sale, Carleton learned he owed approximately $34,000 in taxes. Carleton sued the agent for professional negligence in failing to recognize a tax-deferred exchange situation. The Court of Appeal emphasized that a real estate agent has no duty to give tax advice. The listing statement, "A real estate agent is a person qualified to advise about real estate. If legal or tax advice is desired, consult a competent professional," strengthened the agent's defense.
>
> *Note*: If the agent had given tax advice, the agent could have been found negligent and liable for damages.

Net Listings

Under a **net listing**, the agent's commission is all money received for a property over a net amount set in the listing. Illegal in a number of other states, net listings are legal in California. However, serious conflict-of-interest problems can arise. The broker is no longer working simply to consummate a sale but wants a sale at as much over the listing price as possible. In setting the net price, the agent's best interest therefore is served by as low a price as possible. That is contrary to the principal's best interests.

Prior to or at the time of acceptance of an offer on a net listing, the broker must disclose to the principal the amount of commission to be received [Business and Professions Code Section 10176(g)]. If the licensee makes an extraordinary profit from a net listing, the owner may claim that the agent, in helping to set the list price, was acting in a self-serving manner and therefore breached his or her duties of financial trust. A net listing could very well be an invitation to a lawsuit.

The ethical conflict of net listings, the danger of being successful without earning a fee as well as the greater likelihood of an expensive lawsuit and ill will has resulted in very few brokers being willing to accept a net listing.

Option Listings

In an **option listing** the broker takes a listing combined with an option to purchase. This places the broker in the dual role of agent and principal. To exercise the option, the agent would have to reveal all offers received. This probably extends to oral offers as well as written ones.

Section 10176(h) of the Business and Professions Code requires the agent to reveal fully, in writing, the amount of profit and to obtain the principal's written consent to the amount of profit. The withholding of approval could prevent the exercise of the option.

In a combined listing-option agreement, the broker also should make certain that the owner understands that the exercise of the option is at the broker's discretion.

The listing-option agreement is not a guaranteed sales agreement in which the broker agrees to purchase in the event a buyer is not found.

Agent as Buyer

When a licensee is acting as a principal, the agent should inform the buyers and sellers that he or she, while a licensed real estate agent, is dealing as a principal and not in an agency capacity.

Full disclosure could extend beyond revealing that the purchaser is an agent and is associated with the listing firm to revealing the motives or intentions of the purchaser. If the agent intends to purchase the property for resale, the agent should disclose not only that fact but also what the agent hopes to obtain and any possible purchasers then known to the agent. If the agent intends to do work on the property to make the property more valuable, the agent should disclose these intentions.

Many firms will not allow any of their salespeople or brokers to purchase office listings because they feel that the firm and purchaser also could be buying litigation. Because the agent has the duty to represent the owner and the owner's best interests, the principal should have the opportunity to use the expertise of the agent to the principal's advantage and not have the principal's property used by the agent in a self-serving manner. In purchasing an office listing, the agent appears to be putting self-interest above the interests of a client, which violates the agent's fiduciary duties. Courts are likely to determine that an agent was acting in a self-serving manner rather than protecting the interests of the principal if there is evidence that the purchase price was substantially below market value.

If the agent helped set the list price and purchased at the list price or less and then sold at a profit, a court very likely would determine that the agent purposely set the price too low. Action such as this could result in not only compensatory damages but punitive damages as well.

Even if the owner set the list price, the agent would have a duty of financial trust to inform the owner of the property's value. If the agent accomplished a rapid resale at a profit, the courts would be more likely to determine that the agent breached his or her duty of full disclosure. The courts could determine that the agent made a secret profit, which would then have to be turned over to the principal.

When property is purchased by an agent and resold at a profit, the courts are likely to burden the agent with proving that full disclosure has been made. As a means of protection, the agent should prepare a complete disclosure of all material facts, including his or her intentions, and have it signed by the sellers prior to the purchase agreement.

Even with full disclosure, courts could determine that undue influence was used to obtain an agreement based on the principal-agent relationship of trust. Additional protection against such claims would require that the seller obtain independent legal counsel and that the seller's attorney also receive all disclosures.

Disclosures also should be made when the purchaser is related to the agent by blood or marriage or connected by a strong business or social relationship. If an appearance of impropriety exists, courts are likely to determine that a duty was breached.

Even if an agent prevails in a lawsuit, a suit by a client can damage a firm's reputation and be costly in time and money.

Case Study

The case of *Horning v. Shilberg* (2005) 13 C.A.4th 197, involved a licensed broker, Horning who prepared a purchase agreement whereby Horning would buy Shilberg's property as a principal and receive 3 percent of the purchase price as compensation for services at close of escrow.

After a breach of contract, the appellate Court noted in its affirmation of the trial court, that although Shilberg breached the contract, "Horning suffered no damages because a broker acting as principal in a transaction is not entitled to receive a commission as a matter of law." Because Horning suffered no damages, the court ruled that Shilberg was the prevailing party entitled to attorney fees and costs.

Note: A real estate licensee acting in his or her own behalf in a real estate transaction is not acting as a broker within the meaning of Business and Professions Code 10131. A purported commission is simply a reduction in price to be paid.

■ AGENT'S DUTIES TO BUYERS

Caveat Emptor

Let the buyer beware was formerly a precept of business. It was the buyer's duty to inspect the property and his or her own fault if there were any problems with the property.

Caveat Emptor is not the law of California, which requires disclosure of known defects. While ignorance was once bliss in that an agent did not have to disclose what the agent did not know, the agent now has duties to know about property offered for sale.

Case Study

In the case of *In re Estate of De Harte* (1961) 196 C.A.2d 452, a broker neglected to inform the administrator of an estate that the purchaser was his mother. Seventeen days after the sale was approved for $9,600, the purchaser entered into an agreement to sell the property for $11,900. The agreement was arranged by the broker. The court held that the good-faith duties of an agent preclude the agent from taking an adverse position. The court considered this sale a fraud on the court and the administrator. The sale and the prior confirmation of the broker's commission were vacated by the court.

The *Easton* Case

Now, not only must an agent disclose detrimental facts known about a property, but the case of *Easton v. Strassburger* (1984) 152 C.A.3d 90 determined that the agent also has an *affirmative duty* to find out material facts. A broker's duty of disclosure applies to facts that should be known as well as known facts. In this case, a home was sold for $170,000 through a broker. After the sale, the property suffered extreme damage in a landslide. The cost to repair was estimated at $213,000.

The court held that the duties of the real estate broker include "the affirmative duty to conduct a reasonably competent and diligent inspection of the residential property listed for sale and to disclose to prospective purchasers all facts materially affecting the value of the property that such an investigation would reveal."

In the *Easton* case a reasonable inspection would have revealed the problem because testimony indicated that

- a listing agent had seen netting on a hill used to repair a prior landslide,

- at least one agent knew the house was built on filled land, and

- the floor of the guesthouse was known not to be level.

The court in the *Easton* case indicated that its decision did not necessarily apply to commercial transactions, in which buyers are likely to be more sophisticated. (This was later confirmed in the *Smith v. Rickard* case referenced on the following page, which refused to extend *Easton* to commercial property.)

The California Supreme Court declined to hear the *Easton* case, which makes the decision an authority for the duties of licensees.

California Civil Code Section 2079 et seq. was passed to codify, clarify, and modify the duties imposed by the *Easton* decision. According to the *Department of Real Estate Bulletin*, the impact of the bill can be summarized as follows:

- It (the bill) mandates only a reasonably competent visual inspection of the property. The decision in *Easton* does not clearly indicate the type of inspection required.

- The duty to make the visual inspection is limited to residential real property of one to four units. The duty in *Easton* was limited to residential property.

- It defines the standard of care owed by a broker to a prospective purchaser as the degree of care a reasonably prudent real estate licensee would exercise and is measured by the degree of knowledge through education, experience, and examination required to obtain a real estate license under California law. *Easton* did not clearly define the measure of the standard of care owed by a broker to the buyer.

- It would apply the duty only to a broker who has entered into a written contract with the seller to find or obtain a buyer, and to a broker who acts in cooperation with such a (listing) broker to find and obtain a buyer. *Easton* did not limit its application to brokers with written contracts, nor did it impose a duty on cooperating brokers.

- It provides that the duty of inspection does not include or involve areas that are reasonably and normally inaccessible to such inspection or to inspection of common areas in common-interest subdivisions if the seller or broker supplies the prospective buyer with the documents and information specified in Civil Code Section 1360. *Easton* did not address the issue of the scope of the inspection.

- It established a two-year statute of limitations that runs from the date of recordation, close of escrow, or occupancy, whichever occurs first.

- It provides that the buyer or prospective buyer has a duty to exercise reasonable care to protect himself or herself, including knowledge of adverse facts that are known to or within the diligent attention and observation of the buyer or prospective buyer. *Easton* stated that a buyer has a duty to make a reasonable inspection but did not limit its application to cases where the facts were not known but determinable by a diligent inspection or observation by the buyer.

- Although not directly related to the duties imposed under *Easton*, the bill provides that no professional liability insurer may exclude under its policy coverage for liability arising as a result of a breach of the duty established by the bill and the *Easton* decision.

In the case of *Smith v. Rickard* (1989) 205 C.A.3d 1354, the court indicated that the affirmative duty to conduct a reasonable inspection does not extend to non-residential or agricultural property.

Oral and Written Disclosures

The duty of a seller to disclose relevant facts concerning the property for sale can be found in California statutes, case law, and real estate law.

Section 1102 of the Civil Code requires that a seller of one to four residential units provide a written disclosure of known property defects to a purchaser. To comply with this disclosure requirement, the California Association of REALTORS® has developed the Real Estate Transfer Disclosure Statement.

Transfer Disclosure Statement

Shown in Figure 3.1, the **Real Estate Transfer Disclosure Statement (TDS)** requires sellers to disclose defects that are known to them. The seller certifies that the information given is true and correct to the seller's knowledge. Defects are not limited to the physical aspects of the property but also include items such as zoning violations and nuisances in the area. The seller's agent and cooperating agent (if applicable) also execute this disclosure statement, indicating the existence of defects based on a reasonable competent and diligent visual inspection of the accessible areas of the property. The form also advises the purchasers that they may wish to obtain professional advice or their own inspection of the property.

Case Study

The case of *Realmuto v. Gagnard* (2003) 110 C.A.4th 193 involved two investors who signed a purchase contract to buy a residence for $683,000 with the intention of assigning the property to an Indian tribe for a casino. Because the tribe never agreed to buy the property, the buyers did not complete their purchase. The seller sued the buyers for specific performance to force the buyers to complete the purchase (the liquidated damages clause in the purchase agreement was not initialed by the parties). The purchasers responded that the seller had never delivered the TDS as required by Civil Code 1102 for sellers of one to four residential units.

The superior court granted summary judgment for the buyers because the TDS had never been delivered and failure to deliver cannot be waived. The Court of Appeal affirmed.

"The delivery of a TDS is a nonwaivable condition precedent to the buyer's duty of performance." The buyer not requesting a TDS cannot be construed as a waiver. The court noted that after delivery of the TDS, the buyer has three days to rescind the sale.

Note: Specific performance was likely sought because the purchase price was significantly greater than the value of the property as a residence.

The disclosure of known facts includes any negative fact that would be likely to influence a purchaser's decision. The presence of minority group members in the area is not considered a detrimental fact and should not be revealed. In fact, providing such information to a buyer likely would be considered steering, which would be a violation of the Civil Rights Act of 1968.

Case Study

In the case of *Michel v. Moore & Associates* (2007) 156 C.A. 4th 756, Kirkpatrick was an agent for Larry Moore & Associates and made a prelisting inspection of a home, noting pool cracks. The listing was not awarded to Kirkpatrick but given six months later to Fred Sands. Buyer Michel made an offer through Larry Moore & Associates. Kirkpatrick, a transaction coordinator at Larry Moore & Associates, reviewed the transfer disclosure statement but did not include information on the pool based on his prior inspection. Cracks later appeared in the house and pool. A soil report revealed settling of 3½ inches. Costs to repair property would be $500,000. Michel sued the seller, Fred Sands, and Larry Moore. The seller went bankrupt, Fred Sands settled for $50,000, and the case against Larry Moore & Associates went to trial. The jury decided in favor of Larry Moore & Associates, ruling they did not conceal a material fact and did not fail to reveal material facts disclosed by a reasonably competent visual inspection.

The Court of Appeal reversed and ordered the case retried, holding that the jury should have been instructed as to negligent concealment. While a broker could conduct a competent inspection and reveal all material facts, the broker still could be liable as to fiduciary duty to fail to disclose other finds that the broker knew or should have known.

Note: This case expands broker liability for disclosure beyond the T.D.S. to knowledge gained from other sources.

The Real Estate Transfer Disclosure Statement is not required for business and income property. In the sale of income property or business opportunities, reliance by the buyer on false information likely could result in a lawsuit involving the broker. The broker, whenever possible, should attempt to verify figures from the owner's income tax returns and/or sales tax reports. The broker should never report income and expense figures as fact but should state that they come only from the owner and should note if and how they were verified.

An agent cannot avoid full disclosure by using words such as "**as is**" in the sale of residential property. "As is" means the property is being sold in its present condition and the seller will not pay for any repairs. Courts generally have held that "as is" applies only to specific named items or to obvious defects that would be seen by a buyer (**patent defects**). Courts have held that "as is" does not protect an agent from known **latent defects**—those unlikely to be disclosed by an inspection. Exceptions include probate, tax, and foreclosure sales where the sale may be "as is."

If a seller required disclosure is received by the buyer after execution of a purchase agreement, the buyer has three days after delivery in person (five days after mail delivery) to terminate the offer or agreement.

FIGURE 3.1

Real Estate Transfer Disclosure Statement

REAL ESTATE TRANSFER DISCLOSURE STATEMENT
(Statutory Form)

THIS FORM FOR USE
IN CALIFORNIA ONLY

Real Estate Forms
Since 1966

THIS DISCLOSURE STATEMENT CONCERNS THE REAL PROPERTY SITUATED IN THE CITY OF _____,
COUNTY OF _____, STATE OF CALIFORNIA, DESCRIBED AS _____

THIS STATEMENT IS A DISCLOSURE OF THE CONDITION OF THE ABOVE DESCRIBED PROPERTY IN COMPLIANCE WITH SECTION 1102 OF
THE CIVIL CODE AS OF (DATE) _____. IT IS NOT A WARRANTY OF ANY KIND BY THE SELLER(S) OR ANY AGENT(S)
REPRESENTING ANY PRINCIPAL(S) IN THIS TRANSACTION, AND IS NOT A SUBSTITUTE FOR ANY INSPECTIONS OR WARRANTIES THE
PRINCIPAL(S) MAY WISH TO OBTAIN.

I. COORDINATION WITH OTHER DISCLOSURE FORMS

This Real Estate Transfer Disclosure Statement is made pursuant to Section 1102 of the Civil Code. Other statutes require disclosures,
depending upon the details of the particular real estate transaction (for example: special study zone and purchase-money liens on residential
property).

Substituted Disclosures: The following disclosures and other disclosures required by law, including the Natural Hazard Disclosure Report/Statement
that may include airport annoyances, earthquake, fire, flood, or special assessment information, have or will be made in connection with this real
estate transfer, and are intended to satisfy the disclosure obligations on this form, where the subject matter is the same:

☐ Inspection reports completed pursuant to the contract of sale or receipt for deposit.

☐ Additional inspection reports or disclosures: _____

II. Seller's information

The Seller discloses the following information with the knowledge that even though this is not a warranty, prospective Buyers may rely on
this information in deciding whether and on what terms to purchase the subject property. Seller hereby authorizes any agent(s) representing
any principal(s) in this transaction to provide a copy of this statement to any person or entity in connection with any actual or anticipated sale
of the property.

**THE FOLLOWING ARE REPRESENTATIONS MADE BY THE SELLER(S) AND ARE NOT THE REPRESENTATIONS OF THE AGENT(S), IF ANY. THIS
INFORMATION IS A DISCLOSURE AND IS NOT INTENDED TO BE PART OF ANY CONTRACT BETWEEN THE BUYER AND SELLER.**

Seller ☐ is, ☐ is not occupying the property.

A. The subject property has the items checked below (read across): *

☐ Range	☐ Oven	☐ Microwave
☐ Dishwasher	☐ Trash Compactor	☐ Garbage Disposal
☐ Washer/Dryer Hookups		☐ Rain Gutters
☐ Burglar Alarms	☐ Carbon Monoxide Device(s)	☐ Fire Alarm
☐ T.V. Antenna	☐ Satellite Dish	☐ Intercom
☐ Central Heating	☐ Central Air Conditioning	☐ Evaporator Cooler(s)
☐ Wall/Window Air Conditioning	☐ Sprinklers	☐ Public Sewer System
☐ Septic Tank	☐ Sump Pump	☐ Water Softener
☐ Patio/Decking	☐ Built-in Barbecue	☐ Gazebo
☐ Sauna		
☐ Hot Tub ☐ Locking Safety Cover	☐ Pool ☐ Child Resistant Barrier	☐ Spa ☐ Locking Safety Cover
☐ Security Gate(s)	☐ Automatic Garage Door Opener(s)	☐ Number Remote Controls _____
☐ Garage: ☐ Attached	☐ Not Attached	☐ Carport
☐ Pool/Spa Heater: ☐ Gas	☐ Solar	☐ Electric
☐ Water Heater: ☐ Gas		
☐ Water Supply: ☐ City	☐ Well	☐ Private Utility, or
☐ Gas Supply: ☐ Utility	☐ Bottled	Other _____
☐ Window Screens	☐ Window Security Bars,	
	☐ Quick Release Mechanism on Bedroom Windows	

Exhaust Fan(s) in _____ 220 Volt Wiring in _____ Fireplace(s) in _____

Gas Starter _____ Roof(s): Type: _____ Age: _____ (approx.)

Other: _____

Are there, to the best of your (Seller's) knowledge, any of the above that are not in operating condition? ☐ Yes ☐ No. If yes, then describe.
(Attach additional sheets if necessary.): _____

* Installation of a listed appliance, device, or amenity is not a precondition of sale or transfer of the dwelling. The carbon monoxide device, garage door
opener, or child-resistant pool barrier may not be in compliance with the safety standards relating to, respectively, carbon monoxide device standards of
Chapter 8 (commencing with Section 13260) of Part 2 of Division 12 of, automatic reversing device standards of Chapter 12.5 (commencing with Section
19890) of Part 3 of Division 13 of, or the pool safety standards of Article 2.5 (commencing with Section 115920) of Chapter 5 of Part 10 of Division 104
of, the Health and Safety Code. Window security bars may not have quick-release mechanisms in compliance with the 1995 edition of the California
Building Standards Code.

Buyer acknowledges receipt of a copy of this page. [_____] [_____] Date _____

Page 1 of 3

FORM 110.21 CAL (07-2010) COPYRIGHT BY PROFESSIONAL PUBLISHING, NOVATO, CA

Form generated by: **TrueForms™**   www.TrueForms.com   800-499-9612

PROFESSIONAL PUBLISHING

Source: Professional Publishing

FIGURE 3.1
Real Estate Transfer Disclosure Statement, Continued

Property Address _____

B. Are you (Seller) aware of any significant defects/malfunctions in any of the following? ☐ Yes ☐ No. If yes, check appropriate box(es) **below.**

☐ Interior Walls ☐ Ceilings ☐ Floors ☐ Exterior Walls ☐ Insulation ☐ Roof(s) ☐ Windows ☐ Doors ☐ Foundation ☐ Slab(s) ☐ Driveways ☐ Sidewalks ☐ Walls/Fences ☐ Electrical Systems ☐ Plumbing/Sewers/Septics ☐ Other Structural Components (Describe: _____
_____).

If any of the above is checked, explain. (Attach additional sheets if necessary):

_____
_____
_____
_____
_____
_____
_____
_____

C. Are you (Seller) aware of any of the following:

1. Substances, materials, or products which may be an environmental hazard such as, but not limited to, asbestos, formaldehyde, radon gas, lead-based paint, mold, fuel or chemical storage tanks, and contaminated soil or water on the subject property . . . . ☐ Yes ☐ No
2. Features of the property shared in common with adjoining landowners, such as walls, fences, and driveways, whose use or responsibility for maintenance may have an effect on the subject property . . . . ☐ Yes ☐ No
3. Any encroachments, easements or similar matters that may affect your interest in the subject property . . . . ☐ Yes ☐ No
4. Room additions, structural modifications, or other alterations or repairs made without necessary permits . . . . ☐ Yes ☐ No
5. Room additions, structural modifications, or other alterations or repairs not in compliance with building codes . . . . ☐ Yes ☐ No
6. Fill (compacted or otherwise) on the property or any portion thereof . . . . ☐ Yes ☐ No
7. Any settling from any cause, or slippage, sliding, or other soil problems . . . . ☐ Yes ☐ No
8. Flooding, drainage or grading problems . . . . ☐ Yes ☐ No
9. Major damage to the property or any of the structures from fire, earthquake, floods, or landslides . . . . ☐ Yes ☐ No
10. Any zoning violations, nonconforming uses, violations of "setback" requirements . . . . ☐ Yes ☐ No
11. Neighborhood noise problems or other nuisances . . . . ☐ Yes ☐ No
12. CC&R's or other deed restrictions or obligations . . . . ☐ Yes ☐ No
13. Homeowners' Association which has any authority over the subject property . . . . ☐ Yes ☐ No
14. Any "common area" (facilities such as pools, tennis courts, walkways, or other areas co-owned in undivided interest with others) . . . . ☐ Yes ☐ No
15. Any notices of abatement or citations against the property . . . . ☐ Yes ☐ No
16. Any lawsuits by or against the Seller threatening to or affecting this real property, including any lawsuits alleging a defect or deficiency in this real property or "common areas" (facilities such as pools, tennis courts, walkways, or other areas co-owned in undivided interest with others) . . . . ☐ Yes ☐ No
17. Any Mello-Roos special tax levy lien or fixed lien assessment pursuant to Improvement Bond Act of 1915 on subject property. (If yes, disclosure notice should be obtained from levying agency.) . . . . ☐ Yes ☐ No
18. Any former federal or state ordnance locations (as defined in C.C. 1102.15) within one mile of the subject property . . . . ☐ Yes ☐ No
19. Whether subject property is affected by or zoned to allow certain manufacturing or commercial or airport use as set forth in CCP 731a . . . . ☐ Yes ☐ No
20. An order from a local health officer prohibiting the use or occupancy of portions of the property contaminated by methamphetamine. (If so, a copy of the order must be delivered to any prospective purchaser.) . . . . ☐ Yes ☐ No

If the answer to any of these is yes, explain. (Attach additional sheets if necessary.): _____
_____

D. 1. The Seller certifies that the property, as of the close of escrow, will be in compliance with Section 13113.8 of the Health and Safety Code by having operable smoke detectors(s) which are approved, listed, and installed in accordance with the State Fire Marshal's regulations and applicable local standards.

2. The Seller certifies that the property, as of the close of escrow, will be in compliance with Section 19211 of the Health and Safety Code by having the water heater tank(s) braced, anchored, or strapped in place in accordance with applicable law.

Seller certifies that the information herein is true and correct to the best of the Seller's knowledge as of the date signed by the Seller.

Seller _____ Date _____ Seller _____ Date _____

Buyer acknowledges receipt of a copy of this page. [_____] [_____] Date _____

Page 2 of 3
FORM 110.22 CAL (07-2010) COPYRIGHT BY PROFESSIONAL PUBLISHING, NOVATO, CA

PROFESSIONAL PUBLISHING

Form generated by: **TrueForms™**   www.TrueForms.com   800-499-9612

Source: Professional Publishing

FIGURE 3.1
Real Estate Transfer Disclosure Statement, Continued

Property Address _____

III. AGENT'S INSPECTION DISCLOSURE (Listing Agent)
(To be completed only if the Seller is represented by an agent in this transaction.)
THE UNDERSIGNED, BASED ON THE ABOVE INQUIRY OF THE SELLER(S) AS TO THE CONDITION OF THE PROPERTY AND BASED ON A REASONABLY COMPETENT AND DILIGENT VISUAL INSPECTION OF THE ACCESSIBLE AREAS OF THE PROPERTY IN CONJUNCTION WITH THAT INQUIRY, STATES THE FOLLOWING:
☐ Agent notes no items for disclosure.
☐ Agent notes the following items:

_____
_____
_____
_____
_____
_____

Agent (Broker
Representing Seller) _____ By _____ Date _____
                (Please Print)   (Associate Licensee or Broker Signature)

IV. AGENT'S INSPECTION DISCLOSURE (Selling Agent)
(To be completed only if the agent who has obtained the offer is other than the agent above.)
THE UNDERSIGNED, BASED ON A REASONABLY COMPETENT AND DILIGENT VISUAL INSPECTION OF THE ACCESSIBLE AREAS OF THE PROPERTY, STATES THE FOLLOWING:
☐ Agent notes no items for disclosure.
☐ Agent notes the following items:

_____
_____
_____
_____
_____
_____

Agent (Broker
Obtaining the Offer) _____ By _____ Date _____
                (Please Print)   (Associate Licensee or Broker Signature)

V. BUYER(S) AND SELLER(S) MAY WISH TO OBTAIN PROFESSIONAL ADVICE AND/OR INSPECTIONS OF THE PROPERTY AND TO PROVIDE FOR APPROPRIATE PROVISIONS IN A CONTRACT BETWEEN BUYER(S) AND SELLER(S) WITH RESPECT TO ANY ADVICE /INSPECTIONS/DEFECTS.

I/WE ACKNOWLEDGE RECEIPT OF A COPY OF THIS STATEMENT.

Seller _____ Date _____ Buyer _____ Date _____

Seller _____ Date _____ Buyer _____ Date _____

Agent (Broker
Representing Seller) _____ By _____ Date _____
                (Please Print)   (Associate Licensee or Broker Signature)
Agent (Broker
Obtaining the Offer) _____ By _____ Date _____
                (Please Print)   (Associate Licensee or Broker Signature)

SECTION 1102.3 OF THE CIVIL CODE PROVIDES A BUYER WITH THE RIGHT TO RESCIND A PURCHASE CONTRACT FOR AT LEAST THREE DAYS AFTER THE DELIVERY OF THIS DISCLOSURE IF DELIVERY OCCURS AFTER THE SIGNING OF AN OFFER TO PURCHASE. IF YOU WISH TO RESCIND THE CONTRACT, YOU MUST ACT WITHIN THE PRESCRIBED PERIOD.

A REAL ESTATE BROKER IS QUALIFIED TO ADVISE ON REAL ESTATE. IF YOU DESIRE LEGAL ADVICE, CONSULT YOUR ATTORNEY.

Page 3 of 3
FORM 110.23 CAL (07-2010) COPYRIGHT BY PROFESSIONAL PUBLISHING, NOVATO, CA

PROFESSIONAL PUBLISHING

Form generated by: **TrueForms™**   www.TrueForms.com   800-499-9612

Source: Professional Publishing

Mobile Home Transfers

A mobile home transfer disclosure statement, similar to the one- to four-unit residential transfer disclosure statement, is required upon transfer of a personal property mobile home or manufactured home. The agents also are required to make a visual inspection.

Natural Hazards

The transferor of one to four residential units built before January 1, 1960, must give a buyer a booklet entitled *Homeowner Guide to Earthquake Safety* prior to the transfer and disclose any known deficiencies, such as absence of anchor bolts, unreinforced masonry walls, unanchored water heater, etc. The seller or his agent must also complete a **Natural Hazards Disclosure Statement** that indicates if the property is in a special flood hazard area, an area of potential flooding, a very high fire hazard severity zone, a wildlife area that may contain substantial fire risks and hazards, an earthquake fault zone, or a seismic hazard zone.

Case Study

In the case of *Geernaent v. Mitchell* (1995) 31 C.A.4th 601, a seller indicated that there were no foundation problems and modifications made were to code. True facts were apparently concealed in order to make the sale. The house was sold and then resold. The buyer sued the original owner for misrepresentation. The trial court held that homeowners could not sue a prior owner for alleged fraudulent misrepresentations because the misrepresentations were not made directly to the plaintiffs.

But the appeals court held that a seller can be liable to subsequent buyers for misrepresentations made to previous buyers even if there is no privity of contract (privity of contract refers to a mutual relationship as to the contract, such as being a party to the contract). The court pointed out that the plaintiff still had the burden of showing that defendants could reasonably expect subsequent purchasers to rely on their misrepresentation.

It is in the best interests of the seller as well as the buyer for the seller to disclose all potential problems of the property. Revealing possible problem areas not only alerts the buyers but also protects the seller against later claims of misrepresentation.

Death on the Premises

After three years, an agent need not disclose a death or the cause of death of a prior occupant. Civil Code 1710.2 states, "No cause of action arises against an owner of real property or his or her agent, or any agent of a transferee for failure to disclose the occurrence of an occupant's death upon the real estate or the manner of death where the death has occurred more than three years prior to the date the transferee offers to purchase . . ." Civil Code Section 1710.2 does not actually require disclosing a death on the premises within the three years before the sale. However, many agents feel that such disclosure is implied by the statute and they should disclose death by murder or suicide within three years of the sale.

If a buyer inquired as to any deaths on the property or cause of death, the agent would have to answer truthfully as to any information the agent had. A fake statement could subject an agent to liability even though the agent had no duty to disclose the information.

Because a buyer's agent has greater disclosure obligations to a buyer, a court could determine that deaths or assaults on the premises, that could reasonably be expected to influence a purchase, must be disclosed.

> **Case Study**
> The case of *Reed v. King* (1983) 145 C.A.3d 261 involved a sale in which the agent did not inform the purchaser that five murders had been committed in the house ten years earlier. The agent was held to have breached the duty of disclosure because the fact of the murders could have been expected to disturb a purchaser and could materially affect a property's value. The rule of the *Reed v. King* case has, however, now been modified by Civil Code Section 1710.2.

AIDS Disclosure

What facts need to be disclosed is an issue that is always evolving. For example, in recent years, the prevalence of AIDS (acquired immunodeficiency syndrome) in the United States has created a new dilemma for real estate agents. Should a broker reveal that a tenant or owner had AIDS or suspected AIDS? The risk of slander if the agent were mistaken and the question of whether the presence of AIDS is a material fact requiring disclosure were discussed at length within the real estate and legal professions. The situation was resolved by Civil Code Section 1710.2, which provides that neither the owner nor the agent shall be liable to the transferee for failing to disclose that an occupant was afflicted with or died of AIDS.

Opinion 95-907 of the California Attorney General indicates that an agent need not disclose the nearby location of a licensed care facility servicing six or fewer people (a larger facility might require disclosure).

WEB LINK @

Megan's Law

Megan's Law concerns the registration of sex offenders and making information regarding sex offenders available to the public. Civil Code Section 2079.10(a) now requires that every lease or rental agreement for residential real property and every contract for the sale of one to four residential units must include a specific notice informing consumers of the available public information regarding registered sex offenders at local police and sheriff offices, as well as at *www.meganslaw. ca.gov.*

> **Case Study**
> A broker neglected to inform a purchaser that there was a due-on-sale clause in a second trust deed being assumed. This clause required that the loan be repaid in full should the property be sold. The property subsequently was lost by foreclosure of the second trust deed. The court held that even though the agent might have believed the loan was assumable despite the due-on-sale clause, the agent breached a duty to inform the purchaser about the clause. The court awarded damages amounting to the difference between the purchase price and encumbrances (purchaser's equity), as well as expenses incurred to prevent foreclosure [*Pepitone v. Russo* (1997) 64 C.A.3d 685].

Other Disclosures

There are a number of other disclosures including the following:

- Mello-Roos bonds
- Farming area disclosure
- State tax withholding requirements
- Foreign investment in real property tax withholding
- Presence of carbon dioxide detectors
- Energy conservation and thermal insulation disclosure
- Importance of home inspection notice
- Smoke detector notice
- Homeowners' association disclosures
- Military ordnance locations
- Window security bar presence
- Water heater bracing
- Septic system disclosure
- Methamphetamine contamination order
- Industrial/airport disclosure
- Title insurance importance
- Supplemental tax bill disclosure
- Negotiability of real estate commission
- Sales price
- Structural pest control inspection and certification report
- Affiliated business arrangement disclosure

There are also a number of finance disclosures.

The California Department of Real Estate publishes a booklet on disclosures. It is available at no charge at *www.dre.ca.gov/pub_disclosures.html.*

The Unsophisticated Buyer

Court decisions seem to indicate that an agent has greater duties when dealing with an unsophisticated party than when dealing with a sophisticated party. With an unsophisticated buyer, the agent should ascertain that the purchaser fully understands the effect of balloon payments, points, and other matters that might not be obvious to such a buyer.

Case Study

The case of *Jue v. Smiser* (1994) 23 C.A.4th 312 involved a late disclosure. Buyers contracted to buy a home represented to have been designed by renowned architect Julia Morgan. The name Julia Morgan added to the prestige value of the property. Apparently, the sellers had some doubt as to their prior representation, because three days before the close of escrow, the sellers asked the buyers to sign a document acknowledging that there were no plans available that verified the architect. The buyers refused to sign but went through with the purchase. Then, discovering the house was not designed by Julia Morgan, the buyers sued the sellers and their broker for misrepresentation. The trial court held that there was no reliance on the misrepresentation because of the disclosure prior to the closing of escrow.

The Court of Appeal reversed the trial court holding that it is not necessary that there be continuing reliance until the contract is executed.

Note: While full disclosure of detrimental facts learned is required prior to closing, the disclosure might not be enough to avoid liability. In a case such as this, the last-minute disclosure could place buyers in a position where they would have to complete the purchase or be homeless.

Case Study

The case of *Salahutin v. Valley of Calif. Inc.* (1994) 24 C.A.4th 555 involved buyers who, in 1979, told a real estate agent that they wanted to buy a home that could eventually be divided into two lots (for each of their children). The agent found a home listed by another agent, and the MLS listing said "1 Acre+."

The agent knew that the Hillsborough property had to be at least 1 acre to allow a future lot split. In 1989, the buyers discovered that the lot contained only 0.998 acres, so it could not be split. The value of the parcel was $175,000 less than it would have been if a split were possible. The court held that the selling broker had a fiduciary duty either to investigate the size of the lot or to tell the buyer he had not done so, as size was of significant importance to the buyers.

Constructive fraud can occur when the broker is merely an innocent conduit of misinformation. The court applied damages based on the value at the time of discovery of the fraud rather than at the time of purchase. (The buyers paid only $274,000 in 1979, but it would have been worth $1,100,000 in 1989 if it could have been subdivided.)

Note: If any representation by the owner or listing broker is of importance to a buyer, the selling broker should check it out or disclose to the buyer that it is the representation of another, which he or she has not verified.

If an unsophisticated buyer requested property tax information, the agent probably would have the duty to explain that past property taxes are not indicative of what property taxes will be in the future because the property will be reassessed upon sale based on the sale price. The base tax will be 1 percent of sale price plus local assessments. The annual tax increase can be up to 2 percent.

Agents should avoid discouraging prospective buyers from obtaining professional help, such as an attorney or a fee appraiser, and should take care not to convey a false sense of urgency. Such actions would adversely affect a broker's defense in a lawsuit involving a breach of duty or fraud.

Even when an agent is not involved in aiding the buyer to obtain a loan, agents should warn unsophisticated buyers about predatory lending tactics that could lead to unnecessary expense and even foreclosure.

If an agent knows that a contemplated use is not allowed or is unlikely to be allowed because of zoning or other restrictions, the agent has an affirmative duty to tell the buyer.

Fraud, Misrepresentation, and Puffing

Agents may not use blind ads to attract buyers. A **blind ad** is one that fails to indicate that the advertiser is an agent and not a principal. (See Table 4.1 on page 106 for advertising requirements.)

Inducing the purchase of a particular property by giving false comparables could subject an agent to damages for fraud. Agents have been known to show overpriced listings to make the property they hope to sell appear to be a bargain. Courts conceivably could treat this practice as a fraudulent representation of value.

Fraud is intentional deceit to induce a party to act to his or her detriment. Courts might award punitive as well as compensatory damages for an agent's fraud. In addition, fraud could result in criminal prosecution.

> ### Case Study
> In *U.S. v. Peterson* (2008) 538 F 3d 1064, it was shown that a developer falsified 43 gift letters showing gifts to homebuyers of the 3 percent down payment necessary to obtain FHA insurance. The down payments were actually advanced by the developer to allow no-down-payment loans. The defendants were found guilty of making false material statements to a federal agency. Defendants were sentenced to 18 months in prison, fined $50,000, and ordered to pay restitution of over $1 million for losses suffered by HUD because of foreclosures.
>
> *Note:* Other developers have attempted to skirt the law by making gifts to charities that in turn would make gifts to the homebuyers.

An agent who showed a prospective buyer only a few units in an apartment complex probably would be implying that they were representative of all of the units. If in fact the units shown were only the few updated units, the broker's action might be considered fraud even though specific representations were not made.

Misrepresentation is the intentional or unintentional misstatement or concealment of a material fact. Misrepresentation could result in civil damages to compensate the injured party as well as other contractual remedies.

The case of *Ford v. Cournale* (1974) 36 C.A.3d 172 held that providing income data based on 100 percent occupancy was misrepresentation for which the broker could be held liable.

There is some question about the broker's liability to a buyer when repeating false information provided by the owner. If the broker knew or should have known the information was false, the broker likely would be liable. It is not known if the *Easton* decision could be expanded to extend to a duty to check facts provided by an owner. As minimum protection, when supplying facts that have not been verified, a broker should indicate the source of the facts and that they have not been verified.

Puffing is a statement of opinion that, while it may be optimistic, is not a statement of fact or a promise, that if false, would be misrepresentation or fraud. An example of such a statement would be, "You will be happy in this house."

This would not be misrepresentation or fraud even if you were not happy in the house as it is clearly the salesperson's opinion and not a guarantee. There can be a fine line between allowable puffing and misrepresentation or fraud. If an agent were to represent nearly worthless desert property as "a sound investment," a court could determine such a statement to be fraud or misrepresentation rather than mere puffing.

> **Case Study**
>
> The case of *Manderville v. PCG&S Group, Inc.* (2007) 146 C.A. 4th 1486 involved two couples who sought to buy property that could be split for two houses. The agent found a MLS property of 2.62 acres that stated, "1 acre min. lot size could be split." Because a previous MLS listing for the property did not indicate it could be split, the selling agent contacted the listing agents who prepared the MLS language. It was confirmed by the listing agent that the property could be split. An offer was made on a CAR purchase form titled, "Vacant Land Purchase Agreement and Joint Escrow Instructions." The form stated that the buyers and sellers were aware that the brokers did not guarantee "condition" of the property and gave the buyers 21 days to inspect the property. The buyers did not know the county general plan designator "4" required a 4-acre minimum lot size for splitting. The Superior Court granted summary judgment for the brokers ruling that the exculpatory language in the purchase contract absolved the brokers from liability.
>
> The Court of Appeal reversed ruling that neither the exculpatory language of the purchase contract, nor buyers failure to investigate the zoning as to lot splitting, bars their action for the listing brokers intentional misrepresentation (Civil Code Section 1668 bars exculpatory clauses from exempting anyone from his or her fraud).

Referral Fees

When someone is moving from the area, brokers often will recommend that he or she see a particular broker in the new area. The prospective buyer reasonably could believe that the broker is acting as a gratuitous agent in recommending someone who can best meet his or her needs. This often is not the case; the broker may in fact be recommending that the buyer see a particular broker because that broker will give the agent part of any commission upon any resulting sale. A case could be made that this fee is a secret profit being made by the presumed gratuitous agent of the buyer. If the courts agreed to this supposition, the buyer would be entitled to the secret profit paid to the agent. Brokers could protect themselves by making full disclosure of any financial arrangements they have with the recommended firm.

A real estate licensee may not offer premium gifts or anything of value to a purchaser or lender as an inducement to make a loan or buy a promissory note or sales contract. However, the restriction has been removed as to prospective borrowers. (Business and Professions Code Section 10236.1)

■ DUTIES TO OTHER BROKERS

A broker has no legal duty to cooperate with other brokers; however, brokers customarily cooperate with one another because doing so is in their best interests. The various associations serving the real estate business have codes of ethics and rules that help set standards for professional conduct. These are not laws, though statutes cover some of the same areas. The penalties for breaching these rules generally are fines or expulsion from the organization. If the exclusion of a broker from an organization would have a detrimental economic effect on that broker's business, then exclusion can be effected only for good cause.

WEB LINK @

The largest association of brokers is the National Association of REALTORS® (NAR). The state organization of NAR (*www.realtor.org*) is the California Association of REALTORS® (CAR) (*www.car.org*). The word REALTOR® is a trademark word, and it is a violation of the law for a person who is not a member of the NAR to use the REALTORS® designation. The same is true for Realtist, which denotes a member of the National Association of Real Estate Brokers. (*www.nareb.com.*)

The National Association of REALTORS® encourages arbitration of broker disputes, but brokers can sue one another in court.

To work with **subagents**, the broker must have the specific approval of the principal. If the listing authorizes subbrokers (subagents), an agency is created between the seller and the subbroker. The seller is liable to third persons for the subbroker's actions, and the subbroker has a fiduciary responsibility to the owner. (Listings that authorize the listing agent to make the property available to a multiple-listing service really authorize the creation of subagents.)

If a subbroker is appointed properly, the original agent is not responsible to third parties for the acts of the subbroker. If an agent appoints a subbroker without authority to do so, the subbroker is the agent of the listing broker and not of the principal. Because subagency makes the selling broker the agent of the seller, it provides no protection for the buyer. Therefore, cooperating brokers are unlikely to accept subagency. Subagency provisions have been removed from many listing forms.

A broker could be held liable to another broker if the first broker indicated that he or she had an exclusive-right-to-sell listing and the other broker obtained a buyer only to find there was no listing.

Multiple-listing services may not exclude listings that are not exclusive-right-to-sell listings. Such action would be an unreasonable restraint of trade, as would agreements setting minimum commissions among brokers.

Brokers have been known to tell owners that it is in their best interests to prohibit them from cooperating with other brokers. If the reason is that the property is highly saleable and the broker wants to avoid splitting a commission, then this prohibition would be self-serving. If it could be shown that the prohibition worked to the financial detriment of the owner because of offers that would otherwise have been received, the broker could be liable for damages.

Sherman Antitrust Act of 1890

The case of *Marin County Board v. Polsson* (1976) 16 C.3d 920 held that refusal to allow a broker to join the multiple-listing service is an antitrust violation. (The court also ruled that an MLS member need not be a member of the local REAL-TOR® organization.)

WEB LINK @

The **Sherman Antitrust Act** was enacted to prevent businesses from conspiring to control prices and/or competition. Penalties for violations include fines, damages, court costs, and up to three years' imprisonment. The act is enforced by the Federal Trade commission (*www.ftc.gov*).

Antitrust violations include the following four:

1. **Price-fixing.** It would be illegal for a group of brokers to agree on minimum commissions that they would charge.

2. **Market allocation.** Agreements of firms to divide a marketplace geographically or by type of service would be a violation because it would tend to reduce or eliminate competition.

3. **Group boycotting.** Firms may not agree to refuse to do business with a firm or individual. As an example, it would be a violation of the act for two or more firms to agree not to allow another firm to show their listings.

4. **Tie-in agreements.** Agreements that require a business to buy additional goods or services in order to get the goods or services desired would be illegal. An example of a tie-in agreement would be the requirement that the buyer agree to keep the property insured through a firm controlled by the broker as a condition of submitting the buyer's offer.

The **Cartwright Act** (Business & Professions Code 16720) is California's antitrust act that prohibits agreements restraining trade.

■ FEES TO NONLICENSEES

Although finder's fees payments by real estate licensees are not allowed in some states, a California real estate licensee can pay a referral or **finder's fee** to a nonlicensee for an introduction. However, the introduction must be the extent of the finder's involvement; the nonlicensee cannot quote prices, show property, negotiate the transaction, or perform any duty for which a license is required. A broker may not compensate an unlicensed finder who performs any act for which a license is required (Business and Professions Code Section 10137).

Case Study

Tenzer, a director of Superscope, was asked to find a buyer for property owned by the corporation. The president orally agreed to a 10 percent finder's fee, and Tenzer produced a buyer who purchased the property for $16 million. The corporation refused to pay Tenzer a finder's fee. After a summary judgment in favor of Superscope, the case was appealed to the California Supreme Court.

The court held that a finder without a written agreement may recover if the principal is estopped from pleading the statute of frauds.

The court held that if Tenzer was not otherwise obligated to reveal the names of the prospective purchaser and did so upon the verbal promise of a finder's fee, then Superscope would be estopped from raising the defense of the statute of frauds. While licensed brokers cannot get around the statute of frauds by claiming estoppel, Tenzer was not licensed. The supreme court indicated that the trial court should determine if Tenzer was a mere finder or participated in sale negotiations. If he participated, he would have had to have been licensed to collect a fee. The court also indicated that Tenzer could recover based on fraud if Superscope's president never intended to pay him.

Because the plaintiff's claim was based on equity, the court held that the plaintiff must show that the agreement was fair [*Tenzer v. Superscope, Inc.* (1985) 39 C.3d 18].

■ DUTY OF BUYERS

While sellers have a duty of disclosure, buyers have no corresponding duty to disclose material facts that they are aware of, such as why they are buying.

Case Study

The case of *Nussbaum v. Weeks* (1989) 214 C.A.3d 1589 involved a purchase of the plaintiff's land by the general manager of the water district. The sellers sued the buyer for failure to disclose the probability that the water district would increase the availability of water to the land purchased. The Court of Appeal, in reversing a superior court decision, held that a property buyer has no duty to disclose material facts to a seller, and that the buyer had no special duty as general manager of the water district to explain that the board of directors might vote to increase water supplies.

■ SUMMARY

In Chapter 2, you learned about agency rights and duties. This chapter expands the framework established by Chapter 2.

While our laws set the minimum standard of acceptable conduct, ethics go beyond the law to what *should* be. Understanding ethics is important to the real estate licensee because ethics precede the law. What apparently was legal, but unethical at the time of an action, might later be determined to have been illegal by our courts. Licensees who use the law alone as a standard of conduct could find themselves facing great future liability.

Employment contracts between brokers and salespersons often specify that the salesperson is an independent contractor. The reason for this type of contract is to avoid withholding tax and Social Security contributions by the broker. The Department of Real Estate, however, regards a salesperson to be an employee of the broker. The broker is liable for the wrongful acts of the salesperson within the scope of employment.

The agent's primary duty is to his or her principal. The agent's conduct must be governed by what is in the best interests of the principal. The agent not only must be honest with the principal, but also must protect the principal from the dishonest conduct of others. The agent also must be particularly careful to protect the principal's interests when the agent has an interest as well, such as in the case of a net listing, an option listing, or when the agent is also a buyer.

The agent's duty to buyers is much more than simply revealing anything detrimental about a property that the agent is aware of. The agent has an affirmative duty to conduct a reasonably competent and diligent inspection of residential property and to disclose to prospective purchasers all facts materially affecting the value of the property that such an investigation reveals. The seller of one to four residential units also has a duty to disclose known defects to a buyer. Both the seller and the broker must execute the Real Estate Transfer Disclosure Statement.

Neither the principal nor the agent can avoid liability by selling property "as is." "As is" applies only to obvious defects and offers no protection to agents and/or owners from hidden defects that they knew of, but failed to disclose.

Although brokers have no legal duty to cooperate with other brokers, they should be aware of the liabilities and responsibilities imposed by subagency.

The Sherman Antitrust Act makes it illegal for businesses to conspire to control prices or competition through price fixing, market allocation agreements, group boycotting, or tie-in agreements.

Buyers do not have the duty to disclose to sellers material facts that they are aware of.

■ DISCUSSION CASES

1. The sellers' broker obtained one termite report that indicated $971 worth of work was required. A second report indicating termite infestation, dry rot, and fungus estimated correction costs of $1,155. The broker did not disclose the second report to the buyers but provided for paying the buyers the cost of doing the work discovered on the first report. The buyers discovered the extensive dry rot and termite infestation when they moved in. **What is the liability of the broker?**

   Godfrey v. Steinpress (1982) 128 C.A.3d 154

2. Marcos, a minor, moved into the house his mother had purchased. After occupancy, an environmental test showed a dangerous level of mold spores. Marcos became ill and sued the real estate agents alleging breach of statutory duties. **Assuming there was negligence on the part of the agent, should Marcos be entitled to damages?**

   Coldwell Banker Residential Brokerage Co. Inc. v. Superior Court (2004) 117 C.A.4th 158

3. A multiple-listing service refused to accept any listings but exclusive-right-to-sell listings. **Was the action of the multiple-listing service proper?**

   People v. National Association of REALTORS® (1981) 120 C.A.3d 459

4. The defendant, a real estate salesman, failed to recommend a title search when the plaintiffs leased a chicken ranch with an option to purchase. The defendant, without actual knowledge, represented that one trust deed against the property existed and that the payments included interest. In fact there was a second trust deed and the payments on the first trust deed did not include the interest. The plaintiffs indicated that had they known of the condition of the title, they would not have entered into the lease agreement. **What problems does this case present?**

   Wilson v. Hisey (1957) 147 C.A.2d 433

5. A broker fraudulently represented to the purchaser that he was the agent of a property owner. He quoted a price of $1,000 more per acre than was being asked for a 72-acre-plus parcel. The broker presented his own offer of $4,000 per acre to the owner after he had induced the purchaser to make an offer of $5,000 per acre. **What is the broker's liability, and to whom, if anyone, would he be liable?**

   Ward v. Taggart (1959) 51 C.2d 736

6. Sutherland transferred and sold his house to a relocation company. In the Transfer Disclosure Statement he answered "No" as to any neighborhood noise problems or other nuisances. Shapiro purchased the home and immediately discovered loud disturbances from the family next door (arguments and late-night music). Shapiro learned that the Sutherlands had called the police a number of times about the arguments and late-night music. Shapiro asked for a rescission of the sale. The Sutherlands said that they had no contractual relationship with Shapiro. **Are the Sutherlands liable to Shapiro?**

Shapiro v. Sutherland (1998) 60 C.A.4th 666

7. A broker who was not an attorney advised a husband and wife about the kind of document they should execute to secure a loan. **Was the broker's advice proper?**

People v. Sipper (1943) 61 C.A.2d 844

8. While viewing a property, a prospective tenant thought she was entering a closet and fell down basement stairs behind an inward-swinging door. The stairs had no landing or handrail. **What is the liability of the agent?**

Merrill v. Buck (1962) 58 C.2d 552

9. While the plaintiff did not read the written agreement, the plaintiff asked the loan broker about the loan terms and received misleading and incomplete information. Late charges also were made that could not be justified. **What duties, if any, has the loan broker breached?**

Wyatt v. Union Mortgage Company (1979) 24 C.3d 773

10. A private individual brought suit against a board of REALTORS® because he was denied access to its multiple-listing service. He claimed that refusing him the ability to list his house with the service forced him to deal through a broker, which violated the antitrust laws. **Was his complaint valid?**

Derish v. San Mateo–Burlingame Board (1982) 136 C.A.3d 534

11. Carter, a broker, sold a net listing to his daughter and received a $5,000 commission. The seller had agreed to the list price based on the broker's recommendations. **What are the problems involved in this case?**

Sierra Pacific Industries v. Carter (1980) 104 C.A.3d 579

12. A multiple-listing service provided that disputes among members over commissions be submitted to an arbitration procedure and that members who refused to arbitrate could be expelled. Bernstein refused to arbitrate and was expelled from the service. **Was expulsion proper?**

United Multiple Listing Service v. Bernstein (1982) 134 C.A.3d 486

13. A broker purchased a house listed by another broker. The purchasing broker indicated that he was a broker and would share in the commission. He also indicated that he was purchasing the house as his residence. The broker opened a second escrow because he had a purchaser for the house. **Did the purchasing broker do anything wrong?**

Gray v. Fox (1984) 151 C.A.3d 482

14. Traweek Investment Company promoted and managed a limited partnership. Three months after buying a building for $4 million (including 6 percent commission to Traweek), the company placed the building on the market for $5.7 million. Ballou, a broker, produced an offer for $5.4 million. While Ballou had been promised a 6 percent commission, Traweek indicated that Ballou would have to agree to a $100,000 commission, claiming that was all that could be paid because the general partners had guaranteed returns that had to be met. Later Ballou agreed to a further reduction to $50,000 based on Traweek's assertion that no other commissions were being paid. Ballou later discovered Traweek received $222,000 in commission for the sale. **What are Ballou's rights?**

Ballou v. Masters Props. No. 6 (1987) 189 C.A.3d 65

15. A neighbor operated a tree-trimming business from his home, engaged in noisy activities, poured motor oil on his roof, and had a cabana not in conformance with the subdivision restrictions. Five families sued to abate alleged nuisances. **Does a seller have a duty to disclose these facts to a buyer?**

Alexander v. McKnight (1992) 7 C.A.4th 973

16. A buyer received a seller-disclosure that a house was in a floodplain. It did not disclose that a city ordinance prohibited enlarging such homes or rebuilding them if they were destroyed. **Was the disclosure adequate?**

Sweat v. Hollister (1995) 37 C.A.4th 603

17. A broker suggested to a seller that a lead paint test be made because the home was built in 1860. The test was positive. While the seller completed the lead paint disclosure form that referenced the report, the report was not given to the buyer. The broker, acting as a dual agent, orally advised the buyers of the lead paint and the existence of the report, but the broker was not able to get the report from the sellers. However, it was provided at closing.

A written disclosure of known lead-based paint is required by the Residential Lead-Base Paint Hazards Reduction Act of 1992 and must be signed by the buyer. The act calls for treble damages when a person "knowingly" violates the statute. **Was the broker's oral disclosure adequate?**

Smith v. Coldwell Banker Real Estate Services (2000) 122 F. Supp. 2d 267

18. Cal Fed acquired a condominium unit through its nonjudicial trustee's fore-
     closure sale. Assilzadeh, a tenant in another unit, made a purchase offer
     through Fred Sands Realty who disclosed it was acting as a dual agent. The
     seller's counteroffer stated, "Buyer to be aware that property was acquired
     through foreclosure and Seller is exempt from providing a property disclo-
     sure statement. No warranties expressed or implied are included in this sale.
     Subject property is being sold in its present 'As Is' condition. Buyer will sat-
     isfy himself or herself as to the condition of said property, and their requirement
     regarding permitted and nonpermitted areas of the subject property." Dur-
     ing escrow, Assilzadeh signed an amendment to the purchase contract that
     said, "Buyer hereby acknowledges that there has been no representation by
     the Seller regarding the condition of the property. Buyer is hereby granted
     the right to inspect the Property or to obtain inspection reports from quali-
     fied experts at his own expense . . . If such reports reveal any latent defects
     which are unacceptable to Buyer . . . neither Buyer nor Seller shall have any
     further liability to the other." The dual agent verbally informed Assilzadeh
     of the homeowner's association lawsuit against the developer and its recent
     settlement for $5.1 million.

     Assilzadeh inspected the condo with her son, Amin. She also hired a pro-
     fessional inspector. After escrow closed, Assilzadeh bought marble flooring.
     But the homeowners' association said she could not install it because of
     structural defects affecting the load capabilities of the highrise building.
     She sued Cal Fed, Fred Sands Realty, and the sales agent for rescission and
     restitution, as well as fraudulent concealment, negligence, and breach of
     fiduciary duty against Fred Sands Realty and the agent. **Were adequate
     disclosures made by the agent?**

     Assilzadeh v. California Federal Bank (2000) 82 C.A.4th 399

■ CHAPTER QUIZ

1. Ethics would best be described as

   a. obeying the law.

   b. doing what is right.

   c. an agency duty.

   d. treating all people the same.

2. In selling listings of another broker, a real estate salesperson is directly responsible to

   a. his or her broker.

   b. the owner.

   c. the listing broker.

   d. the multiple-listing service.

3. Which statement is *NOT* an IRS requirement for a real estate salesperson to be treated as an independent contractor so that the employing broker can avoid withholding taxes and Social Security contributions?

   a. That the salesperson have a valid California real estate license

   b. That reimbursement be based solely on sales and not on hours worked

   c. That there be a written contract that the salesperson will be treated as an independent contractor for tax purposes

   d. That the salesperson work without supervision

4. A broker would *MOST* likely be responsible to salespersons for

   a. unemployment compensation.

   b. minimum wages.

   c. workers' compensation.

   d. all of the above.

5. Commission disputes between a broker and salespeople would likely be referred to the

   a. state labor commissioner.

   b. court of appeal.

   c. agency review board.

   d. real estate commissioner.

6. A nonlicensee may properly be paid a finder's fee if he or she

   a. participated in negotiations.

   b. introduced the parties to the licensee.

   c. obtained the offer to purchase.

   d. had a signed agreement to act as an agent of a broker.

7. In presenting two identical offers requiring seller financing to an owner, which act of the broker would be wrong?

    a. Mentioning that one buyer had only recently been hired after a long period of unemployment

    b. Mentioning that one buyer was black

    c. Mentioning that one buyer had substantially greater income

    d. Mentioning that one buyer had not given truthful credit information

8. A prospective buyer knows that the owner is considering accepting an offer from another party. He asks you, the listing broker, the amount of the offer so that he can exceed it. You should

    a. tell him, because it is in the owner's best interests.

    b. tell him, because you must reveal all known facts to a buyer.

    c. notify the owner of the request.

    d. refuse to tell him or to accept any offer unless the present offer is rejected.

9. A seller's broker may *NOT* inform a prospective purchaser that

    a. the owner will accept less than the list price.

    b. the present use of the structure does not conform to zoning.

    c. there are material defects in the improvements.

    d. the building is on filled land.

10. An agent need not disclose to an owner that he or she has received an offer when

    a. the owner has already accepted another offer.

    b. the offer is verbal.

    c. escrow has already closed.

    d. the offer is less than the listing price.

11. Which statement is *TRUE* regarding net listings?

    a. They are illegal in California.

    b. The broker must disclose the amount of commission to be received.

    c. The broker's best interests would be served by setting as high a net price as possible.

    d. None of the above is true.

12. Which statement is *FALSE* regarding option listings?

    a. If a property fails to sell, the broker must exercise the purchase option.

    b. Prior to exercising the option, the broker must reveal all offers received.

    c. The broker must reveal the amount of profit, if any, to the owner to exercise the option.

    d. The owner must consent in writing to the agent's profit should the option be exercised.

13. A broker sold an apartment building to a syndicate of which the broker was a member without informing the seller of this interest. Before closing, the owner discovers the broker's interest and refuses to sell. Which of the following choices would probably result from a suit to collect a commission?

    a. The broker's license would be revoked.

    b. The broker would get the commission.

    c. No commission would be paid.

    d. The buyer would obtain specific performance.

14. During the term of an escrow a listing broker discovered that an addition to the building had been made without a building permit and that the addition was in violation of the building code. The broker should notify

    a. the buyer only.

    b. the seller only.

    c. both the buyer and the seller.

    d. neither, because the broker obtained this knowledge after the contract was entered into.

15. Two brokers agreed that they would not allow a third broker to show their listings. This would be:

    a. price fixing.   b. a tie-in agreement.

    c. a Sherman Act violation.   d. market allocation.

16. Which statement is *TRUE* about required disclosures to residential buyers?

    a. There is a two-year statute of limitations on disclosure.

    b. The buyer also has a duty to exercise reasonable care.

    c. The duty of inspection is limited to one to four residential units.

    d. All the statements above are true.

17. The *Easton* decision about required disclosures does *NOT* apply to

    a. single-family residences.

    b. defects that would be discovered by a reasonably competent inspection.

    c. nonresidential property.

    d. patent defects.

18. An agent would *MOST* likely have to inform a prospective purchaser about the

    a. triple murder in the home six months earlier.

    b. race of the previous occupants.

    c. former owner having died of AIDS five years ago.

    d. present owner having AIDS.

19. Which is an example of blind advertising?

    a. Failure to advertise a location

    b. Failure to indicate that the advertiser is an agent

    c. Failure to include the name of the agent

    d. Failure to include the price

20. In selling a commercial property, an agent's duty to the buyer includes

    a. informing the buyer of the results of a reasonably competent and diligent visual inspection.

    b. informing the buyer that the zoning is not appropriate for the intended use.

    c. telling the buyer the reason the seller is selling.

    d. providing the buyer a disclosure statement regarding agency relationships.

21. I told prospective purchasers, "You will love living in this neighborhood." After experiencing problems with their new neighbors, they sued the broker for this false statement. A court would likely determine the statement was

    a. criminal fraud.   b. misrepresentation.

    c. puffing.   d. none of the above.

22. A listing broker is *NOT* ordinarily responsible for wrongful acts committed in the course of a sale by

    a. his employees.

    b. his salespersons having independent contractor contracts.

    c. other brokers acting as subagents.

    d. none of the above.

23. An agent may pay a fee to an unlicensed party who

    a. shows property.

    b. negotiates sale or lease terms.

    c. takes a deposit from a buyer.

    d. introduces the buyer to the broker.

24. Which statement is *TRUE* of the buyer's duties?

    a. Buyers have the same disclosure duties as sellers.

    b. Buyers are required to complete a disclosure statement only for residential purchases.

    c. Buyers are subject to *Easton* liability for nondisclosure.

    d. Buyers have no duty to disclose material facts to the seller.

25. Buyers *MUST* disclose to sellers

    a. any information they have of which the seller is unaware.

    b. the purpose of their purchase.

    c. other purchases they have made.

    d. none of the above.

CHAPTER FOUR

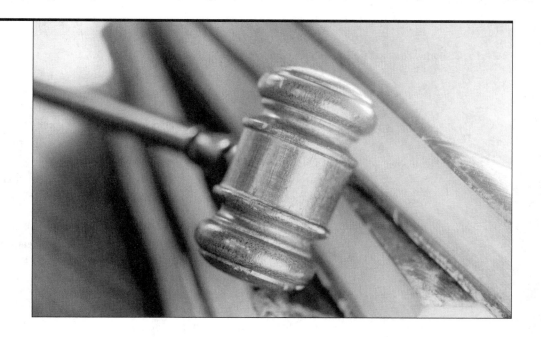

REGULATION OF LICENSEES

■ KEY TERMS

Administrative
  Procedures Act
advance fee
Americans with
  Disabilities Act
Article 5
Article 7
blockbusting
Bulk Sales Act
California Fair
  Employment and
  Housing Act
Civil Rights Act of 1866
Civil Rights Act of 1968
Equal Housing
  Opportunity poster

Fair Housing
  Amendment Act of
  1988
familial status
Federal Personal
  Responsibility and
  Work Opportunity
  Act
Franchise Investment
  Law
MOG brokers
Mortgage Loan
  Disclosure Statement
mortgage loan originator
  (MLO)
Nationwide Mortgage
  Licensing System and
  Registry (NMLS)

Omnibus Housing
  Nondiscrimination
  Act
Real Estate Advisory
  Commission
redlining
restricted license
Rumford Act
SAFE Act
send-out slip
sexual harassment
steering
successor liability
table funding
Unruh Civil Rights Act
usury

■ THE DEPARTMENT OF REAL ESTATE

The purpose of the real estate law is to ensure, as far as possible, that real estate brokers and salespeople will be honest, truthful, and of good reputation. *Brown v. Gordon* (1966) 240 C.A.2d 659.

WEB LINK @

The real estate commissioner is the chief executive of the Department of Real Estate (DRE), *www.dre.ca.gov*. The primary responsibility of the real estate commissioner, who is appointed by the governor, is to enforce the real estate law in such a manner that purchasers of real estate and those persons dealing with real estate licensees are afforded maximum protection.

The commissioner has full authority to control the issuance, suspension, and revocation of real estate licenses. The commissioner also has the authority to adopt or repeal rules and regulations necessary to enforce the real estate law. As mentioned in Chapter 1, these rules and regulations have the force and effect of law.

The real estate commissioner may bring an action in the name of the people of California in the superior court against persons the commissioner believes to be in violation of the real estate law. (The California attorney general is the legal adviser to the real estate commissioner.) In that action, the commissioner may ask the court to enjoin any further violations of the law. The commissioner may include in any action a claim for restitution in the names of persons injured (Business and Professions Code Section 10081). Any criminal action against a licensee for a wrongful act is brought by the district attorney in the county where the offense took place, not by the commissioner.

If the commissioner believes, from satisfactory evidence, that trust funds are not being accounted for properly or are in danger, the commissioner may ask the superior court for an injunction. If the commissioner has conducted an audit that indicates a conversion of funds in excess of $10,000, the court may order the broker to refrain from further exercising the privileges of his or her real estate license. After a hearing, the court may appoint a receiver.

Before revoking, suspending, or denying any real estate license, the commissioner must hold a hearing (see Figure 4.1 for hearing procedures) in accordance with the **Administrative Procedure Act**.

■ ACTIVITIES REQUIRING A LICENSE

A real estate broker is a person who, for compensation or the expectation of compensation, does one or more of the following acts for others:

- Sells or offers to sell, buys or offers to buy, solicits prospective sellers or purchasers of, solicits or obtains listings of, or negotiates the purchase, sale, or exchange of real property or a business opportunity [Business and Professions Code 10131(a)]

- Leases or rents or offers to lease or rent, or places for rent, or solicits listings of places for rent, or solicits for prospective tenants, or negotiates the sale, purchase, or exchange of leases on real property or on a business opportunity, or collects rents from real property or improvements thereon or from business opportunities [Business and Professions Code Section 10131(b)]

FIGURE 4.1

License Discipline Hearing Procedures

The following is reprinted from the California DRE Real Estate Bulletin, summer 1990:

Disciplinary hearings are conducted under the Administrative Procedure Act (Government Code Sections 11500-11528) and are presided over by an administrative law judge who is employed by a state agency independent of the Department of Real Estate. The hearings are conducted in a manner similar to court trials without a jury. At the hearing, the department has the burden of proving the charges contained in the accusation and usually does so by calling witnesses and presenting documents in evidence. The department is represented by its own attorneys at the hearing, and the respondent may be represented by his or her attorney or may proceed without an attorney. There is no provision of law which allows the respondent to be represented by an attorney at state expense similar to the public defender in criminal cases. The respondent has the right to object to evidence offered by the department and to cross-examine witnesses called by the department. The respondent also has the right to present evidence and to call witnesses to testify on his or her behalf.

The document which initiates the process to determine whether a licensee should be formally disciplined is known as an accusation. The accusation sets forth in ordinary and concise language the acts or omissions with which the licensee (referred to as the respondent) is charged. After the accusation has been filed as a formal document with the department, it must be served on the respondent. Service is effected by personal delivery or by certified mail to the respondent's last known business, residence or mailing address on file with the department. After being served, the respondent has 15 days to file a notice of defense with the department. The notice of defense serves two functions: first, as a formal denial of the charges in the accusation and secondly, as a request for a hearing. A failure to file a notice of defense allows the department to proceed to disciplinary action (usually a license revocation) without hearing. After a notice of defense is filed, the department asks the Office of Administrative Hearings to schedule a hearing. Depending on the length of time required, the hearing will generally be held from two months to 12 months from the date the notice of defense is filed. The respondent has the right under the discovery provisions of the law to examine evidence in the department's investigative file and to be told the names and addresses of witnesses who may be called.

After the hearing is concluded, the administrative law judge prepares a proposed decision which is sent to the real estate commissioner. The commissioner has three options: adopt the proposed decision as his/her own, reduce the penalty or reject the decision. If rejected, the commissioner must obtain a complete transcript and record of the hearing and issue a decision based on review of the transcript and exhibits.

If an adverse decision is issued by the commissioner, the respondent may petition the commissioner for reconsideration or may seek judicial review of the decision in Superior Court. After the decision becomes final, the respondent may petition the commissioner for reinstatement of a license one year after the effective date of the decision.

This brief overview of the process is provided to give you a greater understanding of what takes place in license disciplinary actions. As you can see, the law provides a number of rights to a respondent in a disciplinary action to insure that a fair hearing has been held.

Those interested in learning more about Administrative Procedure Act hearings should refer to Section 11500 et seq. of the Government Code.

- Assists or offers to assist in filing an application for the purchase or lease of or in locating or entering upon lands owned by the state or federal government [Business and Professions Code Section 10131(c)]

- Solicits borrowers or lenders for or negotiates loans or collects payments or performs services for borrowers or lenders or note owners in connection with loans secured directly or collaterally by liens on real property or on a business opportunity [Business and Professions Code Section 10131(d)]

■ Sells or offers to sell, buys or offers to buy, or exchanges or offers to exchange a real property sales contract or a promissory note secured directly or collaterally by a lien on real property or on a business opportunity and performs services for the holders thereof [Business and Professions Code Section 10131(e)]

■ Collects an **advance fee** in connection with promoting the sale, lease, or exchange of real property or of a business opportunity or to arrange a loan thereon (Business and Professions Code Section 10131.2)

■ Issues, sells, exchanges, negotiates, or solicits sellers or purchasers of securities specified in Section 25206 of the Corporations Code (shares in real estate syndicates). These syndicate interests also may be sold by broker/dealers licensed by the commissioner of corporations (Business and Professions Code Section 10131.3)

■ Buys and sells or offers to buy and sell, negotiate for, or solicit purchasers or sellers of mobile homes. Dealers licensed by the Department of Housing and Community Development are also authorized to sell mobile homes (Business and Professions Code Section 10131.6)

■ WHEN LICENSING IS NOT REQUIRED

Exempt from real estate licensure are

■ those dealing in their own property as principals, except those buying, selling, or exchanging eight or more notes per year secured by deeds of trust or sales contracts;

■ officers dealing for a corporation in corporation property for which they receive no special compensation;

■ those dealing under an executed power of attorney;

■ attorneys-at-law rendering services while acting as attorneys-at-law;

■ those operating under court order (receivers, trustees in bankruptcy, executors of estates, etc.);

■ trustees selling under a power of sale in a trust deed;

■ banks, trust companies, savings associations, industrial loan companies, pension trusts, credit unions, insurance companies, or their employees;

■ auctioneers who merely "cry" an auction need not be licensed, but soliciting buyers and sellers for a real estate auction or presenting documents to be signed after the auction requires a license;

■ lenders making loans insured by an agency of the federal government or for which such a commitment has been made;

- nonprofit agricultural cooperatives engaged in lending and marketing;

- persons licensed as personal property brokers, consumer finance lenders, or commercial finance lenders, while acting in that capacity;

- cemetery authorities and their agents;

- those who make real estate loan collections for the owners, provided they collect $40,000 or less from ten or fewer loans in one year or they are corporations licensed as escrows;

- unlicensed assistants who do not show property, solicit business, or negotiate or encourage a purchase or utilization of a broker;

- stenographers, bookkeepers, receptionists, and other clerical help carrying out normal clerical duties;

- resident managers of apartment complexes (Business and Professions Code Section 10131.01 has expanded the resident manager exception to include employees of a property management firm retained to manage a residential apartment building—potentially including nonresident employees—working under the supervision of a licensed broker or salesperson. Also exempt are persons renting transient accommodations.);

- condominium association managers who do not rent or sell units;

- homeowners' association managers may be certified—in order to be certified, prescribed educational requirements must be met; and

- finders who receive a fee for introducing the parties.

Case Study

A power of attorney cannot be used to circumvent licensing requirements. In *Sheetz v. Edmonds* (1988) 201 C.A.3d 1432, the Court of Appeal upheld the real estate commissioner's order to Sheetz to stop managing 23 properties. Sheetz, who was not licensed as a broker, performed management services for compensation and claimed to be exempt from Business and Professions Code Section 10133 because she held a power of attorney from the owner. The exemption was judged to apply only to a particular or isolated transaction and cannot be used as a substitute for a broker's license. The court considered the fact that the owner was a close friend of Sheetz's to be irrelevant

---

■ LICENSE REQUIREMENTS

WEB LINK @

Applicable sections of the California Business and Professions Code as well as regulations of the real estate commissioner dealing with licensing requirements can be found in the *Real Estate Law* volume published by the Department of Real Estate. (The book may be accessed free of charge at *www.dre.ca.gov*.)

Salesperson's License

To qualify for a salesperson's license, the applicant must

- provide proof of U.S. citizenship or legal presence in the United States (**The Federal Personal Responsibility and Work Opportunity Act** denies public benefits, including professional licenses, to illegal immigrants.);

- be at least 18 years of age;

- take and pass the real estate examination for salespersons;

- be fingerprinted;

- have an employing broker at the time the license is issued (broker affiliation is not required to sit for the examination);

- apply for a license within one year after passing the salesperson's examination;

- have completed three college-level courses including real estate principles, real estate practice, and a third course from an approved list (members of the State Bar of California are exempt from course requirements);

- be honest and truthful (conviction of a felony or crime involving moral turpitude may result in denial of license); and

- pay the applicable fee.

Note: U.S. citizenship is not required for either the salesperson or the broker license; however, proof of legal presence in the United States must be shown, such as a U.S. birth certificate, U.S. passport, or resident alien card.

Broker's License

An applicant for a broker's license must

- provide proof of U.S. citizenship or legal presence in the United States (The Federal Personal Responsibility and Work Opportunity Act denies public benefits, including professional licenses, to illegal immigrants.);

- be at least 18 years of age;

- have two years' experience or the equivalent as a real estate salesperson within the prior five-year period or a valid four-year college degree (one year experience with a two-year AA degree);

- have successfully completed eight college-level courses including real estate practice, legal aspects of real estate, real estate finance, real estate appraisal, and accounting or real estate economics (plus three additional courses from an approved list);

- pass the broker's examination;

- be fingerprinted;

- be honest and truthful (conviction of a felony or crime involving moral turpitude may result in denial of license);

- pay the applicable fee; and

- for a California real estate broker, applicant must maintain an office location within California (can be a home office).

Partnership Licenses While there is no specific partnership license, a broker can be a partner with a salesperson in a real estate brokerage business. However, every partner through whom the partnership acts must be a licensed real estate broker. A broker may be a partner with a nonlicensee in business activities where real estate licenses are not required.

Corporation Licenses A real estate sales corporation must have one real estate broker who has a corporation officer license. The broker also can have a separate individual license.

A salesperson can be an officer and a stockholder of a corporation. The salesperson can be a majority stockholder only if the responsible corporate broker is also an officer and director of the corporation.

Nonresident Licensees A new license will be issued to a nonresident of California only if California residents can obtain licenses in the applicant's state. Nonresidents holding California real estate licenses must agree that they can be sued in California courts. Legal service to institute a lawsuit may be made on the Secretary of State if by using reasonable diligence; process cannot be personally served on the licensee in California.

License Identification Real estate licensees must place their identification number on their first point of contact marketing material (e.g., cards, Web sites, flyers) as well as home purchase agreements.

■ LICENSE RENEWALS

The original real estate license and each renewal are in effect for four years. There is no examination for license renewal. For their first license renewal, both salesperson and brokers, licensees must complete 45 hours of continuing education that includes

- five courses of 3 hours each in ethics, agency, fair housing, trust fund handling, and risk management. At least 18 hours of the 45 hours must be in consumer protection with the remaining clock hours in either consumer service or consumer protection courses.

Renewals, after the first renewal, for both salespersons and brokers require 45 hours of continuing education including

- 12 hours of continuing education courses in ethics, agency, trust fund handling, and fair housing, or one 6-hour survey course covering these subjects (ethics, agency, trust fund handling, and fair housing)

- 3-hour course in risk management

- Minimum of 18 clock hours of consumer protection courses

- The remaining clock hours, to total 45, in either consumer service or consumer protection courses

The Department of Real Estate (DRE) can withhold issuance or renewal of a real estate license of a party who has been placed on a certified list of persons who are delinquent in child or family support payments. The DRE can issue a temporary license for a period of 150 days during which period the licensee must comply with required payments.

Under the 70/30 rule, licensees who are at least 70 years of age and have been licensed in good standing in California for 30 continuous years are exempt from continuing education requirements for license renewal.

■ LATE RENEWALS

For late license renewals, there is a two-year grace period. The licensee cannot act as a real estate agent while the license is expired.

■ GROUNDS FOR DISCIPLINARY ACTION

All real estate licensees are subject to disciplinary proceedings by the real estate commissioner for

- making a substantial misrepresentation;

- making a false promise likely to influence, persuade, or induce;

- engaging in a continued and flagrant course of misrepresentation or making false promises;

- acting for more than one party to a transaction without the knowledge and written consent of all the parties (undisclosed dual agency);

- commingling with his or her own money or property the money or property of others entrusted to the agent's care;

- claiming or receiving a fee for any exclusive listing that does not include a definite termination date;

- making a secret profit;

- exercising an option coupled with a listing where the licensee failed to reveal the amount of profit and obtain the consent of the owner for the amount of profit;

- engaging in any conduct that constitutes fraud or dishonest dealing;

- obtaining the agreement of a prospective purchaser that the purchaser will deal only through the agent with regard to a particular property (**send-out slip**) without the written authorization of the owner (must have written authorization to sell from the business owner before having purchaser agree to pay compensation if the purchase is completed);

- procuring or attempting to procure a real estate license by fraud, misrepresentation, or deceit, or by a material misstatement of fact in an application for a license, license renewal, or license reinstatement (within 90 days after issuance the commissioner can suspend a license so obtained, without a hearing);

- entering a plea of guilty or nolo contendere to, or being found guilty of, a felony or misdemeanor where the crime bares a substantial relationship to the duties of a real estate licensee and the time for appeal has expired.

- knowingly aiding in the publication or circulation of a material false statement concerning the licensee's business or any business opportunity, land, or subdivision;

- willfully disregarding any provision of the real estate law;

- making any false statement concerning their business or designation, certificate, special education, or trade organization membership, including using the terms REALTOR®, *Realtist*, or any trade name or insignia when not entitled to such use;

- improperly influencing or attempting to improperly influence an appraisal through coercion, extortion or bribery;

- performing any action that would have warranted the denial of a license;

- demonstrating negligence or incompetence in performing any act requiring a real estate license;

- failing to exercise reasonable supervision over the acts of salespersons;

- using his or her employment by a government agency in such a way as to violate the confidentiality of the access provided;

- violating any terms, conditions, or limitations of a restricted license;

- inducing the listing of residential property because of increase in crime, decline of quality in the schools, or loss of value caused by the entry or prospective entry into the community of persons of another race, color, religion, ancestry, or national origin (blockbusting);

- violating any provision of the Franchise Investment Law (discussed later in this chapter);

- violating any provision of the Corporate Securities Code; and

- failing, as agent for the buyer, to disclose any direct or indirect ownership in the property being purchased;

- violating Article VI of the Real Estate Law;

- intentionally delaying the closing of a mortgage loan for the sole purpose of increasing interest, cost fees, or charges payable by the borrower;

- providing the lender an inaccurate opinion of value in a debt forgiveness sale (short sale) to obtain a financial advantage (listing or sale commission);

- influencing or attempting to influence an appraisal through coercion, extortion, or bribery;

- failing to deliver mortgage loan funds (mortgage broker) in accordance with a commitment to do so when the broker is the lender or is authorized to do so by the lender; and

- any act that indicates an applicant is not honest or truthful. (This would include acts that resulted in denial or revocation of a license by any other governmental agency.)

To revoke or suspend a license, the Department of Real Estate must show "convincing proof to a reasonable certainty," not proof beyond a reasonable doubt [*Realty Projects Inc. v. Smith* (1973) 32 C.A.3d 204].

> **Case Study**
> In *Madrid v. Department of Real Estate* (1984) 152 C.A.3d 454, an applicant for a real estate license neglected to disclose an out-of-state conviction five years earlier for bingo fraud but did disclose a 20-year-old conviction for contracting without a license. The plaintiff claimed to have forgotten about the conviction and claimed license revocation was improper. While failure to disclose a minor matter could be excused, the court held this to be a major matter and a recent conviction that was omitted knowingly. Because knowledge of the conviction would have justified denial of license, revocation of the plaintiff's license was held to be proper.

Statute of Limitations

Disciplinary action must be brought within three years of the wrongful act except in the case of fraud, where it is three years after the act or one year after discovery, whichever comes later, but in no event later than ten years from the wrongful act (Business and Professions Code Section 10101).

Criminal Liability

The grounds for disciplinary action also are considered a misdemeanor subject to criminal prosecution (Business and Professions Code Section 10185).

Restricted Licenses

Probationary or restricted real estate licenses may be granted by the commissioner after a license has been revoked, suspended, or denied subsequent to a hearing.

The **restricted license** can be restricted to a period of time, to the type or area of activity, or to employment by a particular broker (salesperson). The commissioner can require detailed reports of each transaction, a surety bond, other conditions, or a combination of conditions.

The restricted licensee has no automatic right to renewal. The commissioner can suspend a restricted license for a violation prior to a formal hearing; however, revocation requires a hearing.

As a condition of issuance of a regular license, the commissioner can require that the continuing education requirements be met.

Education, Research, and Recovery Allocation

Twenty percent of license fees go into a special fund that in turn is divided into two separate accounts. Twelve percent of all fees go into a recovery account that provides restitution to members of the public who suffer a loss because of a wrongful act of a real estate licensee. Eight percent of all fees go into the Education and Research Account.

An aggrieved party who obtains an uncollectible judgment against a licensee because of fraud, misrepresentation, deceit, or conversion of trust funds can apply to the DRE for recovery from the fund. The fund will pay only if the wrongful act required a real estate license.

Up to a maximum of $50,000 will be paid to the claimants because of any one transaction, regardless of the number of persons injured or the number of licensees involved [Business and Professions Code Section 10471(b)].

No more than $250,000 will be paid out for multiple claims against one licensee [Business and Professions Code Section 10474(c)].

Should the fund pay a claim because of a licensee, the licensee's license automatically will be suspended. No reinstatement will be made until the fund has been repaid, including prevailing interest. A discharge in bankruptcy will not relieve a person from the repayment requirements for reinstatement. Repayment to the fund will not nullify or modify any other disciplinary action that is brought because of the licensee's actions.

An illegal alien is not entitled to compensation from the recovery account.

■ MORTGAGE BROKERS

WEB LINK @

Rules and regulations regarding mortgage loan broker activities can be found on the DRE Web site, *www.dre.ca.gov/pub_categories.html*. RE7 is the **Mortgage Loan Broker Compliance Manual** and includes the RE7A **Mortgage Loan Broker Compliance Checklist**.

Mortgage loan brokers make or arrange loans for compensation. The mortgage loan broker is thus a middleman, matching borrowers and lenders. The mortgage loan broker has the duty of fair dealing to both lenders and borrowers.

Business and Professions Code Section 10131(d) requires that a person who solicits borrowers and lenders, makes loans, or performs services for borrowers and lenders when such loans are secured by real property be licensed as a real estate broker and be subject to the regulations of the real estate commissioner. While an owner normally can sell his or her own property without a license, an owner who engages in eight or more trust deed transactions within one year must have a broker's license.

Case Study

The case of *Direnfield v. Stabile* (1988) 198 C.A.3d 126 involved an unemployed licensed real estate salesman who arranged loans in which Direnfield was the lender. While previously employed by a broker, Stabile had arranged other loans for Direnfield. The loans he arranged while unemployed were for 30 percent interest. Two years later, the borrowers sued Direnfield for usury because the loans were not made through a real estate broker. A settlement allowed Direnfield only the return of principal. Direnfield sued Stabile for failing to disclose that he was not employed by a broker. Stabile could not pay the judgment granted, so Direnfield requested payment from the recovery fund.

The Court of Appeal held that the recovery fund can be required to pay for an action of an unemployed salesperson because the salesperson's license was not terminated while the salesperson was unemployed. (Direnfield was limited to interest at the statutory rate [7 percent], not the 30 percent rate of the loan.).

The license requirements apply to the sale, exchange, and servicing of existing loans as well as to arranging new loans [Business and Professions Code Section 10131(e)].

Persons who make loan collections on ten or fewer loans and do not negotiate loans need not be licensed as brokers. A person who collects on more than ten loans or collects an amount exceeding $40,000 per year must either have a broker's license or apply to the real estate commissioner for an exemption. To obtain the exemption, the person must agree to comply with the provisions of the real estate law and the commissioner's regulations and must post a bond or other security to protect client funds.

Article 5 of the real estate law (Business and Professions Code Sections 10230–10236.1) governs transactions in trust deeds and real property sales contracts. The provisions of Article 5 do not apply to one- to four-residential-unit sales involving seller carryback financing. The provisions of Article 5 also do not apply when the broker has a direct or an indirect monetary interest as a party to the transaction [Business and Professions Code Section 10230(a)].

Article 5 provisions include the following:

- Brokers cannot accept funds from prospective real property lenders unless the broker has a specific loan arranged for the funds (Business and Professions Code Section 10231).

- In servicing a real property loan, the broker cannot retain funds for more than 25 days unless there is a written agreement with the purchaser or lender, in which case the interest must be paid on the funds retained.

- A real estate broker is prohibited from advertising or giving gifts or premiums to prospective purchasers or lenders as an inducement for making a loan (Business and Professions Code Section 10236.1).

- Any real estate licensee who undertakes to service a loan must have a written authorization from the purchaser or lender of the loan (Business and Professions Code Section 10233).

- If a broker who is servicing a loan remits funds other than the funds of the obligor (the broker advances the funds), then within ten days of such payment, the broker must notify the holder of the loan as to the source of the funds and the reason for making the advance (Business and Professions Code Section 10233.1).

- If the broker is going to benefit directly or indirectly by the loan, other than commission or fees, the broker must notify the Department of Real Estate and lender or purchaser of the facts (Business and Professions Code Section 10231.2).

- The mortgage broker who places a loan must deliver copies of any deed of trust to the investor or lender and to the borrower.

- Real estate licensees who negotiate loans secured by real property must have the instruments recorded prior to the disbursement of funds unless the lender authorizes prior release, in which case within ten days of the release of funds the broker must either record the trust deed or deliver it to the lender with a written recommendation that it be recorded immediately.

- If the licensee arranges an assignment of an existing trust deed or sales contract, he or she must have the assignment recorded within ten working days after close of escrow or deliver the trust deed or sales contract to the purchaser with the written recommendation that it be recorded immediately (Business and Professions Code Section 10234).

Advertising

Advertising a specific yield greater than the rate stated on the note is misleading advertising unless the ad also includes the actual interest rates and purchase discount.

Mortgage loan brokers must include their license number in their advertising soliciting borrowers or investors. They must also include a telephone number, established by the DRE, to enable consumers to check on the broker's licensed status. The advertising requirements for loan and investor solicitation, as well as for other broker ads, are set forth in Table 4.1.

Costs and Charges

Article 7 of the real estate law (Business and Professions Code Sections 10240–10248.3) covers loan broker maximum costs and commissions as well as loan payment requirements. This article applies only to regulated loans (first trust deeds of less than $30,000, and second trust deeds of less than $20,000). Larger loans have no upper limit on costs and fees.

Mortgage Broker Costs for Regulated Loans

Loan broker costs for a regulated loan (first loans of less than $30,000 and second loans of less than $20,000) cannot exceed actual costs and expenses, and are limited to 5 percent of the loan or $390, whichever is greater, but in no event more than $700. For example, for a loan of $2,000, the costs can be up to $390 (5 percent or $390, whichever is greater), and for a $19,000 loan the costs cannot exceed $700 (5 percent is $950, but the maximum that can be charged is $700). Examples of costs are appraisal fees, escrow charges, title insurance, notary fees, and credit report charges.

Maximum $700
5% of loan
Minimum $390

Mortgage Broker Commissions for Regulated Loans

The loan broker commission for negotiating a regulated loan also is limited. For first trust deeds up to three years, the maximum commission is 5 percent of the amount borrowed; and for three years or more it is 10 percent. For second trust deeds up to two years the maximum commission is 5 percent; for more than two years but less than three years it is 10 percent; and for three years or more it is 15 percent.

	2 Years	3 Years
First Trust Deeds		5%	10%
Second Trust Deeds	5%	10%	15%

If a broker charges more than the maximum allowable fees or costs, the borrower may recover three times the excess fees or costs charged (Business and Professions Code Section 10246).

TABLE 4.1
Advertising Requirements for Mortgage Brokers

Required Information for Ads	Soliciting for Borrowers	Soliciting for Investors (Lenders)	All Other Broker Advertising
Phrasing	CA Dept. of Real Estate—Real Estate Broker; or Real Estate Broker—CA Dept. of Real Estate	Broker, agent, REALTOR®, loan correspondent, or abbreviations bro., agt., or other similar terms or abbreviations	Broker, agent, REALTOR®, or abbreviations bro., agt., or other similar terms or abbreviations
Identification Number	8-digit broker license ID	8-digit broker license ID	N/A
Telephone Number	DRE "license information" telephone number: 877-373-4542		N/A

The broker may not enter into an exclusive agreement with a prospective borrower to procure a loan that ties up the borrower for more than 45 days (Business and Professions Code Section 10243).

The licensee may not condition the granting of a loan on the purchase of credit group life or disability insurance.

Late Charges

Late charges after ten days may not exceed 10 percent of the installment due, with a minimum late charge of $5. (For loans not made through loan brokers, the late charge generally is limited to 6 percent.) Late charges may not be pyramided.

Prepayment Fees

Loans on owner-occupied single-family dwellings may be prepaid at any time, but prepayments within seven years may be subject to prepayment penalties. (For residential loans made by other than loan brokers, prepayment penalties may not be imposed after five years, but if owner occupied, the prepayment penalties are limited to three years.) Prepayment penalties may not exceed six months' interest. Up to 20 percent of the loan always can be prepaid in any 12-month year without penalty (Business and Professions Code Section 10242.6).

When loans are made without consideration of borrowers' ability to pay (predatory lending), prepayment penalties are limited to the first 36 months.

Loans made by loan brokers must have substantially equal payments.

Balloon payments (payments greater than twice the amount of the smallest payment) may not be imposed on a loan secured by an owner-occupied dwelling if the loan is for six years or less.

Case Study

The case of *Carboni v. Arrospide* (1991) 2 C.A.4th 76 involved a $4,000 broker loan bearing interest at 200 percent that was originally due in three months. Additional advances were made by the broker totaling $99,346, all at the 200 percent rate. By the time of trial for judicial foreclosure and deficiency judgment, accumulated interest was nearly $390,000. The trial court wrote, "While in regard to short-term loans of 90 days or so, as was anticipated here, interest at the rate of 200 percent per annum may or may not shock the conscience of the court, interest at that rate for one and one-half years does." The trial court set the interest at 24 percent. The Court of Appeal affirmed, explaining that Civil Code Section 1670.5 allows a court to refuse to enforce an unconscionable contract or to modify it to avoid an unconscionable result.

Usury laws (laws setting the maximum interest rates that can be charged) do not apply to loans made or arranged by loan brokers. Even though loans made by real estate brokers may be exempt from usury limits, they are not necessarily without limits.

If the broker uses his or her own funds wholly or in part for the loan, the broker must notify the borrower prior to the close of escrow (Business and Professions Code Section 10241.2).

Every loan broker who negotiates a loan to be secured by real estate must deliver to the borrower a statement in writing containing all of the cost information as well as loan terms. This statement must be delivered within three business days after receipt of a completed written loan application, or before the borrower becomes obligated, whichever is earlier. The broker must keep a copy of the statement, signed by the borrower, for three years.

Disclosures

Article 7 requires a real estate broker who makes or arranges a mortgage loan of any kind or in any amount to present a **Mortgage Loan Disclosure Statement** to the borrower within three days of receipt of a completed loan application. The borrower's signature on the disclosure must be obtained prior to the time that the borrower becomes obligated to make the loan. The disclosure requires that specific important features of the loan be set forth.

Brokers who arrange loans must provide the purchaser with a Lender/Purchaser Disclosure Statement providing information regarding the loan, and a statement of the property's fair market value, as determined by an appraisal, as well as a copy of the appraisal. The lender or purchaser must also be given a copy of the loan application and credit report, and the option of purchasing a title policy.

■ REAL PROPERTY SYNDICATES

The Department of Corporations has jurisdiction over both corporate and non-corporate syndicates. Broker/dealers licensed by the Department of Corporations can sell syndicate interests.

The Department of Corporations has transferred control of noncorporate syndicates having 100 or fewer investors to the Department of Real Estate. Real estate brokers are exempt from licensing requirements of the Corporations Code when selling these interests.

A real estate broker's violation of the Corporations Code can be the basis of disciplinary action by the real estate commissioner.

■ MINERAL, OIL, AND GAS BROKERS

New mineral, oil, and gas (MOG) licenses have not been issued since 1993. However, existing MOG licenses may be renewed every four years for the life of the holder. A person holding a real estate broker's license can engage in MOG transactions without additional licensing or qualifications. Anyone engaged in a MOG transaction without holding a valid MOG or real estate license could be fined up to $500 and/or face imprisonment for up to six months. Grounds for revocation or suspension of MOG licenses are similar to the grounds for revocation or suspension of real estate licenses and are set forth in Section 10561 of the Business and Professions Code.

The permits and licenses once necessary to handle MOG transactions are no longer required. This special licensing was initially established due to past sales abuses. Investors were sold parcels in oil and gas subdivisions that were touted as great investments offering fantastic potential. However, in some cases, the parcels sold had remote if any possibility of containing oil or gas products. Eventually, a number of promoters were convicted of grand theft, and approximately 600 real estate salespersons and brokers had their licenses revoked. The licensing and activities of **MOG brokers** have now been placed under the Department of Real Estate.

■ TABLE FUNDING

Table funding is prohibited for residential loans in California. Under table funding, the broker is named as the lender, but at settlement, the loan is transferred to another lender who advanced the funds for the closing. Table funding was used to hide from the borrower the true cost of the loan in that the loan broker received an undisclosed premium in the loan transfer. The loan broker in table funding is acting as a principal and not in a broker capacity.

■ FEDERAL SECURE AND FAIR ENFORCEMENT FOR MORTGAGE LICENSING ACT OF 2008 (SAFE ACT)

The purpose of the Federal Secure and Fair Enforcement for Mortgage Licensing Act of 2008 (SAFE Act) is to protect borrowers in mortgage loan transactions and to reduce fraud. Every state must have a licensing system for residential mortgage originators. A registry of mortgage originators is maintained by the Nationwide Mortgage Licensing System and Registry (NMLS).

California real estate licensees may engage in business as mortgage loan originators only if they obtain a real estate license endorsement identifying themselves as a licensed mortgage loan originator. License endorsements are valid for a period of one year and expire on December 31 of each year.

Licensing requires specified prelicensing education and a national and state examination.

■ ESCROW AGENT

The regulation of escrows is covered in Division 6 of the California Financial Code and requires that escrow agents be licensed by the commissioner of corporations.

Among those exempted are real estate brokers licensed by the real estate commissioner while performing acts in the course of or incidental to real estate transactions in which the brokers are principals or acting as agents in performing acts for which a real estate license is required [Financial Code Section 17006(d)].

The Department of Corporations has interpreted this exemption to be personal to the broker. The broker cannot set up an association with other brokers to conduct escrows or contract out the escrow services. The broker cannot advertise escrow services without making it clear that the services are only incidental to real estate transactions.

Escrows are covered in detail in Chapter 14.

■ MOBILE HOME SALES

Mobile homes are factory-built housing units that are transported to a site on their own chassis. They are usually set up on a permanent foundation and connected to utilities.

Once considered only temporary homes or for travel, mobile homes have become used as principal residences or stationary vacation homes. Their relatively low cost has resulted in growing numbers of mobile home parks in some communities. They make up a significant portion of single-family housing priced under $100,000.

Since July 1975, real estate licensees have been granted limited rights to act as agents in the sale of mobile homes. They can list and sell these mobile homes in rental spaces, as well as with the land. Salespeople sometimes specialize in mobile home sales in particular, while some specialize in specific mobile home parks. In so acting, they are subject to these limitations:

- The mobile home must be in place. It must be able to remain on its rented lot. If the mobile home is sold with a lot, the lot must be zoned properly so the home can remain.

- Real estate licensees cannot advertise that no down payment is required for a mobile home when in fact secondary financing will be used to finance the down payment.

- Real estate licensees must withdraw all advertising of a mobile home for sale within 48 hours after receipt of notice that the mobile home is no longer available for sale, lease, or financing.

- A real estate broker who is not also licensed as a mobile home dealer may not have an office where two or more mobile homes are displayed and offered for sale. (There is a separate license for mobile home sales.)

■ A real estate licensee is prohibited from prorating license or title fees unless the buyer and the seller agree to the proration, or the licensee was required to pay the fees to avoid penalties for late payment.

■ A licensee may not represent that the mobile home can be transported over California highways unless it meets all physical requirements for such transport. The licensee must reveal any material facts pertaining to the equipment requirements.

■ The licensee must have all transfer papers delivered. Mobile homes must be registered annually with the Department of Housing and Community Development (HCD). Formerly, registration was required with the Department of Motor Vehicles. Exceptions to the annual registration are mobile homes sold new on or after July 1, 1980, mobile homes affixed to a permanent foundation, and mobile homes sold prior to July 1, 1980, that have become more than 120 days delinquent in the payment of license fees.

■ Mobile homes not subject to annual registration are registered only at the time of title transfer. These homes are on local property tax rolls.

■ Not later than ten calendar days after the sale of a used mobile home that is subject to registration, the broker must supply written notice of the transfer to the Department of Housing and Community Development. For details on transferring title and registering a mobile home, see Section 18100.5 et seq. of the Health and Safety Code. The Department of Housing and Community Development has a toll-free number for mobile home transfer information: 800-452-8356.

■ Real estate licensees cannot include any added license or transfer fee if such a fee is not due to the state.

Exceptions to the limitations set forth are mobile homes attached to a permanent foundation so as to have become real property. The four prerequisites for a mobile home to become real property are

1. obtaining a building permit;

2. placing the mobile home on a permanent foundation;

3. obtaining a certificate of occupancy; and

4. recording a document reflecting that the mobile home has been affixed to a foundation.

Section 10177.2 of the Business and Professions Code provides for the discipline of a licensee who

■ used a fictitious name in the registration of a mobile home or knowingly concealed any fact in the registration or otherwise committed fraud in the registration application;

- failed to provide for the delivery of a properly endorsed certificate of ownership or certificate of title from the seller to the buyer;

- knowingly participated in the acquisition or sale of a stolen mobile home;

- submitted a bad check to the Department of Housing and Community Development; or

- violated other provisions of the California codes.

There is a Manufactured Home Recovery Fund similar to the Real Estate Recovery Account. After receiving a final judgment against a dealer or salesperson for failure to honor warranties, fraud, or willful misrepresentation, a claimant can receive a maximum of $75,000 from the fund.

■ ADVANCE FEE RENTAL AGENTS

There is a separate license available to operate a prepaid rental listing service (PRLS). No examination is required for a two-year PRLS license. Licensed real estate brokers are exempt from this requirement (Business and Professions Code Section 10167 et seq.). A $10,000 surety bond is required for each location that a PRLS licensee maintains.

Licensees must provide a prospective tenant with a DRE-approved written contract that describes the services to be provided and the prospective tenant's needs.

If the licensee fails to provide a list of at least three rental properties to the prospective tenant within five days, the advance fee must be refunded in full.

The licensee must refund within ten days of request any amount more than $50 in charges if the prospective tenant does not obtain a rental through the licensee and demands a return within ten days of expiration of the contract. The right to refund must be set forth in boldface type (Business and Professions Code Section 10167.10). For example, if a prospective tenant paid a $100 advance fee and qualified for a refund, $50 would be refunded to the prospective tenant.

The licensee must not knowingly refer a property to a prospective tenant where

- the property does not exist or is not available for occupancy;

- the property has been described by the licensee in a false, misleading, or deceptive manner;

- the licensee has not confirmed the availability of the property during the four-day period preceding the referral (however, it is not a violation to refer property when availability was not confirmed from five to seven days after the last confirmation if the licensee has made a good-faith effort to confirm availability); or

- the licensee has not obtained written or oral permission to list the property from the owner or agent.

■ BUSINESS OPPORTUNITY BROKERS

A business opportunity broker sells or leases an existing business enterprise, including its goodwill. While real estate might be included with a business opportunity sale, generally all that is sold is personal property. At one time, separate licensing was available to those engaged in the sale or lease of business opportunities. Since 1966, however, a real estate license has been required to engage in such transactions.

In business opportunity sales, more than in any other transaction, buyers tend to rely on the broker's expertise. The danger of dual agency is always present. The broker must make his or her status clear to the prospective buyer.

For protection, the broker should not repeat the owner's oral statements about gross or net income, but should instead ask for copies of the seller's federal tax returns and state sales tax returns, and get the seller's permission to disclose the information to prospective purchasers. Even then, the broker must indicate to prospective purchasers that the information was supplied by the owner and that the broker does not warrant its authenticity. The broker could still be liable if a court determined the broker should have doubted the information provided by the owner.

The broker must make sure that the purchaser is protected.

Some of the items for consideration are

- transferability of leases;
- obtaining of necessary licenses and permits;
- compliance with the Bulk Sales Act;
- compliance with the fictitious name requirements (Business and Professions Code Section 17900 et seq.);
- obtaining a clearance receipt from the Board of Equalization certifying that prior sales tax has been paid so that the purchaser is not liable for the unpaid sales taxes (under *successor liability* the purchaser of a business is liable for sales taxes collected but not remitted to the state by the prior owner of the business);
- complete agreement as to terms consistent with such a sale, such as covenant not to compete; and
- obtaining agreement on apportionment of the sales price for tax purposes.

Failure to protect the purchaser might be considered negligence on the part of the broker and subject the broker to damages and/or disciplinary action.

Case Study

In the case of *Salazar v. Interland* (2007) 152 C.A. 4th 1031, Salazar, doing business as Los Angeles Technology, learned that AT&T was interested in selling its small business web hosting. Salazar contacted Host Pro, which was owned by Interland, Inc., and arranged meetings with AT&T. The meetings resulted in Host Pro acquiring 150,000 AT&T customers. Host Pro had agreed to pay Salazar a commission based on fees. Interland, the parent company, refused to pay Salazar because Salazar did not hold a real estate broker's license required to sell a business opportunity. Salazar claimed it was not a business opportunity because it was not the sale of company stock or even a substantial part of AT&T's business.

Salazar sued for $20 million damages. The Superior Court ruled that Salazar was not entitled to any commission because he did not hold a broker's license as required by Business and Professions Code Sections 10030 and 10130 for the business opportunity sales.

The Court of Appeal affirmed ruling a business opportunity sale does not have to involve the sale of an entire business. It can be the sale of business assets, customer contracts, and goodwill. The statute prohibits the collection of compensation by an unlicensed business opportunity broker.

Bulk Sales Act

The **Bulk Sales Act** (Commercial Code Sections 6101–6111) is of particular interest to brokers engaged in the sale of business opportunities. A bulk sale is a sale not in the course of the seller's ordinary business. The sale of the seller's business or a substantial part of the materials, supplies, merchandise, or other inventory would be a bulk sale. The Bulk Sales Act is intended to give notice to the creditors of the seller so that they can protect their interests.

Compliance with the act requires

- recording of a notice of sale at least 12 business days before the sale is to be consummated;

- publishing of a notice in a newspaper of general circulation within the judicial district in which the property is located at least 12 business days prior to the sale; and

- sending of a registered or certified letter to the county tax collector at least 12 business days prior to the sale.

Such notice must include

- the statement that a bulk transfer is to be made;

- the name and address of the transferor and transferee and all other business names and addresses used by the transferor within three years, as far as known by the transferee;

- the location and general description of the property to be transferred;

- the place and date on which the bulk transfer is to be consummated; and

- the name and address of the person with whom claims may be filed and the last date for filing claims.

If the sale is to be made by auction, notice that the sale is to be made by auction must be given, including the name of the auctioneer and the time and place of the auction.

If the bulk sales notice provides for an escrow, the buyer must deposit the full purchase price with the escrow holder.

When statutory notices are not complied with, the sale is fraudulent and void with regard to those creditors who hold claims based on transactions prior to the bulk transfer. In such cases, the creditors could have rights superior to the purchaser.

In the case of an auction, the responsibility for notices rests on the auctioneer. Failure to comply does not render an auction sale fraudulent and void, but the auctioneer is held personally liable to the transferor's creditors up to the reasonable value of the assets sold.

Franchise Sales

A franchise is a contract by which a business operator (franchisee) is granted, for some payment, the right to engage in a business of marketing goods or services under a plan or system prescribed by the seller of the franchise (franchisor) and associated with the franchisor's name, trademark, logo, advertising, or other commercial symbol. Agreements between petroleum companies and distributors and retailers to use brand identification or lease agreements allowing the sale of products under a trade identification are examples of franchises.

Because of the advantages of national advertising and training programs, a tremendous growth in real estate franchises has occurred.

Franchise sales are regulated by the **Franchise Investment Law**, which requires disclosure from the franchisor to the franchisee. The California commissioner of corporations controls sales, and franchise offerings must be registered with the commissioner prior to sale. Exempt from registration are franchisors with a net worth of $5 million or more that have had a minimum of 25 franchises in operation during the five years prior to the sale. Most major real estate franchisors therefore would be exempt from registration.

Required disclosures must be set forth in an offering prospectus, which must be delivered to a prospective purchaser at least ten business days prior to a binding franchise agreement or the receipt of any consideration, whichever comes first.

The disclosure requirements enable prospective franchisees to make a decision based on a full understanding of the duties and rights of the franchisor and franchisee. The purpose of the law is to protect against fraud or the likelihood that the franchisor promises will not be met.

Three groups of people are authorized to sell franchises:

1. The person identified in the application for offering (the franchisor or agent)
2. A person licensed by the Department of Real Estate as a broker or salesperson
3. A person licensed by the commissioner of corporations as a broker/dealer

APPRAISERS

Title XI, Real Estate Appraisal Reform Amendment of the federal Financial Institutions Reform, Recovery, and Enforcement Act (FIRREA) of 1989, requires that appraisers be licensed or certified by the state for real estate transactions involving federal financial and public policy interests. This covers loans made by practically all of our financial institutions.

Every state must enact legislation to provide for certification, which is consistent with criteria established by the Appraisal Foundation, a private nonprofit corporation. Certification must be in residential and general categories (general includes income as well as residential property). An examination is required without exception. For federally related transactions that do not require a certified appraiser, the appraiser must be licensed. The criteria for licensing must be consistent with Title XI. Every state must set minimum appraiser standards, even for appraisals that are not federally related.

WEB LINK @

Business and Professions Code Sections 11300–11421 enact the Real Estate Appraisers Licensing and Certification Law (California). The Office of Real Estate Appraisers (OREA) within the Business, Transportation, and Housing Agency administers and enforces the law. (The website for OREA is *www.orea.ca.gov*.) The law also created a Real Estate Appraisers Regulation Fund, which includes a Recovery Account similar to the Real Estate Recovery Account.

The law prohibits any licensed or certified appraiser from making an appraisal where the appraised value affects the appraiser's compensation.

FAIR HOUSING

Fair housing laws mandate that real estate licensees deal with buyers, sellers, lessors, and lessees in a nondiscriminatory manner. Besides the legal penalties of our various fair housing laws, violations of fair housing legislation may be the basis of disciplinary action by the Department of Real Estate.

Federal Laws

Federal and state fair housing legislation overlaps. A single act can violate more than one fair housing act.

Civil Rights Act of 1866. The Civil Rights Act of 1866 (C.31, 14 Stat. 27) gave citizens of all races the same rights enjoyed by white citizens to inherit, purchase, lease, sell, or hold real and personal property. This act covered only race.

For many years, the act was ineffective because of the narrow court interpretation that it did not apply to private property. The Supreme Court really nullified the effect of this act.

Under the act, an aggrieved party may sue in federal court for damages, obtain an injunction to prohibit the sale to another, or obtain an order forcing the owner to sell.

Case Study
In *Jones v. Mayer* (1968) 392 U.S. 409, the U.S. Supreme Court held the act to be valid under the Thirteenth Amendment. In this case, an owner refused to sell his own house because of race. The court determined that the act prohibits all racial discrimination (both public and private) in the sale or rental of property.

Federal Fair Housing Act

Title VIII of the **Civil Rights Act of 1968** prohibits discrimination in housing based on race, color, religion, or national origin. In 1974, the Housing and Community Development Act added sex to the list of protected classes. In 1988, the **Fair Housing Amendments Act** added disability and familial status. Today, these laws are known as the federal Fair Housing Act. The **Fair Housing Act** prohibits discrimination on the basis of race, color, religion, sex, disability, familial status, or national origin. Real estate licensees must not take part in these activities, regardless of the wishes of their principals. Familial status refers to those under the age of 18 living with a parent or guardian, those in the process of settling legal custody issues, persons in the adoption process, and any pregnant person. Exempt from discrimination on the basis of familial status are communities having at least 80 percent of the units occupied by at least one person 55 years of age or older. Also exempt are housing units intended for and solely occupied by persons 62 years of age or older.

Case Study

The case of *Taylor v. Rancho Santa Barbara* (2000) 206 F.3d 932 involved a buyer of a mobile home who was refused a rental agreement because he was under 55 years of age. The plaintiff challenged the constitutionality of amendments to the Fair Housing Act that eliminated the requirement that senior citizen housing provide special services and facilities for seniors. He also challenged the California Mobilehome Residency Law (MRL) that authorizes age restrictions complying with federal law. The basis of the plaintiff's action was a violation of the 14th Amendment Equal Protection Clause, as well as the 5th Amendment's Due Process Clause. The case was dismissed by the U.S. District Court for failure to state a claim, and the Court of Appeal affirmed that neither the federal nor California laws violate the Constitution. Age-restrictive apartments and mobile home communities are an exception to antidiscrimination statutes based on family status. The court pointed out the rational basis of these laws was to provide inexpensive housing for retirees on fixed incomes.

Even if an apartment complex has a family section, designation of an area as *all-adult* is prohibited. Steering prospective tenants toward a particular area in an apartment complex and away from another area would also violate the act.

Apartments can have rules for children's use of facilities when there is a non-discriminatory reason for the difference in rules. The act does not prohibit owners from setting maximum occupancy of units as long as the rule is enforced without discrimination (unreasonably limited occupancy rules are likely to be unenforceable).

A disability is a physical or mental impairment. The term includes those having a history of, or being regarded as having, an impairment that substantially limits one or more major life activities. Persons who have AIDS are protected by the fair housing laws under this classification. The law specifically prohibits discrimination against guide dogs and support animals.

The landlord must make reasonable adjustments to rules, policies, practices, or services to afford people with disabilities the equal opportunity to enjoy a unit.

The act requires that a landlord allow a person with a disability to make reasonable modifications to the premises, at the tenant's expense, if necessary for the tenant's full use and enjoyment of the premises. The landlord can insist on restoration of the premises at the end of the tenancy if the premises would be undesirable for the general population.

Case Study

In the case of *Auburn Woods I Homeowners Association v. Fair Employment and Housing Council* (2004) 121 C.A.4th 1578, condominium residents who were suffering from depression were precluded from having a dog because it violated rules of the homeowners' association. The California Fair Employment and Housing Commission charged the homeowners' association with disability discrimination by failure to make reasonable accommodations. The administrative law judge ruled that the couple was disabled and the association discriminated against them. The superior court ruled for the homeowners' association because there was no medical evidence that a companion dog was a necessary reasonable accommodation.

The Court of Appeal reversed, ruling that there was substantial evidence to support the CFEHC decision in favor of the condominium owners. Because the couple improved when they had the dog but regressed when they had to give it up, the association must allow the dog.

Note: While this ruling was fact-specific to this situation, which involved a condominium association, it would seem to be applicable to apartment dwellers as well. Even if an animal does not qualify as a service animal, a landlord could apparently be liable for refusing an animal necessary for emotional support.

Case Study

Giebler v. M & B Associates a Limited Partnership (2003) 343 F.3d 1143 involved a plaintiff who has AIDS and is disabled. He had income of $837 per month from Social Security disability and between $300 and $400 per month from Housing Opportunities for People with AIDS.

Plaintiff was denied a rental because his income did not meet the landlord's requirements of three times the monthly rent, although his credit and rental history were good. The plaintiff's mother, who lived nearby and has adequate income and excellent credit, wanted to sign the lease but was rejected because of the landlord's policy of no cosigners.

Giebler brought action under the Federal Fair Housing Amendment Act, California's Fair Employment and Housing Act, and the Unruh Act alleging intentional discrimination for failure to reasonably accommodate Giebler's disability by refusal to accept a cosigner.

The U.S. District Court ruled for the landlord stating, "An accommodation which remedies the economic status of a disabled person is not an accommodation as contemplated by FHAA."

The 9th Circuit reversed, ruling that the FHAA includes reasonable economic accommodations to disabled tenant applicants rather than an inflexible rental policy barring cosigners. The court pointed out that renting to Giebler's mother would not be an economic burden to the landlord and would be a reasonable accommodation to a disabled resident.

The landlord also must allow the tenant, at the tenant's expense, to make reasonable alterations to the common area that is necessary for the tenant's use of that area. However, the tenant does not have to restore the common area at the end of the tenancy.

For four or more new rental units built after March 13, 1991, the act specifies structural requirements for access for people with disabilities.

Discrimination under the act includes charging families higher security fees, requiring additional fees for people with disabilities who modify their units, and, possibly, selective use of advertising media as well as the models used for advertising.

The Civil Rights Act of 1968 prohibits

- discrimination by brokers toward clients and customers;
- refusal to show, rent, or sell through false representation that a property is not available;
- discrimination in access to multiple-listing services;
- **steering**, that is, directing people of different races, religions, etc., away from or toward a particular area;
- discriminatory advertising—prohibited even when related to those activities exempt from the act;
- retaliatory acts against those making fair housing complaints and intimidation to discourage complaints;
- discriminatory sale or loan terms;
- **blockbusting**, that is, inducing panic selling by representing that prices will drop because of the entrance or possible entrance of minority groups; and
- **redlining**, that is, refusal to loan or insure within an area [*Harrison v. Heinzroth Mortgage Co.* (1977) 430 F. Supp. 893].

Exempted from the act are

- religious groups, which can discriminate in providing nonprofit housing, provided that the religion is open to all, regardless of race, sex, or national origin;
- private clubs, which can discriminate or give preference to members when selling or leasing housing for noncommercial purposes;
- owners of single-family homes, who can discriminate when selling or renting without an agent, provided they do not own more than three such homes and are not in the business; and
- owners of one to four residential units who occupy a unit, who can discriminate when renting without an agent.

Note: Neither the Civil Rights Act of 1866 nor California Fair Housing laws include these exemptions.

WEB LINK @

The Federal Fair Housing Act is enforced by the Department of Housing and Urban Development (HUD). The HUD website for the Office of Fair Housing and Equal Opportunity is *www.hud.gov/fairhousing*. While HUD can initiate complaints on its own, the aggrieved party may take either of two courses:

1. He or she may bring a complaint to HUD within one year of the discriminatory action. A hearing on the complaint would be held before an administrative law judge, who can assess civil penalties from $10,000 to $50,000, as well as actual damage and compensation for humiliation suffered because of discriminatory practices.

2. He or she may bring a civil action in state or federal district court within two years after the occurrence. In this case the court could award

   ■ actual damages plus punitive damages, court costs, and attorney fees; and

   ■ a permanent or temporary injunction or restraining order.

Failure of a broker to post in the broker's place of business the equal housing opportunity poster shown in Figure 4.2 can shift the burden onto the broker to prove an act was not discriminatory should a complaint be made.

Case Study

In the case of *Pfaff v. U.S. Dept. of Housing and Urban Development* (1996) 88 F.3rd 739, a family of five was denied a 1,200-square-foot, two-bedroom rental because the owner felt that four persons was the maximum based on size and the fact that the property lacked a basement or a backyard. HUD alleged violations of Title VIII of the Civil Rights Act of 1968, in that there was discrimination based on family size.

An administrative law judge ruled there was prima facie discrimination because the owner had not shown a business necessity for a numerical occupancy requirement and awarded $4,212.61 in compensatory damages and $20,000 in emotional distress damages plus an $8,000 civil penalty. The Court of Appeal reversed, stating that the landlord did not have to rebut any prima facie case against them and did not have to prove a compelling business necessity to justify numerical occupancy guidelines, as HUD has no current occupancy guidelines. The owner's numerical restriction was not unreasonable to prevent dilapidation of the little house. The court held that "HUD's actions were well outside the tenets of good or acceptable government."

While the government was arbitrary in the previous case, the following case involved a landlord who appeared to be arbitrary in a similar situation.

FIGURE 4.2
Fair Housing Poster

U. S. Department of Housing and Urban Development

EQUAL HOUSING OPPORTUNITY

We Do Business in Accordance With the Federal Fair Housing Law

(The Fair Housing Amendments Act of 1988)

It is illegal to Discriminate Against Any Person Because of Race, Color, Religion, Sex, Handicap, Familial Status, or National Origin

---

◼ In the sale or rental of housing or residential lots

◼ In advertising the sale or rental of housing

◼ In the financing of housing

◼ In the provision of real estate brokerage services

◼ In the appraisal of housing

◼ Blockbusting is also illegal

Anyone who feels he or she has been discriminated against may file a compliant of housing discrimination:
    1-800-669-9777 (Toll Free)
    1-800-927-9275 (TDD)

U.S. Department of Housing and Urban Development
Assistant Secretary for Fair Hosuing and Equal Opportunity
Washington, D.C. 20410

Previous editions are obsolete   form HUD-928.1A (2/2003)

FIGURE 4.2
Fair Housing Poster, Continued

U. S. Department of Housing and Urban Development

IGUALDAD DE OPORTUNIDAD
EN LA VIVIENDA

Conducimos nuestros negocios de acuerdo a la Ley Federal de Vivienda Justa

(Acta de enmiendas de 1988 de la Ley Federal de Vivienda Justa)

> # Es ilegal discriminar contra cualquier persona por razon de su raza, color, religion, sexo, incapacidad fisica o mental, la presencia de niños menores de 18 años o de mujer embarazada en su familia o su origen nacional

■ En la venta o renta de vivienda y terrenos residenciales

■ En los anuncios de venta o renta de vivienda

■ En la financiamiento de vivienda

■ Amenazar o interferir con la persona para que no registre su queja

■ En los servicios de corretaje que prestan vendedores de vivienda

■ En la valoracion de vivienda

■ Tambien es ilegal forzarle a vender o rentar su vivienda diciendole que gente de otra raza, religion o grupo etnico se estan mudando en su vecindario

Cualquier persona que sienta que fue discriminada debe de enviar su queja de discriminacion:

    1-800-669-9777 (llamada gratis)
    1-800-927-9275 (TDD llamada gratis)

U.S.Department of Housing and Urban Development
Assistant Secretary for Fair Housing and Equal Opportunity
Washington, D.C. 20410

Previous editions are obsolete

form HUD-928.1A (2/2003)

> ### Case Study
>
> In the case of *Fair Housing Council of Orange County Inc. v. Ayres* (1994) 855 F. Supp. 315, a landlord had an occupancy restriction of two persons per unit. It was alleged to have a disparate impact on families with children and was therefore discriminatory as to familial status. Families with children were denied rental if there were more than two persons in the household. Couples who had children while they were tenants were forced to leave.
>
> The court indicated that this was a prima facie case of discrimination; therefore, the defendant had a burden to show legitimate nondiscriminatory justification for the restriction. The defendant failed to show such a reason. The defendant indicated that the purpose was to protect the units against excessive wear and tear. The court pointed out that this purpose could have been accomplished with higher security deposit, greater care in tenant selection, and more frequent inspections to protect the premises.

Americans with Disabilities Act (ADA)

The **Americans with Disabilities Act** prohibits discrimination in a place of public accommodation based on an individual's physical or mental disabilities. The law also prohibits employers having 15 or more employees from discriminating against employees with disabilities. Employers must alter the workplace to provide reasonable accommodations for disabled employees, unless it creates an undue hardship to the business.

> ### Case Study
>
> The case of *Gilligan v. Jamco Development Corporation* (1997) 108 Fed.3d 246 involved a family who received federal aid to families with dependent children. In applying for a rental, they were denied because the income source was Aid to Families with Dependent Children (AFDC). The defendant never inquired as to the amount of income the Gilligan's were receiving, nor did they tell Gilligan the monthly rent. Instead, they were told that Verduga Gardens is not a "welfare building," and they were refused the right to inspect a unit.
>
> The court held that prospective tenants must be allowed to inspect, as well as apply for, residential units, and to refuse to accept a rental application from an AFDC or welfare recipient is illegal discrimination. While a review of their finances might reveal that they are unqualified to rent, their status as AFDC recipients does not make them unqualified to apply.

A "place of public accommodation" refers to a facility with a nonresidential, commercial use (stores, offices, etc.). Owners and operators of commercial facilities, including property managers and lessees, must make the facilities accessible to the extent readily achievable. "Readily achievable" is defined as easily accomplished without a great deal of expense and is based on the relationship of the costs involved to the total property value, as well as the financial abilities of the person(s) involved. Under the ADA, new construction must be readily accessible and usable by people with disabilities as well, unless it is structurally impractical to do so.

The ADA may be enforced by an action by the U.S. Attorney, or through a civil action by a private citizen. Penalties include $50,000 in civil penalties for the first violation, and $100,000 for each subsequent violation, including compensatory damages and attorney fees.

Case Study

The case of *Madden v. Del Taco, Inc.* (2007) 150 C.A.4th 294, involved a customer, Madden, who was unable to navigate his wheelchair around a concrete trash can in the middle of a 42-inch wide sidewalk in order to enter a Del Taco.

The trial court granted summary judgment for Del Taco based on the fact that there was another entrance that was handicapped accessible and the blockage of the one entrance was temporary.

The Court of Appeal reversed ruling that the Americans with Disabilities Act imposed a duty to remove architectural barriers to places of public accommodation, and in this case, removal of the barrier was readily achievable. This is a prima facie violation of ADA.

Case Study

In the case of *Southern California Housing Rights Center v. Los Feliz Towers* (2006) 426 C.A. 2d 1061, an individual with disabilities used a motorized scooter, had a van specially equipped for her, and lived in a condominium where she had a deeded garage parking space. She requested an accessible parking space—either the manager's space or one of the visitor spaces. While her request was denied, management policy allowed her to park in the front of the building, and a security guard would then park her car. The condominium board did offer to park her car every morning in one of the guest spaces where it would remain easily accessible to her. She felt the parking service diminished her independence. Because of a bladder control problem, she felt humiliated having to turn her keys over to an employee after she had wet the seat. After moving out and renting her unit, she filed action for housing discrimination under the Americans with Disabilities Act.

While the court did not rule as to whether reserving a specific space was necessary for compliance with ADA, and whether the association's proposal was a reasonable accommodation, they granted summary judgment for the association ruling that ADA did not apply because this was private property and not a place of public accommodation. However, the court did rule that the condo association was a business, and the Unruh Act prohibited discrimination. The court, however, denied the claims for negligence and punitive damages.

Note: The condominium association could have avoided legal fees and the cost of their alternative solutions by simply reserving several parking spaces for people with disabilities.

Case Study

The case of *Long v. Coast Resorts Inc.* (2002) 267 F.3d 918 involved the Orleans Hotel and Casino in Las Vegas. The hotel was built in 1997, well after the enactment of the Americans with Disabilities Act. There were 819 bathroom doors 28 inches wide, but ADA requires a 32-inch width for new construction. In addition, the casino bar areas were not accessible for people with disabilities.

The Court of Appeals ruled that the hotel must modify 819 of its rooms to expand the bathroom doors, as well as make the casino bar areas accessible.

Note: While architects should understand ADA requirements and building inspectors should check plans for ADA compliance, they don't always do so. In this case, it was a costly oversight.

Case Study

The case of *Lonberg v. Sanborn Theatres, Inc.* (2001) 259 F.3d 1029 involved a multiplex cinema that was not fully wheelchair accessible. The wheelchair-bound plaintiffs sued the theater operators, the lessor, and the architect based on the Americans with Disabilities Act.

The U.S. District Court granted partial summary judgment for the architect, as Title III of ADA does not name architects as possibly liable for discrimination. The Court of Appeals affirmed, since the architect was not the owner, lessee, lessor, or operator.

Note: It appears that owners cannot rely on architects for compliance with ADA. Perhaps architects' contracts should contain an owner indemnity clause for failure to comply with ADA requirements.

Case Study

In the case of *Coronado v. Cobblestone Village Community Rentals L.P.* (2008) 163 C.A. 4th 831, a tenant was injured when his wheelchair toppled over a curb as he was trying to reach his parking space. The tenant alleged an Unruh Act and an Americans with Disabilities Act violation.

The trial court concluded that neither the Unruh Act nor the ADA applied because an apartment parking lot was a private common area and not a place of public accommodation.

The appeals court affirmed the ruling that apartment owners are not liable for failure to install a curb cut because it was not a place of public accommodation.

Note: The tenant could have modified the common area at the tenant's expense under the Fair Housing Amendment Act of 1988.

Advertising

The Civil Rights Act of 1968 prohibits discriminatory advertising; however, there has been little guidance as to what is discriminatory. The problem is that words may have different meanings to different ethnic groups, different meanings geographically, and meanings may even change by usage. The Department of Housing and Urban Development, which enforces fair housing laws, gave a partial clarification in a 1995 internal memo with the following 5 points.

1. *Race, Color, National Origin.* Complaints should not be filed for use of "master bedroom," "rare find," or "desirable neighborhood." Some groups felt that "master" indicated slavery and "rare find," and "desirable neighborhood" indicated areas without minorities.

2. *Religion.* Statements such as "apartment complex with chapel" or "services" such as "kosher meals available" do not, on their face, state a preference for persons who might use such facilities. Prior to HUD's memo, groups were advising that any reference in an ad to religion would violate the Federal Fair Housing Act.

3. *Sex.* Use of the term "master bedroom," "mother-in-law suite," and "bachelor apartment" do not violate the act because they are commonly used physical descriptions.

4. *Disability.* Descriptions of properties such as "great view," "fourth-floor walk-up," and "walk-in closets" do not violate the Act. Services or facilities such as "jogging trails" or references to neighborhoods, such as "walk to bus stop," do not violate the Act.

   Because many people with disabilities cannot perform these activities, it was formerly thought that references to walking, biking, jogging, and so on would violate the law. It also is acceptable to describe the conduct required of residents such as "nonsmoking" or "sober." You can't, however, say "nonsmokers" or "no alcoholics" because these describe persons, not barred activities. You can advertise accessibility features such as "wheelchair ramp."

5. *Familial Status.* While advertisements may not contain a limitation on the number or ages of children or state a preference for adults, couples or singles, you are not "facially discriminatory" by advertising the properties as "two-bedroom, cozy, family room," services and facilities with "no bicycles allowed," or neighborhoods with "quiet streets."

A number of organizations have made lists of what they consider acceptable as well as discriminatory advertising terms. Unfortunately, there is disagreement among these lists. The Miami Valley Fair Housing Center Inc. has what many consider a reasonable list that can be viewed at *www.mvfairhousing.com*.

State Laws

Because of the danger that an advertisement might be considered discriminatory, it is wisest to err on the side of caution, because penalties can be severe.

Unruh Civil Rights Act. "All persons within the jurisdiction of this state are free and equal, and no matter what their race, color, religion, ancestry, or national origin, are entitled to the full and equal accommodations, advantages, facilities, or services in all business establishments of every kind whatsoever" (Civil Code Section 51). Gender, disability, medical condition, marital status, and sexual orientation were added in 2006. Because real estate brokerage is a business, discrimination against clients or customers by a broker is a violation of the Unruh Civil Rights Act.

> **Case Study**
>
> The case of *Beliveau v. Caras* (1995) 873 F. Supp. 1393 involved an action brought to federal court based on a claim of **sexual harassment**.
>
> A female tenant alleged a resident manager sexually harassed her. Among other things, the manager allegedly stared at her when she was lying by the pool in her swimsuit and made off-color flirtatious remarks. It was alleged that while making faucet repairs, the manager put his arm around her and told her she was an attractive woman and that he would like to keep her company. He made remarks about her breasts and grabbed her buttock when she walked away. In an action to dismiss, the court held that she had shown a good cause of action.
>
> The court pointed out that discrimination may be based on a sexual harassment case. Offensive touching, if proved, would support a sexual harassment claim. If the manager was found to have sexually harassed the tenant, the owner of the property could be held liable under the doctrine of respondeat superior.
>
> *Note*: This case could open a floodgate of allegations by tenants. To avoid false allegations, landlords and property managers should be careful about being alone with a tenant in an apartment.

The Unruh Act is enforced through civil action for damages.

Victims of discrimination can obtain:

- cease and desist order;
- discriminatory sale or loan terms;
- out of pocket expenses;
- damages for emotional distress;
- exemplary damages three times actual damages, or $1,000, whichever is greater.

Persons who suffer any violence or intimidation can be awarded a civil penalty of $25,000 plus attorney fees.

Thus, the act was extended to cover age discrimination; it has also been extended to include blindness and other physical disabilities, as well as sexual orientation and marital status. The California Supreme Court held that the antidiscrimination provisions of the Unruh Civil Rights Act are not confined only to the limited category of protective classes, but rather protect all persons from any arbitrary discrimination by a business establishment [*Marina Point, Ltd. v. Wolfson* (1982) 30 C.3d 721]. Thus, the act was extended to cover age discrimination; it has also been extended to include blindness and other physical disabilities, as well as sexual orientation and marital status. The California Supreme Court held that the antidiscrimination provisions of the Unruh Civil Rights Act are not confined only to the limited category of protective classes, but rather protect all persons from any arbitrary discrimination by a business establishment [*Marina Point, Ltd. v. Wolfson* (1982) 30 C.3d 721].

The small claims court has jurisdiction in cases involving the Unruh Act whose damages do not exceed $7,500.

Case Study

In the case of *Hubert v. Williams* (1982) 133 C.A.3d Supp.1, a quadriplegic was evicted because his 24-hour-a-day attendant was an alleged lesbian, and the quadriplegic associated with homosexuals. The Unruh Act was held also to extend to discrimination based on sexual preference. The court held that if homosexuals are protected, then persons who associate with this protected group also should be protected.

California Fair Employment and Housing Act (Rumford Act)

The **California Fair Employment and Housing Act** (Government Code Section 12900 et seq.) prohibits discrimination because of race, color, religion, sex, marital status, national origin, or ancestry in supplying housing accommodations. The **Rumford Act** has been expanded to include all housing, including single-family residences. The only exception is renting to a roomer or boarder in a single-family house with no more than one roomer or boarder.

Case Study

The case of *Botosan v. Paul McNally Realty* (2000) 216 F.3d 827 involved a paraplegic who claimed ADA and Unruh Act violations because a Realty World Office lacked parking for people with disabilities, so he was precluded from patronizing the office. Before filing suit, the plaintiff did not notify any local authorities as to the alleged violations. The district court awarded Botosan $1,000 minimum statutory Unruh Act damages. The Court of Appeals affirmed, ruling that prior notification to local authorities is not required, damages need not be proven, nor can an owner avoid liability by transferring compliance responsibility under a lease provision.

Note: This case points out that owners and tenants must take the Americans with Disabilities Act seriously and comply because some people might be looking to profit by failure to do so.

WEB LINK @

Complaints under the act are brought within 60 days of the discriminatory action to the Department of Fair Employment and Housing (*www.dfeh.ca.gov*). The filing of such a complaint does not preclude the injured party from commencing an action under any other law.

The Department of Fair Employment and Housing will investigate and can order the owner to

- sell or rent the unit to the complainant, or
- offer to the complainant the next available unit, or
- pay civil damages up to $10,000 ($25,000 for a second violation, and $50,000 for three or more violations).

Case Study

The case of *Smith v. Fair Employment & Housing Commission* (1996) 12 C.4th 1143 involved a landlord who refused to rent to an unmarried couple based on her religious convictions that to do so would be to condone sin.

The couple filed a complaint with the California Fair Employment and Housing Commission alleging violation of the Unruh Act, as well as California's Fair Employment and Housing Act. While an administrative law judge ruled in favor of the couple and awarded damages, the decision was appealed to the Court of Appeal where it was reversed.

The California Superior Court reversed the Court of Appeal and pointed out that neither federal nor state law allows an exemption to a landlord for discrimination because of a personal contrary religious belief.

A constitutional amendment was enacted that barred the state from interfering with an owner's right to sell or lease his or her property. This amendment, which would have had the effect of repealing the Rumford Act, was held to violate the equal protection clause of the Fourteenth Amendment to the U.S. Constitution.

As of January 1, 2007, all of California's fair housing laws prohibit discrimination based on race, skin color, gender, religion, marital status, national origin, ancestry, familial status, disability, source of income, and sexual orientation. In addition, California courts prohibit discrimination that is arbitrary even when it is against groups not specifically protected by California's law.

Business and Professions Code

Section 125.6 of California's Business and Professions Code provides that "every person who holds a license under the provisions of this code is subject to disciplinary action . . . if, because of the applicant's race, color, sex, religion, ancestry, disability, marital status, or national origin, he or she refuses to perform the licensed activity or aids or incites the refusal to perform such licensed activity by another licensee . . . [or] makes any discrimination or restriction in the performance of the licensed activity." The code would appear to cover any discriminatory practice committed while acting as a licensee.

**California
Omnibus Housing
Nondiscrimination Act**

This act makes all California acts dealing with discrimination consistent with the California Fair Employment and Housing Discrimination Act. Every act will apply to national origin, ancestry, race, color, gender, religion, marital status, familial status, disability, source of income, and sexual orientation.

■ **SUMMARY**

The purpose of the real estate law is to protect the public. The Department of Real Estate administers the licensing of brokers and salespersons, as well as the regulation of their activities. This chapter sets forth the activities requiring licensure, as well as those activities exempt from the real estate licensing requirements.

After a hearing, in accordance with the Administrative Procedure Act, licenses can be revoked, suspended, or denied for a number of specified violations. After a license has been revoked, suspended, or denied, the real estate commissioner has the power to grant a restricted license, which is probationary in nature.

If a member of the public is injured because of his or her dealings with a real estate licensee for an activity for which licensing is required, and the injured party obtains a judgment against the licensee that is uncollectible, the injured party can apply to the Department of Real Estate for reimbursement. Injured parties can collect up to a total of $50,000 from the recovery account for any single transaction.

Besides the listing and sale of real property, licensing allows the broker to engage in a number of specialized activities, including the following:

- Mortgage broker: These brokers solicit borrowers and lenders for loans secured by real estate, and their activities are strictly regulated. (Under the Federal Secure and Fair Enforcement Mortgage Licensing Act [SAFE Act], every state must have a system for licensing mortgage originators.)

- Real property syndicate security dealer: A real estate broker is exempt from the licensing requirements of the corporation's code and may sell both corporate and noncorporate syndicate interests.

- Mineral, oil, and gas broker: While MOG licenses are no longer being issued, a real estate licensee can engage in MOG transactions without additional licensing and without permits.

- Escrow agent: A real estate broker can act as an escrow agent in those transactions in which he or she represented either the buyer or seller, or in which the broker was a principal to the transaction.

- Mobile home sales: With specified restrictions, a real estate licensee can engage in the sale of mobile homes.

- Advance fee rental agent: While there is a separate rental agent license, a real estate broker is exempt from the licensing requirement and may engage in a prepaid rental listing service.

- Business opportunity broker: A real estate licensee can engage in the sale of business opportunities.

- Franchise sales: A real estate licensee is authorized to sell franchise opportunities.

Real estate licensees must comply with all federal and state fair housing laws. These include the following:

- Civil Rights Act of 1866: Citizens of all races shall have the same rights as enjoyed by white citizens to inherit, purchase, lease, sell, or hold real and personal property.

- Civil Rights Act of 1968 (Federal Fair Housing Act): This act prohibits discrimination in housing based on race, color, sex, religion, or national origin. A 1988 amendment extended its coverage to include familial status and disability.

- Unruh Civil Rights Act: This act prohibits discrimination by a business on the basis of race, color, religion, ancestry, national origin, age, sex, and sexual preference.

- Fair Employment and Housing Act (Rumford Act): This act prohibits discrimination based on race, color, religion, sex, marital status, national origin, or ancestry.

- Business and Professions Code: Provides for commissioner disciplinary action against licensees for discriminatory practices.

Because of overlapping coverage, a civil rights violation is likely to be a violation of several acts. The Omnibus Housing Nondiscrimination Act expands the protected categories of all California antidiscrimination acts to conform with the California Fair Employment and Housing Act.

■ DISCUSSION CASES

1. The plaintiff negotiated a lease and an option to extend the lease. The defendant agreed to pay the plaintiff $7,500 if the option was exercised. Prior to the expiration of the lease period, and after the broker's license had lapsed, the lessor and lessee agreed to a new option, and a new lease was entered into at terms different from those originally specified. **Is the former broker entitled to $7,500?**

   Cline v. Yamaga (1979) 97 C.A.3d 239

2. Katz, a broker, purchased a building that he knew had code violations and was subject to an order to demolish an illegal room. Katz advertised the property as a "fixer-upper" that would be sold "as is." Katz asked the buyer's broker if he knew there were code violations. The buyer's broker mentioned he had noticed some. Katz did not inform the buyer's broker of all of the violations or of the city order to demolish the room. The purchaser later discovered the violations. Katz offered to rescind the sale but refused to pay for work already performed by the purchaser. **Was the Department of Real Estate justified in revoking Katz's license?**

   Katz v. Department of Real Estate (1979) 96 C.A.3d 895

3. During a marriage that lasted two months and was subsequently annulled because of fraud, a wife invested in a joint venture with her husband. The wife was defrauded in the joint venture and subsequently obtained a judgment against her former husband, who was a real estate broker. The judgment was uncollectible against the broker. **Is the former wife entitled to compensation from the Recovery Account?**

   Powers v. Fox (1979) 96 C.A.3d 440

4. The recovery account, in determining what to pay, used a setoff of tax benefits received by an investor against the loss. **Was this action proper?**

   Froid v. Fox (1982) 132 C.A.3d 832

5. A mortgage loan broker charged escrow fees based on the maximum allowed by law. **Was this action proper?**

   Pacific Plan of California v. Kinder (1978) 84 C.A.3d 215

6. A landlord had a minimum income policy for rentals. The requirement was a gross income at least three times greater than the rent. The plaintiff claimed that the policy arbitrarily discriminated against persons with lower incomes regardless of their actual ability to pay, and that it discriminated against women because of disparate earnings. **Does this income test violate the Unruh Act?**

   Harris v. Capital Growth Investors XIV (1991) 52 C.3d 1142

7. The real estate commissioner denied a license on the grounds that the applicant had been convicted of distributing cocaine. **Was the action of the real estate commissioner proper?**

   Brandt v. Fox (1979) 90 C.A.3d 737

8. The plaintiff was arrested after landing an airplane containing between 800 and 1,000 pounds of marijuana. He pleaded guilty to possession for the purpose of sale. **Was the commissioner's action to revoke the plaintiff's license proper?**

   Golde v. Fox (1979) 98 C.A.3d 167

9. Pieri pleaded guilty to obtaining unemployment benefits by fraud. He was placed on probation, and the charge was dismissed at the end of the probationary period. Pieri's application for a broker's license three years later was denied because of a conviction for a crime involving moral turpitude. **Was the commissioner's action proper?**

   Pieri v. Fox (1979) 96 C.A.3d 802

10. A landlord had a policy allowing two adults and two children to occupy an apartment only if the second child was born after the family had taken possession. **Is the landlord's policy proper?**

    Smith v. Ring Bros. Management Corp. (1986) 183 C.A.3d 649

11. A real estate salesman falsely represented himself as a real estate broker to induce the plaintiff to invest in short-term loans secured by trust deeds. The salesperson took the money but did not invest in the trust deeds. After a judgment that could not be collected, the plaintiff asked for reimbursement from the recovery account. The commissioner took the position that the defendant was not licensed as a broker and so could not engage in the transactions; therefore the account should not be liable. **Do you agree?**

    Vinci v. Edmonds (1986) 185 C.A.3d 1251

12. **Is a creditor who has obtained a judgment entitled to recover from the recovery account when the broker's debt was discharged in bankruptcy?**

    Armenta v. Edmonds (1988) 201 C.A.3d 464

13. The town of Huntington, New York, has about 200,000 residents, of which 95 percent are white and less than 4 percent are black. A private developer sought to change the zoning from single-family housing to multifamily rental to build a project fostering integration. The town refused to rezone. **Does the town's action violate the Civil Rights Act of 1968?**

    Town of Huntington v. Huntington Branch, NAACP (1989) 488 U.S. 15

14. A mobile home park charged a per diem guest fee, as well as a parking fee, for a home health-care aide required for an infant with respiratory problems. **Is there any problem as to these fees?**

    U.S. v. California Mobile Home Park Management Co. (1994) 29 F.3d 1413

15. The real estate commissioner automatically suspended the license of a broker who failed to reimburse the recovery fund. The broker alleged that due process was violated because he did not have a hearing. **Is the broker correct?**

    Rodriguez v. Calif. Dept. of Real Estate (1997) 51 C.A.4th 1289

16. A title insurer paid a lender's claim after a mortgage broker embezzled the funds that were to pay off existing trust deeds. The title insurer then sued the broker and obtained a judgment that could not be collected. The title insurer then filed a claim with the California Department of Real Estate recovery fund. **Does the title insurer have a valid claim against the recovery fund?**

    Stewart Title Guaranty Co. v. Park (2001) 250 F.3d 1249

17. Using a business visitor pass, Jankey frequently visited the Twentieth Century Fox film and production lot in Los Angeles. Because he was confined to a wheelchair, he was unable to access the commissary, studio store, or automatic teller machine. Jankey alleged violation of the Americans with Disabilities Act. **Was the act violated in this case?**

    Jankey v. Twentieth Century Fox Film Corporation (2000)
    212 F.3d 1159

18. A quadriplegic who was confined to a wheelchair was denied access to the California Center for the Arts in Escondido because of her small dog who was able to retrieve small dropped items. The dog had barked during intermission at several prior concerts. **Was the refusal to allow the dog to attend events justified?**

    Lentini v. California Center for the Arts, Escondido (2004)
    370 F.3d 837

19. An investor renamed apartment buildings Korean World Towers, Wilshire Korean Towers, The Sterling Korean Plaza, Windsor Square Korean Towers, Fremont Place, Korean Plaza, and Hancock Asian Towers. While the buildings were near the Koreatown area of Los Angeles, the residents of these buildings were primarily African American.

    It was alleged that the use of Korean in the names, as well as the Korean flag in their advertising, indicated a preference for Korean and Asian tenants. **Should the court grant a preliminary injunction against the use of "Korean" in the names of the buildings? Why?**

    Housing Rights Center v. Donald Sterling Corp. (2003)
    274 Fed. Supp. 2nd 1129

20. A "for sale by owner" Internet listing service charged a flat fee for Internet listings but not sales commissions. They were notified by the Real Estate Commissioner that they must be represented by a California Real Estate Broker. **Do you agree with the commissioner?**

    forsalebyowner.com Corporation v. Zinnemann (2005)
    347 Fed. Supp. 2nd 868

21. A licensed broker who managed over 1,000 apartments pleaded guilty to three misdemeanor code violations. Before the guilty plea, he had been convicted of 50 code violations and had been disciplined by the State Bar. The DRE revoked the broker's license, contending that the violations were done with the intent of financial gain. **Was the revocation proper?**

    Robbins v. Davi (2009) 175 C.A. 4th 118

22. A jury determined that a broker had negligently misrepresented square footage of a home. The jury did not find that there was clear and convincing evidence that the broker acted fraudulently. The Department of Real Estate suspended the brokers license based on the jury verdict of negligent misrepresentation. **Was the DRE suspension justified?**

    The Grubb Co. Inc. v. Department of Real Estate (2011) 194 C.A. 4th 1494

■ CHAPTER QUIZ

1. A person would MOST likely contact the real estate commissioner to

   a. resolve a salesperson/broker commission dispute.

   b. report fraud of a licensee.

   c. obtain an opinion of the legality of a course of action.

   d. arbitrate disputes between brokers.

2. Which persons would require a real estate license?

   a. An attorney-in-fact selling property of another

   b. An attorney-at-law taking a listing

   c. A paid administrator of an estate selling the decedent's property

   d. None of the above

3. A broker for a corporation who also wants to conduct a separate brokerage business MUST

   a. sell his or her corporate stock.

   b. obtain a separate broker's license.

   c. operate through another licensee.

   d. return the corporate license to the commissioner.

4. A nonresident who wishes to obtain a California real estate license MUST

   a. first establish California residency.

   b. consent to process service on the secretary of state if the prospective licensee cannot be located within the state.

   c. also be licensed in his or her state of residency.

   d. be 21 years of age.

5. A three-hour course in ethics is required to be taken

   a. prior to taking the real estate broker examination.

   b. within 18 months of obtaining a salesperson's license.

   c. prior to a salesperson's first license renewal.

   d. for license renewals, but only after the first renewal for salespersons.

6. Which is *NOT* sufficient cause for the revocation of a real estate license?

    a. Commingling of principal and personal funds

    b. Acting for more than one party in a transaction

    c. Making a substantial misrepresentation

    d. Making any false promises of a character likely to influence, persuade, or induce

7. Which is *NOT* grounds for disciplinary action by the real estate commissioner?

    a. Failure of an agent to disclose an ownership interest in property being sold

    b. Failure to exercise reasonable supervision over the acts of salespersons

    c. Violation of the Franchise Investment Law

    d. Revealing to a buyer problems that make the property unsuited to his purpose

8. Broker Thomas, who was a member of the city planning commission, told his friend broker Jones that an area was to be rezoned from agricultural use to commercial use. Broker Thomas did not receive any consideration for this information. Broker Jones purchased several parcels in the area and made a profit when the zoning was changed. Which broker has placed his license in jeopardy?

    a. Thomas

    b. Jones

    c. Both Thomas and Jones

    d. Neither Thomas nor Jones

9. The maximum amount a person can obtain from a licensee after obtaining a judgment against the licensee for a fraudulent act is

    a. $20,000.

    b. $50,000 for each offense.

    c. $250,000.

    d. the amount of the judgment.

10. Which activity requires a real estate license?

    a. Being the resident manager of an apartment building

    b. Selling more than eight parcels of one's own real estate in one year

    c. Subdividing one's own property

    d. Acting as a mortgage loan broker

11. A $5,000 fee that a broker charged for negotiating a three-year second trust deed for $20,000 is

   a. usurious.   b. voidable.

   c. illegal.   d. legal.

12. A broker's loan statement is prepared for the benefit of the

   a. broker.   b. Department of Real Estate.

   c. lender.   d. borrower.

13. In advertising a mobile home, a broker used "no down payment" in the ads because he had arranged a separate loan to cover the down payment. The advertising was

   a. proper, because there was 100 percent financing.

   b. expressly prohibited by law.

   c. unethical but not illegal.

   d. proper, if all loan terms were included in the ad.

14. In selling mobile homes, a real estate broker may *NOT*

   a. have an office where six model homes are displayed.

   b. advertise "no down payment" if the payment is to be borrowed.

   c. fail to withdraw advertising within 48 hours of receipt of notice of nonavailability.

   d. do any of the above

15. After collecting an advance rental fee of $75, you are unable to provide your client with a rental that suits her. When she requests a refund, upon expiration of her rental contract, you must return

   a. nothing, if you provided a list of at least three rentals.

   b. $50.

   c. $25.

   d. $40.

16. Which of the following is *NOT* required to be included in the notice required under the Bulk Sales Act?

   a. Name of seller   b. Date and place of sale

   c. Sales price and terms   d. All of the above

17. In cases of noncompliance with the Bulk Sales Act, the party likely to be MOST adversely affected would be the

    a. seller.
    b. purchaser.

    c. creditors of the seller.
    d. Franchise Tax Board.

18. As a licensee dealing with people of other races, you should

    a. suggest that they could be better served by dealing with agents of their own race.

    b. be frank and honest in explaining the problems of locating in areas having few people of their race.

    c. be proper and helpful, even though you would prefer they seek help elsewhere.

    d. be completely "color-blind" regarding race.

19. The federal case that upheld fair housing was

    a. *Jones v. Mayer.*

    b. *Brown v. Board of Education.*

    c. *Shelley v. Kraemer.*

    d. *Wellenkamp v. Bank of America.*

20. A nonprofit women's organization intends to develop housing for members. It will limit rentals to women and will give preference to unmarried mothers. This action would likely be a violation of the

    a. Civil Rights Act of 1866.
    b. Civil Rights Act of 1968.

    c. Rumford Act.
    d. Acts in b and c.

21. The Civil Rights Act of 1968, as amended, does NOT prohibit

    a. sex discrimination.

    b. age discrimination.

    c. housing reserved for the elderly.

    d. discrimination against people with disabilities.

22. A broker takes listings in an area where property values are going down because the neighborhood is changing, and there is a mass exodus of whites. Which of the following actions by the broker would be a violation of fair housing laws?

    a. Advertising "Sell your property fast before you lose equity"

    b. Offering whites a lower commission rate to sell their property

    c. Both a and b

    d. Neither a nor b

23. Which of the following is an example of steering?

    a. Directing whites away from mixed-race areas

    b. Advertising properties in black areas only in newspapers aimed at black readers

    c. Both a and b

    d. Neither a nor b

24. Refusal to make a mortgage loan within a designated area is known as

    a. steering.   b. redlining.

    c. blockbusting.   d. none of the above

25. For a broker's violation of the Civil Rights Act of 1968, the courts would *NOT*

    a. issue a restraining order.

    b. award actual damages.

    c. award punitive damages.

    d. revoke or suspend the broker's license.

CHAPTER FIVE

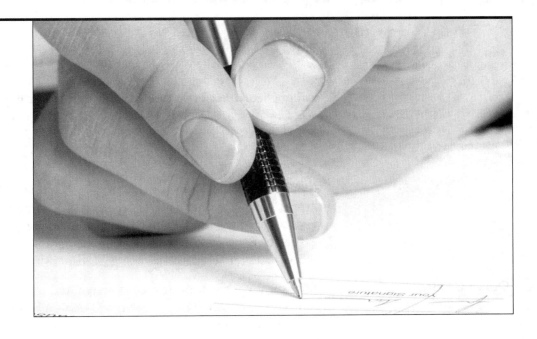

LAW OF CONTRACTS

■ KEY TERMS

accord and satisfaction
anticipatory breach
assignment of contract
bilateral contract
breach of contract
commercial frustration
contract of adhesion
divisible contract
duress
emancipated minor
estoppel
executed contract
executory contract

express contract
illusory contract
implied contract
judgment
laches
liquidated damages
menace
novation
option
parol evidence rule
quasi contract
right of first refusal
seals

statute of frauds
third-party beneficiary
time is of the essence
undue influence
Uniform Electronic
    Transactions Act
    (UETA)
unilateral contract
valid contract
voidable contract
void contract
waiver

■ TYPES OF CONTRACTS

A contract is an agreement between two or more parties to do or not to do something. Valid contracts are generally enforceable under the law.

Express Versus Implied   Contracts are either express or implied. An **express contract** is an agreement stated in words. The terms of the agreement may be set forth, either orally or in writing. An agreement whereby a buyer agrees to buy, and a seller agrees to sell a property at an agreed-on price and terms, would be an express contract. Later in this chapter, you will learn why most real estate contracts must be express contracts.

An **implied contract** is an agreement that, while not specifically stated, is understood by the parties. Section 1621 of the Civil Code states, "An implied contract is one, the existence and terms of which are manifested by conduct." For example, assume that you ask a pest control firm to make a termite inspection of a property. While you never agreed to pay a particular amount, or even any amount, for the termite inspection, a reasonable person would understand that the pest control firm will expect to be paid for its services. The party ordering the report should expect to be charged for the work, and the party performing the work should expect to be paid. Therefore, an implied contract to pay the reasonable value of the services rendered exists.

Quasi Contract

In a **quasi contract**, no real contractual intent exists. The law implies the existence of a contract. The law often will imply a contract when one party benefited but did not really consent to any agreement. For example, suppose by mistake your neighbor paid the real estate taxes on your property. You would be obligated, as a matter of equity or fairness, in a quasi contract to reimburse your neighbor for the amount of taxes paid for your benefit.

Bilateral Versus Unilateral

Contracts may be bilateral or unilateral agreements. A **bilateral contract** is an agreement in which a mutual exchange of promises occurs—a promise for a promise. If a pest control firm offered to provide a termite inspection for a property at a stated price and you agreed to have it performed at the price stated, you would have formed a bilateral contract. This is an example of an express (stated) bilateral contract.

Offers to purchase real estate, when accepted, form bilateral contracts. The buyer, who is usually the *offeror*, agrees to buy at a specified price and terms, and the seller, usually the *offeree*, agrees to sell at that price and those terms.

Exclusive-right-to-sell listings are bilateral contracts. The owners promise to pay a fee to the broker if the broker obtains a ready, willing, and able buyer according to the terms of the listing or any other terms the sellers are willing to accept. In exchange, the broker promises to use diligence to obtain a buyer.

A **unilateral contract** is a promise for an act; one party makes a promise to induce another party to act. The second party (offeree) is not bound to act, but if the offeree accepts the offer by performing the requested act, a binding contract is formed. For example, suppose you offered to pay a painter $800 if he would repair the stucco on your garage and paint the exterior with two coats of paint. The painter would not be obligated to perform because you cannot bind another party to a contract without that party's assent. However, if the painter were to repair the stucco and paint the garage as requested, he would have accepted your offer by his performance and would be entitled to be paid as agreed.

An open (nonexclusive) listing is a unilateral contract. Under an open listing, an owner promises to pay a broker should the broker succeed in procuring a buyer. The broker is under no obligation to use diligence to look for a buyer, but if the broker does procure a buyer, the broker would, by performance, be accepting the offer. If the listing required that a broker use due diligence to seek a buyer, it would be a bilateral contract (promise for a promise) and not an open listing (promise for an act).

Executory Versus Executed

A contract is either executory or executed. An **executory contract** is one that has not yet been fully performed. An agreement between a buyer and seller for the sale of land would be executory until escrow was closed. The agreement would be executory until title was transferred and the consideration was paid.

An **executed contract** is one in which everything that was required to be performed has been performed. After escrow closes on a sales agreement, the contract becomes an executed one. (Do not confuse an executed contract with the execution of a document, which is the signing of the document.)

■ ESSENTIALS OF A VALID CONTRACT

For a **valid contract** to exist, four elements are necessary:

1. Competent parties
2. Mutual consent
3. Legal purpose
4. Consideration

Valid contracts generally are enforceable. Exceptions are contracts outlawed by the statute of limitations or discharged in bankruptcy, which, while valid agreements, are nevertheless unenforceable.

Competent Parties

A minor is anyone under the age of 18. Contracts for the purchase or sale of real property entered into by unemancipated minors are void. A void contract is the same as having no agreement at all because the agreement does not bind either of the parties to it. (For information about void contracts, refer to Void and Voidable Contracts later in this section.) A minor can contract only for necessities—items required for support, such as food and clothing.

Most contracts by minors for other than necessities are subject to disaffirmance (annulment) by the minor within a reasonable time after reaching the age of 18. In California, only the former minor has this right to disaffirm and not the person with whom the minor contracted. A minor who claimed to be of contractual age is not prevented from disaffirming the contract. Therefore, parties who deal with individuals who could be minors have a duty to ascertain the status of the person they are dealing with.

After reaching the age of 18, a person can ratify contracts made as a minor so that the contracts no longer can be disaffirmed. After the age of 18, any action indicating that the person intended to be bound—payment on a property, repairing, altering, renting, or offering the property for sale—would be a ratification.

An **emancipated minor** is an exception to the general rule that minors cannot contract for other than necessities. Emancipated minors can contract as adults and cannot disaffirm their contracts. Minors can be emancipated if they

- are married or unmarried (widowed or divorced);
- enter military service on active duty; or
- receive a declaration of emancipation from the court (Civil Code Section 62).

If a broker arranges a sale to a minor and the minor later disaffirms the purchase agreement, the minor could be entitled to the return of consideration paid to the seller. The broker could be liable to the seller for the damages suffered.

A person adjudged insane cannot contract. Any contract entered into would be void. The same holds true for persons not adjudged insane but who are wholly without understanding. Both minors and incompetents can, however, convey, mortgage, lease, or acquire real property following a superior court order obtained through appropriate guardianship or conservatorship proceedings.

A person who is of unsound mind but not wholly without understanding and who has not been adjudged insane can void contracts they entered into. These contracts are valid unless voided. After regaining sanity, a person can ratify or disaffirm a contract made while of unsound mind.

A person of unsound mind who has not been adjudged insane and who has lucid periods could enter into a binding contract during a lucid period.

A person who is under the influence of alcohol and/or drugs and as a result is wholly without understanding cannot contract. However, merely being under the influence of alcohol and/or drugs generally is not sufficient by itself to void a contract.

Persons sentenced to imprisonment in state prisons are deprived of their civil rights to the extent necessary for the security of the institution in which they are confined and for the reasonable protection of the public. Convicts do not forfeit their property. They may acquire property by gift, inheritance, or will under certain conditions, and they may convey their property or acquire property through conveyance. The Department of Corrections may restrict conveyances made for business purposes.

Aliens have contractual capacity in California.

The existence of a meeting of the minds is decided by the courts based on how a reasonable person would view the words and actions of the parties. Therefore, a secret intent of a different performance by a party would have no effect.

Mutual Consent

An offer and acceptance that indicate a meeting of the minds on a definite and certain agreement usually are considered evidence of mutual consent.

The Offer.   The offer must be a clear and definite offer made with the intent that when it is accepted, there will be a binding agreement.

A letter of intent is a nonbinding expression of interest. Even though definite terms may be expressed, it is not an offer. Breach of a letter of intent would not entitle the other party to damages.

Acceptance.   A contract is formed when the offeree (person to whom a definite and certain offer is made) accepts the offer of the offeror (person making the offer). An offer can specify the manner of acceptance, but if no form for acceptance is specified, the offer can be accepted in any reasonable manner.

In the case of *Hofer v. Young* (1995) 38 C.A.4th 52, the court held that a FAX is "a reasonable and increasingly common means of modern communication." While acceptance may be by FAX, unless the offer prescribes the means of acceptance, records should be kept to prove that the FAX was sent as well as the time it was received.

Professional Publishing Corporation's Standard Residential Purchase Agreement provides that a document is to be considered delivered at the time the FAX is transmitted, provided a transmission report is generated reflecting the accurate transmission of the document.

Acceptance is possible by e-mail because e-mail is "a reasonable and increasingly common means of modern communication." Pads are available that allow signatures to be electronically attached to documents. A person can scan documents and send them by e-mail as long as that person can show the original signed document. California is one of 47 states that have passed the **Uniform Electronic Transactions Act** that gives legal recognition to electronic signatures in business transactions.

At an auction, the persons who are bidding are the offerors. They make their bids to the auctioneer, who is the offeree. The auctioneer does not have to accept any offer unless the auction is being conducted *without reserve*, which means the seller has agreed in advance that the highest bid will be accepted. A bidder at a real estate auction that is not held "without reserve" should realize that the high bid does not mean the bidder has made a purchase unless the bid is accepted.

Acceptance takes place when the offeree notifies the offeror or the offeror's agent of the acceptance. Communicating acceptance to a third party who is not an agent of the offeror is not an acceptance. At an auction, the fall of the auctioneer's hammer signifies acceptance and is considered notification to the bidder. The act of mailing a written acceptance constitutes notification (effective upon posting, Civil Code 1583). Because it might become necessary to prove mailing, a postal receipt is desirable.

Case Study
In the case of *Gibbs v. American Savings* (1990) 217 C.A.3d 1372, the buyers gave their acceptance of a seller's counteroffer to a company mail clerk at 10 A.M. The mail clerk failed to take it promptly to the post office. At 11 A.M., the seller called to revoke the counteroffer. The buyers sued the seller for damages and specific performance. The court held that a contract would have been formed if the acceptance had been deposited in the U.S. Mail beyond the buyers' further control, but in this case, a contract had not been formed because the acceptance had not been mailed.

The acceptance must be made by the offeree. A third person who has knowledge of an offer to sell cannot, by acceptance, form a binding contract because the offer was not made to that party.

Silence to an offer generally is regarded as neither acceptance nor rejection. Even if an offer states, "Failure to reply within ten days will be considered acceptance," failure to reply will not in fact be acceptance of the offer. Only if the parties by their prior dealings have established silence as acceptance might silence be construed as acceptance.

Intent to enter into a contract must be present. Acceptance of an offer obviously made in jest will not form a binding agreement.

Newspaper advertisements of real estate are not offers to sell; they are merely invitations to negotiate. A buyer's acceptance does not form a binding contract because newspaper advertisements are really announcements that the property is being placed on the market. Therefore, a buyer cannot accept an "offer" made in an ad. Similarly, providing information to a multiple-listing service is an invitation to negotiate only and not an offer to sell.

If an offer fails to state how long it will remain open for acceptance, it can be accepted within a reasonable period of time. Even if the offer does state a period for acceptance, courts often will allow acceptance after that period unless the offer indicates that time is critical, usually accomplished by including the words "**time is of the essence.**"

Although several cases have held that a "time is of the essence" clause does not always make time essential in a contract [*Nash v. Superior Court* (1978) 86 C.A.3d 690], these decisions have applied to contractual performance and not to the period for acceptance of an offer.

Counteroffer. An acceptance that varies from the offer is not an acceptance but a counteroffer. A counteroffer is, in fact, a rejection of the original offer. Assume an offer calls for a 90-day escrow. An acceptance that states, "Accepted provided the escrow period be 30 days," represents a material change in the offer. The offeror really is making a counteroffer and rejecting the original offer. After such rejection, the offeree no longer can form a binding contract by later accepting the original offer.

In a counteroffer, the offeree becomes the new offeror. The original offeror is now the offeree and can accept the counteroffer and form a binding contract, reject it, or make a new counteroffer.

A request for a change in the proposed contract that does not condition the acceptance is not a counteroffer. For example, in an accepted offer that has the notation, "It would be appreciated if escrow could be closed before December 30th," the acceptance forms a binding contract because acceptance is not conditioned on this request. That is, the offeror is not bound to the December 30th date.

> ## Case Study
>
> The case of *Roth v. Malson* (1998) 67 C.A.4th 552 involved an acreage parcel that was listed for sale at $47,600. A buyer offered $41,650 cash and a close of escrow within 30 days of acceptance. The seller made a counteroffer of $44,000. The buyer signed and dated the counter to counteroffer portion of the counteroffer form and wrote, "Price to be $44,000 as above. Escrow to close on or before December 6, 1995. All cash."
>
> Subsequently, the seller notified the buyer that the property was being withdrawn from the market. The buyer then sued for specific performance. The superior court granted judgment for seller Malson, concluding that no sale contract was ever formed.
>
> The Court of Appeal affirmed because Roth, the buyer, failed to accept the counteroffer. Civil Code 1585 requires that an acceptance must be "absolute and unqualified." The buyer changed the close of escrow from "Within 30 days of acceptance" to "on or before December 6th." This was a counter to the seller's counteroffer requiring the seller's acceptance.

Revocation. Prior to notification of acceptance, an offeror can withdraw the offer. This generally is true even if the offeror promised to keep the offer open for a specified period of time. Unless consideration is given to keep an offer open (this would be an option), the offer generally can be revoked. One exception is that the offeror can no longer revoke the offer after performance has started on a unilateral contract.

Revocation must be made to the offeree or the offeree's agent to be effective.

Revocation takes place upon receipt, so contrary to an acceptance, mailing a revocation has no effect until it is received. Assume a revocation was mailed on the first of the month and the offeree mailed an acceptance on the third of the month. The revocation was received on the fourth of the month, and the acceptance was received on the fifth of the month. A valid contract would result because acceptance took place on the third (upon mailing), and the revocation had no effect because it was not effective (received) until after the offer was accepted.

Case Study

The case of *Ersa Grae Corp. v. Fluor Corp.* (1991) 1 C.A.4th 613 involved a firm that had negotiated simultaneously with two different buyers. It communicated to its broker that it was withdrawing the counteroffer it had made to one of the buyers. However, the broker did not communicate the revocation to the buyer. The court found that while the property owner had communicated revocation of its counteroffer to the broker before the counteroffer was accepted, the broker was not acting as the buyer's agent and had not communicated the revocation to the buyer. Accordingly, the buyer's acceptance of the seller's counteroffer constituted a contract. The seller sold the same property twice and was liable to Ersa Grae Corp. for nondelivery damages.

When an offeror dies or becomes mentally incapacitated prior to acceptance, the offer is dead, and a later acceptance will not form a binding contract. When the offeror is a corporation, the death of the officer making the offer will not affect the offer, because the corporation is a separate legal entity and does not die with the death of its officers.

Unless a contract calls for personal services, death or mental incapacity after acceptance will not affect a contract. The contract will bind the heirs or estates.

The destruction of the subject matter terminates an offer. If a house is destroyed by fire prior to acceptance of an offer, acceptance by the seller after the destruction will not form a binding contract.

When the acceptor fails to fulfill a condition precedent to acceptance, such as verifying gross or net income within a stated period of time, the offer is revoked.

Definiteness. An agreement must be definite. An agreement to buy "the house on Third Street" probably would be definite enough if the seller owned only one house on Third Street. However, if the seller owned several houses on Third Street, the agreement might not be binding.

> ### Case Study
>
> In the case of *Sterling v. Taylor* (2007) 40 C.A. 4th 757, Sterling and Taylor drafted a handwritten memorandum entitled "Contract for Sale of Real Property." The contract stated, "approx. 10.468 × gross income. Estimated income $1,600,000, Price $16,750.00." While Sterling dated and initialed the memorandum as "buyer," the seller space was left blank. Later, Sterling wrote Taylor confirming the contract of sale and Taylor signed the letter "agreed, accepted, and approved."
>
> Sterling determined the actual income was $1,375,404, not $1,600,000 as estimated and wanted the sales price lowered to $14,404,841 based on actual rents and the 10.468 multiplier. Taylor refused and Sterling sued.
>
> The trial court granted the defendants motion for summary judgment based on the fact that, under the Statute of Frauds, the terms were too uncertain to be enforced. The Court of Appeal reversed ruling that while price was ambiguous, it could be clarified by extrinsic evidence.
>
> The Supreme Court reversed ruling that the terms were unclear. While Sterling claimed that "approx" applied to the total price not the multiplier and the missing zero was a simple error, the extrinsic evidence was at odds with the memorandum. The memorandum did not indicate the parties contemplated any change to the price based on actual income.
>
> *Note:* While Sterling and Taylor are mega-real estate investors who are sophisticated as to contracts, it is unusual that a deal of this magnitude should be made without consultation with real estate attorneys.

Agreement to buy a property at "a price to be agreed on" would not be binding because it would lack definitiveness. An agreement to buy real estate at a price to be determined by a definite formula would be binding, even though the exact price is not known at the time the agreement is entered into. For example, an agreement to buy at the average appraisal price of three named appraisers could be binding.

The case of *Goodyear Rubber Corporation v. Munoz* (1985) 170 C.A.3d 919 held that an option to buy at "fair market value" was valid. However, the case of *ETCO Corporation v. Hauer* (1984) 161 C.A.3d 1154 held that a lease at a rent to be mutually agreed upon rendered the option unenforceable.

When a purchase is subject to the purchaser's or seller's later decision about whether to complete the transaction, the contract is an **illusory contract**, and neither party is bound. "I will pay you $100,000 for the lot if I decide to buy it" is not an agreement. Prospective tenants often sign letters of intent that indicate they will seriously negotiate with the owner for space. While letters of intent from quality tenants might influence a construction lender, they are not valid contracts. Again, these are illusory contracts and are agreements only that the parties will attempt to agree.

"Subject to" provisions do not make a contract illusory. Offers are frequently written subject to zoning changes, appraisals, financing, and other contingencies.

Requirements that work is to be performed to a person's satisfaction have been held to mean that dissatisfaction must be exercised in good faith and not merely to break the agreement.

For a contract to be valid, the parties not only must be identified but also must exist. Parties may use fictitious names or pseudonyms, but they must be real people or business entities. An agreement by an entity that does not exist, such as a nonexistent corporation, would not be enforceable. However, the parties can agree that a party will be designated later to perform or to receive performance, as in naming a designee to receive the deed.

The manner and time of payment do not have to be specified in the contract. Payment in cash at the time of closing is implied unless specified otherwise. When a closing date is not specified in an agreement, a closing within a reasonable period of time is implied. Similarly, in the absence of a stated time for possession to be given to the buyer, it is implied that possession will transfer upon close of escrow.

Also implied is that the seller will convey marketable title and that any work to be performed will be performed in a workmanlike manner.

Mistakes. A contract can be voided on the basis of a mutual mistake as to fact. For example, if both buyer and seller believed that a trust deed was assumable but discovered that it was not after the sales agreement had been signed, the buyer would be able to void the agreement because of the mutual mistake.

A unilateral mistake, in contrast, will not be the basis for voiding a contract. In the preceding example, if only the purchaser believed that the loan was assumable and the seller was unaware of the buyer's intent to assume the loan and had done nothing to warrant the buyer's belief, the contract would be enforceable.

Case Study
In the case of *Levy v. Wolff* (1956) 46 C.2d 367, a buyer paid $16,500 for a parcel of land that both the buyer and seller believed to be subject to a valid lease. Subsequent to the sale, the tenant brought an action that resulted in a court determination that the lease "had never been binding or in force." The court held that the mutual mistake as to fact would allow rescission. In this case, the purchaser wanted to keep the land, so the court allowed the purchaser to recover damages (the difference between the value of the land with the lease and the value without the lease).

A party who realizes that the other party is mistaken cannot take advantage and hold the mistaken party to the agreement. This is an exception to the rule that a unilateral mistake is not grounds to void a contract.

Legal Purpose

If parties enter into a contract in violation of the law, they generally cannot ask for enforcement of the agreement. A lease of premises for a specified illegal purpose, for example, could not be enforced by the lessor or lessee.

Neither party can enforce an illegal executory contract. If executed, either party can rescind the agreement because of its illegal purpose.

A change in the law that results in an agreement becoming illegal voids a contract. It also revokes an unaccepted offer.

If an illegality is minor or not related directly to the agreement, the courts ordinarily will allow enforcement. For example, a masonry contractor who builds a proper block wall with building permits and in accordance with the contractual specifications will not be barred from collecting the value of his work because a business permit in the community where the wall was constructed has expired or because he paid a laborer less than minimum wage.

Where the law was intended to protect a party from a wrongdoer, the law cannot be used to protect the wrongdoer. A broker who sold an unregistered real property security would be liable to the purchaser for any misrepresentations even though the sale violated the law because the registration requirement was intended to protect purchasers of securities, not sellers.

When one party is less guilty than the other, the less-guilty party might be able to recover. This is especially true if the other person has a greater knowledge of the law and represents the agreement as being legal.

If a contract is composed of several **divisible contracts**, the illegality of one part will not void the balance of the agreement. For example, assume a lease agreement covered several properties with separate rents. If one of the leases provided for a percentage of the gross from a specified illegal activity, that portion would be unenforceable, but the rest of the contract could be enforceable.

When an agreement is subject to two interpretations, one that is lawful and another that is illegal, in the absence of other evidence as to intent, the court will determine that the agreement should be given the legal interpretation.

Contracts that unreasonably restrain a person from engaging in business are against public policy and are unenforceable. In the sale of a barbershop, an agreement that the seller never will open another barbershop anywhere would be unenforceable because it is too severe a restraint. An agreement that the seller would not open another shop within a five-mile radius of the shop for a period of three years, however, probably would be considered reasonable and therefore enforceable.

An agreement between a real estate salesperson and a broker that the salesperson would never become a broker or never would work for any other broker would not only be against public policy but would likely be in violation of antitrust legislation.

Consideration

Consideration is anything of value given in exchange for a promise or performance of another. Consideration could be forbearance from acting, as well as a promise to act. For example, a creditor's agreeing not to start foreclosure for 90 days, when the creditor was entitled to foreclose, would be consideration for the transfer of other property.

A promise unsupported by consideration generally is considered unenforceable. It is merely a promise to make a gift. While an enforceable promise requires consideration, an executed transfer requires no consideration. Such a transfer is a completed gift.

The reason that an offeror can withdraw an offer anytime prior to acceptance is that an offer is unsupported by consideration. On the other hand, the presence of consideration requires that the offeror keep the offer open. In an option, the optionor receives consideration from the optionee so that the offer cannot be withdrawn.

Courts ordinarily will not get involved in evaluating the adequacy of consideration. The courts will, however, consider the amount of consideration when a party claims fraud, undue influence, or a mutual mistake as to a material fact. If a court determines that a contract is so unfair as to be unconscionable, the court may refuse to enforce it and allow the injured party to rescind the agreement or provide the injured party with other appropriate relief.

In cases involving specific performance, adequacy of consideration is essential. Without fair consideration, specific performance cannot be enforced (Civil Code Section 3391). (Specific performance, as stated in Chapter 1, is an equitable remedy. Therefore, unless the consideration is fair, this equitable remedy will be denied.)

A third party can enforce a contract even when that third party did not pay consideration: "A contract made expressly for the benefit of a third party may be enforced by him at any time before the parties thereto rescind it" (Civil Code Section 1559). For example, Alfred agreed to build a shed for Baker. Assume that Alfred then paid Charley to build the shed. If Charley failed to perform, then Baker, who is a third-party beneficiary of the contract between Alfred and Charley, could enforce the contract.

Past consideration cannot be used as consideration to enforce a present promise in excess of the promisor's duty. For example, a past gift given freely will not be consideration for a new promise, because the promisor was under no obligation or duty to act, forbear to act, or make any promise.

The promise to honor an existing obligation or to pay a just debt also is not consideration for a new promise. However, an agreement to pay a debt before it is due or after it was uncollectible or discharged in bankruptcy will be consideration for a new promise.

A contract does not need to cite the consideration. However, when a contract does recite a consideration, the consideration is presumed to have been given. This presumption can, however, be rebutted by evidence to the contrary.

■ VOID AND VOIDABLE CONTRACTS

A *void contract* is one that never had any legal existence or effect. A void contract cannot be enforced. It is treated as if it were never made. A contract that lacks one of the four required contractual elements is void.

A *voidable contract* is a valid contract unless or until voided. What this means is that a wronged party has the right or election to void the contract or let it stand as an enforceable agreement against the wrongdoer.

Fraud

Fraud is an intentional misrepresentation of fact by words, conduct, or concealment that is intended to deceive another to act to their detriment and that does in fact so deceive the other party. Making false statements without knowing whether they are true also could be considered fraud.

To make a contract voidable, the fraud must have been material; that is, it must induce a party to contract. When one party knows that the other party is lying, fraud does not exist because the party who was lied to did not rely on the false statements in contracting.

A statement made in a contract that the parties are not relying on any oral statements or promises does not relieve the parties of responsibility for fraud.

Only the injured party can cancel the contract for fraud. Failure to void the contract within a reasonable period of time after learning of the fraud could be regarded as affirmation of the agreement.

A seller can be liable for failure to disclose the buyer's fraud to a third party.

Case Study

The case of *U.S. v. Cloud* (1989) 872 F.2d 846 involved the sale of the Cal-Neva Lodge by Cloud. The sales price was $17 million. At a preclosing conference, Cloud discovered that the escrow agreement indicated a $27.5 million price and showed $7.5 million had been paid outside of escrow. The figures had been inflated so that the buyer could obtain a $20 million loan.

Cloud did not tell the escrow officers of the fraud but did insist that the escrow instructions reflect he was netting only $17 million from the loan. The lender eventually lost more than $24.5 million because of this loan. Cloud appealed his conviction for bank fraud and conspiracy. The Court of Appeal upheld the conviction because Cloud knew that the sales price was inflated and that he had not received money outside of escrow. His amendment to the escrow instructions did not exonerate him. In fact. it indicated that he fully understood and knowingly agreed to be part of a fraudulent scheme that was a conspiracy.

Misrepresentation

Misrepresentation is a civil wrong that differs from criminal fraud in that it is not intentional. While there are no criminal penalties for misrepresentation, it, like criminal fraud, makes a contract voidable and may induce civil damages.

People who honestly believed that their false assertions of fact were true but had no reasonable grounds for this belief will have committed the tort of negligent misrepresentation.

Duress and Menace

Duress generally is regarded as force. The wrongful confinement of a person or detention of property is duress. **Menace** is the threat of (1) confinement of a person, (2) detention of property, or (3) injury to the person, property, or character of another. A contract made under duress or menace makes the contract voidable at the election of the injured party.

Undue Influence

Undue influence is improper persuasion based on the relationship of the parties whereby a person really is not acting under his or her own free will. An example might be a nephew's persuading an elderly uncle to transfer property to him for a token consideration. Contracts entered into because of undue influence are voidable.

■ OPTIONS TO CONTRACT

An **option** is a contract to make a contract. The optionor (the owner) gives the optionee (potential purchaser or lessee) the right to buy or lease the property during a stated period of time for a specified price and terms.

An option is a contract and as such requires consideration be given to the optionor. The consideration must actually change hands. Reciting "in consideration of $1 and other good and valuable consideration" is not sufficient.

Case Study

The case of *Steiner v. Thexton* (2010) 48 C. 4th 411 involved a purchase contract that provided the contract was subject to a feasibility study to determine whether the land could be divided for multiple homesites. The contract also stated that the "buyer may, at its sole discretion during this period, elect not to continue in this transaction and this purchase contract will become null and void."

While the seller was seeking approval from the courts of the tentative parcel map, the seller cancelled the escrow (approximately one year after the purchase contract was entered into). The buyer sued for specific performance.

The trial court rules that, because of the election to void the agreement, this was an option not a purchase contract. The option to buy was unenforceable because no consideration had been paid for it. The trial court awarded the seller $85,000 in attorney fees as the prevailing party.

The Supreme Court reversed, ruling that there was consideration for the option to be enforced. The buyer took substantial steps involving considerable expense to obtain a parcel split. The Superior Court held that the otherwise illusory contract was cured by the part performance.

Note: The Supreme Court sent the matter back to the trial court to determine whether specific performance should be granted (could determine that money damages are adequate).

If the option to buy is part of a lease agreement, part of the rent would suffice as consideration for the option. Because consideration is present, the optionor cannot revoke the option after it has been given. However, if the purchase price were not adequate, a court would not grant the optionee the remedy of specific performance. (Further discussion of options is included in Chapter 6.)

Right of First Refusal

A **right of first refusal** differs from an option in that the prospective buyer is not given the absolute right to purchase but only the right to match an offer from a third party. A right generally is given to buy only if the owner decides to sell. Before the owner can sell, the owner must offer the property to the holder of the right of first refusal at the price and terms that the owner wishes to accept from a buyer. The holder of the right of first refusal loses that right if the holder does not meet the price and terms of the offer within a certain period of time.

A tenant with a right of first refusal might have difficulty exercising that right when consideration offered by another buyer is other than cash.

Case Study

In the case of *Ellis v. Chevron U.S.A., Inc.* (1988) 201 C.A.3d 132, Chevron's lease gave it the right of first refusal as to lease proposals made by third parties when its own lease expired. Ellis, the owner, received a lease offer of $3,000 a month; the lessee was to construct a new building on the site, acquire the adjacent site, and give Ellis the right to buy the adjacent site at the end of the lease.

Chevron offered to meet the rent but took the position that it had no need for a new building or the adjacent site, and so these provisions should not be included. The Court of Appeal held that Chevron's right of first refusal was set forth in a lease it had prepared, and therefore any ambiguities should be resolved against Chevron. Chevron claimed that an implied covenant of good faith and fair dealings restricted the term of offers that Ellis could entertain. The court, however, held that as long as a landlord solicited reasonable offers, the covenant was not breached.

Case Study

The case of *Hartzheim v. Valley Land & Cattle Co.* (2007) 153 C.A. 4th 383, involved a lessor, Hartzheim, who leased a parcel of land from a partnership. The lease gave Hartzheim a right of first refusal to purchase if the lessor received a "bona fide offer from any third party."

Because of tax concerns, the lessor partners transferred ownership to their grandchildren in exchange for their grandchildren's interest in their home ranch.

Hartzheim sued because he was not given an opportunity to purchase the property. The trial court determined that the transfer was part of estate planning and was not the result of a "bona fide" offer, so it did not trigger a right of first refusal.

The Court of Appeal affirmed ruling that a right of first refusal does not become an option until the owner decides to sell and receives a third-party offer. The intent was to keep the property in the family. There was no evidence that a purpose of the transfer was to deprive Hartzheim of any rights he had.

Note: Even if the sale was the result of a bona fide offer, Hartzheim could not make the purchase, as he could not transfer the home ranch interest in exchange.

■ INTERPRETATION OF CONTRACTS

Courts ordinarily will try to interpret contracts in accordance with the intent of the parties. Words will be given the general meaning they hold within the trade or profession involved.

In the event of an ambiguity, the courts generally will resolve the ambiguity against the party drafting the instrument if it was not drafted as a mutual effort.

> ### Case Study
> The case of *Wilson v. Gentile* (1992) 8 C.A.4th 759 involved a lease option that provided for the exercise of the option "within thirty (30) days prior to the expiration of this option." Seven days prior to the expiration of the option, the optionee notified the optionor in writing of the exercise of the option. The optionor claimed the language required that the option be exercised at least 30 days prior to lease expiration. The Court of Appeal ruled that while the optionor may have had another intent, there was no ambiguity. The clause had to be interpreted in accordance with its plain meaning. The wording meant that there was a beginning date and an ending date to exercise the option.
>
> *Note*: The optionor sued the real estate broker who drafted the clause. If the owner intended that the option be exercised only up to a specified date (30 days prior to the expiration of the lease), that should have been stated clearly. Precise drafting of legal instruments can be critical. This case points out the need for legal review.

If printed numerals differ from the words, the words generally will govern. So if a contract provided for monthly payments of "Four hundred dollars ($40.00)," the monthly payment will be $400.

In an ambiguity involving something added in typewriting to a printed form, the typewritten addition governs. If the ambiguity involves a handwritten portion, handwriting takes precedence over the printed or typed portions because it more clearly indicates intent.

Typographical errors ordinarily can be disregarded. See the case of *Gutzie Assocs. v. Switer* (1989) 215 C.A.3d 1636.

If conflicting agreements are present, the last one in time generally governs because it indicates the final intent of the parties. For example, if a purchase agreement and later-signed escrow instructions differ, the escrow instructions generally will govern. Because they were signed later, they more clearly indicate the final intent of the parties.

■ DISCHARGE OF CONTRACTS

Impossibility of Performance

A party is excused from performance because of impossibility. For example, a property manager who has a long-term contract to manage a structure that is now being taken by the city under eminent domain will be excused from performing for the remainder of the term.

Commercial Frustration

Performance will be excused in cases where the court determines commercial frustration is present. That is, performance is not impossible but has become impractical because of an unforeseen occurrence. The nonoccurrence of the event or act actually was an implied condition of the contract. The doctrine of commercial frustration does not apply to situations in which the event reasonably could have been foreseen.

An example of commercial frustration would be a lease that allowed the premises to be used only for the sale of new automobiles. If a war resulted in new automobiles not being available, the courts probably would allow the lessee out of the lease because of commercial frustration.

Unconscionable Contracts

Courts will refuse to enforce contracts that are so grossly unfair that they offend public conscience. As an example, assume a property was in danger because of a flood and the person owning the only available pump wanted $1,000 per hour for the use of the pump when $50 a day was the normal rental. Even though a property owner agreed to the charge, a court would likely refuse to enforce the agreement as written.

A contract that does not allow a person to modify the agreement (take it or leave it) is considered a **contract of adhesion**. An example of such a contract would be a standard loan agreement used by all banks. If such a contract takes unreasonable advantage of the party who did not prepare it, courts will refuse to enforce the provision against that party.

> ### Case Study
> The case of *Higgins v. Superior Court (Disney/ABC)* (2006) 140 C.A. 4th 1238 involved five orphaned Higgins siblings who were to appear on the ABC TV reality show, "Extreme Makeover: Home Edition." They lived at the home of the Leomitis. The family was chosen to receive a renovated nine-bedroom house and were given about 10 minutes to look over and sign an agreement prepared by the show's producers. Paragraph 69 contained a one-sided arbitration clause. After the show aired, the Leomitis forced the Higgins' siblings to leave. The Higgins' siblings brought action against the TV producers for intentional representation breach of contract, unfair competition, and false advertising. The producers petitioned to compel arbitration.
>
> While the Superior Court ordered arbitration, the Court of Appeal reversed on the grounds that the arbitration clause was unconscionable and therefore unenforceable. The court pointed out that this was a "take it or leave it" contract of adhesion.

Breach of Contract

Most contracts end with performance according to their terms. However, some contracts are breached. A breach of contract is a failure to perform a contractual provision as agreed.

> ## Case Study
>
> *Jaramillo v. JH Real Estate Partners, Inc.* (2003) 3 Cal. Rptr.3d 525 involved a residential lease clause that required binding arbitration of any disputes with the parties equally sharing in the advance payment of arbitration fees for a three-arbitrator panel. The plaintiffs argued the arbitration clause was unconscionable as it was an undue economic burden as well as that the clause was unenforceable as it was a contract of adhesion. The defendant appealed from a superior court ruling that the arbitrations clause was unenforceable.
>
> The Court of Appeal affirmed ruling the clause was unconscionable and lacked mutuality because this was a contract of adhesion where the tenant had no bargaining power.
>
> *Note*: See *Flores v. Transamerica Home First Inc.* (2001) 93 C.A.4th 846. In this case, the court ruled a mandatory arbitration clause in a reverse mortgage is unconscionable and unenforceable by the lender as a contract of adhesion due to lack of bilateralism.

A party does not have to wait to start legal action until an actual breach has occurred if there has been an **anticipatory breach**. Examples of anticipatory breaches are

- renunciation of the agreement by the other party;
- an act that would make performance impossible, such as the seller conveying title to another prior to a scheduled close of escrow.

Often, parties will look for ways to get out of contracts that are disadvantageous. If they disavow the contract by treating an action of the other party as a contractual breach when it was not such a breach, they might be guilty of breaching the contract themselves.

Generally, the only party with a standing to sue for damages would be the injured contracting party. There is an exception in that a **third-party beneficiary** can sue for equitable or monetary remedy. A third-party beneficiary, while not a party to a contract, was intended to be the beneficiary of the contract. As an example, if a close friend paid a painter to paint your house and the painter decided he didn't have to do it because your friend had died, you could sue for damages, the cost of having the house painted, because you were the third-party beneficiary of the contract.

Accord and Satisfaction

Accord and satisfaction is an agreement to accept something different from (usually less than) what a contract provides for in satisfaction of the obligation.

When a debt is in dispute, based on factors such as the condition of the property or the quality of repairs made, the parties can agree to accept a lesser sum. For example, if a debt is in dispute and a check is tendered with a statement that it is in full satisfaction of the debt, endorsing and cashing the check will be considered full satisfaction of the debt. However, Civil Code Section 1526 says the creditor may cross out the words "payment in full" on a check and cash it without agreeing to accord and satisfaction of a disputed amount or debt.

Novation

A **novation** is an agreement to substitute. Usually, it is the substitution of one party for another party under the contract. The prior party, in that case, would be relieved of all obligations under the contract.

Tender

A tender is an offer to perform. A party might refuse a proper tender in the mistaken belief that the tender was improper. As an example, a party might refuse $4,000 to discharge a debt with the mistaken belief that $4,400 was due. The refusal of full payment under a contract does not excuse the debt, but it does prevent future interest from accumulating until the party agrees to accept the proper tender.

If a person's performance is a condition precedent or a concurrent condition for the performance of the other party, the first party must make a tender of performance to hold the other party in default.

Tender is not required to hold another party in default if tender of performance would be an idle act. For example, if a seller under a purchase contract sells the property to another, the buyer does not have to tender the purchase price because the seller is no longer capable of making a conveyance.

Doctrine of Substantial Performance

Substantial performance allows recovery when an unintentional breach has occurred and the noncompliance is not related to substantial matters. Normally, the doctrine of substantial performance involves construction contracts, where a different or less expensive material than was specified was used, but the different material did not endanger the structure. In such a case, a court normally will say that the contract price should be reduced by the difference in value of the structure as built, and the value the structure would have had if the contract had been strictly complied with.

■ CONTRACTUAL REMEDIES

The judicial remedies discussed in Chapter 1 apply to breach of contract.

Monetary Damages

Compensatory Damages. Compensatory damages are awarded to make the injured party whole. They are financial compensation for the loss suffered.

When a real estate purchase contract is breached, the measure of monetary damages would be the difference between the contract price and the property's fair market value at the time of the contract breach. [*Reese v. Wong* (2001) 93 C.A.4th 51]

If a service or construction contract were breached, the measure of damages would be the additional reasonable costs incurred for the work in excess of the original contract price.

An injured party has a duty to keep damages at a minimum or to mitigate them. For example, if a lessee breaches a lease, the lessor has a duty to use reasonable efforts to rerent the premises.

> ### Case Study
>
> The case of *Erlich v. Menezes* (1999) 21 C.4th 543 involved a "dream home" built on an ocean view lot. Two months after occupancy, rain saturated the bedrooms and left three inches of water in the living room. Nearly every window leaked. The garage ceiling liquefied and fell in chunks. Structural engineers found serious construction errors. The Erlichs sued the builder Menezes. The San Luis Obispo County Superior Court awarded them $406,700 for the cost of repairs, $100,000 for emotional distress, and $50,000 for physical pain and suffering. The Court of Appeal affirmed the award.
>
> The California Supreme Court affirmed as to the cost of repair but reversed the award for emotional distress. The court held that negligent breach of contract is not sufficient alone to support a tort action. To find the builder liable for emotional distress, the breach of contract must be accompanied by fraud, or the party must realize the breach will cause serious harm in the form of anguish, etc.
>
> *Note*: Damages for defective construction are limited to repair costs, lost use, and/or relocation expenses, or the diminution in value.

Punitive or Exemplary Damages.   These damages are awarded in addition to compensatory damages to punish the wrongdoer. They are awarded by courts for intentional and outrageous acts. Excessive punitive damages will not be upheld by the courts.

> ### Case Study
>
> In the case of *Storage Services v. C.R. Oosterbaan et al.* (1989) 214 C.A.3d 498, the trial court had awarded $75,000 in punitive damages against an agent because of fraud. This was at least one-third of the agent's net worth and more than the agent's annual gross income. The court pointed out that generally punitive damage awards exceeding 10 percent of a defendant's net worth have been considered excessive. The court ordered a new trial on the damages unless the plaintiff agreed to a reduced award of $20,000.

Nominal Damages.   Nominal damages are a token sum, such as $1 or $10, awarded for a breach where no real compensatory damages were warranted.

Liquidated Damages.   Liquidated damages are agreed to at the time of contracting. Typically, purchase agreements call for the forfeiture of the down payment as liquidated damages in the event the buyer defaults. Construction contracts often have a per-day charge as liquidated damages in the event of a delay in completion.

Since July 1, 1978, liquidated damages on residential purchase agreements of one to four units where the buyer intends to occupy a unit have been limited by law. The liquidated damages to be forfeited if the buyer defaults cannot exceed 3 percent of the sales price or the actual deposit amount, whichever is less if both parties so agreed in the contract. The defaulting buyer is entitled to a further refund if the buyer proves that the retained amount is unreasonable, such as a sale at an equal or higher price to another party within six months.

Liquidated damages for commercial property and for more than four residential units are not subject to these limitations. They are allowed so long as they are reasonable and reflect what possible damages could be anticipated if a breach of the contract were to occur. If, however, the damages are unreasonably high, the court will consider them a penalty and will not enforce the damages.

> ### Case Study
> In the case of *Kuish v. Smith* (2010) 181 C.A. 4th 1419, the purchase contract for $14 million provided that the $620,000 deposit was "nonrefundable." (There was no liquidated damages provision.) The buyer cancelled and the seller resold the property for $15 million. The seller refused to return the original buyer's deposit.
>
> The trial court ruled that the seller could keep the deposit, which was not an unlawful forfeiture.
>
> The Court of Appeal reversed. The seller had not incurred damages because the property was resold at a higher price. In the absence of a liquidated damages provision, "nonrefundable" means that the seller can retain deposit only to the extent of actual damages incurred.

Waiver of Damages.   In a contract, a person cannot waive his or her rights to hold another personally liable for damages for fraud, willful acts, or violations of the law, either willful or negligent (Civil Code Section 1668). Nevertheless, some contracts still contain such waivers of this type, apparently based on the reasoning that if people do not think they have any rights, they will not seek to enforce them.

> ### Case Study
> In the case of *Salton Bay Marina v. Imperial Irr. Dist.* (1985) 172 C.A.3d 914, the plaintiffs had a written agreement with the irrigation district that shielded the irrigation district from liability and gave the district the right to flood the plaintiffs' property. According to Civil Code Section 1668, contracts affecting public interest that purport to exempt a party from liability for negligence are against public policy and void. The court held that the flooding agreements were contracts affecting the public interest that attempted to exempt the district from its own negligence. The agreement was therefore against public policy and void.

Equitable Remedies

Specific Performance.   Specific performance forces a party to perform as agreed and is awarded only when compensating damages are inadequate.

Because land is a unique commodity, specific performance will be enforced for the sale or lease of land, agreements to convey easements, and lease assignments. Specific performance would most likely be granted to buyers or lessees when there is a compelling need for a particular property. Property sellers normally resell and sue for consequential damages from the defaulting first buyer rather than seek specific performance; however, sellers may be granted specific performance.

> **Case Study**
> The case of *B D Inns v. Pooley* (1990) 218 C.A.3d 289 involved an agreement by Pooley to buy an 840-unit motel built by B D Inns for $6,825,000. The court held that, while B D Inns could have sued for monetary damages, it still had a legal remedy of specific performance to which it was entitled.

Because specific performance is an equitable remedy, it will not be granted if

- there has not been adequate consideration;
- it is not just and reasonable;
- the agreement was obtained by unfair practices; or
- the agreement was entered into under a misapprehension (Civil Code Section 3391).

> **Case Study**
> In the case of *Gilbert v. Mercer* (1960) 179 C.A.2d 29, an owner agreed to sell 65 acres of land for $325. Before the title was transferred, the prospective purchaser gave a listing on the property for $3,750 and received an offer for $3,500. The court refused to grant the buyer specific performance. The court held that there was sufficient evidence that the consideration was not adequate, and that in an action for specific performance, the plaintiff must plead and prove adequacy of consideration.

Reformation.   In asking for the equitable remedy of reformation, a party is requesting that the contract be modified to reflect what was intended by the parties. Reformation will be granted only when there was a complete understanding between the parties that was not properly reflected because of fraud or a mutual mistake in drafting the contract, such as a typographical error in a legal description in a deed that provides a transfer of property other than what was intended to be conveyed.

Injunction.   An injunction is a remedy in equity that orders a party to cease an activity, such as trespass. Prohibiting an action prevents future harm. Courts may order a permanent injunction or simply a temporary restraining order. As an example, a court might order a person to cease an activity that is in violation of a deed restriction.

Declaratory Relief.   The remedy of declaratory relief results in a court order determining the rights and duties of the parties. This remedy can be sought before actual damages occur.

Rescission.   Rescission is a retroactive cancellation or annulment of a contract. Cancellation terminates future obligations, but rescission returns parties to their position prior to contracting. The basis for rescission can be fraud, mutual mistake of fact, impossibility of performance, undue influence, or lack of contractual capacity.

Statutes also provide for rescission in a number of specific cases, including the following:

- Time-share purchasers in California have 72 hours after contracting to rescind their contracts.

- Purchasers in undivided interest subdivisions have a right of rescission within three days of executing the contract.

- Civil Code Section 1689.6, dealing with home solicitation sales, provides a three-business-day right of rescission.

- Civil Code Sections 1695.13–1695.14 provide for rescission within two years on home equity sales where a buyer of one to four residential units took unconscionable advantage of an owner in foreclosure.

- Section 66499.32 of the Government Code allows buyers to rescind within one year of discovery that a parcel was wrongfully divided according to the Subdivision Map Act.

- The Interstate Land Full Disclosure Sales Act, 15 U.S. Code Section 1703(b), gives purchasers the right to rescind within seven days after signing for purchase of undeveloped land covered by the act.

- According to the Truth-in-Lending Act, 15 U.S. Code Section 1635(a), buyers may rescind up until midnight on the third business day following a transaction that places a lien on the borrower's residence. The rescission rights do not apply to purchase money, primary loans, or loans in which a state agency is the lender.

For a minor breach, courts ordinarily will allow only compensatory damages, not rescission.

Waiver.   Waiver is the act of giving up a right. A party to a contract can waive a breach and accept the performance as received. A party also can waive any contractual condition that was for his or her sole benefit. For example, if a contract required a termite report prior to closing, the purchaser could waive the noncompliance because the report was for the purchaser's sole benefit.

■ ASSIGNMENT OF CONTRACT

In an **assignment of a contract**, the assignor transfers the assignor's interest in the contract to a third-person assignee. In an assignment, the assignee becomes primarily liable under the contract, while the assignor retains secondary liability should the assignee default on required performance (to avoid this contingent liability, see "Novation" earlier in the chapter). The assignee takes all of the rights and duties of the assignor.

In the absence of an agreement to the contrary, all or part of the performance under a contract can be assigned to another. The nature of some contracts, however, precludes their assignment. When a person contracts for another person's skill, such as an architect's services, the architect generally cannot assign the contract to another. If an agreement required taking an unsecured personal note, the person giving the note would not be able to assign that function to another. Because an agency agreement is considered personal in nature, agencies generally cannot be assigned.

Delegation of Duties

The obligations under a contract can be delegated to another when they are not personal services and are standardized in nature. Unlike an assignment, the person obligated under the contract retains liability for the performance of the duties, although the person to whom the duties have been delegated can also be held liable.

■ STATUTE OF FRAUDS

The **statute of frauds** comes from English common law and was designed to prevent people from committing fraud by claiming to have orally agreed to purchase the land of another person. Because land was considered the basis of all wealth, it was determined that agreements concerning land were too important to be oral. The California Statute of Frauds (Civil Code Section 1624) requires the following agreements to be in writing:

- Contracts for the transfer of real property or any interest therein

- Real property leases for more than one year (an oral lease for six months therefore could be valid)

- Contracts that cannot be performed within one year (an agreement for a six-month lease starting in seven months would have to be in writing because it could not be performed within one year of the agreement)

- Sales of personal property for more than $500

- Contracts by executors or administrators of estates

- Agreements to answer to the debt or default of another

- Listing agreements for the sale or lease of real property for more than one year [Civil Code Section 1624(5)]

The statute of frauds applies significantly to executory contracts because contracts that fail to comply are unenforceable. After a contract has been fully performed (executed contract), however, the statute of frauds cannot be raised.

The statute of frauds does not require a formal contract, but a note or letter memorandum or a series of notes and memorandums must show a complete agreement. A telegram, for example, can satisfy the statute of frauds.

The agreement need not be signed by all the parties. It need be signed only by the party who is sought to be bound to the agreement or by that person's agent. The signature on the document need not be handwritten as long as it was intended as a signature. For example, if it could be shown that a person used a rubber stamp to sign an agreement, the rubber stamp signature would satisfy the statute of frauds.

Foreign Language Negotiations

If a contract is negotiated in Spanish, Chinese, Tagalog, Vietnamese, or Korean, a translation of the contract must be furnished prior to execution in the language in which it was negotiated.

Parol Evidence Rule

The **parol evidence** rule provides that oral extrinsic evidence may not be introduced to modify a written document that is complete on its face. While parol evidence cannot be used to modify a clearly written contract, it is admissible to show a later oral modification of the written contract.

Parol evidence also can be used to clarify an ambiguity; to show fraud, undue influence, or a mutual mistake of fact; or to show that the instrument was represented to be other than a contract.

> **Case Study**
> In *Seck v. Foulks* (1972) 25 C.A.3d 556, the memorandum in Figure 5.1 was written on the back of the broker's business card and was initialed by the owner.
>
> The court held that the memorandum need not be a complete contract, provided it showed authority to act. The other terms may be shown by parol (oral) evidence. In this case, parol evidence indicated that "Sitten" referred to the seller's attorney, to whom the offer was to be presented. "310 M/L" referred to the parcel size, 310 acres, more or less. The agreement was entered into on 3/24/65 and was to terminate on 10/1/65. The court determined in this case that the writing was sufficient to satisfy the statute of frauds.

Estoppel

The doctrine of **estoppel** or promissory estoppel means that a person may not assert a right when that person's previous statements, actions, or silence caused another party to act to their detriment. For example, assume that an oral agreement had been made for the sale of a lot, and the purchaser, with the knowledge of the seller, made extensive improvements to the lot. The seller would be estopped (prevented) from raising the defense of the statute of frauds because the seller's statement caused the purchaser to act to his detriment (acceptance could be inferred by conduct). If the seller could have voided the sale, then the seller would have been unjustly enriched.

FIGURE 5.1

The "Sitten" Memorandum

> "Sitten"
> 310 m/x
> $2,000 per acre
> ½ down
> bal 5 years
> 5% int
> 3-24-65
> quarterly with int.
> Keep taxes up to date
> ½ mineral rights
> 6% comm.
> 10/1/65
> GWF

Case Study

The case of *ARYA Group, Inc. v. Cher* (2000) 77 C.A.4th 610 involved a partially completed oral construction contract. The entertainer, Cher, negotiated with the ARYA Group, Inc., to design and build a house on her Malibu property for $4,217,529 with progress payments. The contract was delivered to Cher and, despite her promise to do so, the contract was never signed by Cher and delivered to the contractor. The contractor was induced to begin work and did receive some progress payments.

Cher requested that ARYA meet with Janet Bussell of Tuft Design Group, who had previously worked with Cher on a speculative residential project. It was alleged that the purpose of the meetings was to obtain proprietary information from ARYA. Cher then terminated the "oral" contract with ARYA and failed to pay $415,169.41 due to ARYA. Cher contacted ARYA's subcontractors to induce them to work directly with her and had ARYA's building permits transferred to her name. It was alleged that Cher never intended to sign the contract with ARYA. ARYA sued Cher for breach of contract. Cher demurred on the grounds that the statute of frauds (B&PC 7164) required a written contract. The Los Angeles County Superior Court dismissed the lawsuit because ARYA did not have a signed contract.

The Court of Appeal reversed, ruling that ARYA's allegations were sufficient to support a claim of unjust enrichment. While the court noted that "generally speaking" a contract made in violation of a regulatory statute is void, the rule is not inflexible. The court noted that Cher is a highly sophisticated homeowner with previous involvement in residential construction projects and that legal representatives assisted Cher in negotiating the construction agreement. The court pointed out substantial work had been completed and Cher would be unjustly enriched if she were not required to pay ARYA. The court distinguished this case from *Phillipe v. Shapell Indus*. because construction is tangible and the benefit is apparent while a broker's services are intangible. The court noted that if failure to compensate the contractor would not have resulted in unjust enrichment, then the contractor would not have been entitled to collect.

■ STATUTE OF LIMITATIONS

> ### Case Study
>
> The case of *Phillippe v. Shapell Indus. Inc.* (1987) 43 C.3d 1247 involved an oral promise to pay a commission. Prince, the director of land acquisitions for Shapell, orally agreed to pay Phillippe, a licensed real estate broker, a commission for land found by Phillippe that was acquired by Shapell. Phillippe showed a parcel of land to Shapell that was rejected because of zoning. When the zoning was amended a year later, Shapell purchased the parcel for $2.7 million.
>
> While the trial court awarded Phillippe $125,000 in commission, the California Supreme Court reversed the judgment. Civil Code Section 1624(d) requires that a broker employment agreement be in writing. The fact that Shapell was itself a broker does not alter the statute (this was not an agreement between brokers to split a commission). The court stated that, except for a few narrow exceptions, a broker may not assert estoppel as a defense against the statute of frauds. While the broker had been promised a commission, Phillippe knew the rules and was not entitled to any commission due to a lack of a written sales commission agreement.

If an action is not brought within a prescribed period of time, it becomes barred by the statute of limitations. Thus, a contract may be valid but unenforceable. A person who ignores his or her rights can lose them through the passage of time.

In California, various statutes of limitations provide the following time periods:

- 90 days—actions by former tenants to recover belongings left in furnished quarters

- Two years—personal injury

- Two years—actions based on oral contracts

- Three years—actions for damages due to trespass

- Three years—attachment lien

- Three years from date of discovery—actions for relief under a contract based on fraud or mistake

- Three years—replevin actions (to recover goods wrongfully held by another)

- Three years—disciplinary actions against a real estate licensee (if the action is based on fraud, the time period is three years or one year after discovery of fraud, whichever is later)

- Four years—most actions based on written contracts (the statute of limitations for contracts runs from the time the agreement was breached, not from the date of the agreement)

- Five years—actions for recovery of real property and the profits from the property

- Five years—to challenge a void or voidable deed or other document (20 years if the claimant is a minor or insane)

- Ten years—actions based on judgments and latent defects in real property

- Code of Civil Procedure §323—unless otherwise stated, the statute of limitations is four years

If a partial payment is made and accepted on a debt, the statute of limitations period on the debt would start again from the date of the partial payment.

■ LACHES

Laches is preventing a person from asserting a right or claim when that person's delay in asserting that right causes or results in disadvantage, injury, injustice, detriment, or prejudice to the defendant in a lawsuit. For example, a person could be estopped by laches from having an encroachment removed if the person were aware of the construction and waited until it was completed to demand its removal. To grant the landowner rights would not be equitable, based on the delay in bringing action. (Unlike the statute of limitations, laches is considered an equitable defense.)

■ SEALS

Seals—marks or impressions—were required on certain contracts in England to authenticate the execution of a document. Their use grew out of a period when most individuals were illiterate and had to make their "mark."

States that require seals accept a simple "(Seal)" or "L.S.," which stands for "Locus Sigilli" (the place of the seal).

California does not require seals on any documents, but if a corporation that has a seal uses it on a document, it is presumed that the person(s) signing did so with corporate authority.

■ JUDGMENTS

When a court adjudicates a dispute, the final order of the court is a **judgment**. Unless the order is appealed to a higher court, the judgment is enforceable. Most judgments are for a monetary payment.

Recording an abstract of a monetary judgment creates a lien on all of the debtor's property in the county where it is recorded. A judgment lien is good for ten years and may be renewed. Judgment liens for child or spousal support remain enforceable until paid in full without the necessity of renewal.

If the debtor fails to pay after a judgment has been entered, the creditor can get a writ of execution whereby the sheriff seizes and sells assets of the debtor to satisfy the debt. (Judgments will be covered in greater detail in Chapter 11.)

Attorneys often tell clients that there are three necessities for a successful lawsuit. There must be (1) a wrongful act or omission that (2) has resulted in a loss or injury to the plaintiff and (3) the defendant must have assets or insurance coverage. Without number 1, the defendant has no liability. Without number 2, there are no damages to be compensated. Without number 3, time and money would be expended to gain an uncollectible judgment.

■ SUMMARY

Contracts are either express (stated) or implied, bilateral (promise for a promise) or unilateral (promise for an act), or executory (not yet fully performed) or executed (fully performed).

Contracts that meet all contractual requirements are valid contracts; contracts that do not are void. Voidable contracts are valid unless voided by the injured party.

Most contracts can be disaffirmed by minors within a reasonable period after reaching the age of 18, or by persons lacking mental capacities to contract but not declared incompetent.

Other reasons for voiding a contract include

- fraud,
- misrepresentation,
- duress and menace, and
- undue influence.

Options to contract are agreements whereby one party has the right to contract. A right of first refusal is a first right to purchase should a seller decide to sell to another.

Courts ordinarily will try to interpret contracts in accordance with the intent of the parties.

Excuses for nonperformance include impossibility of performance and commercial frustration.

A breach of a contract is a failure to perform a contractual provision as agreed.

A party can waive a breach by the other party or waive any contractual condition that is for his or her sole benefit.

Parties can agree to accept something other than what was agreed to. This is known as accord and satisfaction. A novation is an agreement to substitute one party for another under the contract and relieves the original party of all obligations under the contract.

A tender is an offer to perform a contract.

The doctrine of substantial performance excuses a minor unintentional breach of a contract. While the breach would not be a basis for terminating the agreement, the contract price would be reduced to reflect the difference in performance.

Contractual remedies for a breach of contract are monetary or equitable.

Monetary remedies include compensatory damages, punitive or exemplary damages, and nominal damages, as well as liquidated damages.

Equitable remedies include specific performance, reformation, injunction, declaratory relief, and rescission.

Contracts that do not by their terms prohibit assignment and are not personal in nature can be assigned. Under an assignment, the assignee becomes primarily liable under the contract. Obligations under a contract can be delegated to another. Unlike an assignment, the person obligated retains primary liability for the contractual performance.

The statute of frauds requires certain contracts, including contracts for the transfer of real property and leases for more than one year, to be in writing.

Copies of contracts in the language used for negotiations must be provided for designated languages.

Parol or oral evidence cannot be used to show that a contract that appears complete upon its face means other than what it says. Parol evidence can be used to show fraud or to clarify an ambiguity.

Persons can be estopped from raising the defense of the statute of frauds if, by their words or actions, they caused another to act to his or her detriment.

The statute of limitations deals with statutory time limitations on bringing legal action.

Laches is an equitable defense that prevents a party from asserting a claim if his or her unreasonable delay in bringing action worked to the prejudice of the other party.

A judgment is the final order of a court. When recorded, an abstract of judgment becomes a judgment lien on all of the debtor's property in the county where the judgment is recorded.

■ DISCUSSION CASES

1. A notation on a check stated, "Down payment on Lot 16 of Berwyn Heights. Full Price to be $4,000." The check was endorsed by the payee. **In the absence of any other written document, has the statute of frauds been complied with?**

2. In the sale of four lots, the escrow inadvertently left out the necessary reservation of a right-of-way from one of the lots. A subsequent holder requests reformation. **Will it be granted?**

    Shupe v. Nelson (1967) 254 C.A.2d 693

3. The plaintiff acted as a rental agent and informed the owner that he would like to represent him in selling the property. No written agreement was drawn up, although several offers were submitted. The plaintiff received an offer for $100,000 and requested authorization to sell. The owner sent a telegram to the plaintiff stating, "This will confirm that I will sell 608 South Bay Front Balboa Island for $100,000 cash. This offer good until noon 1-19-60. Chas. P. Hansen." The owner subsequently refused to sign a standard form deposit receipt providing for a 5 percent commission. **Is the plaintiff broker entitled to a commission?**

    Franklin v. Hansen (1963) 59 C.2d 570

4. A purchase agreement provided for $20,000 in liquidated damages should the buyer resell the property to an uncle of the seller. After purchase, the buyer resold to the seller's uncle. The purchaser claimed that the prohibition against resale to the uncle was an unreasonable restraint on alienation (conveyance). **Do you agree?**

    Zlotoff v. Tucker (1984) 154 C.A.3d 988

5. A purchaser of a property was given the preemptive right to purchase an adjoining parcel for $10,000. The owner subsequently sold the lot for $22,000 without offering it to the holder of the preemptive right to purchase. Was there a valid right to purchase? **If so, what would the damages be?**

    Mercer v. Lemmens (1964) 230 C.A.2d 167

6. The lessee leased premises for a restaurant. The greater portion of the premises (on the second floor) had not been used for 14 years. The lease specified that the premises were taken "as is." After entering into the lease, the lessee discovered that extensive and expensive work had to be done inside and outside the premises to meet the building codes. Because of basic structural weaknesses in the building, the second floor could not support a restaurant operation. **Is the lessee liable under the lease?**

    William v. Puccinelli (1965) 236 C.A.2d 512

7. A contractor, in working to stabilize soil, broke a sewer pipe causing concrete to spread into the sewer system. The owners sued for damages, but the contractor brought a motion to compel arbitration. The preprinted contract required that controversies be settled "with the Uniform Rules for Better Business Arbitration" The rules, which were not attached to the contract, limit damages to refunds, completion of work, or expenses not to exceed $2,500. **Should arbitration be required?**

Harper v. Ultimo (2004) 113 C.A.4th 1402

8. The defendants gave the broker an unsigned typewritten document entitled "Re Beverly Wilshire Hotel." It included a description of the hotel, the price of $2,000,000, and the commission that the hotel would pay. After extensive work by the plaintiff, the defendants gave the plaintiff a carbon copy on a hotel letterhead that included a description of the property and the sale terms. This copy indicated a price of $2,250,000 and provided for a broker's commission of 5 percent on $50,000 and 2½ percent on the balance. This memo also was unsigned. Testimony was given that the broker protested that the price was being raised, which would make the sale more difficult, and that the commission was being lowered. An oral agreement was made to a $57,500 commission, and an unsigned note later was given indicating a $57,500 commission. The plaintiff was the procuring cause of the sale, and the defendants refused to pay a commission. **What are the rights of the broker?**

Marks v. Walter G. McCarty Corp. (1949) 33 C.2d 814

9. A lessee of a property authorized repairs, and the owner of the property failed to post a notice of nonresponsibility, which would have protected him against mechanics' liens. In an action to foreclose on a mechanic's lien, the owner raised the fact that he was under the age of 18. **Is this a good defense?**

Burnand v. Irigoyen (1947) 30 C.2d 861

10. A deposit receipt provided that the payment terms were to be arranged after new financing was obtained. **Was there an enforceable contract?**

Burgess v. Rodom (1953) 121 C.A.2d 71

11. The vice president of a bank told both buyers and sellers that the bank would make a $40 million loan to the purchasers of 11 acres on Wilshire Boulevard in Los Angeles. Based on the oral promise, the buyer and seller agreed to a sales contract of $1 million down, $2 million in 30 days, and $7 million in 50 days. While the bank covered the first two payments, it rejected the loan application five days prior to the $7 million becoming due, which caused the purchasers to default. **Is the bank liable for breach of its oral agreement to make the loan?**

Landes Constr. Co. v. Royal Bank (1987) 833 F.2d 1365

12. A lender agreed to provide financing if the borrower's parents would provide security. The parents agreed to execute a trust deed on property in Sebastopol that they owned with their son. The lender's cover letter referred to the Sebastopol property, but the trust deed prepared by the lender described the parents' residence in Petaluma. **After the son defaulted, what are the rights of the parties?**

Balistreri v. Nevada Livestock Prod. Credit Ass'n (1989) 214 C.A.3d 635

13. An arbitration clause in a purchase contract was initialed by the buyer but not the seller. The clause stated "buyer, seller, and agent agree that such controversy shall be settled by final binding arbitration . . ." **Is arbitration mandatory?**

Marcus Millichap Real Estate Investment Brokerage Co. v. Hock Investment Co. (1998) 68 C.A.4th 83

14. A husband, who had a stroke, made an oral promise to his wife that if she would care for him at home, so he didn't end up in a nursing home, he would leave her specified property. The wife performed her part of the agreement but discovered, upon his death, that the property was willed to his daughter. **Does the wife have rights as to the property?**

Borelli v. Brusseau (1993) 12 C.A.4th 647

15. A seller reneged on a sale contract. The buyer intended to renovate the property for resale. The trial court ruled that the buyer was entitled to return of deposit, planning costs of $90,000, and $600,000 in lost profits. **Was the award for lost profits proper?**

Greenwich S.F. LLC v. Wong (2010) 190 C.A. 4th 739

■ CHAPTER QUIZ

1. A written contract whereby the seller agrees to convey at an agreed price at a definite time in the future, and the buyer agrees to buy at said time and price would be a(n)

   a. executory, express, bilateral contract.

   b. executed, implied, unilateral contract.

   c. valid, express, unilateral contract.

   d. enforceable, bilateral, executed contract.

2. When a person, while not of sound mind but not declared insane or wholly without understanding, contracts to buy real property, the contract likely is

   a. void.   b. voidable.

   c. illegal.   d. valid.

3. Mutuality in a contract would ordinarily be indicated by

   a. consideration.   b. offer and acceptance.

   c. execution.   d. waiver.

4. An offer would *NOT* be terminated by

   a. revocation by the offeror.

   b. a counteroffer.

   c. request for an extension for acceptance by the offeree.

   d. the death of the offeror.

5. In which situation can an offer *NOT* be withdrawn?

   a. When the seller has not yet had an opportunity to accept it

   b. When the stated period for which it would remain open has not expired

   c. When notification of acceptance has been made

   d. When the deposit has not been forfeited

6. Which is *TRUE* regarding acceptance and/or revocation of an offer?

   a. Revocation takes place upon receipt.

   b. Acceptance takes place upon mailing.

   c. Both a and b are true.

   d. Neither a nor b is true.

7. Albert gave his friend Baker a deed to a property, which Baker recorded. A year later, Albert and Baker had a dispute. Albert demanded the return of the property because Baker had not given any consideration for the property transfer. Assuming there was no consideration, which statement is correct?

    a. Albert can obtain revocation because of lack of consideration.

    b. The agreement is void because of lack of consideration.

    c. Albert is entitled to the fair market value of the property conveyed.

    d. Baker can keep the property, which was a completed gift.

8. An example of fraud would be

    a. a promise made by one who did not intend to keep it.

    b. a false statement of fact by one who does not know if it is fact or not.

    c. the act of hiding a defect so another party will not know of it.

    d. all of the above.

9. Albert knew that Keith was lying about the property's income, but Albert nevertheless completed the purchase. When Albert changed his mind, Albert could

    a. void the contract.   b. collect damages for the fraud.

    c. do either a or b.   d. do neither a nor b.

10. Which statement about options is *FALSE*?

    a. Consideration is necessary for a valid option.

    b. The optionee has the option to exercise or refrain from exercising the option.

    c. The optionor can revoke the option by returning the consideration.

    d. Options can be assigned unless personal in nature or prohibited by the option terms.

11. Which statement describes how a court will interpret an ambiguous contract?

    a. Words take precedence over numerals.

    b. Parol evidence can be admitted to show intent.

    c. Handwritten takes precedence over typed.

    d. All of the above describe how a court will interpret an ambiguous contract.

12.   An agreement whereby one party to a contract is discharged and another party becomes obligated is a(n)

a.   accord and satisfaction.   b.   reformation.

c.   novation.   d.   rescission.

13.   Which is NOT an equitable remedy?

a.   Reformation   b.   Compensatory damages

c.   Rescission   d.   Specific performance

14.   Forfeiture of agreed damages in a contract is known as

a.   mitigated damages.   b.   subordination.

c.   liquidated damages.   d.   punitive damages.

15.   Liquidated damages on a duplex that the buyer intended to occupy called for the forfeiture of a $10,000 deposit on a $100,000 purchase price. After the buyer's default, the seller must return

a.   the entire deposit.   b. $7,000.

c. $23,000.   d.   nothing.

16.   The fact that every parcel of real estate is unique is the reason for the remedy of

a.   specific performance.   b.   injunction.

c.   reformation.   d.   punitive damages.

17.   When, after close of escrow, the purchaser discovered that the seller's broker had materially misrepresented the income, the purchaser could

a.   sue for rescission.

b.   accept the property as is.

c.   sue the seller and the broker for damages.

d.   do any of the above.

18.   Which is TRUE regarding the difference between waiver and rescission?

a.   Waiver leaves the parties as they are.

b.   Rescission puts the parties back the way they were.

c.   Both a and b are true.

d.   Neither a nor b is true.

19. Which is *NOT* a requirement of every valid contract?

    a. Consideration

    b. Meeting of the minds

    c. Writing

    d. Legal purpose

20. An oral real estate lease for six months starting in six months is

    a. valid.

    b. void.

    c. voidable.

    d. illegal.

21. After Albert agreed orally to sell to Smith, Smith made extensive improvements to the property with the knowledge of Albert. Albert now refuses to sell because the sales agreement was oral. What will be the result?

    a. Albert does not have to sell, based on the statute of frauds.

    b. Albert must sell, because of the doctrine of estoppel.

    c. Albert must sell, because of laches.

    d. Albert's only remedy is compensatory damages.

22. The passage of time can make a valid contract

    a. invalid.

    b. illegal.

    c. unenforceable.

    d. voidable.

23. In California, the statute of limitations for verbal contracts is

    a. two years.

    b. three years.

    b. four years.

    d. ten years.

24. Losing a right because of failure to assert it in a timely manner is known as

    a. rescission.

    b. laches.

    b. estoppel.

    d. specific performance.

25. Which is a *TRUE* statement about judgments?

    a. They are good for ten years.

    b. They can be renewed.

    c. When recorded, they create a general lien in the county of recordation.

    d. All the statements above are true.

CHAPTER SIX

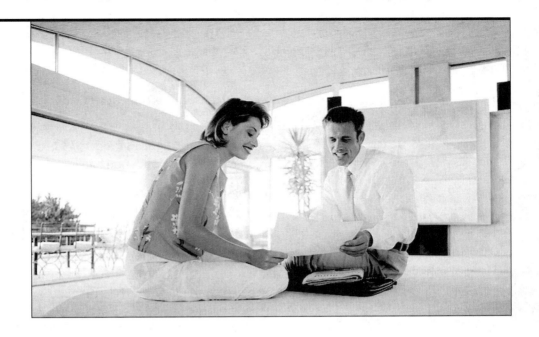

REAL ESTATE
CONTRACTS

■ KEY TERMS

advance costs
advance fee addendum
burden of proof
buyer listing
cooperating broker fee
  agreements
due diligence
exclusive-agency listing

exclusive authorization
  and right-to-sell
  listing
good faith
hold harmless clauses
interim occupancy
  agreement
loan broker listing

no deal–no commission
open listings
privity of contract
procuring cause
safety clause

■ LISTINGS

A listing is an agency contract whereby a principal (usually the property owner) appoints an agent (a real estate broker) to perform some task. Customarily, the principal gives the agent a listing to procure a buyer or lessee for specified property. Listings also can be created for the purpose of locating property for a buyer or obtaining financing. A listing can also be for a loan modification.

An agent who is to procure a buyer generally is not given the power to obligate the principal contractually. The agent solicits offers; the principal accepts or rejects them.

A buyer's agent locates property for the buyer's consideration. The buyer makes any purchase decision.

To be enforceable, listing agreements for real estate must be in writing [Civil Code Section 1624(5)].

The case of *Franklin v. Hansen* (1963) 59 C.2d 570 makes it clear that a broker cannot enforce a verbal commission agreement.

Because listings are contracts, they require all the elements of a valid contract to be enforceable: mutual consent (for an exclusive listing, discussed later in this chapter), consideration, legal purpose, and competent parties.

Listings must be specific about the subject matter of the agency. They also should be specific about price and terms, if any. If no price is specified, the principal will not be obligated to the agent if the principal refuses an offer at a fair price. If no terms are specified, the principal can refuse a full-price offer if not for cash, and the principal will not be obligated to any commission.

Listings usually authorize an agent to place a For Sale sign on the property. Without such authorization, the agent does not have the right to place a sign.

An agent is not entitled to compensation if not provided for in the listing agreement. Authorizing an agent to procure a buyer does not imply that the owner will pay a fee if the agent is successful. There can be a gratuitous agency.

Unless the listing authorizes the agent to accept a deposit, the agent will have to take deposits as the agent of the buyer.

Hold harmless clauses customarily are included in listings. The owner agrees to hold the agent harmless and indemnify the agent for losses in the event the owner fails to provide a disclosure or fails to provide correct information. Such a clause probably would not entitle the broker to recover a loss if he or she knew, or should have known, an owner was mistaken. Like most contracts, listings usually provide that, in the event of legal action, the prevailing party will be entitled to legal fees.

Unless a listing authorizes an agent to employ subagents, the agent has no authority to do so. An agency is a personal relationship that requires consent, and the principal is responsible for the acts of the agent within the scope of the agency. The agent therefore has no authority to expand the liability of the principal to acts of subagents without the express authority of the principal. The CAR listing form in Figure 6.1 does not provide for subagency but provides for cooperation with other brokers.

The listing agreement is between the principal and the agent and cannot be enforced by third parties. For example, a prospective buyer could not force an owner to accept an offer at a property's listed price because no **privity of contract** (contractual relationship) exists between the owner and the prospective buyer. The agent, however, might be entitled to a commission. An exception would be refusal of the owner to accept an offer on the terms of the listing because of unlawful discrimination (see the discussion of fair housing in Chapter 4).

If the consummation of a sale is prevented by the default of the agent's principal or by the principal's inability to convey marketable title, the sales agent will be entitled to a commission because the agent fully performed as required by the agency.

The **burden of proof** of performance is on the agent. To collect a commission, the agent must show full compliance with the agent's obligations according to the contract or the principal's wrongful breach of obligations.

The rate or amount of commission may not be preprinted in a listing contract for the sale of a building with one to four residential units. This includes mobile homes. The agreement also must contain the following statement in ten-point boldface type: "**Notice: The amount or rate of real estate commissions is not fixed by law. They are set by each Broker individually and may be negotiable between Seller and Broker.**" You will find this notice on the sample listing agreement.

A commission customarily is earned under a valid listing upon the execution of a valid purchase agreement unless conditions remain to be fulfilled. The commission normally is paid upon close of escrow, which could be some time after the commission is earned.

If a listing requires consummation of the sale, the sale must be consummated for the broker to earn a commission (**no deal–no commission**). If in such a case the buyer breaches the contract and the owner does not pursue legal remedies for the breach, the broker gets nothing.

If the owner breaches the agreement, the broker is entitled to a commission because the principal's action violated the implied condition of **good-faith** dealings. Similarly, if the buyer's obligation was conditional and the seller prevented the satisfaction of the conditions, the broker would be entitled to his or her commission.

> **Case Study**
>
> In the case of *City of Turlock v. Paul M. Zagaris Inc.* (1989) 209 C.A.3d 189, a real estate contract signed only by the buyer and seller acknowledged that the seller owed the broker a 6 percent sales commission to be paid as the price was received. This was the sole agreement on commission. Because the city acquired the property by condemnation, escrow never closed. The broker asserted his commission in the condemnation action, alleging "vested contractual rights." The Court of Appeal held that the broker's right was contingent on the escrow closing, so the broker lost his rights when the escrow failed to close.

Case Study

The case of *R.J. Kuhl Corp. v. Sullivan* (1993) 13 C.A.4th 1589 involved a buyer's agent who entered into negotiations for a purchase. The buyer's agent contract called for a commission if a sale was consummated. The negotiations failed and a third party purchased the property. The third party gave the broker's client (Sullivan) an option to buy the property and also agreed to share in paying any commission that the buyer might owe.

The broker sued Sullivan and the third party for breach of contract, failure to pay a commission, and interference and conspiring to interfere with a contractual relationship.

The court held that Sullivan's obligation was subject to the covenant of good faith and fair dealing. The client benefited from the broker's services and profited unfairly. Even though the sale was never consummated, the breach of the covenant of good faith and fair dealing excused the consummation of the sale as a condition of payment.

Exclusive Listings

Most listings are exclusive listings, in which the owner makes the agent his or her exclusive agent to procure a buyer and agrees to pay a commission should the agent succeed. The agent promises to use **due diligence** in procuring a buyer. As mentioned in Chapter 5, this mutual exchange of promises makes exclusive listings bilateral contracts.

Exclusive listings must be signed by the owner. While the signature of one spouse alone on any listing is sufficient to obligate the community property to a commission, both spouses must sign the deed to sell community property. A spouse who has signed the listing will be less likely to refuse to convey; therefore, the signatures of both spouses are desirable.

Agents are required to give a copy of an exclusive listing to the owners at the time they sign. Failure to do so does not void the listing, but it does subject the agent to disciplinary action. Listings normally include a statement above the principal's signature that the principal acknowledges having received a copy of the listing. This acknowledgment serves as protection against later claims by principals that they did not receive a copy as required. (Notice the statement above the signature space in Figure 6.1.)

Exclusive listings must have a definite termination date. Stating that the listing shall expire within a stated period after a notice is given to terminate is not enough. In the absence of a definite termination date, the listing can be terminated by the owner without notice, provided the owner has not benefited from the listing by a sale. The absence of a termination date on an exclusive listing also subjects the agent to disciplinary action that could include suspension or revocation of his or her license.

FIGURE 6.1

Exclusive Authorization and Right To Sell

CALIFORNIA
ASSOCIATION
OF REALTORS®

RESIDENTIAL LISTING AGREEMENT
(Exclusive Authorization and Right to Sell)
(C.A.R. Form RLA, Revised 11/11)

1. **EXCLUSIVE RIGHT TO SELL:** _____ ("Seller")
   hereby employs and grants _____ ("Broker")
   beginning (date) _____ and ending at 11:59 P.M. on (date) _____ ("Listing Period")
   the exclusive and irrevocable right to sell or exchange the real property in the City of _____,
   County of_____, Assessor's Parcel No. _____,
   California, described as:_____ ("Property").

2. **ITEMS EXCLUDED AND INCLUDED:** Unless otherwise specified in a real estate purchase agreement, all fixtures and fittings that are attached to the Property are included, and personal property items are excluded, from the purchase price.
   ADDITIONAL ITEMS EXCLUDED: _____.
   ADDITIONAL ITEMS INCLUDED: _____.
   Seller intends that the above items be excluded or included in offering the Property for sale, but understands that: **(i)** the purchase agreement supersedes any intention expressed above and will ultimately determine which items are excluded and included in the sale; and **(ii)** Broker is not responsible for and does not guarantee that the above exclusions and/or inclusions will be in the purchase agreement.

3. **LISTING PRICE AND TERMS:**
   A. The listing price shall be: _____
   _____ Dollars ($ _____).
   B. Additional Terms: _____
   _____

4. **COMPENSATION TO BROKER:**
   Notice: The amount or rate of real estate commissions is not fixed by law. They are set by each Broker individually and may be negotiable between Seller and Broker (real estate commissions include all compensation and fees to Broker).
   A. Seller agrees to pay to Broker as compensation for services irrespective of agency relationship(s), either ☐ _____ percent of the listing price (or if a purchase agreement is entered into, of the purchase price), or ☐ $ _____,
   AND _____, as follows:
     (1) If during the Listing Period, or any extension, Broker, cooperating broker, Seller or any other person procures a buyer(s) who offers to purchase the Property on the above price and terms, or on any price or terms acceptable to Seller. (Broker is entitled to compensation whether any escrow resulting from such offer closes during or after the expiration of the Listing Period, or any extension).
   OR (2) If within _____ calendar days **(a)** after the end of the Listing Period or any extension; or **(b)** after any cancellation of this Agreement, unless otherwise agreed, Seller enters into a contract to sell, convey, lease or otherwise transfer the Property to anyone ("Prospective Buyer") or that person's related entity: **(i)** who physically entered and was shown the Property during the Listing Period or any extension by Broker or a cooperating broker; or **(ii)** for whom Broker or any cooperating broker submitted to Seller a signed, written offer to acquire, lease, exchange or obtain an option on the Property. Seller, however, shall have no obligation to Broker under paragraph 4A(2) unless, not later than **3 calendar days** after the end of the Listing Period or any extension or cancellation, Broker has given Seller a written notice of the names of such Prospective Buyers.
     (3) If, without Broker's prior written consent, the Property is withdrawn from sale, conveyed, leased, rented, otherwise transferred, or made unmarketable by a voluntary act of Seller during the Listing Period, or any extension.
   B. If completion of the sale is prevented by a party to the transaction other than Seller, then compensation due under paragraph 4A shall be payable only if and when Seller collects damages by suit, arbitration, settlement or otherwise, and then in an amount equal to the lesser of one-half of the damages recovered or the above compensation, after first deducting title and escrow expenses and the expenses of collection, if any.
   C. In addition, Seller agrees to pay Broker: _____.
   D. Seller has been advised of Broker's policy regarding cooperation with, and the amount of compensation offered to, other brokers.
     (1) Broker is authorized to cooperate with and compensate brokers participating through the multiple listing service(s) ("MLS") by offering to MLS brokers out of Broker's compensation specified in 4A, either ☐ _____ percent of the purchase price, or ☐ $_____.
     (2) Broker is authorized to cooperate with and compensate brokers operating outside the MLS as per Broker's policy.
   E. Seller hereby irrevocably assigns to Broker the above compensation from Seller's funds and proceeds in escrow. Broker may submit this Agreement, as instructions to compensate Broker pursuant to paragraph 4A, to any escrow regarding the Property involving Seller and a buyer, Prospective Buyer or other transferee.
   F. **(1)** Seller represents that Seller has not previously entered into a listing agreement with another broker regarding the Property, unless specified as follows: _____.
     (2) Seller warrants that Seller has no obligation to pay compensation to any other broker regarding the Property unless the Property is transferred to any of the following individuals or entities: _____
     (3) If the Property is sold to anyone listed above during the time Seller is obligated to compensate another broker: **(i)** Broker is not entitled to compensation under this Agreement; and **(ii)** Broker is not obligated to represent Seller in such transaction.

RLA REVISED 11/11 (PAGE 1 OF 4)   Print Date

Seller's Initials (_____)(_____)

Reviewed by _____ Date _____

EQUAL HOUSING OPPORTUNITY

RESIDENTIAL LISTING AGREEMENT - EXCLUSIVE (RLA PAGE 1 OF 4)

FIGURE 6.1

Exclusive Authorization and Right to Sell, Continued

Property Address: _____ Date: _____

5. **OWNERSHIP, TITLE AND AUTHORITY:** Seller warrants that: **(i)** Seller is the owner of the Property; **(ii)** no other persons or entities have title to the Property; and **(iii)** Seller has the authority to both execute this Agreement and sell the Property. Exceptions to ownership, title and authority are as follows: _____
    _____ .

6. **MULTIPLE LISTING SERVICE:** All terms of the transaction, including financing, if applicable, will be provided to the selected MLS for publication, dissemination and use by persons and entities on terms approved by the MLS. Seller acknowledges that Broker is required to comply with all applicable MLS rules as a condition of entry of the listing into the MLS and Seller authorizes Broker to comply with all applicable MLS rules. MLS rules require that the listing sales price be reported to the MLS. MLS rules allow MLS data to be made available by the MLS to additional Internet sites unless Broker gives the MLS instructions to the contrary. MLS rules generally provide that residential real property and vacant lot listings be submitted to the MLS within 48 hours or some other period of time after all necessary signatures have been obtained on the listing agreement. However, Broker will not have to submit this listing to the MLS if, within that time, Broker submits to the MLS a form signed by Seller (C.A.R. Form SEL or the locally required form).
    Information that can be excluded:
    A. Internet Display;
        (1) Seller can instruct Broker to have the MLS not display the Property on the Internet. Seller understands that this would mean consumers searching for listings on the Internet may not see information about the Property in response to their search; **(2)** Seller can instruct Broker to have the MLS not display the Property address on the Internet. Seller understands that this would mean consumers searching for listings on the Internet may not see the Property's address in response to their search.
    B. Features on MLS Participant and Subscriber Websites;
        (1) Seller can instruct Broker to advise the MLS that Seller does not want visitors to MLS Participant or Subscriber Websites that display the Property listing to have **(i)** the ability to write comments or reviews about the Property on those sites; or **(ii)** the ability to hyperlink to another site containing such comments or reviews if the hyperlink is in immediate conjunction with the Property. Seller understands **(i)** that this opt-out applies only to Websites of MLS Participants and Subscribers who are real estate broker and agent members of the MLS; **(ii)** that other Internet sites may or may not have the features set forth herein; and **(iii)** that neither Broker nor the MLS may have the ability to control or block such features on other Internet sites. **(2)** Seller can instruct Broker to advise the MLS that Seller does not want MLS Participant or Subscriber Websites that display the Property listing to operate **(i)** an automated estimate of the market value of the Property; or **(ii)** have the ability to hyperlink to another site containing such automated estimate of value if the hyperlink is in immediate conjunction with the Property. Seller understands **(i)** that this opt-out applies only to Websites of MLS Participants and Subscribers who are real estate brokers and agent members of the MLS; **(ii)** that other Internet sites may or may not have the features set forth herein; and **(iii)** that neither Broker nor the MLS may have the ability to control or block such features on other Internet sites.
    Seller acknowledges that for any of the above opt-out instructions to be effective, Seller must make them on a separate instruction to Broker signed by Seller (C.A.R. Form SEL or the locally required form). Information about this listing will be provided to the MLS of Broker's selection unless a form instructing Broker to withhold the listing from the MLS is attached to this listing Agreement.

7. **SELLER REPRESENTATIONS:** Seller represents that, unless otherwise specified in writing, Seller is unaware of: **(i)** any Notice of Default recorded against the Property; **(ii)** any delinquent amounts due under any loan secured by, or other obligation affecting, the Property; **(iii)** any bankruptcy, insolvency or similar proceeding affecting the Property; **(iv)** any litigation, arbitration, administrative action, government investigation or other pending or threatened action that affects or may affect the Property or Seller's ability to transfer it; and **(v)** any current, pending or proposed special assessments affecting the Property. Seller shall promptly notify Broker in writing if Seller becomes aware of any of these items during the Listing Period or any extension thereof.

8. **BROKER'S AND SELLER'S DUTIES: (a)** Broker agrees to exercise reasonable effort and due diligence to achieve the purposes of this Agreement. Unless Seller gives Broker written instructions to the contrary, Broker is authorized to **(i)** order reports and disclosures as necessary, **(ii)** advertise and market the Property by any method and in any medium selected by Broker, including MLS and the Internet, and, to the extent permitted by these media, control the dissemination of the information submitted to any medium; and **(iii)** disclose to any real estate licensee making an inquiry the receipt of any offers on the Property and the offering price of such offers. **(b)** Seller agrees to consider offers presented by Broker, and to act in good faith to accomplish the sale of the Property by, among other things, making the Property available for showing at reasonable times and referring to Broker all inquiries of any party interested in the Property. Seller is responsible for determining at what price to list and sell the Property. **Seller further agrees to indemnify, defend and hold Broker harmless from all claims, disputes, litigation, judgments and attorney fees arising from any incorrect information supplied by Seller, or from any material facts that Seller knows but fails to disclose.**

9. **DEPOSIT:** Broker is authorized to accept and hold on Seller's behalf any deposits to be applied toward the purchase price.

Copyright © 1991-2011, CALIFORNIA ASSOCIATION OF REALTORS®, INC.
RLA REVISED 11/11 (PAGE 2 OF 4)

Seller's Initials (_____)(_____)

Reviewed by _____ Date _____

RESIDENTIAL LISTING AGREEMENT - EXCLUSIVE (RLA PAGE 2 OF 4)

Source: Reprinted with permission, California Association of REALTORS®. Endorsement not implied.

FIGURE 6.1

Exclusive Authorization and Right to Sell, Continued

Property Address: _____ Date: _____

10. **AGENCY RELATIONSHIPS:**
    A. **Disclosure:** If the Property includes residential property with one-to-four dwelling units, Seller shall receive a "Disclosure Regarding Agency Relationships" form prior to entering into this Agreement.
    B. **Seller Representation:** Broker shall represent Seller in any resulting transaction, except as specified in paragraph 4F.
    C. **Possible Dual Agency With Buyer:** Depending upon the circumstances, it may be necessary or appropriate for Broker to act as an agent for both Seller and Buyer, exchange party, or one or more additional parties ("Buyer"). Broker shall, as soon as practicable, disclose to Seller any election to act as a dual agent representing both Seller and Buyer. If a Buyer is procured directly by Broker or an associate-licensee in Broker's firm, Seller hereby consents to Broker acting as a dual agent for Seller and such Buyer. In the event of an exchange, Seller hereby consents to Broker collecting compensation from additional parties for services rendered, provided there is disclosure to all parties of such agency and compensation. Seller understands and agrees that: **(i)** Broker, without the prior written consent of Seller, will not disclose to Buyer that Seller is willing to sell the Property at a price less than the listing price; **(ii)** Broker, without the prior written consent of Buyer, will not disclose to Seller that Buyer is willing to pay a price greater than the offered price; and **(iii)** except for (i) and (ii) above, a dual agent is obligated to disclose known facts materially affecting the value or desirability of the Property to both parties.
    D. **Other Sellers:** Seller understands that Broker may have or obtain listings on other properties, and that potential buyers may consider, make offers on, or purchase through Broker, property the same as or similar to Seller's Property. Seller consents to Broker's representation of sellers and buyers of other properties before, during and after the end of this Agreement.
    E. **Confirmation:** If the Property includes residential property with one-to-four dwelling units, Broker shall confirm the agency relationship described above, or as modified, in writing, prior to or concurrent with Seller's execution of a purchase agreement.

11. **SECURITY AND INSURANCE:** Broker is not responsible for loss of or damage to personal or real property, or person, whether attributable to use of a keysafe/lockbox, a showing of the Property, or otherwise. Third parties, including, but not limited to, appraisers, inspectors, brokers and prospective buyers, may have access to, and take videos and photographs of, the interior of the Property. Seller agrees: **(i)** to take reasonable precautions to safeguard and protect valuables that might be accessible during showings of the Property; and **(ii)** to obtain insurance to protect against these risks. Broker does not maintain insurance to protect Seller.

12. **KEYSAFE/LOCKBOX:** A keysafe/lockbox is designed to hold a key to the Property to permit access to the Property by Broker, cooperating brokers, MLS participants, their authorized licensees and representatives, authorized inspectors, and accompanied prospective buyers. Broker, cooperating brokers, MLS and Associations/Boards of REALTORS® are **not** insurers against injury, theft, loss, vandalism or damage attributed to the use of a keysafe/lockbox. Seller does (or if checked ☐ does not) authorize Broker to install a keysafe/lockbox. If Seller does not occupy the Property, Seller shall be responsible for obtaining occupant(s)' written permission for use of a keysafe/lockbox (C.A.R. Form KLA).

13. **SIGN:** Seller does (or if checked ☐ does not) authorize Broker to install a FOR SALE/SOLD sign on the Property.

14. **EQUAL HOUSING OPPORTUNITY:** The Property is offered in compliance with federal, state and local anti-discrimination laws.

15. **SUCCESSORS AND ASSIGNS:** This Agreement shall be binding upon Seller and Seller's successors and assigns.

16. **MANAGEMENT APPROVAL:** If an associate-licensee in Broker's office (salesperson or broker-associate) enters into this Agreement on Broker's behalf, and Broker or Manager does not approve of its terms, Broker or Manager has the right to cancel this Agreement, in writing, within **5 Days** After its execution.

17. **ADDITIONAL TERMS:** ☐ REO Advisory Listing (C.A.R. Form REOL) ☐ Short Sale Information and Advisory (C.A.R. Form SSIA)

_____

_____

_____

_____

_____

_____

18. **ATTORNEY FEES:** In any action, proceeding or arbitration between Seller and Broker regarding the obligation to pay compensation under this Agreement, the prevailing Seller or Broker shall be entitled to reasonable attorney fees and costs from the non-prevailing Seller or Broker, except as provided in paragraph 20A.

19. **ENTIRE AGREEMENT:** All prior discussions, negotiations and agreements between the parties concerning the subject matter of this Agreement are superseded by this Agreement, which constitutes the entire contract and a complete and exclusive expression of their agreement, and may not be contradicted by evidence of any prior agreement or contemporaneous oral agreement. If any provision of this Agreement is held to be ineffective or invalid, the remaining provisions will nevertheless be given full force and effect. This Agreement and any supplement, addendum or modification, including any photocopy or facsimile, may be executed in counterparts.

Seller's Initials (_____)(_____)

Reviewed by _____ Date _____

RESIDENTIAL LISTING AGREEMENT - EXCLUSIVE (RLA PAGE 3 OF 4)

FIGURE 6.1

Exclusive Authorization and Right to Sell, Continued

Property Address: _____ Date: _____

20. DISPUTE RESOLUTION:

    A. MEDIATION: Seller and Broker agree to mediate any dispute or claim arising between them out of this Agreement, or any resulting transaction, before resorting to arbitration or court action, subject to paragraph 20B(2) below. Paragraph 20B(2) below applies whether or not the arbitration provision is initialed. Mediation fees, if any, shall be divided equally among the parties involved. If, for any dispute or claim to which this paragraph applies, any party commences an action without first attempting to resolve the matter through mediation, or refuses to mediate after a request has been made, then that party shall not be entitled to recover attorney fees, even if they would otherwise be available to that party in any such action. THIS MEDIATION PROVISION APPLIES WHETHER OR NOT THE ARBITRATION PROVISION IS INITIALED.

    B. ARBITRATION OF DISPUTES: (1) Seller and Broker agree that any dispute or claim in law or equity arising between them regarding the obligation to pay compensation under this Agreement, which is not settled through mediation, shall be decided by neutral, binding arbitration, including and subject to paragraph 20B(2) below. The arbitrator shall be a retired judge or justice, or an attorney with at least 5 years of residential real estate law experience, unless the parties mutually agree to a different arbitrator, who shall render an award in accordance with substantive California law. The parties shall have the right to discovery in accordance with California Code of Civil Procedure §1283.05. In all other respects, the arbitration shall be conducted in accordance with Title 9 of Part III of the California Code of Civil Procedure. Judgment upon the award of the arbitrator(s) may be entered in any court having jurisdiction. Interpretation of this agreement to arbitrate shall be governed by the Federal Arbitration Act.

    (2) EXCLUSIONS FROM MEDIATION AND ARBITRATION: The following matters are excluded from mediation and arbitration: (i) a judicial or non-judicial foreclosure or other action or proceeding to enforce a deed of trust, mortgage, or installment land sale contract as defined in California Civil Code §2985; (ii) an unlawful detainer action; (iii) the filing or enforcement of a mechanic's lien; and (iv) any matter that is within the jurisdiction of a probate, small claims, or bankruptcy court. The filing of a court action to enable the recording of a notice of pending action, for order of attachment, receivership, injunction, or other provisional remedies, shall not constitute a waiver of the mediation and arbitration provisions.

        "NOTICE: BY INITIALING IN THE SPACE BELOW YOU ARE AGREEING TO HAVE ANY DISPUTE ARISING OUT OF THE MATTERS INCLUDED IN THE 'ARBITRATION OF DISPUTES' PROVISION DECIDED BY NEUTRAL ARBITRATION AS PROVIDED BY CALIFORNIA LAW AND YOU ARE GIVING UP ANY RIGHTS YOU MIGHT POSSESS TO HAVE THE DISPUTE LITIGATED IN A COURT OR JURY TRIAL. BY INITIALING IN THE SPACE BELOW YOU ARE GIVING UP YOUR JUDICIAL RIGHTS TO DISCOVERY AND APPEAL, UNLESS THOSE RIGHTS ARE SPECIFICALLY INCLUDED IN THE 'ARBITRATION OF DISPUTES' PROVISION. IF YOU REFUSE TO SUBMIT TO ARBITRATION AFTER AGREEING TO THIS PROVISION, YOU MAY BE COMPELLED TO ARBITRATE UNDER THE AUTHORITY OF THE CALIFORNIA CODE OF CIVIL PROCEDURE. YOUR AGREEMENT TO THIS ARBITRATION PROVISION IS VOLUNTARY."

        "WE HAVE READ AND UNDERSTAND THE FOREGOING AND AGREE TO SUBMIT DISPUTES ARISING OUT OF THE MATTERS INCLUDED IN THE 'ARBITRATION OF DISPUTES' PROVISION TO NEUTRAL ARBITRATION."

| Seller's Initials _____ / _____ | Broker's Initials _____ / _____ |

By signing below, Seller acknowledges that Seller has read, understands, received a copy of and agrees to the terms of this Agreement.

Seller _____ Date _____

Address _____ City _____ State _____ Zip _____

Telephone _____ Fax _____ E-mail _____

Seller _____ Date _____

Address _____ City _____ State _____ Zip _____

Telephone _____ Fax _____ E-mail _____

Real Estate Broker (Firm) _____ DRE Lic. # _____

By (Agent) _____ DRE Lic. # _____ Date _____

Address _____ City _____ State _____ Zip _____

Telephone _____ Fax _____ E-mail _____

Published and Distributed by:
REAL ESTATE BUSINESS SERVICES, INC.
a subsidiary of the California Association of REALTORS®
525 South Virgil Avenue, Los Angeles, California 90020

Reviewed by _____ Date _____

RLA REVISED 11/11 (PAGE 4 OF 4)

RESIDENTIAL LISTING AGREEMENT - EXCLUSIVE (RLA PAGE 4 OF 4)

Case Study
In *Nystrom v. First National Bank of Fresno* (1978) 81 C.A.3d 759, a 90-day exclusive listing was not to be effective until a deed was acquired at a forthcoming trustee's sale. In an action to collect a commission where a sale was consummated by another broker, the court held that, while the beginning date was uncertain, the listing did have a definite date for termination.

Exclusive listings generally provide that if the seller cancels the listing, leases, or rents the property without the approval of the agent, or otherwise adversely affects its marketability, the agent is entitled to his or her commission.

While owners usually cannot cancel an exclusive listing without obligation, courts have held that an owner may properly cancel an exclusive listing if the agent has failed in his or her duty to use good-faith efforts to procure a buyer.

There are two types of exclusive sale listings: exclusive-right-to-sell listings and exclusive-agency listings.

Exclusive Authorization and Right-To-Sell Listing.   With an **exclusive authorization and right-to-sell listing**, the owner agrees to pay a commission to an agent if the agent, any other agent, or the owner procures a buyer in accordance with the price and terms of the listing, or for any other price or terms that the owner accepts. The broker will not be entitled to a commission if the buyer located lacks the financial ability to complete the purchase because the broker has failed to procure a ready, willing, and able buyer.

Because the listing agent earns a commission no matter who sells the property, this is the most desirable listing for brokers.

Exclusive-right-to-sell listings frequently contain a **safety clause**. This clause customarily provides that the owner is obligated to pay a commission if a sale is made within a stated period after expiration of the listing to any person the agent negotiated with and whose name was furnished in writing to the owner within three days after the expiration of the listing. Sometimes, these clauses provide that in the event another listing is entered into, the owner no longer is obligated under the safety clause. Without such an exception, an owner could be obligated to pay more than one commission. Notice the safety clause, paragraph 4.A.2, in the listing agreement (Figure 6.1). Often the rules of a local board of REALTORS® have the effect of a safety clause on subsequent listings.

Paragraph 12 covers keybox authorization, and the owner is advised to obtain appropriate insurance coverage. If an agent recommends a keybox without any warnings to the owner, conceivably the agent could be held liable for any resulting loss.

Paragraph 14-B provides that by initialing, the parties agree to arbitration of any disputes arising from the agreement (mandatory arbitration).

Exclusive-Agency Listing. Under an **exclusive-agency listing**, the named broker is the exclusive agent for the owner, and if the listing broker or any other agent procures a purchaser in accordance with the terms of the listing, or any other price and terms the owner might agree to, the agent has earned a commission. The owner can, however, sell the property by himself or herself without any obligation to pay a commission.

Exclusive-agency listings usually are entered into when an owner might have one or more prospective buyers. A better arrangement, however, would be to write an exclusive-right-to-sell listing that excludes named individuals for a set period of time. This would encourage the seller's prospects to buy if they are serious buyers. After the expiration of the stated period of time, the exception would be removed.

Exclusive-agency listings usually require that the owner notify the agent of any sale and identify the purchasers. They usually also prohibit the owner from offering the property at a lower price than that offered by the agent.

Under an exclusive-agency listing, the owner might be encouraged to subvert the agent's efforts. Problems arise as to who really was the procuring cause of a sale when the agent had contact with the owner's buyer (procuring cause is discussed further below). Because of the possible problems of exclusive-agency listings, many brokers refuse to accept them.

Open Listings

Open listings are nonexclusive listings; they may be offered to one or more brokers. The broker who earns the commission is the first agent to bring the owner an offer that meets the terms of the listing or that the owner accepts. A sale under one open listing automatically cancels all other open listings. The principal has no duty to notify the agents under other open listings of the sale.

An open listing may be simply a note or memorandum that describes the property and states the price wanted and that a stated commission will be paid. The agent need not sign the open listing, but it must be signed by the principal (property owner).

The open listing is really a unilateral contract. The agent makes no promise to use diligence to obtain a buyer. By procuring a buyer the agent accepts the owner's promise to pay a commission.

Unlike exclusive listings, open listings need not have a definite termination date. An owner generally can cancel the open listing at any time without obligation but cannot cancel an open listing to avoid paying a commission and then accept the benefits of the agent's efforts by consummating a sale to a buyer procured by the agent. An owner who cancels an open listing in good faith is not obligated to the agent simply because a sale later was made to a buyer whom the agent had contacted.

Open listings often lead to disagreements between owners and agents as well as among agents over who was the procuring cause of a sale. Several legal form providers offer open listing forms. An advantage of a formal listing is the broker protection of the safety clause.

Procuring Cause

The agent who is the **procuring cause** of a sale is that agent who initiated an uninterrupted series of events that led to the sale. Under open listings and exclusive-agency listings, an agent who was the procuring cause of the sale is entitled to a commission.

If a break in the chain of events occurred, such as failure to contact a prospective buyer for several months or failure to obtain financing, the original agent who failed for lack of diligence or effort generally would not be considered the procuring cause. Simply telling a person about a property or giving a buyer a list in which a property is included would not qualify an agent as a procuring cause.

> **Case Study**
> In the case of *Coldwell Banker and Co. v. Pepper Tree Office Center Assocs.* (1980) 106 C.A.3d 272, the plaintiff had an exclusive-agency listing. The court held that submitting a one-page brochure and forwarding floor plans to the broker of a prospective tenant did not reasonably constitute procuring cause.

The agent who claims that he or she was the procuring cause has the burden of proof. When the broker's efforts led directly to the buyer and seller getting together, the courts generally will consider the broker to have been the procuring cause.

Procuring cause problems often arise when a prospective buyer fails to inform an agent that he or she has already been exposed to a particular property by another agent. An agent who discovers after a sale that the buyer had previous contact with another agent should have the buyer make a written statement about the nature of the contact and the dates, as well as the reason the buyer did not continue to negotiate with the original agent. If this statement shows that another agent might have a reasonable claim to being the procuring cause, the selling agent should consider negotiating a fair settlement.

An owner who has given multiple open listings may assume, unless notified otherwise, that the broker presenting the offer is the procuring cause.

The safety clause in a listing appears only to require that the agent introduced the buyer to the property. This is much less than the requirement under procuring cause. Therefore, a broker could be in a better position claiming notification under the safety clause than making a claim as to procuring cause. A prior offer made by the ultimate purchaser has been held to satisfy the notification requirements of the safety clause.

Oral Listings

While listings of real property are required to be in writing to be enforceable, one exception may exist. If, after a listing expires, the owner encourages the broker to continue to work on the sale of the property, the owner may have waived his or her rights to claim the statute of frauds as a defense against paying a commission. The doctrine of estoppel might apply.

See *Filante v. Kikendall* (1955) 134 C.A.2d 695 for an example.

Buyer Listings

As discussed earlier, the agent can represent the buyer only rather than the seller. A **buyer listing**, like a listing from owners, can be exclusive: the broker has the sole right to locate property for a buyer. In a buyer exclusive-agency listing, the buyer can locate property for himself or herself, but the broker is the exclusive agent. In an open-buyer listing, the broker is given nonexclusive authorization to locate property.

Like a seller's listing, a buyer's listing, to be enforceable, must be in writing and signed to satisfy the statute of frauds. An oral agreement by a buyer to pay a commission is unenforceable.

Like a seller's listing, a buyer's listing would authorize the broker to cooperate with other brokers. The terms in the buyer's listing are very similar to those found in the usual listings given by owners. One difference is the fee structure. Buyers' listings for residential property generally provide that the buyer will pay the agent's commission; however, any commission paid to the agent by third parties (commission splits) will be credited against the fee owed by the buyer. Buyers' listings frequently provide a fee for obtaining an option to purchase and another fee when exercised. Buyers' listings sometimes include an hourly fee as well as an advance against expenses.

> **Case Study**
> In the case of *Schaffter v. Creative Capital Leasing Group LLC* (2008) 166 C.A. 4th 745, a buyer agency listing provided for a 2.3 percent commission less fees paid to the broker by the developer. The buyer purchased 16 units and received $89,000 from the developer. He was still owed $38,400 when the buyer defaulted and refused to close on the remaining units. The agent sued the buyer.
>
> The trial court ruled that the commission was earned when the contract was entered into. Because the buyer defaulted, the broker was entitled to the full remaining commission on all units totaling $147,000 as well as attorney fees. The Court of Appeal affirmed.

Net Listings

Net listings refer to the commission payment only and provide that all money received over a stated or net amount shall be the agent's commission. They are illegal in many states because they create a serious conflict of interest. The agent under a net listing really is dealing more as a principal than as an agent. The agent is closer to being an optionee (with an option to buy) than a representative of the owner.

Even though net listings are legal in California, agents should be aware that the seller is likely to allege fraud or misrepresentation should the sales price result in a commission that is greater than customary.

A net listing does not relieve the broker from informing the owner of offers at or less than the list price. When an owner accepts such an offer, the broker is not entitled to a commission.

The agent must disclose the amount of his or her net commission prior to or at the time the principal commits to the transaction. Failure to do so could be grounds for disciplinary action.

Because of the ethical problems involved with net listings, a net listing form has not been included in this chapter.

Other Listing Forms

Advance Fee Addendum.   The growth of professionalism in real estate has led to a growing acceptance of advance fees. While more common in buyer listings, they also are gaining acceptance in seller listings, especially listings involving larger residential, commercial, or industrial property where a great deal of professional effort and expense will be required prior to a sale.

The **advance fee addendum** usually sets forth specific activities that the agent is to be compensated for, as well as an hourly rate (or set rate) for the compensation. The agreement is very similar to an agreement that an attorney makes with his or her client.

The Department of Real Estate requires approval of all advance fee forms (approval does not extend to photocopies of approved forms). Any additions or deletions to an approved form must be submitted to the Department of Real Estate at least ten days prior to entering into an agreement. Failure to do so could result in disciplinary action.

Advance fees must be placed in the broker's trust account until they are earned.

Advance Costs.   **Advance costs** differ from advance fees in that they are paid to the agent to cover cash outlays in carrying out the agency. They are not intended to cover brokerage fees or general overhead expenses. As an example, if an owner wanted an expensive ad in the *Wall Street Journal*, the broker might require cost in advance.

Monies collected to cover advance costs must be treated as trust money and must be placed in the broker's trust account. The trust fund remains the property of the principal until disbursed by the agent for the principal.

The broker must provide the principal with a quarterly accounting of all disbursements, and any remaining funds must be returned to the principal at the expiration of the agreement along with a final accounting.

Listing Modification.   While it is possible for a broker and a principal to enter into a new listing agreement that by its terms supersedes an existing listing, it is far simpler to enter a simple modification. Brokers can use an all-purpose addendum form or a specific listing addendum form for this purpose.

Loan Broker Listing Agreement.   A mortgage loan broker represents a borrower, as his or her agent, to obtain a loan. The agency agreement setting forth the rights and obligations of the parties is known as a **loan broker listing agreement**.

Loan brokers' commissions and costs on regulated loans are limited by law (see Chapter 4). Loan brokers' listings cannot exceed 45 days when seeking a residential loan of $2,000 or less.

A loan broker listing agreement generally allows the broker to work with other agents, provides a safety clause pertaining to loans made after the expiration of the listing, and contains other provisions that are similar to those found in exclusive-right-to-sell listings.

Seller's Net.   Often, sellers do not understand the effect of escrow costs, prorations, prepayment penalties, title insurance costs, seller's points, and other matters. Surprises can result in sellers refusing to sell, filing a complaint against the agent, and even suing the agent.

Estimated Seller's Net Sheet forms are available that allow the agent to estimate seller's actual net after loans, liens, costs, and fees are deducted from the sale price. An Estimated Seller's Net Sheet form can be used at the time a listing is taken, when an offer is received, or in preparing a counteroffer. The more open an agent is in his or her dealings, the less chance the agent has of creating animosity and/or being sued by a party to a transaction.

■ OPTIONS

As pointed out in Chapter 5, an option is a contract to make a contract. The option must clearly show the price if the option is exercised. (The price can be determined by a formula; however, it cannot be ambiguous.) Time is considered to be of the essence in options in that the option *must* be exercised within the period provided.

Generally, option-to-purchase forms provide for the method of exercising the option, include any agreed-on sales terms, and contain provisions for escrow and delivery of title, as well as for brokerage fees. The form in Figure 6.2 protects the broker during any extensions to the option as well as for a safety period of one year after the expiration of the option or extensions thereto. Some option forms provide for option extensions upon the payment of additional consideration.

An owner cannot avoid a commission by giving an option during the listing period that is to be exercised after the listing expires. See *Anthony v. Enzler* (1976) 61 C.A.3d 872.

FIGURE 6.2

Standard Option to Purchase Form

STANDARD OPTION TO PURCHASE
Irrevocable Right-to-Buy

| Prepared by: Agent _____ | Phone _____ |
| Broker _____ | Email _____ |

DATE: _____, 20_____, at _____, California.

Items left blank or unchecked are not applicable.

1. OPTION MONEY:

Optionor herewith receives from Optionee option money in the amount of $_____, evidenced by: ☐ cash, ☐ check, or ☐ _____, given in consideration for this option to purchase real property.

2. REAL PROPERTY UNDER OPTION:

Address _____

Legal description/Assessor's parcel number _____

3. ADDITIONAL CONSIDERATION:

As further consideration for this option, Optionee is to obtain at his expense and deliver to Optionor prior to expiration of this option the following checked items regarding the property:

☐ Property survey report by licensed California surveyors   ☐ Off-site improvement plans
☐ Architectural plans and specifications   ☐ Soil engineer's report
☐ Zoning ordinance request   ☐ Land use study
☐ On-site engineering plans   ☐ Application for a conditional use permit
☐ Application for a parcel map or waiver   ☐ _____

4. OPTION PERIOD:

Optionor hereby grants to Optionee the irrevocable option to purchase the Optionor's right, title and interest in the property on the terms stated, for a period commencing with the acceptance of this option and expiring _____, 20_____, or ☐ on termination of the optionee's leasehold interest in the property.

5. EXERCISE OF OPTION:

Optionee may exercise this option during the option period by:

5.1   Signing escrow instructions identical in provisions to those attached as **Exhibit A** and delivering the instructions to escrow [See **ft** Form 401];

5.2   Depositing cash in escrow of $_____; and

5.3   Delivering an escrow-certified copy of the signed escrow instructions to Optionor within the option period, in person or by both certified and regular mail.

6. ESCROW CONTRACT:

In the event this option is exercised, the transaction shall be escrowed with _____.

6.1   Escrow shall close within _____ days after exercise.

7. DELIVERY OF TITLE:

On Optionee's exercise of this option, Optionor shall timely place all documents and instruments into escrow required of the Optionor as necessary for escrow to close as scheduled.

8. BROKERAGE FEE:

Optionor agrees to pay a brokerage fee of $_____, or _____% of the selling price, IF:

8.1   This option is exercised;

8.2   Within one year after expiration of option period and any extension or renewal, Optionor enters into an agreement to option, sell, lease or exchange with Optionee, or their assigns or successors; or

8.3   Optionor wrongfully prevents the exercise of this option;

8.4   Payable to Broker(s) _____

9. SALE TERMS:

Price of $_____ payable as follows:

9.1   ☐ All cash.

9.2   Cash down payment in the amount of $_____.

9.3   ☐ Take title subject to, or ☐ Assume, an existing first trust deed note held by _____, with an unpaid principal balance of $_____, payable $_____ monthly, including interest not exceeding _____%, ☐ ARM, type _____, plus a monthly tax/insurance impound payment of $_____. _____

     a.   At closing, loan balance differences per beneficiary statement(s) to be adjusted into:
         ☐ cash, ☐ carryback note, or ☐ sales price.

     b.   The impound account to be transferred: ☐ charged, or ☐ without charge, to Optionee.

9.4   ☐ Take title subject to, or ☐ Assume, an existing second trust deed note held by _____, with an unpaid principal balance of $_____, payable $_____ monthly, including interest not exceeding _____%, ☐ ARM, type _____, due _____, 20_____.

— — — — — — — — — — — — — — — — *PAGE ONE OF TWO — FORM 161* — — — — — — — — — — — — — — — — — —

Reprinted with permission from first tuesday.

FIGURE 6.2

Standard Option to Purchase Form, Continued

— — — — — — — — — — — — — — — — *PAGE TWO OF TWO — FORM 161* — — — — — — — — — — — — — — — — — —

9.5 A note for the balance of the purchase price in the amount of $_____ to be executed by Optionee in favor of Optionor and secured by a trust deed on the property junior to the above referenced financing, payable $_____ monthly, or more, beginning one month after closing, including interest at _____% per annum from closing, due _____ years after closing.

    a. This note and trust deed to contain provisions to be provided by Optionor for:

        ☐ due-on-sale, ☐ prepayment penalty, ☐ late charges, ☐_____

    b. ☐ The attached Financial Disclosure Statement is an addendum to this agreement (mandatory on four-or-less residential units). [See **ft** Form 300]

    c. ☐ Optionee to provide a Request for Notice of Default and Notice of Delinquency to senior encumbrancers. [See **ft** Form 412]

10. GENERAL PROVISIONS:

10.1 ☐ **See attached addendum for additional provisions.** [See **ft** Form 250]

10.2 Attached as addenda are the following checked disclosures mandated on four-or-less residential units:

    a. ☐ Condition of Property Disclosure — Transfer Disclosure Statement (TDS) [See **ft** Form 304]

    b. ☐ Natural Hazard Disclosure Statement [See **ft** Form 314]

    c. ☐ Disclosure of Sexual Predator Database [See **ft** Form 319]

    d. ☐ Hazard Disclosure Booklet, and related Optionor disclosures, containing Environmental Hazards, Lead-based Paint and Earthquake Safety [See **ft** Forms 313 and 315]

    e. ☐ Documentation on any Homeowners' Association (HOA) involved.

    f. ☐ Notice of Supplemental Property Tax Bill [See **ft** Form 317]

10.3 Possession of the property to be delivered on:
☐ close of escrow, or ☐ see attached Occupancy Agreement. [See **ft** Forms 271 and 272]

10.4 Both parties reserve their rights to assign, and agree to cooperate in effecting an Internal Revenue Code §1031 exchange prior to close of escrow, on either party's written notice.

11. EXPIRATION OF OPTION:

This offer to sell shall be deemed expired if not accepted by exercise during the option period.

11.1 This option contract shall automatically terminate by expiration on _____, 20_____.

OPTIONOR'S BROKER: _____	**OPTIONEE'S BROKER:** _____
Broker's DRE Identification #: _____	Broker's DRE Identification #: _____
Agent's Name: _____	Agent's Name: _____
Agent's DRE Identification #: _____	Agent's DRE Identification #: _____
Signature: _____	Signature: _____
Is the agent of: ☐ Optionor exclusively.	Is the agent of: ☐ Optionee exclusively.
☐ Both Optionor and Optionee.	☐ Both Optionor and Optionee.
Address: _____	Address: _____
Phone: _____ Cell: _____	Phone: _____ Cell: _____
Email: _____	Email: _____
I hereby grant this option and agree to the terms stated above.	**I hereby accept this option and agree to the terms stated above.**
Date: _____, 20_____	Date: _____, 20_____
Optionor: _____	Optionee: _____
Signature: _____	Signature: _____
Signature: _____	Signature: _____
Address: _____	Address: _____
Phone: _____ Fax: _____	Phone: _____ Fax: _____
Email: _____	Email: _____

FORM 161   11-10   ©2010 **first tuesday**, P.O. BOX 20069, RIVERSIDE, CA 92516 (800) 794-0494

Reprinted with permission from first tuesday.

> **Case Study**
>
> The case of *Patel v. Liebermensch* (2008) 45 C. 4th 344 involved a lease with a purchase option. The lessees notified the owner that they wished to exercise their purchase option. The owners sent a contract with a 90-day escrow. Lessees demanded a 30-day escrow.
>
> The Court of Appeal reversed, ruling that there was no meeting of the minds so the option could not be exercised.
>
> The Supreme Court reinstated the trial court order and held that failure to state a time period for close of escrow was not a fatal flaw. It could be implied in an option that escrow should close within a reasonable period of time.

As discussed in Chapter 3, in California, an agent with a listing may also obtain an option to purchase the property. However, because the broker is dealing as an agent under the listing and as a principal under the option, a serious conflict of interest arises. As stated earlier, before the option can be exercised, the agent must disclose fully if he or she has an offer, the amount of the offer, and his or her profit. The agent also must obtain the owner's written consent after said disclosure to exercise the option.

Because of the serious ethical questions raised by options combined with listings, the authors strongly advise against the use of these agreements.

> **Case Study**
>
> The case of *Rattray v. Scudder* (1946) 28 C.2d 214 involved a listing-option agreement. The broker located a buyer but indicated to the owner that he was unable to find one. He then negotiated a lower purchase price for himself. The court held that a broker, when pursuing his own interests, cannot ignore those of his principal. The broker cannot be allowed to enjoy the fruits of an advantage taken under a fiduciary relationship.

■ BROKER'S FORMS

Finder's Fee

An agent may not pay a commission to an unlicensed party for any act that requires a real estate license. Finders' fees, however (discussed in Chapter 3), are legal. They are not paid for an act requiring a real estate license; they are paid for a referral or introduction to a buyer, seller, borrower, or lender. Sharing part of a sales commission with an unlicensed person nevertheless is illegal.

Oral agreements made with brokers have been enforced on the theory that the broker does not need the protection of the statute of frauds. For the protection of both the broker and the finder, a written agreement should be prepared.

Generally, in finder's fee agreements, the finder agrees not to participate in or conduct negotiations with prospective clients or to solicit loans on behalf of prospective clients.

Cooperating Broker Agreements

Agreements between brokers to split commissions are not required by the statute of frauds to be in writing. They deal in dollars and not real estate.

To avoid misunderstandings, brokers may enter into written agreements setting forth the commission split. Some **cooperating broker fee agreements** require that the nonlisting broker identify prospective buyers so that the listing broker can notify the owner of these prospective purchasers (to be protected under the safety clause of the listing). Brokers seldom use these agreements, however, because generally both listing and selling brokers are members of a trade group, such as a multiple-listing service, that enforces commission split agreements.

■ REAL ESTATE PURCHASE CONTRACT

The California Association of REALTORS® (CAR) has prepared several real estate purchase contract forms. We have included a California Residential Purchase Agreement and Joint Escrow Instructions as Figure 6.3. This form provides for most contingencies and avoids the necessity of agent-drafted provisions that might not clearly reflect the intentions of the parties. The form also serves as joint escrow instructions. Included here are comments on the paragraphs to aid in your understanding of the purpose and applications of the provisions of this contract.

Paragraph 1: Defines the form as an offer from offeror, describes the property, sets the purchase price, and specifies the closing time.

Paragraph 2: Reiterates the agency disclosure and confirms the agency of the listing and selling agent.

Paragraph 3: Provides for initial and increased deposits, financing contingency and terms of loans, appraisal contingency, and other finance terms. By checking the appropriate block, the offer can be made without a loan contingency.

Paragraph 4: Indicates who is responsible for which costs.

Paragraph 5: Includes buyer's intention to occupy premises as a principal residence (see Para. 25 Liquidated Damages), when possession shall be given, if tenant occupied, providing assignable warranties as well as keys and other openers.

Paragraph 6: The requirements of the Transfer Disclosure Statement, Natural Hazard Disclosures, Subsequent Disclosures, Mello-Roos notice, lead paint, tax withholding, and additional required disclosures, which include the "Megan's Law" disclosure as to the availability of information of known sex offenders in the community.

Paragraph 7: Sets forth disclosures required if the property is in a common interest subdivision.

Paragraph 8: Provides that fixtures and fittings shall remain with the property (free of liens), as well as additional items to be included with the sale or items to be excluded from the sale.

Paragraph 9: Sets forth that the property is sold in its present condition, it will be maintained, and personal property and trash will be removed by close of escrow. The paragraph reiterates that the seller will disclose known material facts and defects. The seller's right to inspect and request for repairs is also set forth. If the seller refuses or is unable to make repairs, the buyer has cancellation rights. The buyer is strongly advised to conduct an inspection, as the seller may not be aware of all problems.

Paragraph 10: Sets forth buyer's rights to conduct inspections and tests and states that utilities shall be on for the inspection. Buyer agrees to indemnify seller for any damage or injury resulting from the inspection as well as to keep the property free of liens from work or inspection.

Paragraph 11: Sets forth the disclosures that the seller shall provide.

Paragraph 12: Provides that buyer shall receive a grant deed, preliminary title report, and homeowners' policy of title insurance. Seller must also disclose all known matters affecting title.

Paragraph 13: By checking the appropriate block, the offer is either contingent upon the sale of another property or there is no such contingency. If there is a contingency, the addendum allows the seller the right to offer the property for sale and give buyer the opportunity to remove the contingency if seller accepts another offer.

Paragraph 14: Provides time periods for removal of contingencies as well as cancellation rights. In the event of cancellation, release of funds requires mutual agreement. If a party refuses to release funds when there is no good-faith dispute, the party may be subject to $1,000 in civil damages.

Paragraph 15: Provides that seller repairs shall be prior to final verification of condition and work will be done properly and in accordance with applicable law.

Paragraph 16: Provides for a final inspection of the property prior to close of escrow to determine if the property has been maintained and that the seller has completed agreed-upon repairs and complied with other obligations.

FIGURE 6.3
Residential Purchase Agreement

CALIFORNIA ASSOCIATION OF REALTORS ®

CALIFORNIA
RESIDENTIAL PURCHASE AGREEMENT
AND JOINT ESCROW INSTRUCTIONS
For Use With Single Family Residential Property — Attached or Detached
(C.A.R. Form RPA-CA, Revised 4/10)

Date _____

1. OFFER:
  A. **THIS IS AN OFFER FROM** _____ ("Buyer").
  B. **THE REAL PROPERTY TO BE ACQUIRED** is described as _____
    _____, Assessor's Parcel No. _____, situated in
    _____,-County of _____, California ("Property").
  C. **THE PURCHASE PRICE** offered is _____
    _____ (Dollars $ _____).
  D. **CLOSE OF ESCROW** shall occur on _____ (date) (or ☐ _____ **Days** After Acceptance).

2. AGENCY:
  A. **DISCLOSURE:** Buyer and Seller each acknowledge prior receipt of a "Disclosure Regarding Real Estate Agency Relationships" (C.A.R. Form AD).
  B. **POTENTIALLY COMPETING BUYERS AND SELLERS:** Buyer and Seller each acknowledge receipt of a disclosure of the possibility of multiple representation by the Broker representing that principal. This disclosure may be part of a listing agreement, buyer representation agreement or separate document (C.A.R. Form DA). Buyer understands that Broker representing Buyer may also represent other potential buyers, who may consider, make offers on or ultimately acquire the Property. Seller understands that Broker representing Seller may also represent other sellers with competing properties of interest to this Buyer.
  C. **CONFIRMATION:** The following agency relationships are hereby confirmed for this transaction:
    Listing Agent _____ (Print Firm Name) is the agent of (check one):
    ☐ the Seller exclusively; or ☐ both the Buyer and Seller.
    Selling Agent _____ (Print Firm Name) (if not the same as the Listing Agent) is the agent of (check one): ☐ the Buyer exclusively; or ☐ the Seller exclusively; or ☐ both the Buyer and Seller. Real Estate Brokers are not parties to the Agreement between Buyer and Seller.

3. FINANCE TERMS: Buyer represents that funds will be good when deposited with Escrow Holder.
  A. **INITIAL DEPOSIT:** Deposit shall be in the amount of . . . .$ _____
    (1) Buyer shall deliver deposit directly to Escrow Holder by personal check, ☐ electronic funds transfer,
    ☐ Other _____ within 3 business days after acceptance
    (or ☐ Other_____);
    OR (2) (If checked) ☐ Buyer has given the deposit by personal check (or ☐ _____)
    to the agent submitting the offer (or to ☐ _____), made payable to
    _____. The deposit shall be held uncashed until Acceptance and
    then deposited with Escrow Holder (or ☐ into Broker's trust account) within **3** business days after
    Acceptance (or ☐ Other_____).
  B. **INCREASED DEPOSIT:** Buyer shall deposit with Escrow Holder an increased deposit in the amount of . . . .$ _____
    within _____ **Days** After Acceptance, or ☐ _____.
    If a liquidated damages clause is incorporated into this Agreement, Buyer and Seller shall sign a
    separate liquidated damages clause (C.A.R. Form RID) for any increased deposit at the time it is
    deposited.
  C. **LOAN(S):**
    (1) FIRST LOAN: in the amount of . . . .$ _____
    This loan will be conventional financing or, if checked, ☐ FHA, ☐ VA, ☐ Seller (C.A.R. Form SFA),
    ☐ assumed financing (C.A.R. Form PAA), ☐ Other _____. This loan shall be at a fixed
    rate not to exceed _____% or, ☐ an adjustable rate loan with initial rate not to exceed ____%.
    Regardless of the type of loan, Buyer shall pay points not to exceed ____% of the loan amount.
    (2) ☐ SECOND LOAN in the amount of . . . .$ _____
    This loan will be conventional financing or, if checked, ☐ Seller (C.A.R. Form SFA), ☐ assumed
    financing (C.A.R. Form PAA), ☐ Other _____. This loan shall be at a fixed rate not to
    exceed _____% or, ☐ an adjustable rate loan with initial rate not to exceed ____%. Regardless
    of the type of loan, Buyer shall pay points not to exceed ____% of the loan amount.
    (3) FHA/VA: For any FHA or VA loan specified above, Buyer has **17 (or ☐ _____) Days** After
    Acceptance to Deliver to Seller written notice (C.A.R. Form FVA) of any lender-required repairs or
    costs that Buyer requests Seller to pay for or repair. Seller has no obligation to pay for repairs or
    satisfy lender requirements unless otherwise agreed in writing.
  D. **ADDITIONAL FINANCING TERMS:** _____
    _____
  E. **BALANCE OF PURCHASE PRICE OR DOWN PAYMENT** in the amount of . . . .$ _____
    to be deposited with Escrow Holder within sufficient time to close escrow.
  F. **PURCHASE PRICE (TOTAL):** . . . .$ _____

Buyer's Initials (_____)(_____)   Seller's Initials (_____)(_____)

RPA-CA REVISED 4/10 (PAGE 1 OF 8) Print Date BD Apr 10   Reviewed by _____ Date _____

CALIFORNIA RESIDENTIAL PURCHASE AGREEMENT (RPA-CA PAGE 1 OF 8)

FIGURE 6.3
Residential Purchase Agreement, Continued

Property Address: _____   Date: _____

    G. VERIFICATION OF DOWN PAYMENT AND CLOSING COSTS: Buyer (or Buyer's lender or loan broker pursuant to 3H(1)) shall, within **7 (or ☐ _____) Days** After Acceptance, Deliver to Seller written verification of Buyer's down payment and closing costs. (If checked, ☐ verification attached.)

    H. LOAN TERMS:
        (1) LOAN APPLICATIONS: Within **7 (or ☐ _____) Days** After Acceptance, Buyer shall Deliver to Seller a letter from lender or loan broker stating that, based on a review of Buyer's written application and credit report, Buyer is prequalified or preapproved for any NEW loan specified in 3C above. (If checked, ☐ letter attached.)
        (2) LOAN CONTINGENCY: Buyer shall act diligently and in good faith to obtain the designated loan(s). Obtaining the loan(s) specified above **is a contingency** of this Agreement unless otherwise agreed in writing. Buyer's contractual obligations to obtain and provide deposit, balance of down payment and closing costs **are not contingencies** of this Agreement.
        (3) LOAN CONTINGENCY REMOVAL:
            (i) Within **17 (or ☐ _____) Days** After Acceptance, Buyer shall, as specified in paragraph 14, in writing remove the loan contingency or cancel this Agreement;
        OR (ii) (If checked) ☐ the loan contingency shall remain in effect until the designated loans are funded.
        (4) ☐ NO LOAN CONTINGENCY (If checked): Obtaining any loan specified above is NOT a contingency of this Agreement. If Buyer does not obtain the loan and as a result Buyer does not purchase the Property, Seller may be entitled to Buyer's deposit or other legal remedies.

    I. APPRAISAL CONTINGENCY AND REMOVAL: This Agreement is (**or,** if checked, ☐ is NOT) contingent upon a written appraisal of the Property by a licensed or certified appraiser at no less than the specified purchase price. If there is a loan contingency, Buyer's removal of the loan contingency shall be deemed removal of this appraisal contingency (**or,** ☐ if checked, Buyer shall, as specified in paragraph 14B(3), in writing remove the appraisal contingency or cancel this Agreement within **17 (or ____) Days** After Acceptance). If there is no loan contingency, Buyer shall, as specified in paragraph 14B(3), in writing remove the appraisal contingency or cancel this Agreement within **17 (or ☐ ____) Days** After Acceptance.

    J. ☐ ALL CASH OFFER (If checked): Buyer shall, within **7 (or ☐ _____) Days** After Acceptance, Deliver to Seller written verification of sufficient funds to close this transaction. (If checked, ☐ verification attached.)

    K. BUYER STATED FINANCING: Seller has relied on Buyer's representation of the type of financing specified (including but not limited to, as applicable, amount of down payment, contingent or non contingent loan, or all cash). If Buyer seeks alternate financing, (i) Seller has no obligation to cooperate with Buyer's efforts to obtain such financing, and (ii) Buyer shall also pursue the financing method specified in this Agreement. Buyer's failure to secure alternate financing does not excuse Buyer from the obligation to purchase the Property and close escrow as specified in this Agreement.

4. ALLOCATION OF COSTS (If checked): Unless otherwise specified in writing, **this paragraph** only determines who is to pay for the inspection, test or service ("Report") mentioned; it **does not determine who is to pay for any work recommended or identified in the Report.**

    A. INSPECTIONS AND REPORTS:
        (1) ☐ Buyer ☐ Seller shall pay for an inspection and report for wood destroying pests and organisms ("Wood Pest Report") prepared by _____ a registered structural pest control company.
        (2) ☐ Buyer ☐ Seller shall pay to have septic or private sewage disposal systems inspected _____.
        (3) ☐ Buyer ☐ Seller shall pay to have domestic wells tested for water potability and productivity _____.
        (4) ☐ Buyer ☐ Seller shall pay for a natural hazard zone disclosure report prepared by _____.
        (5) ☐ Buyer ☐ Seller shall pay for the following inspection or report _____.
        (6) ☐ Buyer ☐ Seller shall pay for the following inspection or report _____.

    B. GOVERNMENT REQUIREMENTS AND RETROFIT:
        (1) ☐ Buyer ☐ Seller shall pay for smoke detector installation and/or water heater bracing, if required by Law. Prior to Close Of Escrow, Seller shall provide Buyer written statement(s) of compliance in accordance with state and local Law, unless exempt.
        (2) ☐ Buyer ☐ Seller shall pay the cost of compliance with any other minimum mandatory government retrofit standards, inspections and reports if required as a condition of closing escrow under any Law. _____.

    C. ESCROW AND TITLE:
        (1) ☐ Buyer ☐ Seller shall pay escrow fee _____.
        Escrow Holder shall be _____.
        (2) ☐ Buyer ☐ Seller shall pay for **owner's** title insurance policy specified in paragraph 12E _____.
        Owner's title policy to be issued by _____.
        (Buyer shall pay for any title insurance policy insuring Buyer's **lender,** unless otherwise agreed in writing.)

    D. OTHER COSTS:
        (1) ☐ Buyer ☐ Seller shall pay County transfer tax or fee _____.
        (2) ☐ Buyer ☐ Seller shall pay City transfer tax or fee _____.
        (3) ☐ Buyer ☐ Seller shall pay Homeowners' Association ("HOA") transfer fee _____.
        (4) ☐ Buyer ☐ Seller shall pay HOA document preparation fees _____.
        (5) ☐ Buyer ☐ Seller shall pay for any private transfer fee _____.
        (6) ☐ Buyer ☐ Seller shall pay for the cost, not to exceed $ _____, of a one-year home warranty plan, issued by _____, with the following optional coverages:
        ☐ Air Conditioner ☐ Pool/Spa ☐ Code and Permit upgrade ☐ Other: _____.
        Buyer is informed that home warranty plans have many optional coverages in addition to those listed above. Buyer is advised to investigate these coverages to determine those that may be suitable for Buyer.
        (7) ☐ Buyer ☐ Seller shall pay for _____.
        (8) ☐ Buyer ☐ Seller shall pay for _____.

Buyer's Initials (_____)(_____)　　　　Seller's Initials (_____)(_____)

RPA-CA REVISED 4/10 (PAGE 2 OF 8)

Reviewed by _____ Date _____

EQUAL HOUSING OPPORTUNITY

CALIFORNIA RESIDENTIAL PURCHASE AGREEMENT (RPA-CA PAGE 2 OF 8)

FIGURE 6.3

Residential Purchase Agreement, Continued

Property Address: _____ Date: _____

5. **CLOSING AND POSSESSION:**
   A. Buyer intends (or ☐ does not intend) to occupy the Property as Buyer's primary residence.
   B. **Seller-occupied or vacant property:** Possession shall be delivered to Buyer at 5 PM or (☐ _____ ☐ AM/☐ PM), on the date of Close Of Escrow; ☐ on _____; or ☐ no later than _____ **Days** After Close Of Escrow. If transfer of title and possession do not occur at the same time, Buyer and Seller are advised to: **(i)** enter into a written occupancy agreement (C.A.R. Form PAA, paragraph 2); and **(ii)** consult with their insurance and legal advisors.
   C. **Tenant-occupied property:**
      (i) **Property shall be vacant** at least 5 (or ☐ _____) **Days** Prior to Close Of Escrow, unless otherwise agreed in writing. **Note to Seller: If you are unable to deliver Property vacant in accordance with rent control and other applicable Law, you may be in breach of this Agreement.**
      OR (ii) (if checked) ☐ **Tenant to remain in possession.** (C.A.R. Form PAA, paragraph 3)
   D. At Close Of Escrow, **(i)** Seller assigns to Buyer any assignable warranty rights for items included in the sale, and **(ii)** Seller shall Deliver to Buyer available Copies of warranties. Brokers cannot and will not determine the assignability of any warranties.
   E. At Close Of Escrow, unless otherwise agreed in writing, Seller shall provide keys and/or means to operate all locks, mailboxes, security systems, alarms and garage door openers. If Property is a condominium or located in a common interest subdivision, Buyer may be required to pay a deposit to the Homeowners' Association ("HOA") to obtain keys to accessible HOA facilities.
6. **STATUTORY DISCLOSURES (INCLUDING LEAD-BASED PAINT HAZARD DISCLOSURES) AND CANCELLATION RIGHTS:**
   A. **(1)** Seller shall, within the time specified in paragraph 14A, Deliver to Buyer, if required by Law: **(i)** Federal Lead-Based Paint Disclosures (C.A.R. Form FLD) and pamphlet ("Lead Disclosures"); and **(ii)** disclosures or notices required by sections 1102 et. seq. and 1103 et. seq. of the Civil Code ("Statutory Disclosures"). Statutory Disclosures include, but are not limited to, a Real Estate Transfer Disclosure Statement ("TDS"), Natural Hazard Disclosure Statement ("NHD"), notice or actual knowledge of release of illegal controlled substance, notice of special tax and/or assessments (or, if allowed, substantially equivalent notice regarding the Mello-Roos Community Facilities Act and Improvement Bond Act of 1915) and, if Seller has actual knowledge, of industrial use and military ordnance location (C.A.R. Form SPQ or SSD).
      (2) Buyer shall, within the time specified in paragraph 14B(1), return Signed Copies of the Statutory and Lead Disclosures to Seller.
      (3) In the event Seller, prior to Close Of Escrow, becomes aware of adverse conditions materially affecting the Property, or any material inaccuracy in disclosures, information or representations previously provided to Buyer, Seller shall promptly provide a subsequent or amended disclosure or notice, in writing, covering those items. **However, a subsequent or amended disclosure shall not be required for conditions and material inaccuracies** of which Buyer is otherwise aware, or which are **disclosed in reports provided to or obtained by Buyer or ordered and paid for by Buyer.**
      (4) If any disclosure or notice specified in 6A(1), or subsequent or amended disclosure or notice is Delivered to Buyer after the offer is Signed, Buyer shall have the right to cancel this Agreement within **3 Days** After Delivery in person, or **5 Days** After Delivery by deposit in the mail, by giving written notice of cancellation to Seller or Seller's agent.
      (5) Note to Buyer and Seller: Waiver of Statutory and Lead Disclosures is prohibited by Law.
   B. **NATURAL AND ENVIRONMENTAL HAZARDS:** Within the time specified in paragraph 14A, Seller shall, if required by Law: **(i)** Deliver to Buyer earthquake guides (and questionnaire) and environmental hazards booklet; **(ii)** even if exempt from the obligation to provide a NHD, disclose if the Property is located in a Special Flood Hazard Area; Potential Flooding (Inundation) Area; Very High Fire Hazard Zone; State Fire Responsibility Area; Earthquake Fault Zone; Seismic Hazard Zone; and **(iii)** disclose any other zone as required by Law and provide any other information required for those zones.
   C. **WITHHOLDING TAXES:** Within the time specified in paragraph 14A, to avoid required withholding, Seller shall Deliver to Buyer or qualified substitute, an affidavit sufficient to comply with federal (FIRPTA) and California withholding Law (C.A.R. Form AS or QS).
   D. **MEGAN'S LAW DATABASE DISCLOSURE:** Notice: Pursuant to Section 290.46 of the Penal Code, information about specified registered sex offenders is made available to the public via an Internet Web site maintained by the Department of Justice at www.meganslaw.ca.gov. Depending on an offender's criminal history, this information will include either the address at which the offender resides or the community of residence and ZIP Code in which he or she resides. (Neither Seller nor Brokers are required to check this website. If Buyer wants further information, Broker recommends that Buyer obtain information from this website during Buyer's inspection contingency period. Brokers do not have expertise in this area.)
7. **CONDOMINIUM/PLANNED DEVELOPMENT DISCLOSURES:**
   A. **SELLER HAS: 7 (or ☐ _____) Days** After Acceptance to disclose to Buyer whether the Property is a condominium, or is located in a planned development or other common interest subdivision (C.A.R. Form SPQ or SSD).
   B. If the Property is a condominium or is located in a planned development or other common interest subdivision, Seller has **3 (or ☐ _____) Days** After Acceptance to request from the HOA (C.A.R. Form HOA): **(i)** Copies of any documents required by Law; **(ii)** disclosure of any pending or anticipated claim or litigation by or against the HOA; **(iii)** a statement containing the location and number of designated parking and storage spaces; **(iv)** Copies of the most recent 12 months of HOA minutes for regular and special meetings; and **(v)** the names and contact information of all HOAs governing the Property (collectively, "CI Disclosures"). Seller shall itemize and Deliver to Buyer all CI Disclosures received from the HOA and any CI Disclosures in Seller's possession. Buyer's approval of CI Disclosures is a contingency of this Agreement as specified in paragraph 14B(3).
8. **ITEMS INCLUDED IN AND EXCLUDED FROM PURCHASE PRICE:**
   A. **NOTE TO BUYER AND SELLER:** Items listed as included or excluded in the MLS, flyers or marketing materials are **not** included in the purchase price or excluded from the sale unless specified in 8B or C.
   B. **ITEMS INCLUDED IN SALE:**
      (1) All EXISTING fixtures and fittings that are attached to the Property;
      (2) EXISTING electrical, mechanical, lighting, plumbing and heating fixtures, ceiling fans, fireplace inserts, gas logs and grates, solar systems, built-in appliances, window and door screens, awnings, shutters, window coverings, attached floor coverings, television antennas, satellite dishes, private integrated telephone systems, air coolers/conditioners, pool/spa equipment, garage door openers/remote controls, mailbox, in-ground landscaping, trees/shrubs, water softeners, water purifiers, security systems/alarms; (If checked) ☐ stove(s), ☐ refrigerator(s); and
      (3) The following additional items:_____.
      (4) Seller represents that all items included in the purchase price, unless otherwise specified, are owned by Seller.
      (5) All items included shall be transferred free of liens and without Seller warranty.
   C. **ITEMS EXCLUDED FROM SALE:** Unless otherwise specified, audio and video components (such as flat screen TVs and speakers) are excluded if any such item is not itself attached to the Property, even if a bracket or other mechanism attached to the component is attached to the Property; and _____.

Buyer's Initials (_____)(_____)   Seller's Initials (_____)(_____)

RPA-CA REVISED 4/10 (PAGE 3 OF 8)

| Reviewed by _____ Date _____ |

EQUAL HOUSING OPPORTUNITY

FIGURE 6.3

Residential Purchase Agreement, Continued

Property Address: _____   Date: _____

9. **CONDITION OF PROPERTY:** Unless otherwise agreed: **(i) the Property is sold (a) in its PRESENT physical ("as-is") condition as of the date of Acceptance and (b) subject to Buyer's Investigation rights; (ii)** the Property, including pool, spa, landscaping and grounds, is to be maintained in substantially the same condition as of the date of Acceptance; and **(iii)** all debris and personal property not included in the sale shall be removed by Seller by Close Of Escrow.
   A. Seller shall, within the time specified in paragraph 14A, DISCLOSE KNOWN MATERIAL FACTS AND DEFECTS affecting the Property, including known insurance claims within the past five years, and make any and all other disclosures required by law.
   B. Buyer has the right to inspect the Property and, as specified in paragraph 14B, based upon information discovered in those inspections: (i) cancel this Agreement; or (ii) request that Seller make Repairs or take other action.
   C. **Buyer is strongly advised to conduct investigations of the entire Property in order to determine its present condition. Seller may not be aware of all defects affecting the Property or other factors that Buyer considers important. Property improvements may not be built according to code, in compliance with current Law, or have had permits issued.**
10. **BUYER'S INVESTIGATION OF PROPERTY AND MATTERS AFFECTING PROPERTY:**
   A. Buyer's acceptance of the condition of, and any other matter affecting the Property, is a contingency of this Agreement as specified in this paragraph and paragraph 14B. Within the time specified in paragraph 14B(1), Buyer shall have the right, at Buyer's expense unless otherwise agreed, to conduct inspections, investigations, tests, surveys and other studies ("Buyer Investigations"), including, but not limited to, the right to: **(i)** inspect for lead-based paint and other lead-based paint hazards; **(ii)** inspect for wood destroying pests and organisms; **(iii)** review the registered sex offender database; **(iv)** confirm the insurability of Buyer and the Property; and **(v)** satisfy Buyer as to any matter specified in the attached Buyer's Inspection Advisory (C.A.R. Form BIA). Without Seller's prior written consent, Buyer shall neither make nor cause to be made: **(i)** invasive or destructive Buyer Investigations; or **(ii)** inspections by any governmental building or zoning inspector or government employee, unless required by Law.
   B. Seller shall make the Property available for all Buyer Investigations. Buyer shall **(i)** as specified in paragraph 14B, complete Buyer Investigations and, either remove the contingency or cancel this Agreement, and **(ii)** give Seller, at no cost, complete Copies of all Investigation reports obtained by Buyer, which obligation shall survive the termination of this Agreement.
   C. Seller shall have water, gas, electricity and all operable pilot lights on for Buyer's Investigations and through the date possession is made available to Buyer.
   D. **Buyer indemnity and Seller protection for entry upon property:** Buyer shall: **(i)** keep the Property free and clear of liens; **(ii)** repair all damage arising from Buyer Investigations; and **(iii)** indemnify and hold Seller harmless from all resulting liability, claims, demands, damages and costs of Buyer's Investigations. Buyer shall carry, or Buyer shall require anyone acting on Buyer's behalf to carry, policies of liability, workers' compensation and other applicable insurance, defending and protecting Seller from liability for any injuries to persons or property occurring during any Buyer Investigations or work done on the Property at Buyer's direction prior to Close Of Escrow. Seller is advised that certain protections may be afforded Seller by recording a "Notice of Non-responsibility" (C.A.R. Form NNR) for Buyer Investigations and work done on the Property at Buyer's direction. Buyer's obligations under this paragraph shall survive the termination or cancellation of this Agreement and Close Of Escrow.
11. **SELLER DISCLOSURES; ADDENDA; ADVISORIES; OTHER TERMS:**
   A. **Seller Disclosures (if checked):** Seller shall, within the time specified in paragraph 14A, complete and provide Buyer with a:
      ☐ Seller Property Questionnaire (C.A.R. Form SPQ)   **OR**   ☐ Supplemental Contractual and Statutory Disclosure (C.A.R. Form SSD)
   B. **Addenda (if checked):**   ☐ Addendum # _____ (C.A.R. Form ADM)
      ☐ Wood Destroying Pest Inspection and Allocation of Cost Addendum (C.A.R. Form WPA)
      ☐ Purchase Agreement Addendum (C.A.R. Form PAA)   ☐ Septic, Well and Property Monument Addendum (C.A.R. Form SWPI)
      ☐ Short Sale Addendum (C.A.R. Form SSA)   ☐ Other
   C. **Advisories (If checked):**   ☑ Buyer's Inspection Advisory (C.A.R. Form BIA)
      ☐ Probate Advisory (C.A.R. Form PAK)   ☐ Statewide Buyer and Seller Advisory (C.A.R. Form SBSA)
      ☐ Trust Advisory (C.A.R. Form TA)   ☐ REO Advisory (C.A.R. Form REO)
   D. **Other Terms:** _____
      _____

12. **TITLE AND VESTING:**
   A. Within the time specified in paragraph 14, Buyer shall be provided a current preliminary title report, which shall include a search of the General Index. Seller shall within 7 Days After Acceptance give Escrow Holder a completed Statement of Information. The preliminary report is only an offer by the title insurer to issue a policy of title insurance and may not contain every item affecting title. Buyer's review of the preliminary report and any other matters which may affect title are a contingency of this Agreement as specified in paragraph 14B.
   B. Title is taken in its present condition subject to all encumbrances, easements, covenants, conditions, restrictions, rights and other matters, whether of record or not, as of the date of Acceptance except: **(i)** monetary liens of record unless Buyer is assuming those obligations or taking the Property subject to those obligations; and **(ii)** those matters which Seller has agreed to remove in writing.
   C. Within the time specified in paragraph 14A, Seller has a duty to disclose to Buyer all matters known to Seller affecting title, whether of record or not.
   D. At Close Of Escrow, Buyer shall receive a grant deed conveying title (or, for stock cooperative or long-term lease, an assignment of stock certificate or of Seller's leasehold interest), including oil, mineral and water rights if currently owned by Seller. Title shall vest as designated in Buyer's supplemental escrow instructions. THE MANNER OF TAKING TITLE MAY HAVE SIGNIFICANT LEGAL AND TAX CONSEQUENCES. CONSULT AN APPROPRIATE PROFESSIONAL.
   E. Buyer shall receive a CLTA/ALTA Homeowner's Policy of Title Insurance. A title company, at Buyer's request, can provide information about the availability, desirability, coverage, survey requirements, and cost of various title insurance coverages and endorsements. If Buyer desires title coverage other than that required by this paragraph, Buyer shall instruct Escrow Holder in writing and pay any increase in cost.
13. **SALE OF BUYER'S PROPERTY:**
   A. This Agreement is NOT contingent upon the sale of any property owned by Buyer.
   OR B. ☐ (If checked): The attached addendum (C.A.R. Form COP) regarding the contingency for the sale of property owned by Buyer is incorporated into this Agreement.

Seller's Initials (_____)(_____)

RPA-CA REVISED 4/10 (PAGE 4 OF 8)

Reviewed by _____ Date _____

CALIFORNIA RESIDENTIAL PURCHASE AGREEMENT (RPA-CA PAGE 4 OF 8)

FIGURE 6.3

Residential Purchase Agreement, Continued

Property Address: _____   Date: _____

14. **TIME PERIODS; REMOVAL OF CONTINGENCIES; CANCELLATION RIGHTS: The following time periods may only be extended, altered, modified or changed by mutual written agreement. Any removal of contingencies or cancellation under this paragraph by either Buyer or Seller must be exercised in good faith and in writing (C.A.R. Form CR or CC).**
   A. **SELLER HAS: 7 (or ☐ _____) Days** After Acceptance to Deliver to Buyer all Reports, disclosures and information for which Seller is responsible under paragraphs 4, 6A, B and C, 7A, 9A, 11A and B, and 12. Buyer may give Seller a Notice to Seller to Perform (C.A.R. Form NSP) if Seller has not Delivered the items within the time specified.
   B. **(1) BUYER HAS: 17 (or ☐ _____) Days** After Acceptance, unless otherwise agreed in writing, to:
      (i) complete all Buyer Investigations; approve all disclosures, reports and other applicable information, which Buyer receives from Seller; and approve all other matters affecting the Property; and
      (ii) Deliver to Seller Signed Copies of Statutory and Lead Disclosures Delivered by Seller in accordance with paragraph 6A.
      (2) Within the time specified in 14B(1), Buyer may request that Seller make repairs or take any other action regarding the Property (C.A.R. Form RR). Seller has no obligation to agree to or respond to Buyer's requests.
      (3) Within the time specified in 14B(1) (or as otherwise specified in this Agreement), Buyer shall Deliver to Seller either (i) a removal of the applicable contingency (C.A.R. Form CR), or (ii) a cancellation (C.A.R. Form CC) of this Agreement based upon a remaining contingency or Seller's failure to Deliver the specified items. However, if any report, disclosure or information for which Seller is responsible is not Delivered within the time specified in 14A, then Buyer has **5 (or ☐ _____) Days** After Delivery of any such items, or the time specified in 14B(1), whichever is later, to Deliver to Seller a removal of the applicable contingency or cancellation of this Agreement.
      (4) Continuation of Contingency: Even after the end of the time specified in 14B(1) and before Seller cancels this Agreement, if at all, pursuant to 14C, Buyer retains the right to either (i) in writing remove remaining contingencies, or (ii) cancel this Agreement based upon a remaining contingency or Seller's failure to Deliver the specified items. Once Buyer's written removal of all contingencies is Delivered to Seller, Seller may not cancel this Agreement pursuant to 14C(1).
   C. **SELLER RIGHT TO CANCEL:**
      (1) Seller right to Cancel; Buyer Contingencies: If, within time specified in this Agreement, Buyer does not, in writing, Deliver to Seller a removal of the applicable contingency or cancellation of this Agreement then Seller, after first Delivering to Buyer a Notice to Buyer to Perform (C.A.R. Form NBP) may cancel this Agreement. In such event, Seller shall authorize return of Buyer's deposit.
      (2) Seller right to Cancel; Buyer Contract Obligations: Seller, after first Delivering to Buyer a NBP may cancel this Agreement for any of the following reasons: **(i)** if Buyer fails to deposit funds as required by 3A or 3B; **(ii)** if the funds deposited pursuant to 3A or 3B are not good when deposited; **(iii)** if Buyer fails to Deliver a notice of FHA or VA costs or terms as required by 3C(3) (C.A.R. Form FVA); **(iv)** if Buyer fails to Deliver a letter as required by 3H; **(v)** if Buyer fails to Deliver verification as required by 3G or 3J; **(vi)** if Seller reasonably disapproves of the verification provided by 3G or 3J; **(vii)** if Buyer fails to return Statutory and Lead Disclosures as required by paragraph 6A(2); or **(viii)** if Buyer fails to sign or initial a separate liquidated damages form for an increased deposit as required by paragraphs 3B and 25. In such event, Seller shall authorize return of Buyer's deposit.
      (3) Notice To Buyer To Perform: The NBP shall: **(i)** be in writing; **(ii)** be signed by Seller; and **(iii)** give Buyer at least **2 (or ☐ _____) Days** After Delivery (or until the time specified in the applicable paragraph, whichever occurs last) to take the applicable action. A NBP may not be Delivered any earlier than **2 Days** Prior to the expiration of the applicable time for Buyer to remove a contingency or cancel this Agreement or meet an obligation specified in 14C(2).
   D. **EFFECT OF BUYER'S REMOVAL OF CONTINGENCIES:** If Buyer removes, in writing, any contingency or cancellation rights, unless otherwise specified in a separate written agreement between Buyer and Seller, Buyer shall with regard to that contingency or cancellation right conclusively be deemed to have: **(i)** completed all Buyer Investigations, and review of reports and other applicable information and disclosures; **(ii)** elected to proceed with the transaction; and **(iii)** assumed all liability, responsibility and expense for Repairs or corrections or for inability to obtain financing.
   E. **CLOSE OF ESCROW:** Before Seller or Buyer may cancel this Agreement for failure of the other party to close escrow pursuant to this Agreement, Seller or Buyer must first Deliver to the other a demand to close escrow (C.A.R. Form DCE).
   F. **EFFECT OF CANCELLATION ON DEPOSITS:** If Buyer or Seller gives written notice of cancellation pursuant to rights duly exercised under the terms of this Agreement, Buyer and Seller agree to Sign mutual instructions to cancel the sale and escrow and release deposits, if any, to the party entitled to the funds, less fees and costs incurred by that party. Fees and costs may be payable to service providers and vendors for services and products provided during escrow. **Release of funds will require mutual Signed release instructions from Buyer and Seller, judicial decision or arbitration award. A Buyer or Seller may be subject to a civil penalty of up to $1,000 for refusal to sign such instructions if no good faith dispute exists as to who is entitled to the deposited funds (Civil Code §1057.3).**

15. **REPAIRS:** Repairs shall be completed prior to final verification of condition unless otherwise agreed in writing. Repairs to be performed at Seller's expense may be performed by Seller or through others, provided that the work complies with applicable Law, including governmental permit, inspection and approval requirements. Repairs shall be performed in a good, skillful manner with materials of quality and appearance comparable to existing materials. It is understood that exact restoration of appearance or cosmetic items following all Repairs may not be possible. Seller shall: **(i)** obtain receipts for Repairs performed by others; **(ii)** prepare a written statement indicating the Repairs performed by Seller and the date of such Repairs; and **(iii)** provide Copies of receipts and statements to Buyer prior to final verification of condition.

16. **FINAL VERIFICATION OF CONDITION:** Buyer shall have the right to make a final inspection of the Property within **5 (or _____) Days** Prior to Close Of Escrow, NOT AS A CONTINGENCY OF THE SALE, but solely to confirm: **(i)** the Property is maintained pursuant to paragraph 9; **(ii)** Repairs have been completed as agreed; and **(iii)** Seller has complied with Seller's other obligations under this Agreement (C.A.R. Form VP).

17. **PRORATIONS OF PROPERTY TAXES AND OTHER ITEMS:** Unless otherwise agreed in writing, the following items shall be PAID CURRENT and prorated between Buyer and Seller as of Close Of Escrow: real property taxes and assessments, interest, rents, HOA regular, special, and emergency dues and assessments imposed prior to Close Of Escrow, premiums on insurance assumed by Buyer, payments on bonds and assessments assumed by Buyer, and payments on Mello-Roos and other Special Assessment District bonds and assessments that are a current lien. The following items shall be assumed by Buyer WITHOUT CREDIT toward the purchase price: prorated payments on Mello-Roos and other Special Assessment District bonds and assessments and HOA special assessments that are a current lien but not yet due. Property will be reassessed upon change of ownership. Any supplemental tax bills shall be paid as follows: **(i)** for periods after Close Of Escrow, by Buyer; and **(ii)** for periods prior to Close Of Escrow, by Seller (see C.A.R. Form SPT or SBSA for further information). TAX BILLS ISSUED AFTER CLOSE OF ESCROW SHALL BE HANDLED DIRECTLY BETWEEN BUYER AND SELLER. Prorations shall be made based on a 30-day month.

Buyer's Initials (_____)(_____)

Seller's Initials (_____)(_____)

RPA-CA REVISED 4/10 (PAGE 5 OF 8)

Reviewed by _____ Date _____

CALIFORNIA RESIDENTIAL PURCHASE AGREEMENT (RPA-CA PAGE 5 OF 8)

FIGURE 6.3

Residential Purchase Agreement, Continued

Property Address: _____   Date: _____

18. **SELECTION OF SERVICE PROVIDERS:** Brokers do not guarantee the performance of any vendors, service or product providers ("Providers"), whether referred by Broker or selected by Buyer, Seller or other person. Buyer and Seller may select ANY Providers of their own choosing.

19. **MULTIPLE LISTING SERVICE ("MLS"):** Brokers are authorized to report to the MLS a pending sale and, upon Close Of Escrow, the sales price and other terms of this transaction shall be provided to the MLS to be published and disseminated to persons and entities authorized to use the information on terms approved by the MLS.

20. **EQUAL HOUSING OPPORTUNITY:** The Property is sold in compliance with federal, state and local anti-discrimination Laws.

21. **ATTORNEY FEES:** In any action, proceeding, or arbitration between Buyer and Seller arising out of this Agreement, the prevailing Buyer or Seller shall be entitled to reasonable attorney fees and costs from the non-prevailing Buyer or Seller, except as provided in paragraph 26A.

22. **DEFINITIONS:** As used in this Agreement:
    A. **"Acceptance"** means the time the offer or final counter offer is accepted in writing by a party and is delivered to and personally received by the other party or that party's authorized agent in accordance with the terms of this offer or a final counter offer.
    B. **"C.A.R. Form"** means the specific form referenced or another comparable form agreed to by the parties.
    C. **"Close Of Escrow"** means the date the grant deed, or other evidence of transfer of title, is recorded.
    D. **"Copy"** means copy by any means including photocopy, NCR, facsimile and electronic.
    E. **"Days"** means calendar days. However, after Acceptance, the last **Day** for performance of any act required by this Agreement (including Close Of Escrow) shall not include any Saturday, Sunday, or legal holiday and shall instead be the next Day.
    F. **"Days After"** means the specified number of calendar days after the occurrence of the event specified, not counting the calendar date on which the specified event occurs, and ending at 11:59 PM on the final day.
    G. **"Days Prior"** means the specified number of calendar days before the occurrence of the event specified, not counting the calendar date on which the specified event is scheduled to occur.
    H. **"Deliver"**, **"Delivered"** or **"Delivery"**, regardless of the method used (i.e. messenger, mail, email, fax, other), means and shall be effective upon (i) personal receipt by Buyer or Seller or the individual Real Estate Licensee for that principal as specified in paragraph D of the section titled Real Estate Brokers on page 8;
    OR (ii) if checked, ☐ per the attached addendum (C.A.R. Form RDN).
    I. **"Electronic Copy"** or **"Electronic Signature"** means, as applicable, an electronic copy or signature complying with California Law. Buyer and Seller agree that electronic means will not be used by either party to modify or alter the content or integrity of this Agreement without the knowledge and consent of the other party.
    J. **"Law"** means any law, code, statute, ordinance, regulation, rule or order, which is adopted by a controlling city, county, state or federal legislative, judicial or executive body or agency.
    K. **"Repairs"** means any repairs (including pest control), alterations, replacements, modifications or retrofitting of the Property provided for under this Agreement.
    L. **"Signed"** means either a handwritten or electronic signature on an original document, Copy or any counterpart.

23. **BROKER COMPENSATION:** Seller or Buyer, or both, as applicable, agree(s) to pay compensation to Broker as specified in a separate written agreement between Broker and that Seller or Buyer. Compensation is payable upon Close Of Escrow, or if escrow does not close, as otherwise specified in the agreement between Broker and that Seller or Buyer.

24. **JOINT ESCROW INSTRUCTIONS TO ESCROW HOLDER:**
    A. **The following paragraphs, or applicable portions thereof, of this Agreement constitute the joint escrow instructions of Buyer and Seller to Escrow Holder,** which Escrow Holder is to use along with any related counter offers and addenda, and any additional mutual instructions to close the escrow: 1, 3, 4, 6C, 11B and D, 12, 13B, 14F, 17, 22, 23, 24, 28, 30, and paragraph D of the section titled Real Estate Brokers on page 8. If a Copy of the separate compensation agreement(s) provided for in paragraph 23, or paragraph D of the section titled Real Estate Brokers on page 8 is deposited with Escrow Holder by Broker, Escrow Holder shall accept such agreement(s) and pay out of Buyer's or Seller's funds, or both, as applicable, the respective Broker's compensation provided for in such agreement(s). The terms and conditions of this Agreement not specifically referenced above, in the specified paragraphs are additional matters for the information of Escrow Holder, but about which Escrow Holder need not be concerned. Buyer and Seller will receive Escrow Holder's general provisions directly from Escrow Holder and will execute such provisions upon Escrow Holder's request. To the extent the general provisions are inconsistent or conflict with this Agreement, the general provisions will control as to the duties and obligations of Escrow Holder only. Buyer and Seller will execute additional instructions, documents and forms provided by Escrow Holder that are reasonably necessary to close the escrow.
    B. A Copy of this Agreement shall be delivered to Escrow Holder within **3** business days after Acceptance (or ☐ _____). Escrow Holder shall provide Seller's Statement of Information to Title company when received from Seller. Buyer and Seller authorize Escrow Holder to accept and rely on Copies and Signatures as defined in this Agreement as originals, to open escrow and for other purposes of escrow. The validity of this Agreement as between Buyer and Seller is not affected by whether or when Escrow Holder Signs this Agreement.
    C. Brokers are a party to the escrow for the sole purpose of compensation pursuant to paragraph 23 and paragraph D of the section titled Real Estate Brokers on page 8. Buyer and Seller irrevocably assign to Brokers compensation specified in paragraph 23, respectively, and irrevocably instruct Escrow Holder to disburse those funds to Brokers at Close Of Escrow or pursuant to any other mutually executed cancellation agreement. Compensation instructions can be amended or revoked only with the written consent of Brokers. Buyer and Seller shall release and hold harmless Escrow Holder from any liability resulting from Escrow Holder's payment to Broker(s) of compensation pursuant to this Agreement. Escrow Holder shall immediately notify Brokers: **(i)** if Buyer's initial or any additional deposit is not made pursuant to this Agreement, or is not good at time of deposit with Escrow Holder; or **(ii)** if either Buyer or Seller instruct Escrow Holder to cancel escrow.
    D. A Copy of any amendment that affects any paragraph of this Agreement for which Escrow Holder is responsible shall be delivered to Escrow Holder within **2** business days after mutual execution of the amendment.

Buyer's Initials (_____)(_____)

Seller's Initials (_____)(_____)

RPA-CA REVISED 4/10 (PAGE 6 OF 8)

Reviewed by _____ Date _____

EQUAL HOUSING OPPORTUNITY

CALIFORNIA RESIDENTIAL PURCHASE AGREEMENT   (RPA-CA PAGE 6 OF 8)

FIGURE 6.3

Residential Purchase Agreement, Continued

Property Address: _____ Date: _____

25. **LIQUIDATED DAMAGES: If Buyer fails to complete this purchase because of Buyer's default, Seller shall retain, as liquidated damages, the deposit actually paid. If the Property is a dwelling with no more than four units, one of which Buyer intends to occupy, then the amount retained shall be no more than 3% of the purchase price. Any excess shall be returned to Buyer. Release of funds will require mutual, Signed release instructions from both Buyer and Seller, judicial decision or arbitration award. AT TIME OF THE INCREASED DEPOSIT BUYER AND SELLER SHALL SIGN A SEPARATE LIQUIDATED DAMAGES PROVISION FOR ANY INCREASED DEPOSIT (C.A.R. FORM RID).**

Buyer's Initials _____/_____	Seller's Initials _____/_____

26. **DISPUTE RESOLUTION:**
    A. **MEDIATION:** Buyer and Seller agree to mediate any dispute or claim arising between them out of this Agreement, or any resulting transaction, before resorting to arbitration or court action. **Buyer and Seller also agree to mediate any disputes or claims with Broker(s) who, in writing, agree to such mediation prior to, or within a reasonable time after, the dispute or claim is presented to the Broker.** Mediation fees, if any, shall be divided equally among the parties involved. If, for any dispute or claim to which this paragraph applies, any party (i) commences an action without first attempting to resolve the matter through mediation, or (ii) before commencement of an action, refuses to mediate after a request has been made, then that party shall not be entitled to recover attorney fees, even if they would otherwise be available to that party in any such action. THIS MEDIATION PROVISION APPLIES WHETHER OR NOT THE ARBITRATION PROVISION IS INITIALED. **Exclusions from this mediation agreement are specified in paragraph 26C.**
    B. **ARBITRATION OF DISPUTES:**
    Buyer and Seller agree that any dispute or claim in Law or equity arising between them out of this Agreement or any resulting transaction, which is not settled through mediation, shall be decided by neutral, binding arbitration. Buyer and Seller also agree to arbitrate any disputes or claims with Broker(s) who, in writing, agree to such arbitration prior to, or within a reasonable time after, the dispute or claim is presented to the Broker. The arbitrator shall be a retired judge or justice, or an attorney with at least 5 years of residential real estate Law experience, unless the parties mutually agree to a different arbitrator. The parties shall have the right to discovery in accordance with Code of Civil Procedure §1283.05. In all other respects, the arbitration shall be conducted in accordance with Title 9 of Part 3 of the Code of Civil Procedure. Judgment upon the award of the arbitrator(s) may be entered into any court having jurisdiction. Enforcement of this agreement to arbitrate shall be governed by the Federal Arbitration Act. **Exclusions from this arbitration agreement are specified in paragraph 26C.**
    "NOTICE: BY INITIALING IN THE SPACE BELOW YOU ARE AGREEING TO HAVE ANY DISPUTE ARISING OUT OF THE MATTERS INCLUDED IN THE 'ARBITRATION OF DISPUTES' PROVISION DECIDED BY NEUTRAL ARBITRATION AS PROVIDED BY CALIFORNIA LAW AND YOU ARE GIVING UP ANY RIGHTS YOU MIGHT POSSESS TO HAVE THE DISPUTE LITIGATED IN A COURT OR JURY TRIAL. BY INITIALING IN THE SPACE BELOW YOU ARE GIVING UP YOUR JUDICIAL RIGHTS TO DISCOVERY AND APPEAL, UNLESS THOSE RIGHTS ARE SPECIFICALLY INCLUDED IN THE 'ARBITRATION OF DISPUTES' PROVISION. IF YOU REFUSE TO SUBMIT TO ARBITRATION AFTER AGREEING TO THIS PROVISION, YOU MAY BE COMPELLED TO ARBITRATE UNDER THE AUTHORITY OF THE CALIFORNIA CODE OF CIVIL PROCEDURE. YOUR AGREEMENT TO THIS ARBITRATION PROVISION IS VOLUNTARY."
    "WE HAVE READ AND UNDERSTAND THE FOREGOING AND AGREE TO SUBMIT DISPUTES ARISING OUT OF THE MATTERS INCLUDED IN THE 'ARBITRATION OF DISPUTES' PROVISION TO NEUTRAL ARBITRATION."

Buyer's Initials _____/_____	Seller's Initials _____/_____

    C. **ADDITIONAL MEDIATION AND ARBITRATION TERMS:**
    (1) **EXCLUSIONS: The following matters shall be excluded from mediation and arbitration: (i) a judicial or non-judicial foreclosure or other action or proceeding to enforce a deed of trust, mortgage or installment land sale contract as defined in Civil Code §2985; (ii) an unlawful detainer action; (iii) the filing or enforcement of a mechanic's lien; and (iv) any matter that is within the jurisdiction of a probate, small claims or bankruptcy court. The filing of a court action to enable the recording of a notice of pending action, for order of attachment, receivership, injunction, or other provisional remedies, shall not constitute a waiver or violation of the mediation and arbitration provisions.**
    (2) **BROKERS: Brokers shall not be obligated or compelled to mediate or arbitrate unless they agree to do so in writing. Any Broker(s) participating in mediation or arbitration shall not be deemed a party to the Agreement.**
27. **TERMS AND CONDITIONS OF OFFER:**
    This is an offer to purchase the Property on the above terms and conditions. The liquidated damages paragraph or the arbitration of disputes paragraph is incorporated in this Agreement if initialed by all parties or if incorporated by mutual agreement in a counter offer or addendum. If at least one but not all parties initial such paragraph(s), a counter offer is required until agreement is reached. Seller has the right to continue to offer the Property for sale and to accept any other offer at any time prior to notification of Acceptance. If this offer is accepted and Buyer subsequently defaults, Buyer may be responsible for payment of Brokers' compensation. This Agreement and any supplement, addendum or modification, including any Copy, may be Signed in two or more counterparts, all of which shall constitute one and the same writing.
28. **TIME OF ESSENCE; ENTIRE CONTRACT; CHANGES:** Time is of the essence. All understandings between the parties are incorporated in this Agreement. Its terms are intended by the parties as a final, complete and exclusive expression of their Agreement with respect to its subject matter, and may not be contradicted by evidence of any prior agreement or contemporaneous oral agreement. If any provision of this Agreement is held to be ineffective or invalid, the remaining provisions will nevertheless be given full force and effect. Except as otherwise specified, this Agreement shall be interpreted and disputes shall be resolved in accordance with the laws of the State of California. **Neither this Agreement nor any provision in it may be extended, amended, modified, altered or changed, except in writing Signed by Buyer and Seller.**

Buyer's Initials (_____)(_____)   Seller's Initials (_____)(_____)

RPA-CA REVISED 4/10 (PAGE 7 OF 8) | Reviewed by _____ Date _____ |

CALIFORNIA RESIDENTIAL PURCHASE AGREEMENT (RPA-CA PAGE 7 OF 8)

FIGURE 6.3
Residential Purchase Agreement, Continued

Property Address: _____   Date: _____

29. EXPIRATION OF OFFER: This offer shall be deemed revoked and the deposit shall be returned unless the offer is Signed by Seller and a Copy of the Signed offer is personally received by Buyer, or by _____, who is authorized to receive it, by 5:00 PM on the third Day after this offer is signed by Buyer (or, if checked, □ by _____ □AM/□PM, on _____(date)).
Buyer has read and acknowledges receipt of a Copy of the offer and agrees to the above confirmation of agency relationships.

Date _____   Date _____
BUYER _____   BUYER _____
_____   _____
(Print name)   **(Print name)**
_____
(Address)
□ Additional Signature Addendum attached (C.A.R. Form ASA).

30. ACCEPTANCE OF OFFER: Seller warrants that Seller is the owner of the Property, or has the authority to execute this Agreement. Seller accepts the above offer, agrees to sell the Property on the above terms and conditions, and agrees to the above confirmation of agency relationships. Seller has read and acknowledges receipt of a Copy of this Agreement, and authorizes Broker to Deliver a Signed Copy to Buyer.
□ (If checked) **SUBJECT TO ATTACHED COUNTER OFFER (C.A.R. Form CO) DATED:** _____.

Date _____   Date _____
SELLER _____   SELLER _____
_____   _____
(Print name)   **(Print name)**
_____
(Address)
□ Additional Signature Addendum attached (C.A.R. Form ASA).

(____/____) **CONFIRMATION OF ACCEPTANCE:** A Copy of Signed Acceptance was personally received by Buyer or Buyer's
(Initials) authorized agent on (date) _____ at _____ □AM/□PM. **A binding Agreement is created when a Copy of Signed Acceptance is personally received by Buyer or Buyer's authorized agent whether or not confirmed in this document. Completion of this confirmation is not legally required in order to create a binding Agreement. It is solely intended to evidence the date that Confirmation of Acceptance has occurred.**

REAL ESTATE BROKERS:
A. Real Estate Brokers are not parties to the Agreement between Buyer and Seller.
B. Agency relationships are confirmed as stated in paragraph 2.
C. If specified in paragraph 3A(2), Agent who submitted the offer for Buyer acknowledges receipt of deposit.
D. **COOPERATING BROKER COMPENSATION:** Listing Broker agrees to pay Cooperating Broker **(Selling Firm)** and Cooperating Broker agrees to accept, out of Listing Broker's proceeds in escrow: **(i)** the amount specified in the MLS, provided Cooperating Broker is a Participant of the MLS in which the Property is offered for sale or a reciprocal MLS; or **(ii)** □ (if checked) the amount specified in a separate written agreement (C.A.R. Form CBC) between Listing Broker and Cooperating Broker. Declaration of License and Tax (C.A.R. Form DLT) may be used to document that tax reporting will be required or that an exemption exists.

Real Estate Broker (Selling Firm) _____ DRE Lic. #_____
By _____ DRE Lic. # _____ Date _____
Address _____ City _____ State _____ Zip _____
Telephone _____ Fax _____ E-mail _____
Real Estate Broker (Listing Firm) _____ DRE Lic. #_____
By _____ DRE Lic. # _____ Date _____
Address _____ City _____ State _____ Zip _____
Telephone _____ Fax _____ E-mail _____

ESCROW HOLDER ACKNOWLEDGMENT:
Escrow Holder acknowledges receipt of a Copy of this Agreement, (if checked, □ a deposit in the amount of $ _____),
counter offer numbered _____, □ Seller's Statement of Information and □ Other _____
_____, and agrees to act as Escrow Holder subject to paragraph 24 of this Agreement, any supplemental escrow instructions and the terms of Escrow Holder's general provisions if any.

Escrow Holder is advised that the date of Confirmation of Acceptance of the Agreement as between Buyer and Seller is _____.

Escrow Holder _____ Escrow # _____
By _____ Date _____
Address _____
Phone/Fax/E-mail _____
Escrow Holder is licensed by the California Department of □ Corporations, □ Insurance, □ Real Estate. License # _____

PRESENTATION OF OFFER: (_____) Listing Broker presented this offer to Seller on _____(date).
                           Broker or Designee Initials

REJECTION OF OFFER: (_____)(_____) No counter offer is being made. This offer was rejected by Seller on_____(date).
                         Seller's Initials

THIS FORM HAS BEEN APPROVED BY THE CALIFORNIA ASSOCIATION OF REALTORS® (C.A.R.). NO REPRESENTATION IS MADE AS TO THE LEGAL VALIDITY OR ADEQUACY OF ANY PROVISION IN ANY SPECIFIC TRANSACTION. A REAL ESTATE BROKER IS THE PERSON QUALIFIED TO ADVISE ON REAL ESTATE TRANSACTIONS. IF YOU DESIRE LEGAL OR TAX ADVICE, CONSULT AN APPROPRIATE PROFESSIONAL.

This form is available for use by the entire real estate industry. It is not intended to identify the user as a REALTOR®. REALTOR® is a registered collective membership mark which may be used only by members of the NATIONAL ASSOCIATION OF REALTORS® who subscribe to its Code of Ethics.

R E B S / I N C   Published and Distributed by:
REAL ESTATE BUSINESS SERVICES, INC.
a subsidiary of the CALIFORNIA ASSOCIATION OF REALTORS®
525 South Virgil Avenue, Los Angeles, California 90020

Reviewed by _____
Broker or Designee _____ Date _____

EQUAL HOUSING OPPORTUNITY

REVISION DATE 4/10

CALIFORNIA RESIDENTIAL PURCHASE AGREEMENT   (RPA-CA PAGE 8 OF 8)

Paragraph 17: Provides that taxes and assessments will be paid current and prorated.

Paragraph 18: Provides that brokers do not guarantee performance of any service provider referred by a broker or any other party. Parties may choose any service providers.

Paragraph 19: Allows for broker reporting of sale terms to a multiple-listing service (MLS). Without this authorization, such reporting could be a breach of agent's duty of confidentiality.

Paragraph 20: Asserts that the sale is in compliance with fair housing laws.

Paragraph 21: Provides that in the event of any legal action or arbitration, the prevailing party shall be entitled to reasonable attorney fees (this paragraph also serves to reduce the likelihood of frivolous lawsuits).

Paragraph 22: Provides definition of terms used.

Paragraph 23: Provides for broker compensation from seller or buyer (where broker represents buyer).

Case Study

The case of *Paul v. Schoellkopf* (2005) 128 C.A.4th 147 involved a successful plaintiff's entitlement to attorney fees. While the purchase contract did not have any provision for attorney fees, the escrow instructions signed by the parties did include an attorney fee clause. The Los Angeles Superior Court awarded damages to the plaintiff totaling $105,499.92, as well as attorney fees of $371,942.

The Court of Appeal affirmed the award of monetary damages but reversed on the award of plaintiff's attorney fees. The court ruled that the attorney fee clause in the escrow agreement only applied to an escrow dispute, not any dispute involving enforcement of details of the purchase agreement.

Note: For attorney fees to be awarded, there must be an attorney fee clause in the documents that are the basis of the lawsuit, not in a separate document that is not involved in the dispute.

Paragraph 24: Provides that this agreement constitutes joint escrow instructions but that broker's compensation can only be amended with broker's agreement.

Paragraph 25: Limits liquidated damages to 3 percent of purchase price in the event of buyer default. The limitation only applies where buyer intended to occupy the premises as a principal residence (1–4 units) and both parties initialed this paragraph.

Note: If the purchaser can show the amount retained is unreasonable, the court can reduce or eliminate liquidated damages. (An example would be an immediate sale to another party at a greater price.)

Paragraph 26: The parties agree to mediate any dispute arising from this agreement. Disputes involving brokers shall be mediated if brokers agree to mediation. By initialing the arbitration clause, the parties agree to give up their rights for court litigation and agree to arbitration of disputes if mediation was not successful.

Paragraph 27: Reiterates that this is an offer to purchase. Paragraphs requiring initials of parties must be initialed by all parties to be incorporated in the agreement. Seller can continue to offer property until notified of acceptance of any counter offer. If buyer defaults, buyer may be responsible for paying broker commission.

Paragraph 28: Provides that time is of the essence for all performance, that this agreement is the final and complete expression of this agreement and may not be contradicted by a prior or contemporaneous oral agreement, and that if any portion is invalid, the remaining portions remain valid. Extension modifications, alterations, and changes require the signature of both buyer and seller.

Paragraph 29: Specifies the time limitation for acceptance and provides for buyer's signatures to the offer.

Paragraph 30: This is seller's acceptance of offer, or it may provide for a counteroffer. Seller warrants ownership and right to accept offer. Seller's acceptance signatures are part of this paragraph.

The CAR form includes a confirmation of acceptance and agreement if the broker is to pay cooperating broker compensation. The escrow holder acknowledges receipt of agreement and deposit.

If a purchase offer fails to provide a period for acceptance, the offer will terminate after the expiration of a "reasonable period of time." Because an offeror normally does not receive consideration to keep an offer open, the offer can be withdrawn by the offeror any time prior to acceptance even if the offeror agreed to keep the offer open for a stated period of time.

Additions to the Purchase Agreement

Contingencies.   Offers to purchase often are contingent on something happening, such as receiving an appraisal for a stated amount or more, obtaining a loan to stated specifications, or the sale or purchase of another property. The most common contingency is an offer contingent on financing.

When an offer is contingent on financing, failure of the buyer to use good faith in seeking financing would be a breach of contract. See *Fry v. George Elkins Company* (1958) 162 C.A.2d 256 for an example of this.

Contingencies can tie up a property for months. To avoid such a situation, the seller would be in a better position if he or she agreed to a contingency, such as the one shown in Figure 6.4. This agreement allows the seller to continue to offer the property. A subsequent offer could be accepted conditioned on the original buyer's waiving his or her contingency within a stated period of time. If the original buyer fails to waive the contingency, his or her offer becomes null and void and the deposit is returned.

A contingency can be removed by signing a Removal of Contingency Form.

The person who benefits from a contingency can always waive the contingency. For example, if an offer were contingent on an appraisal of $100,000 by a lender, the offeror could waive this contingency and go ahead with the purchase if the appraisal came in for a lower amount. The refusal to waive a contingency that cannot be corrected would end the agreement.

Case Study
In *Beverly Way Associates v. Barham* (1990) 226 C.A.3d 49, a buyer of a $3,900,000 apartment building had a purchase agreement that provided the buyer with the contingency to approve specified documents. The ALTA survey showed an electrical room that reduced parking by one space from what had been shown on a tract map. The buyer wrote to the seller, "We reluctantly disapprove of the matters disclosed on the survey and relating to the property." The letter later stated, "Advise as to how you wish to proceed with this transaction." The seller did not answer. The buyer later agreed to waive the objections. When the seller refused to sell, the buyer filed a lis pendens, a notice of a pending lawsuit regarding a claim involving an interest in a property. The court held that the buyer had a right not to consummate the purchase as long as he acted reasonably. However, once the agreement was rejected, the contract was terminated and the buyer could not later waive its objection even though the contract lacked a "time is of the essence" clause.

FIGURE 6.4

Contingency for Sale or Purchase of Other Property

CALIFORNIA ASSOCIATION OF REALTORS ®

CONTINGENCY FOR SALE OR PURCHASE OF OTHER PROPERTY
(C.A.R. Form COP, Revised 11/08)

This is an addendum to the ☐ California Residential Purchase Agreement, ☐ Counter Offer, ☐ Other _____ _____ ("Agreement"), dated _____, on property known as _____ ("Seller's Property"), between _____ ("Buyer") and _____ ("Seller").

A. ☐ (If checked) **SALE OF BUYER'S PROPERTY:**
1. **(a)** The Agreement is contingent on the close of escrow of Buyer's property, described as: _____ _____ ("Buyer's Property").
   (b) If Buyer's Property does not close escrow by the earliest of: **(i)** the scheduled close of escrow of Seller's Property; **(ii)** the date specified in paragraph A3; or **(iii)** Other ☐ _____, then either Seller, after first giving Buyer a Notice to Buyer to Perform (C.A.R. Form NBP), or Buyer may cancel the Agreement in writing.
2. ☐ (If checked) Buyer's Property is **not** now in escrow and (check boxes as applicable):
   (a) ☐ is not yet listed for sale.
   (b) ☐ is listed for sale with _____ company and is offered for sale in the _____ MLS, # _____.
   (c) Buyer shall, within **17 (or** ☐ _____ **) Days** After Acceptance, provide Seller with Copies of the contract, escrow instructions and all related documents ("Escrow Evidence") for the sale of Buyer's Property showing that Buyer's Property has entered escrow.
3. ☐ (If checked) Buyer's Property **is in escrow** with _____ escrow holder, (escrow # _____) scheduled to close escrow on _____ (date). Buyer shall, within **5 Days** After Acceptance, deliver to Seller Escrow Evidence that Buyer's Property is in escrow.
4. If Buyer fails to provide to Seller Escrow Evidence within the time specified in A2(c) or A3, Seller, after first giving Buyer a Notice to Buyer to Perform, may cancel the Agreement in writing.
5. If Buyer's Property is in or enters escrow, Buyer shall give Seller written notice if either party to that escrow gives notice to the other of intent to cancel. In such event, either Buyer or Seller may cancel the Agreement in writing.
6. After Acceptance, Seller shall have the right to continue to offer the Property for sale for Back-up Offers. If Seller accepts a written back-up offer:
   (a) **Immediate Right to Notify Buyer to Remove Sale of Property Contingency:** Seller shall have the right to immediately give written notice to Buyer to, in writing: **(i)** remove this contingency; **(ii)** remove the loan contingency, if any; **(iii)** provide verification of sufficient funds to close escrow without the sale of Buyer's Property; and **(iv)** comply with the following additional requirement(s): _____. If Buyer fails to complete these actions within **72 (or** ☐ _____ **) hours** after receipt of such notice, Seller may then immediately cancel the Agreement in writing.
   OR (b) ☐ (If checked) **Delayed Right to Notify Buyer:** Seller shall not invoke the notice provisions in paragraph A6(a): **(i)** within the first **17 (or** ☐ _____ **) Days** After Acceptance; or **(ii)** (if checked) ☐ during the term of the Agreement.

B. ☐ (If checked) **SELLER'S PURCHASE OF REPLACEMENT PROPERTY:**
1. The Agreement is contingent on Seller entering a contract to acquire replacement property.
2. Seller shall, within **17 (or** ☐ _____ **) Days** After Acceptance, remove this contingency or cancel the Agreement. If Seller does not remove this contingency in writing within that time, Buyer, after first giving Seller a Notice to Seller to Perform (C.A.R. Form NSP), may cancel the Agreement in writing.
3. **(a)** Time periods in the Agreement for inspections, contingencies, covenants and other obligations shall begin: **(i)** as specified in the Agreement; **(ii)** (if checked) ☐ the day after Seller delivers to Buyer a written notice removing this contingency; or **(iii)** (if checked) ☐ Other _____
   (b) Buyer and Seller agree that Seller may, by providing Buyer written notice at the time Seller removes this contingency, extend the Close Of Escrow date for a maximum of _____ additional Days or until ☐ _____ (date).
4. Even after the expiration of the time specified in B2, Seller retains, until Buyer cancels pursuant to B2, the right to remove in writing this contingency or cancel the Agreement. Once Buyer receives Seller's written removal of this contingency, Buyer may not cancel pursuant to B2.

By signing below, Buyer and Seller each acknowledge that they have read, understand, accept and have received a copy of this Addendum.

Date_____ Date_____
Buyer _____ Seller_____
Buyer _____ Seller_____

Published and Distributed by:
REAL ESTATE BUSINESS SERVICES, INC.
a subsidiary of the California Association of REALTORS®
525 South Virgil Avenue, Los Angeles, California 90020

Reviewed by _____ Date _____

EQUAL HOUSING OPPORTUNITY

COP 11/08 (PAGE 1 OF 1)

CONTINGENCY FOR SALE OR PURCHASE OF OTHER PROPERTY (COP PAGE 1 OF 1)

Reprinted with permission, California Association of REALTORS®. Endorsement not implied.

Case Study

An offer provided five days for acceptance in the case of *Sabo v. Fasano* (1984) 154 C.A.3d 502. The offer was accepted on the sixth day. The buyer and seller then opened escrow. The seller later refused to sell, claiming that there was no contract because acceptance came after the five-day period. The court held that in this case, the time limit for acceptance was for the benefit of the offeror, not the offeree. The offeror waived the right to object to the late acceptance by opening escrow. Upon the waiver, both buyer and seller were bound to the agreement.

"As Is" Clause

An "as is" clause in a purchase agreement can lead to problems. As discussed in Chapter 3, "as is" generally applies only to patent defects, which are obvious defects, and not to latent or hidden defects known by the seller and/or agent.

A seller who wishes to sell "as is" should make a full disclosure of all defects known to him or her and state that additional defects, which the seller is unaware of, may be found. A seller who is not familiar with the property for any reason (such as occupancy by tenants) should disclose this fact. Doing so puts the purchaser on notice that he or she cannot rely on the very limited knowledge of the seller.

The "as is" clause also should provide a right of the purchaser to inspect the property within a stated number of days and communicate any defects to the seller. The seller then should have the option to cure the defects within a stated period or return the buyer's deposit. The parties also could agree to a change in price, or the purchaser could waive the defect.

If "as is" is to be enforceable as to defects discovered later, full disclosure is important, and the buyer should be given not just the right, but also the responsibility to inspect. Commercial property is treated differently from residential property regarding the effect of an "as is" clause. "As is" can protect a commercial seller who fails to disclose defects but is not guilty of fraud or concealment of the defects. See *Shapiro v. Hu* (1986) 188 C.A.3d 324 for an example of this.

Interim Occupancy Agreement.   At times, a buyer will be given possession prior to closing. It must be fully understood that the buyer's position is as a renter and not a buyer taking early possession.

If a problem such as a defect were to be discovered by the buyer, he or she conceivably could delay closing for many months without payment of rent if he or she were not clearly a renter. Allowing even a few days' early occupancy could create enormous problems.

An **interim occupancy agreement**, such as CAR Form 10A-11, makes it clear that the buyer is in possession as a renter. If the sale is not completed on its designated date, the form allows a different rental amount. By setting an amount that is fairly high, but not so high as to be regarded as a penalty, the buyer is encouraged not to delay the purchase.

Counteroffer.   As discussed in Chapter 5, an acceptance that varies from the original offer on a material term is considered a counteroffer, which is a rejection of the original offer. California Association of REALTORS® Counter Offer (CO-11) Form can be used as a counter to an offer, an exchange agreement, or even another counteroffer.

When separate forms are signed and dated individually for each counteroffer, the sequence of negotiations can be followed from the records, and the final agreement will be clear.

Cancellation of Contract.   The parties to a purchase agreement can agree to release each other from the contract. The agreement could provide for a full return of the deposit to the offeror (a rescission) or forfeiture of the total deposit or partial forfeiture. A release agreement should provide that all further rights and obligations are null and void. California Association of REALTORS® form CC-11 Canc. of Contract, Rel. of Deposit and Joint Escrow Inst. can be used as a joint release.

Because brokers may have commission rights, they should be parties to release agreements.

Seller Financing Disclosure Statement.   When the seller provides carry-back financing on one to four residential units, Section 2956 of the Civil Code requires that a disclosure statement be provided to both buyer and seller. While technically not a contract, it is ordinarily an attachment or addendum to a purchase agreement. California Association of REALTORS® Seller Financing Addendum and Disclosure (SFA-11) complies with the statutory disclosure requirements.

Estimated Buyer's Costs.   The estimated buyer's costs sheet is similar to a seller's net form and is not a contract. It is a disclosure form to show a buyer the funds needed to complete a transaction. The form can be used for purchase agreements, counteroffers, exchange agreements, or even option agreements. California Association of REALTORS® Estimated Buyer's Costs (EBC-11) form provides for the purchaser's signature. The agent is therefore protected against later allegations that the buyer was misled about the cash requirements for purchasing the property.

Mortgage Loan Disclosure Statement.   Before a borrower is obligated to complete a nonfederally-related loan agreement arranged by a real estate broker, the borrower must be given and must sign a mortgage loan disclosure statement setting forth all costs and fees, payments, liens, etc. The disclosure must be made on a form approved by the Department of Real Estate, and the mortgage broker must keep a copy of the disclosure form for three years. The first tuesday Mortgage Loan Disclosure Statement is an approved form for this purpose.

■ LEASES

Listing forms to lease or rent, such as the CAR Exclusive Authorization to Lease or Rent (Form LL), are quite similar to sale listing agreements. When a landlord accepts a deposit on a rental from a prospective tenant, the landlord could be entering a lease agreement unless it is clear it is only an *application* to rent and not an *agreement* to rent. Most standard forms make it very clear that it is an application to rent only and must be approved by the owner.

Many types of leases and lease forms are available. Figure 6.6 provides a simple residential lease form. Agents should seek legal advice for any major modification of a simple lease form. For commercial and industrial leases, using preprinted forms is dangerous because the forms probably will not accurately reflect the needs and intent of the parties.

The cut-and-paste leases that are frequently prepared by agents from other leases could subject an agent to a charge of the unauthorized practice of law, as well as liability for errors or omissions. An agent who assumes the responsibility of preparing a lease has the duty to do so properly.

■ BROKER-SALESPERSON AGREEMENT

A broker is required to have a written contract with his or her salespeople. The broker-salesperson relationship is covered in detail in Chapter 3.

■ RETENTION OF RECORDS

A real estate broker shall retain, for three years, copies of all listings, deposits, receipts, canceled checks, trust records, and other documents executed by the broker or obtained in connection with any transaction for which a real estate license is required. The retention period runs from the date of closing a transaction or, if not closed, from the date of the listing.

■ DISCLOSURES

Figure 6.5 lists some of the disclosures required in real estate.

WEB LINK @

Many of the disclosures referenced in Figure 6.5 are set forth in the California Association of REALTORS® standard forms, although failure of a form to include a required disclosure does not excuse a broker from liability. Further information is available in the pamphlet *Disclosures in Real Property Transactions*, published by the California Department of Real Estate. This information can also be accessed through its Web site, *www.dre.ca.gov.*

FIGURE 6.5
Disclosures in Real Estate

Many disclosures are required by state as well as federal law. The penalty for failure to disclose could be monetary damages or it could allow rescission of a sale. Most disclosures relate to sale or financing of one to four residential units. Some of the disclosures that must be considered include the following:

Physical Aspects of a Property (transfer disclosure statement)

Agency Relationship Disclosure

Negotiability of Real Estate Commission

Disclosure of Sale Price (written disclosure to buyer and seller)

Advisability of Title Insurance

Home Inspection Notice (Buyer must sign receipt for notice, *The Importance of a Home Inspection*)

Agents Visual Inspection Disclosure

Commercial or Industrial Zone Disclosure

Farming Area Disclosure

Toxic Contamination

Methamphetamine Contamination Order (buyers and tenants must be provided a copy of cleanup order for contaminated structures)

Earthquake Hazards Homeowner's Guide (mandatory delivery to *purchaser)*

Flood Hazard Area (federal disclosure)

Natural Hazards Disclosure

> *Special Flood Hazard Area* (California)
>
> *Area of Potential Flooding*
>
> *State Responsibility Areas* (wild land areas where state has responsibility for fire prevention)
>
> *Very High Fire Hazard Severity Zone*
>
> *Seismic Hazard Zone* (subject to earthquake damage)
>
> *Earthquake Fault Zone*

Environmental Hazards Disclosure (Buyer must be given a pamphlet entitled *Environmental Hazards: A Guide for Homeowners, Buyers, Landlords, and Tenants)*

Flood Disaster Insurance (federal requirement as to obtaining *and maintaining this coverage)*

Supplemental Tax Bill Disclosure (disclosure by seller that buyers should expect supplemental property tax reassessment bills)

Home Energy Ratings (delivery of home energy rating booklet when it becomes available)

Home Environmental Hazards (booklet to be provided *homebuyer)*

Lead Paint Pamphlet (Buyer must sign receipt)

Lead Paint Notice (Buyer must be notified as to known *presence of lead* paint)

Megan's Law (Information notice as to access to information *about known* sex offenders in community)

Mello-Roos District (existence of special tax or assessment *district)*

Military Ordnance Location (disclosure of known former *ordnance site that may con*tain explosives)

Mold (actual knowledge of toxic mold)

Notice of Smoke Detector Compliance

Carbon Monoxide Detector Notice

Window Security Bars (the existence of such bars and safety *release mechanism)*

Delivery of Structural Pest Control Inspection and Certification Reports (if there is an inspection)

Water Heater Bracing (certification that it has been complied with)

Subdivided Land Law Disclosure (public report)

Subdivision Map Act (recordation of final map or parcel map)

Disclosure of Rescission Rights (time-shares and undivided *interest subdivisions)*

Disclosure of Blanket Encumbrance

Delivery of Governing Documents (for purchaser of common-*interest developments)*

Association Disclosure (financial disclosures of homeowners' *associations)*

Statement of Defects (disclosure for a common-interest *development conversio*n)

Disclosures by Managing Agent of a Common-Interest Development

Adjustable-Rate Loan Disclosure

Seller Financing Disclosure Statement

Truth-in-Lending Disclosures

Real Estate Settlement Procedures Act Disclosures (lender disclosures)

Agent Disclosure of Compensation from a Lender

Consumer Caution and Home Ownership Counseling Notice (given to loan applicants no later than three days prior to signing loan documents)

Credit Score (a notice to loan applicant)

FIGURE 6.5

Disclosures in Real Estate, Continued

Business Opportunity Disclosures (bulk sales act, tax clearance, license transfer, etc.)Notice of Transfer of Loan Servicing
Disclosure to Borrower of Real Estate Loans (mortgage loan disclosure statement)
Notice to Borrower of Right for Copy of Appraisal
Broker Disclosure to Lender or Loan Purchaser
Equal Credit Opportunity Act (notice of adverse action)
Holden Act Disclosure (antidiscrimination law)
Notice and Disclosure to Buyer of State Tax Withholding on Disposition of California Real Property
Foreign Investment in Real Property Tax Act (federal tax withholding by buyer).

Many of the disclosures referenced in Figure 6.5 are set forth in the California Association of REALTORS® standard forms, although failure of a form to include a required disclosure does not excuse a broker from liability. Further information is available in the pamphlet entitled *Disclosures in Real Property Transactions*, published by the California Department of Real Estate. This information can also be accessed through its Web site, *www.dre.ca.gov.*

Note: Forms are available from the California Association of REALTORS®, 525 South Virgil Avenue, Los Angeles, CA 90020. Sample forms are also available from first tuesday (*www. firstuesday.us/downloads.cfm*) and Professional Publishing Company (*www.trueforms.com*).

■ SUMMARY

The real estate agency agreement is known as the "listing." The types of listings are as follows:

- Exclusive-right-to-sell listing: This listing provides that the broker is entitled to a commission if the listing broker or any other broker or the owner sells the property.

- Exclusive-agency listing: This listing makes the broker the owner's exclusive agent. The broker is entitled to a commission if the listing broker or any other broker sells the property, but the owner can sell the property himself or herself without being obligated to pay a commission.

- Open listing: This is a nonexclusive listing whereby the broker is entitled to a commission only if he or she is successful.

- Oral listing: Generally, a verbal real estate listing is unenforceable because of the statute of frauds. An owner might waive statute of frauds protection if he or she encourages a broker to continue to work on a listing after it has expired.

- Buyer listing: Such listings can be of various types, but the agency is with the buyer.

- Net listing: A net listing can be any of the preceding listing types. *Net* refers to the broker's commission, which is all monies over a net price for the owner.

FIGURE 6.6
Residential Lease or Month-to-Month Rental Agreement

**RESIDENTIAL LEASE OR
MONTH-TO-MONTH RENTAL AGREEMENT**
(C.A.R. Form LR, Revised 4/11)

Date _____, _____ ("Landlord") and
_____ ("Tenant") agree as follows:

1. PROPERTY:
    A. Landlord rents to Tenant and Tenant rents from Landlord, the real property and improvements described as: _____
    _____ ("Premises").
    B. The Premises are for the sole use as a personal residence by the following named person(s) **only:** _____
    _____.
    C. The following personal property, maintained pursuant to paragraph 11, is included: _____
    _____ or ☐ (if checked) the personal property on the attached addendum.
    D. The Premises may be subject to a local rent control ordinance _____.
2. TERM: The term begins on (date) _____ ("Commencement Date"), **(Check A or B):**
    ☐ **A. Month-to-Month:** and continues as a month-to-month tenancy. Tenant may terminate the tenancy by giving written notice at
        least 30 days prior to the intended termination date. Landlord may terminate the tenancy by giving written notice as provided
        by law. Such notices may be given on any date.
    ☐ **B. Lease:** and shall terminate on (date) _____ at _____ ☐ AM/ ☐ PM. Tenant
        shall vacate the Premises upon termination of the Agreement, unless: **(i)** Landlord and Tenant have extended this Agreement
        in writing or signed a new agreement; **(ii)** mandated by local rent control law; or **(iii)** Landlord accepts Rent from Tenant (other
        than past due Rent), in which case a month-to-month tenancy shall be created which either party may terminate as specified
        in paragraph 2A. Rent shall be at a rate agreed to by Landlord and Tenant, or as allowed by law. All other terms and conditions
        of this Agreement shall remain in full force and effect.
3. RENT: "Rent" shall mean all monetary obligations of Tenant to Landlord under the terms of the Agreement, except security deposit.
    A. Tenant agrees to pay $ _____ per month for the term of the Agreement.
    B. Rent is payable in advance on the **1st (or** ☐ _____ **) day** of each calendar month, and is delinquent on the next day.
    C. If Commencement Date falls on any day other than the day Rent is payable under paragraph 3B, and Tenant has paid one full
        month's Rent in advance of Commencement Date, Rent for the second calendar month shall be prorated based on a 30-day period.
    D. PAYMENT: Rent shall be paid by ☐ personal check, ☐ money order, ☐ cashier's check, or ☐ other _____, to
        (name) _____ (phone) _____ at (address)
        _____, (or at any other location
        subsequently specified by Landlord in writing to Tenant) (and ☐ if checked, rent may be paid personally, between the hours of
        _____ and _____ on the following days _____). If any payment is
        returned for non-sufficient funds ("NSF") or because tenant stops payment, then, after that: (i) Landlord may, in writing, require
        Tenant to pay Rent in cash for three months and (ii) all future Rent shall be paid by ☐ money order, or ☐ cashier's check.
4. SECURITY DEPOSIT:
    A. Tenant agrees to pay $ _____ as a security deposit. Security deposit will be
        ☐ transferred to and held by the Owner of the Premises, or ☐ held in Owner's Broker's trust account.
    B. All or any portion of the security deposit may be used, as reasonably necessary, to: **(i)** cure Tenant's default in payment of Rent (which
        includes Late Charges, NSF fees or other sums due); **(ii)** repair damage, excluding ordinary wear and tear, caused by Tenant or by a guest
        or licensee of Tenant; **(iii)** clean Premises, if necessary, upon termination of the tenancy; and **(iv)** replace or return personal property or
        appurtenances. **SECURITY DEPOSIT SHALL NOT BE USED BY TENANT IN LIEU OF PAYMENT OF LAST MONTH'S RENT.** If
        all or any portion of the security deposit is used during the tenancy, Tenant agrees to reinstate the total security deposit within five days
        after written notice is delivered to Tenant. Within 21 days after Tenant vacates the Premises, Landlord shall: **(1)** furnish Tenant an
        itemized statement indicating the amount of any security deposit received and the basis for its disposition and supporting
        documentation as required by California Civil Code § 1950.5(g); and **(2)** return any remaining portion of the security deposit to Tenant.
    C. **Security deposit will not be returned until all Tenants have vacated the Premises and all keys returned. Any security
        deposit returned by check shall be made out to all Tenants named on this Agreement, or as subsequently modified.**
    D. No interest will be paid on security deposit unless required by local law.
    E. If the security deposit is held by Owner, Tenant agrees not to hold Broker responsible for its return. If the security deposit is held
        in Owner's Broker's trust account, **and** Broker's authority is terminated before expiration of this Agreement, **and** security deposit
        is released to someone other than Tenant, **then** Broker shall notify Tenant, in writing, where and to whom security deposit has been
        released. Once Tenant has been provided such notice, Tenant agrees not to hold Broker responsible for the security deposit.
5. MOVE-IN COSTS RECEIVED/DUE: Move-in funds made payable to _____ shall
    be paid by ☐ personal check, ☐ money order, or ☐ cashier's check.

Category	Total Due	Payment Received	Balance Due	Date Due
Rent from _____ to _____ (date)				
*Security Deposit				
Other _____				
Other _____				
Total				

    *The maximum amount Landlord may receive as security deposit, however designated, cannot exceed two months' Rent for
    unfurnished premises, or three months' Rent for furnished premises.

Tenant's Initials (_____)(_____)   Landlord's Initials (_____)(_____)

LR REVISED 4/11 (PAGE 1 OF 6) Print Date

Reviewed by _____ Date _____   EQUAL HOUSING OPPORTUNITY

RESIDENTIAL LEASE OR MONTH-TO-MONTH RENTAL AGREEMENT (LR PAGE 1 OF 6)

FIGURE 6.6

Residential Lease or Month-to-Month Rental Agreement, Continued

Premises: _____ Date: _____

6. **LATE CHARGE; RETURNED CHECKS:**
   A. Tenant acknowledges either late payment of Rent or issuance of a returned check may cause Landlord to incur costs and expenses, the exact amounts of which are extremely difficult and impractical to determine. These costs may include, but are not limited to, processing, enforcement and accounting expenses, and late charges imposed on Landlord. If any installment of Rent due from Tenant is not received by Landlord within **5 (or ☐ _____) calendar days** after the date due, or if a check is returned, Tenant shall pay to Landlord, respectively, an additional sum of $ _____ or _____% of the Rent due as a Late Charge and $25.00 as a NSF fee for the first returned check and $35.00 as a NSF fee for each additional returned check, either or both of which shall be deemed additional Rent.
   B. Landlord and Tenant agree that these charges represent a fair and reasonable estimate of the costs Landlord may incur by reason of Tenant's late or NSF payment. Any Late Charge or NSF fee due shall be paid with the current installment of Rent. Landlord's acceptance of any Late Charge or NSF fee shall not constitute a waiver as to any default of Tenant. Landlord's right to collect a Late Charge or NSF fee shall not be deemed an extension of the date Rent is due under paragraph 3 or prevent Landlord from exercising any other rights and remedies under this Agreement and as provided by law.

7. **PARKING: (Check A or B)**
   ☐ **A.** Parking is permitted as follows: _____
   _____.
   The right to parking ☐ is ☐ is not included in the Rent charged pursuant to paragraph 3. If not included in the Rent, the parking rental fee shall be an additional $ _____ per month. Parking space(s) are to be used for parking properly licensed and operable motor vehicles, except for trailers, boats, campers, buses or trucks (other than pick-up trucks). Tenant shall park in assigned space(s) only. Parking space(s) are to be kept clean. Vehicles leaking oil, gas or other motor vehicle fluids shall not be parked on the Premises. Mechanical work or storage of inoperable vehicles is not permitted in parking space(s) or elsewhere on the Premises.
   OR ☐ **B.** Parking is not permitted on the Premises.

8. **STORAGE: (Check A or B)**
   ☐ **A.** Storage is permitted as follows: _____
   The right to separate storage space ☐ is, ☐ is not, included in the Rent charged pursuant to paragraph 3. If not included in the Rent, storage space fee shall be an additional $ _____ per month. Tenant shall store only personal property Tenant owns, and shall not store property claimed by another or in which another has any right, title or interest. Tenant shall not store any improperly packaged food or perishable goods, flammable materials, explosives, hazardous waste or other inherently dangerous material, or illegal substances.
   OR ☐ **B.** Except for Tenant's personal property, contained entirely within the Premises, storage is not permitted on the Premises.

9. **UTILITIES:** Tenant agrees to pay for all utilities and services, and the following charges: _____,
   except _____, which shall be paid for by Landlord. If any utilities are not separately metered, Tenant shall pay Tenant's proportional share, as reasonably determined and directed by Landlord. If utilities are separately metered, Tenant shall place utilities in Tenant's name as of the Commencement Date. Landlord is only responsible for installing and maintaining one usable telephone jack and one telephone line to the Premises. Tenant shall pay any cost for conversion from existing utilities service provider.

10. **CONDITION OF PREMISES:** Tenant has examined Premises and, if any, all furniture, furnishings, appliances, landscaping and fixtures, including smoke detector(s).
    (Check all that apply:)
    ☐ **A.** Tenant acknowledges these items are clean and in operable condition, with the following exceptions: _____
    _____.
    ☐ **B.** Tenant's acknowledgment of the condition of these items is contained in an attached statement of condition (C.A.R. Form MIMO).
    ☐ **C.** **(i)** Landlord will Deliver to Tenant a statement of condition (C.A.R. Form MIMO) ☐ within **3 days** after execution of this Agreement; ☐ prior to the Commencement Date; ☐ within **3 days** after the Commencement Date.
    (ii) Tenant shall complete and return the MIMO to Landlord within **3 (or ☐ _____) days** after Delivery. Tenant's failure to return the MIMO within that time shall conclusively be deemed Tenant's Acknowledgement of the condition as stated in the MIMO.
    ☐ **D.** Tenant will provide Landlord a list of items that are damaged or not in operable condition within **3 (or ☐ _____) days** after Commencement Date, not as a contingency of this Agreement but rather as an acknowledgment of the condition of the Premises.
    ☐ **E.** Other: _____.

11. **MAINTENANCE:**
    A. Tenant shall properly use, operate and safeguard Premises, including if applicable, any landscaping, furniture, furnishings and appliances, and all mechanical, electrical, gas and plumbing fixtures, and keep them and the Premises clean, sanitary and well ventilated. Tenant shall be responsible for checking and maintaining all carbon monoxide and smoke detectors and any additional phone lines beyond the one line and jack that Landlord shall provide and maintain. Tenant shall immediately notify Landlord, in writing, of any problem, malfunction or damage. Tenant shall be charged for all repairs or replacements caused by Tenant, pets, guests or licensees of Tenant, excluding ordinary wear and tear. Tenant shall be charged for all damage to Premises as a result of failure to report a problem in a timely manner. Tenant shall be charged for repair of drain blockages or stoppages, unless caused by defective plumbing parts or tree roots invading sewer lines.
    B. ☐ Landlord ☐ Tenant shall water the garden, landscaping, trees and shrubs, except: _____
    _____.
    C. ☐ Landlord ☐ Tenant shall maintain the garden, landscaping, trees and shrubs, except: _____
    _____.
    D. ☐ Landlord ☐ Tenant shall maintain _____.
    E. Tenant's failure to maintain any item for which Tenant is responsible shall give Landlord the right to hire someone to perform such maintenance and charge Tenant to cover the cost of such maintenance.
    F. The following items of personal property are included in the Premises without warranty and Landlord will not maintain, repair or replace them: _____.

Tenant's Initials (_____)(_____)   Landlord's Initials (_____)(_____)

Reviewed by _____ Date _____

RESIDENTIAL LEASE OR MONTH-TO-MONTH RENTAL AGREEMENT (LR PAGE 2 OF 6)

FIGURE 6.6

Residential Lease or Month-to-Month Rental Agreement, Continued

Premises: _____ Date: _____

12. **NEIGHBORHOOD CONDITIONS:** Tenant is advised to satisfy him or herself as to neighborhood or area conditions, including schools, proximity and adequacy of law enforcement, crime statistics, proximity of registered felons or offenders, fire protection, other governmental services, availability, adequacy and cost of any wired, wireless internet connections or other telecommunications or other technology services and installations, proximity to commercial, industrial or agricultural activities, existing and proposed transportation, construction and development that may affect noise, view, or traffic, airport noise, noise or odor from any source, wild and domestic animals, other nuisances, hazards, or circumstances, cemeteries, facilities and condition of common areas, conditions and influences of significance to certain cultures and/or religions, and personal needs, requirements and preferences of Tenant.

13. **PETS:** Unless otherwise provided in California Civil Code § 54.2, no animal or pet shall be kept on or about the Premises without Landlord's prior written consent, except: _____

14. ☐ (If checked) **NO SMOKING:** No smoking of any substance is allowed on the Premises or common areas. If smoking does occur on the Premises or common areas, (i) Tenant is responsible for all damage caused by the smoking including, but not limited to stains, burns, odors and removal of debris; (ii) Tenant is in breach of this Agreement; (iii) Tenant, guests, and all others may be required to leave the Premises; and (iv) Tenant acknowledges that in order to remove odor caused by smoking, Landlord may need to replace carpet and drapes and paint the entire premises regardless of when these items were last cleaned, replaced. or repainted. Such actions and other necessary steps will impact the return of any security deposit. The Premises or common areas may be subject to a local non-smoking ordinance.

15. **RULES/REGULATIONS:**
    A. Tenant agrees to comply with all Landlord rules and regulations that are at any time posted on the Premises or delivered to Tenant. Tenant shall not, and shall ensure that guests and licensees of Tenant shall not, disturb, annoy, endanger or interfere with other tenants of the building or neighbors, or use the Premises for any unlawful purposes, including, but not limited to, using, manufacturing, selling, storing or transporting illicit drugs or other contraband, or violate any law or ordinance, or commit a waste or nuisance on or about the Premises.
    B. **(If applicable, check one)**
       ☐ 1. Landlord shall provide Tenant with a copy of the rules and regulations within _____days
       or _____.
       OR ☐ 2. Tenant has been provided with, and acknowledges receipt of, a copy of the rules and regulations.

16. ☐ (If checked) **CONDOMINIUM;PLANNED UNIT DEVELOPMENT:**
    A. The Premises are a unit in a condominium, planned unit development, common interest subdivision or other development governed by a homeowners' association ("HOA"). The name of the HOA is _____
       Tenant agrees to comply with all HOA covenants, conditions and restrictions, bylaws, rules and regulations and decisions ("HOA Rules"). Landlord shall provide Tenant copies of HOA Rules, if any. Tenant shall reimburse Landlord for any fines or charges imposed by HOA or other authorities, due to any violation by Tenant, or the guests or licensees of Tenant.
    B. **(Check one)**
       ☐ 1. Landlord shall provide Tenant with a copy of the HOA Rules within _____ days
       or _____.
       OR ☐ 2. Tenant has been provided with, and acknowledges receipt of, a copy of the HOA Rules.

17. **ALTERATIONS; REPAIRS:** Unless otherwise specified by law or paragraph 29C, without Landlord's prior written consent, **(i)** Tenant shall not make any repairs, alterations or improvements in or about the Premises including: painting, wallpapering, adding or changing locks, installing antenna or satellite dish(es), placing signs, displays or exhibits, or using screws, fastening devices, large nails or adhesive materials; **(ii)** Landlord shall not be responsible for the costs of alterations or repairs made by Tenant; **(iii)** Tenant shall not deduct from Rent the costs of any repairs, alterations or improvements; and **(iv)** any deduction made by Tenant shall be considered unpaid Rent.

18. **KEYS; LOCKS:**
    A. Tenant acknowledges receipt of (or Tenant will receive ☐ prior to the Commencement Date, or ☐ _____):
       ☐ _____ key(s) to Premises,   ☐ _____ remote control device(s) for garage door/gate opener(s),
       ☐ _____ key(s) to mailbox,   ☐ _____,
       ☐ _____ key(s) to common area(s),   ☐ _____.
    B. Tenant acknowledges that locks to the Premises ☐ have, ☐ have not, been re-keyed.
    C. If Tenant re-keys existing locks or opening devices, Tenant shall immediately deliver copies of all keys to Landlord. Tenant shall pay all costs and charges related to loss of any keys or opening devices. Tenant may not remove locks, even if installed by Tenant.

19. **ENTRY:**
    A. Tenant shall make Premises available to Landlord or Landlord's representative for the purpose of entering to make necessary or agreed repairs (including, but not limited to, installing, repairing, testing, and maintaining smoke detectors and carbon monoxide devices, and bracing, anchoring or strapping water heaters), decorations, alterations, or improvements, or to supply necessary or agreed services, or to show Premises to prospective or actual purchasers, tenants, mortgagees, lenders, appraisers, or contractors.
    B. Landlord and Tenant agree that 24-hour written notice shall be reasonable and sufficient notice, except as follows. 48-hour written notice is required to conduct an inspection of the Premises prior to the Tenant moving out, unless the Tenant waives the right to such notice. Notice may be given orally to show the Premises to actual or prospective purchasers provided Tenant has been notified in writing within 120 days preceding the oral notice, that the Premises are for sale and that oral notice may be given to show the Premises. No notice is required: **(i)** to enter in case of an emergency; **(ii)** if the Tenant is present and consents at the time of entry; or **(iii)** if the Tenant has abandoned or surrendered the Premises. No written notice is required if Landlord and Tenant orally agree to an entry for agreed services or repairs if the date and time of entry are within one week of the oral agreement.
    C. ☐ (If checked) Tenant authorizes the use of a keysafe/lockbox to allow entry into the Premises and agrees to sign a keysafe/lockbox addendum (C.A.R. Form KLA).

20. **SIGNS:** Tenant authorizes Landlord to place FOR SALE/LEASE signs on the Premises.

21. **ASSIGNMENT; SUBLETTING:** Tenant shall not sublet all or any part of Premises, or assign or transfer this Agreement or any interest in it, without Landlord's prior written consent. Unless such consent is obtained, any assignment, transfer or subletting of Premises or this Agreement or tenancy, by voluntary act of Tenant, operation of law or otherwise, shall, at the option of Landlord, terminate this Agreement. Any proposed assignee, transferee or sublessee shall submit to Landlord an application and credit information for Landlord's approval and, if approved, sign a separate written agreement with Landlord and Tenant. Landlord's consent to any one assignment, transfer or sublease, shall not be construed as consent to any subsequent assignment, transfer or sublease and does not release Tenant of Tenant's obligations under this Agreement.

Tenant's Initials (_____)(_____)

Landlord's Initials (_____)(_____)

Reviewed by _____ Date _____

☐ EQUAL HOUSING OPPORTUNITY

RESIDENTIAL LEASE OR MONTH-TO-MONTH RENTAL AGREEMENT (LR PAGE 3 OF 6)

Reprinted with permission, California Association of REALTORS®. Endorsement not implied.

FIGURE 6.6

Residential Lease or Month-to-Month Rental Agreement, Continued

Premises: _____ Date: _____

22. **JOINT AND INDIVIDUAL OBLIGATIONS:** If there is more than one Tenant, each one shall be individually and completely responsible for the performance of all obligations of Tenant under this Agreement, jointly with every other Tenant, and individually, whether or not in possession.

23. ☐ **LEAD-BASED PAINT (If checked):** Premises were constructed prior to 1978. In accordance with federal law, Landlord gives and Tenant acknowledges receipt of the disclosures on the attached form (C.A.R. Form FLD) and a federally approved lead pamphlet.

24. ☐ **MILITARY ORDNANCE DISCLOSURE:** (If applicable and known to Landlord) Premises are located within one mile of an area once used for military training, and may contain potentially explosive munitions.

25. ☐ **PERIODIC PEST CONTROL:** Landlord has entered into a contract for periodic pest control treatment of the Premises and shall give Tenant a copy of the notice originally given to Landlord by the pest control company.

26. ☐ **METHAMPHETAMINE CONTAMINATION:** Prior to signing this Agreement, Landlord has given Tenant a notice that a health official has issued an order prohibiting occupancy of the property because of methamphetamine contamination. A copy of the notice and order are attached.

27. **MEGAN'S LAW DATABASE DISCLOSURE:** Notice: Pursuant to Section 290.46 of the Penal Code, information about specified registered sex offenders is made available to the public via an Internet Web site maintained by the Department of Justice at www.meganslaw.ca.gov. Depending on an offender's criminal history, this information will include either the address at which the offender resides or the community of residence and ZIP Code in which he or she resides. (Neither Landlord nor Brokers, if any, are required to check this website. If Tenant wants further information, Tenant should obtain information directly from this website.)

28. **POSSESSION:**
   A. Tenant is not in possession of the Premises. If Landlord is unable to deliver possession of Premises on Commencement Date, such Date shall be extended to the date on which possession is made available to Tenant. If Landlord is unable to deliver possession within **5 (or** ☐ **_____) calendar days** after agreed Commencement Date, Tenant may terminate this Agreement by giving written notice to Landlord, and shall be refunded all Rent and security deposit paid. Possession is deemed terminated when Tenant has returned all keys to the Premises to Landlord.
   B. ☐ Tenant is already in possession of the Premises.

29. **TENANT'S OBLIGATIONS UPON VACATING PREMISES:**
   A. Upon termination of this Agreement, Tenant shall: **(i)** give Landlord all copies of all keys or opening devices to Premises, including any common areas; **(ii)** vacate and surrender Premises to Landlord, empty of all persons; **(iii)** vacate any/all parking and/or storage space; **(iv)** clean and deliver Premises, as specified in paragraph C below, to Landlord in the same condition as referenced in paragraph 10; **(v)** remove all debris; **(vi)** give written notice to Landlord of Tenant's forwarding address; and **(vii)** _____ .
   B. All alterations/improvements made by or caused to be made by Tenant, with or without Landlord's consent, become the property of Landlord upon termination. Landlord may charge Tenant for restoration of the Premises to the condition it was in prior to any alterations/improvements.
   C. **Right to Pre-Move-Out Inspection and Repairs: (i)** After giving or receiving notice of termination of a tenancy (C.A.R. Form NTT), or before the end of a lease, Tenant has the right to request that an inspection of the Premises take place prior to termination of the lease or rental (C.A.R. Form NRI). If Tenant requests such an inspection, Tenant shall be given an opportunity to remedy identified deficiencies prior to termination, consistent with the terms of this Agreement. **(ii)** Any repairs or alterations made to the Premises as a result of this inspection (collectively, "Repairs") shall be made at Tenant's expense. Repairs may be performed by Tenant or through others, who have adequate insurance and licenses and are approved by Landlord. The work shall comply with applicable law, including governmental permit, inspection and approval requirements. Repairs shall be performed in a good, skillful manner with materials of quality and appearance comparable to existing materials. It is understood that exact restoration of appearance or cosmetic items following all Repairs may not be possible. **(iii)** Tenant shall: **(a)** obtain receipts for Repairs performed by others; **(b)** prepare a written statement indicating the Repairs performed by Tenant and the date of such Repairs; and **(c)** provide copies of receipts and statements to Landlord prior to termination. Paragraph 29C does not apply when the tenancy is terminated pursuant to California Code of Civil Procedure § 1161(2), (3) or (4).

30. **BREACH OF CONTRACT; EARLY TERMINATION:** In addition to any obligations established by paragraph 29, in the event of termination by Tenant prior to completion of the original term of the Agreement, Tenant shall also be responsible for lost Rent, rental commissions, advertising expenses and painting costs necessary to ready Premises for re-rental. Landlord may withhold any such amounts from Tenant's security deposit.

31. **TEMPORARY RELOCATION:** Subject to local law, Tenant agrees, upon demand of Landlord, to temporarily vacate Premises for a reasonable period, to allow for fumigation (or other methods) to control wood destroying pests or organisms, or other repairs to Premises. Tenant agrees to comply with all instructions and requirements necessary to prepare Premises to accommodate pest control, fumigation or other work, including bagging or storage of food and medicine, and removal of perishables and valuables. Tenant shall only be entitled to a credit of Rent equal to the per diem Rent for the period of time Tenant is required to vacate Premises.

32. **DAMAGE TO PREMISES:** If, by no fault of Tenant, Premises are totally or partially damaged or destroyed by fire, earthquake, accident or other casualty that render Premises totally or partially uninhabitable, either Landlord or Tenant may terminate this Agreement by giving the other written notice. Rent shall be abated as of the date Premises become totally or partially uninhabitable. The abated amount shall be the current monthly Rent prorated on a 30-day period. If the Agreement is not terminated, Landlord shall promptly repair the damage, and Rent shall be reduced based on the extent to which the damage interferes with Tenant's reasonable use of Premises. If damage occurs as a result of an act of Tenant or Tenant's guests, only Landlord shall have the right of termination, and no reduction in Rent shall be made.

33. **INSURANCE:** Tenant's or guest's personal property and vehicles are not insured by Landlord, manager or, if applicable, HOA, against loss or damage due to fire, theft, vandalism, rain, water, criminal or negligent acts of others, or any other cause. **Tenant is advised to carry Tenant's own insurance (renter's insurance) to protect Tenant from any such loss or damage.** Tenant shall comply with any requirement imposed on Tenant by Landlord's insurer to avoid: **(i)** an increase in Landlord's insurance premium (or Tenant shall pay for the increase in premium); or **(ii)** loss of insurance.

34. **WATERBEDS:** Tenant shall not use or have waterbeds on the Premises unless: **(i)** Tenant obtains a valid waterbed insurance policy; **(ii)** Tenant increases the security deposit in an amount equal to one-half of one month's Rent; and **(iii)** the bed conforms to the floor load capacity of Premises.

Tenant's Initials (_____)(_____)   Landlord's Initials (_____)(_____)

LR REVISED 4/11 (PAGE 4 OF 6)

Reviewed by _____ Date _____

RESIDENTIAL LEASE OR MONTH-TO-MONTH RENTAL AGREEMENT (LR PAGE 4 OF 6)

FIGURE 6.6

Residential Lease or Month-to-Month Rental Agreement, Continued

Premises: _____   Date: _____

35. **WAIVER:** The waiver of any breach shall not be construed as a continuing waiver of the same or any subsequent breach.

36. **NOTICE:** Notices may be served at the following address, or at any other location subsequently designated:
   Landlord: _____   Tenant: _____
   _____ _____
   _____ _____
   _____ _____

37. **TENANT ESTOPPEL CERTIFICATE:** Tenant shall execute and return a tenant estoppel certificate delivered to Tenant by Landlord or Landlord's agent within **3 days** after its receipt. Failure to comply with this requirement shall be deemed Tenant's acknowledgment that the tenant estoppel certificate is true and correct, and may be relied upon by a lender or purchaser.

38. **REPRESENTATIONS:**
   A.   TENANT REPRESENTATION; OBLIGATIONS REGARDING OCCUPANTS; CREDIT: Tenant warrants that all statements in Tenant's rental application are accurate. Landlord requires all occupants 18 years of age or older and all emancipated minors to complete a lease rental application. Tenant acknowledges this requirement and agrees to notify Landlord when any occupant of the Premises reaches the age of 18 or becomes an emancipated minor. Tenant authorizes Landlord and Broker(s) to obtain Tenant's credit report periodically during the tenancy in connection with the modification or enforcement of this Agreement. Landlord may cancel this Agreement: **(i)** before occupancy begins; **(ii)** upon disapproval of the credit report(s); or **(iii)** at any time, upon discovering that information in Tenant's application is false. A negative credit report reflecting on Tenant's record may be submitted to a credit reporting agency if Tenant fails to fulfill the terms of payment and other obligations under this Agreement.
   B.   LANDLORD REPRESENTATIONS: Landlord warrants that, unless otherwise specified in writing, Landlord is unaware of **(i)** any recorded Notices of Default affecting the Premise; **(ii)** any delinqent amounts due under any loan secured by the Premises; and **(iii)** any bankruptcy proceeding affecting the Premises.

39. **MEDIATION:**
   A. Consistent with paragraphs B and C below, Landlord and Tenant agree to mediate any dispute or claim arising between them out of this Agreement, or any resulting transaction, before resorting to court action. Mediation fees, if any, shall be divided equally among the parties involved. If, for any dispute or claim to which this paragraph applies, any party commences an action without first attempting to resolve the matter through mediation, or refuses to mediate after a request has been made, then that party shall not be entitled to recover attorney fees, even if they would otherwise be available to that party in any such action.
   B. The following matters are excluded from mediation: **(i)** an unlawful detainer action; **(ii)** the filing or enforcement of a mechanic's lien; and **(iii)** any matter within the jurisdiction of a probate, small claims or bankruptcy court. The filing of a court action to enable the recording of a notice of pending action, for order of attachment, receivership, injunction, or other provisional remedies, shall not constitute a waiver of the mediation provision.
   C. Landlord and Tenant agree to mediate disputes or claims involving Listing Agent, Leasing Agent or property manager ("Broker"), provided Broker shall have agreed to such mediation prior to, or within a reasonable time after, the dispute or claim is presented to such Broker. Any election by Broker to participate in mediation shall not result in Broker being deemed a party to this Agreement.

40. **ATTORNEY FEES:** In any action or proceeding arising out of this Agreement, the prevailing party between Landlord and Tenant shall be entitled to reasonable attorney fees and costs, except as provided in paragraph 39A.

41. **C.A.R. FORM:** C.A.R. Form means the specific form referenced or another comparable form agreed to by the parties.

42. **OTHER TERMS AND CONDITIONS;SUPPLEMENTS:**   ☐ Interpreter/Translator Agreement (C.A.R. Form ITA);
   ☐ Keysafe/Lockbox Addendum (C.A.R. Form KLA); ☐ Lead-Based Paint and Lead-Based Paint Hazards Disclosure (C.A.R. Form FLD)
   _____
   _____
   The following ATTACHED supplements are incorporated in this Agreement: _____
   _____
   _____

43. **TIME OF ESSENCE; ENTIRE CONTRACT; CHANGES:** Time is of the essence. All understandings between the parties are incorporated in this Agreement. Its terms are intended by the parties as a final, complete and exclusive expression of their Agreement with respect to its subject matter, and may not be contradicted by evidence of any prior agreement or contemporaneous oral agreement. If any provision of this Agreement is held to be ineffective or invalid, the remaining provisions will nevertheless be given full force and effect. Neither this Agreement nor any provision in it may be extended, amended, modified, altered or changed except in writing. This Agreement is subject to California landlord-tenant law and shall incorporate all changes required by amendment or successors to such law. This Agreement and any supplement, addendum or modification, including any copy, may be signed in two or more counterparts, all of which shall constitute one and the same writing.

44. **AGENCY:**
   A.   CONFIRMATION: The following agency relationship(s) are hereby confirmed for this transaction:
   Listing Agent: (Print firm name) _____ is the agent of
   (check one): ☐ the Landlord exclusively; or ☐ both the Landlord and Tenant.
   Leasing Agent: (Print firm name) _____ (if not same as Listing Agent) is
   the agent of (check one): ☐ the Tenant exclusively; or ☐ the Landlord exclusively; or ☐ both the Tenant and Landlord.
   B.   DISCLOSURE: ☐ (If checked): The term of this lease exceeds one year. A disclosure regarding real estate agency relationships (C.A.R. Form AD) has been provided to Landlord and Tenant, who each acknowledge its receipt.

45. ☐ **TENANT COMPENSATION TO BROKER:** Upon execution of this Agreement, Tenant agrees to pay compensation to Broker as specified in a separate written agreement between Tenant and Broker.

Tenant's Initials (_____)(_____)   Landlord's Initials (_____)(_____)

Copyright © 1991-2011, CALIFORNIA ASSOCIATION OF REALTORS®, INC.
LR REVISED 4/11 (PAGE 5 OF 6)

Reviewed by _____ Date _____

RESIDENTIAL LEASE OR MONTH-TO-MONTH RENTAL AGREEMENT (LR PAGE 5 OF 6)

Reprinted with permission, California Association of REALTORS®. Endorsement not implied.

FIGURE 6.6

Residential Lease or Month-to-Month Rental Agreement, Continued

Premises: _____   Date: _____

46. ☐ **INTERPRETER/TRANSLATOR:** The terms of this Agreement have been interpreted for Tenant into the following language: _____. Landlord and Tenant acknowledge receipt of the attached interpreter/translator agreement (C.A.R. Form ITA).

47. **FOREIGN LANGUAGE NEGOTIATION:** If this Agreement has been negotiated by Landlord and Tenant primarily in Spanish, Chinese, Tagalog, Korean or Vietnamese, pursuant to the California Civil Code, Tenant shall be provided a translation of this Agreement in the language used for the negotiation.

48. **OWNER COMPENSATION TO BROKER:** Upon execution of this Agreement, Owner agrees to pay compensation to Broker as specified in a separate written agreement between Owner and Broker (C.A.R. Form LCA).

49. **RECEIPT:** If specified in paragraph 5, Landlord or Broker, acknowledges receipt of move-in funds.

> Landlord and Tenant acknowledge and agree Brokers: **(a)** do not guarantee the condition of the Premises; **(b)** cannot verify representations made by others; **(c)** cannot provide legal or tax advice; **(d)** will not provide other advice or information that exceeds the knowledge, education or experience required to obtain a real estate license. Furthermore, if Brokers are not also acting as Landlord in this Agreement, Brokers: **(e)** do not decide what rental rate a Tenant should pay or Landlord should accept; and **(f)** do not decide upon the length or other terms of tenancy. Landlord and Tenant agree that they will seek legal, tax, insurance and other desired assistance from appropriate professionals.

Tenant agrees to rent the Premises on the above terms and conditions.

Tenant _____   Date _____
Address _____ City _____ State _____ Zip _____
Telephone _____ Fax _____ E-mail _____
Tenant _____   Date _____
Address _____ City _____ State _____ Zip _____
Telephone _____ Fax _____ E-mail _____

☐ **GUARANTEE:** In consideration of the execution of this Agreement by and between Landlord and Tenant and for valuable consideration, receipt of which is hereby acknowledged, the undersigned ("Guarantor") does hereby: **(i)** guarantee unconditionally to Landlord and Landlord's agents, successors and assigns, the prompt payment of Rent or other sums that become due pursuant to this Agreement, including any and all court costs and attorney fees included in enforcing the Agreement; **(ii)** consent to any changes, modifications or alterations of any term in this Agreement agreed to by Landlord and Tenant; and **(iii)** waive any right to require Landlord and/or Landlord's agents to proceed against Tenant for any default occurring under this Agreement before seeking to enforce this Guarantee.

Guarantor (Print Name) _____
Guarantor _____   Date _____
Address _____ City _____ State _____ Zip _____
Telephone _____ Fax _____ E-mail _____

Landlord agrees to rent the Premises on the above terms and conditions.

Landlord _____   Landlord _____
Address _____
Telephone _____ Fax _____ E-mail _____

> **REAL ESTATE BROKERS:**
> **A.** Real estate brokers who are not also Landlord under this Agreement are not parties to the Agreement between Landlord and Tenant.
> **B.** Agency relationships are confirmed in paragraph 44.
> **C.** **COOPERATING BROKER COMPENSATION:** Listing Broker agrees to pay Cooperating Broker (Leasing Firm) and Cooperating Broker agrees to accept: **(i)** the amount specified in the MLS, provided Cooperating Broker is a Participant of the MLS in which the Property is offered for sale or a reciprocal MLS; or **(ii)** ☐ (if checked) the amount specified in a separate written agreement between Listing Broker and Cooperating Broker.

Real Estate Broker (Listing Firm) _____   DRE Lic. # _____
By (Agent) _____ DRE Lic. # _____ Date _____
Address _____ City _____ State _____ Zip _____
Telephone _____ Fax _____ E-mail _____

Real Estate Broker (Leasing Firm) _____   DRE Lic. # _____
By (Agent) _____ DRE Lic. # _____ Date _____
Address _____ City _____ State _____ Zip _____
Telephone _____ Fax _____ E-mail _____

LR REVISED 4/11 (PAGE 6 OF 6)

Reviewed by _____ Date _____

RESIDENTIAL LEASE OR MONTH-TO-MONTH RENTAL AGREEMENT (LR PAGE 6 OF 6)

In open listings and exclusive-agency listings, procuring cause is often an issue. The agent may not be entitled to a commission if the agent failed to initiate an uninterrupted series of events that led to the sale.

Besides listing contracts, other agreements that have relevance between the principal and the agent include the following:

- Advance fee addendum to listing: This agreement sets forth activities for which the agent is to be compensated as well as the fee to be paid in advance.

- Advance costs addendum: This addendum covers costs to be advanced to cover expected broker outlays.

- Listing modification: This agreement allows changes to the listing without an entire new agreement.

- Loan broker listing agreement: This listing gives the loan broker the right to obtain a loan for a prospective borrower.

- Seller's net: This is a statement from the agent that shows what the owner will have after all costs, payments, and expenses.

Options are contracts to make contracts whereby the optionee has an irrevocable right to make a contract if he or she wishes to do so.

A finder's fee agreement sets forth the conduct of the finder and the compensation. It protects both the broker and the finder.

Cooperating broker agreements: While agreements between brokers to split commissions need not be in writing, this form prevents misunderstanding.

Estimated buyer's costs: By using this disclosure form, the broker is protected against later allegations that the buyer was misled regarding financial requirements for purchase.

The real estate purchase contract generally is the buyer's offer to purchase. When accepted by the seller, it becomes a binding contract. Additional forms of interest include the following:

- Contingency removal: When signed by the buyer, this simple form will remove contingencies from his or her offer.

- Interim occupancy agreement: This agreement allows the purchaser early possession of the premises as a tenant, not a buyer.

- Counteroffer: Rather than modify an offer, a party can counter an offer with a separate counteroffer form. The advantage of a counteroffer form is that it helps to reconstruct the events clearly.

- Seller financing disclosure statement: This statement, which is provided to both buyer and seller, warns parties of the effect of terms and provides a full disclosure.

- Release of contract: By signing a release agreement, the parties can agree to cancel an agreement.

- Mortgage loan disclosure statement: This form is required when the broker is arranging credit while acting as a mortgage loan broker.

- Exclusive authorization to lease or rent: This is the listing agreement for rentals.

- Residential lease: Agents should not attempt major modifications of lease forms because of their liability for errors and omissions as well as because it could be the unauthorized practice of law. The use of preprinted forms for other than simple residential leases is dangerous because they are unlikely to reflect the intent of the parties.

- Broker-salesperson contracts: Often, contracts specify independent contractor status rather than employee-employer relationships.

- A great many disclosures are required by state and federal law. While many disclosures are included in standard forms, the failure of forms to include required disclosures does not excuse a broker from liability.

■ DISCUSSION CASES

1. An exclusive listing entered into on August 4, 1966, was revoked by the owners on November 25, 1966, prior to its expiration. It was alleged that the broker failed to advertise, show the property, and present offers. **If the allegations were correct, was the cancellation of the irrevocable exclusive listing proper?**

    Coleman v. Mora (1968) 263 C.A.2d 137

2. While a listing was in force, the broker sent a letter to the owner saying that she had obtained a $500 deposit on the purchase price of the property. She did not reveal the name of the buyer or submit the written offer. The owner never received the offer because he was taken to the hospital and died.

    The broker claimed she was entitled to her commission because she had produced a purchaser who was ready, willing, and able to buy on the listing terms. **Was she right?**

    Duin v. Security First National Bank (1955) 132 C.A.2d 904

3. In February 1955, Hunter authorized Rose, a licensed broker, to sell a motel for $197,500 (open listing). Spratt, a salesman for Rose, showed the property to Schmidt. In April 1955, Spratt sent a letter to Hunter stating, "This letter is being sent to you to put you on notice that this office was the procuring agent and that all brokerage rights are being claimed and in the event of a sale to Mr. Schmidt, a 5 percent brokerage commission of the sales price will be due Robert Rose Realty Company."

    There was no reply to this letter, but on May 5, Hunter notified Rose that the motel was "off the market." On May 31, Hunter sent a letter to Rose saying he could show the property again. A postscript stated, "No Trades Accepted."

In the meantime, Schmidt had continued to negotiate with Hunter and purchased the motel for $165,000 and traded personal property valued at $30,000.

Evidence was introduced to show that another agent first called Schmidt's attention to the motel in September 1954. **Is Rose entitled to a commission?**

Rose v. Hunter (1957) 155 C.A.2d 319

4. **Is an oral agreement of a broker to pay a finder's fee enforceable?**

Grant v. Marinell (1980) 112 C.A.3d 617

5. A broker sued the seller for a commission. The seller's defense was the lack of a written listing. In this case, the seller's attorney had advised the broker that a listing had been prepared and adopted by the seller's board of directors. **Is the broker entitled to a commission?**

Owens v. Foundation for Ocean Research (1980) 107 C.A.3d 179

6. A broker found a buyer under an oral listing. The deposit receipt signed by the parties provided a commission of $8,250, or one-half of the forfeited deposit.

The escrow instructions differed from the deposit receipt and provided, "Pay at close of escrow any encumbrances necessary to place this title in the condition called for and the following: Pay commission of $8,250 to Ruth Lipton Realty Company..."

The sale was never completed. The defendant claimed the close of escrow was a condition precedent to payment of the commission. **Was the broker entitled to a commission?**

Lipton v. Johansen (1951) 105 C.A.2d 363

7. A 20-day exclusive listing provided for $5,000 down. Within the 20 days, the agent brought the owner $1,000 as a deposit. The offer provided for $5,000 in cash 20 days after execution of a contract to purchase.

The owner refused to accept the $1,000 check offered, claiming he was entitled to $5,000, which he demanded in gold. The purchaser then said, "Give me time to step out to the bank, and I'll get the money for you." The seller replied, "You need not, because I don't want to sell the property on those terms anyway." **Is the agent entitled to a commission?**

Merzoian v. Papazian (1921) 53 C.A. 112

8. Under an exclusive-right-to-sell listing, a broker advertised a country club property and contacted members of the club about the property, which was located on a fairway. No offers were received.

    The defendant's fiancé and the broker argued prior to the expiration of the listing. The defendant's fiancé told the broker to remove his sign because his services were no longer wanted. The broker asked the defendant if she concurred, and she said that she did.

    Upon request from the broker's attorney for commission, the defendant softened her position and requested that the broker continue to work on the property.

    The listing provided that the broker was entitled to his commission if the owner withdrew the property from the market. **Is the broker entitled to his commission?**

    Blank v. Borden (1974) 11 C.A.3d 963

9. The plaintiff's help was requested to obtain financing for a shopping center. The plaintiff asked for a 3 percent fee, which was agreed on, and then contacted various lenders.

    The plaintiff located a lender and brought the parties together, but talks broke off. Some months later, after being unable to find financing, the defendant contacted the same lender, and a loan commitment was made for $7 million. The plaintiff was not notified.

    The defendant claimed that the plaintiff was not a licensed real estate broker, so no fee need be paid. **Do you agree?**

    Tyrone v. Kelly (1973) 9 C.A.3d 1

10. A broker had a listing on eight buildings with a commission of $1,000 on each. The broker agreed that no commission would be due if there was no sale. Because of a cloud on the title, escrow could not close. The broker orally agreed to reduce the commission by 50 percent (to $4,000) if the sellers would clear the title. Pursuant to this agreement, the title was cleared, and the broker aided in closing escrow. After receiving a $4,000 check, which the broker cashed, he changed his position and demanded the balance of his commission according to the listing. **Was the broker entitled to additional compensation?**

    Fidler v. Schiller (1963) 212 C.A.2d 569

11. The broker made fraudulent representations about a well. He stated that it could provide sufficient water for a parcel and that it produced at least 60 miner's inches. The escrow instructions stated, "Buyer has inspected well and accepts same 'as is.'" **Are the broker and/or vendor liable because of the insufficiency of the well?**

    Crawford v. Nastos (1960) 182 C.A.2d 659

12. A sale was to be subject to testing the water availability. If the test was not satisfactory to the buyers, the deposit was to be returned to them. The buyer was not satisfied and asked for and was given the deposit without the concurrence of the owner. The seller then sued the broker for wrongfully returning the deposit. **Should the broker have returned the buyer's deposit?**

Lyon v. Giannoni (1959) 168 C.A.2d 336

13. A builder contacted a subdivider to purchase a lot for a client. The subdivider, as a condition of sale, required that the subdivider's broker be paid a commission if the lot was resold within three years. This provision was insisted on even though the builder already had a buyer. After the builder conveyed title to the buyer, he refused to pay the commission. **Was the refusal proper?**

Classen v. Weller (1983) 145 C.A.3d 27

14. A seller agreed to pay a broker's commission out of the payments received. The seller foreclosed on the property but then reconveyed the property to the original buyer on different terms. The broker actively participated in the second sale, but no new listing was entered into. **Is the broker entitled to further commission payments?**

Hughes v. Morrison (1984) 160 C.A.3d 103

15. The owner of a home had a contract with a builder. The builder would take the home in trade at $113,000 for a new home under construction if the owner was unable to sell it. The house was listed for sale, and an offer was received for $115,000. Because this was less than the $113,000 credit the builder had offered (after commissions), the owner turned down the offer. After the listing expired, the offeror was contacted, and the property was transferred to the builder and then immediately to the original offeror by the builder. The listing contained a safety clause requiring a commission if the property was sold during a stated time period to anyone who had made an offer during the listing. **Does this safety clause apply when the sale was made by the builder and not the owner who had listed the property?**

McKay and Company v. Garland (1986) 701 S.W.2d 392

16. Chan was a buyer's broker for Tsang. Chan located a shopping center, and Tsang agreed to pay $4 million. The purchase contract provided that if the buyer defaulted, the seller would retain the $20,000 deposit as liquidated damages. Tsang defaulted on the purchase agreement, and Chan sued Tsang for the commission he would have received had the sale been completed. **Does Chan have a valid claim?**

Chan v. Tsang (1991) 1 C.A.4th 1578

■ CHAPTER QUIZ

1. Which phrase *BEST* describes an owner's oral agreement to pay a real estate sales commission?

   a. Enforceable if the seller benefited by the broker's efforts

   b. Enforceable for commercial property only

   c. Unenforceable

   d. Enforceable only for sales up to $1,000

2. A broker brought an offer to an owner. While the broker did not have a listing, the offer provided for a commission. The owner crossed out the provision for a commission above the signature block and signed the acceptance. Which is *TRUE* regarding the broker's rights?

   a. By signing the acceptance, the owner made the broker his agent.

   b. The broker is entitled to a reasonable commission.

   c. The broker is entitled to a full commission if the sale is completed.

   d. There was no listing, so no commission need be paid.

3. A valid listing agreement *MUST* contain which stipulation?

   a. The preprinted rate of commission

   b. A hold harmless clause

   c. Specific reference to the subject matter of the listing

   d. The right of either party to cancel upon notice

4. The effect of a hold harmless clause is that it

   a. warrants that the property presents no risks.

   b. indicates the property is to be sold "as is."

   c. means the owner agrees to indemnify the agent for losses suffered because of the owner's failure to disclose or the owner's incorrect disclosure.

   d. does none of the above.

5. An exclusive-right-to-sell listing provides for 20 percent down and owner financing at 13 percent interest. The owner received a full-price cash offer that he does not wish to accept. Which is *TRUE* regarding the owner's rights?

   a. He must pay the commission, but can reject the offer.

   b. He must accept the offer and pay the commission.

   c. He may reject the offer without obligation regarding commission.

   d. He may accept the offer without obligation regarding commission.

6. After signing an exclusive-right-to-sell listing, an owner refuses to accept an offer that conforms exactly to the terms of the listing. In this case specific performance can be obtained by

   a. the broker.   b. the offeror.

   c. either a or b.   d. neither a nor b.

7. The rate of commission for the sale of real property is set by

   a. the real estate law.

   b. local real estate boards.

   c. the real estate commissioner.

   d. agreement between the parties.

8. A commission is ordinarily earned by a broker when

   a. escrow closes.

   b. the broker procures a ready, willing, and able buyer.

   c. escrow opens.

   d. the purchaser deposits the full purchase money or liens in escrow.

9. A broker's promise to use diligence makes a listing

   a. a bilateral contract.   b. an illusory contract.

   c. a unilateral contract.   d. voidable.

10. On an exclusive listing of a single-family home a broker can be disciplined for failure to

    a. include a definite termination date.

    b. indicate that the commission is negotiable.

    c. give a copy to the owner.

    d. do all of the above.

11. The exclusive listing that broker Jones had on the Adams farm expired at noon on December 15. At 1 PM on December 15, Adams gave broker Riley an exclusive listing on the farm. At 2:30 PM on December 15, broker Jones procured a buyer at the price and terms of the listing. Who is legally entitled to the commission?

 a. Broker Jones, because a buyer was procured within a reasonable period of time of the listing

 b. Broker Riley

 c. Brokers Riley and Jones, who must split the commission equally

 d. No one above is legally entitled to the commission

12. Which provision would *LEAST* likely be found in a real estate purchase contract?

 a. Safety clause

 b. Occupancy intentions

 c. Financing contingency

 d. Provision for physical inspection

13. A termination date is required for all contracts below *EXCEPT* an

 a. open listing.

 b. exclusive-agency listing.

 c. exclusive-right-to-sell listing.

 d. option.

14. To be the procuring cause of a sale, the broker must have

 a. made the sale.

 b. supplied the owner with the name of the purchaser.

 c. initiated an uninterrupted chain of events that led to the sale.

 d. made first contact with the buyer.

15. Procuring cause is of greatest significance in

 a. options.

 b. oral listings.

 c. open listings.

 d. rights of first refusal.

16. To collect a commission for a sale on an exclusive-right-to-sell listing, the broker must prove all *EXCEPT* that

    a. there was a valid listing.

    b. the sale took place during the listing, an extension of it, or its safety period.

    c. the broker was licensed at the time the commission was earned.

    d. the broker was the procuring cause of the sale.

17. When a listing includes a purchase right and the broker informs the owner that the broker will buy the property, the broker must

    a. disclose all known facts to the seller.

    b. present any offers received.

    c. obtain the seller's written consent to exercise the option.

    d. do all of the above.

18. An oral agreement *MOST* likely to be enforceable would be a(n)

    a. option to purchase.

    b. agreement between brokers to split a commission.

    c. open listing.

    d. real estate purchase contract.

19. A listing broker refuses to split a commission with a cooperating broker after agreeing orally to do so. To collect, the cooperating broker would likely

    a. notify the real estate commissioner.

    b. file a complaint with the state labor commissioner.

    c. start legal action against the other broker.

    d. do nothing, because an oral agreement cannot be enforced.

20. Liquidated damages can exceed 3 percent of the sales price when the subject property is

    a. five residential units.

    b. residential property that the buyer did not intend to occupy.

    c. a commercial building.

    d. any of the above.

21. An offer to purchase stated that it would remain open for 48 hours. Which statement is *TRUE* regarding this offer?

    a. This offer is really an option.

    b. This offer is irrevocable for 48 hours.

    c. This offer can be revoked by the offeror prior to the expiration of 48 hours without penalty.

    d. While the offer is revocable immediately, the offeror must forfeit the deposit.

22. A real estate purchase offer fails to specify a time for acceptance. The offer

    a. must be accepted immediately.

    b. can be accepted within a reasonable period of time.

    c. cannot be withdrawn prior to acceptance.

    d. is void.

23. Which statement is *TRUE* about contingencies in purchase offers?

    a. They must be reasonable to be enforceable.

    b. The person benefiting by the contingency can waive it.

    c. They make the contract illusory.

    d. If one party can be relieved by the failure of a contingency, the other party can also be relieved from performance should the contingency fail.

24. A contract for the sale of a residence stated "as is." Which statement is *TRUE* relating to this provision?

    a. It is void because a buyer has a right to a habitable dwelling.

    b. It applies to visible conditions only.

    c. It applies only to matters of title.

    d. It is a valid disclaimer as to all defects.

25. "As is" would *MOST* likely protect a seller from hidden defects when the sale is

    a. to a buyer who does not intend to occupy the premises.

    b. of a commercial property.

    c. a single-family residence only.

    d. of one to four residential units.

7

PROPERTY, ESTATES, AND RECORDINGS

■ KEY TERMS

acknowledgment	contingent remainder	pur autre vie
actual notice	defeasible estate	real property
after acquired title	emblements	remainder interest
appurtenance	fee simple	restraint against
bundle of rights	fixtures	alienation
chattels	freehold estates	reversionary interest
chattels real	fructus industriales	rule against perpetuities
chose in action	fructus naturales	successive estates
concurrent estates	life estates	trade fixtures
condition precedent	lis pendens	vested remainder interest
condition subsequent	nonfreehold estates	waste
constructive notice	patents	wild document

■ ORIGIN OF CALIFORNIA LAND OWNERSHIP

In 1513, Balboa crossed the Isthmus of Panama and claimed for Spain all of the land washed by the waters of the Pacific Ocean. In 1542, Cabrillo sailed up the Pacific coast and landed in California, again claiming ownership for Spain. Under Spanish domination, title to California land was held in the name of the crown. Some grants of land were made, but they were primarily grants of use (agriculture and grazing) and not of title.

A number of presidios, or military garrisons, were established, as were several pueblos, or towns. The pueblos received four square leagues of land (about 4,400 acres) and had the power to grant city lots.

The Mission period started in 1769 with the establishment of a string of missions along the California coast. Most of the padres returned to Spain after Mexican independence (1822) and the subsequent secularization of the missions.

Under the short period of Mexican control (1822–1848), huge tracts of land, known as ranchos, were granted. As mentioned in Chapter 1, the Treaty of Guadalupe Hidalgo, which ended the Mexican War (1848), provided that the U.S. government would recognize the property rights of Mexican owners, including community property rights.

Most of California was not privately owned. The United States took title to all lands not given by Spanish or Mexican grants that were not cities, towns, or tidelands. Tidelands, between high and low tide lines, belong to the state.

The United States gave tracts of land to private owners under various homestead, timber, and mining acts. The Preemption Act gave a preferential right to occupants of land to purchase it at a low price. Special congressional grants gave land to the State of California. Additional tracts of land were given to Native Americans by treaty. Railroads received sections of land in a checkerboard pattern along their rights-of-way as an inducement to build. Land also has been given to colleges by the federal government and, from time to time, been sold or traded by government agencies. Grants of land from the government were known as **patents**. Today, approximately 50 percent of California land is owned by private citizens or corporations; the balance is owned by federal, state, and local governments.

■ PROPERTY

Property is anything capable of being owned. The two major categories of property are real property and personal property.

Real Property

Real property generally consists of

- land;

- what is affixed to land;

- what is incidental, or an **appurtenance,** to land (appurtenances include rights, privileges, and improvements that transfer with the land); and

- what is immovable by law except that, for the purposes of sale, emblements, industrial growing crops, and things attached to or forming part of the land that are agreed to be severed before sale or under the contract of sale are treated as goods (personal property).

Structures such as buildings, sheds, and fences are affixed to the land and are real property. Examples of incidental rights considered to be real property are riparian rights (the beneficial use of a stream or river by an adjacent landowner, covered in Chapter 12) and the right to lateral support (your neighbor cannot perform any activity, such as excavation that would cause your land to settle or collapse).

Fructus naturales (naturally growing uncultivated trees and crops) are considered real property until severed or constructively severed (sold).

Air rights and mineral, oil, and gas (subsurface) rights generally are considered real property. Easement rights, which are covered in Chapter 12, also are considered real property. These rights, unless specifically excluded, transfer with the real estate.

> **Case Study**
> In the case of *U.S. v. Causby* (1946) 328 U.S. 256, the Supreme Court held that a landowner owns at least as much space above the ground as he or she can occupy or use in conjunction with the land even though the owner does not occupy it in a physical sense. Therefore, low-flying aircraft that interfere with the normal use of property would be interfering with the owner's rights.

Personal Property

Personal property, also known as **chattels**, is any property that is not real property. Personal property generally is considered to be movable. Title to personal property does not automatically pass with the transfer of title to the real property where it is located.

Chattels Real.   **Chattels real** are personal property interests that concern real property. Examples of chattels real are leasehold interests, mortgages, trust deeds, shares in real estate syndicates, and shares in housing cooperatives. While real property oriented, they are considered personal property.

Chose in Action.   **Chose in Action** refers to a right to demand money or other personal property through legal action. The claim is considered personal property.

Fructus Industriales.   Also known as **emblements**, **fructus industriales** are crops resulting from labor. While generally regarded as personal property, in the absence of any agreement between the buyer and seller of real property, they transfer with the land.

If the crops are the fruit of the labor of a tenant, they remain the goods or personal property of the tenant, even though the lease may expire prior to harvest. The former tenant has the right to return to the land to harvest the crops.

Mineral, Oil, and Gas Rights.   As previously stated, mineral, oil, and gas rights are real property. An oil lease for an indefinite period of time also is real property. However, an oil lease for a definite period of time is personal property.

Because oil and gas are considered fluid, no ownership of the actual oil or gas exists until it is extracted from the ground. Ownership of subsurface rights is actually the right to extract the minerals, oil, or gas. After it has been captured, or removed from the ground, it becomes personal property. The owner of rights actually can take fluid oil and gas from under land for which they have no rights. The owner of rights, however, cannot intrude on or under land where they have no rights to do so; for example, they cannot slant-drill into the land of another.

An owner can sell mineral and oil and gas rights but retain a royalty interest as well as land ownership.

> **Case Study**
> In the case of *Geothermal Kinetics Inc. v. Union Oil Co.* (1977) 77 C.A.3d 56, the court held that where the specific intent of the parties cannot be ascertained, a grant of a mineral estate includes all geothermal resources located on or under the property. It held that a general grant of a mineral estate is intended to convey commercially valuable underground resources that are not necessary for the enjoyment of the surface estate.

Fixtures.   **Fixtures** are former items of personal property that have become affixed to realty so that they are now part of the real property. For example, a household furnace is personal property before it is installed in a residence, but becomes real property (a fixture) after it is installed. Title to fixtures generally transfers with the real property.

There are five basic tests for determining whether or not an item is a fixture:

1. *Intent*: This is the most important test. Did the improver intend to make a permanent improvement to the property? If so, it is likely to be a fixture.

> **Case Study**
> In the case of *Larkin v. Cowert* (1968) 263 C.A.2d 27, the court held that the fact that carpets and drapes in an apartment house could be removed without damage was of no significance. The court held that the intent was that they remain as long as they served their purpose of higher rents and rentability.

2. *Method of attachment*: Is the item attached in a permanent manner? Bolts, nails, concrete, and pipe generally are considered permanent, even though an item can be readily removed. If an item is attached by roots (a tree or plant), it generally is regarded as a fixture.

   A fixture could be attached by its weight alone. An example would be a building that is not anchored to a foundation.

> **Case Study**
>
> The case of *Seatrain Terminal of California, Inc. v. County of Alameda* (1978) 83 C.A.3d 69 involved two cargo cranes. The cranes weighed 750 tons each and ran on rails on a wharf. They were not attached to the realty. However, the terminal had been designed for the use of cranes. The court held that even though not attached to the realty, the cranes were fixtures. They were a necessary part of the wharf and were intended to be permanent.
>
> *Note*: Alameda County sought to have the cranes declared real property so that they would be subject to real property taxes.

Personal property does not become a fixture when it has been wrongfully attached—when it is attached by a person who is not the owner of the real property—and who had no right or permission to make the attachment.

3. *Adaptability*: Was the item specifically adaptable to the use of the real property? For adaptability, the item need not be custom made; it need only relate reasonably to the use.

   For example, an argument could be made that an odd-size refrigerator placed in a specially built alcove is a fixture, even though its only connection to the real property is a plug in a wall socket.

> **Case Study**
>
> In *Allstate Ins. Co. v. County of Los Angeles* and *Security Pac. Nat'l Bank v. County of Los Angeles* (1984) 161 C.A.3d 877 (consolidated cases), the plaintiffs had elaborate computer systems placed in rooms with elevated floors (to hide the cables). They also had added supplemental air conditioning. The County of Los Angeles took the position that the systems were real property for taxation purposes.
>
> The buildings had not been specifically designed or substantially modified for the computer systems. There was no evidence that the systems were installed with the intention to affix them to the real estate. The court thus held that standardized general-purpose computers placed in general-purpose office buildings are personal property. The minor alterations required did not make the systems real property.

All three of the preceding tests need not be met for the courts to determine that an item is a fixture. Civil Code Section 1019 added two additional tests for fixtures:

4. *Agreement*: Parties are free to agree on whether an item is real or personal property, and their agreement will govern the nature of the property.

5. *Relationship of the parties*: When it is not clear if an item is a fixture or personal property, the issue will be determined in favor of
   - the tenant between landlord and tenant,

- the buyer between seller and buyer, and
- the lender between borrower and lender.

Trade Fixtures. **Trade fixtures** are fixtures installed for the purpose of trade or business. They remain the property of the tenant and may be removed at any time prior to the expiration of the lease. In California, a tenant may remove from the premises anything the tenant has affixed thereto for the purposes of trade, manufacture, ornament, or domestic use if the removal can be effected without substantial injury to the premises, and unless some agreement to the contrary has been made between the landlord and the tenant.

> **Case Study**
> In the case of *Roberts v. Mills* (1922) 56 C.A. 556, the court held that a building was a trade fixture. The building erected by the tenant was built in such a manner that it could be removed without injury to the premises.

Civil Code Section 1019 restricts tenants' rights to remove trade fixtures if the trade fixture becomes an integral part of the premises.

> **Case Study**
> In the case of *Yokohama Specie Bank Ltd. v. Higashi* (1943) 56 C.A.2d 709, a tenant installed a refrigeration plant in a building. Installation required removal of columns supporting the building and substitution of refrigerating rooms. The court held that, because the refrigerating rooms had become an integral part of the building, they were not subject to removal by the tenant.

For month-to-month leases, courts generally will allow a reasonable period after the end of the lease for removal of trade fixtures.

A "mistaken improver" is allowed to remove the improvements, even though they would otherwise be regarded as fixtures. The mistaken improver will, however, be liable for damages resulting from the removal.

Mobile Homes

Since July 1, 1980, mobile homes attached to a foundation have been taxable as real property. Besides placing the mobile home on a foundation, to have the home considered real property the owner must

- obtain a building permit,
- obtain a certificate of occupancy, and
- record a document reflecting that the mobile home has been affixed to a foundation.

A mobile home may not be removed from a foundation (real property) unless

- all persons who have any interest in the real property consent to its removal, and
- the Department of Housing and Community Development is notified 30 days prior to removal.

Mobile homes sold new after July 1, 1980, that are not attached to a foundation, and mobile homes sold prior to that date whose vehicle license fees are 120 days or more delinquent, are taxed as personal property. While the tax rate and procedure for personal property and real property are virtually indistinguishable, mobile homes attached to permanent foundations have certain advantages over mobile homes that are taxed as personal property. Under Proposition 13, the assessed value for mobile homes taxed as real property can increase only 2 percent each year. If taxed as personal property, the mobile home would be taxed at full market value.

Mobile homes sold new on or before June 30, 1980, continue to be taxed as vehicles. The vehicle fees are now paid to the Department of Housing and Community Development, not the Department of Motor Vehicles.

■ DEGREE OF OWNERSHIP

The degree of ownership a person has in property is known as an *estate*.

Estates where the exact termination date is unknown are considered **freehold estates**. Fee simple estates (indefinite period) and life estates (end with death) are the two types of freehold estates and are considered to be real property.

Fee Simple or Fee Simple Absolute

The **fee simple** or fee simple absolute estate is the highest degree of ownership possible. Normal home ownership would be held in fee simple. There are three characteristics of fee simple ownership:

1. There is no time limit.
2. Owners can transfer title freely.
3. The estate may be inherited (an estate of inheritance).

A grant that does not indicate the extent of the interest being conveyed is presumed to be made in fee simple.

The beneficial rights of ownership are called the **bundle of rights**, and they include the right to convey, lease, use, encumber, inherit, and exclude others. Ownership rights are not, however, absolute. Under the police power of the state, land use can be regulated (see Chapter 13) and property can be taken, with compensation, for public purposes (see "Eminent Domain," Chapter 9).

Defeasible Estates.   A **defeasible estate** is an estate that can be lost. The fee interest is qualified. For example, with a fee on a **condition subsequent**, property is transferred to a grantee with a condition. If the condition is breached, the estate can revert to the grantor by court action. The grantor must bring action within five years of the breach (Civil Code Section 784). The grantor therefore retains a **reversionary interest**.

Grantors sometimes use grants with a condition subsequent to advance their personal convictions. For example, a common condition subsequent is the prohibition of the sale of alcoholic beverages. The deed could provide that the property, if ever used for the sale of alcoholic beverages, shall revert to the grantor or heirs. If a grantor failed to take action within a five-year period after a condition subsequent was breached, the courts could determine that the grantor has waived the right to enforce the reversion.

Property also may be dedicated to a municipality or charity with instructions for its specific use, the condition being that abandonment of that use will result in reversion of the property to the grantor. Courts generally will interpret the specified use quite liberally to avoid forfeiture.

A **condition precedent** precludes a grant from taking place until something happens, such as the grantee reaches the age of 21. Once the condition is met, the grantee has a fee simple interest.

Case Study

In *Springmeyer v. City of South Lake Tahoe* (1982) 132 C.A.3d 375, the city acquired title with a condition subsequent that provided for automatic reversion to the grantor if "the city failed to build office buildings for municipal government use by a specified date or the buildings no longer were used for government office purposes."

The city allowed the county to use the buildings, and the grantor demanded reversion under the second condition. The court held that because reversion is such a harsh penalty, if more than one interpretation is possible, it must fall against triggering a reversion. In this case "government office purposes" was held to include federal, state, county, and local offices, so the property did not revert to the grantor.

Case Study

The case of *Alamo School District v. Jones* (1960) 182 C.A.2d 180 involved a deed given to a school district subject to the right of the grantor to buy back the land at the same price should it ever be abandoned by the school district. The court held that this was not a defeasible estate, but rather was simply a contingent option to purchase. This option was held to be personal, so it did not pass to the heirs of the grantor. It was void upon the grantor's death.

Because the law abhors forfeiture, courts often will determine that a condition is only a covenant so that the remedy for breach will be monetary damages rather than forfeiture.

Restraints Against Alienation.   A restraint in a transfer that unreasonably restricts future alienation (the ability to grant, sell, devise, lease, or encumber) is unenforceable and void because it is contrary to public policy. An example of such a **restraint against alienation** would be a conveyance on the condition that the grantee not convey to other than "heirs of my body."

Life Estates

Life estates are given to a grantee for life. The life tenant has exclusive and absolute use of the property, for their lifetime, is entitled to the rents and profits from the property, and can even file a homestead declaration on their interest.

A life estate is generally granted to a person for the grantee's own lifetime, although it is possible to grant a life estate for the life of another (**pur autre vie**). When it is based on the life of another, the death of the life tenant does not affect the estate. The heirs of the deceased will have the use of the property as long as that third party is alive. Normally, however, the life estate is based on the life of the life tenant.

When the life tenant dies, the property either reverts to the grantor or their heirs (a **reversionary interest**) or passes to a designated third party, who is said to have a **remainder interest**. Upon the death of the life tenant, the reversionary or remainder interest holder customarily holds title in fee simple.

If the remainder interest requires that the third party outlive the life tenant, the third-party interest is a **contingent remainder** (contingent on the third party's being alive to receive the remainder interest). If, however, there are no contingencies, the remainder will, upon the death of the life tenant, pass to the remainder holder or their heirs. This type of estate is called a **vested remainder interest** because someday the life tenant must die, ensuring that the remainder holder will receive the property.

Life estates might be granted to give the grantors a charitable tax deduction while they are alive and allow them to keep all the benefits of ownership. They often are used to care for spouses or others during their lifetime and then go to others to fulfill the wishes of the grantor.

Farmers often give their farmland to a child but retain a life estate. Knowing that they will eventually get the farm, the grantee thus is more likely to stay, and the grantor retains control, along with the income, for life.

Life estates also can be subject to a **condition subsequent**, such as a life estate that goes to a remainder interest holder should the life tenant remarry. This type of estate often is used when the grantor feels that they have a duty to support the life tenant only while the life tenant remains unmarried.

Life estates can be granted to more than one life tenant. The interests of the joint life tenants would be much like a joint tenancy (see Chapter 8) with the last survivor having sole possession [*Green v. Brown* (1951) 37 C.2d 391].

A life tenant cannot use the property in any way that would diminish its value. For example, if tearing down structures or clearing out timber would reduce the property's value, the life tenant would be prohibited from these acts. The life tenant may, however, cut timber as necessary for repairs and fuel. The life tenant also may mine the property, but only if it was mined prior to the life estate.

A life tenant may not commit **waste**; that is, they must maintain the property, pay taxes, and protect the rights of reversionary or remainder interest holders. If a life tenant does commit waste, the court might appoint a receiver.

> ### Case Study
> In the case of *King v. Hawley* (1952) 113 C.A.2d 534, a testator gave a life estate in all of his property to his sister. The will provided that she could "use all of the proceeds of my estate for her comfort and support, but that whatever may be left shall go" to the remainder interest. The life tenant transferred some of the property to friends without consideration and some with inadequate consideration. The life tenant was held to have fraudulently attempted to defeat the remainder interest.

For an extraordinary expense, such as a sewer hookup, the expense will be borne proportionately by the life tenant and the remainder or reversionary rights holders, based on the life of the improvement and the age of the life tenant. Courts prorate extraordinary costs based on the benefits to be received.

The life tenant can borrow against the property but cannot encumber the property beyond their lifetime without the concurrence of remainder or reversionary interest holders. Lenders might lend on the life tenant's interests alone if the loan is coupled with a policy of life insurance payable to the lender.

Remainder and reversionary interest holders also can assign or encumber their interests; however, neither they nor their assignees or creditors will have any right to use the property or receive rents or profits until the life estate ends.

Unless the life tenant's use is restricted, the life tenant can lease the property, but the death of the life tenant will terminate the lease unless the reversionary or remainder interest holders also sign the lease as lessors and thus obligate their interests. Before signing a long-term lease, a prospective tenant who will be making substantial improvements should have a title search conducted to be certain of the lessor's interests.

Unless restricted, a life tenant can sell their interest, but the purchaser will receive no more than the life tenant possessed. Upon the death of the life tenant, the purchaser's interest will cease.

A life tenant has no duty to insure the property. If the life tenant does insure and the property is destroyed, the prevailing view is that the life tenant is entitled to the insurance proceeds. Some courts have held that the insurance was taken out for the joint benefit of the life tenant and the remainder or reversionary interest holder. A remainder or reversionary interest holder who is not specifically named as an insured should obtain insurance to protect their interests.

If a life tenant receives a property with a mortgage or trust deed against it, the principal payments on the mortgage or trust deed will be a charge against the remainder or reversionary holder, but the interest payments will be the responsibility of the life tenant.

> **Case Study**
>
> In the case of *Osborne v. Osborne* (1954) 42 C.2d 358, a deed granting a fee simple estate was deposited into escrow with the provision that it not be delivered to the grantee until the death of the grantor. The court held that, if the grantor intended the transaction to be irrevocable, the deed created a remainder interest in fee simple with a life estate reserved in the grantor.

If a property is taken by eminent domain (see Chapter 9), which requires the payment of "just compensation" by the government, the life tenant and remainder interest owners will share the proceeds based on the benefits to which they are entitled.

A deed transferring the interest of the remainder interest holders to a life tenant will merge the two interests into a fee simple estate owned by the former life tenant.

Rule Against Perpetuities.   The **rule against perpetuities** states that any noncharitable interest must vest without limitations within the lives of persons in being at the time of conveyance, plus 21 years. The interest is further restricted in that it must either vest with an owner or terminate within 90 years of its creation. This rule would prohibit a perpetual trust to support the heirs of the grantor.

Nonfreehold Estates

Nonfreehold estates are leasehold interests (personal property). **Freehold estates** (fee simple) and life estates are real property. Nonfreehold estates are tenancies and are covered in detail in Chapter 15.

Concurrent Estates

Concurrent estates—more than one ownership or estate at the same time—can exist in a property. For example, a tenant can have a leasehold estate while an owner has a fee simple interest. The fee simple owner would have a reversionary interest of possession at the expiration of the leasehold interest.

Air and mineral interests also can be conveyed, creating separate interests. Property can even be divided horizontally, with the mineral, oil, and gas rights being conveyed in layers.

Successive Estates

Estates can be established to succeed existing estates. An example of **successive estates** is a remainder or reversionary estate to follow a life estate.

■ RECORDING OF REAL PROPERTY INTERESTS

Under the Spanish and Mexican governments, California had no system for recording and safeguarding interests in real property. To prove ownership, a person physically had to possess the original grant or deed.

When California became a state in 1850, one of the first acts of the California legislature was to institute a system for recording interests in real property. The system adopted was patterned after that established by the original 13 states. By providing for evidence of title to be collected and made available at central locations, recording statutes protect buyers against secret conveyances and interests and make real property readily and freely transferable.

The basic real property recording laws are found in Civil Code Sections 1169-1220 and Government Code Sections 27201-27383. The recording statutes provide that, after being acknowledged, any instrument or judgment affecting title to, possession of, or rights in real property may be recorded. Real estate listings may not be recorded because the agent has no rights in real property, only rights to compensation.

Prohibitions against recording contained in documents that could otherwise be recorded would be considered contrary to public policy, and the document could be recorded in spite of the attempted prohibition.

Acknowledgment

Before a document can be recorded, it must be acknowledged. **Acknowledgment** is made before a notary or other designated official by the person attesting to the document. That person acknowledges that they are the person claimed and is the one who has signed the instrument as their own free act. The maker of an instrument must appear personally before the notary, and the notary has a duty to ascertain identity by personal knowledge or by identification by a third person under oath. A notary can accept driver's licenses and passports as proof of identity. The notary does not verify the facts of the document.

Notary publics who verify the acknowledgment of a deed or deed of trust must place in the notary's journal the right thumbprint of the person signing the document.

The acknowledgment must include the state and county where acknowledged and the name and capacity of the acknowledging party.

When two or more persons are executing a document requiring acknowledgment, each of their signatures must be acknowledged. Without acknowledgment, constructive notice (discussed in the next section) of that person's interest has not been given.

A person who holds an instrument that otherwise could be recorded except for the lack of acknowledgment can bring an action against the other party to prove the instrument and can then record a certified copy of the judgment (Civil Code Section 1203).

Excepted from the requirement that instruments be acknowledged to be recorded or filed are

- judgments authenticated by the clerk of the court;

- notices of mining claims;

- tax certificates of amount due;

- leases from the federal government; and

- documents required to be signed by an attorney, such as a **lis pendens**, which is a notice of a pending lawsuit involving a claim against real property.

Constructive Notice

Recording a document gives the whole world **constructive notice** of an interest in real property. If Al conveyed to Bert and Bert recorded the deed, subsequent grantees of the property from Al would get nothing because they would have had constructive notice that Al no longer owned the property.

If a document is recorded with a defect, such as the absence of acknowledgment, the recording would not give constructive notice until one year after the recording. A defect, such as a document filed in the wrong county or with a name spelled incorrectly, so that a reasonable search of the records would not reveal the document, does not provide constructive notice.

Possession also gives constructive notice. Assume Art deeded to Ben, who took possession but did not record. If Art later conveyed the same property to Carl, who recorded, title would be with Ben. Carl had constructive notice by Ben's possession of Ben's interest. In failing to check with the party in possession to ascertain the possessor's interests, Carl did not act diligently. If a buyer checks with a party in possession and is not informed of an adverse claim, however, the possession does not provide constructive notice of the interests of the party in possession.

A plaintiff in an action involving real property may file a lis pendens with the county recorder to provide subsequent purchasers or encumbrancers with constructive notice of the plaintiff's claim of interest.

While the law is clear that recording gives constructive notice of the documents recorded, it is not clear whether recording gives constructive notice of all other documents referenced in the recorded document. The prevailing view is that a person should reasonably investigate the referenced document. An improper description of land being conveyed does not give constructive notice as to the land intended to be conveyed.

Case Study

Gates Rubber Co. v. Ulman (1989) 214 C.A.3d 356 involved a tenant under a 25-year lease who also had a separate option to purchase the property for $550,000 during the 20th year of the lease. Neither the lease nor the option was recorded, although a short-form lease was recorded that named the parties and referenced the lease. The landlord sold the property six years later for $633,000. Fourteen years later, in the 20th year of the lease, the tenant sought to exercise the purchase option (the property was now worth $2 million). The Court of Appeal affirmed the trial court's decision that the defendant (Ulman) should prevail if he qualifies as a bona fide purchaser without notice. While in some instances possession places a duty to inquire, the court held that this is the case only when the possession is inconsistent with record title. In this instance, the tenant's possession was consistent with a recorded lease that made no reference to an option to purchase. While Ulman had a duty to check the lease referenced in the recorded lease, there was no duty to inquire as to any other rights the tenant might have. Ulman therefore had taken title free of the option.

Actual Notice

While recording and possession give constructive notice of an interest in real property, **actual notice** is express knowledge of the prior interest. A person who has actual knowledge of a prior interest cannot claim priority of interest because they recorded first. Actual notice has the same effect as the constructive notice of recording.

Figure 7.1 illustrates the difference between actual notice and constructive notice.

Priority

Besides providing constructive notice of an interest, recording determines priority of interests. Recording often has been called "the race of the diligent" because priority of interest in the absence of actual knowledge is determined by time and date of recording and not time and date of execution of an instrument (Civil Code Section 1214). (The first to record is first in right.)

Assume Alvira conveyed to Bryan and Alvira later conveyed the same property to Cindy. If Cindy arrived at the recorder's office ahead of Bryan, then Cindy's deed would be recorded first. As a general rule, Cindy would take title and Bryan would have nothing (other than a claim against Alvira). If Cindy *had* diligently searched the records, Cindy would have found no evidence of Bryan's interest. If anyone should suffer, it should be the one who was negligent in failing to immediately make their interest known as a matter of record rather than a diligent later purchaser, which would mean that Cindy would have good title.

FIGURE 7.1
Notice

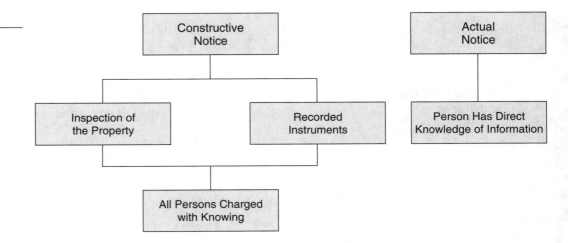

Notice

Recording does not give priority over prior unrecorded conveyances if the person recording is not acting in good faith or has not paid a valuable consideration. For example, a recorded deed given without consideration (a gift deed) would not give the grantee priority over a prior unrecorded deed or trust deed that was given for valuable consideration. Therefore, for recording to give priority it must be done by a bona fide purchaser (or lender) for value without prior notice of other interests. The courts would consider the adequacy of consideration in determining whether a party is a bona fide purchaser. A person who receives notice of a prior interest at any time prior to paying the consideration would not be a bona fide purchaser.

A purchase-money trust deed (a trust deed given to finance the purchase) would take priority over liens against the grantee, even though those liens attach as soon as title is passed.

Failure to Record

The recording act does not require recording; it merely permits recording. Between a grantor and a grantee of an unrecorded deed, the grantee would have title. The grantee's title, however, would not take priority over a later recorded deed or trust deed given for value by the original grantor, provided that the later grantee or beneficiary (lender) had no constructive or actual notice of the prior conveyance.

Recording is required for homestead declarations, mechanics' liens, and judgment liens. Without recording, these instruments have no effect.

Documents Recordable without Owner's Consent

Recording documents in proper form with the owner's notarized signature cannot be prohibited. But the following documents can be recorded without the owner's notarized signature: judgment liens, mining claims against the federal government, tax deeds, trustee's deeds, mechanics' liens, federal and state income tax liens, child support liens, homeowners' association liens, and lis pendens.

After Acquired Title

If a deed is given by a grantor who does not have title, no title would pass to the grantee. However, if the grantor later acquires title, the **after acquired title** would then pass to the grantee. Similarly, a person who gave a deed of trust on property without owning it would find this lien against the property upon later acquiring title. This principle is called the *doctrine of* **after-acquired title**. But, because a reasonable title search by a later lender would not reveal a lien placed prior to ownership, the earlier lien would not take priority over a purchase-money lien.

Wild and Forged Documents

A **wild document**, one outside the chain of title, gives no constructive notice because it would not be discovered by a diligent search of the records.

A recorded assignment or sublease of an unrecorded lease also would be outside the chain of title and therefore would not give constructive notice.

A forged document is void and does not give constructive notice of any interest and has no effect. Knowingly recording a forged or false document is a felony (Penal Code Section 115). Such an action would also be a tort (slander of title).

There have been incidents in which unscrupulous individuals have forged deeds to themselves, using both forged owner signatures and forged notary seals. They have then borrowed on the property. Because a forged document does not transfer any interest, the lenders did not obtain a valid lien interest in the property. Filing a false deed or deed of trust can result in criminal penalties.

The Recording Process

While it is in the best interests of a grantee to record a document as soon as possible, there is no time limit for recording (except in the case of mechanics' liens). A document is deemed recorded when it is deposited in the recorder's office and marked "filed for record." The recorder gives each document a filing number indicating the order in which the document was received and time-stamps the document.

The recorder transfers the document to the appropriate book of records. Documents are indexed alphabetically by grantor-grantee, showing the name, nature of the recording, date of recording, and reference where the document is filed.

Ordinarily, the document is photocopied and the original returned to the person indicated as the recipient in the heading of the document.

If the recorder improperly indexes a document, the recording does not provide constructive notice. The duty to see that a document is recorded properly falls on the person recording.

Case Study

In the case of *Hochstein v. Romero* (1990) 219 C.A.3d 447, an abstract of judgment was improperly indexed. The court held because the abstract was not locatable by search, it did not impart constructive notice. It must therefore be treated as if it were never recorded, and a bona fide purchaser for value took title free of the judgment lien.

The name of the grantor and grantee must be signed legibly or printed for the recorder.

The recorder will not accept for recording a document that is not in English unless a certified English translation is attached to it.

A document can be recorded in more than one county and would apply to the property within the counties where recorded. A certified copy can be used to record in more than one county.

Counties may now allow electronic recording at county option.

The recorder will not record until the recording fee is paid. The county recorder also will require that the documentary transfer tax (tax on seller's equity being conveyed) be paid prior to recording deeds.

The county recorder will require that deeds contain the name and address to which tax statements are to be sent. Failure to comply, however, does not affect constructive notice.

Any person has the right to check the county recorder's records.

Change of Ownership

As provided in Proposition 13, real property is reassessed upon sale. Therefore, transferees of ownership interests are required to file a change of ownership statement with the county recorder or tax assessor within 45 days after receipt of a request from the assessor. Failure to comply could result in a penalty of $100 or 10 percent of the current year's taxes, whichever is greater.

■ SUMMARY

Ownership passed from government to private ownership in California under Spanish rule by the establishment of pueblos or towns. Under Mexican rule, large tracts of land, known as ranchos, were given out. The United States gave tracts of land to private owners under various homestead, timber, and mining acts. Additionally, large tracts were given to railroads and colleges. Government grants were known as patents. Only about half of the land in California is owned privately.

Real property consists of land and what goes with the land. Personal property, known as chattels, consists of movable property that does not automatically transfer with the conveyance of real property. Chattels real are personal property interests in real estate, such as lease interests, mortgages, and trust deeds.

Fixtures are former items of personal property that have become so affixed to real property that they are part of the real estate. In the absence of an agreement, three basic tests are used to determine whether an item is a fixture They are intent, method of attachment, and adaptability.

Trade fixtures installed for the purpose of conducting a business or trade remain personal property and may be removed by the tenant.

While mobile homes attached to a foundation are considered real property, mobile homes not permanently attached are personal property.

A person having property in fee simple, the highest degree of ownership, owns it without time limitation, can convey it freely, and can pass it by inheritance.

Defeasible estates are estates that can be defeated or lost upon the happening of some event (estate on a condition subsequent).

Life estates are given for the life of a person. Upon the death of the life tenant, the life estate either reverts to the grantor or his or her heirs (a reversionary interest) or passes to a third person (a remainder interest). The life tenant cannot encumber the property beyond his or her lifetime.

Both fee simple estates and life estates are known as freehold estates. Nonfreehold estates are leasehold interests.

Recording gives constructive notice of an interest in real property. As a general rule, to be recorded, an instrument must be acknowledged. Possession also provides constructive notice to parties who acquire later interests of the rights of the party in possession.

Recording does not give priority notice when the party recording had actual notice of a prior unrecorded interest. Recording of a deed given without consideration would not take precedence over a prior unrecorded interest given for good and valuable consideration.

Defective recording that would not reveal an interest by a diligent search of the records does not give constructive notice.

The recording process involves depositing the document with the county recorder. It is marked "filed for record" and given a number. The document then is transferred to the appropriate book of records and the original is returned to the person recording. The recorder keeps an alphabetical grantor-grantee index.

■ DISCUSSION CASES

1. The county assessor assessed the plaintiff's leasehold interests in the *Queen Mary* as real property. The plaintiff claimed that it was attached to a floating vessel, so the interests were personal property. **Considering the manner in which the vessel is attached to its pier and its adaptability, is the *Queen Mary* real or personal property?**

Specialty Restaurants Corp. v. County of Los Angeles (1977) 67 C.A.3d 924

2.   Two trust deeds were presented to the recorder at the same time. The trust deed intended to be recorded second was recorded first, and the trust deed intended to be recorded first was recorded second. The trust deed that was recorded second stated on its face that it was to be a first trust deed. **Which trust deed has priority?**

Phelps v. American Mortgage Company (1936) 6 C.2d 604

3.   A dealer negotiated a franchise with a beverage firm. A recorded mortgage showed the dealer to be a corporation. **Was the prior recorded mortgage constructive notice to the beverage firm that the dealer was a corporation?**

Nesbitt Fruit Products Inc. v. Del Monte Beverage Co. (1966) 177 C.A.2d 353

4.   A notary personally did not know the person who it was claimed had acknowledged a document, and the executing party was not present when the notary acknowledged the signature. **Does the recording give constructive notice?**

Thomas v. Speck (1941) 47 C.A.2d 512

5.   A delivered deed provided that it was not to take effect until the grantor died. **Was this a valid conveyance?**

Lowe v. Ruhlman (1945) 67 C.A.2d 828

6.   A recorded mortgage indicated one date for its execution, and the acknowledgment was dated five days later. The trustee in bankruptcy sought to set aside the instrument and make the creditors unsecured. **Does the discrepancy affect the constructive notice of recording?**

Clements v. Snider (1969) 409 F.2d 549

■ CHAPTER QUIZ

1. Real property includes

    a. growing annual crops.   b. mineral rights.

    c. leasehold interests.   d. trust deeds.

2. Which is *NOT* an example of chattels real?

    a. Furniture

    b. Trust deeds

    c. Lease interests

    d. Shares in a housing cooperative

3. Which would be classified as personal property?

    a. Mineral rights   b. An oil lease for ten years

    c. Fixtures   d. Riparian rights

4. Which is *NOT* an important test of a fixture?

    a. Cost   b. Intent

    c. Method of attachment   d. Adaptability

5. Which is *NOT* an appurtenance?

    a. A right of egress   b. Mineral rights

    c. Water rights   d. Trade fixtures

6. A new mobile home located in a rental park in 2008 was not attached to a foundation. It would be taxed

    a. as real property.

    b. as personal property.

    c. as a vehicle with fees to the Department of Motor Vehicles.

    d. with fees paid to the Department of Housing and Community Development.

7. Which is a characteristic of an indefeasible estate?

    a. It cannot be canceled.

    b. It can be lost upon a happening.

    c. It is voidable.

    d. It is a reversionary interest.

8. Which statement *BEST* describes a fee on a condition subsequent?

    a. Ownership interest that does not transfer to grantee until something happens

    b. A qualified interest that may be lost should something happen

    c. A recording charge that need not be paid until the property is sold

    d. A nonfreehold interest

9. The future interest of a grantor of a life estate would likely be a

    a. reversionary interest.

    b. contingent remainder interest.

    c. vested remainder interest.

    d. nonfreehold estate.

10. A future uncertain interest of possession would *MOST* likely be a

    a. personal property interest.

    b. vested remainder interest.

    c. contingent remainder interest.

    d. life estate.

11. Which is a right of a life tenant?

    a. To refuse to pay taxes

    b. To lease the property

    c. To convey the interest by will

    d. To encumber the reversionary interest

12. Which is *NOT* a characteristic of fee simple ownership?

    a. Nonfreehold interest   b. No time limit

    c. Freely transferable by owner   d. Inheritable

13. Henry willed his property in trust with the beneficiaries to be all future heirs of his body. His action is prohibited by

    a. the statute of limitations.   b. the rule against perpetuities.

    c. laches.   d. the recording statutes.

14. Albert received a life estate in property, but the property had a mortgage against it. Which statement is *TRUE* regarding this situation?

    a. Mortgage payments are the responsibility of the remainder interest holder.

    b. The mortgage nullifies the life estate.

    c. The life tenant pays the interest, but the remainder interest pays the principal.

    d. The mortgage payment is split evenly between life tenant and remainder holder.

15. Which is a characteristic of an estate in real property?

    a. It can exist within another estate.

    b. It will always run forever.

    c. It requires possession.

    d. It is a nonfreehold interest.

16. What is the result when the grantee records a deed that states that it *CANNOT* be recorded?

    a. The recordation does not give constructive notice.

    b. The deed has been voided.

    c. The title reverts to the grantor.

    d. The recording gives constructive notice.

17. A person who states that his or her signing is a free act would be making a(n)

    a. affirmation.   b. acknowledgment.

    c. notarization.   d. verification.

18. Anne sold property to Bob. Bob took possession but did not record his deed. Anne learned of this and immediately sold to Claude. Claude recorded his deed. Which decision would a court of law *MOST* likely render?

    a. Claude wins because he did the proper thing by recording his deed.

    b. Claude wins because he had no notice.

    c. Bob wins because he was in possession.

    d. Bob wins because he purchased first.

19.   Which is *NOT* true of recording?

    a.   It provides constructive notice of the recorded instrument.

    b.   It provides actual notice of an interest.

    c.   It determines the priority of liens.

    d.   It creates a presumption of delivery.

20.   Priority of trust deeds can easily be ascertained by the

    a.   date of recording.   b.   date of the instrument.

    c.   heading of the instrument.   d.   date on the note.

21.   Adolph sold to Betty on January 1. Betty took possession on January 15 and recorded her deed on February 1. Adolph obtained a home equity loan on the same property on January 10. The lender, Clement, recorded the same day. On January 20, Adolph sold the same property to Don who recorded on January 21. What are the rights of the parties?

    a.   Don has title subject to Clement's lien.

    b.   Betty has title clear of any lien.

    c.   Betty has title, but Clement has a valid lien against it.

    d.   None of the above are true.

22.   A recorded gift deed would *NOT* take priority over

    a.   subsequent recorded deeds for value.

    b.   a prior unrecorded deed given for valuable consideration.

    c.   subsequent trust deeds.

    d.   prior unrecorded gift deeds.

23.   What would result when Albert deeded to Henry, but Henry inadvertently recorded in the wrong county?

    a.   Albert would retain title.

    b.   Between Henry and Albert, Henry would have title.

    c.   The minor defect in recording would not affect the constructive notice.

    d.   The deed could be voided upon return of consideration.

24.   The county recorder indexes deeds by

   a.   time received.

   b.   location.

   c.   grantor's and grantee's names.

   d.   tax assessor's number.

25.   Which is *TRUE* regarding recordation?

   a.   A document can be recorded in more than one county.

   b.   To be recorded, deeds must include the name and address where tax statements are to be sent.

   c.   The duty to see that the instrument is properly recorded falls with the person recording the instrument.

   d.   All of the above are true.

CHAPTER EIGHT

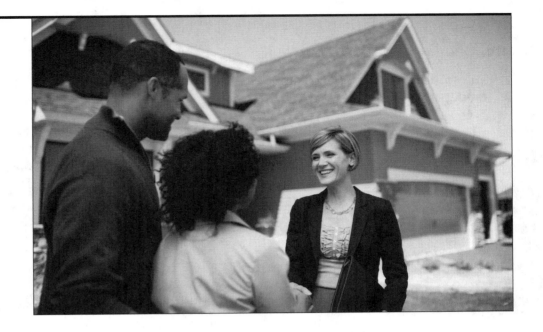

OWNERSHIP OF REAL PROPERTY

■ **KEY TERMS**

attractive nuisance
  doctrine
CERCLA
common elements
common interest
  subdivision
community apartment
  project
community property
community property
  with right of
  survivorship
condominium
corporation
fictitious name

general partner
Homeowner Association
  (HOA)
joint tenancy
joint ventures
limited common
  elements
limited liability
limited liability company
limited partnerships
partition action
partnership
planned unit
  development

recreational user
  immunity
real estate investment
  trust
severalty
standard subdivision
stock cooperative
survivorship
tenancy by the entirety
tenancy in common
time-share
undivided interest
  subdivision
unincorporated
  association

Every property must have an owner. In Pennsylvania, a 600-acre forest that was deeded to God reverted to the state *for nonpayment of taxes.*

■ OWNERSHIP IN SEVERALTY

Ownership in **severalty** is ownership by one individual or corporation. (A corporation is a legal entity.) It is singular ownership with no other party or parties having a common ownership interest. A city (municipal corporation) would own city property in severalty, as would an individual owning property by himself or herself.

■ TENANCY IN COMMON

A **tenancy in common** is undivided ownership—of real or personal property—by more than one party without the right of survivorship. An undivided interest means that the tenant in common has a share in the whole and not ownership of a separate portion. For example, a tenant in common having a one-half interest in ten acres of land would have a one-half interest in the entire ten acres and not one-half of the land (five acres).

The right of **survivorship** means the right of other co-owners to receive one co-owner's interest upon his or her death. Upon the death of a tenant in common, his or her interest does not pass by survivorship to the other tenants in common. The interest passes by will or intestate succession to the heirs of the decedent. If the tenant in common dies intestate (without a will) and leaves no heirs, the interest will escheat (pass) to the state. (Unmarried partners who live together will often choose tenancy in common as their form of ownership when the survivorship feature is not desired.)

Interests of tenants in common do not have to be equal and can be created at different times by different instruments; however, each tenant in common has an equal right of possession. Therefore, if one tenant in common is in sole possession of the premises, that tenant in common will not be obligated to the other tenants in common for rent unless he or she agrees to it. A tenant in common cannot, in the absence of an agreement to the contrary, exclude other tenants in common from the property.

One tenant in common cannot give an exclusive lease to a third party without the agreement of all of the tenants in common because such a lease would be inconsistent with the other tenants' equal rights of possession.

A tenant in common who farms the property does not have to share the crops with the other tenants in common. However, if a tenant in common receives rents or royalties from a third person, the other tenants in common have the right to share in the income based on their proportional ownership.

See *Black v. Black* (1949) 91 C.A.2d 328 for rights of a tenant in possession.

If one tenant in common pays reasonable and necessary property expenses or taxes, that tenant is entitled to recover proportional shares of the expenditures from the other tenant(s) in common.

While a tenant in common can get contributions for repairs, one tenant in common cannot get contributions for improvements from the others if the others have not agreed to the improvements. Otherwise, it would be possible to make unauthorized improvements beyond the payment ability of another tenant in common. The result would be that the tenant in common who could not pay his or her share of the cost could end up losing his or her interest.

One tenant in common can get an injunction against another tenant in common to stop waste. One tenant in common also can force another to make an accounting for rents, royalties, expenses, and profits of a property held in common.

Under extremely unusual circumstances, a tenant in common who has exclusive use may acquire title from the other tenants in common based on adverse possession. Should a tenant in common who has exclusive possession of the jointly owned property clearly indicate that his or her possession is intended to preclude the possession by the other tenants in common, that action could be considered an ouster. The tenant's use would be hostile and would enable him or her to obtain title by adverse possession by continuing the open, notorious, and hostile use continuously for a five-year period and paying the taxes for that period (see Chapter 9).

No consent of the other tenants in common is required to transfer an interest or even a portion of an interest to another.

A tenant in common can encumber his or her own undivided interest. Any subsequent foreclosure by a creditor would apply only to the interest of that tenant in common.

A conveyance to two or more persons, other than spouses, that fails to indicate how title is to be held will pass title as a tenancy in common.

■ JOINT TENANCY

Joint tenancy, like tenancy in common, is an undivided interest in either real or personal property (or both). Unlike a tenancy in common, however, joint tenancy has the right of survivorship. Upon the death of a joint tenant, the interest the deceased joint tenant held ceases to exist. The interest is incapable of being transferred by will or by intestate succession. The surviving joint tenants receive the interest of the deceased joint tenant. Joint tenancy property does not need to be probated, because it could not be part of the estate of the deceased person. Because of survivorship, the property interest passes to the surviving joint tenants free of claims of the personal creditors of the deceased.

Assume Annie, Brenda, and Connie are joint tenants. If Connie dies, Annie and Brenda will be joint tenants. If Brenda then dies, Annie will be an owner in severalty.

Annie_____ Brenda_____ Connie   Joint tenants
Each owns an undivided one-third interest.

Connie dies:
Annie_____ Brenda _____
Annie and Brenda are joint tenants; each owns an undivided ½ interest.

Brenda dies:
Annie _____
Annie owns the entire property in severalty.

Because corporations can live forever, which would defeat survivorship, corporations cannot hold title as joint tenants. Also, because of potential conflicts with community property laws, an unmarried person ordinarily should not own property in joint tenancy with a married person unless the spouse of the married person signs a quitclaim deed or otherwise consents to the joint tenancy.

The legal principle that a murderer cannot inherit from the victim applies to joint tenancies. The courts will not allow the murderer to profit by survivorship. They will view the victim as being a tenant in common, and the interest will pass to the heirs.

In the event of the simultaneous deaths of all of the joint tenants, the Uniform Simultaneous Death Act will treat the interest of each of the joint tenants as if he or she had survived the other(s). This would result in separate probates of each of their interests.

For title purposes, when a joint tenant dies, the survivor(s) should record, in the county where the property is located, either

- a certified copy of a court decree determining the fact of death and describing the property, or
- a certified copy of the death certificate (an affidavit identifying the deceased as one of the joint tenants in described property) and an affidavit of survivorship normally would be attached.

Creation of Joint Tenancy

The conveying instrument must expressly state that ownership will be held in joint tenancy; otherwise any conveyance to two or more persons, other than spouses, will be considered a conveyance to tenants in common.

Two couples could own property as tenants in common with each couple's interest a joint tenancy. A deed could express this through language such as "Tom and Helen Smith (as joint tenants) as tenants in common with Frank and Ethyl Jones (as joint tenants)." Also required to create a joint tenancy are the four unities of

1. time,
2. title,
3. interest, and
4. possession.

Memory Tool: TTIP

Time. Joint tenants must get their interests at the same time. Formerly, if a person who owned property in severalty wished to create a joint tenancy with another, the grantor had to convey interest to a third party (a straw man), who would then convey the property back to the grantor and the other party(ies) as joint tenants. One problem with this procedure was that if any judgments against the straw man existed, they would become encumbrances on the property the instant the straw man took title. The property conveyed as the joint tenancy thereby could be subject to liens. Now, Section 683 of the Civil Code makes it unnecessary to follow this procedure. A joint tenancy can be created by an owner simply deeding the property to himself or herself and the other party(ies) as joint tenants.

Title. Joint tenants must acquire their interests by the same document.

Interest. Joint tenants, unlike tenants in common, must have equal interests. A grant that provides for unequal interests will create a tenancy in common even if it states that the property being conveyed will be owned in joint tenancy.

Possession. Possession is the only one of the four unities that is also applicable to tenants in common. The joint tenants' rights as to use and contributions are identical with those of tenants in common.

Termination of Joint Tenancy

The sale or transfer by a joint tenant of an interest terminates the joint tenancy as it applies to that interest.

Assume Art, Bart, and Curt are joint tenants. If Curt sells to Dirk, then Art and Bart will remain joint tenants, each with an undivided one-third interest, and Dirk will have an undivided one-third interest as a tenant in common.

Art_____ Bart _____Curt   Joint tenants
Art_____ Bart _____Curt
                          ↓

                        Dirk

If Bart dies, Art will take Bart's interest by survivorship, and Art will be a tenant in common with Dirk. The joint tenancy cannot continue because no two owners have the four unities of joint tenancy. Art will have an undivided two-thirds interest as a tenant in common with Dirk, who will be a tenant in common with an undivided one-third interest.

Art _____Dirk   Tenants in common

One of the problems with a joint tenancy is that a joint tenant can convey their interest to another, and the other joint tenant(s) might be completely unaware that the survivorship rights have been defeated.

> **Case Study**
> The case of *Riddle v. Harmon* (1980) 102 C.A.3d 524 held that one joint tenant can terminate the joint tenancy by a conveyance to himself or herself as a tenant in common.

Bankruptcy of a joint tenant terminates the joint tenancy as it applies to the bankrupt party's interest.

A judgment against one joint tenant does not sever the joint tenancy, but levying execution against the property and having a sale does end the joint tenancy. If the joint tenant dies prior to the execution of the judgment against the property, the property will pass free and clear of the debt to the surviving joint tenant(s).

A joint tenant can borrow on their personal interest without destroying the joint tenancy. If the loan is foreclosed, the joint tenancy, of course, will be broken. However, if the borrower dies, the surviving joint tenant(s) will get the interest free and clear. In lending on a joint tenant's interests, a lender would want to couple the loan with a life insurance policy that would pay off the loan in the event of the borrower's death.

Because of changing relationships, a person might no longer wish to remain a joint tenant or tenant in common. In that case, a **partition action** can be brought to break up the joint tenancy or tenancy in common. (By agreement, the parties can give up their rights to a partition action.) If possible, the court will order the property divided among the co-owners.

When division is not possible or practical, the property will be sold under judicial supervision and the sale proceeds divided among the co-owners.

> **Case Study**
> In the case of *Formosa Corp. v. Rogers* (1952) 108 C.A.2d 397, the plaintiff sought a sale of a movie studio where Mary Pickford Rogers owned a 41/80 ownership. The court held that the party seeking partition by sale had the burden of proof that sale was necessary for equitable distribution. In this case, the court determined that the value of the separate properties was less than the value of the whole because the property as a whole had added value resulting from its adaptation for use in making motion pictures.

Note: A number of states, other than California, have a special form of joint tenancy for husband and wife known as **tenancy by the entirety**. It differs from joint tenancy in that neither spouse can separately convey an interest during the lifetime of the other spouse.

■ COMMUNITY PROPERTY

Community property, originally a Spanish concept, holds that property acquired by a husband and wife during marriage is owned equally by the husband and wife. This principle differed greatly from the early English concept that the wife's property became the property of the husband.

As noted earlier, the Treaty of Guadalupe Hidalgo ending the Mexican War in 1848 called for the rights of Mexican ownership of property to be respected. Mexico had adopted the Spanish concept of community property. The California Constitution specifically adopted the community property concept.

There are nine community property sates: Arizona, California, Idaho, Louisiana, Nevada, New Mexico, Texas, Washington, and Wisconsin. Puerto Rico allows ownership of community property, and in Alaska, parties can agree to community property ownership.

Formerly, in California, property acquired in the wife's name alone was presumed to be her separate property. Now, property acquired by either spouse alone during marriage is presumed to be community property. The burden of proving it to be separate property falls on the spouse claiming separate property.

Property that is acquired with community property funds is community property.

Property that is acquired by one spouse using the credit of the other spouse is community property.

Separate property remains separate property unless it becomes commingled so as to be indistinguishable from community property, in which case it could become community property by the commingling. One spouse's use of community property to improve the separate property of the other spouse is considered a gift and is not commingling. One spouse's use of community property to improve their separate property could be commingling, which would convert the separate property to community property. However, the courts are more likely to give a community property interest proportionally based on the community property investment.

Exclusions

In California, excluded from the equal ownership of community property are

- property separately owned by husband or wife prior to marriage,
- rents and profits from separate property,
- property acquired by either spouse by gift or inheritance,
- property acquired with separate property funds,

- damages received for personal injuries, and

- earnings and accumulations of a spouse while living separate and apart (includes legal separation).

Case Study

The case of *Marriage of Rico* (1992) 10 C.A.4th 706 involved a couple who lived together and purchased a house as tenants in common prior to their marriage. After their marriage, they refinanced their home and converted title to joint tenancy. In dividing the community property upon the couple's divorce, the court determined that each party should receive their separate property contribution before the appreciated value was equally divided. However, the court ruled that proper measure of reimbursement was the fair market value of each spouse's separate property at the time of conversion to community property, not the original contribution. This case shows how complicated the division of separate and community property can become upon dissolution of marriage.

Case Study

In re Marriage of Branco (1996) 47 C.A.4th 1621 involved a situation where community property funds were used to pay off a mortgage on the separate property of one spouse. The court held that the community is entitled to its share of the appreciation during the marriage.

Generally, when there is no marriage, there is no community property. When one or both spouses believe that a valid marriage existed, however, the property acquired that would have been community property had a valid marriage existed will be considered quasi-marital property and will be divided as if it were community property.

Domestic Partnerships

As of January 2005, same sex domestic couples, although not married, may register with the California Secretary of State. Property acquired with earned income after registration will be considered equally owned as if community property. This registration is also available to unmarried opposite sex couples where one party is at least 72 years of age.

Note: The purpose of domestic partnerships for older, opposite sex couples was likely to allow couples to retain greater Social Security benefits and also have property rights similar to community property.

> ### Case Study
> *Estate of Leslie* (1984) 37 C.3d 186 involved a couple married in Mexico who lived together for nine years in California. The probate court determined that the marriage was invalid because it was not recorded as required under Mexican law. The supreme court reversed the decision and held that as a matter of fairness, a putative spouse (reputed or commonly established spouse) is entitled to succeed to the property of the deceased spouse in the same manner as a legal spouse.

> ### Case Study
> *Estate of Vargas* (1974) 36 C.A.3d 714 involved a decedent who had led a double life. He had two separate families, neither of which knew of the other's existence. The Court of Appeal affirmed the trial court's finding that the second wife was a putative spouse even though the second marriage of 24 years was void. She had married with the good-faith belief that her husband had been divorced from his first wife. The court deemed it equitable to divide the property equally between the legal and putative spouses.

Premarital and Marital Agreements

Premarital agreements about property rights generally are valid.

Agreements entered into after marriage may be valid if undue influence is not a factor.

Many unmarried people living together enter into contracts concerning their property rights. These agreements may provide community-property-like rights should the relationship terminate, or may otherwise specify property rights and/or division of property. California courts will enforce these nonmarital agreements unless they are based on the consideration of sexual services.

> ### Case Study
> In the case of *In re Marriage of Stitt* (1983) 147 C.A.3d 579, a couple agreed to live together and combine their earnings. During this period, the woman acquired a vacant parcel of land in her name alone, and a residence was constructed with a loan in her name. Payments were made on the loan from a joint account. In a proceeding for dissolution of their subsequent marriage, the court held that the property was community property upon marriage. The parties had purchased the property with the intention that it be co-owned. The court held that unmarried cohabitants may enter into express or implied contracts respecting their property rights and earnings.

Case Study

The case of *Marvin v. Marvin* (1978) C. 3d 660 involved actor Lee Marvin and his live-in girlfriend of six years, Michelle Triola, who changed her name to Marvin. She claimed that Lee Marvin had promised to support her for life at the time they began living together.

The California Supreme Court ruled that Michelle Marvin had not proven the existence of the alleged contract and that California had abolished common law marriage in 1896. While nonmarital contracts—whether oral, implied, or written—may be enforced, they must be provable. The court also held that while unmarried couples can contract as to property division, if the agreement is explicitly based upon sexual services (as Lee Marvin alleged), it will be unenforceable.

Note: This was the "palimony" case that determined that living together did not in itself give property rights.

Community Property Rules

Prior to January 1, 1975, the husband was by law the manager of the community property. Community property assets were subject to the premarital and postmarital debts of the husband, but only the postmarital debts of the wife. Since January 1, 1975, each spouse has had coequal management and control of the community property. Community property now is liable for the debts of either spouse after marriage. The earnings of a spouse are not liable for the debts of the other spouse incurred prior to marriage. An exception to equal rights of management is that one spouse alone can have sole management of a business owned as community property.

Neither spouse can make a gift of community property to a third person without the other spouse's permission, because this could defeat community property rights. A gift of one spouse to the other of property that would otherwise qualify as community property would become the separate property of the donee spouse.

A married person cannot use community property funds to form a joint tenancy with a third person. Despite the language of the deed, a tenancy in common would be formed, with the married person and their spouse owning their shares as community property.

Community real property transfers, as well as leases for more than one year, require the signatures of both spouses. Neither spouse alone can encumber or obligate community real property.

Neither spouse can partition community real property by selling their one-half interest to another.

Neither spouse can encumber or sell the furniture or furnishings of the home without the other spouse. Neither spouse can sell the clothes of the other spouse or of the minor children without the other's approval.

Because community property actually is owned equally by both spouses, either spouse can transfer their one-half interest by will. If a spouse dies intestate (without a will), the community property interest will pass to the surviving spouse without probate.

Community property is divided equally upon dissolution of marriage. For the purpose of division of property or separate maintenance only, joint tenancy property is presumed to be community property. To overcome this presumption, strong and persuasive evidence to the contrary must be present (Civil Code Section 4800.1). However, a spouse is entitled to reimbursement for separate property contributions toward community property assets unless he or she has made a written waiver of that right (Civil Code Section 4800.2).

Case Study

In re Marriage of Campbell (1999) 74 C.A.4th 1058 involved a house owned by the husband prior to marriage. Because the husband had little income during the first years of marriage, the wife contributed money from her separate property to keep the marriage afloat. She also contributed $34,000 to buy equipment for the husband's business, and $66,000 to remodel her husband's house. The wife claimed that she relied on a promise to place her name on the title to the house. At marriage dissolution, she claimed an ownership interest in her husband's house claiming fraudulent conduct. The husband claimed that Family Code Section 852, which requires a written agreement, does not allow oral transmutation from separate to community properties. The wife claimed equitable estoppel as an exception to the statute of frauds.

The Sonoma County Superior Court ruled that the house was the separate property of the husband. The Court of Appeal affirmed, explaining that a writing is required for transmutation (conversion) of separate property to community property and extrinsic evidence could not be allowed. There must be a written agreement if separate property is to become community property.

Note: While contributions did not change separate property to community property, the wife could be entitled to her separate property contributions toward the property.

If property acquired in other states by California residents would have been considered community property had it been in California, it will be treated as community property upon marriage dissolution or death (quasi-community property). New residents of California should understand that once they take California residency, property owned in other states by one or both spouses will be regarded as community property if that property would have been community property had it been acquired in California.

A former advantage of community property over joint tenancy was that community property acquired a new cost basis stepped up to market value upon the death of a spouse, while only the deceased spouse's half interest in joint tenancy property acquired a new cost basis. This distinction has been removed by Revenue Ruling 87–98, which allows both joint tenancy and community property to acquire a new cost basis upon the death of a spouse if the property was acknowledged as community property before the death of the spouse. For property that has appreciated in value, this reduces the taxable income upon a later sale to the difference between the new cost basis and the sales price.

Table 8.1 shows the differences and similarities among tenancy in common, joint tenancy, and community property.

Community Property with Right of Survivorship (CPRS)

This form of ownership applies only to real estate instruments created after July 2, 2001 (Civil Code 682.1). To be effective, the **Community Property with Right of Survivorship** (CPRS) ownership must be expressly declared on the deed. When one spouse dies, the surviving spouse, as in joint tenancy, takes title regardless of any will. CPRS, as in joint tenancy, avoids probate costs and delays. Prior to death, either or both spouses can terminate the tenancy by executing and recording a new deed as to their interests.

- The major reason for using the CPRS form of ownership rather than community property is that the CPRS property is not subject to the will of the deceased and must pass to the surviving spouse.

■ TENANCY IN PARTNERSHIP

Two or more persons associated to carry on a business for profit compose a **partnership**. An agreement to share in the profits and losses would create a presumption of a partnership's existence.

A **general partner** is an active partner in the partnership who has unlimited personal liability for the debts of the partnership. A new general partner to an existing partnership would have unlimited liability for future debts of the partnership, but liability for the existing partnership debts would be limited to the extent of their contribution to capital (partner's investment).

Under the Uniform Partnership Act (Corporation Code Sections 15001–15004) general partners

- have equal rights to use partnership property for partnership purposes,
- cannot transfer their interests to another without the consent of the other partners, and
- the death or bankruptcy of a general partner dissolves the partnership.

Creditors of the partnership have first claim on the assets of a partnership. Partnership assets are not subject to attachment or execution for the private debts of

TABLE 8.1
Common Ownership Forms

	Tenancy in Common	Joint Tenancy	Community Property
Parties	Any number of persons (can be husband and wife).	Any number of persons (can be husband and wife).	Only husband and wife.
Division	Ownership can be divided into any number of interests, equal or unequal.	Ownership interests cannot be divided and must be equal.	Ownership interests are equal.
Title	Each co-owner has a separate legal title to an undivided interest.	There is only one title to the whole property.	Title is the "community" (similar to title being in a partnership).
Possession	Equal right of possession.	Equal right of possession.	Equal right of possession.
Conveyance	Each co-owner's interest may be conveyed separately by its owner.	Conveyance by one co-owner without the others breaks the joint tenancy.	Both co-owners must join in conveyance of real property; separate interests cannot be conveyed.
Purchaser's Status	Purchaser becomes a tenant in common with the other co-owners.	Purchaser becomes a tenant in common with the other co-owners.	Purchaser can acquire only whole title of community, cannot acquire a part of it.
Death	Upon co-owner's death, their interest passes by will to the devisees or heirs; no survivorship right.	Upon co-owner's death, their interest ends and cannot be willed; survivor owns the property by survivorship.	Upon co-owner's death, half goes to survivor in severalty; up to one half goes by will or succession to others (consult attorney with specific questions).
Successor's Status	Devisees or heirs become tenants in common.	Last survivor owns property in severalty.	If passing by will, tenancy in common between devisee and survivor results.
Creditor's Rights	Co-owner's interest may be sold upon execution sale to satisfy a creditor; creditor Purchaser becomes a tenant in common.	Co-owner's interest may be sold upon execution sale to satisfy creditor; joint tenancy is broken, and creditor becomes tenant in common.	Co-owner's interests cannot be seized and sold separately; the whole property may be sold to satisfy debts of either husband or wife, depending on the debt (consult attorney with specific questions).
Presumption	Favored in doubtful cases except husband and wife (see Community Property).	Must be expressly stated and properly formed.	Strong presumption that property acquired by husband and wife is community property.

the partners. However, bankruptcy of a partner would dissolve the partnership as it applies to the bankrupt partner, which would allow the creditors to reach the bankrupt partner's share of partnership assets.

Partners' interests are undivided. The interests need not be equal, but in the absence of any agreement, the partners have equal rights in the partnership.

Spouses of partners do not have a direct community property interest in partnership property. Partnership property can be conveyed by the partnership without the signatures of the spouses of the partners.

The heirs of a deceased partner have no right to the partnership business, because a partnership requires consent. The heirs are entitled only to the value of the deceased partner's share of the assets over the liabilities, or surplus, not to the continuing business.

General partnership agreements need not be in writing to be valid.

A partnership can acquire property in the name of the partnership. The recording of a statement of partnership that has been signed, acknowledged, and verified by two or more partners is proof of membership in the partnership. A bona fide purchaser for value from the partnership can rely on the statement about the identity of all of the partners and be protected against unnamed parties claiming a partnership interest.

If a partner takes title to partnership property in their separate name, other partners can claim their interests by showing it to be partnership property.

While a partner is entitled to an accounting of cash or property from other partners, a partner cannot sue the partnership; in so doing, the partner in effect would be suing himself.

A partner cannot compete with her partnership. See *Leff v. Gunter* (1983) 33 C.3d 508 for an example of this.

Case Study

Enea v. Superior Court (2005) 132 C.A. 4th 1559 involved a falling out between partners when a partner questioned the below-market rent being paid by one of the partners to rent the partnership property (his law office). The defendant moved for summary judgment on the grounds that Corporation Code 16404(b) and (c) state there is no duty or obligation when a partner's conduct furthers the partners own business. The defendant claimed that they owned no fiduciary duty to the plaintiff to pay fair market rent. After judgment for the defendant, the plaintiff appealed.

The Appeal Court reversed ruling that the conduct of the defendant general partnership in charging themselves below-market rent violated their fiduciary duties as partners. They pointed out that a partnership is a fiduciary relationship, and partners cannot take advantages for themselves at the expense of the partnership.

Fictitious Name

A **fictitious name** is a name that does not include the surname of every partner. If a partnership fails to comply with the fictitious name statutes, the partnership cannot sue or defend a suit in the partnership name on contracts made using the fictitious name.

To comply with the fictitious name statutes, the partnership must

- file, within 40 days of beginning business, a fictitious name statement with the county clerk that identifies the principals, the business, and its fictitious name; and

- publish, within 30 days of filing, the fictitious name statement in a newspaper of general circulation within the county where the principal place of business is located, once a week for four successive weeks.

All fictitious name statements expire at the end of five years from December 31 of the year filed with the county clerk. Renewal statements again must be filed, but need not be advertised.

A partnership can abandon a fictitious name by filing a statement of abandonment.

Taxation of Partnerships

An advantage that partnerships have over corporations is that partnerships do not pay income tax. Taxes are paid by the individual partners, while a corporation has double taxation: corporate profit is taxed, and then the stockholders also are taxed on their dividends.

Termination of Partnerships

Partnerships may be terminated by

- agreement,

- bankruptcy of a partner or the partnership,

- court order that results when a partner petitions the court for a dissolution of the partnership, or

- death of a general partner.

Joint Ventures

Joint ventures are partnerships for a single undertaking rather than a continuing business. Because a joint venture is set up for a limited purpose, the implied authority of its members is more limited than in a general partnership.

A joint venturer does not necessarily have the power to bind the other joint venturers. A joint venture is generally considered a partnership. A joint venture is taxed in the same way as a partnership (taxes are paid by the individual joint venturers), and joint venturers also have the joint and several liability of partners as to third parties. Unlike in a partnership, one joint venturer can sue the joint venture. The death of a partner automatically terminates a partnership, but the death of a joint venturer does not necessarily dissolve the joint venture. Control of the joint venture is normally given to a managing partner.

Limited Partnerships

Limited partnerships are partnerships in which the limited partners have limited liability rather than the unlimited liability of a general partnership. Limited partners are liable only to the extent of their investment. However, a limited partnership must have at least one general partner who has unlimited liability.

Limited partnership names must end with "A California Limited Partnership." The agreement must be in writing, and a formal certificate of limited partnership must be filed. A limited partner cannot allow their name to be used in a manner that would indicate he or she is a general partner.

The 1983 Revised Limited Partnership Act (Corporation Code Sections 15611–15721) allows partners to contribute services, but not a promise concerning future services (formerly, a limited partner could not provide anything other than money).

A limited partner can get an accounting from the general partner, and the limited partners can oust the general partner for cause.

> **Case Study**
>
> The case of *BT-1 v. Equitable Life Assurance Society* (1999) 75 C.A.4th 1406 involved a partnership that owned real property. Equitable was the general partner, and BT-1 was the limited partner. Equitable purchased $62.5 million in loans against the property for the discounted price of $38.5 million. Equitable then demanded payment and took sole title to the property by foreclosure. BT-1 sued Equitable for its loss of equity as well as the gain from the discharge of indebtedness.
>
> While the trial court entered judgment for Equitable, the Court of Appeal reversed. It ruled that the acquisition of partnership debt by a general partner is a breach of fiduciary duty and the duty cannot be contracted away in the partnership agreement. Equitable was BT-1's partner, not its lender, and it lost sight of this basic distinction in its haste to pounce upon the loan. A general partner cannot take advantage of a limited partner by self-dealing.

Relatively few new limited partnerships are being formed today because of the advantages offered by another form of operation known as the **limited liability company**, covered later in this chapter.

Syndicates.   Syndicates are generally limited partnerships. Real estate syndicates fall under the jurisdiction of the Department of Corporations.

Real estate brokers are authorized by the Corporation Code to sell real estate security interests without having to obtain a broker/dealer license from the Department of Corporations.

An investor in a real estate syndicate has the advantage of the limited liability of a corporation investor. That is, the investor's liability is limited to the amount invested.

A major attraction of syndicates to investors formerly was their unlimited tax shelter aspect; losses from depreciation could be passed through to the investors. Current tax laws do not allow the use of losses on these passive investments. Consequently, interest in syndicates has greatly diminished.

Trusts.   Property may be held in the name of a trust for a specific purpose, such as for a charitable purpose. Living trusts (revocable) are used for estate planning purposes, as probate can be avoided. Community property placed in a living trust would still entitle each spouse to community property interests.

■ REAL ESTATE INVESTMENT TRUSTS

Real estate investment trusts allow smaller investors to pool their resources for quality investments with limited liability. Under federal law, a **real estate investment trust (REIT)** is an unincorporated trust or association managed by a trustee that meets the following criteria:

- It cannot hold property for sale to customers in the ordinary course of business.

- It must be owned by at least 100 investors.

- Five persons or fewer cannot hold more than a 50 percent interest.

- Interests must be in the form of transferable shares or certificates. California requires that each share carry with it an equivalent vote in determining trust policy.

- Investments must account for at least 90 percent of the trust's gross income.

- Up to 75 percent of the trust's gross income may result from short-term gains on sales of stocks or securities held for less than six months plus sales of real estate held for less than four years. This does not apply to involuntary conversion, such as eminent domain.

If the real estate investment trust distributes 90 percent or more of its ordinary earnings to shareholders, it is taxed only on its retained earnings at the corporate rate.

The trustee in a real estate investment trust must have exclusive power to manage the trust. Trusts are either equity trusts (real estate), mortgage trusts (investments in mortgages and trust deeds), or hybrid trusts (investments in both real estate and mortgages).

Unlike syndicate interests, which are often difficult to resell, many REITs are listed on major stock exchanges so that interests are more readily salable.

■ CORPORATIONS

A **corporation** is a separate legal entity established under state law by the filing of articles of incorporation with the secretary of state. It can own property in the corporate name.

Shareholders of a corporation have limited liability and have no direct management of the corporation.

A disadvantage of corporations is double taxation. The corporation pays income tax on its profits and dividends paid to stockholders from the profits are taxed to the stockholders.

Shareholders elect the directors, who set corporate policy. The directors appoint the corporate officers, who operate the corporation. The authority of the corporate officers is set forth in the corporate bylaws, which are the rules of the corporation.

Because a corporation is a separate legal entity, shareholders can sue the corporation. Also, because it is a legal entity, corporations have an unlimited life and theoretically "live" forever.

A corporate conveyance that involves a sale of all or a majority of the corporate assets must be approved by a majority of the stockholders.

If a corporation exists in name only—that is, individual funds are commingled with corporate funds—the courts will "pierce the corporate veil" and determine that the corporation is in fact a partnership or sole proprietorship, and the limited liability protection of the corporation will be lost.

A closely held, or close, corporation is one in which the stock is held by a few persons who actively control the business. Closely held corporations often are able to avoid significant corporate taxation by not showing a profit. They accomplish this through salaries, benefits, and bonuses to the officers, who are also the stockholders.

Foreign Corporations

A domestic corporation is a corporation organized in California. A corporation organized in any other state is a foreign corporation in California. To do business in California, a foreign corporation must get permission from the secretary of state; otherwise it cannot sue in California courts. The foreign corporation also must file, with the secretary of state, a consent to allow legal process to be served against the corporation by service on the secretary of state; this eliminates the need to go to the state of incorporation to bring suit.

S Corporations

As mentioned earlier, corporations are subject to double taxation. To avoid this, a small corporation can elect to be taxed as a partnership by becoming an S corporation. An S corporation must meet the following criteria:

■ It must have fewer than 75 shareholders.

- Only one category of stock may be issued.

- All stockholders must be individuals, not corporations.

- The business cannot receive more than 20 percent of its income from interest, rents, dividends, and royalties. (This excludes many real estate–related businesses.)

- The corporation cannot be affiliated with any other corporation. It must be independent.

- It must be incorporated in the United States.

Limited Liability Companies (LLC)

Limited liability companies (LLCs) provide the **limited liability** protection of corporations without the regulations associated with S corporations. The advantages offered by an LLC have resulted in fewer decisions to form S corporations or limited partnerships. LLCs have operating agreements that are similar to corporate bylaws, but unlike corporations, they do not have perpetual existence. One or more members can file articles of organization with the secretary of state to engage in any lawful business activity. They must also file annual statements.

While it takes at least two members to form a limited partnership, one person can form an LLC. In a limited partnership, a limited partner would lose the liability protection by actively engaging in business matters. In an LLC, member activity does not affect the protection from personal liability.

■ UNINCORPORATED ASSOCIATIONS

An **unincorporated association** is a nonprofit organization that under common law could not hold title because it is not an entity. In California, however, unincorporated associations for religious, scientific, social, educational, recreational, or benevolent purposes may hold title to real property necessary for their purposes in the name of the organization. Property nonessential to the operation of the organization cannot be held for more than ten years.

An unincorporated association can convey property by a deed executed by the president and secretary or others as authorized by the bylaws. Recording a verified certificate listing the names of officers and other persons authorized to convey would be conclusive proof that a deed so executed was a properly executed conveyance.

In California, members of such associations are not personally liable for leases or purchases of property used by the association unless they agree to liability in writing.

■ MULTIPLE HOUSING DEVELOPMENTS

Under the Subdivided Lands Law, the division of property into five or more parcels for the purpose of sale, lease, or financing is considered a subdivision. Subdivision classifications include the following:

- **Standard subdivision**: A standard subdivision is a land division with no common areas.

- **Common interest subdivision**: A common interest is a division whereby owners own their unit, separate interests, and an area in common with other owners. Common interests include condominiums, planned developments, stock cooperatives, community apartment projects, and time-share projects.

- **Undivided interest subdivision**: An undivided interest is a development in which owners are tenants in common with all other owners without an exclusive right of ownership of a particular lot or unit. An example would be many of the large, member-owned recreational vehicle parks. Purchasers in an undivided interest subdivision have a three-day right of rescission. (The subdivision process and the Interstate Land Sales Full Disclosure Act are covered in Chapter 13.)

There are several types of ownership forms for common-interest and undivided-interest subdivisions.

Condominiums

A **condominium** is an interest in real property consisting of an undivided interest in common in a portion of a parcel together with a separate interest in space. The property can be residential, commercial, or industrial. Most condominium owners own their unit in fee simple.

A condominium is really a vertical subdivision with the unit owner having a separate deed showing ownership of the airspace in fee simple but owning the common areas, including the land, as a tenant in common with the other owners.

Each unit owner can encumber their unit interest separately without affecting the interests of the other owners. Each unit owner pays separate real property taxes that include a share of the common areas. A condominium owner may not sell his or her unit without conveying the rights to the common areas.

Areas for use of all of the owners in a common interest development are known as **common elements**. Common areas for the exclusive use of designated owners (such as a parking space or storage locker) are known as **limited common elements**.

A **homeowners' association** (HOA) board of directors, elected by the owners, is the governing body for the condominium. (Homeowners' associations also govern cooperatives, community apartment projects, planned developments, and time-shares.) Homeowners' associations can place reasonable assessments against the units, which if unpaid are liens against the individual units. Homeowner associations can record their lien against a member's property for unpaid assessments if the amount exceeds $1,800. There is a 90-day redemption right after lien foreclosure. Membership in a homeowners' association is generally a deed covenant that runs with the land. A homeowners' association must prepare an operating budget and must perform a reserve study every three years to determine adequacy of reserves.

What are homeowner responsibilities and what is the responsibility of the homeowners' association can be a matter of contention.

Case Study

The case of *Dover Village Assn. v. Jennison* (2010) 191 C.A. 4th 123 involved a sewer line that ruptured beneath a homeowner's unit. The sewer line exclusively serviced the homeowner's unit and joined to the condominium project's main sewer line. The HOA claimed that the homeowner should bear the repair costs, and the homeowner contended it was common area and the HOA had the duty to maintain it.

The trial judge ruled that sewer pipes within the concrete slab were part of the common area and the HOA had a duty to maintain it. The homeowner was awarded attorney fees and costs.

The Court of Appeal affirmed, pointing out that a sewer system is one of interconnecting pipes and it would be unreasonable to differentiate between parts of the system.

Case Study

In the case of *Sui v. Price* (2011) 196 C.A. 4th 933, homeowners had a disabled vehicle parked in their exclusive parking space for three years before the HOA amended rules to prohibit storage of inoperable vehicles in parking spaces. The homeowners refused to remove the vehicle, and the HOA had it towed away. The homeowners sued for trespass and emotional distress and discrimination because the HOA association rule prohibits discrimination against owners.

The Court of Appeal upheld the trial court in that the new rules were not discriminatory and were reasonable.

Note: Just because only one homeowner is affected by a rule does not in itself make it discriminatory.

Stock Cooperatives

A **stock cooperative** is a corporation formed for the purpose of holding title to an improved property. Each shareholder has the exclusive right to the occupancy of a unit through a proprietary lease with the elected governing body. The transfer of shares also transfers occupancy by a sublease.

While a condominium owner can freely transfer their unit, most cooperative associations have the right to approve the purchaser of stock before the stock seller can sublease to the stock purchaser.

There are two basic disadvantages of cooperatives:

1. The stockholder does not have ownership of a unit, so borrowing on equity can be more difficult.

2. There could only be one tax bill. If tax payments are not made by all owners, a lien can be placed on the entire property. If there is only one deed of trust, the failure of one or more owners to make their share of the payment also could result in the entire cooperative's being foreclosed unless the other owners pay the defaulting owner's share.

Sale of developments of five or more cooperative units fall under the jurisdiction of the real estate commissioner. Cooperatives with four or fewer units are under the jurisdiction of the corporation commissioner.

Community Apartment Projects

In a **community apartment project**, the owners purchase the property together as tenants in common with the right to exclusive occupancy of their units through a lease agreement.

Owners could have difficulty borrowing on their undivided interest. Because there is only one trust deed, the failure of one owner to pay could jeopardize all of the owners. Because of these problems, resale of an owner's interest is often very difficult.

Sale of developments of five or more units are under the jurisdiction of the real estate commissioner.

Planned Developments

A *planned development*, better known as a **planned unit development (PUD)**, is a subdivision with the unit and the land under it owned by the individual unit. Areas for the use of all of the owners, such as recreational facilities or common areas, are owned by all of the owners as tenants in common. The major difference between a planned development and a condominium is that in a planned development, owners actually own their own land and not just airspace. Many California developments are PUDs.

Time-Sharing Projects

A **time-share** is an interval or fractionalized ownership whereby the owner gets the exclusive use of a unit annually for a set period of time. Time-share interests may be in perpetuity, for life, or for a stated number of years.

Twelve or more time-share estates of five years or more are considered a subdivision and fall under the jurisdiction of the real estate commissioner. A real estate license is required to sell any time-share interests in California. Because of abusive sales tactics of some time-share developers, purchasers have a rescission right of seven days following their offer.

Time-shares are often marketed based on exchange privileges with other time-share developments. The buyer must be informed that the purchase does not guarantee a right to use or occupy accommodations other than the unit purchased.

A resort vacation club is similar to a time-share, except the investor does not purchase an ownership interest. The investor has the right to rent a unit and use club facilities. These developments are now under the control of the real estate commissioner and are classified as time-share projects.

Sale of Units

Prior to transfer of title, owners of condominiums, community apartment projects, cooperatives, and planned developments must provide purchasers with a copy of restrictions, bylaws, and articles of incorporation, plus an owners' association financial statement including any delinquent assessments and costs.

An owners' association must furnish the owner with a copy of the latest version of documents within ten days of request by an owner. A reasonable fee for doing this may be charged. A homeowners' association cannot charge a transfer fee when units are sold that exceed their actual cost of changing their ownership records.

■ OWNER LIABILITY

An owner of real property is liable for injuries to other persons and/or property caused by negligence in maintaining or operating the property.

Case Study

In the case of *Salinas v. Martin* (2008) 166 C.A. 4th 1098b, a homeowner who was having construction work done at his residence allowed a contractor to store equipment and material in the fenced backyard. The contractor and his employee, Salinas, had permission to enter the backyard at any time to retrieve equipment and material. The homeowner also hired gardeners who had two pit bulls. The owner consented to the dogs running free in the yard when the gardeners were working. The contractor told the homeowner he was afraid of the dogs and that they should not be on the property. Salinas was attacked and bitten by the dogs when he attempted to retrieve material. He managed to get away by climbing on top of the owner's car.

The trial court granted summary judgment for the homeowner. The trial court used a residential landlord standard of care that requires actual knowledge that the dogs were dangerous.

The Court of Appeal reversed. Even though the homeowner had no knowledge of the danger, he allowed the gardeners to keep the dogs in the yard and permitted the contractor's entry. He could have prevented a problem by requiring the animals to be restrained. The homeowner therefore bears a measure of blame.

Note: The owner has a duty of care as to contractors.

Civil Code Section 1365.9 has given individual owners in a common interest subdivision some protection from liability resulting from injuries relating to the common areas. If the association carries specified minimum liability coverage, then the individual owners will not be held liable. The coverage required is as follows:

- At least two million dollars ($2,000,000) if the common interest development consists of 100 or fewer separate interests

- At least three million dollars ($3,000,000) if the common interest development consists of more than 100 separate interests

If dangerous conditions are obvious, an injured party might be denied relief if he or she could be said to have assumed the risk.

Case Study

The case of *Melton v. Boustred* (2010) 183 C.A. 4th 521 involved a defendant who advertised a house party on Myspace.com with live music and alcoholic beverages. At the party, several guests were stabbed by unknown persons. The victims sued the homeowner for negligence and premises liability. The trial court sustained a demurrer to the complaint.

The Court of Appeal affirmed. The homeowner has no duty to a guest unless the homeowner creates a risk of criminal conduct that could injure a guest. Without knowledge that guests will be violent, the owner has no duty to foresee criminal conduct even though it was an open invitation.

Note: The plaintiffs asserted that the defendant had a duty to hire security guards and to control the number of guests.

Case Study

The case of *Privette v. Superior Court* (1993) 5 C.4th 689 involved an employee of an independent contractor who was injured by hot tar and sought to recover damages from the property owner (in addition to workers' compensation). The California Supreme Court held that employees of independent contractors, even those performing high-risk activity, can recover only their workers' compensation benefits and cannot receive damages from the property owner.

The duty of care an owner of real property owes to others extends beyond tenants or invitees. An owner's liability could extend to trespassers as well as neighbors who are injured because of dangerous conditions on the property.

> **Case Study**
> In the case of *Preston v. Goldman* (1986) 42 C.3d 108, the California Supreme Court held that a former landlord is not liable for patent defects after he or she relinquishes possession and control. In this case, the Kubichans built a pond and then sold the property to the Goldmans, who leased it with an option to buy to the Reids. The two-year-old son of the visiting plaintiff fell into the pond and suffered brain damage. While the Court of Appeal held that a landowner who creates a dangerous condition is liable for resulting injuries after transfer, the California Supreme Court reversed, ruling that the controlling factors are possession and control as to liability for patent defects, so the previous owner was not liable.

An owner is not liable for "trivial" defects and need not maintain property in an absolutely perfect condition. See *Ursino v. Big Boy Restaurants of America* (1987) 192 C.A.3d 394.

> **Case Study**
> The case of *Brunelle v. Signore* (1989) 215 C.A.3d 122 involved a weekend houseguest who was bitten by a brown recluse spider. The guest sued the homeowner for damages. The court held that negligence exists only when there has been a breach of duty. In this case, brown recluse spiders had not previously been seen on the premises, so the defendant was held not to have a duty to prevent the spider bite. The court pointed out that an owner or occupier of a property is not an insurer of the safety of persons on the premises.

Recreational User Immunity

Under Civil Code Section 846, an owner of an interest in real property owes no duty of care to keep the premises safe for entry by others for recreational purposes or to give warning of hazardous conditions. This does not apply to willful or malicious failure to guard or warn against a known dangerous condition, use, structure, or activity that is not obvious.

Recreational user immunity is not limited to rural property, as indicated in *Ornelas v. Randolph* (1993) 4 C.4th 1095.

Attractive Nuisance

California has abandoned the **Attractive Nuisance Doctrine** that placed strict requirements on property owners to protect children trespassers from dangerous conditions on their property. In California, owners are generally not liable for natural dangers and are only liable if they create or maintain a specified dangerous situation where there would be a reasonable expectation that children would be attracted. The requirement of forseeability has reduced owner liability.

Owner liability for injuries to tenants and invitees is covered in Chapter 15.

Case Study

The case of *Shipman v. Boething Treeland Farms Inc.* (2000) 77 C.A.4th 1424 involved trespassers who were injured when their all-terrain vehicle collided with a vehicle driven by a farm employee. The accident occurred at a tree-obstructed intersection on the property. The trespasser, Shipman, sued for negligent operation of a motor vehicle and premises liability. The superior court granted summary judgment for the defendant ruling that Civil Code Section 846 bars liability to recreational user trespassers.

The Court of Appeal affirmed, explaining that Section 846 affords broad immunity protection to property owners from liability to trespassers.

Note: Apparently, the immunity would extend even if the owner's employee had been driving negligently.

Case Study

The case of *Miller v. Weitzen* (2005) 133 C.A. 4th 732 involves an equestrian who was injured when her horse lost its footing while crossing a paved driveway that the riding trail went across. The property owner had paved the driveway without a permit. The rider belonged to the Rancho Santa Fe Association and her dues included a trail maintenance fee. She sued both the property owner and the Rancho Santa Fe Association for negligence.

The trial court ruled that Civil Code Section 846 (Recreational user immunity) protects both the property owner and the association from liability. However, there is an exception where a fee was paid. The trial court ruled that since the association received a fee, they were liable for the injury.

The Court of Appeals affirmed the ruling that the property owner was protected from liability and the fact that a paving permit was not obtained was irrelevant. The owners received no consideration, but the association was not so protected.

Note: There are two exceptions to the recreational user immunity statute:

1. When consideration is paid to the land owner for entrance.

2. When the property owner knows of a dangerous condition that is not obvious, not clearly marked, or not disclosed.

Case Study

In *New v. Consolidated Rock Prods.* (1984) 171 C.A.3d 681, two motorcyclists were injured when they drove their motorcycle over a 20-foot cliff at the end of an abandoned road. The owner had posted "no trespassing" signs, but the signs had little deterrent effect on motorcyclists. The court held that the defendant had acted willfully or in conscious disregard of the duty to warn plaintiffs of a dangerous condition under Civil Code Section 846 and was therefore liable for the resulting injury.

Hazardous Substance Disclosure

Health and Safety Code Section 25359.7(a) requires that owners of nonresidential real property before they sell or lease give notice to buyers or lessees of the release of hazardous substances that they know of; they also must give notice when they have reasonable cause to believe hazardous substances are located on or beneath the property.

Section 25359.7(b) requires that lessees (both nonresidential and residential) give written notice to owners regarding hazardous substances they know to have been released or believe to exist on or beneath the property. Failure to disclose constitutes a default by the tenant under the lease.

Lead Paint

Purchasers (and renters) of one to four residential units built prior to 1978 must be given a *Watch Out for Lead-Based Paint* booklet, and they have up to ten days after signing the sales contract to have the residence inspected for lead-based paint. While sellers cannot refuse to allow this inspection, this right can be waived by the buyer. Foreclosed residences and housing designed for the elderly or disabled, where children under six years old are unlikely to reside, are exempt. Penalties include fines up to $10,000, criminal prosecution, and/or treble damages to the buyer and renter.

When a landlord who receives federal subsidies or loans is confronted with deteriorating paint in a pre-1978 housing unit, the landlord must alert affected tenants to the possible health dangers and use government-certified workers and special containment practices to abate any risk of public exposure.

CERCLA

Under the Federal Comprehensive Environmental Response, Compensation, and Liability Act of 1980, CERCLA owners, operators, and lessees of real property have cleanup liability for actual or threatened release of hazardous substances. Also liable are those who generated, transported, or disposed of the hazardous substances. Under federal law, landowners may raise the defense of innocence when they conducted appropriate inquiry prior to acquiring the property. Because California law requires prior owner and lessee disclosure, the defense of innocence will likely be removed if any disclosure was made.

Case Study

The case of *Wiegmann & Rose International Corp. v. NL Industries, Inc.* (1990) 735 F. Supp. 957 involved a sale of land where the seller had dumped hazardous waste. The sale provision included an "as is" clause. The court held that the "as is" provision in the deed did not absolve the seller because the purchaser of the contaminated property had no knowledge, actual or constructive, of the presence of hazardous waste. Applying federal law, the U.S. district court ruled that NL Industries was strictly liable for cleanup costs. The liability imposed by CERCLA (Comprehensive Environmental Response, Compensation and Liability Act of 1980) is not absolved by an "as is" clause.

In several states the hazardous substance removal liens take precedence over all other liens, which could effectively wipe out a lender's interests. While both California and federal laws set forth landowner liability for removing hazardous substances, neither California nor federal law provides for such super liens.

> **Case Study**
>
> The case of *United States of America v. Maryland Bank & Trust* (1986) 632 F. Supp. 573 involved a bank that foreclosed on a mortgage it held. At the foreclosure sale, the bank bid $381,500 and took title to the property. The prior owners had used the site as a dump for hazardous waste. The EPA ordered the bank to clean up the site, and when it failed to do so, the EPA removed the toxic material at a cost of $551,713.50. The bank was held liable for the cleanup costs. The court's ruling indicates that lenders must protect themselves. Before lenders foreclose, they should consider possible liability from activities of former owners and tenants.

In California, Code of Civil Procedure Section 726.5 allows a lender to waive its security interest (lien) on environmentally impaired property and to proceed directly against the borrower for the debt. In this way the lender is spared the possible liability of cleanup costs.

Disclosures are also required for natural hazards (see Chapter 6).

■ SUMMARY

Ownership of property can be held in the following forms:

- Ownership in severalty: This is ownership by one person or corporation alone.

- Tenancy in common: This is an undivided ownership by two or more persons without the right of survivorship.

- Joint tenancy: This is an undivided interest by two or more persons with the right of survivorship. Upon the death of a joint tenant, their interest immediately passes to the surviving joint tenant(s). To form a joint tenancy, the four unities of time, title, interest, and possession are necessary.

- Community property: Property acquired by husband or wife during marriage is, with some exceptions, considered to be owned jointly and equally by the spouses. Both spouses must agree to the transfer or encumbrance of community real property.

- Community Property with Right of Survivorship: Community property where neither spouse can will their portion to a third party.

- Domestic partnerships: In California, domestic partnerships that are registered have property rights similar to community property.

- Partnership: A partnership is two or more persons associated to carry on a business for profit. Property can be held in the name of the partnership.

- Joint venture: A joint venture is a partnership for a particular undertaking rather than a continuing business.

- Limited partnership: This is a partnership that has limited partners who are inactive and have limited liability. They are liable only to the extent of their investment. Limited partnerships must have at least one general partner who is active and has unlimited liability.

- Real estate investment trust (REIT): This type of trust, having 100 or more investors, issues certificates or shares to the investors. The shares are freely transferable.

- Corporation: A corporation is an artificial person created by law that can own property. Corporations pay taxes on their profits, and the dividends paid to the shareholders are taxed to the shareholders (double taxation). S corporations are small corporations that have elected to be taxed as partnerships to avoid double taxation.

- Limited liability company (LLC): Because of ease of formation (e.g., they can be formed by a single individual) and fewer restrictions, LLCs are becoming more popular with investors than limited partnerships and S corporations.

- Unincorporated associations: These are nonprofit organizations. In California, unincorporated associations for specific purposes can hold title to real property.

Following are a number of forms of ownership for housing developments:

- Condominium: A condominium interest is a separate interest in the airspace of a unit coupled with an undivided interest in common in the common areas.

- Stock cooperative: A stock cooperative is a corporation in which each shareholder also has a lease interest that entitles him or her to occupancy of a unit.

- Community apartment project: A community apartment project is an undivided tenancy-in-common interest in the real property, with each owner having the right to occupy a unit.

- Planned development: A planned development is a subdivision in which some areas are owned in common. Individual unit owners own their own units and the land under the units.

- Time-share: A time-share is a fractionalized ownership in which each owner has exclusive use of the property for a set time period.

Owners of real property are liable for injuries to other persons and/or property resulting from negligence in maintaining their property. Owners, however, are not absolute insurers regarding the safety of others.

Owners generally have no duty of care to keep their premises safe for recreational users, but must warn against known dangers.

Owners and lessees have duties of disclosure regarding hazardous substances, and owners can be held liable for removal of hazardous waste even when they were not responsible for the waste being on their property.

■ DISCUSSION CASES

1. **When a property is given to two or more parties as life tenants, what is the relationship between the life tenants?**

    Green v. Brown (1951) 37 C.2d 391

2. One joint tenant used a property for 22 years, paid the taxes, and maintained the property. In a quiet title action, he claimed title to the entire property by adverse possession. **Does his claim have merit?**

    Dimmick v. Dimmick (1962) 58 C.2d 417

3. A property settlement between joint tenants gave the former husband exclusive possession for life. The husband agreed not to convey his interest and to pay the taxes and maintain the property. **What is the form of ownership, and what are the rights of the former wife?**

    Cole v. Cole (1956) 139 C.A.2d 691

4. A cyclist was injured in the Los Angeles National Forest when he was hit by a U.S. service truck. **Does the California recreational immunity protect the U.S. government?**

    Klein v. United States of America (2010) 50 C. 4th 68

5. A corporation authorized to enforce the provisions of a recorded declaration of restrictions assessed residents for expenses incurred in suing the city to abate airport noise. The restrictions covered activities within the complex but not those outside the complex. **Was the assessment proper?**

    Spitzer v. Kentwood Home Guardians (1972) 24 C.A.3d 215

6. Several investors purchased a 300-acre tract for $71 million. The tract was to be broken up with parcels sold by the managing partner. It was agreed that the managing partner was not to receive any sales commissions. The managing partner marked up invoices by 5 percent without notifying his partners and received sale commissions in the form of kickbacks from brokers. **What, if any, damages are the other investors entitled to?**

   Bardis v. Oates (2004) 119 C.A.4th 1

7. A man purchased a tenant in common's interest in an island-type property used for waterfowl hunting. He wanted the entire parcel, but the other tenant in common refused to sell. He brought a partition action and asked that the property be sold. **Should the court order a sale?**

   Butte Creek Island Ranch v. Crim (1982) 136 C.A.3d 360

8. A trespasser crawled through a hole in the fence of a paint-stripping plant. He climbed on top of a vat and fell through a thin plywood cover into acid. The owner who leased the premises to the operator was unaware of the vats of acid. **Is the owner liable for the injuries to the trespasser?**

   Bisetti v. United Refrigeration Corp. (1985) 174 C.A.3d 643

9. A husband whose wife was in a mental hospital acquired an interest in real property with a woman with whom he was living. He used community property for his contribution, and she used her separate property. **Can they hold title as joint tenants?**

   Yeoman v. Sawyer (1950) 99 C.A.2d 43

10. During the process of marriage dissolution, a husband alone gave a trust deed to property held in joint tenancy. The court later gave the wife title to the property. **What would be the effect of foreclosure of the trust deed?**

    Kane v. Huntley Financial (1983) 146 C.A.3d 1092

11. While standing outside the door of an arcade, the plaintiff was shot by a security guard who had been hired by a tenant of the landlord. The guard was a convicted felon who was unlawfully in possession of the gun. **Is the landlord liable for the plaintiff's injury?**

    Leakes v. Shamoun (1986) 187 C.A.3d 772

12. A law student was assaulted after leaving the school property and walking in a public area toward his car. The student alleged the school did not properly light the area. **Assuming the area was dark and the darkness allowed the student to be assaulted, is the school liable?**

    Donnell v. California Western School of Law (1988) 200 C.A.3d 715

13. After leaving a convenience store, a customer was assaulted and injured in a vacant lot adjacent to the store, where customers often parked. The defendants had a nonexclusive right to use the lot for extra parking under their lease and knew customers used the lot. On several occasions, they had sought police assistance to remove loiterers from the lot. **What, if any, were the duties of the defendants?**

   Southland Corp. v. Superior Court (1988) 203 C.A.3d 656

14. A husband signed a contract to sell community property. The buyer was unaware of the existence of the wife, who refused to perform, that is, sell. **Can the buyer obtain specific performance?**

   Andrade Development Co. v. Martin (1982) 138 C.A.3d 330

15. A motorcyclist fell into a percolation test hole and sued the landowner as well as the responsible contractor and subcontractor. **Are the defendants entitled to raise the recreational use immunity?**

   Jensen v. Kenneth Mullen Co. (1989) 211 C.A.3d 653

16. A wife quitclaimed her interest in a community property residence to her husband for value while separated. During subsequent reconciliations, she lived in the house with her husband, and community funds were used to pay the mortgage. **In a subsequent marriage dissolution, would the wife have a community property interest in the residence?**

   Marriage of Broderick (1989) 209 C.A.3d 489

17. A lessee of 40,000 acres under a U.S. Forest Service grazing permit placed a barbed wire gate across a forest service road to control his cattle. The land was also open for recreational users. The plaintiff drove his off-road motorcycle into the wire and was injured. **Is the lessee liable?**

   Hubbard v. Brown (1990) 50 C.3d 189

18. A passerby slipped on dog feces on the public sidewalk in front of a store. The owner of the store did not create the hazard; however, a municipal ordinance required landlords to keep city sidewalks clean. **Is the landlord liable for the pedestrian's injuries?**

   Selger v. Steven Bros. Inc. (1990) 222 C.A.3d 1585

19. A park brochure described a trail as safe for cycling and advertised its bikes. A tourist died from a cycling accident. **Does recreational immunity protect the defendant?**

   Pau v. Yosemite Park (1991) 928 F.2d 880

20. Migrant farmworkers built a camp without the permission or knowledge of the owner. A fire in the encampment led to personal injury. **Should the owner of the property be held liable?**

   Lucas v. Pollock (1992) 7 C.A.4th 668

21. A wife used $40,000 of her separate property to extinguish a $53,000 debt against community property. (The debtor agreed to settle for $40,000.) **What were the wife's rights upon marriage dissolution?**

   In re Marriage of Tallman (1994) 22 C.A.4th 1697

22. A five-year-old girl was jumping up and down on her bed in a second-story apartment. She sustained injuries when she fell through a window screen, dropping 30 feet. (The window ledge was 44 inches from the floor.) The building was in compliance with local codes, but the tenant claimed that the window should have had bars. **Is the landlord liable?**

   Pineda v. Ennabe (1998) 61 C.A.4th 1403

23. Two couples owned a beachfront town house as partners. On default on the trust deed, one couple purchased the property at the lender's trustee's foreclosure sale. **Was this a breach of fiduciary duty?**

   Jones v. Wagner (2001) 90 C.A.4th 466

24. A mother and her child were visiting a friend who had a pool. The mother and homeowner were watching the children play in the front yard. When the mother went to make a phone call, her child went in the back yard and drowned in the pool. **Did the homeowner have a duty to supervise the child?**

   Padilla v. Rodas (2008) 160 C.A.4th 742

25. A private farm road led to public road 172. There was no evidence of the public using the farm road. Because the road ran through rows of trees, farm vehicles traveled the road at relatively slow speeds. A truck from another farm used the private road to get to 172. It was moving at excessive speed and hit a van full of agricultural workers upon entering 172. **Was the farm owner negligent in failing to install a stop sign where the private road entered 172?**

   Garcia v. Paramount Citrus Assn. (2008) 161 C.A.4th 321

■ CHAPTER QUIZ

1. What would be the ownership form for property that is solely owned by a married woman?

   a. Community property

   b. Tenancy in common

   c. Ownership in severalty

   d. Ownership in partnership

2. Which ownership form is matched with an incorrect characteristic?

   a. Joint tenancy/undivided interest

   b. Tenancy in common/survivorship

   c. Community property/equal ownership

   d. Severalty/alone

3. To convey your property to a son and daughter on a one-third/two-thirds basis, you would want to convey title as

   a. community property.   b. tenancy in severalty.

   c. tenancy in common.   d. joint tenancy.

4. Agnes and Alfred, who were recently married, want to purchase a house together. They each want their interest to pass to their individual children from previous marriages in the event of death. They should buy the house

   a. in partnership.   b. in severalty.

   c. as tenants in common.   d. as joint tenants.

5. A single tenant in common may NOT

   a. sell her interest without approval of the other tenants in common.

   b. will her interest to her children.

   c. use the property without compensating the other tenants in common.

   d. give exclusive possession to another.

6. Which statement accurately describes a tenancy in common?

   a. Interests must be equal.

   b. There is an equal right of possession.

   c. Interests must be acquired at the same time.

   d. Interests must be acquired from the same documents.

7. Albert, Baker, Charlie, and David are joint tenants. What form of owner-ship exists when David sells to Edith and Albert then dies?

    a. Baker, Charlie, and Edith are tenants in common.

    b. Baker and Charlie are joint tenants, and Edith is a tenant in common.

    c. Albert's heirs, Baker, Charlie, and Edith are tenants in common.

    d. None of the above describes the existing ownership.

8. Thomas and Andrew own property in joint tenancy. Thomas put a $50,000 mortgage on his interest. A short time later Thomas died. Who owns the property and how?

    a. Andrew owns the property clear of the mortgage.

    b. Andrew owns the property with a mortgage against it.

    c. Because the mortgage destroyed the joint tenancy, Andrew and the heirs of Thomas own the property as tenants in common.

    d. Andrew and the mortgagee own the property as tenants in common.

9. Which is an example of a partition action?

    a. Dividing an apartment building into condominiums

    b. Any land subdivision

    c. A court proceeding to divide jointly owned property

    d. Breaking large apartments into smaller units

10. After Albert and Helen were married, they purchased a home. The $40,000 down payment was the separate property of Helen. Payments on the home were made with community property funds. Upon marriage dissolution, what are the rights of the parties to the sale proceeds from the house?

    a. Albert and Helen share the proceeds equally.

    b. Albert gets one-half of the payments made, but Helen gets the remainder.

    c. Helen is entitled to $40,000 plus one-half of the balance of the sale proceeds (if any).

    d. None of the above is true.

11. Without the consent of the other spouse, one spouse can

a. buy real estate using community property funds.

b. sell community real property.

c. give community real property away.

d. lease community real property for 18 months.

12. According to community property rules, one spouse alone may

a. sell community real property interest.

b. encumber community real property interest.

c. will community real property interest.

d. None of the above

13. Jim and Tom are general partners in a real estate office. Jim dies, leaving all of his property to his wife, Lois, who is also a real estate broker. What is the result?

a. Lois and Tom are general partners.

b. Lois has an interest in the partnership assets but not in the business.

c. Lois becomes a limited partner.

d. Lois has no interest in the business or the assets of the business.

14. A partnership that has *NOT* complied with the fictitious name statute

a. would be a limited partnership.

b. cannot sue in the partnership name.

c. is an unincorporated association.

d. is all of the above.

15. Which statement is *TRUE* of a joint venture?

a. One joint venturer can sue the joint venture.

b. The death of a joint venturer automatically dissolves the joint venture.

c. Joint venturers have the same power to bind other joint venturers as partners have to bind other partners.

d. All are true.

16.   A new limited partnership *MUST*

    a.   end its name with "A Limited Partnership."

    b.   have a written agreement.

    c.   file a formal certificate of limited partnership.

    d.   do all of the above.

17.   Under federal law, a real estate investment trust must have

    a.   a corporate charter.   b.   fewer than 100 investors.

    c.   100 or more investors.   d.   1,000 or more investors.

18.   Two separate corporations could hold title together as

    a.   tenants in severalty.   b.   joint tenants.

    c.   community property.   d.   a partnership.

19.   Which is (are) true regarding income tax?

    a.   Partnerships do not pay income tax.

    b.   A disadvantage of corporations is double taxation.

    c.   An S corporation does not pay taxes.

    d.   All of the above are true.

20.   Rights of occupancy of owners in a cooperative are based on

    a.   a proprietary lease.

    b.   the articles of incorporation.

    c.   the bylaws of the association.

    d.   individual deeds to each unit.

21.   Ownership as tenants in common with a right to occupy a unit describes a

    a.   cooperative.

    b.   community apartment project.

    c.   planned development.

    d.   None of the above

22. Interval exclusive occupancy coupled with a joint ownership likely refers to a(n)

    a. cooperative.

    b. community apartment project.

    c. undivided interest subdivision.

    d. time-share.

23. The seller of a condominium property must provide the purchaser with

    a. a copy of the restrictions.

    b. the association bylaws.

    c. the owners' association financial statement showing delinquent assessments.

    d. all the documents above.

24. An owner is likely to be liable to a recreational user of his or her property when

    a. he or she failed to post "No Trespassing" signs.

    b. he or she failed to warn against a dangerous condition.

    c. the property is urban in nature.

    d. all of the conditions above exist.

25. Notice of known hazardous substances on the premises must be given by

    a. owners to buyers.   b. owners to lessees.

    c. lessees to owners.   d. all of the above.

CHAPTER NINE

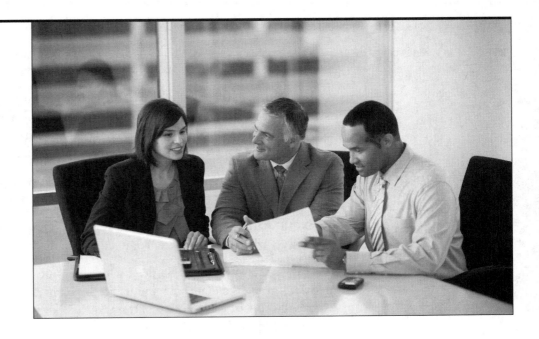

ACQUISITIONS AND CONVEYANCES

■ **KEY TERMS**

ademption
administrator
adverse possession
after-acquired title
codicil
color of title
dedication
deed
devise
eminent domain
escheat
exception in a deed
executor

formal will
gift deed
grant deed
holographic will
Independent
    Administration of
    Estates Act
intestate succession
inverse condemnation
marketable title
per stirpes
police power
probate

Proposition 99
quitclaim deed
reservation in a deed
sheriff's deed
simultaneous death
tacking on
tax deed
trustee's deed
valid will
warranty deed
will

■ **VOLUNTARY TRANSFERS OF REAL PROPERTY**

Deeds

Prior to the statute of frauds, title was passed by a voluntary ceremony known as *livery of seisin*. The parties would physically indicate transfer of title through the symbolic transfer of a clod of earth, a twig, or a key. It became common for unscrupulous individuals, using perjured testimony, to claim a transfer when in fact a livery of seisin had not taken place. The statute of frauds was really enacted to defeat this type of fraud.

The statute of frauds requires that transfers of real property interests be in writing (Civil Code Section 1624). The **deed** is the transfer instrument in a voluntary transfer. When the deed is properly executed, delivered, and accepted, it transfers title to real property from a grantor to a grantee.

Requirements of a Deed

Written. The statute of frauds requires that every instrument dealing in rights in real estate, other than a lease for one year or less, be in writing.

Execution. The deed must be executed—that is, signed—by the grantor. The grantee, who receives the deed, need not sign the deed.

The grantor must sign the deed with the same name in which the grantor took title. If there is a material variance in the name, the recording of the deed will not provide constructive notice of the transfer. For example, a married woman who is conveying a title that she took before her marriage must identify the maiden name or different married name under which title was taken.

An attorney-in-fact may convey marketable title only if the power of attorney under which the deed is executed is acknowledged and recorded.

A deed that is executed in blank does not transfer title when a property description is inserted at a later date by another person unless that person was authorized to insert the description.

A forged deed is void and transfers no interest. A deed containing unauthorized alterations also is void.

Case Study

The case of *People v. Sanders* (1998) 67 C.A.4th 1403 involved forgery of deeds. Wesley Sanders III forged 10 deeds on 11 parcels of property in Los Angeles County. He located property from tax collector lists of property to be sold at tax collector sales. He forged the owners' signatures (owners were deceased in most cases) and used a forged notary public stamp. He then redeemed the property by paying the taxes. Because of the large number of deeds transferred to him, the tax collector became suspicious and a sheriff's investigation resulted in Sanders being arrested, charged, and convicted of grand theft. Sanders was sentenced to five years in prison.

The Court of Appeal reversed the decision, and Sanders was released. The basis of the decision was that a forged deed is void so no transfer of real estate was possible. In addition, Sanders had no contact with the owners, and there was no evidence of false pretense or misrepresentation.

Note: Sanders should have been charged with forgery and possibly conspiracy to defraud, but not theft.

Description. The property must be described sufficiently so that no doubt exists about the identity of the property being conveyed, and the boundaries must be positively located. A legal description is not required on a deed, although title insurance cannot generally be obtained in the absence of a legal description.

Delivery. To transfer title, a deed must be delivered. The most important element of delivery is the intent of the grantor. The grantor must intend to transfer title irrevocably to the grantee or a trustee and to divest the grantor of title immediately. The grantor's intent can be determined by words or acts before, at the time of, and after execution of the deed. In an actual delivery, the grantee receives the deed.

Although an agreement for a future transfer of title is not a delivery, a legal delivery is possible, even if the grantee's rights to possession and enjoyment of the property are to accrue at a future date. For example, a deed could be given in an irrevocable trust to be given to a grantee at a later date. The delivery of a deed to a third party where the grantor cannot get the property back is considered a constructive delivery.

Recording the deed creates a presumption that the deed was delivered. A deed also is presumed to have been delivered if it is in the possession of the grantee. However, if the grantor is in possession of the deed, it is presumed not to have been delivered. These presumptions can be overcome by evidence to the contrary, and legal delivery can be made even if the deed was not physically transferred.

A deed to more than one grantee need be delivered to only one of them for effective delivery. Delivery must be absolute; it cannot be conditional. For example, assume a deed is given to a third party to hold with the provision that it should be given to the grantor's son upon the grantor's death but it should be returned to the grantor upon the grantor's request. In that case, title would not pass because the transfer was conditioned on the grantor's not voiding it before death.

See *Stone v. Daily* (1919) 181 C. 571.

Acceptance. To be valid, a deed must be accepted. The law will not force a person to take title. Acceptance generally is presumed if the grant is to the benefit of the grantee. Failure to repudiate a transfer within a reasonable period of time also will imply its acceptance. Acts, words, or conduct of the grantee could show an intent to accept. Any exercise of dominion over the property, such as repairing it, occupying it, placing a sign on it, putting the property on the market, or borrowing on the property would show acceptance of the grant.

> **Case Study**
> In the case of *Brown v. Sweet* (1928) 95 C.A. 117, when the grantee received a deed in the mail, she immediately returned it to the grantor. Because she did not accept the deed, title was held not to have passed to the grantee.

If the grantee conditionally accepts the grant, title does not pass to the grantee until the conditions set are satisfied.

Granting Clause. While particular wording is not required, the language of the deed must clearly indicate a transfer of title.

Competent Parties.   The grantor must be a competent party. In the case of a gift deed, however, the grantee can be an incompetent or a minor. In this situation, the legal representative of the incompetent or minor would accept the deed or acceptance could be presumed on the basis that the grant was beneficial.

Grantee.   The grantee must be identified. While a grant may be made to a real person using an assumed name, title cannot pass to a nonexistent person.

Not Required for Deeds   **Acknowledgment.**   Acknowledgment is made by a grantor before a notary public or another authorized person. The grantor acknowledges that the signing of the deed is the grantor's own free act. The notary has a duty to determine the identity of the person executing the document. The notary and the notary's sureties would be liable for negligence in ascertaining the identity of the person signing.

A deed need not be acknowledged to be a valid transfer, but without acknowledgment, the deed will not be accepted for recording. California notaries must now obtain the right thumbprint of the grantor of any deed in their record books.

> **Case Study**
> In the case of *Cordano v. Wright* (1911) 159 C. 610, a deed described the grantor as John McDonald, but it was signed and acknowledged by both John and Catherine McDonald. The court held that the grantee did not get the interests of Catherine McDonald because a deed acknowledged by a person not named in the instrument as a grantor does not transfer that person's interest.

Recording   Between the parties, an unrecorded deed can convey good title. However, an unrecorded deed does not give constructive notice to the world of the grantee's interest.

Besides acknowledgment, a deed to be recorded must contain the name and address to which future tax statements are to be sent. The recorder also will require that the documentary transfer tax be paid prior to recording. The county tax assessor requires filing a "Change of Ownership" form.

Consideration.   While a promise to give a deed would require consideration to be enforceable, a deed is not a contract. It is a completed transfer, and consideration generally is not required. However, consideration is required for deeds by personal representatives (executors, guardians, attorneys-in-fact, etc.).

If a deed is given without consideration or for inadequate consideration while the grantor is insolvent, creditors of the grantor or a trustee in bankruptcy might be able to reach the property because the transfer would have constituted fraud against the creditors. While the courts ordinarily are not concerned with the adequacy of consideration, inadequate consideration would be admissible to show fraud or undue influence.

The recording of a deed given without consideration would not give the grantee priority over prior unrecorded conveyances and encumbrances for value.

The conveyance of a deed given on the promise of later consideration will remain valid, even in the event of failure to give the consideration.

Manner of Taking Title.   The deed need not indicate how title is being taken. If the grantee is a single individual, the grantee would take title in severalty. In the case of more than one grantee, it would be presumed that they are taking title as tenants in common. An exception to this is that deeds to husbands and wives that do not indicate how title is to be taken pass title as community property.

Witnesses and Seals.   In California, deeds need not be witnessed (unless they are signed with an X), nor are seals required. As for other documents, the presence of a seal on a corporate deed creates the presumption that the person signing had corporate authority.

Dated.   A deed need not be dated. The deed takes effect on delivery. A mistake in the date on the deed does not affect its validity. However, the date of a deed could be important in the case of a conflicting claim.

Types of Deeds

Grant Deed.   The deed used most commonly in California to transfer title, the **grant deed**, has two implied covenants:

1. That prior to the time of execution of such conveyance, the grantor has not conveyed the same estate or any right, title, or interest therein to any person other than the grantee

2. That such estate is at the time of execution of the conveyance free from encumbrances done, made, or suffered by the grantor or any person claiming under him or her (other than those declared)

If one of the grantor's implied covenants in a grant deed is breached, the grantee will be entitled to either rescission or damages.

A grant deed customarily is used along with a policy of title insurance.

Grants by grant deed are presumed to be in fee simple (Civil Code Section 1105). When a person purports to grant real property in fee simple and subsequently acquires any claim or title to the real property, the claim or title passes to the grantee or successors (Civil Code Section 1106). Grant deeds, therefore, convey **after-acquired title** as if the grant deed stated ". . . and all interest that I may at any time hereafter acquire." For example, suppose a grantor executes a grant deed to property the grantor thinks he inherited from a distant relative. However, the relative is still alive! When the relative later dies and the grantor inherits title, the grantee would thereby receive after-acquired title.

Figure 9.1 is a sample of a Grant Deed.

FIGURE 9.1

Sample Grant Deed

RECORDING REQUESTED BY

AND WHEN RECORDED MAIL TO

Name

Street
Address

City &
State

SPACE ABOVE THIS LINE FOR RECORDER'S USE

MAIL TAX STATEMENTS TO:

Name

Street
Address

City &
State

DOCUMENTARY TRANSFER TAX $ _____

☐ Computed on the consideration or value of property conveyed; or

☐ Computed on the consideration or value less liens or encumbrances remaining at time of sale.

☐ Unincorporated area _____

☐ City of _____ ,

_____
(Signature of Agent determining tax)

GRANT DEED

Prepared by: Agent _____   Phone _____
Broker _____   Email _____

I/We, _____ ,

grant to _____

the real property in the City of _____ ,

County of _____ , State of California,

referred to as _____

APN # _____

☐ See attached Signature Page Addendum. [ft Form 251]

Date: _____, 20_____   _____   _____
(Print Name)   ture)

Date: _____, 20_____   _____   _____
(Print Name)   ture)

STATE OF CALIFORNIA
COUNTY OF _____   _____

On _____   before me,

_____
(Name and title of officer)

personally appeared _____
_____ ,

who proved to me on the basis of satisfactory evidence to be the person(s) whose name(s) is/are subscribed to the within instrument and acknowledged to me that he/she/they executed the same in his/her/their authorized capacity(ies), and that by his/her/their signature(s) on the instrument the person(s), or the entity upon behalf of which the person(s) acted, executed the instrument.

I certify under PENALTY OF PERJURY under the laws of the State of California that the foregoing paragraph is true and correct.

WITNESS my hand and official seal.

Signature _____
(Signature of notary public)

_____
(This area for official notarial seal)

TAX STATEMENTS TO BE MAILED AS DIRECTED ABOVE

FORM 404   03-11   ©2011 first tuesday , P.O. BOX 20069, RIVERSIDE, CA 92516 (800) 794-0494

Reprinted with permission from first tuesday.

Quitclaim Deed.   A grantor under a **quitclaim deed** transfers only the interest that the grantor has and makes no warranties of title. If the grantor has a fee simple title, then that is the title conveyed. If the grantor has only a life estate, then only the life estate will be conveyed.

Quitclaim deeds often are used to clear title from grantors who have a possible or disputed interest.

Warranty Deed.   Under a **warranty deed,** the grantor expressly guarantees a good title and agrees to defend the title and to be liable if the title is defective. Because of the use of title insurance in California, warranty deeds are not commonly used.

Sheriff's Deed.   A **sheriff's deed** is given at execution of a judgment under a sheriff's sale. It transfers only the former owner's interest and contains no warranties (see Chapter 10).

Case Study

The case of *L & B Real Estate v. Housing Authority* (2007) 149 C.A. 4th 950 involved a low income housing project that was sold by the developer to the state but an error in draftsmanship resulted in the omission of two parcels from the legal description. The state subsequently sold the property to the county housing authority. This deed also omitted the two parcels. The county assessor continued to send tax bills to the developer. The two parcels were sold at tax sale. The buyer at the tax sale failed to make payments and L & B purchased the property at a later tax sale. The county housing authority had no notice of any tax assessments or tax sales. Property of the housing authority is exempt from property taxes.

L & B brought a quiet title action against the housing authority. The authority was granted summary judgment on the grounds that L & B's deed was void because it had constructive notice of the authority's ownership. L & B was therefore not a good faith purchaser because the property was tax exempt.

The Court of Appeal affirmed. Because public property is exempt from real estate taxation, tax deeds that purport to convey such property are void. A prerequisite of a valid tax deed is that the property be legally subject to property tax.

Note: L & B sought to take title to a large low income housing development based on their tax deed.

Tax Deed.   A **tax deed** is given when property is sold by the tax collector to the public for nonpayment of taxes. After one year from date of purchase, the property is acceptable for title insurance. Because real estate taxes are a priority lien, a tax sale removes junior encumbrances.

Trust Deed.   A trust deed is given by a borrower to a third party to hold in trust as security for a lender. It is covered in detail in Chapter 10.

Trustee's Deed.   A trustee's deed is given to the highest bidder at a nonjudicial foreclosure sale on a deed of trust (see Chapter 10).

Gift Deed.   Any deed where no valuable consideration was given is considered a **gift deed**. The deed is valid unless it was given to defraud creditors, in which case it can be voided.

Void and Voidable Deeds.   A void deed transfers no interest whatsoever, even if a purchaser paid value and acted in good faith. The following would make a deed void:

- Forgery
- Alteration
- The fact that the grantor is a minor
- The fact that the grantor has been declared insane or is entirely without understanding
- Failure of delivery

Voidable deeds are valid deeds unless or until they are voided. The following would allow a deed to be voided:

- Fraud
- Undue influence
- Duress or menace
- The grantor's not being of sound mind (but not declared insane or entirely without understanding)

The statute of limitations to challenge a void or voidable deed is five years, 20 years if the claimant is a minor or insane (Civil Code Sections 318, 319, and 328).

> **Case Study**
>
> The case of *Lee v. Lee* (2009) 175 C.A. 4th 1553 involved a deed that was altered by other than the grantee after the deed was delivered to the grantee. The alteration added two more persons to the grantees. The grantors brought action to void the deed. The trial court ruled the deed was valid and the Court of Appeal affirmed the decision.
>
> If the deed had been altered before delivery to the grantee, it would have been void. Once delivered, it is valid, and an alteration by a third party will not invalidate it.

Case Study

The case of *Anderson v. Reynolds* (1984) 588 F. Supp. 814 involved a plaintiff who had befriended the defendant, an aspiring opera singer. The defendant became a trusted adviser to the plaintiff. The plaintiff wished to sell her Lake Tahoe estate, which was valued between $1 million and $1.6 million. The defendant told the plaintiff that several movie stars he knew, including Paul Newman, were interested in her property. The defendant convinced the plaintiff to deed the property to him so he could market the property for her as a principal. He indicated that the movie stars would not deal through agents because they wanted to avoid claims for real estate commissions. The plaintiff lost faith in the defendant, who had failed to procure a buyer, and asked for the return of her deed. The defendant gave excuses and subsequently recorded the deed. The defendant issued a trust deed to his attorney for $375,000 for the apparent purpose of encumbering the property. Other trust deeds were given to further cloud the title. There was no evidence that anything of value was given for the trust deeds.

In an action for cancellation of the deed and revocation of the trust deeds, the court stated that the elements of fraudulent representation are

- false representation,
- knowledge or belief that the representation was false,
- intent to induce another to act or refrain from acting in reliance on the representation,
- justifiable reliance on the misrepresentation, and
- damages resulting from reliance.

The court held that the deed was induced by intentional fraud, so it should be considered null and void and of no force whatsoever and should be set aside along with the trust deeds.

Reservation in a Deed.   A reservation in a deed gives the grantor a right that did not exist separately prior to the grant. For example, a grantor could reserve an easement over the property conveyed, retain a life estate, and retain oil and mineral rights, and so on.

Exception in a Deed.   An exception withdraws part of the described property from the grant. For example, the grantor, after describing the deeded property, could except the south 20 feet from the grant. Exceptions in deeds often use the word "sans," which means "without."

Dedication

A **dedication** is a donation of land for public use. Because it is a donation, the donor receives no consideration.

A person cannot dedicate more than that person owns. One cotenant cannot dedicate land to public use without the consent of the other cotenants.

To obtain Subdivision Map Act approval (local control over subdivisions), subdividers might donate land for streets, bike paths, parks, schools, etc., in fee as well as easement rights.

Dedication may be accomplished through a grant deed or by recording a subdivision map showing the publicly owned areas, which would be implied dedication. A deed dedicating property to a government body must be accepted by the government body.

If property is given for a particular purpose only, the dedication should state clearly that the property shall revert to the grantor if the use ceases or is abandoned. Otherwise, courts likely would determine it really was given for any public purpose.

Formerly, if an owner knew that a government entity was using the owner's private property by spending public funds on improvements, clearing, or performing maintenance related to the public good for five years, an implied dedication of the property could result. In response, the state legislature enacted Civil Code Section 1009, which states that future public use of private property shall not ripen into public use by implied dedication.

Dedication cannot be required as a condition of obtaining a building permit where the purpose of the use of the dedicated land does not relate to the new structure.

Case Study

The case of *Dolan v. City of Tigard* (1994) 114 S. Ct. 2309 involved a property owner who wished to redevelop a property by tearing down an existing structure and erecting a new building. The proposed development conformed to zoning. The planning commission granted the permit subject to the dedication of a 15-foot pedestrian and bike path along an adjacent creek. This dedication amounted to 10 percent of the property. The city claimed that the dedication would help mitigate traffic. The U.S. Supreme Court ruled that the dedication requirement violated the Fifth Amendment as it was a taking of property. The city had failed to prove that additional traffic generated by the new building had any relationship to the dedication of a bike/pedestrian path.

■ INVOLUNTARY TRANSFERS OF REAL PROPERTY

Besides foreclosure sales, sheriff's sales, tax sales, and property that escheats to the state (discussed later in this chapter), title can be passed involuntarily—without the consent of the owner—in several ways.

Adverse Possession

A user of land can acquire title to the land of another by **adverse possession**. The rationale is that property should be used productively and taxes should be paid. Several conditions must be met:

- The possession must be an actual occupation. A person need not actually live on the property to get title by adverse possession. The person must, however, use or fence the property. Title cannot be claimed for more than what a person exercises dominion over, except when a person claims title under a defective deed. Title to all the property described in the deed could be obtained under adverse possession, even if all of the property were not used. There also must be exclusive use. If another adverse user or the owner is also in possession, an adverse user cannot gain title by adverse possession.

■ A claim of occupancy can be based on the occupancy of a tenant of the person claiming the adverse interest.

■ Possession must be open, notorious, and hostile to the true owner's title. If a person uses property with permission, that person will not be able to get title by adverse possession because the use is not hostile. A tenant, therefore, could not obtain title by adverse possession because the tenant would be in possession with permission.

■ Use must be under a claim of right or color of title. A claim of right for adverse possession does not mean that a person believes they have title; it means only that that person claims title against others. Any hostile use would be regarded as a claim of right. **Color of title** could be a claim under a defective document; for example, a forged deed or a deed that is void because of a defect.

■ Possession must be continuous and uninterrupted for a period of five years. The five-year period is satisfied if an adverse user uses the property for two years and a successor in interest to the adverse user uses the property for an additional three years (tacking on). For **tacking on**, there must be some sort of privity (mutual or successive relationship) between the two users. While the use does not have to occur every day, it must be of a continuous nature. If the use is interrupted, a new five-year period will start.

■ The adverse user must pay all property taxes for five years. If the owner continues to pay the taxes, the adverse user cannot obtain title unless the user also paid the taxes. Use based on a mistaken boundary probably would not give the adverse user title because no taxes would have been paid. However, a prescriptive easement might arise.

Title cannot be taken from a government entity, public utility, or railroad by adverse possession. Title also cannot be taken from a minor or an insane person. The five-year continuous use must occur when an owner is competent.

An adverse user cannot get greater rights than the true owner had. For example, the adverse possession of the surface would not include any mineral rights previously separated from the land.

A user cannot defeat future interests by obtaining an interest by adverse possession. If the true owner had a life estate, by adverse possession all the adverse user could obtain would be an estate for the life of the former life tenant.

To obtain a **marketable title**, an adverse user either would have to obtain a quit-claim deed from the title owner of record or would have to commence a quiet title action to have the court determine ownership. An adverse user who recorded a court's determination of title in the adverse user would have a marketable title.

> ### Case Study
> The case of *Preciado v. Wilde* (2006) 139 C.A. 4th 321 involved co-owners who brought a quiet title action claiming that they were entitled to a 3/10th interest of a co-owner based on adverse possession.
>
> Wilde admitted that after 1992, Preciado paid the property taxes. Preciado had planted crops on one-third of the property for personal use and erected a fence to keep a horse on the property. Wilde said she never was told not to enter the property and she visited it several times per year and was never excluded.
>
> The Superior Court ruled that the Preciados had not established title to their co-owners' portion.
>
> The Court of Appeal affirmed because Preciado failed to prove ouster of Wilde.
>
> *Note*: It is rare that adverse possession is successful against a co-owner because the adverse user has to show that the other owner was excluded from the property for the required five years.

Eminent Domain

The power of the government to take private property for the public good is called **eminent domain** and is set forth in the Fifth Amendment to the U.S. Constitution as well as the California Constitution. Eminent domain may be exercised at any level of government. It may be delegated to schools, hospitals, and public utilities.

The condemning entity must compensate the owner for the property taken. The power of eminent domain should not be confused with the exercise of police power. The exercise of **police power** to protect health, safety, morals, and general welfare generally cannot be delegated, and it does not entitle an owner to compensation. Examples of police power would be enforcement of zoning ordinances or fire, building, and health codes.

The owner is entitled to the fair market value of the property at the time it is taken. Any increase in value because of the use by the condemning entity is not considered in determining value.

An owner who is not satisfied with the compensation offered has the right to have the value determined by the court. In that event, a jury will determine market value as a question of fact. The condemnation award should be based on the highest and best use of the property, even if the property is being used for another purpose (Code of Civil Procedure Section 1250.410).

Relocation expenses are allowed by statute in cases of eminent domain. Compensation also is allowed for goodwill of a business if the loss cannot be prevented by relocation.

Tenants are entitled to be compensated for their remaining leasehold interests unless the lease provides that it terminates upon condemnation.

Case Study

The case of *People ex rel. Caltrans v. Woodson* (2002) 93 C.A.4th 954 involved a condemnation offer of $1,400,000 based on its current use as a trailer park, rather than its highest and best use for storage rentals. The trial court awarded $1,876,750 but refused to award litigation costs.

The Court of Appeal explained that Civil Code Procedure Section 1250.410 requires awarding litigation costs where the final offer is unreasonable in relation to the final award. The court emphasized that to determine reasonableness, the guidelines are (1) the amount of the difference between the offer and the compensation awarded; (2) the percentage of the difference between the offer and award; and (3) the good faith, care, and accuracy of how the amount of the offer and owner's demand were determined. In this case, there was a $476,750 difference between positions, the offer was only 74 percent of the final award, and Caltrans's offer was based on the obviously wrong current property use. Litigation costs were awarded.

Case Study

The case of *City of San Diego v. Sobke* (1998) 65 C.A.4th 379 involved a condemnation for street improvements. Baja-Mex Insurance and Money Exchange in San Ysidro, near the Mexican border, had to move, thus increasing operating costs. The move, which was to a less-desirable and more-costly location, coincided with a peso devaluation that resulted in Baja-Mex showing an increase in monthly earnings of 400 percent.

Baja-Mex sought a condemnation award for loss of goodwill. In affirming the trial court decision, the Court of Appeal pointed out that while tenants are entitled to goodwill damages in cases of eminent domain, the damages must be proven by a change in pre-taking and post-taking positions. Increased expenses was not the proper measurement of lost goodwill.

Note: With business up 400 percent, Baja-Mex had an impossible task to prove a loss of goodwill resulting from relocation.

Every taking of property in fee or a lesser interest (easement) means that an owner is entitled to compensation for the value of the property or interest taken. The taking for a street or a utility easement could result in a benefit to the remaining property so that the owner would not be entitled to compensation for any detriment caused to the balance of the parcel.

Even if a property is not used for the purpose for which it was taken under eminent domain, the former owner has no right to reclaim the property.

Proposition 99 (Homeowner and Private Property Protection Act) prohibits the taking of private property by eminent domain when the intention is to turn the property over to a private party rather than take it for public use.

Private parties can obtain an easement for utility services over the land of others by eminent domain, provided

- there is a great necessity for the easement,
- the easement location provides the most reasonable service and is consistent with the least damage to the burdened property, and
- the hardship of the owner of the appurtenant property, if the taking is not permitted, clearly outweighs any hardship to the owner of the burdened property [Civil Code Section 1001(c)].

Inverse Condemnation.   If an owner is unable to use the property as a result of public action, an action could be brought for **inverse condemnation**: to force condemnation proceedings. For example, if the construction of a new airport caused jets to pass 500 feet over the roof of a house, the noise might destroy the owner's peaceful use of the premises, and an action for inverse condemnation would be proper.

If a public entity delays for more than six months in commencing eminent domain after announcing it will take the property, an owner can bring an action for inverse condemnation (Code of Civil Procedure Section 1245.260).

Case Study

In the case of *Regency Outdoor Advertising, Inc. v. City of Los Angeles* (2006) 39 C.A. 4th 507, it was alleged that trees on city property grew to the point where they partially blocked billboards from the view of motorists, thus decreasing their value. This lawsuit was for inverse condemnation. The city offered to remove one tree and pay $1,000 in damages, but Regency refused.

The trial court denied any damages and ordered Regency to pay the city's $99,145.64 expert witness fees.

On appeal, the trial court decision was affirmed ruling that roadside businesses do not have a right to be seen. Impairment of commercial visibility from the road is not compensable.

Case Study

The case of *Dina v. People ex rel Dept. of Transp*. (2007) 151 C.A. 4th 1029 involved homeowners in the City of La Verne who sued the Dept. of Transportation for inverse condemnation, nuisance, and negligence alleging that an adjacent I-210 freeway extension caused physical damage to their homes by compromising structural integrity and causing subsurface erosion that resulted in cracks in patio and garage floors. They also alleged damage from noise and dust.

The trial court dismissed the action because the homeowners failed to demonstrate that the property suffered peculiar and substantial damages or that the freeway construction or operation was unreasonable.

The Court of Appeal affirmed noting that the homeowners failed to demonstrate that their property suffered a direct substantial or peculiar burden from the freeway. The homeowners failed to produce any causal connection between the cracking and construction or maintenance of the freeway. The nuisance claim was barred because CC3482 provides that nothing done or maintained under express authority of statute can be deemed a nuisance. The court also noted that there is no authority for the proposition that noise and dust emulating from the freeway constituted a dangerous condition.

Note: For this suit to have been successful, the homeowners would have had to show a relationship of construction and maintenance with their physical damage, and/or that the construction or maintenance placed a particular dangerous burden on the homeowners.

Severance Damage. If the taking of property results in a lower value to the remaining property that has not been taken, the owner will be entitled to severance damage (Code of Civil Procedure Section 1240.150).

Case Study

Gilbert v. State (1990) 218 C.A.3d 234 involved a moratorium on new water connections because of a water shortage. The owners of the property alleged inverse condemnation. The court held that California law does not recognize potential water use as a compensable property right. While the court indicated a regulation effects a taking if it does not substantially advance legitimate state interests, in this case, the conditions imposed were in the state's interest in ensuring a potable water supply. Further, because the land was purchased without a water supply, the state did nothing to diminish the value of the land.

Government Seizure

The government can seize property without compensation to the owners when the property was used with the owner's knowledge for unlawful acts, such as the sale, manufacture, or distribution of controlled substances, or was purchased with revenue derived from drug traffic.

The Financial Institutions Reform, Recovery, and Enforcement Act (FIRREA) provides for the forfeiture to the United States of any real or personal property derived from proceeds traceable to violation of 18 U.S. Code Section 1014, which prohibits "knowingly making any false statement . . . for the purpose of influencing in any way the action of . . . any institution the accounts of which are insured by the Federal Deposit Insurance Corporation upon any application for a loan." Falsifying a loan application could, therefore, result in the forfeiture of the property securing the loan.

> **Case Study**
>
> The case of *U.S. v. 3814 N.W. Thurman St.* (1999) 164 F.3rd 1191 involved a fraudulent loan application. Three-year income was shown as $308,106, when it was actually $27,286, and $108,356 in outstanding liabilities was not disclosed. Based on the false loan application, the U.S. government filed an action in rem (against the property) in a forfeiture action for knowingly making false statements to a federally insured financial institution. The district court granted judgment in favor of the government and ordered the property forfeited. The trial court refused to consider if the forfeiture was excessive under the Eighth Amendment.
>
> The Ninth Circuit Court of Appeals reversed, ruling that forfeiture was an excessive fine because there was no loss to the bank and the owner had not been involved in other criminal activity. If this were a criminal case, the penalty would have been six months imprisonment and a fine of $500 to $5,000. The court held that forfeiture of 40 times the maximum fine violates the excessive fines clause of the Eighth Amendment to the U.S. Constitution.

The Fourth Amendment protects property owners against seizure without a notice and hearing.

> ### Case Study
>
> The case of *U.S. v. James Daniel Good* (1993) 114 S. Ct. 492 involved a drug seizure in which a quantity of marijuana was found in a home. Good pleaded guilty to a state drug offense. In an ex parte proceeding (without the defendant being present), the federal magistrate ordered the immediate seizure of the property. The tenants who were in possession were ordered to pay their rent to the government rather than to Good.
>
> The Ninth Circuit Court of Appeals held that the civil seizure without prior notice or hearing violated the Fifth Amendment's due process clause. The U.S. Supreme Court agreed that the property interests of Good were protected by the Fifth Amendment. The Fourth Amendment also protected Good against wrongful search and seizure. While seizure could be justified to protect evidence and prevent it from being moved, this was not the situation, as real property is not movable. A lis pendens notice would have served to protect government interests. The court held that absent a pressing reason, seizure requires a notice and hearing.

■ TRANSFERS OF REAL PROPERTY UPON DEATH

Upon an owner's death, the owner's property can be transferred voluntarily to the heirs—by will—or involuntarily by the laws of intestate succession to relatives, or by escheat to the state.

Testate Succession

A **will** is a testamentary declaration about the disposition of a person's property, to take effect upon the maker's death. A will is said to be an *ambulatory instrument* because it can be changed any time prior to the maker's death. The maker of a will is a testator (*trix*, formerly added as a suffix to designate a woman, is not used in this book). Anyone 18 or older and of sound mind may make a will. The testator must understand the nature of the testator's property and the disposition of the property.

A later **valid will** that makes a complete disposition of the property of the testator in a manner different from an earlier will completely revoke the earlier will.

A **codicil**, an amendment to a will, requires the same formalities as a will.

A **devise** is a transfer of real property by will. A *bequest* is a transfer of personal property. *Legacy* refers to money.

Types of Wills

Formal Will. A **formal will** must be signed in the presence of at least two witnesses who, at the maker's request, attest to the testator's declared will. Beneficiaries under the will should not be witnesses. While a formal will need not be dated, an undated will could create a problem when more than one will is found because the dated will is presumed to be the latest in time.

Holographic Will (Probate Code Section 6111). A holographic will is hand-written by the testator. For such a will to be valid, the material provisions must be in the handwriting of the testator, and it must be signed by the testator, but neither witnesses nor a date are required. A letter could meet the requirements of a valid holographic will if it were handwritten with testamentary intent.

Nuncupative Will. Oral, or nuncupative, wills are no longer valid in California.

Ademption

Disposition of property prior to a person's death revokes the portion of the will giving that property to a named beneficiary (i.e., **ademption**). For example, if a man's will gave a specific property to his cousin, but he sold that property prior to his death, the devise to the cousin would be revoked. The proceeds from the sale would go to residual beneficiaries and not to the cousin.

Simultaneous Death

When spouses die in a common disaster, **simultaneous death**, and there is insufficient evidence to conclude that one spouse survived the other, the estate of each spouse will be distributed as if each had survived the other (Uniform Simultaneous Death Act, California Probate Code Sections 220–230). For this reason, joint tenant property owners should each have wills.

Intestate Succession

When a deceased leaves no will, the property passes to the deceased's heirs by the law of **intestate succession**: All community property passes to the surviving spouse. Separate property passes as follows:

- No spouse, no children—property passes to the parents.
- No spouse, no children, no parents—property passes to siblings (or their heirs).
- No spouse, no children, no parents, no siblings—property passes to blood heirs going back through a common ancestor.
- Spouse, no children—half of the property passes to the spouse and half to the parents (or blood heirs).
- Spouse, one child—half of the property passes to the spouse and half to the child.
- Spouse, more than one child—one-third passes to the spouse and two-thirds to the children.
- No spouse, child (or children)—all passes to the child (children).

Heirs take by right of representation (*per stirpes*). That is, children would share equally in the share their deceased parent would have received had their parent survived.

Inheritance is by blood (or adoption). In-laws do not inherit.

Figure 9.2 will aid in the understanding of intestate succession.

FIGURE 9.2
Intestate Succession

CALIFORNIA LAW OF INTESTATE SUCCESSION

Community Property

If there is a surviving spouse:
- One-half already belongs to surviving spouse
- Remaining one-half goes to surviving spouse after decedent's liabilities have been paid

Community Property with Right of Survivorship
If there is a surviving spouse, surviving spouse takes entire property

Separate Property
If there is a surviving spouse and no child:
- Surviving spouse takes one-half
- Surviving parent, brother or sister; or child of deceased brother or sister; or (if none of these) spouse takes one-half

If there is a surviving spouse and one child:
- Surviving spouse takes one-half
- Child takes one-half

If there is a surviving spouse and more than one child:
- Surviving spouse takes one-third
- Children divide two-thirds equally

If there is no surviving spouse or child:
- Property is distributed to next of kin in order prescribed by California law; if no heirs can be located, the property will escheat to the state

Escheat. If a person dies intestate and that person's representative is unable to locate an heir within two years after death, the attorney general will bring an action to declare title to be vested in the state. If heirs fail to come forward within five years of the person's death, the property will **escheat** to the state (Probate Code Sections 220–231), and it can then be sold.

Probate

Probate is the legal procedure that provides for the transfer of the real and personal property of the deceased, as well as the payment of the debts of the deceased.

The person appointed under the will to serve as the personal representative of the deceased during probate is commonly referred to as the **executor**.

If the deceased died intestate (without a will), the court will appoint a personal representative (commonly referred to as an **administrator**) to represent the deceased.

Upon a person's death, the person's property becomes immediately vested in the beneficiaries named in the will or the heirs if there is no will. Theoretically, they immediately could encumber or transfer their interests; however, title would not be insurable because the property would be subject to the control of the deceased's representative until probate was concluded. Heirs and beneficiaries often will transfer their interests for consideration prior to completion of probate. Some people are in the business of buying the interests of heirs and beneficiaries.

Real property is probated in the state where the property is located. Probates in the state where the deceased resided are domiciliary probates. Probates in other states are ancillary probates. In California, estates are probated in superior court in the county where the real property is located or the deceased resided.

Probate starts with a petition for probate (if a will) or letters of administration (if intestate). A hearing is held, and a representative is appointed or confirmed. Creditors generally have four months from publication of notice to file their claims. An inventory and appraisal are filed with the court clerk. The representative files an accounting of all receipts and disbursements and requests court approval. Finally, the representative petitions the court to distribute the remaining assets to the proper heirs and devisees.

If a deceased had a pending contract for the sale of real property, the court would have to confirm the sale.

When it is in the best interests of the estate, property may be sold in probate. Money may be needed to pay debts, taxes, costs, or simply to allow the division of assets among heirs or beneficiaries.

The representative of the estate can grant an exclusive listing for a period not to exceed 90 days. Generally, sales by the representative of the deceased are subject to court approval.

Bids usually would be taken to the court for an approval hearing. Late bids from other parties will be considered. However, for a late bid to be considered, it must be at least 10 percent higher on the first $10,000, and 5 percent higher on the balance of the bid being considered. For example, if the bid being considered were for $90,000, a late bid would have to be $5,000 higher:

10 percent of	$10,000 =	$1,000
5 percent of	$80,000 =	$4,000
	$90,000 =	$5,000

(An easy way to remember this formula is 5 percent plus $500.)

The court can set increments for further bids and then confirm the sale.

The probate code requires completion of the probate sale for the broker to earn a commission.

> **Case Study**
>
> At a confirmation hearing on an estate sale, the person who made the successful overbid listed broker Henry Tong as the person entitled to a real estate commission.
>
> Tong's license had expired at the time of the purchase, although it was subsequently renewed. The superior court held that Tong was not entitled to a commission because he was not licensed at the time the cause of action arose (the time of the bid).
>
> The Court of Appeal reversed because the Probate Code states that an estate is not liable for a commission unless the sale is consummated. While the general rule is that a broker is entitled to a commission when an offer from a ready, willing, and able buyer is accepted by the property owner, that rule is superseded by Probate Code Section 10160, which requires completion of the probate sale for the broker to earn a commission. Because Tong was licensed when the commission was earned (the sale was completed), Tong was entitled to his commission [*Estate of Lopez* (1992) 8 C.A.4th 317].

Probate sales are one of the few instances where commissions are subject to court review. When the probate court confirms the bid and there is no overbid in court, the listing agent receives all of the sales commission. When there is no listing, but a real estate agent procures an acceptable offer that is confirmed by the probate court, the agent receives all the sales commission (the rate is set by the court).

If there is no agent on the original offer and there is an agent for the late bid, the agent's commission cannot exceed 50 percent of the difference between the original offer and the accepted offer.

If an agent procures a bid that is overbid in probate court by a buyer represented by an agent, the two agents split the commission on the original amount, and the agent who obtains the overbid receives all of the commission on the overbid amount, but is limited to 50 percent of the increased bid, with the court determining the commission rate.

If the original offer was made through the listing agent and the overbid is made by a buyer not represented by an agent, the listing broker earns a commission on the amount of the original bid, with the court determining the commission rate.

The **Independent Administration of Estates Act** allows a private sale of property in probate without a court proceeding allowing later bids. The heirs must agree to this procedure and court approval is required.

Living Trusts

A living trust may be used in addition to a will. Under the living trust, the trustor(s) generally transfer their property to themselves as trustees for the beneficiaries, who are usually the same persons. The living trust, which is a revocable trust, avoids probate because the trustors have already conveyed their property to the trust. The trust provides for the division of the property after the death of the last trustor. The successor trustee makes the conveyance, thus avoiding probate costs and delays.

By use of more involved A-B living trusts, it is possible for a married couple to reduce their federal estate taxes on large estates by doubling the individual exemption. The federal estate tax exemption for individuals dying in 2011 and 2012 is $5,000,000 so a couple using an A-B Trust could exempt $10,000,000. Unless changed by statute, the exemption is scheduled to be reduced to $11,000 in 2013.

■ SUMMARY

Title can be transferred by both voluntary and involuntary conveyances. The most common way is by deed.

Deed requirements include

- writing (because of the statute of frauds),
- execution,
- description of the property,
- delivery,
- acceptance,
- granting clause,
- competent grantor, and
- definite grantee.

The following are *not* required for a valid deed:

- Acknowledgment (although a deed must be acknowledged to be recorded)
- Recording (although an unrecorded deed does not give constructive notice to later purchasers for value)
- Consideration (a valid deed can be given for love and affection)
- Manner of taking title (if not specified, conveyances to spouses transfer title as community property, conveyances to two or more parties who are not spouses transfer title as tenants in common, conveyances to one party transfer title in severalty)
- Witnesses and seals
- Date (deed takes effect on date of delivery)

The types of deeds include the

- grant deed, in which the grantor implies that the grantor previously has not conveyed the property and that the grantor has not encumbered the property other than what has been disclosed; grant deeds convey after-acquired title;

- quitclaim deed, which conveys whatever interest the grantor has but makes no warranty of title;

- warranty deed, through which the grantor expressly warrants that the grantor has good title and agrees to defend the title and be liable should it be defective (not used in California);

- sheriff's deed, which is given after a sheriff's sale and transfers only the interest a former owner had;

- tax deed, which is given when property is sold for nonpayment of taxes (because taxes are a priority lien, the sale wipes out junior encumbrances); and

- gift deed, given for love and affection.

Dedication is the voluntary transfer of real property through donation for public use.

Involuntary transfers include

- adverse possession, through which a user can acquire title by open, notorious, hostile, adverse occupation for a period of five years, as well as paying the taxes during that period; and

- eminent domain, through which the government can take property for the public good but must pay the former owner the fair market value of the property taken.

A will is a testamentary declaration to dispose of the property of a deceased. A formal will requires the signature of the testator and two witnesses. A holographic will, a handwritten will signed by the testator, also is valid in California, but a nuncupative (oral) will is not.

If a person dies intestate with no heirs, the person's property is transferred involuntarily to the state by escheat.

Probate is the legal procedure to carry out the wishes of the deceased and pay the debts.

■ DISCUSSION CASES

1. **Under what circumstances could a life tenant transfer their interests by will?**

2. Grantors conveyed title to grantees, retaining a life estate in a portion of the property conveyed. The description of the portion reserved was ambiguous. **What are the rights of the grantors?**

    Lehman v. Kamp (1969) 273 C.A.2d 701

3. A cotenant conveyed the entire fee title. Subsequently, the cotenant acquired the interest of his cotenant. **What are the rights of the parties?**

    Emeric v. Alvarado (1891) 90 C. 444

4. A deed was given to a grantee with the request that it not be recorded until the grantor died. **Is this a valid transfer?**

    McCarthy v. Security Trust & Savings Bank (1922) 188 C. 229

5. After a deed was delivered, it was placed in the grantor's deposit box. The grantor continued to collect the rents and pay expenses on the property. **Did a valid transfer occur?**

    Huth v. Katz (1947) 30 C.2d 605

6. The federal government took all of the land bordering a lake by eminent domain. Condemnees had three cabin barges on the lake that were used in their business. The cost of moving the barges would have been excessive. The government refused to pay for the barges because they were personal property. **Are the condemnees entitled to the value of the barges?**

    U.S. v. 967.905 acres of land (1969) 305 F. Supp. 83

7. The United States condemned three summer camps. The camps, owned by nonprofit organizations, had a fair market value of less than $1 million, but the replacement cost was approximately $6 million. **What are the owners entitled to?**

    U.S. v. 564 acres of land (1979) 99 S. Ct. 1854

8. Muller owned property that he rented to his veterinary corporation. The state condemned the building. Muller built another building in the same area, which he also rented to his corporation. Because of higher costs, Muller charged the corporation a higher rent. Because of the higher rent, the corporation suffered a decrease in profits. **Is the corporation entitled to compensation for this loss?**

    People ex rel. Dept. of Transportation v. Muller (1984) 36 C.3d 263

9. A deed was placed in escrow for one-half of a lot. The evidence was conclusive that the deed later was altered to convey the entire lot. **Are the sellers entitled to the value of the property they did not intend to convey?**

   Montgomery v. Bank of America (1948) 85 C.A.2d 559

10. A redevelopment agency acquired a junkyard by eminent domain. The owner was unable to relocate her business. She was forced to sell her inventory as scrap for far less than its value for parts. **Is this a compensable loss?**

    Baldwin Park Redev. Agency v. Irving (1984) 156 C.A.3d 428

11. A foreclosure was imminent, and one joint tenant signed the name of the other joint tenant on a deed because the other joint tenant was not available. **Was the transfer valid?**

    Handy v. Shiells (1987) 190 C.A.3d 512

12. When the Johnsons were purchasing their home, their son suggested he be the purchaser so they could take advantage of his GI financing. The parents supplied the down payment and treated the home as their own. Upon the father's death the son asked his widowed mother to leave so he could sell his house. **Is the son's action proper?**

    Johnson v. Johnson (1987) 192 C.A.3d 551

13. A decedent's will left a valuable piece of property to you. However, before her death, she sold the property. The sale did not close until three days after her death. Both you and the residual beneficiary claim the sale proceeds. **What are your rights?**

    Estate of Worthy (1988) 205 C.A.3d 760

14. A dedication of property was made to the City of Palm Springs for specific use as a library. The city wished to convey a portion of the property to a developer for access to a proposed neighboring commercial development. The conveyance would require that a portion of the library be demolished. **Was the proposed conveyance to the developer proper?**

    Save the Welwood Murray Memorial Library Comm. v. City Council (1989) 215 C.A.3d 1003

15. A development plan called for B.F. Goodrich to consolidate its holdings. B.F. Goodrich was unable to reach an agreement to purchase 3.2 acres adjacent to its corporate offices. The redevelopment agency brought an eminent domain action so it could then convey title to B.F. Goodrich. **Was this action proper?**

    Redevelopment Agency of the City of Chula Vista v. Rados Bros. (2002) 95 C.A.4th 309

■ CHAPTER QUIZ

1. After a deed was signed by the grantor, the grantee made a slight unauthorized alteration that increased the size of the property conveyed from 600 acres to 620 acres. The effect of this modification was that

    a. the entire deed became void.

    b. only 600 acres would be transferred because the alteration cannot pass title.

    c. 620 acres were transferred, but the grantee could be liable for damages.

    d. the grantor has one year to discover the forgery and void the transfer.

2. Title transfers with a deed at the time of

    a. delivery.   b. signing.

    c. acknowledgment.   d. recording.

3. The most important factor in the delivery of a deed is

    a. the intent of the grantor.   b. physical conveyance.

    c. possession.   d. recording.

4. After a man's death, a deed giving his home to a nephew is discovered in the same envelope as his will. The will, dated prior to the deed, gave the house to his church. Who gets the house?

    a. The church, because the will was dated prior to the deed

    b. The church, because the deed was never delivered

    c. The nephew, because the deed was dated later and thus modified the will

    d. The nephew, because deeds have priority over wills

5. Which deeds would fail to transfer title?

    a. A deed to John Jones using his stage name "Mr. Marvelous"

    b. A deed made to Henry Schmidt and wife

    c. A deed made to Henry or Henrietta Schmidt

    d. A deed to Tom Brown, an emancipated minor

6. Acknowledgment is necessary to

    a. deliver a deed.   b. validate a deed for recording.

    c. have a formal will.   d. convey legal title.

7. Which is(are) characteristic(s) of a recorded deed?

    a. It must be acknowledged.

    b. It is presumed to have been delivered.

    c. It provides constructive knowledge of the transfer.

    d. All the above are characteristics of a recorded deed.

8. Which is a requirement of a valid deed?

    a. Acknowledgment   b. Dated

    c. Witnesses   d. None of the above

9. Which is a characteristic of a quitclaim deed?

    a. It conveys after-acquired interests.

    b. It can convey a partial interest.

    c. It warrants that the grantor has not previously conveyed the property.

    d. It warrants that there is nothing against the property that the grantor knows about that has not been disclosed.

10. What type of deed is received by a purchaser after a sheriff's sale?

    a. Limited warranty deed   b. Quitclaim deed

    c. Sheriff's deed   d. Grant deed

11. When you receive and record a gift deed, which could adversely affect your title?

    a. Creditors of the grantor

    b. Rights of parties in possession

    c. Prior unrecorded deeds given for valuable consideration

    d. All of the above

12. A grantor retained an easement over conveyed land. What is this called?

    a. A reservation   b. An exception

    c. A codicil   d. An after-acquired interest

13. In obtaining title by adverse possession, it is *NOT* necessary to

    a. live on the property.

    b. actually pay taxes.

    c. have open and notorious occupation

    d. have occupation that is hostile to the interests of the owner.

14. *Tacking on* refers to

    a.   an additional party to an agreement.

    b.   additionally acquired security.

    c.   adverse use of a previous or subsequent user.

    d.   none of the above.

15. Able's property was taken by the city for a new civic center. Baker was Able's tenant in the property and had five years remaining on an advantageous lease. Which statement is *TRUE* of Baker's rights?

    a.   Baker's only right is to 30-day notification.

    b.   Baker has rights against Able for the value of his lease interest.

    c.   Baker has rights against the city for the value of his lease interest.

    d.   Both b and c are true of Baker's rights.

16. Loss of value of remaining land caused by a taking under eminent domain is known as

    a.   inverse condemnation.   b.   the police power of the state.

    c.   severance damage.   d.   exemplary damage.

17. An owner's property was seized because it was used for drug sales. Which statement is correct?

    a.   The owner is entitled to the fair market value of the property.

    b.   If the owner is not found guilty of a felony, the property must be returned.

    c.   Innocence of any knowledge of the use would be a defense against seizure.

    d.   None of the statements above is correct.

18. A codicil providing for transfer of real property is a(n)

    a.   type of deed.

    b.   amendment to a deed.

    c.   original government transfer.

    d.   amendment to a will.

19. Alex's inheritance of a house from his uncle George would be called a

    a.   bequest.   b.   devise.

    c.   legacy.   d.   dedication.

20. Which is a requirement of a holographic will?

    a.   Verbal disposition   b.   Handwritten

    c.   Witnessed   d.   Dated

21. Agnes sold her house and purchased stocks and bonds with the proceeds. Upon her death, a will was found giving her house to her best friend, Mildred. What is Mildred entitled to?

    a.   The stocks and bonds

    b.   The value of the house at the time Agnes died

    c.   The price Agnes received for the house

    d.   Nothing

22. Alice and Jack, a married couple, hold all of their property as community property. When Alice dies intestate, each of the couple's five children will receive

    a.   one-fifth of her property.

    b.   one-fifth of two-thirds of her property.

    c.   one-tenth of her property.

    d.   nothing.

23. A woman died intestate, leaving one living son and two grandchildren (by a deceased daughter) as her only living relatives. The disposition of her property would be

    a.   one-half to her son and one-quarter to each of the grandchildren.

    b.   one-third to her son and one-third to each grandchild.

    c.   to the state by escheat.

    d.   none of the above.

24. A will provided that all of an unmarried testator's estate would go to his only child. His child predeceased the testator, but the child left a spouse and three children. The estate would

    a.   escheat to the state.

    b.   pass one-third to the spouse and two-thirds to the grandchildren.

    c.   pass one-half to the spouse and one-half to the grandchildren.

    d.   pass one-third to each of the grandchildren.

25. The executor brought a bid of $190,000 to the probate court for approval. The court will not consider late bids less than

   a. $190,001.

   b. $191,000.

   c. $200,000.

   d. $209,000.

REAL PROPERTY
SECURITY DEVICES

■ **KEY TERMS**

annual percentage yield (APY)
antimerger clause
assignment of rent
bait and switch advertising
balloon payment
beneficiary statement
blanket encumbrance
California Housing Financial Discrimination Act of 1977
certificate of sale
controlled business arrangement
Covered Loan Act
defeasance clause
deficiency judgment
dragnet clause
due-on-sale clause

Equal Credit Opportunity Act
Fair Credit Reporting Act
fictitious trust deed
financing statement
Garn Act
good faith estimate
holder in due course
hypothecate
lock-in clause
mortgage
Mortgage Forgiveness Debt Relief Act
negotiable instruments
notice of delinquency
obligatory advances
or more clause
partially amortized note
predatory lending
promissory note

Real Estate Settlement Procedures Act
real property sales contract
rent skimming
request for notice of delinquency
right of redemption
security agreement
Servicemembers Civil Relief Act
subject to
trust deed
Truth-in-Lending Act
Truth in Savings Act
uniform settlement statement
wraparound loan

■ PROMISSORY NOTES

A **promissory note** is the evidence of the debt. It is an unconditional written promise signed by the maker to pay a certain sum in money now or at a specific time in the future.

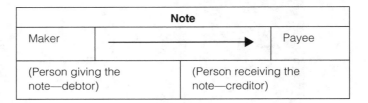

Classification of Promissory Notes

Straight Note.   A straight note is an interest-only payment note with the principal to be paid in full when due. The advantage to the borrower is a lower payment than for an amortized note.

Installment Note.   An installment note provides for regular payments of principal and interest.

Amortized Note.   The regular payments for a fully amortized installment loan pay off the entire principal as well as the interest during the loan term. A **partially amortized note** would have payments based on an amortization schedule, but it would have to be paid in full at a date prior to the end of the amortization schedule (balloon payment).

Negotiable Instruments

While not money, **negotiable instruments** are freely transferable and are used in lieu of money. They are either promises to pay (notes) or orders to another to pay (drafts).

To be a negotiable instrument, a note or draft must be

- in writing,
- signed by the maker,
- an unconditional promise or order to pay another, and
- payable on demand or at a specific time in the future, for a certain sum in money, and payable to the order of the payee or to the bearer.

Whether an instrument is negotiable is of great importance to holders. Assume Anthony gave a note to Bertrand:

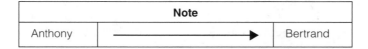

Anthony could have valid personal defenses against paying Bertrand. These defenses could include

- lack of consideration for the promise,
- fraud on the part of Bertrand,
- prior payment or cancellation,

- setoffs from other claims Anthony has against Bertrand, or
- the fact that the note was never delivered to the payee.

Holder in Due Course.   If the note was negotiable, Anthony could not raise these personal defenses against a transferee (Clark) from Bertrand who was a **holder in due course**, often called a *BFP*—bona fide purchaser:

Anthony	→	Bertrand	→	Clark
Maker		Payee		Holder in due course

For a party to be a holder in due course,

- the instrument must be proper and complete on its face,
- the holder must have acquired the instrument prior to its due date without any notice as to previous dishonor,
- the transferee must have been a good-faith purchaser for value, and
- the transferee must have had no notice of any defenses of the maker or any defects in the title of the transferor of the paper.

Assume that the maker (Anthony) had already paid the payee (Bertrand) but had failed to get back the note. While Anthony would have a valid defense against any efforts by Bertrand to collect again on the note, Anthony could not use the prior payment defense against Clark, a transferee from Bertrand who is a holder in due course. Because a holder in due course is not subject to the personal defenses of the maker, the holder in due course has greater rights than the payee (Bertrand).

Some defenses are valid against even a holder in due course. These are known as *real defenses* and include

- incapacity—the maker lacked legal or mental capacity;
- illegality—the note was executed for an illegal purpose;
- forgery; and
- material alteration by the holder. (If the note were raised by a prior holder, a holder in due course could collect on the original terms.)

Case Study

The case of *Wilson v. Steele* (1989) 211 C.A.3d 1053 involved a note secured by a trust deed that was given by a homeowner for remodeling work performed by an unlicensed contractor. The assignee of the note claimed to be protected as a holder in due course. Business and Professions Code Section 7031 requires contractors to be licensed. The Court of Appeal held that because the contractor was not licensed, the contract was illegal and unenforceable. Commercial Code Section 3305 (2)(b) provides that a holder in due course takes free from defenses, but one of the exceptions is illegality of the transaction, which renders the obligation a nullity.

Common Provisions of Notes

Balloon Payments. Often, installment notes provide that the entire balance shall be due at a date prior to the note's being fully amortized. Such notes are called *partially amortized notes*, and the large payment is known as a *balloon payment*. A balloon payment is described as a payment more than twice the amount of the smallest payment (Business and Professions Code Section 10244).

Balloon payments are limited for regulated loans made or arranged by loan brokers. These restrictions do not apply to first trust deeds of $30,000 or more, or to second trust deeds of $20,000 or more (Business and Professions Code Section 10245), nor do they apply to construction loans or notes given by the buyer to the seller to finance the purchaser or to loans made by institutional investors.

A loan with a term of less than three years for nonowner-occupied property may not have a balloon payment. A loan with a term under six years on an owner-occupied dwelling of fewer than three units may not have a balloon payment.

The holder of a balloon note secured by an owner-occupied dwelling of four or fewer units must give from 90 to 150 days' warning of the due date of the balloon payment. Construction loans and loans where seller financial disclosures have been made are exempt from the notification requirement.

Due-on-Sale Clause. Also known as an *alienation clause*, the **due-on-sale clause** calls for the note to be paid in full upon sale of the property. (It accelerates the payments.)

Loans with due-on-sale clauses cannot be assumed. A number of state courts determined that loans made by private individuals and state-licensed lenders were assumable loans despite the language in the notes. In California, in *Wellenkamp v. Bank of America* (1978) 21 C.3d 943, the court determined that an institutional lender could not automatically enforce a due-on-sale clause unless the sale increased the risk of default or impaired the lender's security. Based on California decisions, a huge number of loans with due-on-sale clauses were assumed.

Decisions in California and other states seemed to indicate that all loans were assumable (including those made by federally chartered lenders) unless the assumption impaired the lender's security or otherwise increased the lender's risk.

In 1982, the U.S. Supreme Court, in *Fidelity Federal Savings & Loan v. de la Questa* (1982) 458 U.S. 141, determined that due-on-sale clauses were fully enforceable by federally licensed lenders.

After the *de la Questa* decision, savings associations chartered by states were requesting federal charters to be able to enforce their due-on-sale clauses. Congress then passed the **Garn Act** (Garn–St. Germain Depository Institution Act). The act allowed lenders to enforce due-on-sale clauses unless the loan was made or assumed under state law that allowed loan assumptions at that time. Such loans remained assumable until October 15, 1985 (a three-year window period for assumptions). The due-on-sale full enforcement by federally chartered lenders was not affected by the act.

Because due-on-sale clauses are now considered to be fully enforceable by lenders, a number of methods have been devised to get around the assumption prohibitions. They are at best of questionable legality and at worst could subject the property owner and broker to criminal liability for fraud against a lender. These methods include

- long-term unrecorded lease options,

- unrecorded land contracts,

- friendly foreclosures, in which the lender is really the buyer and the seller does not make payments, so the lender forecloses and obtains the buyer's interest, and

- land trusts.

Not all transfers trigger the due-on-sale provision of notes. Exceptions include transfers resulting from the death of one of the coborrowers and from the dissolution of a marriage, as well as transfers resulting from the foreclosure of a junior lien. A lender knowing of a transfer and failing to act might waive its rights to enforce the due-on-sale clause.

> **Case Study**
> In *Rubin v. Los Angeles Federal Savings and Loan et al.* (1984) 159 C.A.3d 292, the Court of Appeal refused to allow enforcement of the due-on-sale clause because the lender knew of the transfer for four years before it demanded the full payment. The court stated, ". . . although waiver is frequently said to be the intentional relinquishment of a known right, waiver may also result from 'conduct' which according to its natural import is so inconsistent with the intent to enforce the right in question as to induce a reasonable belief that such a right has been relinquished. . . ."

Due-on-Encumbrance Clause.   The due-on-encumbrance clause accelerates the payments on a loan if the owner places a further encumbrance on the property. Civil Code Section 2949, however, prohibits such acceleration for single-family owner-occupied dwellings. For other than a single-family dwelling, a lender can accelerate payments only if the encumbrance endangers the lender's security. (This would be a very unusual situation.)

Acceleration upon Default.   Even when a note states that all payments on the note become due upon default, a borrower can cure a debt that becomes accelerated because of default of payment on principal, interest, taxes, or insurance by paying the amount in arrears plus costs up to five days before sale under a trust deed power-of-sale foreclosure, or at any time prior to entry of a decree on a mortgage foreclosure by court action. Trustee or attorney fees are limited by statute.

Late Charges.   Late charges for a single-family dwelling loan made after January 1, 1976, cannot exceed 6 percent of the principal and interest due; however, a $5 minimum late charge is allowed. No late charge is allowed for payments less than ten days late (Business and Professions Code Section 10242.5).

However, regulated loans of first trust deeds of less than $30,000 and second trust deeds of less than $20,000, made or arranged by a loan broker, can charge 10 percent of the principal and interest as a late charge or $5, whichever is greater.

Late charges for loans not regulated must be reasonable. A late charge that is not reasonably related to the expenses incurred because of the late payment will be considered a penalty and will be unenforceable.

Prepayment Penalties.   The justification for prepayment penalties is that prepayment means an interest loss for the lender until the money has been placed in a new loan, as well as the expense of placing a new loan.

The prepayment fee must be reasonable, based on when the loan was made. An unreasonably high prepayment penalty could be considered an unreasonable restraint on alienation and would not be collectible.

Prepayment penalties are not allowed on FHA-insured or VA-guaranteed loans.

On real property contract sales (land contracts) of one to four residential units, the buyer has the right to prepay; however, the lender can prohibit prepayment for 12 months after the sale.

A clause that provides for payments of a specified amount "*or more*" allows prepayment without penalty.

The absence of any provision allowing prepayment would have the effect of being a **lock-in clause**, locking the borrower in to the full interest for the term of the loan even if the loan is prepaid. To avoid this harsh effect, prepayment is allowed by statute on one to four residential units.

Loans on one to four residential units that were not negotiated by a real estate broker can be prepaid at any time, but prepayment penalties can be assessed for only five years. Twenty percent of the loan can be prepaid in any 12-month period without penalty. Prepayment penalties can be for only the amount prepaid in excess of 20 percent of the original loan amount, and the penalty cannot exceed six months' advance interest on that amount (Civil Code Section 2954.9).

When the loan is for other than one to four residential units, a prepayment fee can be collected only if the borrower expressly waived the right to prepay or agreed in writing to a penalty for prepayment. The borrower must sign this waiver separately.

If the lender does not elect to accelerate the loan upon sale, but the buyer wanted to prepay, a prepayment penalty would appear to be proper (even for one to four residential units), because the lender has not accelerated the payments.

A lender may not collect a prepayment penalty when the lender accelerates the payments upon default for one to four residential units (Civil Code Section 2954.10).

Business and Professions Code Section 10242.6 and Civil Code Section 2954.9 prohibit prepayment penalties for residences that have been damaged by a natural disaster for which the governor has declared a state of emergency and that cannot be occupied when the prepayment is causally related to the disaster.

For loans negotiated by a real estate broker on single-family owner-occupied dwellings, prepayment may be made at any time, but prepayment within seven years of the date of execution could be subject to a prepayment charge. The charge can be imposed only on that portion of the prepayment in excess of 20 percent of the unpaid balance paid in any 12-month period, and the prepayment charge is limited to six months' advance interest on that amount (Business and Professions Code Section 10242.6).

Under the Civil Code, 20 percent of the original amount can be repaid in any 12-month period, but under the Business and Professions Code, it is 20 percent on the unpaid balance.

Usury Interest Rate.   Usury is charging a rate of interest greater than allowed by law. The rate of interest individuals (not exempt from usury limitations) can charge for loans to purchase, construct, or improve real estate cannot exceed 10 percent, or 5 percent greater than the rate designated by the Federal Reserve Bank of San Francisco to member banks for advances as of the 25th day of the month preceding the loan.

This usury rate does not apply to individuals who sell their property and carry back paper (purchase-money loans).

The usury rate also does not apply to loans made or arranged by real estate brokers. The broker is exempt from usury restrictions, even though a loan made by a broker is outside the scope of activity requiring a real estate license (Civil Code Section 1916.1).

Case Study

The case of *Stickel v. Harris* (1987) 196 C.A.3d 575 involved a real estate broker who borrowed money at 30 percent interest for himself and his partners to buy property. The lender sued to recover principal and interest after foreclosure by a prior lienholder. The borrowers argued that the loan rate exceeded the 10 percent usury limit and was not within the usury exemption because the borrower was not acting as a real estate broker. The Court of Appeal upheld the trial court's award to the lender. In this case, the broker acted for both himself and his partners and expected compensation in the form of profit. Therefore, the loan was exempt from the usury limitation.

The broker's usury exemption does not extend to real estate salespeople. See *People v. Asuncion* (1984) 152 C.A.3d 422 for an example where a 288 percent interest rate was held to be usurious.

The usury rate applies to cash loans or forbearance (agreements granting additional time after a loan is due).

Points charged by nonlicensed lenders are considered to be interest in determining whether a loan is usurious.

If a contract is usurious, that portion of the contract calling for interest is void (interest cannot be collected). If a borrower has paid usurious interest, the borrower is entitled to recover the entire amount of the interest paid in the last two years plus treble damages (three times the interest paid) for the last year of the loan.

Impound Accounts.   Impound accounts are trust account reserves kept by the lender for advance payments made by the borrower for property taxes and insurance. The impound account protects the lender in that funds will be available for the taxes and insurance when they are due.

Impound accounts cannot be required for single-family residences unless

- they are required by state or federal law (such as FHA and VA loans), or
- the trustor has failed to pay two consecutive tax payments, or
- the loan is 90 percent or more of the property value or sales price, and the lender requires impounds.

Civil Code Section 2954.1 prohibits excessively large impound accounts. The borrower cannot be required to deposit more than would be required in a federally related loan under the Real Estate Settlement Procedures Act (RESPA), discussed in detail later in this chapter. The section also requires that any sum in excess of monies reasonably necessary to pay obligations must be refunded to the borrower within 30 days unless agreed otherwise. The lender also must make payments in such a manner that insurance is not canceled or property taxes are not allowed to become delinquent.

RESPA (12 U.S. Code §2609) limits the amount of impound accounts for federally related lenders (lenders with Federal Deposit Insurance Corporation [FDIC] insurance). The accounts, when established, can be no more than the prorated taxes and insurance plus an estimated two months' advance charges.

Impound accounts are required for FHA loans. Lenders on FHA loans can require a tax reserve of six months and an insurance reserve of one year.

Impound accounts are not required on VA-guaranteed loans, although the lenders customarily require them.

For impound accounts for one to four residential units, state-licensed lenders must pay interest of at least 2 percent.

Attorney Fees.   Notes frequently provide that the maker agrees to pay reasonable attorney fees if legal action becomes necessary for collection.

■ MORTGAGES AND TRUST DEEDS

While a promissory note is the evidence of the debt, a security device, such as a mortgage or a trust deed, provides security for the note. Mortgages and trust deeds **hypothecate**, or pledge, the property (the borrower keeps possession but gives a security interest).

Mortgages

A **mortgage** is a two-party security instrument in which the mortgagor is the owner or buyer who gives a lien to the mortgagee. The mortgagee is the lender in cases of a hard-money loan (where money actually is advanced) or the seller in cases of a purchase-money loan (where the seller finances the buyer).

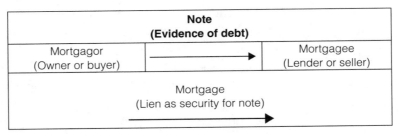

Mortgages are the most common real estate financing instrument in the United States. California, however, favors trust deeds, and mortgages are seldom encountered.

In California, Civil Code Section 2924 provides that a transfer of title given for security purposes is considered a mortgage (a sale with an option of the seller to repurchase). Parties will enter agreements such as this in an attempt to evade the mortgagor's legal rights.

When a mortgage is recorded, it becomes a lien on the property. When the note is paid, the mortgagee gives the mortgagor a "satisfaction of mortgage." The satisfaction, when recorded, removes the lien. The **defeasance clause** in the mortgage provides for the cancellation of the lien upon full payment.

Mortgage		
Mortgagor (has title and possession)	→ creates lien	Mortgagee (has lien)
Satisfaction		
Mortgagor	← removes lien	Mortgagee

After payment of the note, if the mortgagee fails to record a satisfaction of mortgage within 21 days of a written request by the mortgagor, the mortgagee is liable for all damages, as well as the sum of $500.

Mortgage Foreclosure. Under common law, the mortgagee received the property without a sale upon the mortgagor's default. This so-called strict foreclosure is not permitted in California.

In the event of nonpayment by the mortgagor, the mortgagee can enforce the lien and foreclose by court action. Because foreclosure is considered an equitable action, it must be brought in superior court.

The property is sold at a public sale conducted by the county sheriff. The mortgagee can bid the amount of the mortgage lien. Other bidders have to bid cash. Because a foreclosure sale would wipe out all liens junior to the foreclosing mortgage, a junior lienholder who wanted to protect his or her interest would have to bid against the foreclosing mortgagee.

> **Case Study**
>
> In the case of *Webber v. Inland Investments Inc.* (1999) 74 C.A.4th 884, Hyatt Land Development sold four properties to Forecast Mortgage Corporation, carrying back a $754,000 second deed of trust that was later sold to Webber. Sanwa Bank made a $3,653,650 first trust deed loan. Title was transferred to All Cities Mini-Storage. Inland Empire Investments bought the Sanwa Bank note and first trust deed. After default, Inland Empire Investments foreclosed, wiping out Webber's second trust deed. Forecast Mortgage Corporation, All Cities Mini-Storage, and Inland were all owned or controlled by James Previti.
>
> Webber sued all of the companies and Previti for declaratory relief and conspiracy to intentionally interfere with a contractual relationship.
>
> The Riverside County Superior Court awarded Webber $1,254,946 in compensatory damages and $50,000 punitive damages.
>
> The Court of Appeal affirmed as to interference with the contract.
>
> *Note:* This case holds that it is an intentional interference with a contractual relationship for a borrower to use a corporate entity to acquire a senior lien, default on that lien, and foreclose in order to wipe out a junior lien. Because Previti owned or controlled all the corporations, the court had little difficulty in finding this to be a sham foreclosure with the intent of eliminating a junior lien.

When a junior lienholder forecloses, the foreclosure does not affect prior liens, but liens junior to the foreclosing lien are eliminated (the priority of liens, as discussed in Chapter 7, is based on time of recording).

In the event the proceeds of the sale exceed the costs of the sale and the foreclosing mortgagee's lien, the excess goes to pay off junior lienholders in the order of their priority. If any money is left after paying off all of the lienholders, it goes to the mortgagor.

The foreclosure sale is made by sheriff's sale in the same manner as a sale when execution is obtained on a judgment. The property is sold to the highest bidder. Notice of the sale must be posted on the property for 20 days and published once a week for three weeks in a newspaper of general circulation.

The mortgagor can stop the foreclosure anytime prior to the sale date by paying past delinquencies plus costs and fees. Even if the note has an acceleration clause making the entire balance due if a payment is late, the mortgagor need only make the payments current.

The title that is given to the successful bidder is said to *relate back* to the date of the foreclosing lien. The result of this relating-back doctrine is that all subsequent liens other than liens for taxes or special assessments are eliminated by the foreclosure.

Right of Redemption.   California statutes allow a mortgagor to recover the property after a judicial foreclosure sale. This is called the **right of redemption**. If the sale proceeds are less than the foreclosing mortgage debt, the mortgagor has a one-year period of redemption. If the sale proceeds satisfy the foreclosing mortgagee's debt, the period of redemption is three months. By paying the purchaser at foreclosure the sale costs plus interest within the redemption period, the mortgagor can regain title. The mortgagor cannot waive this right of redemption.

Purchasers at mortgage foreclosure sales will have difficulty disposing of property while the mortgagor can still redeem.

The mortgagor has the right to occupy the property during the redemption period, although the mortgagee is entitled to reasonable rent during this period. In reality, the mortgagee might have difficulty collecting the rent, and courts tend to be reluctant to evict a mortgagor during the redemption period.

Mortgages and trust deeds for income property often provide for an **assignment of rent**, which allows the mortgagee to take over the property during the redemption period and apply the rents received to the debt. Without this provision, the mortgagor would keep possession and would be collecting the rents.

Only the mortgagor or successors in interest (heirs or assignees) can redeem after the foreclosure sale.

After the sale, the sheriff provides the high bidder a **certificate of sale** stating that the property is subject to redemption rights. This certificate of sale is recorded. Within one week of the sale, the sheriff must inform the debtor of the right to redeem.

If the property is not redeemed during the redemption period, the sheriff issues a *sheriff's deed*. The grantee receives all of the rights of the foreclosed mortgagor without the foreclosing lien and liens junior to it. Liens senior to the foreclosing lien will still be in force against the property. At this point, the grantee can evict the mortgagor or tenant in possession.

Deficiency Judgments.   Should the judicial foreclosure sale bring less than the amount owed on the mortgage, the foreclosing lienholder can apply for a **deficiency judgment** for the difference, but must do so within three months of the sale. Only after the judicial foreclosure sale can the mortgagee sue the mortgagor for any deficiency amount. Very few deficiency judgments are granted, however, because they are not possible in the following four situations:

1. **Foreclosure is under a power-of-sale clause.** (No deficiency judgments for mortgages or trust deeds foreclosed under power of nonjudicial sale are allowed.) However, a lender on a VA-guaranteed home loan can seek a deficiency judgment after a trustee's sale [*Jones v. Turnage* (1989) 699 F. Supp. 795]. This exception may also apply to FHA home loans.

2. **The foreclosing lien is a purchase-money loan.** There can be no deficiency judgment when the seller provided credit. The seller started out owning the property and ends up owning it, a situation called a *purchase-money mortgage*.

3. **Money advanced by a third-party lender for purchase purposes is also a purchase-money loan.** A mortgagee who provides funds to purchase one to four residential units for occupancy by the mortgagor cannot obtain a deficiency judgment. Purchase-money third-party lenders can obtain deficiency judgments for five or more residential units, nonowner-occupied residential property, or nonresidential property.

4. **The fair market value of the property is equal to or greater than the amount of the lien.** A deficiency judgment is possible only for the difference between the fair market value of the property and the amount of the lien. This prohibits a mortgagee from bidding much less than is owed to manufacture a deficiency.

Anti-deficiency-judgment protection does not extend to debtors when the loan was procured by fraud.

A borrower cannot waive their anti-deficiency-judgment protection in advance or at the time of the loan or loan renewal when the buyer is likely to be under the coercion of the lender.

A sold-out junior lienholder whose rights were lost by the foreclosure may sue the mortgagor directly for his or her note. However, if the junior lienholder had made a purchase-money loan, which would have been precluded from a deficiency judgment, no further collection would be possible.

Case Study

The case of *First Commercial Mortgage Co. v. Reece* (2001) 89 C.A.4th 731 involved a purchase-money loan of $207,593 that was allegedly made based on an inflated $215,000 appraisal. The lender, First Commercial, sold the loan to First Nationwide Mortgage Co. with the agreement that First Commercial would repurchase any bad loans.

After default of the buyer, First Nationwide foreclosed and purchased the property with a full credit bid. As agreed, First Commercial repurchased the property, which they subsequently sold for $79,252. First Commercial then sued the mortgage broker alleging fraud and negligent representation, as well as breach of contract.

The superior court ruled that the full credit bid rule at foreclosure satisfied the loan debt; therefore, this plaintiff could not prove damages. The Court of Appeal reversed, ruling that the full credit bid does not bar a repurchasing lender who suffers damages by misrepresentation, fraud in the inducement, or breach of contract.

Note: If First Commercial had been the one making the full credit bid, then it would have been an admission of property value, so damages could not be shown.

Even though a deficiency judgment is not possible, it could be a mistake for a creditor to bid the full amount owed under the foreclosing lien.

Case Study

The case of *Altus Bank v. State Farm Fire and Cas. Co.* (1991) 758 F. Supp. 567 involved a fire loss. After the loss, there was a foreclosure sale and the lender bid its full-credit amount owed. The lender then brought action against the insurance carrier for acting in bad faith by refusing to pay the insurance loss.

The court held that the mortgagee's full credit bid at foreclosure extinguished the mortgagee's right to make a claim against the homeowner's insurer for the fire loss. In this case, the loss exceeded the debt. By bidding the full amount of the debt owed, the bank cut off any chance of other offers relating to true value. By a full credit bid, the bank was stating that the property was worth what they paid. The court also pointed out that the insurer had no duty to tell the mortgagee the effect of a full-credit bid.

During the early 1980s, some purchasers were buying property without down payments, and then renting the property. They were pocketing the rent receipts and not making payments on the mortgages. Because the sellers' financing constituted purchase-money loans, they felt immune from deficiency judgments.

Civil Code Sections 890–895 were enacted to provide criminal penalties for using rental income during the first year after purchase without first applying it to payments on debts secured by the property (**rent skimming**).

Deed in Lieu of Foreclosure. Often a mortgagee, instead of foreclosing, will have the mortgagor deed the property to the mortgagee. The mortgagee benefits by saving time and foreclosure costs, as well as by avoiding the mortgagor's rights of redemption. The mortgagor benefits by avoiding having their credit report show a foreclosure. Deeds in lieu of foreclosure often are given in exchange for cash or several months' free rent.

A foreclosure of a prior lien will wipe out tenant leases entered into after the lien was created. When rents may have declined on commercial property, creditors have been negotiating deeds in lieu of foreclosure to hold the tenant to leases that are advantageous to the lessor. While a foreclosure wipes out the tenancy, a deed merely transfers the lessor's interest.

A deed in lieu of foreclosure should not be used without a title search. The mortgagee could end up getting the property back subject to a number of liens, such as recorded judgments against the mortgagor. These junior liens would have been eliminated by a foreclosure but now could be in a priority position and able to foreclose on the property. A grantee of a deed in lieu of foreclosure could be buying litigation.

An **antimerger clause** in a mortgage provides that the senior lienholder will retain priority over junior liens in the event of merger. Normally, a lien is extinguished by merger when the lienholder acquires title. If there is an antimerger clause, a foreclosing junior lienholder will be paid only after the sale proceeds have satisfied the senior encumbrances.

A deed in lieu of foreclosure that really was intended as a security device, giving the creditor greater security, rather than as a title transfer, will be considered invalid because it attempted to defeat the debtor's statutory redemption rights.

Some mortgages have sale provisions that provide for a nonjudicial sale in the event of default. These sales would be similar to the sale provision of trust deeds.

Mortgage Forgiveness Debt Relief Act of 2007. Forgiveness of a debt is considered a taxable gain to the debtor. This act provides that debt forgiveness to avoid foreclosure (a short sale) when the property is the principal residence of the debtor will no longer be taxed as imputed income by the federal government (it is still income under California law).

Trust Deeds

Because of the lengthy and costly foreclosure associated with mortgages, as well as the redemption rights that can accrue after the foreclosure sale, the **trust deed** is the most common real estate financing instrument in California.

While a mortgage is a two-party instrument, a trust deed is a three-party transaction. Naked legal title is transferred by the buyer or borrower (the *trustor*) to a

FIGURE 10.1

Trust Deed Flowchart

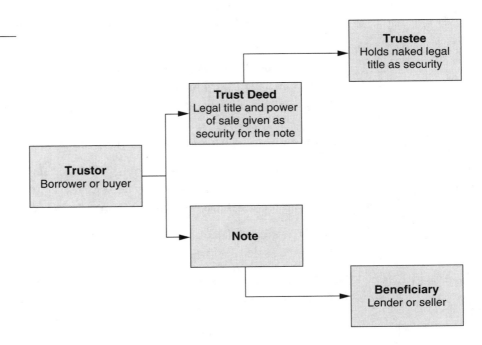

third person (a *trustee*) as security for a note that is given to the lender or seller (the *beneficiary*).

Figure 10.1 shows a trust deed flowchart.

When the trustor finishes paying off the note, the beneficiary delivers the note and trust deed to the trustee with a request for a full reconveyance. Failure to provide the deed of reconveyance within 21 to 30 days of demand can subject the trustee to damages plus a $500 penalty (the same penalty as for failure to provide satisfaction of a mortgage). Failure to provide the deed of reconveyance could, however, result in more than a $500 penalty.

> **Case Study**
> The case of *Pintor v. Ong* (1989) 211 C.A.3d 837 involved a lender who refused to deliver a deed of reconveyance after the note had been paid. The failure to remove the lien made it impossible for the plaintiffs to refinance a first trust deed, which would have allowed them a lower interest rate. They sued for damages for emotional distress and were awarded $15,000, which was upheld upon appeal.

Trust Deed Foreclosure.   In the event the trustor defaults on trust deed obligations, foreclosure is made by private sale and is relatively quick and inexpensive, because the trustee—not the trustor—has the legal title. Default can occur for a number of reasons, such as failure to make loan payments, pay taxes, to keep the property insured, or maintain the property.

Upon the direction of the beneficiary, the trustee forecloses by taking the following actions:

Three-Month Notification of Default   Within 10 days of recording the notice of default, a copy must be sent by registered mail to all persons who recorded a request for notice, and at least 20 days prior to sale the person authorized to make the sale must send, by registered mail, a copy of the notice (often called *special notice*) of the time and place of sale to all those who recorded requests for notification.

According to Civil Code Section 2924b(3), within one month of recording the notice of default, notice must be sent by registered or certified mail to parties whose recorded interests provide constructive notice to the trustee.

The notice of default must advise the trustor of his or her right to sell prior to the trustee's sale.

Notice of Sale   The trustor can stop the sale up to five business days prior to the sale by curing any deficiency and paying costs. To cure the default, in addition to the amount shown in the notice of default, the debtor must also cure all "recurring obligations"—current payments, property taxes, insurance, senior lien payments, etc.—not shown in the notice. If the sale is extended for more than five business days, the reinstatement period is revived.

Notice of sale must be published once a week (3 times) for 20 days and not more than 7 days apart. Notice also must be recorded and posted in a public place, such as city hall or the courthouse, and on the property.

Foreclosure Avoidance   At least 30 days before filing a notice of default, a party seeking to foreclose an owner-occupied residential property must contact the owner to explore options to avoid foreclosure. The notice of default must indicate that such contact was made. There is no requirement that an agreement be reached.

Case Study

California Civil Code Section 2923.5 requires the mortgagee to contact the homeowner to explore options to avoid foreclosure. In the case of *Mabry v. Superior Court* (2010) 165 C.A. 4th 208, the notice of default indicated that Section 2923.5 had been complied with. The debtors sued to postpone foreclosure, alleging they had not been contacted to explore options to avoid foreclosure. The trial court denied the request, ruling that federal law that prohibited states from impairing lenders' ability to transfer loans preempted state mortgage law.

The Court of Appeal reversed, ruling that the state law did not impair federal law. Civil Code Section 2923.5 merely affected the procedure of foreclosure not substantive rights.

Trustee's Sale   A trustee's sale is a public sale in which title is given in the form of a trustee's deed to the highest bidder.

Because deficiency judgments are not possible when foreclosure is made under the sale provisions of a trust deed, the beneficiary generally bids only the amount of his or her lien. However, when a suit for waste is contemplated, the bidder can bid less than the amount of their lien. Other bidders are required to bid cash or by certified check.

Trustee's sales, like mortgage sales, wipe out all junior encumbrances, except a mechanic's lien, where work commenced prior to the trust deed or mortgage being recorded (in which case the mechanic's lien would have priority; see Chapter 11).

The trustee may postpone the sale any number of times at the trustee's discretion without published notice and announce a new sale at the same location. However, the sale may not be postponed beyond 365 days from the original sale date.

The sale must be on a business day between 9:00 a.m. and 5:00 p.m. in a public place within the county where the property is located.

A trustee may reject all bids if he or she believes they are inadequate.

Criminal penalties can be imposed for bid-fixing or offering or accepting consideration for not bidding (bid chilling).

Case Study

The case of *Melendrez v. D&I Investments Inc.* (2005) 127 C.A. 4 th 1238 involved a trustor who was behind in payments. After a Notice of Default, the trustor allegedly reached an oral agreement with the lender as to a payment schedule. Despite the agreement and a $5,000 payment, a foreclosure sale was held and the defendant purchased the property for $197,100 (Evidence indicated the property was worth $375,000).

The trial court held that the sale was to a bona fide purchaser for value and the sale was not subject to being set aside for fraud. The court held that even though the defendant was a foreclosure sale speculator, the purchase was a bona fide purchase for value. The Appellate Court affirmed the decision.

Note: It is important for borrowers to obtain written evidence of repayment agreements. With strong evidence of such an agreement, a lawsuit against the lender would be appropriate.

Case Study

The case of *Lo v. Jensen* (2001) 88 C.A.4th 1093 involved a foreclosure sale by a condominium association for $5,412 in assessments. The day before the sale, one defendant called the other defendant to ascertain interest in the sale. Both defendants regularly competed at sales for similar property. They decided to bid together and share expenses and profits. Both had been considering bids around $100,000. They estimated the fair market value of the condominium at between $150,000 and $160,000. The partners were able to buy the property for $5,412. There were no other liens against the property.

After the sale, the foreclosed owners sued the buyers for violation of the Civil Code Section 2924h(g), which states, "It shall be unlawful for any person, acting alone or in concert with others, to (1) to offer to accept from another, any consideration of any type not to bid, or (2) to fix or restrain bidding in any manner, at a sale of property conducted pursuant to a power of sale in a deed of trust or mortgage."

The trial court vacated the sale ruling that the defendants violated Civil Code 2924h(g) by restraining bidding. The Court of Appeal affirmed, noting that there was unfairness and an inadequate price. The plaintiffs were denied the benefit of competition that they were entitled.

Case Study

In the case of *CTC Real Estate Services v. Lepe* (2006) 140 C.A. 4th 856, Lepe was the victim of identity theft. An unknown perpetrator used her name, social security number, and credit to purchase real estate and obtain two loans against the property. Lepe's signature was forged. The loans were not paid, but foreclosure resulted in an excess of $51,333.87 over the amount due on the two trust deeds. While the attorneys for the trustee believed it would be equitable for Lepe to have the surplus, the Superior Court ordered that the money be paid to the Los Angeles County General Fund.

The Court of Appeal reversed ruling that the surplus should be paid to Lepe. She had been the victim of identity theft and is entitled to the assets stolen even if the value now exceeds that which was stolen.

Note: This decision was really based on equity rather than law. Mrs. Lepe's credit was damaged and the court felt she should be entitled to any surplus.

After the trustee's sale, the trustor has no redemption rights and the purchaser is entitled to immediate possession. (Reinstatement rights are rights of the debtor prior to the foreclosure sale, while redemption rights are rights to regain the property after the sale, such as in a mortgage foreclosure by court action.)

Foreclosure by Court Action If a trust deed failed to include the power of sale, foreclosure would have to be made by judicial sale, the same as for a mortgage.

Any trust deed can be foreclosed by court action rather than by sale under its sale provisions. The reason for foreclosing a trust deed by court action would be to obtain a deficiency judgment. If the trust deed is foreclosed as a mortgage, the trustor has the same redemption rights as a mortgagor.

A creditor can sue directly on the note for the full amount due; however, a creditor who does so gives up the right to foreclose on any security interest.

Case Study

In the case of *Bank of America v. Daily* (1984) 152 C.A.3d 767, a borrower defaulted on a loan secured by real property. The Bank of America seized the amount in the borrower's checking account as a setoff against the loan. The bank then attempted to foreclose on the property. The borrower raised the defense that the bank had waived its security interest. The court held that a creditor is entitled to only one form of action. In this case, the bank elected to forgo its right to the security in taking the defendant's bank account. The Bank of America lost its substantial security in a valuable property by seizing a relatively small checking account.

Junior Lienholders. Because beneficiaries of second trust deeds would be wiped out by senior liens foreclosing, the second trust deed beneficiary would want to know of the senior lien foreclosure to protect their junior interests.

By recording a *Request for Notice of Default*, the junior lienholder will be notified of any "Notice of Default" by the trustee. The junior lienholder can then stop foreclosure and cure the trustor's deficiency by making the trustor's payments. The junior lienholder can then start a foreclosure (based on the monies advanced) and give a three-month notice of default and notice of sale and have a trustee's sale. By buying at the sale, the second trust deed beneficiary owns the property subject to senior encumbrances but wipes out all encumbrances that were junior to it.

Delay by the senior lienholder in foreclosing could result in the junior lienholder's having to cure a significant delinquency. However, with the borrower's written consent, the junior lienholder can request notice from the senior lienholder when the trustor becomes more than four months delinquent (**notice of delinquency**). For a $40 fee, the right to notice is good for five years. Five-year renewals can be obtained by paying a $15 fee.

Liens by Nonowners. Persons who give a mortgage or trust deed on property they do not own will have created a valid lien if they later acquire title. As an example, if a son gives a mortgage or trust deed on a property owned by his father, the lienholder will have no right against the property because the lien was not given by the owner. If the son later acquires title to the property from the father, the lienholder will be able to make a claim against the property to satisfy the lien.

Fictitious Trust Deed.   Recording costs are charged per page. To reduce such costs, lenders record what is known as a master **fictitious trust deed** that includes all of their special provisions (boilerplate). Each trust deed then can be a simple one-page document that incorporates by reference all of the provisions of the fictitious trust deed.

Repossession of Mobile Homes.   Mobile homes that have become real property are foreclosed in accordance with the trust deed. Mobile homes that are not real property are foreclosed in accordance with the Commercial Code.

If the creditor repossesses a mobile home, any person liable under the contract can reinstate the contract by paying the amount in default plus costs and expenses. This right continues until the mobile home is sold in foreclosure. This right of reinstatement may be exercised only once in any 12-month period and only twice during the period of the contract.

The buyer may be precluded from reinstatement if

- the buyer provided false credit information to obtain the loan,
- the buyer moved the mobile home to avoid repossession, or
- waste has been committed on the mobile home.

In these cases, the buyer must pay the entire balance due plus costs.

Any sale proceeds in excess of liens and repossession and sale costs are paid to the former owner.

> **Case Study**
> A deficiency judgment from the sale is possible only if substantial damage to the mobile home has occurred [*Cornelison v. Kornbluth* (1975) 15 C.3d 590].

Real Property Sales Contract

A **real property sales contract**, contract of sale, or land contract is a two-party instrument whereby the seller (vendor) retains legal title and transfers possession to the buyer (vendee).

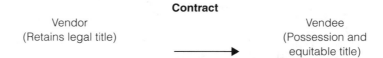

Contract

Vendor
(Retains legal title)

Vendee
(Possession and
equitable title)

The vendee does not get a grant deed until the vendor has been fully paid. A real property sales contract can prohibit prepayment for one year. Therefore, the grantor would not be required to convey legal title for one year. The buyer on a land contract for one to four residential units has the right to prepay a land contract without penalty after 12 months.

The danger for the vendee in a real property sales contract is that the vendor might be unable to transfer marketable title to the vendee when the contract is paid. Vendees can, however, protect themselves by ensuring that the contract is recorded (the vendor must acknowledge the contract for it to be recorded) and obtaining title insurance. (Title insurance is now available for buyers under land contracts.) If a contract were not recorded, the vendor could encumber the property beyond the amount due by the vendee.

A land contract must state the number of years required to pay it off. If taxes are included with the payments, the land contract must include the basis for the tax payment, and the taxes must be kept in a separate escrow account. Land contracts also must include a legal description of the property and must indicate all existing encumbrances.

The risk of loss in a land contract sale is with the buyer, even though the seller retains the legal title. Without the written permission of the buyer, a seller under a land contract cannot encumber the property in an amount exceeding the amount owed on the contract. The seller must apply payments received from the buyer to the encumbrances so that the encumbrances will be paid up when the purchaser has finished paying.

If the seller sells their interest in the contract to another party, the seller also must convey title so that the buyer can get title when he or she finishes paying off the contract.

The case of *Tucker v. Lassen Savings and Loan Association* (1974) 12 C.3d 629 held that a sale by a land contract was not an alienation because title did not pass. Therefore, a land contract sale would not automatically trigger the due-on-sale clause. This decision created a revival of interest in land contracts. Since the passage of the Garn Act, land contracts are no longer a means to avoid due-on-sale provisions, although unrecorded land contracts are still used for this purpose. The benefits probably are outweighed by the dangers to the buyer. As an example, if a land contract were not recorded, an unscrupulous vendor could borrow against the property. When the vendee finished paying on the land contract, the vendee could find that there was still a substantial lien against the property.

A former advantage land contracts had over trust deeds was quick foreclosure. Because of this feature, they often were used when the purchaser had a very low down payment. Courts no longer allow the automatic forfeiture provisions of land contracts, which means that sellers require a quiet title action.

Case Study

The California Supreme Court held in *MacFadden v. Walker* (1971) 5 C.3d 809 that a buyer's default could not be used by a seller to terminate a land contract automatically even though the default was intentional.

Case Study

The California Supreme Court, in *Smith v. Allen* (1968) 68 C.2d 93, allowed a land contract purchaser to get back payments that exceeded the fair rental because the payments unjustly enriched the seller.

> **Case Study**
> In the case of *Petersen v. Hartell* (1985) 40 C.3d 102, the California Supreme Court held that a purchaser who willfully defaulted but had made substantial payments or improvements could redeem prior to a judgment in a quiet title action and within a reasonable period after such judgment as set by the court.

The time and expense of a quiet title action plus the fact that the purchaser may be entitled to a refund or redemption has made the land contract disadvantageous to California sellers.

If the vendor under a land contract violates the law in impairing the rights of the vendee, the vendor could be subject to a fine of up to $10,000 and/or up to one year in county jail or state prison.

Sales in Foreclosure

It is illegal for any person to take unconscionable advantage of a property owner in default. The owner-occupant trustor may void an unconscionable sale of a residence within two years of the date of transaction (Civil Code Section 2945 et seq.), unless the owner-occupant was given a five-day written right to rescind.

Many individuals and firms have gone into the foreclosure consultant business claiming to be able to delay or halt foreclosures. Consumers have a three-day cancellation right after signing a consultant agreement. Consultants must post a $100,000 bond and register with the California Department of Justice.

Consultants may not charge or demand an advance fee before completion of the services contracted for.

Real estate brokers are exempt from the Mortgage Foreclosure Consultants Act. They may arrange loan modification but cannot charge an advance fee. Fee arrangements must state, "It is not necessary to pay a third party to arrange for a loan modification or other form of forbearance from your mortgage lender or servicer. You may call your lender directly and ask for a change in your loan terms. Nonprofit housing counseling agencies also offer these services. . . ."

Real estate agents must take particular care when dealing with owner-occupants who have received notification of default. As a special precaution for the agent, the property owner should have legal representation. Civil Code Sections 1695.15 et seq. and 2945.95 et seq. require that buyer's agents of property in foreclosure and representatives of foreclosure consultants who will not be occupying the one- to four-unit property as their residence must provide written proof to the seller that

- they have a real estate sales license and
- there is a surety bond for twice the fair market value of the property being purchased (such bonds are not widely available in California).

An equity purchaser or foreclosure consultant is liable for all damages from statements made by the equity purchaser's or foreclosure consultant's agent. Violations of the law make the sales contract void and may require damage payments to the seller (no time limit is set).

The effect of these statutes is that buyers' agents for investors/buyers should avoid property in foreclosure unless the parties will agree to an agent's representing the seller only, as a surety bond is then not required.

Case Study

In re Wallace Reed Phelps (2001) 93 C.A.4th 451, the case involved an owner who moved out of her residence while it was in foreclosure. She was subsequently contacted by criminal defendant, Wallace Reed Phelps, and induced to sell the home to him. On the advice of his attorney, the defendant plead guilty of violating the Home Equity Contracts Act. The defendant was not allowed to withdraw his guilty plea and he was sentenced for a felony violation.

The Court of Appeal reversed ruling that Phelps could not have violated the Home Equity Sales Contract Act or the Mortgage Foreclosure Consultants Act because at the time he contacted the homeowner, she was not living in her home. The statutes apply to owner-occupants, and the court held that Phelps was wrongfully convicted.

Case Study

The case of *Garcia v. World Savings* (2010) 183 C.A. 4th 1031 involved a mortgage broker who was aiding a homeowner in default on a mortgage. The mortgage broker notified the lender that the homeowner was in the process of refinancing other property to pay off the loan. The lender agreed to postpone the foreclosure sale until August 29. On August 27, the broker informed the lender that the refinance might not close until early September. On August 29, messages were left with the lender that the loan would be closed within a week. The creditor did not respond but sold the home on foreclosure on August 30.

The homeowner sued the creditor, and the trial court entered summary judgment against the homeowner.

The Court of Appeal reversed and sent the case back for trial on the promissory estoppel cause of action. A lender who promises not to foreclose when the lender is legally entitled to may still foreclose if there was no consideration for postponement. However, if debtors do something they were not obligated to do based on the lender's promise, they have acted to their detriment and the doctrine of promissory estoppel applies.

■ LOAN TYPES, CONDITIONS, AND REGULATIONS

Construction Loans

Construction loans are normally short-term loans for a term of from one to three years, depending on the type of building and customarily bear a higher rate of interest than permanent financing. Loan payments ordinarily are released based on performance of construction tasks. The final payment usually is not made until the mechanic's lien period has expired.

If the builder has not protected the lender through a bond, the lender will insist on lien waivers from all material suppliers and subcontractors. Otherwise, the money might not be sufficient to finish construction.

The payments under construction loans are known as **obligatory advances** because the lender is obligated to make the payments.

The advances made under the loan are covered in a **dragnet clause** that includes the future advances and prevents a subsequent lien from taking priority over the loan advances.

Obligatory advances take precedence over intervening liens, but an optional advance (not required by the original loan agreement) would be junior to intervening liens if the lender had actual notice of the intervening liens.

Seller Financing

Besides mortgages, trust deeds, and real property purchase contracts, several additional financing methods are available exclusively to sellers.

Wraparound Trust Deed. When a property has an assumable below-market-interest-rate loan, the seller could be better off using a wraparound loan than letting a buyer assume the loan and taking back a second trust deed.

A **wraparound loan** (all-inclusive trust deed) is written for the amount of the existing loan as well as for any seller financing. For example, assume a home is to be sold for $70,000, the seller has an existing $30,000 assumable loan at 6 percent, and the buyer has a $10,000 down payment. The wraparound loan would be written for $60,000 at 12 percent interest. The seller would then get 12 percent over the entire $60,000.

$60,000 at 12 percent { $30,000 first trust deed on which seller pays 6 percent
$30,000 seller's equity at 12 percent

The seller, by getting a 6 percent interest differential on the first trust deed, is getting the equivalent of 18 percent interest on his or her equity.

Because wraparound loans involve seller financing, usury limitations do not apply.

If the buyer assumed the first trust deed and gave a second at 12 percent, this situation would exist:

First trust deed, $30,000—buyer assuming at 6 percent
Second trust deed, $30,000—buyer paying seller 12 percent

If the first trust deed had a balloon payment and the seller failed to include one in the wraparound loan, the seller could find that costly refinancing was necessary, and the interest rate being paid might end up exceeding the interest rate being received.

Besides interest differentiation, another advantage that a wraparound loan offers to a seller is that the seller actually makes the payment on the priority loan so he or she knows it is not in default. Because the buyer is not making the payments on the first trust deed, some buyers require lender verification that payments are being made.

Lease Options.   Lease options are often subterfuges to avoid the due-on-sale clause as well as keep the property from being reassessed for property taxes.

These leases might have a large down payment (fee for the option), high rent, and an option to buy at a very low purchase price at a particular time when the existing loan is almost paid off. The courts could be expected to regard such an arrangement as a sale that triggers the due-on-sale clause.

In determining whether a lease option is really a sale, the courts will consider the option cost, purchase price, and rental arrangements.

A disadvantage to the buyer on a lease option agreement is that rent for a residence is not a deductible expense, but interest on a loan as well as property taxes is deductible on personal income tax returns. Because a normal loan payment is mostly interest, the purchaser on an option could be giving up a great deal more than the benefits sought.

Seller Financing Disclosure.   When the seller provides carryback financing for a sale involving one to four residential units, the arranger of credit (broker) must comply with special disclosure requirements set forth in Civil Code Sections 2956–2967. (See Chapter 6.)

The disclosure requirements include

- identification of the note or other credit documents and of the property securing the transaction;
- description of the terms of the note or other credit document or a copy thereof;
- disclosure of the principal terms and conditions of each recorded lien that is or will be senior to the financing being arranged;

- a warning that if refinancing is required because of less than full amortization, such refinancing might be difficult or impossible to obtain in the conventional mortgage marketplace;

- clear disclosure of the fact, when applicable, that a negative amortization is possible as a result of a variable or adjustable interest rate and an explanation of its potential effect;

- an indication, when financing involves an all-inclusive trust deed, of who is liable for payments or responsible for defense in the event of attempted acceleration of a prior encumbrance and what the rights of the parties are in the event of a loan prepayment that results in refinancing, prepayment penalties, or a prepayment discount;

- disclosure of the date and amount of the balloon payment, when involved, and a statement that there is no assurance that new financing or loan extensions will be available at the time of occurrence;

- a disclosure, when the financing involves an all-inclusive trust deed or real property sales contract, of the party to whom payments will be made and who will be responsible for remitting these funds to payees under prior encumbrances and that if that person is not a neutral third party, the parties may wish to have a neutral third party designated for these purposes;

- a statement that no representation of the creditworthiness of the prospective purchaser is made by the arranger and a warning that Section 580b of the Code of Civil Procedure may limit any recovering by the vendor of the net proceeds of the sale of the security in event of foreclosure (no deficiency judgment);

- a statement that loss payee clauses have been added to property insurance to protect the seller or that instructions have or will be given to the escrow or appropriate insurance carrier or a statement that if such provisions have not been made the vendor should consider protecting himself or herself by securing such clauses;

- a statement that a Request for Notification of Default has been recorded or that, if it has not, the vendor should consider recording one;

- a statement that a policy of title insurance has been or will be obtained and furnished to the vendor and purchaser insuring their respective interests or that the vendor and purchaser should consider individually obtaining a policy of title insurance;

- a statement that a tax service has been arranged to report to the vendor whether property taxes have been paid on the property and who will be responsible for the continued retention and compensation of the tax service or that the vendor should assure himself or herself that all taxes have been paid;

- a statement about whether the security documents on the financing have been or will be recorded or a statement that the security of the vendor may be subject to intervening liens if the documents are not recorded; and

- a statement, when applicable, that the purchaser is to receive cash from the proceeds of the transaction (a cash-out buyer), and disclosure of the amount and source of the funds and the purpose of disbursement as represented by the purchaser.

Subordination Agreements.   When a seller agrees to subordinate seller interests, the purchaser can put a later loan on the property that has priority over the seller's lien.

Builders often have sellers agree to a subordinate loan. The builder then can obtain a construction loan that takes precedence over the purchase loan. In effect, the builder is using the seller's equity as collateral for the construction loan. If a loan simply states that it will be subordinate, it will always be last in line. If it says it will be subordinate to a particular loan, then when that particular loan is paid off, it will regain priority.

Subordination clauses have been used in many fraud situations in past years. For example, suppose a person owned a home worth $250,000 free and clear. A purchaser would offer the full price with $100,000 down and the balance to be carried by the seller on a subordinate trust deed at 10 percent interest, all due and payable in six months. The seller might think it was an offer too good to be true and accept it. The buyer could then get a first trust deed for $175,000, pay the seller $100,000, and be a cash-out buyer with $75,000. The buyer would not make any payments on the loan and would let the lender foreclose. To protect his or her interest, the seller would have to make the payments and foreclose on the second trust deed (subordinate). The seller would now have a house encumbered by a $175,000 trust deed. Because it was a purchase-money loan, the buyer would not be liable for a deficiency judgment.

Courts are determining in these cases that the buyer is guilty of fraud and has both civil and criminal liability.

One small protection for sellers who subordinate their interest is to include limitations on the amount and the terms of any loan to which they agree to be subordinate.

A licensee who fails to explain the effects of a subordination agreement fully to a seller could be liable for resulting damages.

Security Agreements— Personal Property

Under the Uniform Commercial Code, a security agreement (often called a *chattel lien* or *chattel mortgage*) creates a security interest in personal property. The security interest is then perfected when a **financing statement** has been filed with the secretary of state. Security agreements for consumer goods, growing crops, and growing timber are filed with the county recorder.

A financing statement, after filing, becomes a lien on the personal property for five years. Continuation statements can be filed for additional five-year periods. A termination statement, when filed, would remove the lien.

Personal property liens are extremely important in the sale of business opportunities and real property containing personal property, such as furnished motels and apartments. Besides a normal title search, a purchaser would want to check for possible liens against the personal property.

Taking Title with a Loan

When a property is sold **subject to** a mortgage or a trust deed, the purchaser takes title with the encumbrance but assumes no personal obligation to pay. While the purchaser must make the payments if he or she is to keep the property, failure to do so would not subject the purchaser to any deficiency judgment. The seller is the individual personally liable on the loan.

Loan Assumption.   When a purchaser assumes an existing loan, the purchaser agrees to be primarily liable on the loan and could therefore be subject to a deficiency judgment in the event of default. The seller remains secondarily liable on the loan.

If a deficiency judgment is possible, it is in the best interest of a buyer to take a "subject to" loan, but it is in the best interest of a seller to insist that a buyer "assume" the loan.

There are currently very few loans that are assumable.

Blanket Encumbrances

A **blanket encumbrance** is a lien (mortgage, trust deed, or real property sales contract) that covers more than one property. In the absence of a release clause, which provides for the release of properties from the blanket encumbrance upon the payment of agreed sums, the debtor would have to pay off the entire blanket encumbrance to convey a property free of the lien.

Lenders often insist on blanket encumbrances to provide themselves with greater security.

Condition of Debt

Borrowers are entitled to know the amount owed (**beneficiary statement**). Beneficiaries and mortgagees must provide this information within 21 days of request. Failure to do so can result in a $300 penalty. There can be a charge for this information, but the borrower must be given an annual statement without cost.

Statute of Limitations

The statute of limitations of four years on written agreements is applicable to mortgages. If a mortgagor has not made any payment within four years of a payment being due, the debt will be outlawed (not legally collectible) because of the statute of limitations.

Civil Code Sections 882.020–882.040 established a statute of limitations on trust deed powers of sale of 10 years from the due date of the obligation (last payment), or 60 years from creation of the obligation if the due date cannot be ascertained.

■ CONSUMER PROTECTION ACTS

Bankruptcy

Debtors frequently use bankruptcy to delay foreclosure. Filing of a bankruptcy petition stops the enforcement of any lien against the bankrupt's property [11 U.S.C. 362a(4)]. In a Chapter 7 bankruptcy, the title to the bankrupt's nonexempt property would pass to a trustee. The creditor would have to either get the trustee to release the property (if the debtor had no equity) or bring a motion for release of the property from the automatic stay.

Real Estate Settlement Procedures Act (RESPA)

The **Real Estate Settlement Procedures Act (RESPA)** is a federal loan disclosure act (12 U.S.C. 2601 et seq.) applicable to federally related first mortgage loans (loans made by lenders insured by FDIC or regulated by the Federal Home Loan Bank or any other federal agency).

The purpose of the act is to provide consumers with information on settlement costs in a timely fashion. The act applies to mortgage loans on one to four residential units, including mobile homes.

The lender is required to supply a **good-faith estimate** of loan costs as well as a Department of Housing and Urban Development (HUD) loan information booklet *Settlement Costs and You* to the borrower within three business days of loan application.

The RESPA disclosure requirements do not apply to

1. loan assumptions, novations, or purchases subject to existing loans;
2. construction loans, unless the construction loan is also the permanent loan;
3. permanent loans for construction when the borrower already owns the land;
4. loans where the purpose of the purchaser is resale (dealer loans);
5. home improvement loans;
6. land contracts; or
7. second mortgages or trust deeds.

The lender cannot charge for compliance with the act. The act prohibits kickbacks and referral fees from service providers. Persons giving or receiving kickbacks or referral fees are liable for civil damages and criminal prosecution, with penalties of up to one year's imprisonment and/or up to a $10,000 fine.

A justifiable service must be provided for every fee charged, and the lender cannot require that the borrower purchase insurance from any particular firm.

The reserve for taxes and insurance (impound account) at closing cannot exceed a prorated estimate plus two months' impound payments.

Upon request, the borrower shall have the right to inspect the settlement statement during the business day preceding settlement. The **Uniform Settlement**

Statement must be mailed or delivered to the borrower and the seller (or their agents) at or before settlement.

RESPA allows a **controlled business arrangement**. A broker can refer business to service providers that the broker has a financial interest in. However, a disclosure must be made as to charges and relationships. The broker may only receive compensation based on profit sharing of the controlled business arrangement, not based on referrals. The controlled business arrangement must function as a separate business.

Equal Credit Opportunity Act

The **Equal Credit Opportunity Act** (15 U.S.C. 1691 et seq.), enforced by the Federal Trade Commission, prohibits credit discrimination because of sex, marital status, age, race, color, religion, or national origin, or because income comes from a public assistance program or because applicant has in good faith exercised any right under the Consumer Credit Protection Act. Credit considerations are limited to income, net worth, employment stability, and credit rating. Individuals may file a discrimination complaint with HUD or sue for damages. The Department of Justice may file a lawsuit when they believe a pattern of discrimination exists.

Fair Credit Reporting Act

The **Fair Credit Reporting Act** (15 U.S.C. 1681 et seq.) restricts credit reports to those with a legitimate need. It also provides that

- an investigative report cannot be made unless it is disclosed to the consumer;

- the consumer has a right to know the substance of the material in their credit file as well as the names of the recipients of reports;

- the consumer has the right to have disputed material investigated;

- the consumer can place a statement of explanation of a dispute in his or her file; and

- the consumer is entitled to a statement of the reasons for adverse action regarding their credit.

California Housing Financial Discrimination Act of 1977

The **California Housing Financial Discrimination Act of 1977**, also called the *Holden Act*, states that a lender cannot deny a loan or change loan terms for reasons unrelated to the credit of the loan applicant. Thus, redlining is prohibited, as it is under the Civil Rights Act of 1968. All other discrimination also is prohibited (Health and Safety Code Sections 35800 et seq.). The Business and Transportation Agency enforces the act and can require compliance as well as a $1,000 payment to persons discriminated against. The act applies to owner-occupied residences of one to four units.

Truth in Savings Act

The **Truth in Savings Act** (12 U.S.C. 4301) is a disclosure act requiring that term, fees, and interest yield on savings, checking, money market account, and certificates of deposit be revealed. Free checking cannot be used if there are any fees. The interest yield must be expressed as **annual percentage yield (APY)**, which is based on a one-year deposit considering compounding of interest.

Truth-in-Lending Act (Regulation Z)

Part of the federal Consumer Protection Act of 1968, the **Truth-in-Lending Act** (15 U.S.C. 1601 et seq.) provides a uniform manner of calculating and presenting the terms of consumer loans to enable borrowers to compare the annual percentage rates and finance costs.

The act's application to real estate is to advertisements for residential property that is to be owner-occupied. The disclosures of the act do not apply if there are to be fewer than four payments. Use of the following terms (*trigger terms*) in the ad requires full disclosure:

- Monthly payment
- Term of loan
- Dollar amount of any finance charges
- Down payment (if the seller is the creditor)

The full disclosure includes the interest rate at an annual percentage rate (APR), the down payment, the monthly payment, and the term of the loan.

Advertising the APR by itself does not trigger full disclosure.

The law makes **bait-and-switch advertising** (advertising property that is not available or that the advertiser will not sell, in an attempt to switch prospects to other property) a federal offense.

While all of the facts must be disclosed in a disclosure statement, the total dollar amount of finance charges need not be included for first mortgages or trust deeds or purchase-money loans. The lender cannot charge for preparation of the disclosure statement.

When a loan is for consumer credit secured by a borrower's residence, a rescission right applies until midnight of the third business day following the completion of the loan. The borrower can waive rescission rights if the loan is needed for a bona fide emergency.

Case Study

In *Jackson v. Grant* (1989) 876 F.2d 764, Union Home Loan gave borrower Jackson the Truth-in-Lending Disclosure Statement and three-day Notice of Right to Cancel on February 18. However, Union was not able to fund the loan until April 29. Almost three years later, Jackson elected to rescind the loan because of the lender's failure to comply with the three-day right of rescission and improper truth-in-lending disclosure. The Ninth Circuit Court of Appeals allowed Jackson to rescind and not to pay any interest on the use of the money for three years.

Case Study

The case of *Jones v. E* Trade Mortgage Corporation* (2005) 397 F 3d 810 involved a prospective borrower who wished to exercise the three-day right to cancel a loan under the Truth-In-Lending Act. The lender told the borrower that he would have to forfeit his $400 "lock-in" fee that assured the interest rate (The reason the borrower wished to cancel was the fact that rates had fallen below the rate that had been "locked in". The borrower then went through with the loan at the higher rate. Jones commenced the lawsuit alleging E* Trade failed to provide a "clear and conspicuous" disclosure of rescission rights.

The Court of Appeals in reversing the District Court dismissal of the claim held that E* Trade cannot be allowed to subvert the rescission right, including the right to return of all the property and money tendered in this transaction.

Note: This case means that "all" money paid to lender must be refunded if rescission right is exercised.

Case Study

The case of *Pacific Shore Funding v. Lozo* (2006) 138 C.A. 4th 1342 concerned Lozo who obtained a $28,000 mortgage on their home from Pacific Shore Funding. Two years later, Pacific Shore refinanced the loan for $71,500 to pay off the first loan as well as prepayment penalties. It is undisputed that Pacific Shore violated the Truth-In-Lending Act by failing to deliver notice of right to rescind with the deadline for rescission.

The Appellate Court stated that "Lenders who omit the disclosures are subject to liability equal to the sum of all finance charges and fees paid by the consumer, unless the failure to comply with the statute is not material." While the Lozos must repay the mortgage balance, Pacific Shore must refund all interest and fees paid, such as loan points, closing charges, and prepayment penalty.

Note: There is a split among federal circuit courts as to the right to rescind a loan, under Truth-In-Lending after a refinance. The court commented, "There is no statutory authority for concluding that a refinance terminates the consumers' rights to rescind the original loan."

Willful violation of the Truth-in-Lending Act is punishable by a fine of not more than $10,000 or imprisonment for not more than one year, or both. It is enforced by the Federal Trade Commission.

Predatory Lending

Predatory lending laws were enacted to protect homeowners from unfair and costly practices that stripped homeowners of their equity and often resulted in foreclosures. These **predatory lending** practices were frequently targeted at lower income and minority homeowners. California's Predatory Lending Law applies to refinancing and home equity loans. California's **Covered Loan Act** (Financial

Code 4970) defines a covered loan as one that does not exceed the conforming loan limit for a single-family mortgage loan established by the Federal National Mortgage Association (FNMA) and either the APR is more than 8 percent above the yield for Treasury securities or the total points and fees exceed 6 percent of the loan. For covered loans,

- prepayment fees are limited to specified conditions and then only during the first three years of the loan;

- loans for five years or less must be fully amortized;

- negative amortization is limited to first loans and must be clearly declared;

- advance loan payments from the loan proceeds are not allowed;

- borrower default cannot trigger increases in interest rate;

- the loan originator must reasonably believe that the borrowers will be able to make payments from sources other than their equity in the property;

- payments from loan proceeds cannot be made directly to a home improvement contractor (can be made jointly to homeowner and contractor);

- lender cannot recommend borrower default on any existing loan;

- lender may not accelerate debt at lender's discretion (call provision);

- refinancing without discernible benefit to the borrowers is prohibited;

- steering a borrower to a higher-risk-rated or higher cost loan product than the borrower is qualified for is prohibited;

- structuring a loan as a line of credit as an attempt to circumnavigate predatory lending restrictions is prohibited; and

- any loan fraud is prohibited.

WEB LINK @

For more information on predatory lending provisions and to review the law, check the California Department of Real Estate site: *www.dre.ca.gov/predatory2.htm.*

Servicemembers Civil Relief Act of 2003

The act protects citizen soldiers and sailors called to active military duty (it does not apply to career military). Protections offered by the act include

- credit obligation entered into before active duty is limited to 6 percent (interest over 6 percent is permanently forgiven);

- the court has the power to stay mortgage and trust deed foreclosure until 90 days after active military service ends;

- families of service personnel may not be evicted without court order for rentals up to $2,400 per month; and

- service personnel may terminate residential leases if transferred.

■ SUMMARY

A promissory note is the evidence of a debt. It is an unconditional written promise to pay a certain sum in money now or at a definite date in the future.

Some common provisions of notes are

- balloon payments, whereby the balance is due in full at a set date;
- due-on-sale clause, whereby the loan must be paid should the property be sold;
- due-on-encumbrance clause, which requires the loan to be paid if an additional loan is placed against the property;
- prepayment penalties for early payment;
- interest provisions—interest rates that are usurious cannot be collected;
- impound accounts, accounts for taxes and insurance that are kept by the lender; and
- attorney-fee clauses, which provide that the borrower pay legal fees necessary for collection.

A mortgage is a two-party security instrument whereby a mortgagor (borrower) gives a lien (the mortgage) to a mortgagee (lender). The mortgage lien is given as security for a note.

Deficiency judgments are judgments for any deficiency between the amount of the foreclosing lien and the foreclosure sale price. Deficiency judgments will not be granted when

- foreclosure is under a power of sale (thus trust deeds foreclosed under the sale provisions cannot result in deficiency judgments, except for VA-guaranteed home loans);
- the foreclosing lien is a purchase-money loan; or
- the fair value of the property exceeds the foreclosing lien.

Trust deeds are three-party instruments in which the trustor (borrower) gives a note to a beneficiary (lender) and, to secure the note, gives a trust deed (naked legal title) to a third party (trustee). When the trustor pays the note in full, the trustee gives the trustor a deed of reconveyance, which, when recorded, removes the lien.

If the trustor defaults on payments, the trustee gives a three-month notification of default, which is followed by a 20-day notice of sale. At the end of this period, the trustee has a sale and gives the purchaser a trustee's deed. After this sale, no redemption by the trustor is possible. However, the trustor can stop the foreclosure by catching up on payments and paying costs anytime within five business days of the sale.

Junior lienholders would be wiped out by a trustee's sale. To protect their interests, they could record a request for notification of default. Upon being notified of default, they could stop foreclosure by making the trustor's payments and then foreclosing on their junior lien. They then could end up owning the property subject to the prior trust deed.

A real property sales contract is a two-party instrument whereby the vendor (seller) keeps the title as security and gives the vendee (buyer) possession. The vendee does not get a deed until the contract is paid up. Real property sales contracts must include a legal description, state the number of years required to pay it up, indicate all encumbrances against the property, and if the payments include taxes, state the basis for the tax payment.

When a seller provides buyer financing, disclosure is required.

Subordination agreements are agreements that seller financing will be secondary to later-acquired liens. They place the seller's interest at risk.

Personal property is secured by a security agreement. A financing statement is filed with the secretary of state and becomes a lien on property for five years. Continuation statements can be filed for additional five-year periods. A termination statement, when filed, releases the lien.

When property is sold subject to a loan, the buyer is under no obligation to pay the loan; but when the loan is assumed, the buyer agrees to be obligated for the loan, making a deficiency judgment possible.

There are a number of consumer protection acts, including the

- bankruptcy laws,
- Real Estate Settlement Procedures Act (RESPA),
- Fair Credit Reporting Act,
- Truth-in-Lending Act,
- Soldiers and Sailors Civil Relief Act, and
- seller financing disclosure laws. Predatory lending practices are prohibited for covered loans.

The Equal Credit Opportunity Act and California Financial Discrimination Act of 1977 prohibit discrimination against borrowers, and the Servicemembers Civil Relief Act prohibits foreclosure within three months after a person leaves active military service.

■ DISCUSSION CASES

1. A mortgagee paid less than the amount owed on the mortgage at a foreclosure sale. The mortgagor subsequently assigned his rights to his wife, who redeemed the property by paying the amount bid. **What are the rights, if any, of the mortgagee?**

   Fry v. Bihr (1970) 6 C.A.3d 248

2. A plaintiff gave a first trust deed to her brother. On the same date, she gave a second trust deed. The second trust deed beneficiary did not know of the first trust deed. The brother foreclosed on the plaintiff, and the plaintiff subsequently filed for bankruptcy. The plaintiff later purchased the property from her brother. The beneficiary of the original second trust deed then foreclosed. **Was the foreclosure proper?**

   Barberi v. Rothchild (1939) 7 C.2d 537

3. The mortgagee assigned the note and mortgage to the mortgagor. The mortgagor then sold the note and mortgage to the plaintiff. **What defenses does the mortgagor have against the foreclosing plaintiff?**

   O'Meara v. De La Mater (1942) 52 C.A.2d 665

4. The beneficiary of a purchase-money trust deed gave an additional loan to the trustor. Prior to this additional loan, the trustor had given a second trust deed to another beneficiary. The trustor defaulted, and the purchase-money loan beneficiary foreclosed. **What are the rights of the parties?**

   Pike v. Tuttle (1971) 18 C.A.3d 746

5. The defendant helped owners in default. He agreed to stop foreclosure actions against their homes. Houses were deeded to the defendant, who then deeded them to straw men who refinanced the property with larger loans. The property then was deeded back to the original owners clear of their default. The defendant kept the difference in the loans as his fee. **Has the defendant done anything wrong?**

   United States v. Miller (1982) 676 F.2d 359

6. **Instead of a definite dollar amount, may a late charge be a percentage of the unpaid principal?**

   Garrett v. Coast & Southern Federal Savings & Loan Ass'n. (1973) 9 C.3d 731

7. A vendor did not wish to go through with a contract of sale. The contract called for the contract of sale to be subordinate and imposed no limitations on subsequent loans. The vendees were not to make their first payment for three years. **Can the vendee get specific performance for this agreement?**

    Handy v. Gordon (1967) 65 C.2d 578

8. The mortgagor was deceased. During foreclosure, the court appointed a receiver, who harvested the crops and applied the proceeds toward the mortgage deficiency judgment. The mortgage decree was not entered into until after the crops had been harvested. **Was the action of the receiver proper?**

    Locke v. Klunker (1898) 123 C. 231

9. In a sale with an option to repurchase, the substantial disparity between the sales price and the option price provided the buyer with an adequate return on his money. **Does the usury law apply to this transaction?**

    Orlando v. Berns (1957) 154 C.A.2d 753

10. **Would the fact that the broker is the borrower exempt a loan from usury limits?**

    Winet v. Roberts (1986) 179 C.A.3d 909

11. **If a trustee's sale results in a sale for far less than the property's value, should the sale be set aside?**

    Moller v. Lien (1994) 25 C.A.4th 822

12. The defendant borrowed $7,060,000 from California Federal Bank (Cal Fed). The note provided for a prepayment clause. Cal Fed sold the loan to the Federal National Mortgage Association (Fannie Mae) at origination, but retained the loan servicing. The defendant inquired if a prepayment penalty would be charged for paying the loan off early. Cal Fed said there would be none. The defendant refinanced without penalty, paying off the Cal Fed loan and receiving the canceled note and deed of reconveyance. Subsequently, Cal Fed had to pay Fannie Mae a prepayment penalty of $653,998.74, which Fannie Mae refused to waive. **Is the defendant liable to Cal Fed for the prepayment penalty?**

    California Federal Bank v. Matreyek (1992) 8 C.A.4th 125

13. A buyer gave a broker a promissory note as a finder's fee. The note was secured by property other than the property purchased. After the security property was foreclosed, the holder of the note sought a deficiency judgment. **Is the note holder entitled to a deficiency judgment?**

    Kurtz v. Calvo (1999) 75 C.A.4th 191

14. A borrower on a $73 million loan defaulted on loan payments and failed to pay property taxes. The owner continued to collect rent during the default period. After the lender foreclosed, the lender sued the borrower for bad-faith waste in failure to pay the property taxes as well as for punitive damages. **Should the lender be entitled to these damages?**

Nippon Credit Bank v. 1333 N. California Blvd. (2001) 86 C.A.4th 486

15. A mortgage servicing firm mistakenly notified a default service that the minimum bid for the trustee's sale should be $10,000. This was a clerical error since $100,000 was intended (the loan balance was $144,656.17). The trustee opened bidding at $10,000 and the high purchasing bid was $10,000.01. **Should the sale be set aside?**

6 Angels, Inc. v. Stuart-Wright Mortgage, Inc. (2001) 85 C.A.4th 1279

16. Prior to a sheriff's sale, a property was damaged by fire. The owner's claim was denied based on a belief the owner was involved in arson. The sheriff's sale proceeds paid off the lender, who also received a check from the insurer because the lender, who was a named insured, was not barred by arson. **Is the lender entitled to be paid twice?**

Washington Mutual Bank v. Jacoby (2009) 120 C.A. 4th 639

■ **CHAPTER QUIZ**

1. To be a negotiable instrument, a note or draft need *NOT* be

    a. a sum certain.

    b. signed by the payee.

    c. an unconditional promise or order.

    d. in writing.

2. Refinancing without a discernable benefit to a borrower is

    a. prohibited by the Servicemembers Civil Relief Act of 2003.

    b. a violation of the Truth in Savings Act.

    c. considered predatory lending.

    d. a violation of the Mortgage Forgiveness Debt Relief Act of 2007.

3. A maker could *NOT* use which as a defense against a holder in due course?

    a. A raised note

    b. Prior payment of the maker to a previous holder

    c. A note given for an illegal purpose

    d. Legal incapacity of the maker

4. The usury law interest regulations do *NOT* apply to

    a. seller purchase-money financing.

    b. cash loans.

    c. loans made or arranged by mortgage loan brokers.

    d. both a and c.

5. For loans on one to four residential units not made or arranged by a real estate broker, prepayment charges can

    a. be charged only for five years.

    b. not be charged on payments up to 20 percent of the original loan in one year.

    c. not exceed six months' interest.

    d. be all the above.

6. The maximum period after a judicial foreclosure sale during which a mortgagor has the right to possession is

    a. 30 days.   b. 90 days.

    c. 6 months.   d. 1 year.

7. Which is more closely related to trust deeds than to mortgages?

   a. Redemption rights after sale

   b. Nonjudicial sale

   c. Deficiency judgments

   d. Legal title with borrower

8. Which constitutes default by a trustor?

   a. Failure to pay taxes

   b. Failure to make monthly payments

   c. Failure to pay insurance

   d. Any of the above

9. Which is a *TRUE* statement regarding trust deeds?

   a. A trust deed is a two-party instrument.

   b. Legal title is held by the beneficiary.

   c. Trustor can reinstate up to five business days prior to sale.

   d. Foreclosure would wipe out all other encumbrances.

10. The total required foreclosure time under a trust deed (power of sale) is most nearly

    a. 4 months.

    b. 9 months.

    c. 1 year.

    d. 18 months.

11. The beneficiary of a second trust deed would be MOST likely to insist on a

    a. subordination clause.

    b. request for notification of default.

    c. subrogation clause.

    d. financing statement.

12. A junior lienholder was worried that a prior lienholder would delay foreclosure until the amount owed was so great that redemption by the junior lienholder would be difficult. To protect against this situation, the junior lienholder should record a

    a. request for notice of default.

    b. request for notice of delinquency.

    c. notice of nonresponsibility.

    d. lis pendens.

13. A financing instrument whereby the seller retains the legal title is a

    a. trust deed.   b. mortgage.

    c. real property sales contract. d. subordination agreement.

14. Which element need NOT be included in a real property sales contract?

    a. The number of years required to pay it off

    b. A legal description

    c. A subordination agreement

    d. The basis for tax payments when taxes are included

15. A dragnet clause in a trust deed covers

    a. any contingency.   b. future advances.

    c. additional parties.   d. increases in the interest rate.

16. A subordinate loan that includes the amount of other loans is known as a(n)

    a. purchase-money loan.   b. wraparound loan.

    c. open-end loan.   d. usurious loan.

17. Seller financing disclosure requires that the broker disclose

    a. whether the purchaser will receive cash from the transaction.

    b. the date and amount of any balloon payment.

    c. both a and b.

    d. neither a nor b.

18. A subordination clause in a trust deed is of greatest benefit to the

    a. trustor.   b. beneficiary.

    c. trustee.   d. tenant.

19. The Servicemembers Civil Relief Act of 2003 protects citizen soldiers by

    a. limiting credit obligations entered into before active duty to 5 percent.

    b. allowing courts to stay foreclosure for up to one year after active service ends.

    c. allowing service personal to terminate residential leases if transferred.

    d. prohibiting any eviction of a service member's family while the service member is on active duty.

20. A financing statement is removed from the records by

    a. final payment of the debt.

    b. a reconveyance deed.

    c. a notice of abandonment.

    d. the filing of a termination statement.

21. Which is *TRUE* of beneficiary statements?

    a. There can be a charge by the beneficiary.

    b. Failure to provide a statement within 21 days of request could result in a $300 penalty.

    c. Both a and b are true.

    d. Neither a nor b are true.

22. RESPA disclosure is the responsibility of the

    a. lender.   b. broker.

    c. escrow holder.   d. title insurer.

23. A lender can properly refuse to grant a loan to a borrower based on

    a. the high rate of loan defaults in the area.

    b. the borrower's public assistance income.

    c. the fact that the borrower is a single person.

    d. none of the above.

24. The Truth-in-Lending Act (Regulation Z) requires that the lender provide the borrower with

    a. the annual percentage rate.   b. the finance charges.

    c. the taxes.   d. both a and b.

25. The Truth-in-Lending Act (Regulation Z) provides that a borrower under a contract that places a lien on his or her residence has a period of rescission of

    a. 24 hours.   b. 3 business days.

    c. 48 hours.   d. 30 days.

CHAPTER ELEVEN

11

INVOLUNTARY LIENS AND HOMESTEADS

■ KEY TERMS

abstract of judgment
ad valorem taxes
affirmation
attachment
cessation of work
declaration of homestead
general lien
homestead

homestead exemption
judgment lien
mechanics' liens
notice of cessation
notice of completion
notice of
   nonresponsibility
preliminary notice

specific liens
stop notice
tax liens
verification
writ of execution

■ INVOLUNTARY LIENS

Involuntary liens are liens against real property that are imposed by the law, as opposed to voluntary liens, such as trust deeds, which are the result of agreement. Liens are a charge against real property, and real property can be foreclosed to satisfy liens.

Judgment Liens

A judgment is a final order of a court. A court's declaration that money is owed does not in itself create a **judgment lien** against the debtor's property. Recording a certified abstract of the court's judgment with the county recorder creates a **general lien** on all of the debtor's nonexempt real property within the county where the judgment is recorded. Certified copies of the **abstract of judgment** might be recorded in additional counties where the debtor has property. An unrecorded judgment or a judgment filed in the wrong county does not create a lien on the debtor's property.

Recording an instrument generally gives it priority over prior unrecorded conveyances and liens. Civil Code Section 1214, which gives this priority, requires that the later conveyance be made in good faith (without notice of the prior conveyance) and for valuable consideration. Judgment creditors are not considered to be bona fide purchasers or encumbrance holders [*Wells Fargo Bank v. PAL Investments Inc.* (1979) 96 C.A.3d 431]. Therefore, a recorded judgment lien would not take priority over a prior unrecorded deed or trust deed given for value.

Judgment liens are good for ten years from the entry of the judgment. Judgment liens based on alimony or child support are good for ten years from the date of recording.

Judgment liens apply to property owned by the debtor at the time the judgment is recorded as well as to postjudgment property acquisitions. While the priority of judgments ordinarily is based on the time of recording, all existing judgments have equal priority as to after-acquired property. A judgment lien applying to after-acquired property is secondary to any purchase-money liens against the property.

Termination of Judgment Liens

Judgment liens can be terminated by the following events:

- Expiration of ten years: The statute of limitations would preclude any action for collection after that period. However, a judgment can be extended for an additional ten years by again recording the abstract of judgment.

- Discharge of the debt in bankruptcy (Debts based on fraud of debtor will not be discharged.).

- Payment and satisfaction: When the debtor has paid, the judgment creditor must give a satisfaction of the judgment within 15 days of demand or be subject to a $100 penalty as well as actual damages. When recorded, the satisfaction releases the lien. Because a judgment is a general lien against all of the debtor's property, a creditor might agree to release a particular property from the general lien in consideration of a partial payment. Because a judgment can be appealed to a higher court, judgment creditors often will agree to accept a lesser sum to satisfy a judgment so as to avoid the risk, time, and expense of an appeal. The judgment creditor also could give a satisfaction without consideration. This would be a gift.

When a debtor has no property, the lien's only value would be against possible future acquisitions. Before commencing a costly lawsuit, creditors ordinarily seek to ascertain whether a resulting judgment will likely be collectible at present or in the future.

Writ of Execution. A judgment creditor, after locating and identifying property of the debtor, can obtain a writ from the court directing the sheriff to seize and sell the debtor's property to satisfy the judgment. This **writ of execution** is a separate lien on the debtor's property for a period of one year.

The judgment creditor who levies execution is given priority over other judgment creditors.

Prior to any sale, the court will hold a hearing at which the debtor will have an opportunity to show why an execution sale should not take place.

When the execution applies to a homesteaded dwelling (discussed later in this chapter), the court will determine the value of the property. The executing creditor can force a sale only if the homeowner's equity exceeds the statutory homeowner's exemption. The property will not be sold unless the bid received is at least equal to an amount that will pay off all liens plus the amount of the homestead exemption and the lien of the judgment creditor enforcing the execution sale. If the highest bid is insufficient, the sale will not be approved, and the judgment creditor will not be able to subject the property to another sale for at least one year.

Case Study

The case of *Little v. Community Bank* (1992) 234 C.A.3d 355 involved a sheriff's sale of homesteaded property. After the sale, the purchaser discovered three IRS liens against the property that had not been listed on the title report relied on by Community Bank in obtaining court approval for the sale. The purchaser, Little, paid the IRS $125,882.94 and sued Community Bank for negligence. The Court of Appeal noted that a sheriff's sale to satisfy a judgment debt can be approved only if (1) the sale proceeds are 90 percent or more of the property value and (2) the sum exceeds the homestead exemption plus any extra amount needed to satisfy all liens. The court ruled that Community Bank was negligent in not discovering the IRS liens before the sale and was liable to Little, who was entitled to a clear title.

The validity of a homestead can be attacked by the judgment creditor. If the homestead declarant did not actually reside on the property or had no actual interest in the property at the time of filing, the homestead will not be valid.

A judgment by itself is not a lien on a homesteaded property. The lien does not attach until levy of execution takes place (Code of Civil Procedure Section 704.950).

Notice of Execution Sale   Notice of an execution sale must be given by

- posting notice of the sale on the property for 20 days prior to the sale,
- publishing notice of the sale once a week for 20 days in a newspaper of general circulation within the county where the property is located, and
- mailing notice to anyone who requests notification from the clerk of the court.

The Execution Sale   The sale must be made at public auction by sheriff's sale in the county where the property is located on a business day between 9:00 AM and 5:00 PM.

The purchaser at the sale receives a certificate of sale.

Redemption Rights   The debtor is allowed to redeem the property from an execution sale within 12 months of the sale (three months if the indebtedness was paid in full by the sale proceeds). The debtor can assign their redemption rights to a third party.

To redeem, the debtor (or assignee) must pay the sales price plus statutory interest, plus taxes, insurance, repairs, and maintenance that were reasonably necessary for the property.

Another judgment creditor also can redeem, but their redemption still will be subject to the redemption rights of the debtor.

A sheriff's deed will be issued to the purchaser if a redemption does not occur within the 12-month period. The purchaser will get no greater interest than the debtor had, so the property could be subject to trust deeds, tax liens, easements, etc.

Section 701.680 of the Code of Civil Procedure provides that an action to set aside the sale must be made within 90 days (if the purchaser is a judgment creditor).

Attachment

Attachment is a process by which real or personal property of a defendant in a lawsuit is seized and kept in the custody of the law to satisfy a judgment that the plaintiff hopes to obtain. The attachment is a prejudgment seizure while a case is pending that ensures the availability of property for execution after a judgment is rendered. One effect of an attachment action is that it can expedite the settlement of claims.

Attachment is now limited to claims arising from the conduct of a business, trade, or profession. Because attachment is based on the theory that only the amount of the debt, not its existence, is in dispute, attachments are limited to actions rising out of express or implied contracts requiring the payment of money.

The attachment lien is in force for three years from the date of levy. The court can extend an attachment lien for an additional two years. The lien can be released by court order, by order of the plaintiff, or by the levying officer.

There is no right of sale with an attachment lien. A sale must be made under an execution after a judgment has been rendered.

Prior to an attachment, a hearing must be held. Property cannot be taken without due process [*Randone v. Appellate Dept.* (1971) 5 C.3d 536]. Before a hearing, the court can issue a temporary restraining order to prohibit the sale of the property.

To obtain an attachment, the plaintiff will have to convince the court that it is needed to protect the plaintiff's interests and that the claims of the plaintiff are likely to be valid.

The court will allow the defendant to post a bond or make a deposit rather than have the property attached; similarly, the court might require the plaintiff to post a bond as a condition to obtain a prejudgment writ of attachment.

The attachment lien will be lost if the defendant prevails in the lawsuit. If the plaintiff obtains a judgment, the attachment lien merges with the judgment lien as of the date of attachment for priority purposes, which would give the creditor priority over liens that otherwise could have priority.

Homeowner Association Liens

Homeowner associations can file liens for unpaid assessments. Assessments that exceed $1800 and have been delinquent for over one year can be foreclosed. The foreclosure sale is subject to a 90-day right of redemption.

Real Property Taxes and Assessments

Property taxes are **ad valorem taxes** in that they are based on property value. Assessments are costs associated with an improvement that benefits a property, such as paving a street.

Proposition 13, enacted in 1978, provides that the assessed value of real estate shall be based on the 1975 tax rolls. Property shall be reassessed upon a purchase by a new owner or other changes of ownership. Changes of ownership that do not trigger reassessment are

- property passing to a surviving spouse or registered domestic partner;
- transfers to children by sale, gift, or inheritance of a parent's principal residence; and
- transfers to children by sale, gift, or inheritance of property other than a principal residence (limited to $1,000,000 in assessed valuation to be excluded from reassessment).

As opposed to general liens, which apply to all of a debtor's property in the county where recorded, liens for property taxes and special assessments are **specific liens** attaching to the particular property on which they are due. Special assessments are for public improvements benefiting the property, such as water, sewers, streets, curbs and gutters, etc.

Property **tax liens** and assessment liens have equal priority and take priority over all other liens, regardless of purpose or when recorded. Because they are priority liens, a tax sale would wipe out not only junior encumbrances but also purchase-money first trust deeds and mechanics' liens.

Taxes on personal property also can be liens against real property if assessed on the secured assessment roll. The personal property tax assessment must be against the owner of the real property.

Real property tax rates are determined on or before September 1. One-half of the tax is due on November 1 and delinquent at 5:00 pm on December 10. The other half is due on February 1 and delinquent at 5:00 pm on April 10.

Real property on which taxes are delinquent goes on the tax-defaulted property rolls after June 30, at which time a five-year redemption begins. (For commercial property, the redemption period is three years.) If the property is not redeemed within the five-year period, the tax collector can sell the property to taxing agencies, revenue districts, certain nonprofit organizations, or anyone at public auction. The tax collector must attempt to sell the property within two years. However, as long as the state retains title, the former owner's redemption rights continue. The property may not be sold for less than 50 percent of its market value. The minimum bid must be approved by the board of supervisors. The purchaser at a tax sale receives a tax deed.

Low income seniors citizens (62 years of age and older) and disabled persons can defer payment of taxes on their residence, in which case the state takes a lien on the property and recovers the taxes plus interest when the owners die or sell the residence.

Federal and State Tax Liens

Liens for federal income tax are general liens and arise when the taxpayer refuses to pay a tax assessment. To have any effect against purchasers or other lienholders, the lien must be recorded.

Liens for state taxes are general liens on all property within the state. Recording is required to establish priority over subsequent liens.

Mechanics' Liens

Mechanics' liens are statutory liens, but they are provided on the basis of equity. That is, improvers of property should have a charge against the property for the value of their improvements; otherwise, owners could receive undeserved enrichment. Mechanics' lien rights are set forth in the California State Constitution (Article XIV, Section 3).

Mechanics' liens are specific liens; they apply only to the property for which labor, material, or services were provided. They play an important role in both construction law and consumer law.

Persons of every class who perform labor, bestow services, or furnish material or equipment that contributes to the construction of, alteration of, addition to, or repair of any building or other structure or work of improvement can file mechanics' liens against the real property. Grading, landscaping, and demolition are included in this definition. Mechanics' liens may not, however, be filed against work contracted for by a public entity (a public work).

Generally, mechanics' liens result when the owner has contracted for services directly or through an architect, general contractor, or subcontractor (regarded as agents of the owner for the purpose of the lien law). A direct privity of contract or even knowledge by the owner of the specific mechanic is not necessary for a mechanic to have lien rights. In California, a worker can file a lien even when their own employer does not file a lien. An unlicensed contractor, however, cannot file a mechanic's lien.

There is an exception in cases where an unlicensed worker performs contracting work where the total price is less than $500 and the owner was made aware that the contractor was not licensed.

Case Study

The case of *Opp v. St. Paul Fire & Marine Ins. Co.* (2007) 154 C.A 4th 71 involved Opp, a California licensed contractor who was President of Mountain Connection, a Montana Corporation that did not have a California contractor's license. Opp, as President of Mountain Connection, Inc., signed a subcontract with a general contractor for work at California State University, Stanislaus. In documentation, Opp put down his personal contractor license. The prime contractor went bankrupt before Mountain Connection was paid. St. Paul Fire and Marine had issued a payment bond for the general contractor. St. Paul refused to pay Mountain Connection because they were an unlicensed contractor. Opp then sued as "William Opp dba Mountain Connection." Opp alleged that Mountain Connection was merely a fictitious name used by Opp. Mountain Connection dropped out of the lawsuit.

St. Paul moved for summary judgment based on the fact that Opp had no standing to sue, as Opp was not a party to the contract.

The court determined that Mountain Connection was the contracting party, not Opp, and the use of Opp's contractor license number did not make him a party. Mountain connection could not recover on the bond because Business & Professions Code Section 7031 precludes unlicensed contractors from enforcing payment.

The Court of Appeal affirmed the trial court decision. The court pointed out that a contractor's license is not required for the person who did the work (Opp claimed to have done the work), but for the party that is the contractor. Mountain Connection was the contractor.

As to Opp's claim that Mountain Connection was simply a fictitious name, B & P.C. Section 17910.5 (a) prohibits use of "Incorporated" or "Inc." in a fictitious name.

Note: Opp wanted corporate immunity but wished to set it aside when it became inconvenient for him.

Case Study

The case of *MW Erectors, Inc. v. Niederhauser Ornamental and Metal Works, Inc.* (2005) 36 C.A. 4th 412 involved failure to have the proper contractor's license. MW Erectors did not have a structural steel contractors' license at the time a contract was entered into with a subcontractor of Disney Corporation, Niederhauser. Anthony Niederhauser was paid by Disney. They refused to pay MW because MW was not licensed before entering the contracts. There were two contracts, one for structural steel work ($955,552.89) and one for ornamental work ($366,694). Work on the structural steel contract began on December 3, 1999, but the contractor was not licensed until December 21, 1999. The work on the ornamental steel contract began after MW was licensed, but MW was not licensed at the time the contract was entered into. The Business and Professions Code requires that a contractor be licensed at all times during performance of the contract.

After Superior Court Summary Judgment in favor of the defendant, MW appealed. The Court of Appeals reversed the decision and Niederhauser appealed to the California Supreme Court.

The Supreme Court ruled that B&PC Section 70316 bars MW from recovery if it were unlicensed at any time during performance of the work. (The doctrine of substantial performance does not apply.) Therefore, MW could not recover for the structural steel contract. However, MW was not barred from recovery for the ornamental steel work ($366,699) because MW was licensed during performance.

Apparently, if any work is done while a contractor is unlicensed, the contractor is barred from recovery for the entire contract.

The decision, while strictly in accordance with the law, seems unjust in that Niederhauser, which was paid in full by Disney, ended up with a windfall of $955,553.

Even when an unlicensed contractor performs the work because of fraudulent representations of the owner, the unlicensed contractor cannot sue in California courts for money owed.

Not only is the unlicensed contractor unable to sue for the contract price, a person who paid an unlicensed contractor may sue for recovery of amounts paid (Business and Professions Code Section 7031).

> ### Case Study
> *Hydrotech Systems v. Oasis Waterpark* (1991) 52 C.3d 988 involved a New York corporation hired as a subcontractor to install surfing pool equipment for a price of $850,000. The water park knew that Hydrotech Systems was not a licensed California contractor. Hydrotech sued for the $110,000 balance owed, and the defense raised was that Hydrotech was not a licensed contractor. Hydrotech amended its complaint alleging fraud. The California Supreme Court pointed out that an unlicensed contractor cannot sue in California courts for any act requiring a contractor's license (Business and Professions Code Section 7031). The court refused to allow any exceptions for fraud or any other reason.

While a contractor must be licensed to file a lien, an employee need not be. The person claiming to be an employee would have the burden to prove that they were not an unlicensed contractor.

To avoid workers' compensation, Social Security contributions, and tax withholding, contracts will sometimes state that a person is an independent contractor and not an employee. Such a contract, by itself, would not disqualify an unlicensed employee from filing a mechanic's lien.

> ### Case Study
> In the case of *Sanders Construction Co. v. Cerda* (2009) 175 C.A. 4th 430, an unlicensed drywall contractor failed to pay workers who filed claims with the state labor commission. The prime contractor was ordered to pay the wages. He appealed and the superior court affirmed the award of wages.
>
> The Court of Appeal affirmed, holding that a general contractor is liable for unpaid wages of unlicensed subcontractors.
>
> *Note:* This sends a message to contractors: do not use unlicensed subcontractors.

> ## Case Study
> In the case of *White v. Cridlebaugh* (2009) 175 C.A. 4th 1535, the responsible licensed contractor manager was in Peru, and the unlicensed manager in charge signed a contract on behalf of the contractor to build a log home. The homeowner sued the contractor for negligent breach of contract, and the contractor sued for $14,000, which was alledgedly still owed.
>
> The trial judge dismissed the contractor claims because the contractor's license was legally suspended because there was no licensed contractor. The trial judge also awarded the homeowner $84,000, which was the amount paid by the homeowner. The trial judge then reversed itself on the $84,000 award.
>
> The Court of Appeal reinstated the $84,000 award, citing the importance of deterring violations of the contractor law.
>
> (Business and Professions Code 7031(b) provides that the homeowner can recover all monies paid to an unlicensed contractor and the amount is not subject to any offset for the value of the work done even if it adds to the value of the property.)
>
> *Note:* This case points out the importance of having the licensed contractor physically available.

Notice of Nonresponsibility

A mechanic's lien also can arise if a property owner discovers unauthorized work being done on their property and fails to give notice that they will not be responsible for the work. The most common situations would be work authorized by tenants or vendees under real property sales contracts. There is often a notice of nonresponsibility posted on stores in shopping centers to protect the owner of the center from liens should the lessee fail to pay contractors.

Within ten days of obtaining knowledge of an actual commencement of work, the owner must post a **notice of nonresponsibility** on the property in a conspicuous place and record a verified copy. Failure to verify has been held not to be a fatal defect [*Baker v. Hubbard* (1980) 101 C.A.3d 226]. Even if a notice is recorded properly, it is ineffective unless it also is posted. If the notice is posted and recorded properly, the owner's interest cannot be liened.

The notice of nonresponsibility must contain

- a property description,
- the name of the person giving notice and the nature of their interest,
- the name of the vendee under the contract or tenant, and
- a statement that the person signing will not be obligated.

While a vendor under a real property sales contract must file a notice of nonresponsibility to be protected against mechanics' liens, the beneficiary under a trust deed need not post or record notice because any mechanics' liens would be subject to prior interest.

If a vendor under a real property sales contract or a lessor under a lease requires the vendee or lessee to make repairs, improvements, or alterations as a condition of the contract or lease, a notice of nonresponsibility will not offer protection from mechanics' liens.

> **Case Study**
> In the case of *Los Banos Gravel Company v. Freeman* (1976) 58 C.A.3d 785, a lease required the lessee to construct a service station and restaurant. Rent was to be based on the gross receipts. The lessor posted a notice of nonresponsibility. The court held that because the property owners were participating with the lessee in the construction of the premises, they were precluded from exempting the property from mechanics' liens by the filing and posting of a notice of nonresponsibility.

Preliminary Notice.   To prevent secret liens or lien claimants, a **preliminary notice** must be given prior to the recording of a mechanic's lien. To fully protect lien rights, the mechanic should file a preliminary notice that the work is subject to lien rights within 20 days of starting work. If the notice is given later, any subsequent liens will cover only the work starting 20 days prior to filing.

The preliminary notice may be served in person or by first class, registered, or certified mail. It must be sent to the owner, the construction lender, and the prime contractor. If the owner contracted directly with the party filing, no notice need be served on the owner. The lender's copy must contain an estimate of the total price of labor, services, and/or material to be furnished.

The preliminary notice must contain

- material to be furnished;
- the name and address of the potential claimant and the name and address of the person who contracted for the purchase of labor, service, equipment, or material;
- a description of the job site; and
- a statement that if the bills are not paid in full, the improved property may be subject to a mechanic's lien.

Period to File a Lien.   A recorded notice filed by an owner that work has been completed, known as a **notice of completion**, sets the exact time of completion. Completion can also be either occupation by the owner or the owner's agent coupled with cessation of labor or acceptance of the work by the owner or the owner's agent. If no notice of completion is filed, any lien claimant can file his or her lien within 90 days of the actual completion of work.

If a notice of completion has been filed, all claimants other than the original contractor have 30 days to file their liens. The original contractor (prime contractor) has 60 days after the recording of the notice of completion to file a lien. The notice of completion must be filed within ten days of completion of work.

Cessation of Work.   If work is stopped and no **notice of cessation** is filed, all lien claimants have 90 days from **cessation of work** to file their liens. Cessation is defined as 60 continuous days without any work being conducted.

If a notice of cessation is filed, all contractors other than the prime contractor have 30 days to file their liens, and the prime contractor has 60 days (the same as for notice of completion).

An owner who files a notice of completion or cessation must notify the original contractor and any subcontractor who has filed a 20-day preliminary notice, within 10 days of recording the notice. Failure to do so would extend the period to file a lien to 90 days.

Figure 11.1 illustrates the time frame for filing mechanics' liens.

FIGURE 11.1
Time Frame for Filing a Mechanic's Lien

TIME FRAME FOR FILING A MECHANIC'S LIEN

- Preliminary Notice – within 20 days of starting work to be fully covered
- Period for filing lien

Notice of Completion filed
    Original contractor has 60 days
    Subcontractors have 30 days

Notice of cessation file
    Original contractor has 60 days
    Subcontractors have 30 days

No notice fled (Completion or Cessation)
    All contractors have 90 days

Recording Mechanics' Liens.   Liens must be verified to be recorded. **Verification** is provided by the mechanic, who swears to the truthfulness of the facts stated. If for religious reasons a mechanic cannot make a public oath, the mechanic will make an **affirmation**, which is a formal declaration that a statement is true. The lien also must

- describe the work of the claimant,
- describe the property covered by the lien,
- state who hired the claimant,

- list the name of the owner or person claiming ownership,
- include the balance due (an intentional overstatement can invalidate the lien), and
- allege that the claimant was licensed at all times during his or her performance.

Enforcing Mechanics' Liens.   Mechanics' liens are enforced through a foreclosure action brought by the lienholder. If they are not satisfied, the property will be sold. The redemption rights from the sale are similar to those in a mortgage foreclosure.

If a lienholder fails to commence an action to enforce a mechanic's lien within 90 days, the property owner can petition the court to remove the lien and may recover up to $2,000 for attorney fees.

Priority of Mechanics' Liens.   All mechanics' liens have equal priority and relate as a whole back to the date on which work actually commenced on the project. When each mechanic started or completed his or her work makes no difference. For the starting time, some work must be apparent to anyone who checks the property. In *Simons Brick Company v. Hitzel* (1925) 72 C.A. 1, the court held that starting time was indicated by "some work and labor on the ground, the effects of which are apparent, easily seen by everyone, such as beginning to dig the foundation, or work of like description that everyone readily can see and recognize as the commencement of a building."

Mechanics' liens, after filing, have priority over other liens attached subsequent to the time of commencement of work. Mechanics' liens also have priority over prior liens that were unrecorded at the time of commencement of work.

The holder of a subsequent mortgage or trust deed can obtain priority over mechanics' liens by posting a bond of not less than 75 percent of the amount of the mortgage or trust deed. The purpose of the bond is to pay judgments in suits to foreclose on mechanics' liens.

Termination of Mechanics' Liens.   Mechanics' liens are lost if no action is taken to enforce them within 90 days of filing. The failure to start action or to file a lien extinguishes only lien rights, not the debt.

Mechanics' liens could be wiped out by a priority lien foreclosing; for example, a trust deed that was recorded prior to the commencement of work.

An owner can get a mechanic's lien released by filing a surety bond of 1½ times the amount of the lien claimed. This is common when an amount due is in dispute.

A tender of full and proper payment that is refused by the mechanic will serve to release the lien. (The debt will still exist.)

Voluntary release of a lien terminates the lien (usually after payment of the debt). A judicial sale also terminates the lien.

Stop Notice. This is a notice to a lender or an owner that a mechanic claimant has not been paid. It is served on the parties (not recorded). To serve a stop notice, the mechanic first must have filed a preliminary notice.

A **stop notice** is a lien on the balance of the funds the lender is holding. It has priority over the lender's using the funds remaining for completion. While a mechanic's lien could be wiped out by a lender's foreclosing, a stop notice protects the mechanic with a lien on the unexpended funds.

Upon receipt of a stop notice, the lender must withhold monies due or to become due in the amount of the claim. If the owner, lender, or prime contractor disputes the validity of the stop notice, a bond in the amount of 125 percent of the amount claimed can be posted; the funds then would be released from the lien.

Lis Pendens

As previously stated, a lis pendens is a notice of a pending lawsuit involving rights concerning real property. When recorded, it is notice to anyone to examine the proceedings because title is in litigation. Any purchaser after the filing takes subject to the adverse claims; however, a lis pendens has no effect on any prior interests.

A lis pendens, while not a lien, protects claimants from a transfer of property that could affect their interests. Wrongfully recording a lis pendens could subject the recording party to damages for slander of title.

Before a lis pendens can be recorded, it must be signed by an attorney or approved by a judge, and all adverse parties must be served with notice. A lis pendens can be expunged (removed from the record) if a court finds that the claimant has not established by a preponderance of evidence the probable validity of the claim.

■ DECLARATION OF HOMESTEAD

Article XX, Section 1.5, of the California Constitution provides for homestead rights. The purpose of a **homestead** is to provide a home free from the fear and anxiety that it will be lost to creditors. A **declaration of homestead** may be recorded by an owner (or lessee under a lease for 30 years or more) to protect the homesteaded property from execution by subsequent judgment creditors.

Case Study

In the case of *Palmer v. Zaklama* (2003) 109 C.A.4th 1367, Mr. and Mrs. Zaklama, both physicians, purchased a home in 1984. In 1989, they moved to New Jersey but hired a property management firm. When the Zaklamas refused to pay for repairs made, the management firm sued and obtained a $9,000 judgment against the house. Execution of the judgment resulted in a sale to the plaintiffs for $10,000, subject to an existing loan. When the Zaklamas learned of the sheriff's sale, they filed a lis pendens, which prevented the buyers from selling the property. They also moved into the house without permission and were arrested and removed by the police. The Zaklamas sued, alleging the buyers were in "cahoots" with the property management firm and the sheriff to acquire title. After the civil suit, the lis pendens was expunged in July 1995.

The foreclosure-sale buyers then sued the Zaklamas for malicious prosecution, abuse of process, and slander of title to recover their losses suffered during the four-year period when the lis pendens prevented them from selling or refinancing the house. The superior court found Esmat Zaklama liable for $235,463 in compensatory damages plus $125,000 punitive damages. Selvia Zaklama was found liable for $235,463 in compensatory damages.

The Court of Appeal affirmed, ruling that slander of title and malicious prosecution are the proper legal remedies for wrongful recordation of a lis pendens. The showing of good faith and a proper purpose are not sufficient for filing a lis pendens. The claimant must also show a probable valid claim. Note that Civil Code section 701.680(a) makes a sheriff's sale absolute and cannot be set aside for any reason unless the purchaser at the sale was the judgment creditor.

A homestead declaration does not protect an owner from voluntary liens, such as trust deeds or from tax liens, mechanics' liens, or homeowners' association assessments. It also does not protect the homesteaded property against judgment creditors whose liens were perfected by recording of the abstract of judgment prior to the recording of the homestead.

To file a homestead declaration, the person recording must reside on the property homesteaded. Actual title is not necessary. Besides a lessee on a lease for 30 years or more, a buyer on a real property sales contract also can file a homestead declaration. A homestead can be filed on any property used as a residence (single-family dwelling, apartment building, farm, condominium, cooperative, mobile home, boat, etc.).

The **homestead exemption** is $75,000 for a single person and $100,000 for a family unit. A $175,000 exemption is available for persons 65 or older, people who have physical or mental disabilities, and low-income persons over the age of 55 ($15,000 or less annual income for a single person and $20,000 or less if married).

> **Case Study**
> In the matter of *In re Rabin* (2006) 336 B. R. 459, the U.S. Bankruptcy Court ruled that registered domestic partners qualify for one $75,000 head of household homestead exemption, not two exemptions. They should be treated the same as married couples since the Domestic Partners Act gives registered domestic partners the same rights and duties of spouses except for filing joint income tax returns.
>
> *Note:* The $75,000 family unit is now $100,000.

The homestead exemption is available in bankruptcy even though a homestead declaration was not filed.

> **Case Study**
> In the case of *In re Howell* (1980) 638 F.2d 81, a father who lived with his 23-year-old unemployed son, who was dependent on the father for support, qualified as a family unit for the homestead exemption.

The homestead exemption applies to an owner's equity. If a home had a fair market value of $100,000 and a $10,000 trust deed against it, the homeowner's equity would be $90,000. If the owner filed as a family unit, the homestead exemption would be $100,000. Subsequent judgment creditors could not force the sale of the property because the homestead exemption exceeds the owner's equity.

Assume that the same homeowner was single and under the age of 65. The homestead exemption then would be $75,000. Because the owner's equity of $90,000 exceeds the $75,000 homestead exemption, subsequent judgment creditors could force the sale.

The proceeds from a creditor's sale of homesteaded property first go to pay off the secured liens ($10,000 first trust deed). Next, the owner receives the amount of their exemption ($75,000) in cash, and the balance, after deducting sale costs, goes to the creditors. The owner has six months to change the cash proceeds into another homesteaded property (the cash cannot be reached by creditors during this period). The homestead exemption does not, however, extend to loan proceeds from refinancing homesteads.

Proceeds from the sale of homesteaded property are protected from creditors for six months. Similarly, if the homestead is destroyed by fire, the proceeds of the insurance are exempt from creditors' claims for six months. In either case, the money can be reinvested in a new dwelling and a new homestead declaration can be filed.

When the owner's equity would allow a sale, the court could partition the property to create a smaller protected homestead. For example, a farm home and a few acres could be partitioned from the balance of the property.

If a husband and wife own separate interests as their separate property, each spouse can file a separate homestead declaration, but their combined exemption cannot exceed that of a family unit.

Either spouse can file a valid homestead on property jointly owned by both spouses. While one spouse formerly could file a declaration of homestead on property separately owned by the other spouse, after July 1, 1983, this was no longer possible. Code of Civil Procedure Section 704.910(b)(1) requires an ownership interest to file a homestead declaration.

Unmarried parties who have an ownership in the same dwelling can file separate homestead exemptions.

Section 6520 of the Probate Code provides that if no homestead property is selected during life, a court can select a probate homestead for the spouse and minor children. This homestead would be effective against the creditors in probate. This homestead protection is limited to the lifetime of the spouse.

When a homesteaded property is sold and a new one is purchased immediately, the new homestead rights take priority as of the date of the prior homestead declaration.

To be valid, a declaration of homestead must be recorded in the county where the property is located. A homestead is not valid unless it is acknowledged. However, Civil Code Section 1207 provides that a recorded instrument that is otherwise valid gives constructive notice after it has been recorded for one year, notwithstanding any defect in or omission of an acknowledgment.

A declaration of homestead must include the following:

- The name of the declared homestead owner (can be both husband and wife if each owns an interest)

- A description of the declared homestead

- A statement that the property is the principal dwelling of the homestead owner and that the homestead owner is residing in the declared homestead at the time the homestead is recorded

Case Study

In the case of *Skinner v. Hall* (1886) 69 C. 195, an owner had rented out his house. He leased one room back from his tenant, where he slept for one night. (His family did not join him.) He then filed his declaration of homestead. The court in this case held that one may file a homestead after residing for one day, a month, or a year. It held that one can have a residency even when one's family resides elsewhere and even in property partially rented out.

A person may have more than one homestead but only one at a time. To terminate a homestead, the owner must either sell the property or file a declaration of abandonment. Moving from the property does not end the homestead.

If a person files a homestead while heavily in debt, creditors may become very nervous. Filing a homestead at the time of purchase generally should not have a significant negative effect on credit.

■ SUMMARY

Involuntary liens are imposed by law, as opposed to voluntary liens, which are created by agreement. Involuntary liens include judgment liens, attachment liens, tax liens, and mechanics' liens.

Judgment liens are general liens against all of the property of the debtor in the county where the abstract of judgment is recorded. A judgment creditor can obtain execution on the judgment, in which case the sheriff seizes and sells the property. The purchaser at the sale receives a certificate of sale. If the debtor fails to redeem the property within 12 months of the sale, the purchaser will receive a sheriff's deed.

An attachment is a prejudgment lien to ensure the availability of property for execution if a judgment is rendered. The attachment is a lien against real property for three years from the date of levy. A hearing must be held, and the court will grant an attachment only if it believes it is necessary to protect the creditor and that the creditor's claim is valid. The defendant can post a bond in lieu of the attachment; an attachment would tie up the property.

Liens for real property taxes and special assessments are specific priority liens. A tax sale will wipe out trust deeds and mechanics' liens.

Federal and state tax liens are general liens, and recording determines their priority.

Mechanics' liens are statutory liens for the value of improvements by a contractor, subcontractor, equipment and material supplier, or laborer. An unlicensed contractor cannot file a mechanic's lien.

Prior to filing a lien, a mechanic who does not have a direct contract with the owner must provide a preliminary notice that the work is subject to a lien. The notice covers work subsequent to the notice and up to 20 days prior to the notice.

If no notice of completion is filed, all mechanics have 90 days after work stops on the project to file their liens. If a notice of completion is filed, subcontractors have 30 days to file and the prime contractor has 60 days. Within 90 days of filing a mechanic's lien, action must be brought under the lien to foreclose the property, or the lien will be lost. A homeowner, or a lessor on a lease for 30 years or more, can record a declaration of homestead, which provides protection against subsequent judgment creditors in the following amounts:

■ Single person: $75,000

- Family unit: $100,000

- 65 or older (or unable to work because of physical or mental disability): $175,000

To file a homestead declaration, the person must live there at the time of filing. To terminate a homestead, the owner must either file a declaration of abandonment or sell the property.

■ DISCUSSION CASES

1. A building corporation also owned a lumberyard. The building corporation sought to foreclose on its own property because the lumber had not been paid for. Why would a company want to foreclose on its own property? **What was the court's probable reaction to this action?**

   Superior Lumber Co. v. Sutro (1979) 92 C.A.3d 954

2. An owner leased property to a convalescent hospital. After the lease was entered into, it was discovered that a great deal of work would be required if the property were to be approved and used for a convalescent home. The owner refused to pay for the work. The tenant authorized the work. The owner filed a notice of nonresponsibility. **Should the property be subject to a mechanic's lien?**

   Baker v. Hubbard (1980) 101 C.A.3d 226

3. A broker furnished trucks, drivers, and equipment for excavating and grading. The broker was not the owner of the equipment provided. **Is the broker entitled to a mechanic's lien?**

   Contractors Dump Truck Service Inc. v. Gregg Construction Co. (1965) 237 C.A.2d 1

4. **Should a mechanic be allowed to foreclose on valuable property when the lien is for a relatively insignificant amount?**

   Robinett v. Brown (1914) 167 C. 735

5. A spouse contracted for work on the separate property of the other spouse. **Is the other spouse liable for the work?**

   Loviet v. Seyfarth (1972) 22 C.A.3d 841

6. After an attachment lien but before a judgment was recorded, a property owner filed a declaration of homestead. **Does the declaration of homestead take priority over the attachment and judgment liens?**

   Becker v. Lindsay (1976) 16 C.3d 188

7. A contractor abandoned a job before the work was substantially completed in accordance with the plans and specifications. The contractor filed a mechanic's lien for the value of material and services he had rendered. **Was the lien proper?**

Marchant v. Hayes (1897) 117 C. 669

8. Prior to filing voluntary bankruptcy, a debtor conveyed her homesteaded property to her daughter for no consideration. **What are the rights of the creditors?**

Gardner v. Johnson (1952) 195 F.2d 717

9. A judgment was entered for child support. After the judgment, the father was absent from the state for most of the time. Twenty-two years later, the wife sought execution of the judgment. **Was she entitled to execution?**

Nutt v. Nutt (1966) 247 C.A.2d 166

10. An engineering firm made aerial topographic maps and studies of a property for a proposed subdivision. It placed engineering stakes and aerial markers on the property. While they could be seen from the air or by walking the property, they could not be seen from the street because of weeds. The engineering firm claimed priority over a loan because of a priority in staking the property and placing the markers. **Does the engineering work constitute commencement of work in terms of the priority of mechanics' liens?**

South Bay Engineering Corp. v. Citizens Sav. & Loan Assn. (1975) 51 C.A.3d 453

11. At the time a landscaper started a job, he was not licensed. In April 2007, the landscaper obtained a license. The homeowner sued for return of $57,500 paid to the landscaper by May 2007. The landscaper appealed a judgment in favor of the homeowner, asserting that the homeowner knew he was unlicensed when the job stared and that $20,000 covered materials that the homeowner retained. **What will the Court of Appeal decide?**

Alatriste v. Cesar's Exterior Designs (2010) 183 C.A. 4th 656

■ CHAPTER QUIZ

1. Involuntary liens include all *EXCEPT*

   a. judgment liens.

   b. tax liens.

   c. attachment.

   d. trust deeds.

2. Which is *NOT* a specific lien?

   a. Property tax lien

   b. Judgment lien

   c. Special assessment lien

   d. Mechanic's lien

3. Henry was injured while swimming in the pool of his neighbor Tom. Henry obtained a $100,000 judgment against Tom. As applied to Tom's house, this would be a(n)

   a. unenforceable lien.

   b. general lien.

   c. specific lien.

   d. priority lien.

4. To create a lien after judgment, the creditor would file

   a. a writ of attachment.

   b. an execution of judgment.

   c. an abstract of judgment.

   d. none of the above.

5. A judgment lien is effective

   a. only in the county where rendered.

   b. only in the county where the debtor resides.

   c. in every county where it is recorded.

   d. for 25 years from recordation.

6. Which is *TRUE* about a judgment that has been enforced by an execution sale?

   a. The buyer receives a certificate of sale.

   b. The former owner has a 12-month period of redemption.

   c. The sale need not be held at the property being sold.

   d. All of the above are true.

7. Which is an example of a prejudgment lien?

   a. Mechanic's lien

   b. Attachment

   c. Homestead declaration

   d. Lis pendens

8. An attachment is a lien for

    a. three years from the date of levy.

    b. four years from the date of levy.

    c. ten years from the date of levy.

    d. ten years from recordation.

9. Which sequence shows the proper legal order for these events?

    a. Execution, attachment, judgment

    b. Judgment, execution, attachment

    c. Attachment, execution, judgment

    d. Attachment, judgment, execution

10. Which is *TRUE* of priority of liens?

    a. Tax liens take priority over prior liens for special assessments.

    b. Tax liens take priority over prior trust deeds.

    c. Judgment liens take priority over prior mechanics' liens.

    d. None of the above is true.

11. Unpaid real estate taxes have a lien priority superior to

    a. prior judgment liens.   b. prior trust deeds.

    c. both a and b.   d. neither a nor b.

12. An unpaid contractor would file which type of lien?

    a. General   b. Specific

    c. Voluntary   d. Attachment

13. An unlicensed person who has mechanic's lien rights would be a(n)

    a. general contractor.   b. subcontractor.

    c. independent contractor.   d. employee of the contractor.

14. A notice of nonresponsibility would *NOT* be filed by a

    a. vendor under a real property sales contract.

    b. lessor.

    c. beneficiary of a prior recorded trust deed.

    d. any of the above.

15. A preliminary notice was filed by a contractor 40 days after work started. The period covered by a subsequent lien would start

    a. with the notice.

    b. 20 days prior to notice.

    c. 20 days after notice.

    d. at no time above.

16. If there is no notice of completion, subcontractors have how many days to file their liens after completion?

    a. 30

    b. 60

    c. 90

    d. 180

17. A contractor started a foundation for a new dwelling, but the owner was not satisfied with his work and paid him off. Three weeks later, the owner got a construction loan secured by a trust deed, which was recorded. The owner proceeded to hire another contractor to build his home, and when the building was finally completed, a painting subcontractor filed a mechanic's lien against the property. What is the result in this case?

    a. The trust deed takes priority over the mechanic's lien.

    b. The mechanic's lien will take priority because a mechanic's lien always takes priority over a trust deed.

    c. The subcontractor will not be able to file against the property but will be able to file a lien against the contractor's property.

    d. The mechanic's lien will take priority over the trust deed because some work was done before the trust deed was recorded.

18. A stop notice

    a. requires that a contractor stop work.

    b. is a lien on construction funds held by a lender.

    c. is equivalent to a lis pendens notice.

    d. is none of the above.

19. A notice of a pending lawsuit involving rights in a property is known as a(n)

    a. attachment.

    b. lis pendens.

    c. execution.

    d. judgment.

20. By filing a valid homestead declaration, the homeowner receives protection against

    a. subsequent mechanics' liens.

    b. prior judgments.

    c. tax liens.

    d. subsequent unsecured claims by creditors.

21. A purchaser of a condominium unit filed a declaration of homestead. The purchaser refused to pay his assessment fees, and the owners' association filed a lien. The lien would be

    a. void because homesteaded property is protected against liens.

    b. enforceable only if the owner's equity exceeds his homestead exemption.

    c. collectible as if there were no homestead.

    d. valid but collectible only when the homestead is sold.

22. A recorded abstract of judgment has priority over a homestead declaration when

    a. it was recorded prior to the homestead.

    b. the homestead is invalid.

    c. the homestead is abandoned.

    d. any of the above occurs.

23. A declaration of homestead would NOT be valid if filed by

    a. a spouse without the other spouse's permission on community property.

    b. a tenant on a 35-year lease.

    c. an owner of a 60-unit apartment complex.

    d. a husband and wife at the start of construction of their future residence.

24. A search of the county records would always show a valid recorded

    a. judgment lien.   b. mechanics' lien.

    c. homestead.   d. all of the above.

25. To give up a valid homestead, the owner would

    a. change residency.   b. rent the premises.

    c. change marital status.   d. do none of the above.

CHAPTER TWELVE

12

ADJACENT PROPERTY RIGHTS

■ **KEY TERMS**

abatement
accretion
affirmative easement
avulsion
doctrine of agreed
   boundaries
dominant tenement
easement
easement by estoppel
easement by necessity

easement by prescription
easement in gross
encroachment
implied easement
lateral support
license
littoral rights
merger
negative easement
nuisance

reliction
right of correlative use
right of prior
   appropriation
riparian rights
servient tenement
spite fence
subjacent support
trespass

■ **BOUNDARY DISPUTES**

When exact property boundaries are uncertain or in dispute, the parties involved can mutually agree to set a fixed line that is clear to both parties. According to the **doctrine of agreed boundaries**, agreed-on boundaries are binding on successors in interest after the boundary has been accepted by the parties for five years. An agreement about the placement of a wall or fence is, however, not necessarily an agreement setting the boundary lines.

In the event of an ambiguity, a boundary reference to a natural monument will prevail over angles or distances.

> **Case Study**
> In the case of *Armitage v. Decker* (1990) 218 C.A.3d 887, a property owner argued on the basis of the doctrine of agreed boundaries that the boundary should be set along a fence. The neighbors successfully argued that the neighbors had not agreed that the boundary should be the fence and that the true boundary was not uncertain but could be proved by legal descriptions and surveys.

When a boundary is clear, an oral agreement setting a different boundary will not bind the parties because it is a grant, which is required to be in writing under the statute of frauds.

The following are additional boundary rules:

- If a boundary is a road, the boundary line ordinarily will be the center of the road.

- If a boundary is a nonnavigable river, the boundary will be the center of the river.

- If a boundary is a navigable nontidal river, the boundary will be the average low-water mark.

- If a boundary is tidelands, the boundary will be the average high-tide line.

Division Fences and Party Walls

Division fences are fences on the boundary line. A fence that rests entirely on the land of one owner is not a division fence. A long-standing fence can imply agreed division.

Party walls can be either on the boundary line or entirely on the land of one owner. Generally, they are the support walls of row-type housing. Party walls are established by express or implied agreement.

For division fences and party walls on the boundary line, each owner owns that portion of the wall or fence on his or her property and also has the right of support of the rest of the wall or fence. Either owner can alter his or her part of the wall or fence but cannot weaken it.

Parties can reach express agreements on the costs of maintaining party walls and division fences, and these agreements will govern. In the absence of any agreement, costs for a division fence will be borne equally by the parties unless one party decides to leave his or her land unfenced. However, if that party fences the land in the future, he or she could be liable for the share of the original cost of the division fence.

It is a misdemeanor to leave a gate open willfully or tear down the fence of another [Penal Code Section 602(h)] that is on the boundary line because part of the fence is owned by another.

Spite fences—fences more than ten feet high that are erected or maintained for the purpose of annoying an adjoining owner—are a private nuisance and can be abated (nuisances and abatement are explained later in the chapter).

> **Case Study**
>
> The case of *Wilson v. Handley* (2002) 97 C.A.4th 1301 involved a row of cypress trees that were planted by the Handleys parallel to a property line. The trees were within two feet to ten feet of the property line and were a hybrid variety designed as a screening barrier or windbreak. Their neighbors, the Wilsons, sued the Handleys relying on Civil Code 841.4 that "any fence or other structure in the nature of a fence" that unnecessarily exceeds ten feet in height and is maliciously erected or maintained for the purpose of annoying a neighbor is a private nuisance.
>
> While a superior court ruled that a naturally growing row of trees is not within the scope of the spite fence nuisance law, the Court of Appeal reversed ruling that the trees could be regarded as a spite fence. The case was remanded for trial on the issue of whether the fence was maliciously erected or maintained for the purpose of annoying the Wilsons.
>
> *Note:* The court pointed out that California has no recognized property right to a view. The court also pointed out that a fence higher than ten feet may be justified if it serves some additional purpose.

Trees

Trees or shrubs whose trunks are on a boundary line are known as *line trees* and belong to both owners. While either owner can remove branches that overhang his or her property (this rule applies to all trees), both owners are liable for the maintenance of line trees and both must agree to the removal of line trees.

■ ENCROACHMENT

An **encroachment** is an intrusion into, under, or over the land of another. Unless the encroacher has taken title by adverse possession or obtained use by a prescriptive easement, a property owner can go to the courts for relief in the form of an injunction prohibiting the continued encroachment or an ejectment, which is an action for ouster and/or damages.

> **Case Study**
>
> The case of *Booska v. Patel* (1994) 24 C.A.4th 1786 involved a defendant who had a contractor sever the roots of a neighbor's tree at the lot line causing the tree to die. The trial court held for the defendant. But the Court of Appeal reversed. While the owner has the right to the surface and everything beneath it (Civil Code Section 829), "one must so use his own rights as not to infringe on the rights of others" (Civil Code Section 3514). The court ruled that Patel did not have an absolute right to sever the roots of Booska's tree if he could have protected his own property interest by taking less severe action. A rule of reasonableness applies, the court explained.

The courts will consider the degree of encroachment, the intent of the parties, the value of the encroaching structure, and the effect on the parties in determining appropriate relief.

An encroaching party might have to remove the encroaching structure, as well as pay damages caused by its removal.

When an encroachment is unintentional and the value of the structure is great compared with the value of the land encroached, the courts and statutes will allow the encroachment to remain, but will have the encroacher pay appropriate damages. While the courts in some instances will allow a good-faith improver of the property of another to retain the use as a matter of equity, such relief will not be available if the encroachment was intentional (Code of Civil Procedure Section 871.1 et seq.).

> **Case Study**
> The case of *Raab v. Casper* (1975) 51 C.A.3d 866 involved improvers who were warned by the plaintiff that they were building a cabin on the plaintiff's land. The defendant disregarded the warning and completed the cabin without a survey. Code of Civil Procedure Section 871.3 requires that the improver's degree of negligence be taken into account in determining his or her good faith and in formulating the relief. The court held in this case that the law should not allow an improver to worsen an owner's position after being warned of a possible trespass. Because of failure to heed the warning, the improver failed to act in good faith.

California courts have applied a relative hardship rule in determining whether to grant an injunction to enjoin a trespass encroachment on another's land.

> **Case Study**
> The case of *Hirshfield v. Schwartz* (2001) 91 C.A.4th 749 involved an unclear boundary line. The defendants built waterfalls, a koi fishpond, stone decking, a putting green, etc., over an area later determined to encroach on the plaintiff's property in three places. The trial court refused to order the encroachment removed and set monetary damages in lieu of removal. The Court of Appeal determined that the cost of removal of the improvements would be substantial but the benefits of removal to the plaintiff would be minimal. The court, therefore, upheld the superior court's decision.

While the courts in some instances will allow a good-faith improver of the property of another to retain the use as a matter of equity, such relief will not be available if the encroachment was intentional (Code of Civil Procedure Section 871.1 et seq.).

Under the common law, the improvements of the improver, even though made in good faith, belong to the landowner. Under California law, a good-faith improver who under mistake of fact or law made improvements believing he or she had the right to do so can remove the improvements; however, the improver will be liable to the owner for any damages to the property.

If an owner knew of the improvements and allowed the innocent improver to continue adding on the improvements, the improver could be allowed the value of his or her labor and materials.

An action to remove a permanent **trespass** (encroachment), such as a building, must be taken within three years of the encroachment, or the encroachment will be allowed to remain. The encroacher will have no right to expand his or her use, nor will the encroacher have the right to rebuild should the encroachment be destroyed.

While a permanent trespass involves taking possession of the land of another with the intent to remain, a continuing trespass is use only. An example of a continuing trespass would be using the land of another for ingress and egress. In the continuing trespass, each repetition is considered a separate wrong. Therefore, the statute of limitations cannot be raised as a defense by a user whose use is continuing. The landowner could sue for an injunction to force the user to cease his or her trespass, as well as for damages for the wrongful use.

■ NUISANCE

Ownership does not carry with it the right to use property in any manner the owner wishes. A person cannot use property in such a manner as to interfere with the reasonable use and enjoyment of others. Such unreasonable use would be considered a nuisance.

A **nuisance** is normally a nonphysical invasion that affects the use or enjoyment of others. It could be smell, dust, light, noise, vibrations, radio interference, dangerous activity, indecent acts, or hours of operation.

In California, the difference between a public and a private nuisance is based on degree. Civil Code Section 3480 states, "A public nuisance is one which affects at the same time an entire community or neighborhood, or any considerable number of persons, although the extent of the annoyance or damage inflicted upon individuals may be unequal."

Any nuisance that is not a public nuisance is considered a private nuisance. While there is no statute of limitations on public nuisances, there is a three-year statute of limitations on private nuisances. Laches is not a defense against the party bringing an action to abate a nuisance.

Courts consider reasonableness in determining whether a use is a nuisance. Livestock noises in an area of farms probably would not be considered a nuisance merely because several suburban residents were disturbed by the noise. Similarly, noise during construction is reasonable and nonpermanent and would not be considered a nuisance, although the noise could constitute a nuisance if the work were done at unreasonable hours.

> **Case Study**
>
> The case of *Lew v. Superior Court* (1993) 20 C.A.4th 866 involved a nuisance. The Lews were the owners of a 36-unit, HUD-insured, Section-8 apartment complex. Seventy-five small claims actions were filed by neighbors each requesting $5,000 damages for allowing illegal drug activity to occur on the premises causing the neighbors emotional and mental distress.
>
> The small claims court awarded each complainant $5,000 plus costs. The superior court set total damages at $218,325, finding that the Lews knew or should have known of the problems generated by their building and failed to remedy the situation. The award was based on the theory of both public and private nuisance.
>
> The Court of Appeal affirmed, holding that by California statute, a drug house is a nuisance and small claims court damages by private parties is a proper remedy. The fact that a nuisance is public does not deprive an individual of his action because, as to him, it is private and obstructs free use and enjoyment of private property.
>
> *Note*: The *Lew* case provides a strong private remedy for neighbors to fight a neighborhood problem.

The fact that zoning permits a use does not mean the use is not a nuisance; it will be considered a nuisance if it unreasonably interferes with the rights of others. It also is not a defense in California that the nuisance was present before the plaintiff moved in.

Action involving a nuisance could be money damages, injunction, or **abatement** (removal) of the nuisance.

A public nuisance that affects the entire community or neighborhood must be abated by a public body or an officer authorized by law. An individual may not abate a public nuisance unless it materially deprives use of private property.

If the roots of a line tree or neighboring tree cause problems, an owner can abate the nuisance. Civil Code Section 3502 provides that, "A person injured by a private nuisance may abate it by removing, or, if necessary, destroying the thing which constitutes the nuisance without committing a breach of the peace or doing unnecessary injury."

This "self help" remedy can be extremely risky, however, because a party whose actions are not justified or reasonable could be liable for damages.

An owner cannot abate the nuisance if it is weeds that are on neighboring land.

Courts will consider the economic effects of the nuisance abatement or injunction compared with the damages caused by the nuisance. Courts also will consider the motives of the parties, such as a personal feud. If an interference is not substantial, courts are unlikely to enjoin a use.

■ WATER RIGHTS

Water is an extremely valuable resource in California, and water rights frequently are subject to litigation. The courts are authorized to refer all water litigation to the state Water Resources Control Board for either investigation and report, or hearing and preliminary determination, subject to final court decision.

Surface water rights depend on whether water is flowing in a defined channel. A property owner generally cannot obstruct the flow of surface water not in a defined channel. An owner can, however, dike against overflow water from a defined channel, which is floodwater, even when such actions cause flooding to land of another.

To dam or divert water in a defined channel requires approval of the local flood control district.

Runoff Damage

Under common law, an owner who changed natural surface water runoff was liable for resulting damages. However, because the development of buildings and paved areas has dramatically increased the amount of runoff, California has modified this liability. While an upper-land owner may be liable if he or she fails to exercise reasonable care, the lower-land owner also must take reasonable precautions to avoid or reduce potential damage.

The rule of reasonableness applies to the use of the upper-land owner. The fact that runoff from use causes some damage to a lower-land owner's land does not in itself make the upper-land owner liable.

See *Keys v. Romley* (1966) 64 C.2d 396.

Water-Related Terms

Following are important water-related legal concepts:

- **Riparian rights** are rights of owners to the reasonable use of water flowing adjacent to, under, or through the property (rivers or streams). Riparian rights are held in common with other riparian owners, even though an owner might never use them.

- **Littoral rights** are rights of owners of property bordering lakes, seas, or oceans (nonflowing water) to a reasonable use of the water.

- The **right of correlative use** holds that an owner does not have absolute use of the ground water not in a defined water course under his or her property. When water is scarce, an owner must share the water table with other owners. The use of underground percolating water in relation to the other owners must be reasonable according to the right of correlative use.

- The **right of prior appropriation** is a concept in several western states that whoever takes water first gets a priority right to future use. While California courts have followed this concept, it has not been followed by the federal courts. One who does not own riparian rights can get rights of prior appropriation through either an easement by grant or an easement by prescription (discussed later in the chapter). An easement by prescription would require the open, notorious, and hostile taking of water under some claim of right for five years without interruption.

- **Accretion** is the gradual and imperceptible buildup of soil by natural causes, such as by action of wind or water. The addition to the land, known as alluvion, belongs to the property to which it is joined. Title is acquired by accession.

- **Avulsion** is the sudden loss of land by action of water, such as a change in a river's course. A property owner has one year to reclaim his or her property. (The river could be diverted back to its original course.)

- **Reliction** is a right holding that when a lake, sea, or river permanently recedes, the adjoining property owners can take title to the adjacent land created by the withdrawal of the water.

■ SUPPORT

Lateral Support

An owner has a right to have his or her land supported in its natural state by the land of neighbors. This support by adjoining property is known as **lateral support**. However, an owner cannot prohibit excavation on a neighbor's property.

A person who is negligent in excavating his or her property will be liable in tort for the resulting damages. In the absence of negligence, an owner does not have absolute liability for damages caused to the property of others by excavations.

Civil Code Section 832 requires that an owner give reasonable notice to neighboring owners of the date of excavation and the depth intended. An excavator who fails to notify adjoining owners of the excavations will have absolute liability for any resulting damages. If the depth is below the neighbors' foundations, the owner must allow the neighbors 30 days to protect their property. An owner has the right to enter the land to be excavated to extend his or her foundations.

If an excavation is to be deeper than nine feet from the curb, the excavator will be liable for damages to neighboring structures. The excavator can enter the neighboring property to protect the structures.

The excavator will not be liable for minor settlement cracks. Heavy rains will not excuse an excavator, because rains can be anticipated.

Because damage might appear later, there is a three-year statute of limitations for damages caused by excavations.

Subjacent Support

Subjacent support is support from below. An underground excavator has an absolute duty to support the surface regardless of any negligence. Cases generally involve owners of mining rights and tunnels for utilities or subways.

■ EASEMENTS

An **easement** is a legal interest in the land of another that entitles the owner of the easement to a limited use or enjoyment in the land of another. It is a nonpossessory interest of one who does not control possession as an owner or tenant. Most residential properties are subject to easements, with utility easements being the most common.

An easement right is for a specific purpose, such as ingress or egress. The easement right could be for continuous use or for intermittent use at specific times. The owner of the property may not interfere with the reasonable exercise of the easement right by the easement holder. Unless the easement specifies exclusive use, it can be used as well by the owner.

> **Case Study**
> In the case of *VanKlompenberg v. Berghold* (2005) 126 C.A. 4 th 345, plaintiff had an easement over defendant's property. The indenture provided that the right-of-way was "to be kept open as a private roadway and be wholly unobstructed."
>
> The defendants had several burglaries and had observed trespassers and illegal dumping. They subsequently installed two locked gates across their easement. While keys to the gates were provided to the plaintiffs, the plaintiffs sought a court order to dismantle the gates. The trial court enjoined the defendants from maintaining gates and the defendants appealed.
>
> The Court of Appeal affirmed the ruling that the easement expressly required the roadway to be "kept open" and "wholly unobstructed." The language of the easement determines the scope of the easement.
>
> *Note*: This case shows that modification of the easement requires concurrence of the easement holder.

Servient Tenement

The land being used by another is in servitude, or serves the needs of another. The land being used, therefore, is known as the **servient tenement**. Because the use by another necessarily places restrictions on an owner's use, a servient tenement is an encumbrance on the land. If the location of an easement is not specified, the servient tenement holder can reasonably designate the easement area.

Dominant Tenement

Normally, an easement benefits other land. For example, ownership of a parcel of land could carry with it the right to cross another parcel. The land being benefited by the easement dominates the servient tenement and is known as the **dominant tenement**. Because a dominant tenement carries benefits with it in the use of the land of another, the easement is considered an appurtenance to the land. Easement rights run with the land, so transfer of title also transfers the rights and/or obligations. The rights of the dominant tenement cannot be separated or conveyed without the land, nor can the dominant tenement holder extend the easement benefit to additional property.

The dominant tenement need not be adjacent to the servient tenement.

Maintenance of Easement

In the absence of any agreement on the maintenance of a right-of-way, the responsibility rests on the dominant tenement. The dominant tenement holder has the right to enter the servient tenement for the purpose of repair and maintenance.

If an easement is jointly used with the landowner and/or with other easement users, the costs of maintaining and repairing the easement will be based on the percentage of use of each user.

Easement in Gross

An **easement in gross** is an easement right that is not joined to any dominant tenement. It is considered personal in nature. Examples of easements in gross would be a right to erect a sign on the land of another or a utility company's right to run lines over a property.

Because an easement in gross is personal in that it does not go with the land, it is considered an assignable right unless the right is expressly or impliedly made personal to an individual. An easement in gross must be expressly transferred to be assigned.

> ### Case Study
> Pacific Telephone had an easement "for the stringing of telephone and electric light and power wires" over the property of Salvaty. A cable television company obtained a license from Pacific Telephone to use its poles. In *Salvaty v. Falcon Television* (1985) 165 C.A.3d 798, Salvaty brought an action for trespass, inverse condemnation, and unfair business practice against the cable company and Pacific Telephone. The court held that inclusion of cable television fell within the scope of the original easement. It was part of the natural evolution of communication and did not increase the burden on the servient tenement.

Figure 12.1 is included to help visualize the above material.

FIGURE 12.1
Easements

The owner of Lot B has an appurtenant easement across Lot A to gain access to the lake. Lot B is dominant and Lot A is servient. The utility company has an easement in gross across both parcels of land for its power lines. Note that Lot A also has an appurtenant easement across Lot B for its driveway. Lot A is dominant and Lot B is servient.

Affirmative and Negative Easements	An **affirmative easement** gives the owner of the dominant tenement the right to do something, normally the right to enter and cross the land of the servient tenement.
	A **negative easement** gives the owner of the dominant tenement the right to prohibit the owner of the servient tenement from some action. For example, the owner of the dominant tenement could impose a height limitation so that the servient tenement owner does not block a view.
Private and Public Easements	Most easements are given to specific property or persons and so are said to be private easements. An easement given to the general public to cross the property is a public easement.
Creation of Easements	**Easement by Grant.** An easement can be created by an actual grant, such as when a person purchases an easement right. Sometimes, easements are needed to obtain map act approval of a subdivision; these easements by dedication also are really easements by grant. Owners might agree to grant easements to each other for a common good, such as a private road serving their properties. Besides grants for ingress or egress, easement can be granted for use, such as seasonal storage. Solar easements protect sunlight for solar collectors. A view easement would pro-

hibit the servient tenement from building or allowing trees to interfere with the view.

Easement by Reservation. An easement can be created by a reservation whereby the grantor retains an easement right over the property granted.

Easement by Prescription. An **easement by prescription** is an easement obtained by use. For the user to obtain the easement, the use must be open, notorious, hostile, under some claim of right, and continuous for five years. Courts hold that a claim of right does not require a belief or claim that the use is legally justified. It merely means that the property was used without the permission of the owner. [*Felgenhauer v. Soni* (2004) 121 C.A.4th 17.] An easement by prescription cannot be obtained against a state, federal, or local governmental unit.

The five-year use need not, however, be by the same user but could be by successors in interest. Tacking on—where, for example, one user uses property for two years and a successor uses it, based on a privity relationship, for three years—will constitute the five years necessary for a prescriptive easement.

Any interference in the use by the legal owner of the property will cause a new five-year period to begin, because the five-year use must be continuous.

The principal difference in establishing an easement by prescription and title to an entire parcel by adverse possession is an easement requires no property tax payment, whereas adverse possession title requires tax payment for five years.

An easement established by prescription is the only easement that is lost by nonuse. Five years of nonuse will end the easement right.

An easement by prescription obtained against a tenant-occupied property applies only to the tenant's interest.

Case Study
In the case of *Dieterich International Truck Sales v. J.S. & J. Services, Inc.* (1992) 3 C.A.4th 1601, a truck sales and repair business had used part of an adjoining property for trucks entering service bays for 22 years. The adjoining truck stop property lessee fenced off the property to install underground tanks for its service station. The truck sales business claimed a prescriptive easement. The court held that while the truck sales and service business had a prescriptive easement against the tenant, who was on a 49-year lease, there was no prescriptive easement against the owner, who would not get possession until 2005.

An easement by prescription applies to the use established during the prescriptive period and may not be expanded for greater use. If the nature of the use changes, a new five-year prescriptive use period will be required to obtain easement rights.

In other easements (by grant or reservation) the courts take a liberal view of use. See *Connolly v. McDermott* (1984) 162 C.A.3d 973.

Civil Code 1009 bars a recreational user from acquiring a prescriptive easement over private land. Therefore, the use would have to be for other than recreational purposes.

The fact that others also are using the property does not defeat an easement by prescription, because multiple easements are possible. However, permission defeats an easement by prescription because the use is not hostile.

A prescriptive easement could be an exclusive easement if the use of others would not be compatible with the prescriptive easement.

Case Study

The case of *Otay Water District v. Beckwith* (1991) 1 C.A.4th 1041 involved a water district that sought quiet title to a prescriptive easement. The water district had purchased property for a reservoir. A grant deed that it received included property that the grantor did not own. The water district then built a reservoir.

The court held that the district's use was hostile and under a claim of right. Its use created a prescriptive easement. The easement was held to be exclusive use since the owner's planned recreational use would have interfered with the use of the reservoir.

Note: While the water district could not obtain title by adverse possession because it did not pay the taxes, an easement of exclusive use gives it all the benefits of ownership.

An implied dedication of an easement to the public is possible if the public, with the owner's knowledge and without consent, uses the right-of-way for five years.

An owner can protect against unauthorized user interests by recording: "The right of the public or any person to make any use whatsoever of the above-described land or any portion thereof (other than use expressly allowed by a written or recorded map, agreement, deed, or dedication) is by permission and subject to control of owner" (Civil Code Section 813). This recording would be conclusive proof that the use was permissive in any lawsuit claiming dedication to public use. For use by other than the general public, the notice must be served by registered mail on the user to be effective.

Owners also can protect themselves from prescriptive easements by posting, at intervals of 200 feet or less, "Right to pass by permission and subject to control of owner, Section 1008, Civil Code."

A servient tenement owner can get title by adverse use against a dominant tenement's easement. Assume a servient owner builds across an easement so that use will be impossible; after five years this adverse use by the servient tenement holder could defeat the prior easement.

> ### Case Study
> In the case of *Masin v. LaMarche* (1982) 136 C.A.3d 687, a servient tenement owner used a road for the storage of material and equipment so that access was denied to the dominant tenement. After seven years' nonuse the dominant tenement holder wished to have the road cleared so it could be used. The court held that the easement had been lost because of the adverse possession by the servient tenement.

Easement by Implication

Besides being expressly created, an easement can be created by implication. An **implied easement** is one that was probably intended, but not expressed. The following are necessary to create an easement by an implied grant:

- There must be a separation of title (prior to separation, the dominant and servient tenements were under the same or common ownership).

- Prior to separation of title, there must have been a use that was obvious and of such duration to indicate it was intended to be permanent.

- The use must have been reasonably necessary for the beneficial enjoyment of the land conveyed.

> ### Case Study
> *Dubin v. Robert Newhall Chesebrough Trust* (2001) 96 C.A.4th 465 involved a landowner who blocked an access driveway to the plaintiff's property that was over other land owned by the defendant. The access over the driveway was not mentioned in the lease. After the death of lessor, the successor owner asked Dubin not to use the driveway. When Dubin did not comply, the owner erected crash posts to block the driveway, which had been used by heavy trucks and trailers. Dubin sued the landlord alleging an implied easement appurtenant, an easement by necessity, and a prescriptive easement. While the superior court granted the landlord's demurrer, the Court of Appeal reversed.
>
> Although other access precluded an easement by necessity and a prescriptive easement was not present as the use was for less than five years, the court ruled that Dubin did state a claim for implied easement appurtenant. The court indicated the easement use was reasonably necessary for use of the premises.
>
> *Note:* The court seemed to be saying that if the landlord and tenant had thought about it, they would have included the easement in the lease. Because they did not, an implied easement appurtenant was created.

If an owner sells a lot that in the past has been reached through land retained by the grantor, the courts could say that an easement right was implied. The courts would consider whether the use was reasonably necessary for proper use, whether it was apparent at the time of sale, and whether the parties intended an easement to exist.

For an implied easement by reservation, the use must have been necessary (not reasonably necessary) for the reasonable enjoyment of the property retained by the grantor. An example would be the owner selling a house on a street while retaining a house on the back portion of the lot but failing to reserve an easement right over a driveway on the portion of the land conveyed.

Oil and mineral rights carry with them an implied easement to enter and drill or mine unless the right is clearly excluded (in which case entry would have to be made outside the property).

A former tenant has an implied easement to enter and harvest the crops that were the fruit of his or her labor (emblements).

California generally does not recognize the common-law-implied easement of light and air. An exception is the Solar Shade Act (California Public Resources Code Sections 25980–25986), which provides an implied easement of light in special cases. After a party has installed a solar collector in compliance with the act, a neighbor cannot permit trees to shade more than 10 percent of the solar collector between the hours of 10:00 AM and 2:00 PM.

To defeat the possibility of an easement by implication, the parties can specify that no easement by grant or reservation will arise by implication.

Easement by Necessity

California courts will in some instances create an **easement by necessity** when an easement is required to allow reasonable use of a property. The dominant and servient tenements must have been under common ownership at time of conveyance. A grantor must have conveyed a portion of a property, retaining a portion, and have created a landlocked parcel. There also can be no other way to get to the property, no matter how inconvenient or difficult. It is a strict necessity concept. Once granted, an easement by necessity runs with the land but will be lost if another access becomes available.

No payment is required when an easement by necessity is created, under the theory that the prior common owner just forgot about creating an easement.

Easement by Eminent Domain

Easements can be obtained by condemnation for any public purpose. This right has been given to utilities for rights-of-way. The landowner is entitled to be compensated for any loss in value caused by the taking of the easement.

It is possible for a property owner to use condemnation to obtain an easement for utility services over the land of another. It does not have to be the only way to obtain utilities, just the most practical.

Easement by Estoppel

An **easement by estoppel** can be created when an owner, by words or acts, causes another party to act to his or her detriment. For example, if an owner told a prospective purchaser of a neighboring parcel that there was an easement to it over his road, the owner could be estopped (prevented) from denying the existence of the easement after the other party purchased the land.

Termination of Easements

Easements are lost upon the following events:

- Destruction of the servient tenement: If there is no longer a servient tenement, there can be no easement.

- **Merger**: If the dominant and servient tenements become owned by the same person, the easement can be lost. A person would not have an easement over his or her own property. When a lesser interest and a greater interest are joined, the lesser interest is lost by merger.

- Nonuse: Nonuse terminates only an easement by prescription (five years' nonuse).

- Deed: A quitclaim deed from the holder of the dominant tenement to the holder of the servient tenement ends the easement. This would be an express release of the easement.

- Prior lien foreclosure: If a prior lien against the property exists at the time an easement is granted, the subsequent foreclosure of that lien will wipe out the easement. The dominant tenement holder could have obtained an agreement with the lienholder to subordinate his or her interest to the easement.

- Estoppel: If a dominant tenement holder indicates to the servient tenement holder that the easement will not be used or has been abandoned and the servient lienholder relies on this statement to his or her detriment, the dominant tenement holder will be estopped from claiming an easement right.

- End of purpose: An easement ends when the stated purpose of the easement ends. An easement to enter so as to hunt game will end with the urbanization of the area.

- End of necessity: An easement granted because of necessity ends when the necessity no longer exists.

- Eminent domain: The taking of the property for a public purpose ends the easement. The dominant tenement holder will, however, have a claim for his or her interest based on just compensation for the fair market value.

- Misuse: An easement can end by misuse, although an injunction and/or monetary damages, not forfeiture, would be the normal remedy granted by the courts.

■ LICENSE

Unlike an easement, a **license** is not an interest in land; it is a permissive use. What would otherwise be a wrongful trespass would be permissible with a license. Unauthorized use or trespass does not create a license. A license always requires permission and is revocable.

While a license can be an exclusive privilege, in the absence of any agreement it will be nonexclusive.

A license is personal to the licensee. It does not transfer with real property, cannot be assigned by the licensee, and cannot be inherited. Transfer of ownership of the property over which the licensee has permission will revoke the license.

A licensee is not a tenant. A tenant has possession and can assign his or her interests. A licensee does not have possession, but merely a revocable privilege to use.

Because a license is not an interest in real property, the statute of frauds does not prohibit the creation of oral licenses.

An owner has a duty to keep the property in a safe condition for the licensee. The licensee should be warned of any danger.

While a license generally can be revoked, courts have held that where the licensee has expended capital and labor in reliance on the license, it would not be equitable to allow the owner to revoke the license. The principle of estoppel will apply.

> **Case Study**
> In the case of *Cooke v. Ramponi* (1952) 38 C.2d 282, a license was granted to use a road. The licensee expended a great deal of money and energy improving the road and building culverts. The court held that the license was irrevocable. Using the doctrine of equitable estoppel, the court determined that to decide otherwise would allow the licensor to perpetrate fraud against the licensee.

■ SUMMARY

Parties can agree on fixed boundaries when exact boundaries are in dispute. Such agreements bind successors in interest to the parties (doctrine of agreed boundaries).

In the event of an ambiguity in a boundary, reference to a natural monument will take precedence over angles or distances.

An encroachment is an intrusion into, under, or over the land of another. An action to remove a permanent encroachment must be taken within three years of the encroachment, or it will be allowed to remain. A good-faith improver of the property of another will be allowed to remove his or her improvements but will be liable for damages to the property of another. If the improvement is costly, however, the court might allow the unintentional encroachment to remain intact.

A nuisance is a use that interferes with the use or enjoyment of the land of another. An abatement action would be taken to remove a nuisance, and an injunction would require a use to cease.

An upper-land owner may be liable if he or she fails to exercise reasonable care and runoff consequently causes damage to a lower property. The courts will consider the utility of the upper-land owner's use compared to the harm caused.

Riparian rights are the rights of an owner to reasonable use of water flowing through, under, or adjacent to a property. Littoral rights are the rights to reasonable use of nonflowing water (lakes or seas).

The right of correlative use is the reasonable right to use, in conjunction with others, the underground percolating water.

California follows the doctrine of prior appropriation. The first user of water has priority over later users.

Owners have duties toward others, which include lateral and subjacent support of other lands.

An easement is an interest in the land of another (normally for ingress and egress). The property using the land of another is the dominant tenement, and the property being used is considered the servient tenement. If there is no dominant tenement—that is, no other property is being benefited—it is an easement in gross. An easement in gross specifically must be transferred by the easement holder, while a normal easement runs with the land.

Easements allowing use of the land of another are affirmative easements, and easements that prohibit the owner of the servient tenement from a use are negative easements.

Easements may be created by grant or reservation in a deed, prescription (adverse use), implication, necessity, eminent domain, or estoppel.

Easements may be lost by destruction of the servient tenement, merger, nonuse (easements by prescription), and deed, foreclosure of a prior lien, estoppel, end of purpose, and end of necessity, eminent domain, or forfeiture for misuse.

A license is a revocable permission that is personal in nature and does not run with the land.

■ DISCUSSION CASES

1. A general right-of-way was granted, but its location was not specified. **Who would decide where the easement would be located?**

   Collier v. Oelke (1962) 202 C.A.2d 843

2. A tenant leased 2,400 acres. The landlord plaintiff claimed that the defendant failed to remove millions of pounds of waste rocket fuel material and other hazardous substances from the property. The complaint alleged causes of action for nuisance and trespass. **Were these proper causes for relief?**

   Mangini v. Aerojet General Corp. (1991) 230 C.A.3d 1125

3. A lessee of property in a quiet rural area invited others to use the oil dump on the property for wastes. One hundred fifty to 200 heavy trucks would use the easement in a ten-hour period. The owners of the servient tenements objected. **Was their objection valid?**

   Wall v. Rudolph (1961) 198 C.A.2d 684

4. An easement to use a common stairway for two buildings stated that the stairway "shall be perpetually kept open." The building with the stairway was destroyed. **Must the owner rebuild?**

   Muzio v. Erickson (1919) 41 C.A. 413

5. An owner cut down trees on the boundary line to use them for firewood. **Was this action proper?**

   Scarborough v. Woodill (1907) 7 C.A. 39

6. Weeds were growing on the banks of a drainage ditch. Seeds from the weeds invaded the neighboring property. An action was brought to abate a nuisance. **Must an owner remove his or her weeds?**

   Boarts v. Imperial Irrigation District (1947) 80 C.A.2d 574

7. A home slid into a neighbor's home. This loss was caused by natural conditions. **Should the upper-land owner be liable for the loss?**

   Sprecher v. Adamson Cos. (1981) 30 C.3d 358

8. A shopping center's drainage runoff went through a concrete drainage ditch and eventually led to a 15-foot-wide natural stream. The natural stream crossed the plaintiff's land, and some of the water flowed across the land, leaving mud and debris. **Assuming that the volume of water from the shopping center caused the stream to overflow, is the shopping center liable for resulting damages?**

   Deckert v. County of Riverside (1981) 115 C.A.3d 885

9. Bel Air Country Club used a strip of land adjacent to the sixth fairway as a rough for 40 years. The plaintiff had actual knowledge that balls were hit and retrieved from the area daily but had never erected permissive use signs or taken steps to halt the use. **What are the rights of the Bel Air Country Club?**

   MacDonald Properties Inc. v. Bel Air Country Club (1977) 72 C.A.3d 693

10. Drivers to the plaintiff's warehouse would trespass on adjacent property to turn around and back into loading docks. Depending on individual drivers' habits and skills, drivers utilized different portions of the adjacent property. **After use for the statutory period, does the plaintiff have a prescriptive easement?**

    Warsaw v. Chicago Metallic Ceilings Inc. (1984) 35 C.3d 564

11. An easement holder lined a ditch with Gunite to stop the water seepage. The result was that vegetation that had flourished in the soil from water percolating through the walls of the ditch died from lack of water. **Was the easement holder's action proper?**

    Krieger v. Pacific Gas & Electric Co. (1981) 119 C.A.3d 137

12. A property owner brought an action against a neighbor to prevent the neighbor from cutting out his light. **Does a property owner have a right to light?**

    Ingwersen v. Barry (1897) 118 C. 342

13. Underground telephone lines were installed outside the easement area. These lines were intended to remain in place for 100 years. After 25 years, the landowner wants their removal because they are a continuing nuisance/trespass. **Must the lines be moved?**

    Spar v. Pacific Bell (1991) 235 C.A.3d 1480

14. The San Diego Gas and Electric Company added power lines on an easement adjacent to plaintiff's home, resulting in increased levels of electromagnetic radiation. **Should the San Diego Gas and Electric Company have any liability to the homeowner?**

    San Diego Gas and Electric Co. v. Superior Court (1996) 13 C.4th 893

15. An oral agreement was made between two property owners where one owner would build a wall on the top of a slope rather than on the property line at the bottom. The party building the wall would do so at his own expense, but it would be on the neighbor's property. The reason for the agreement was that a wall on the bottom of the slope would not afford either property owner any privacy. **Can a later owner of the upper property require the removal of the wall?**

    Noronha v. Stewart (1988) 199 C.A.3d 485

16. Because of a mistaken belief as to boundary locations, a nursery owner planted cactuses on a neighbor's property. A survey revealed the correct boundary, and the neighbor sued for quiet title. The cactuses were worth an estimated $180,000. **Is the neighbor entitled to keep the cactuses?**

    Tremper v. Quinones (2004) 115 C.A.4th 944

17. A property owner piped water from a spring a mile away. **By meeting the requirements of prescriptive use, does the owner obtain rights to take the water?**

    Brewer v. Murphy (2008) 161 C.A. 4th 928

■ CHAPTER QUIZ

1. Which correctly matches the boundary with its boundary line?

    a. Road/center of the road

    b. Non-navigable river/center of the river

    c. Navigable river/average low-water mark

    d. All of the above are correctly matched

2. When a tree trunk is on the boundary line

    a. both owners must agree to its removal.

    b. it belongs to both owners.

    c. either owner can trim branches over his or her property.

    d. all of the above are correct.

3. An action for the removal of a permanent encroachment MUST be commenced within

    a. three years of the encroachment.

    b. four years of the encroachment.

    c. ten years of the encroachment.

    d. a reasonable period of time.

4. A nonphysical invasion of the property of another would likely be a(n)

    a. encroachment.   b. trespass.

    c. nuisance.   d. easement.

5. What is TRUE regarding nuisances?

    a. There is a three-year statute of limitations on a private nuisance.

    b. A public nuisance cannot be abated by the action of a private citizen.

    c. Nuisances that are not private nuisances are considered public nuisances.

    d. All of the above are true.

6. A dispute between riparian rights holders would likely be heard by the

    a. federal district court.

    b. local water agency.

    c. Water Resources Control Board.

    d. none of the above.

7. After an owner developed his property, water runoff from it damaged a lower property. Which statement about liability for this damage is *TRUE*?

    a. The upper-land owner is strictly liable.

    b. The upper-land owner is liable for only the percentage of damage based on the percentage of increase in runoff.

    c. If the development was reasonable use of the land with reasonable care, the upper-land owner is not liable.

    d. None of the above is true.

8. Riparian rights can *BEST* be described as

    a. the absolute right to adjacent water.

    b. reasonable use of flowing water.

    c. reasonable use of nonadjacent water.

    d. reasonable use of nonflowing water.

9. Littoral rights refer to

    a. the underground water table.

    b. water within a defined flowing channel.

    c. nonflowing water.

    d. the right of ingress and egress.

10. Which are rights in nonflowing surface water?

    a. Right of correlative user   b. Avulsion rights

    c. Riparian rights   d. Littoral rights

11. "Acquired by accession" *MOST* likely refers to

    a. a prescriptive easement.   b. accretion.

    c. an encroachment.   d. an easement in gross.

12. A boundary stream suddenly changed course, resulting in removal of land from one owner to another. This is an example of

    a. accretion.   b. avulsion.

    c. erosion.   d. reliction.

13. An owner who excavates on her property below the level of a neighbor's foundation is

    a. always responsible for damages to her neighbor's structure.

    b. required to give notice to the neighbor of the proposed excavation.

    c. both a and b.

    d. neither a nor b.

14. "It goes with the land" *BEST* describes a(n)

    a. homestead right.   b. license right.

    c. appurtenant easement.   d. easement in gross.

15. A sign company that has a right to place a billboard on the land of another would *MOST* likely hold a(n)

    a. license.   b. easement in gross.

    c. appurtenant easement.   d. fee simple.

16. John had all of the elements of an easement by prescription for four years. The owner then gave permission to others for similar use of the property. What are John's rights?

    a. A new five-year period would start.

    b. Multiple use defeats the user's rights to an easement by prescription.

    c. The permission granted to others defeats John's chances of obtaining an easement right.

    d. With one more year of open, notorious, and hostile use, John can obtain an easement.

17. Owners may *NOT* protect themselves against users obtaining prescriptive easements by

    a. recording a permissible use statement.

    b. posting "right to pass by permission and subject to control of owner."

    c. ordering wrongful users to cease their trespass.

    d. doing any of the above.

18. A grant of mineral rights made no mention of an easement to enter the property. What are the rights of the mineral rights holder?

    a. The holder must make a subterranean entrance from outside the property.

    b. The holder has no right of entrance.

    c. The holder has an implied easement to enter and mine.

    d. The holder can obtain an easement by necessity but must pay the fee owner for all resulting damages and loss of use.

19. A landlocked property owner would likely ask the court for

    a. an easement by prescription.   b. an easement in gross.

    c. an easement by necessity.   d. adverse possession.

20. An easement by necessity requires

    a. payment for the easement right.

    b. former common ownership of the dominant and servient tenements.

    c. both a and b.

    d. neither a nor b.

21. In the course of a sale, the seller told the buyer there was an easement to the property over other land the seller owned. The seller CANNOT deny the easement, because of

    a. prescriptive use.   b. estoppel.

    c. the statute of frauds.   d. necessity.

22. An easement by grant will be lost through

    a. nonuse.

    b. foreclosure of a prior lien.

    c. merger of the dominant and servient estates.

    d. both b and c.

23. Which would NOT terminate an easement created by grant?

    a. The destruction of the servient tenement

    b. A merger

    c. Nonuse

    d. A quitclaim deed to the encumbered property from the dominant tenement to the servient tenement

24. For six years, Alfred, with Smith's permission, used a shortcut over Smith's land to get to his home. Alfred likely now has a(n)

    a. easement by necessity.   b. easement in gross.

    c. easement by prescription.   d. license.

25. What is *FALSE* regarding a license?

    a. It goes with the land.   b. It is an interest in real estate.

    c. It can be inherited.   d. All of the above are false.

CHAPTER THIRTEEN

LAND USE CONTROLS

■ KEY TERMS

aesthetic zoning
Alquist-Priolo Special
    Studies Zone Act
bulk zoning
California
    Environmental
    Quality Act
Coastal Zone
    Conservation Act
comprehensive zoning
conditional public report
conditional-use permit
conditions
covenants
covenants, conditions,
    and restrictions

cumulative zoning
declaration of
    restrictions
downzoning
Endangered Species Act
environmental impact
    report
exclusionary zoning
general plan
historical designations
incentive zoning
inclusionary zoning
Interstate Land Sales
    Full Disclosure Act
National Environmental
    Policy Act

negative declaration
nonconforming uses
noncumulative zoning
partial zoning
preliminary public report
public report
rezoning
special-use permit
spot zoning
Subdivided Lands Law
Subdivision Map Act
upzoning
variance
zoning

■ ZONING

Zoning is public control of land use and is permitted under the constitutional doctrine of police power. Police power allows government units to enact legislation for the health, safety, morals, and general welfare of the community. Besides covering use, zoning sets standards for height, open space, setbacks, parking, lot size, building size, and similar issues. Zoning can even cover aesthetics and serve to limit growth.

California has no uniform requirement for zoning symbols. For example, uses allowable under the designation M-3 could vary greatly from area to area. Therefore, one who wants to determine how land in a particular area is zoned must first determine the meaning of the zoning symbols in that city or county.

Every city and county in California is required to develop a **general plan**. This plan, when approved by the local legislative body, becomes the comprehensive zoning for the area. Enabling legislation gave cities and counties the right to control land use through zoning. Adoption of zoning and changes in zoning require public hearings. Cities are required to bring their zoning into conformance with their general plan.

Zoning can be appealed to the courts, but the plaintiffs first must exhaust all administrative appeals. Zoning must be a reasonable exercise of the police power of the state. The courts therefore will not uphold arbitrary zoning or restrictions that tend to create a monopoly.

Case Study

The Pennsylvania case of *National Land and Investment Co. v. Kohn* (1965) 215 A.2d 597 involved a zoning ordinance that required four-acre lots. The developer wanted to reduce the lot size to one acre. The court conceded that there is a presumption of validity to a zoning ordinance and that the burden of proving it invalid falls on the one challenging it. It further indicated that the fact that a developer will suffer an economic loss is not a reason to declare zoning unconstitutional. Nevertheless, the court held that the zoning in this case was invalid because zoning must bear a substantial relationship to police power purposes and must not be unreasonable, arbitrary, or confiscatory. Keeping the area exclusive was not a proper exercise of police power. The court indicated that evidence of protection from pollution could have supported the reasonableness of four-acre sites, but such evidence was not introduced.

Case Study

Zoning can have the effect of keeping the poor and minorities out of an area. The federal case of *Hope v. County of DuPage* (1983) 717 F.2d 1061 concerned zoning regulations of DuPage County, Illinois. This wealthy county regulated lot size, setbacks, and parking, which effectively precluded housing for the poor and minorities. The court determined that the regulations were discriminatory and enjoined the enforcement of the ordinances. The county was ordered to develop a plan that would provide more housing for the poor.

> ### Case Study
>
> In *Southern Burlington County NAACP v. Township of Mount Laurel* (1975) 336 A.2d 713, the New Jersey Supreme Court required a township to redo zoning to provide a fair share of housing for the poor. A similar California case was *Associated Homebuilders Inc. v. City of Livermore* (1976) 18 C.3d 582, in which the court held that zoning must respond to regional welfare.

California courts will not award owners damages when a change in zoning reduces property value. California courts treat zoning as a police power regulation, not eminent domain, which is a taking of property. Several federal courts have taken a contrary position and have awarded damages when zoning change adversely affected value.

> ### Case Study
>
> The case of *Lake Nacimiento Ranch v. San Luis Obispo County* (1987) 830 F.2d 977 involved 1,500 acres of land bordering a lake that had been zoned for recreational use. In 1980, the county rezoned the property as "rural lands," which limited the use. The ranch claimed the rezoning was a taking.
>
> The court pointed out that rezoning is invalid if it does not advance legitimate state interests or if it denies an owner economically viable use of the land. The fact that the restriction does not allow an owner to recover the initial investment does not mean the restriction is constitutionally defective. "Disappointed expectations in that regard cannot be turned into a taking. . . ." Because the ranch failed to show there was no other beneficial use for the land, it was not proved that there had been a taking of property without compensation.

> ### Case Study
>
> In the case of *Lingle v. Chevron U.S.A. Inc.* (2005) 544 U.S. 528, the Supreme Court indicated that zoning would be a "taking" under the Fifth Amendment requiring compensation if it completely deprives the owner of all economically beneficial use in the property or results in a permanent physical invasion of the property.

Case Study

The case of *Lucas v. South Carolina Coastal Council* (1992) 112 S. Ct. 2886 involved a real estate developer, Lucas, who paid $975,000 for two residential lots 300 feet from the beach. While Lucas was developing plans, the legislature enacted the Beachfront Management Act that created the South Carolina Coastal Council. The council prohibited development on the Lucas lots, which were within a "baseline critical area." There were homes on the adjoining lots.

The trial court found that the new law rendered the lots valueless and ordered compensation to Lucas. The South Carolina Supreme Court reversed, holding that payment to Lucas was not required because the primary purpose of the law was to prevent the nuisance of public harm from storm or water damage. The U.S. Supreme Court reversed, holding that this was a total regulatory taking and it must be compensated. This ruling requires payments when government regulations prohibit all economically beneficial use of land. It does not, however, allow an owner to use their land for activities that will harm adjacent landowners, nor will it stop regulations that prohibit specific uses as long as some other economic use is available.

Types of Zoning

Besides zoning categories, such as residential, commercial, and industrial, there are a number of types of zoning.

Cumulative zoning allows all more restrictive uses. For example, an area zoned for multiple-family use would allow single-family homes as well if the zoning were cumulative.

Noncumulative zoning allows only the use specified. Most zoning today is noncumulative.

Exclusionary zoning prohibits specified uses. Restrictions on condominium conversions are exclusionary zoning.

Cities and counties cannot prohibit mobile homes on foundations on lots that are zoned for single-family dwellings.

Restrictions that prohibit an owner or his or her agent from erecting a For Sale sign of reasonable dimensions are void as unreasonable restraints on alienation.

Case Study

In *City of Cleburne v. Cleburne Living Center, Inc.* (1985) 473 U.S. 432, a city ordinance required special-use permits for hospitals for the mentally disabled. Cleburne Living Center wished to operate a group home for 13 men and women with mental disabilities. The center was required to apply for a special-use permit. The city denied the application.

The U.S. Supreme Court rejected the argument that people with mental disabilities were a "quasi-suspect classification." The city did not require conditional-use permits for other types of group housing, such as boardinghouses, fraternity houses, and apartment houses. The Supreme Court held that requiring a special permit was unconstitutional in that it violated the equal protection clause of the Constitution by discriminating against people with mental disabilities.

Note: The dissenting opinion indicated that the case could require a city to justify distinctions in its zoning.

Case Study

The case of *Hernandez v. City of Hanford* (2007) 41 C. 4th 279 involved the City of Hanford, which amended its general plan to provide for a planned commercial district. The new zoning ordinance prohibited sale of furniture in the district with the exception that department stores having at least 50,000 square feet could sell furniture within a 2,500 square foot display area.

Hernandez leased space within the district prior to the new zoning, but the certificate of occupancy granted several months later included the prohibition as to furniture sales.

The alleged purpose of the zoning was to preserve a downtown furniture district. (There were 12 furniture stores in the downtown area and the new district was planned to attract large chain stores.)

While the Superior Court upheld the constitutionality of the ordinance, the Court of Appeal reversed. The court indicated that while the general prohibition of the sale of furniture was related to the legitimate government purpose of retaining the economic viability of a downtown area, its exception permitting large department stores to sell furniture violated equal protection principles in that distinction was made between large and small stores.

The California Supreme Court reversed. They held that preservation of a downtown district for the benefit of the municipality is a legitimate exercise of police power.

Determining where a particular type of business can locate is a traditional zoning objective. The limited exception was for a second legitimate purpose, to attract and retain large department stores that typically carry furniture.

The court determined that the equal protection clause (14th Amendment) does not preclude a government entity from adopting legislation to achieve multiple objectives even when the objectives are partially in conflict.

Inclusionary zoning requires that a development include some feature, such as a percentage of units designated for low income housing.

Bulk zoning is zoning for density through height restrictions, open-space requirements, parking requirements, ratios of floor space to total area, etc.

Comprehensive zoning is zoning of a large area. A broad plan of zoning, such as a general plan, would be included in this category.

Partial zoning is zoning one area without considering its effect on the rest of the community.

Aesthetic zoning is zoning for beauty through regulations governing signs, architectural styles, and even colors.

Incentive zoning can be a boost to building by allowing a use, such as commercial stores on the first floor of a multistory office or residential structure, or a greater height if a public plaza is included.

Spot zoning allows the zoning of individual parcels that are not in conformance with the general-area zoning. Spot zoning is often the result of political influence. Spot zoning that is arbitrary and discriminatory will not be upheld by California courts.

Case Study

Ross v. City of Yorba Linda (1991) 1 C.A.4th 954 involved a family that owned a home on a 1.117-acre lot with zoning for one house per acre. The family wished to divide the property into two lots and build an additional home. Its request for rezoning was denied despite the fact that most of the surrounding property was zoned for one house per one-half acre. The court held that the restriction requiring one acre was arbitrary and discriminatory and therefore unconstitutional. The Court of Appeals affirmed the trial court, pointing out that spot zoning is one of the zoning categories that California courts typically hold as invalid and unreasonable.

Downzoning is a change in zoning to a more restrictive use.

Upzoning is a change in zoning to a less-restrictive use, such as allowing more units.

Rezoning is an actual change in the zoning category.

Variance

A **variance** is a special exception to the zoning, although the zoning is not changed. It usually is granted to prevent hardship, where strict application of the zoning would deprive an owner of benefits available to other, similar property owners. For example, a preexisting lot that does not meet the size requirements to build a home under the zoning might be granted a variance.

Conditional-Use Permit

Unlike a variance, which is simply an exception to the zoning, a **conditional-use permit**, or **special-use permit**, allows a use not permitted to every parcel. It is not granted because of owner hardship but because allowing the use in the area is considered to be in the best interest of the community. An example would be to allow warehouses in an area that was designated for dock use and ship repair.

> ### Case Study
>
> In *Griffin Dev. Co. v. City of Oxnard* (1985) 39 C.3d 256, an Oxnard city ordinance required every condominium to contain at least 1,000 square feet; have two separate bedrooms; have space for a washer and a dryer; have two garage spaces plus one visitor parking space; and have a private storage area.
>
> Griffin wished to convert his 72 apartment units into condominiums and was denied a special-use permit.
>
> The California Supreme Court rejected Griffin's argument that denial of a permit denied him due process because it was not a change in use. The court held that the city had legitimate objectives in preserving rental houses as well as justification for different standards for condominiums and apartments. Because condominiums were expected to be a major source of housing for low-income and moderate-income buyers, the city could impose standards for condominiums different from those for apartments. The court held the regulations to be the proper exercise of police power and not confiscatory.

> ### Case Study
>
> The case of *Autopsy/Post Services, Inc. v. City of Los Angeles* (2005) 129 C.A. 4th 521 involved APS, which purchased a building in a zone on Foothill Boulevard that required at least 70 percent of the first floor to be used for retail, restaurants, or offices. APS obtained a building permit for a medical laboratory. APS applied for a sign permit for a sign showing, "1-800-Autopsy." The sign application was rejected, and the city revoked the previous granted permit that was approved in error.
>
> APS sued, alleging it had a vested right to the building permit. The Superior Court ruled that APS had no vested right to a building permit because it did not act in good faith in omitting that it intended to conduct autopsies on the site. The trial court observed that the common understanding of a medical laboratory includes examination and testing of bodily tissue and bodily fluids, delivered in little bottles, not inside a corpse.
>
> APS appealed and the Court of Appeal affirmed ruling that APS would be operating a morgue or mortuary, which city zoning requires be in an industrial zone. The court noted that there was no offstreet parking, so bodies would be transported in an out of the building on the public sidewalk. (APS attempted to mislead the city building permit officials by not fully disclosing the prohibited intended use of the property.)

Nonconforming Use

Zoning generally is not retroactive. Uses that exist prior to zoning are not automatically excluded by the zoning. These **nonconforming uses** generally are allowed to continue if they were legal when started. They are said to be covered by the laws of that time (grandfather clause).

> ### Case Study
>
> The case of *Jones v. City of Los Angeles* (1930) 211 C. 304 involved a city ordinance that excluded sanitariums within a designated district. The City of Los Angeles sought to enforce the removal of a sanitarium erected prior to the ordinance. The court held that a properly conducted sanitarium for the care and treatment of persons affected with mental or nervous diseases cannot be held to constitute a nuisance. Where a retroactive zoning ordinance causes substantial injury and the prohibited business is not a nuisance, zoning that is retroactive was determined to be an unreasonable and unjustifiable exercise of police power.

The owner of a nonconforming use does not have the right to expand the use. Generally, if the use is abandoned, it cannot be resurrected later. If a nonconforming structure is destroyed, it generally cannot be rebuilt. Courts will uphold zoning that allows nonconforming uses to continue for a stated amount of time (amortization period).

> ### Case Study
>
> In the case of *City of Stanton v. Cox* (1989) 207 C.A.3d 1557, a municipal zoning ordinance prohibited adult bookstores within 1,000 feet of another similar use or within 500 feet of a school, park, playground, or residence. This left only six available sites in the city. The court held that the ordinance was invalid because it did not provide the owner of an adult bookstore a reasonable opportunity to operate a business in the city. The number of available sites would rapidly decrease if any site were occupied by an adult business.

> ### Case Study
>
> In the case of *Ebel v. City of Corona* (1985) 767 F.2d 635, the city passed an ordinance prohibiting adult bookstores and requiring that existing adult bookstores be closed down within 60 days. Ebel, the owner of an adult bookstore, brought this action. The Ninth Circuit Court of Appeals held that the ordinance left Ebel no alternative relocation site and therefore restricted free speech. The court also indicated that 60 days was too short because it did not consider the length of Ebel's lease or her investments.

While zoning does not immediately eliminate a previously existing use, a use that is also a nuisance can be eliminated by an abatement action.

Insuring Zoning

Title insurance is not available to protect owners from changes in zoning. Endorsements are available that ensure that a present use is not in violation of the then-current zoning or that the current zoning is as stated.

In an action for declaratory relief, an owner can ask the courts to determine the extent of their rights regarding the zoning.

■ COVENANTS, CONDITIONS, AND RESTRICTIONS

Covenants are private, voluntary restrictions that run with the land. They are promises among landowners that are mutually enforceable. The remedy for a breach of a covenant will be damages or an injunction.

Conditions differ from covenants in that they create a defeasible estate. A breach of a condition subsequent means that title will be lost (usually it will revert to the original grantor or his or her heirs). Because of the harsh penalty of forfeiture, courts will construe conditions narrowly, and if at all possible, will determine that a covenant rather than a condition was intended.

Covenants, conditions, and restrictions (CC&Rs), also known as *restrictive covenants*, can cover setbacks, lot size, height, building size, outbuildings, materials, colors, landscaping, signs, pets, antennae, etc. CC&Rs can go beyond zoning because they are private agreements not limited to health, safety, morals, and the general welfare. CC&Rs might set up architectural review committees for approval of plans. The committees' actions must be in good faith to prevail if they are challenged in court. CC&Rs are generally beneficial restrictions in that they tend to keep up property values. CC&Rs can be enforced by anyone subject to them.

Case Study

In the case of *Martin v. Bridgeport Community Association* (2009) 173 C.A. 4th 1024, homeowners allowed their daughter and son-in-law to occupy a property in exchange for making the mortgage payments. The tenants had a dispute with the homeowners' association (HOA) about landscape issues and claimed a breach of the CC&Rs. The tenants sued and claimed they had an assignment of rights from the owners. The trial judge ruled against the tenants and awarded the HOA $30,000 in attorney fees.

The Court of Appeal affirmed. The tenant had no standing to sue. You must have a real interest to litigate. CC&Rs are an equitable servitude running with the property. Assignment of rights is meaningless without transfer of the property.

CC&Rs usually are negative covenants, where parties promise not to do something. They are like negative easements because others who are subject to the covenant can get an injunction to make a party cease violating a covenant.

Case Study

In *Edmond's of Fresno v. McDonald Group, Ltd.* (1985) 171 C.A.3d 598, the lease on a jewelry store in a shopping mall provided that the lessor would not permit more than one more jewelry store at the Fresno Fashion Fair. The lessor built an addition to the mall and intended to lease to other jewelry stores.

The restriction on additional jewelry stores was a bargained-for-restrictive covenant, and allowing additional competitors would reduce the benefits bargained for. The court held that the covenant of good faith and fair dealing required that the restrictive covenant apply to the addition. If an ambiguity in what constituted "Fresno Fashion Fair" were present, the court held it should be resolved against the lessor, who drafted the instrument. A permanent injunction prohibiting the lessor from entering into additional jewelry store leases was granted.

CC&Rs also can be affirmative covenants, where a party is required to do something, such as build a structure or construct a fence within a stated period of time.

When CC&Rs and the zoning are at variance, whichever is more restrictive generally will prevail.

Creation of CC&Rs

CC&Rs involve rights in real property, so the statute of frauds requires that they be in writing.

Normally, CC&Rs are created by subdividers, who record the CC&Rs as a **declaration of restrictions** and then incorporate them by reference into every deed. After they are made a matter of record, the CC&Rs run with the land. Unless stated otherwise, CC&Rs have no time limitation.

Case Study

The case of *Cunningham v. Superior Court* (1998) 67 C.A.4th 743 involved a homeowner association that was displeased with the housekeeping of a homeowner, although a city inspection found no building or fire code violations. Under threat of litigation, Cunningham allowed homeowner association representatives to inspect the interior of his unit. Association lawyers wrote to Cunningham demanding he clear his bed of all papers and books, remove paper and cardboard boxes from the floor around the bed and dresser, remove unused boxes and paper in the living and dining rooms, clear boxes and objects from the interior stairs, cease using the downstairs bathroom for storage, and maintain a functioning electrical light in the downstairs bathroom. The letter also suggested that Cunningham remove clothing that had not been used for five years and donate it to the Salvation Army.

A lawsuit resulted in a jury verdict in favor of Cunningham because the association had acted unreasonably. The association moved for a new trial and a judgment notwithstanding the verdict. The trial judge granted a new trial stating that the association had acted "totally reasonably."

The Court of Appeal set aside the new trial and remanded the case to trial as to the amount of damages. The association had clearly gone beyond any legitimate interest it may have had. The homeowner association cannot tell the homeowner how to maintain the interior of his or her unit.

The CC&Rs might provide for new restrictions or changes in the restrictions by agreement of a stated percentage of the property owners. In the absence of any such agreement, any change could require unanimous agreement. Owners of parcels also can agree among themselves to restrictions on use.

To become a matter of record and binding on future owners, the CC&Rs must be recorded in the county where the property is located. Thus, CC&Rs can be discovered through the county recorder's office or through a title company. Buyers of condominiums must be given a copy of the CC&Rs as well as the bylaws of the condominium association and the articles of incorporation. An owners' association must furnish an owner with a copy of the CC&Rs within ten days of the owner's request.

Unenforceable Restrictions

Courts will not enforce some restrictive covenants, as follows:

- A restriction against public policy will not be enforced. For example, a restriction whose purpose is to give one party a monopoly will not be upheld.

- A restriction barring solar energy systems would be unenforceable in that it conflicts with Govt. Code Section 65850.5 et seq. That requires city or county governments to permit solar energy systems unless they adversely affect public health or safety.

- Common interest developments may not prohibit the posting or display of noncommercial posters that are 9 feet square or less in size, or banners and flags that are not more than 15 feet square in size. Civil Code Section 1353.6 was enacted to protect free speech.

- Racial restrictions are void and unenforceable. They have been held to violate the equal protection clause of the Fourteenth Amendment [*Shelley v. Kraemer* (1948) 334 U.S. 1, 68 S.C. 836]. (When providing CC&Rs containing racial restrictions, the real estate agent must stamp in 20-point, boldface, red type that such restrictions are void. Homeowners' associations are also required to remove racial restrictions from their CC&Rs.)

A property owner may have an unlawful restrictive covenant that is based on race, color, religion, sex, sexual orientation, familial status, marital status, disability, national origin, source of income, or ancestry stricken from their deed by the county recorder.

- Unreasonable restraints on alienation will not be upheld. In addition, the rule against perpetuities prohibits restrictions on alienation beyond the life of a living person plus 21 years. The interest must also vest (become definite) or terminate within 90 years of its creation. Therefore, a grantor may not require that a property remain with his or her blood heirs forever.

- Restrictions that require an illegal use are invalid.

- If a person seeking to require another to comply with the restrictive covenants is also in violation of the restrictive covenants, the courts will not grant relief. The person must be in compliance to enforce CC&Rs on others. This equitable principle is known as the "clean hands doctrine."

- Failure to enforce other violations in a timely manner may waive the right to enforce a violation of the CC&Rs later.

- Laches can prevent enforcement. If, because of a failure to enforce, a party acts to their detriment, the court might consider that allowing enforcement would not be equitable. An example of laches would be allowing another to build a structure, with your knowledge, that is not in compliance with the CC&Rs. Waiting until the building was completed before objecting could be considered laches, as the delay allowed another to act to their detriment.

- The statute of limitations for bringing action against a restriction is five years from the time of discovery (or when it should have been discovered using reasonable diligence). (Civil Code Section 784.)

- Courts will not allow enforcement of CC&Rs when conditions have changed. For example, what was previously a rural area with CC&Rs allowing only residential use could now be in the center of a commercial area where taxes would make residential use impractical. A zoning change by itself would not be enough to prove changed conditions, but a change in zoning is evidence of changed conditions.

- Tenants, as well as homeowners subject to restrictive covenants, may not be prohibited from installing satellite dishes within the area of the homeowners' or tenants' control.

> ### Case Study
> The case of *Liebler v. Point Loma Tennis Club* (1995) 40 C.A.4th 1600 involved the plaintiff, Liebler, who owned a condo unit. Liebler leased the unit. The lease provided that Liebler was a co-tenant even though Liebler did not live in the unit. Based on this lease, Liebler used the tennis courts. The CC&Rs provided that the tennis courts were only for residents and their guests. The Association fined Liebler in accordance with their rules.
>
> The superior court found that the rules were reasonable and that the association acted properly in fining Liebler. The Court of Appeal pointed out that when CC&Rs are uniformly enforced, they are presumed to be reasonable. The nonresident-use restriction was therefore reasonable and fairly enforced against all owners.
>
> *Note*: The co-tenancy in the lease was an obvious attempt to avoid the restriction on use.

Ending Restrictions

Restrictive covenants automatically cease with

- time, if they were set up for a particular number of years;
- merger, when all of the parcels are brought together under one ownership;
- agreement, when the owners, subject to the restrictions, agree to end them;
- foreclosure of a prior encumbrance; a trust deed against the property prior to the CC&Rs would remove them by its subsequent foreclosure; and
- condemnation by government authority; taking by eminent domain would remove all private restrictions.

■ REGULATION OF SUBDIVISIONS

The Subdivision Map Act

The **Subdivision Map Act** provides for local control of subdivisions. Every city and county is required to adopt an ordinance to regulate subdivisions. According to the Subdivision Map Act, a subdivision is any division of contiguous land for the purpose of sale, lease, or financing. The map act is concerned with the physical aspects of a subdivision, such as access, streets, drainage, sewage, water, electricity, phones, gas, and schools. Dedication of land for streets, parks, and school sites can be a requirement for map act approval. For school sites, the subdivider may be paid his or her actual site costs for the land dedicated.

If a subdivision contains 50 or fewer parcels, the subdivider can be required to pay a dollar amount per parcel for recreational areas rather than dedicate land.

For subdivisions of fewer than five parcels, the local control is limited to the dedication of rights-of-way, easements, and the construction of reasonable off-site and on-site improvements.

Condominiums and community apartment projects, as well as conversions to these uses, are covered by the map act.

Exceptions.   A tentative and a final map must be prepared for all subdivisions creating five or more parcels. Excepted are

- original parcels of fewer than five acres where each parcel to be created will abut a publicly maintained road and no dedications or improvements are required,

- subdivisions in which each parcel created has a gross area of 20 acres or more and has an improved access to a publicly maintained road,

- commercial or industrial developments that have approval of streets and access, and

- parcels of 40 acres or more.

These exceptions apply only to the filing of a map, not to obtaining local approval. In cases where a tentative and a final map are not required, a parcel map is required.

Conveyances to a government body are not considered conveyances of land for the purpose of the map act.

Tentative Map.   The tentative map will contain

- a legal description sufficient to ascertain the boundaries;

- the location, names, and widths of all adjoining streets;

- the width and proposed grades of all streets within the proposed subdivision;

- the width and location of all existing and proposed easements for roads, drainage, sewers, and other public utilities;

- tentative lot layout and dimensions of each lot;

- the approximate locations of all areas subject to inundations or storm water overflow, and the locations, widths, and direction of flow of all watercourses;

- the source of water supply;

- the proposed method of sewage disposal;

- the proposed use of the property;

- the proposed public areas, if any; and

- the approximate contours when the topography controls street layout.

After the tentative map is submitted, the planning agency investigates and reports on the proposed tract. Copies are submitted to the health department, road department, flood control district, recreation department, school authority, and other governmental bodies, as well as to any adjacent communities so they can make recommendations. The department reports are studied, and the subdivider may be required to meet with representatives of interested departments.

The planning commission (a local advisory agency) makes a written report to the local legislative body within 50 days of the filing of the tentative map. It may approve, conditionally approve, or disapprove the map. If no action is taken by the local advisory agency, the tentative map is considered approved.

The subdivider may appeal actions of the advisory agency to any appeal agency or, if none, to the city council or county board of supervisors. Before going to the courts, a subdivider must have exhausted all administrative remedies. Courts generally will overrule administrative determinations only if they were arbitrary or capricious.

Final Map.   After approval or conditional approval, a final map is prepared under the direction of a registered civil engineer. Prior to approval of the final map, the subdivider may be required to make improvements, provide bonds, or provide some other security so that improvements will be made.

The final map, along with all required signed certificates, is filed, and the governing body approves it at the meeting following filing. The final map is then recorded. By filing the final map, the local agency certifies that its requirements have been met.

Conveyances that do not comply with the map act are voidable, at the option of the grantee, within one year of the date of discovery of the violation. The grantee can recover damages.

Local agencies will not issue any permit to develop real estate that was divided without approval unless the local agency determines that the division complies with all requirements.

Government Code Section 66499.30 (e) allows property to be sold or leased prior to the issuance of the final map as long as the final closing is conditioned on the filing of the final subdivision or parcel map.

Subdivided Lands Law   Subdivided land sales fall under the jurisdiction of the Department of Real Estate. The primary purpose of the **Subdivided Lands Law** (Business and Professions Code Section 11000 et seq.) is to protect purchasers in new subdivisions from fraud, misrepresentation, or deceit in the marketing of subdivided lots, parcels, units, and undivided interests. The disclosures provide the buying public with knowledge of essential facts so that an informed decision to purchase can be made.

A subdivision under the Subdivided Lands Law is a division of five or more parcels for the purpose of sale, lease, or financing. The law applies to subdivisions located within the State of California, as well as subdivisions located outside California that are sold within the state. For out-of-state subdividers, the real estate commissioner must make a determination that the offering is fair, just, and equitable.

The differences and similarities between the Subdivision Map Act and the Subdivided Lands Law are shown in Table 13.1.

"Four-by-fouring" is an attempt to evade the subdivision laws by breaking a parcel into four parcels and selling them to separate people or entities who again break them into four parcels, and so on. This is regarded as a violation of the subdivision laws and will subject the violator to both civil and criminal penalties.

Case Study

The case of *People v. Byers* (1979) 90 C.A.3d 140 involved a father who attempted to avoid the subdivision requirements by transferring portions of his property to his son and others. The grantees then broke each parcel into four parcels, and they were sold, with the father receiving the proceeds. The father fled to avoid prosecution, but the son and two others were tried. The court indicated that the object of the subdivision law was to prevent sharp practices and fraud. The court refused to excuse the acts on the grounds that the parties believed that their actions were lawful. The defendants were found guilty of aiding and abetting a criminal act.

Public Report

Generally, no subdivision can be offered for sale in California until the real estate commissioner has issued a **public report**. The public report will not be issued until the commissioner is satisfied that the subdivider has met all statutory requirements, with particular emphasis on the financial arrangements to ensure completion and maintenance of improvements and facilities included in the offering, and shown that the parcel can be used for the purpose offered. Map act requirements also must be met prior to the issuance of the public report.

Public reports are disclosure statements. They include information on location, the size of the offering, the identity of the subdivider, and the interest to be conveyed to the purchaser or lessee, as well as provisions for handling deposits, purchase money, taxes, assessments, etc. Also included are use restrictions, unusual costs that a buyer will have to bear at the time of purchase or in the future, hazards or adverse environmental findings, special permits required, and utilities availability. The report is intended to provide information to aid a potential buyer in making a purchase decision.

TABLE 13.1 **Subdivision Map Act and** **Subdivided Lands Law**	**Subdivision Map Act**	**Subdivided Lands Law**
	• Local control	• Department of Real Estate control
	• Improved residential subdivisions within city limits (lots sold with residencies) included	• Excluded
	• Two or more lots or parcels	• Five or more lots or parcels
	• "Proposed division" excluded	• "Proposed division" included
	• Parcels must be contiguous	• Parcels need not be contiguous
	• No exemptions for 160 acres and larger	• Parcels of 160 acres or more exempt
	• Community apartments included	• Included
	• Condominiums included	• Included
	• Stock cooperatives not included unless a conversion of five or more existing dwelling units	• Stock cooperatives included
	• Leasing of apartments, offices, stores, or similar space in apartment buildings not included; industrial and commercial buildings are not included	• Leasing of apartments, offices, stores, or similar space in apartment buildings included; industrial and commercial buildings not included
	• Long-term leasing of space in mobile home parks or trailer parks exempt	• Included
	• Undivided interests exempt	• Included
	• Expressly zoned industrial and commercial subdivisions included	• Exempt
	• Agricultural leases exempt	• Included
	• Time-shares exempt	• Included
	• Limited-equity housing cooperatives exempt	• Included
	• Out-of-state subdivisions sold in California exempt	• Included

Prior to being obligated, the purchaser must sign a receipt that they have received and read a copy of the public report. Public reports also must be given to any member of the public upon request. A copy and notice of its availability must be posted in the subdivision sales office.

A public report is good for five years from the date of issuance. Material changes that would cause the public report no longer to reflect the true facts must be reported to the commissioner. Material changes also would include changes in sales contracts or instruments of conveyance. The commissioner would revise the public report to reflect the true conditions.

Business and Professions Code Sections 11016.6 and 11018.1 provide that at the same time a public report is provided, a specified statement entitled "Common Interest Development General Information" must be given to the purchaser. Note that the term *common interest development* is now being used for subdivisions having areas in common, such as condominiums.

Preliminary Public Report. A **preliminary public report** (known as the "pink slip"), which allows the subdivider to take refundable deposits or reservations for sales, may be issued by the commissioner.

A preliminary public report is good until the final report is issued, but not for more than one year.

Conditional Public Report. Section 11018.12 was added to the Business and Professions Code to provide for a new category of public report. In the past, the subdivider could not enter into any binding contract until the public report ("white slip") was issued. Now, however, the **conditional public report** allows a subdivider to enter into a binding contract with a buyer, but an escrow must be opened, and the funds are not to be released to the subdivider or escrow closed until the final public report is issued. The requirements for the conditional public report are more stringent than for the preliminary public report. The term for the conditional public report cannot exceed six months and may be renewed for one additional six-month period if the commissioner determines that the conditions for issuance of the public report are likely to be satisfied during the renewal term.

If the final public report is not issued within the term of the conditional public report, or if the purchaser is dissatisfied with the final public report because of a material change in the setup of the offering, the entire sum of money paid or advanced by the purchaser must be returned to the purchaser.

Interstate Land Sales Full Disclosure Act

The federal **Interstate Land Sales Full Disclosure Act** is administered by the Office of Interstate Land Sale Registration (OILSR) of HUD. A disclosure statement known as the *property report* is required for subdivisions of 25 or more unimproved residential lots offered for sale in interstate commerce. Exempt from the act are parcels of five acres or more, cemetery lots, and sales to builders. The disclosure statement sets forth material facts about the development that must be provided to the purchaser prior to sale. The California public report satisfies this disclosure requirement.

Purchasers have a seven-day right of rescission after signing the purchase agreement.

The act provides civil and criminal remedies for its willful violation. Purchasers have three years after discovery of violations to bring actions for fraud.

■ ENVIRONMENTAL LAW

National Environmental Policy Act (NEPA)

The federal **National Environmental Policy Act** (42 U.S.C. 4321 et seq.) applies to federal agencies and legislation "significantly affecting the quality of human environment."

WEB LINK @

Federal action requires an environmental impact statement (EIS) if the action significantly affects the quality of life. The EIS gathers relevant data along with an analysis of its effects. The website of the Environmental Protection Agency is *www.epa.gov.*

> **Case Study**
> In *No GWEN Alliance v. Aldridge* (1988) 855 F.2d 1380, the Ninth Circuit Court of Appeals held that an environmental impact statement prepared by the U.S. Air Force for the installation of a communications system need not address the environmental impact of nuclear war. (The communications system was intended to transmit messages during and after a nuclear attack.)

California Environmental Quality Act (CEQA)

California's law, the **California Environmental Quality Act** (Public Resources Code 21000 et seq.), allows local government agencies to require environmental impact reports for private and government projects that may have a significant effect on the environment (Public Resources Code Section 21151).

The city or county authorities are responsible for determining whether an **environmental impact report** (**EIR**), which analyzes any adverse impact of development, how it can be reduced, and alternatives, is needed. The Phase 1 report is the draft report submitted for evaluation, and the Phase 2 report is the final version.

A **negative declaration** is a declaration by the city or county that the development will not have a significant adverse effect on the environment. When such a declaration is filed, an environmental impact report is not required.

An important feature of the California act is that private citizens can challenge a project in court if they feel that proper procedures were not followed, or the report was incomplete.

Alquist-Priolo Special Studies Zone Act

A special studies zone is a geological hazard zone on a potentially active earthquake fault line. Zones customarily are one-quarter of a mile or more wide, centering on the fault. The **Alquist-Priolo Special Studies Zone Act** (Public Resources Code Section 2621 et seq.) requires that geological reports be obtained for project approvals within the zones and that prospective purchasers of property in the zones be made aware of the facts.

Coastal Zone Conservation Act

To develop land within a designated coastal zone, either a coastal development permit or an exemption from the provisions of the **Coastal Zone Conservation Act** (Public Resources Code Section 27000 et seq.) is required. The coastal zone includes about 1,800 square miles. It averages approximately 1,000 yards in width, with wider spots in coastal estuaries, marine habitat, and recreational areas. The purpose of the act is to protect the coastal zone and the marine environment, and to ensure public access to the coast.

Case Study

In *Grupe v. California Coastal Common* (1985) 166 C.A.3d 148, Grupe wanted to build a single-family home on coastal land. The coastal commission issued a permit conditioned on Grupe's offering to dedicate an access easement to the coast over two-thirds of his land.

Grupe argued that requiring the dedication would be valid only if it related to a public need. The court held that while Grupe's house alone did not create a need for public access, the house was but one of several projects that collectively would create a need for public access.

The local government agency must issue a permit prior to development within the coastal zone. A person can appeal local rulings to the state coastal commission.

Case Study

In the case of *Nollan v. California Coastal Commission* (1987) 107 S. Ct. 3141, Nollan wished to demolish an oceanfront cottage to build a new residence. The California Coastal Commission conditioned its approval on Nollan's granting a public easement along the beach area. The U.S. Supreme Court held that in this case, the requiring of the easement was a taking of property, which requires consideration, because there was no connection between the building permit and the easement.

This case differs from the *Grupe* case because *Grupe* involved access to the ocean. In *Nollan,* the public had access to the beach, but the coastal commission wished to establish public use of beach area belonging to *Nollan*.

Case Study

In the case of *Ocean Harbor House Homeowners Association v. California Coastal Commission* (2008) 163 C.A. 4th 215, the California Coastal Commission imposed a mitigation fee of $5 million upon a homeowners' association as a condition for approval of a permit to build a seawall to protect condo units.

The Court of Appeal pointed out that a permit condition was derived from the power to deny a permit. However, the permit condition must be related to the impact of permit approval. In this case, the Court of Appeal determined that the fee was proper considering loss of recreational use, effect on sand erosion, and costs. The fee requirement was proper.

Case Study

The case of *AVCO Community Developers Inc. v. South Coast Regional Commission* (1976) 17 C.3d 785 concerned a developer who spent more than $2 million for storm drains, culverts, streets, utilities, etc., based on county zoning and map act approval. The developer also had sold 11 acres of prime sand beach to the county at a price below market value and had dedicated additional land for access. When the coastal commission act became effective, the developer was denied the right to develop the property. The California Supreme Court held that a developer is not considered to have a vested right to develop unless a building permit has been issued, which was not the case.

The legislature apparently considered the *AVCO* decision inequitable. It enacted Sections 65864–65869.5 of the Government Code, which provides for development agreements where the developer and the city agree to use, density, height, size, dedications, etc. These agreements are to be enforceable notwithstanding subsequent changes to the specific plan, zoning, subdivision, or building regulations.

Case Study

The case of *Feduniak v. California Coastal Commission* (2007) 148 C.A. 4th 1346 involved the enforceability of coastal zone regulations. In 1983, the California Coastal Commission issued a permit for a new house located in an environmentally sensitive habitat area. The permit, given to the Bonannos, required an open-space easement and the use of native landscaping on the property. After receiving their permit, the Bonannos changed their approved landscaping plan to include a three-hole golf course. They did not seek approval for this change.

In 2000, the Feduniaks purchased the property because they loved the golf course. The Bonannos did not inform them of the easement and permit requirements. Although they were recorded, the title report failed to disclose the easement and restrictions.

In 2003, the California Coastal Commission issued a cease-and-desist notice and directed the Feduniaks to remove the golf course and restore the grounds to the dunes vegetation native to the Monterey County Coast.

The Feduniaks petitioned for a Writ of Mandamus claiming the commission's actions were invalid. The claim that designated the property as an environmentally sensitive habitat area was improper and even if valid, the commission was estopped from enforcing the restrictions and easement. The trial court held that the Commission should have known that the golf course violated the easement and permit restrictions, and that an 18-year delay in inspecting for compliance was unreasonable.

The Court of Appeal reversed. The court pointed out that the Commission had no duty to inspect the property for compliance, nor did the evidence support the fact that the Feduniaks could reasonably rely on failure to enforce restrictions as abandoning the right to do so. The failure to enforce the law does not estop the government from subsequent enforcement.

Note: The Feduniaks likely had legal remedies against the Bonnanos and the title company.

Endangered Species

The federal **Endangered Species Act** can halt development if, for example, a family of owls, a rare bird, or a new specie of lizard are discovered. Even an obscure minnow can prohibit the construction of a dam. Once a plant or animal is placed on the endangered list, it can place onerous restrictions on the owner of the property.

Historical Designations

Federal law and local ordinances provide for **historical designations**—the designation of structures having historical significance could prohibit redevelopment. In some cases, redevelopment or exterior modification is allowed if the structure is relocated to an approved site.

■ BUILDER AND DEVELOPER LIABILITY

A developer who manufactures a lot has strict liability in tort for damages that are the proximate cause of any defect in design or manufacture. The manufacturer (subdivider) will be liable even in the absence of any fault on his or her own part [AVNER v. *Longridge Estates* (1982) 272 C.A.2d 607].

Because product liability law applies to the manufacture of lots, neither precautions, nor care, nor warnings to a purchaser will protect the manufacturer from resultant damages.

Suits for latent defects in the development of lots can be brought for up to ten years after the completion of improvements (but within three years of discovery of damage) (Code of Civil Procedure Section 338). California Civil Code Section 900 requires that a builder provide a homebuyer with a minimum of a one-year written warranty covering standards set forth in Civil Code Section 896. Builders who offer an "enhanced protection agreement" beyond the one-year minimum may not limit the standards of Section 896.

Besides express warranties, a builder can be held liable for breach of implied warranties that the construction was done in a workmanlike manner and is fit for the intended use.

A homeowner cannot sue a builder for construction deficiencies until the builder has been notified of the defect and given the opportunity to correct (Civil Code Section 910).

For builder liability, there is a four-year statute of limitations for patent defects (Code of Civil Procedure Section 337.1) and a ten-year statute for latent defects (Code of Civil Procedure Section 337.15).

Builder liability would not apply for speculative losses where risks of harm are not foreseeable.

Case Study

The case of *Aas v. Superior Court* (2000) 24 C.4th 627 involved a housing project that allegedly suffered from a variety of construction defects that violated building codes but did not result in property damages or personal injury. Among other items, tile did not have the overlap required by the manufacturers, flashing was not properly lapped, and the nailing pattern failed to comply with the Uniform Building Code. Plaintiffs sued for the defects including diminution in value of their property. The trial court granted defendants' motion to exclude evidence of defects that did not cause personal injury or property damage. The Court of Appeal denied plaintiffs' petition for a writ of mandate, and the California Supreme Court affirmed. The supreme court stated that construction defects that have not ripened into property damage, or at least into involuntary out-of-pocket losses, do not comfortably fit the definition of "appreciable harm." Breaches of duty causing only speculative harm, or the threat of future harm, do not normally create a cause of action. Developers of mass housing projects have been held strictly liable for defects, even to subsequent purchasers who had no privity of contract with the developer.

Case Study

In the 1989 case of *La Jolla Village Homeowners' Assn. Inc. v. Superior County*, the court refused to extend the strict liability of mass producers of homes to their subcontractors. In this case, the California Supreme Court extended the strict liability of mass builder to component manufacturers. The court held that a manufacturer of defective window units was liable for damages caused as the result of the defect. In this case, damages extended to the stucco, insulation, framing, drywall, paint, wall coverings, floor coverings, and other parts of the homes.

■ SUMMARY

Zoning is public control of land use enacted under the police power of the state for the health, safety, morals, and general welfare of the population. Zoning can be appealed to the courts but will be overturned only if found to be arbitrary or capricious.

When zoning is changed to a more restrictive use, California courts will not award the owner damages; they do not consider it a taking of property.

Types of zoning include

- cumulative zoning (zoning that allows more restrictive uses),
- noncumulative zoning (zoning that allows only the uses provided by the zoning category),

- exclusionary zoning (zoning that prohibits specified uses),

- bulk zoning (zoning for density),

- comprehensive zoning (zoning of a large area),

- partial zoning (zoning of an area without considering its effect on other areas),

- aesthetic zoning (zoning for beauty),

- incentive zoning (zoning that allows a greater use as an incentive to build or to provide some desired feature),

- spot zoning (zoning a parcel so it is not in conformance with surrounding property),

- downzoning (a zoning change to a more restrictive, use such as from R-4 to R-2), and

- rezoning (a change in the zoning category).

A conditional-use permit allows an exception to the zoning in the best interests of the community.

Zoning will not be retroactive. A nonconforming use will be allowed to continue, although the zoning could provide an amortization period, after which the use must cease.

Covenants, conditions, and restrictions are private restrictions that run with the land. Normally, they are created by subdividers, who record a declaration of restrictions and then incorporate the declaration by reference in every deed. They also could be created by a recorded agreement of a group of owners.

The Subdivision Map Act allows local control of subdivisions. A tentative map is prepared by the subdivider. Local recommendations may be made for modifications. After all approvals, a final map is prepared and recorded.

The Subdivided Lands Law, a disclosure law intended to protect the public, provides for Department of Real Estate approval of subdivisions having five or more parcels. A person is not required to go through with a transaction until he or she has read (and signed that he or she has received) a copy of the public report (disclosure report). Purchase reservations may be taken with a preliminary report, which is good for one year or until the public report is issued. Binding contracts can be made with buyers after a conditional public report is issued, but funds will not be released and escrow closed until the final public report is filed.

The Interstate Land Sales Full Disclosure Act is a federal law for 25 or more unimproved residential lots offered for sale in interstate commerce. The California public report satisfies the disclosure requirement. Purchasers have a seven-day right of rescission after signing a purchase agreement.

Federal projects significantly affecting the environment require an environmental impact statement that includes an analysis of the project's effect.

California provides that local agencies can require an environmental impact report on projects that will have a significant effect on the environment. Private citizens can challenge the failure to require a report, as well as the completeness of the report.

Purchasers in geological hazard zones must be notified of the proximity of a fault line. Developments within special study zones require special approval.

The Coastal Zone Conservation Act requires approval for coastal zone projects to protect the coastline and environment, and to provide public access.

A developer who manufactures lots has strict liability for defects in design or manufacture. Also subject to strict liability are mass producers of homes.

■ DISCUSSION CASES

1. A community rezoned a parcel as "high flood danger," which prohibited all development. A purpose of the rezoning was to make the property available for public use. **What, if any, are the owners' rights?**

    Annicelli v. Town of South Kingston, R.I. (1983) 463 A.2d 133

2. Landowners attacked the validity of a zoning ordinance that rezoned their property as agricultural. They claimed the zoning was arbitrary and inconsistent with the general plan and represented the taking of their property without just compensation. **Considering that the new zoning significantly lowered property values, was this a taking without compensation?**

    Pan Pacific Properties Inc. v. Santa Cruz (1978) 81 C.A.3d 244

3. A zoning ordinance prohibited outdoor advertising other than those signs related to the businesses conducted on the site. An outdoor advertising company brought an action claiming that the zoning was unreasonable. **Is the zoning reasonable? If it is not, should it be set aside?**

    United Advertising Corp. v. Borough of Metuchen (1964) 198 A.2d 447

4. A zoning ordinance required the discontinuance of a plumbing business after five years. At the time the business was established, the zoning was proper. The owner claimed that the property was suited for this type of business and requiring its removal would be a taking of property. **Do you agree?**

    City of Los Angeles v. Gage (1954) 127 C.A.2d 442

5.   A deed executed in 1917 contained a covenant that the land was to be used for residential purposes. The restriction was for a period of 50 years. Due to the growth of the area, the property became part of a business district. **Can the restriction on use be enforced?**

Norris v. Williams (1947) 54 A.2d 331

6.   The plaintiff wished to operate a rock and gravel operation on land contiguous to an operation that had become substantially depleted. The adjacent property was zoned for agricultural and residential use, which did not permit a gravel operation.

The trial court determined that the property had great value for rock, gravel, and sand excavation, but very little value for any other purpose. The plaintiff maintained that the zoning was a taking of property without compensation, was discriminatory, was a denial of equal protection, and made the plaintiff's property worthless. **Was the zoning a proper exercise of police power?**

Consolidated Rock Products v. City of Los Angeles (1962) 57 C.2d 515

7.   The city denied the plaintiff a building permit on the basis of the plaintiff's refusal to dedicate land for a street extension that would go through the plaintiff's property. The plaintiff wanted to build over some of this land. **Was the action of the city proper?**

Selby Realty v. City of San Buenaventura (1973) 10 C.3d 110

8.   To obtain a landowner's approval to annexation in 1965, the city agreed that the county zoning would remain in effect. In 1971, the city rezoned the property so that a shopping center would not be allowed. **Was the city's action proper?**

Carty v. Ojai (1978) 77 C.A.3d 329

9.   A Los Angeles city ordinance provided that approval would not be granted for a condominium conversion if more than 50 percent of the units were occupied by the elderly, the disabled, or minors, and no reasonable relocation assistance plan was provided.

The plan submitted by the plaintiff allowed continued occupancy by the special tenants until they could be relocated. The city disapproved the conversion because the plan's implementation was prevented by a scarcity of comparable units. **Was the city's action proper?**

Krater v. City of Los Angeles (1982) 130 C.A.3d 839

10. The City of Oakland passed a zoning ordinance that prohibited adult entertainment facilities within 1,000 feet of a residential zone. Existing uses would be allowed to continue for one year, after which they would have to obtain a conditional-use permit. The zoning also provided for an additional two-year period for hardship situations (the lessee was tied to a long lease, or the user had a substantial investment in the structure). **Was the zoning reasonable?**

Castner v. City of Oakland (1982) 129 C.A.3d 94

11. Ten unrelated adults lived in a 24-room house that had ten bedrooms and six baths, plus ample parking. The city sought an injunction for violating a zoning ordinance. The area provided for single-family use and defined a family as either two or more persons related by blood, marriage, or adoption living as a housekeeping unit, or up to five unrelated persons. **Is this zoning valid?**

City of Santa Barbara v. Adamson (1980) 27 C.3d 123

12. A subdivision's CC&Rs restricted occupancy to single-family residential use. It sought to exclude a residential care facility. (Section 1566.5 of the Health and Safety Code provides that a residential care facility serving six or fewer people should be considered single-family use.) **Can the subdivision exclude this use under its restrictions?**

Welsch v. Goswick (1982) 130 C.A.3d 398

13. The City of Camarillo and Pardee Construction Co. entered into a stipulated judgment that Pardee had vested rights to develop a 1,150-acre tract in accordance with approved zoning and the master plan. The city agreed not to adopt any zoning inconsistent with that previously approved.

In reliance on this agreement, Pardee Construction Co. spent approximately $13.5 million for development costs. In June 1981, a voters' initiative limited the number of building permits for the entire city to 400 per year and provided a detailed plan for allocation of permits. **Was Pardee Construction limited in its development by the initiative?**

Pardee Construction Co. v. City of Camarillo (1984) 37 C.3d 465

14. A condominium restriction prohibited the parking of any truck, camper, trailer, or boat of any kind. The carports were restricted to passenger automobiles. The defendant owned a clean, noncommercial pickup truck. The condominium association sued to enjoin the defendant from parking his truck in the carport. **Will the restrictive covenant be enforced?**

Bernardo Vilas Mgmt. Corp. v. Black (1987) 190 C.A.3d 153

15. A homeowners' association knew of lighting problems and that crimes had been committed, including a burglary, at the plaintiff's unit. The plaintiff installed her own lighting but was not permitted to use it because it violated the CC&Rs. The plaintiff was subsequently robbed and raped. **Is the homeowners' association liable?**

    Francis T. v. Village Green Owners Ass'n. (1986) 42 C.3d 490

16. The CC&Rs of a condominium prohibited renting units to tenants (with the exception of roommates). **Is this restriction enforceable by the association?**

    City of Oceanside v. McKenna (1989) 215 C.A.3d 1420

17. Carmel-by-the-Sea enacted an ordinance prohibiting residential rentals of less than 30 days. **Was this ordinance a proper exercise of police power?**

    Ewing v. City of Carmel-by-the-Sea (1991) 234 C.A.3d 1579

18. A San Diego ordinance limited the maximum number of renters that can occupy a residence. It was based on square footage, bedroom, and bathroom requirements, as well as off-street parking. **Were the restrictions proper?**

    College Area Renters and Landlord Association v. City of San Diego (1994) 43 C.A.4th 677

19. A San Francisco ordinance required that owners of residential hotels could not convert them to another type of hotel use. A hotel owners' association brought action claiming that the ordinance violated their Fifth Amendment rights in that it was taking without compensation. **Do you agree?**

    Golden Gate Hotel v. San Francisco City and County (1993) 836 F. Supp. 707

20. A homeowners' association brought action for an injunction against the operation of a residential care facility for nonambulatory adults based on CC&Rs that prohibit commercial use. **Should an injunction be granted?**

    Broadmoor San Clemente Homeowners Assn. v. Nelson (1994) 25 C.A.4th 1

21. A hotel was substantially destroyed by fire in November 1988. The owner applied for a demolition permit. The city withheld the permit because it claimed the hotel was an SRO building (Single Room Occupancy permanent housing). A city ordinance prohibited SRO demolition unless repair was not feasible and the owner agreed to replace the SRO with similar housing. The demolition permit was finally issued in August 1990, when the city determined the hotel was not an SRO.

    During the period prior to issuance of the permit, the hotel experienced a series of fires. The city determined that the owner was not providing proper security and, therefore, the city contracted for 24-hour security. The owner was assessed the costs of $399,000.

The owner sued for refund of the security costs as well as lost income. **Should the owner be entitled to this reimbursement?**

Ali v. City of Los Angeles (1999) 77 C.A.4th 246

22. A homeowner's trees blocked an uphill homeowner's view of the Pacific Ocean. The city issued an order compelling the owner to trim the trees and restore the view under a view restoration act. (Under the act, the upper property owner was required to pay for the trimming.) **Is this an uncompensated taking of private property?**

Echevarrieta v. City of Rancho Palos Verdes (2001) 86 C.A.4th 472

23. **Because of the social and economic effects, may a city use its design review ordinance to exclude nationwide retail chains from shopping malls?**

Friends of Davis v. City of Davis (2000) 83 C.A.4th 1004

24. A homeowner built a 200-foot-long, five-foot-high wrought iron fence around her lot, but the homeowner associations' unrecorded regulations specify fences require advance association approval with exceptions only for low, wooden split rail fences. The association sought a court order to require the woman to seek proper permits or remove the fence. **Is the association regulation enforceable?**

Rancho Santa Fe Association v. Dolan-King (2004)115 C.A.4th 28

■ CHAPTER QUIZ

1. The power to zone was given to cities and counties by

   a. the U.S. Constitution.
   b. the Thirteenth Amendment.
   c. enabling acts.
   d. the U.S. Supreme Court.

2. *LEAST* likely to be upheld by California courts is rezoning that would

   a. eliminate any beneficial use of the land.
   b. result in a reduction of value.
   c. reduce the use density.
   d. be downzoning.

3. Zoning that allows a single-family home to be built in an area zoned for apartments is an example of

   a. downzoning.
   b. cumulative zoning.
   c. spot zoning.
   d. bulk zoning.

4. Zoning that allows more restrictive uses would likely be

   a. cumulative zoning.
   b. noncumulative zoning.
   c. exclusionary zoning.
   d. bulk zoning.

5. Zoning that prohibits adult entertainment within an area is

   a. inclusionary zoning.
   b. exclusionary zoning.
   c. illegal.
   d. downzoning.

6. Zoning for density is known as

   a. incentive zoning.
   b. bulk zoning.
   c. exclusionary zoning.
   d. inclusionary zoning.

7. Which is *TRUE* of a nonconforming use?

   a. It can be retroactive.
   b. It refers to private restrictions.
   c. It was a legal use prior to zoning.
   d. The use must be allowed to continue for the owner's lifetime.

8. New zoning that prohibits an existing use would *NOT* provide for

    a. immediate closure.

    b. the time period for closure.

    c. prohibition of expansion.

    d. continuation of use by a nonconforming user.

9. The *MOST* likely action for violation of a deed covenant would be

    a. action for injunction.

    b. forfeiture.

    c. action for specific performance.

    d. liquidated damages.

10. Which is *TRUE* of restrictive covenants?

    a. They run with the land.

    b. If not recorded, they are not binding on a subsequent purchaser without notice.

    c. They are usually negative covenants.

    d. All of the above are true.

11. Deed restrictions are created by

    a. the local building commission.

    b. the planning commission.

    c. action of law.

    d. the grantors.

12. A copy of the CC&Rs requested by an owner in a condominium, cooperative, or community apartment project *MUST* be furnished within

    a. 10 days.   b. 20 days.

    c. 30 days.   d. 45 days.

13. Which CC&R would *MOST* likely be enforceable?

    a. One that prohibits resale

    b. One that prohibits resale for more than a stated price

    c. One that prohibits resale to a minority buyer

    d. One that requires property to be used only for religious purposes

14. The Subdivision Map Act is concerned with

    a. physical aspects of the subdivision.

    b. protection of the title in the purchaser.

    c. prevention of seller fraud.

    d. all of the above.

15. The Subdivided Lands Law is concerned primarily with

    a. preventing objectionable uses.

    b. providing adequate space.

    c. protecting purchasers.

    d. protecting brokers.

16. The Subdivided Lands Law does NOT apply to

    a. California subdivisions.

    b. Nevada subdivisions sold in California.

    c. division into four parcels for the purpose of sale.

    d. condominiums.

17. When three one-acre parcels are to be sold from a nine-acre parcel each year for three years, the sellers must comply with

    a. the map act.   b. the Subdivided Lands Law.

    c. both a and b.   d. neither a nor b

18. The Subdivided Lands Law covers

    a. undivided interests.

    b. out-of-state subdivisions sold in California.

    c. time-shares.

    d. all of the above.

19. The Subdivision Map Act applies to

    a. agricultural leases.   b. two or more parcels.

    c. out-of-state subdivisions. d. time shares.

20. Public reports expire

    a. five years from the date of the first sale.

    b. five years from the date of the last sale.

    c. five years from the date of issuance.

    d. one year after issuance.

21. A subdivider who has not received a final public report but is able to enter into binding contracts with purchasers has a

    a. preliminary public report.   b. conditional public report.

    c. variance.   d. conditional-use permit.

22. Seven parcels of land were subject to a restrictive covenant limiting use for residential purposes. A woman acquired all seven parcels and intends to build a commercial property in conformance with zoning. Which of the following describes her rights?

    a. She will not be issued a building permit because the use would violate the restrictions.

    b. The restrictive covenant is terminated by merger.

    c. Any former owner can obtain an injunction to stop the project.

    d. Anyone can enforce the restrictions.

23. Which is TRUE of the Interstate Land Sales Full Disclosure Act?

    a. There is a 14-day right of rescission.

    b. It applies to 50 or more parcels.

    c. The California public report can be used to satisfy the disclosure requirements.

    d. All of the above are true.

24. The statute of limitations for builder liability is

    a. four years for patent defects and ten years for latent defects.

    b. one year.

    c. three years.

    d. ten years for patent defects and four years for latent defects.

25. Excluded from strict liability for defects are

    a. latent defects.   b. developers of lots.

    c. builders.   d. subcontractors.

CHAPTER FOURTEEN

ESCROW AND TITLE INSURANCE

■ KEY TERMS

abstract of title
amendments to the
    escrow instructions
American Land Title
    Association
closing
elder abuse law
escrows

escrow instructions
extended-coverage
    policy of title
    insurance
interpleader action
opinions of title
preliminary title report
rebate law

relation-back doctrine
standard policy of title
    insurance
title insurance
title plant
Uniform Vendor and
    Purchaser Risk Act

■ ESCROWS

In many states, real estate settlements are conferences attended by buyers and sellers, their attorneys, the real estate agent, and sometimes the agent's attorney. At this **closing**, all documents are signed and monies are paid.

In California, the closing process is simplified by using an independent depository to handle the closing process. **Escrows** are neutral third-party depositories that are limited in authority to the instructions given by the principals.

Section 1057 of the Civil Code defines an escrow as follows: "A grant deed may be deposited by the grantor with a third person to be delivered on the performance of a condition, and on delivery by the depository, it will take effect. While in the possession of the third person, and subject to condition, it is called an escrow."

Figure 14.1 illustrates the primary function of the escrow.

FIGURE 14.1
Escrow Function

While the escrow is the process, the escrow agent is the individual holder of the funds (usually an employee of the escrow company). An escrow agent is not an arbitrator or a mediator of disputes. Prior to the fulfillment of the escrow conditions, the escrow is the dual agent of the buyer and the seller. After the fulfillment of the conditions, the escrow agent is the agent of each of the parties, with separate obligations to deliver the deed to the buyer and to deliver the consideration paid to the seller.

Because an escrow is an agency, the escrow agent should not have any discretionary powers. An essential element of an escrow is the irrevocability of the deposit of both the deed and the purchase money. An escrow never acquires title; the escrow is always an agency.

Within one month of closing, brokers must inform the buyer and the seller of the final selling price. In actual practice, the broker does not do so, because the escrow provides this information in the closing statement.

Escrows are required by law in cases of court-ordered sales, bulk sales, and sales involving the transfer of a liquor license.

Escrow Instructions

In Southern California, both the buyer and the seller customarily sign the escrow instructions. In Northern California, the escrow instructions often are separate documents separately signed by the buyer and the seller. The separate documents cannot contain any difference regarding the escrow's duties. The escrow is not effective until both the buyer and the seller have signed identical or conforming escrow instructions.

In Southern California, the escrow instructions are customarily signed upon opening of the escrow. In some areas of Northern California, the escrow instructions, while given at the opening of escrow, are not signed until escrow closes.

The widely used CAR form *California Purchase Agreement and Joint Escrow Instructions* makes the escrow instructions part of the purchase agreement, so separate escrow instructions are not required (see Chapter 6).

Because the real estate broker is not a party to the escrow, the escrow agent cannot change the escrow instructions at the direction of the broker.

For a valid escrow, the signed instructions must be returned to the escrow holder.

Escrow instructions include

- names of purchasers and sellers;
- how title is to be taken;
- terms;
- any contingencies;
- date of closing;
- date of possession (if not specified, possession will be given on the date of closing);
- prorations;
- what documents are to be delivered to escrow;
- the authority to accept documents and funds;
- disbursements to be made;
- costs and charges;
- designation of the title insurance company; and
- items of personal property to be included.

When new financing is involved, the lender will submit its own escrow instructions, so the lender becomes an additional party to the escrow.

The escrow instructions should be clear and unambiguous. It is possible for the escrow instructions to be the only agreement between the parties. The signed escrow instructions could meet the requirements of the statute of frauds and form the contract for sale. In fact, escrows frequently are opened without a prior buy-sell agreement. Escrow instructions often are prepared based on the oral instructions of the real estate agent.

Any changes in the escrow instructions (**amendments to the escrow instructions**) should be signed by both buyer and seller.

Escrow agents that violate their instructions are liable to their principals for losses suffered, but are not liable if the principals do not suffer a loss [*Mains v. City Title Insurance Company* (1949) 34 C.2d 580].

Conflict Between Purchase Agreements and Escrow Instructions.

Escrow instructions are actually independent of any purchase agreement between the parties. If a difference exists between the instructions and the purchase agreement, the escrow instructions generally will prevail because, signed at a later date, they more clearly show the final agreement of the parties. However, escrow instructions might state that the purchase contract will govern in the event of an ambiguity. In such a case, the purchase contract would prevail. If the escrow instructions and a later amendment by the parties are in conflict, the later amendment will govern.

Escrow Duties

Escrow duties might include

- ordering preliminary title reports;

- accepting structural pest control reports and other reports as required by escrow for delivery to the buyer;

- obtaining beneficiary statements on existing loans so balances can be ascertained, as well as actual payoff amount (demand statement);

- accepting instructions for new loans and obtaining the buyer's signature to satisfy the lender;

- ascertaining amounts in impound accounts;

- arranging for the transfer of insurance;

- obtaining deeds of reconveyance;

- drafting grant deeds, trust deeds, notes, etc.;

- preparing closing statements showing all receipts, expenditures, costs, and prorations;

- requesting necessary funds for closing;

- recording all documents, disbursing funds, and issuing closing statements; and

- reporting sale to IRS on form 1099-S.

Escrow Agents

Designating the Escrow Holder. The designation of the escrow holder is the responsibility of the buyer and seller. Normally, the buyer designates the escrow holder in the offer; the seller, by the seller's acceptance, has agreed to the escrow.

Real estate brokers cannot nominate an escrow holder as a condition precedent to the transaction but may recommend an escrow holder to the parties.

Licensing. Escrows must be licensed by the commissioner of corporations. Exempt from the licensing requirements of the escrow law are

- banks and savings associations;

- title insurance companies;

- attorneys (attorneys essentially are unregulated unless they operate an escrow company); however, they must have had a bona fide client relationship with one of the parties; and

- real estate brokers. (This exemption applies only to transactions where the broker was either a principal or the listing or selling agent.)

Individuals cannot be licensed as escrows. Escrows must be corporations. Applicants for escrow licenses must furnish a $25,000 surety bond, and all directors, trustees, and employees of an escrow who have access to money or valuable securities must have a $125,000 fidelity bond. All money deposited in escrow must be placed in a trust account that is exempt from execution or attachment for any claim against the escrow agent.

Prohibitions.   Licensed escrows are prohibited from

- paying referral fees to anyone except for the normal compensation of their employees;

- accepting escrow instructions or amendments containing any blanks to be filled in after signing or initialing of the instructions;

- turning over buyer funds to the seller without buyer authorization or until the seller has conveyed title (some of the creative financing arrangements with extremely long escrows providing for funds to be turned over to the seller prior to the close of escrow can be dangerous because intervening liens could attach to the property); and

- permitting any party to unilaterally change or amend signed instructions.

Prohibitions on Broker/Escrow.   While a real estate broker can act as an escrow agent in transactions where the broker represented the buyer, represented the seller, or acted as a principal to the transaction, Section 2950 of the real estate commissioner's regulations prohibits the following acts by a broker/escrow. The following acts are considered to be grounds for disciplinary action:

- Soliciting or accepting an escrow instruction or amendment containing blanks to be filled in after signing or initialing

- Permitting any person to make an addition, a deletion, or an alteration to escrow instructions or amendments unless signed or initialed by all the parties to the escrow instructions

- Failing to provide a copy, at the time of signing, to persons executing escrow instructions or amendments

- Failing to maintain books, records, and accounts in accordance with accepted principles of accounting and good business practice

- Failing to maintain all records relating to escrows freely accessible for audits, inspections, and examination by the commissioner

- Failing to deposit all money received, as an escrow agent and as part of an escrow transaction, in a bank trust account or escrow account on or before the close of the next full working day after receipt thereof

- Withdrawing or paying out any money deposited in such trust account or escrow account without the written instructions of the party or parties paying the money into escrow

- Failing to advise all parties, in writing, that any licensee, acting as such in the transaction, has any interest in the escrow agency—stockholder, partner, officer, owner, etc. (prohibits a broker from having any undisclosed interest in the escrow)

- Failing to provide a written closing statement to the principals showing all receipts and disbursements and to whom they were made

Section 2995 of the Civil Code prohibits a real estate developer from requiring, as a condition precedent for a sale of a single-family dwelling, that escrow be provided by an escrow entity in which the developer has a financial interest. (A financial interest is defined as 5 percent or more.) The penalty for a violation is the greater of $250 or three times the escrow charge, plus attorney fees and costs. This provision cannot be waived by the purchaser.

The Department of Corporations has interpreted Section 17006(d) of the Financial Code (broker's exemption) as follows:

- The exemption is available only to the real estate broker.
- The exemption is personal to the broker and cannot be delegated to others (other than ministerial functions).
- In a purchase and sale agreement, the broker must be either a party to the transaction or the listing or selling broker.
- The exemption is not available for any association of brokers for the purpose of conducting escrows.
- The broker escrow function must only be an ancillary part of the broker's business.
- When the broker's escrow business is a substantial factor in the utilization of the broker's services, the broker may not delegate or contract out any services that may be provided pursuant to the exemption. (This apparently covers the ministerial functions.)

Brokers cannot advertise that they conduct escrows without specifying in the advertisement that such services are only in connection with the real estate brokerage business.

A broker may not use a fictitious name or a corporate name containing the word *escrow* or advertise in any other manner that would tend to be misleading to the public.

A broker who acts as an escrow agent must put aside any agency relationship with the buyer or seller as well as any special interests. The broker must maintain the position of a neutral depository, as would any other escrow agent.

Disclosure.   The escrow agent has a duty to both parties to keep the escrow matters confidential. There is some disagreement among the courts, however, as to an escrow agent's duty to warn the parties of possible fraud, or to advise them to take actions to protect their interests. At present, the majority of the cases indicate that an escrow holder need not warn a seller of exceptional risk or likely fraud. A broker acting as escrow agent still, however, has the duty to protect the parties through full disclosure of any detrimental fact or risk involved in the transaction.

Case Study

In *Lee v. Escrow Consultants, Inc.* (1989) 210 C.A.3d 915, an escrow paid out $100,000 to a seller upon a forged amendment to the escrow instructions authorizing the release of the funds. The court held that the plaintiff had stated a valid cause of action and indicated the escrow agent had a duty to verify the signatures when the escrow instructions require amendments to be in writing.

Case Study

In *Christenson v. Commonwealth Land Title Insurance Company* (1983) 666 P.2d 302, a party to an escrow requested that the escrow agent provide information to a creditor. The escrow agent provided the wrong information, with the result that the creditor suffered a loss. The court held that while the escrow agent had no duty to supply information to third parties, after it did so, it had a duty of reasonable care. The escrow agent was therefore liable for the loss suffered by its negligence.

While an escrow has duties to parties to the escrow, it has no duties to other parties.

Case Study

The case of *Summit Financial Holdings Ltd. v. Continental Lawyers Title Co.* (2002) 27 C.4th 705 involved a loan that was assigned and subsequently paid off with the monies going to the original lender, not the assignee.

Dr. Furnish borrowed $425,000 from Talbert Financial secured by a note and deed of trust. Talbert assigned the note and deed of trust to Summit Financial Holdings. Dr. Furnish was never notified of the recorded assignment, and Talbert apparently continued to service the loan.

Dr. Furnish obtained a new loan from Dundee Securities that was to pay off the existing loan. Continental Lawyers Title Co. acted as escrow. Neither Talbert nor Summit was a party to the escrow. Although the preliminary Title Report showed an assignment to Summit, CLTC paid the loan off to Talbert, but Talbert failed to remit the proceeds to Summit.

Dr. Furnish filed Chapter 11 bankruptcy and ordered the property sold to pay off Dundee and another secured creditor. The bankruptcy court rejected Summit's claim because Dr. Furnish did not receive a notice of the assignment, and he had paid off Talbert. Summit sued CLTC, contending that the escrow was negligent in paying Talbert rather than Summit.

While the superior court awarded judgment to Summit, the Court of Appeal reversed. On appeal, the California Supreme Court upheld the Court of Appeal. They ruled that an escrow holder has a fiduciary duty only to the parties to the escrow, and that CLTC could not foresee any harm in paying off Talbert as directed, because there was no evidence that Talbert would not remit the funds to Summit.

Case Study
In the case of *In re Marriage of Cloney* (2001) 91 C.A.4th 429, the court ruled that an escrow agent had a duty to disclose to its principal, First American Title, and the purchaser that the seller had used alternative names and that the agent's knowledge can be imputed to the principal. (First American Title failed to check records as to liens for other names used by the seller.)

The Elder Abuse Law.   Welfare and Institutions Code Section 15610.30 (the **elder abuse law**) requires that escrow holders, realty agents, and others report elder financial abuse, fraud, or undue influence. The county public guardian is authorized to take control of the elder's assets to prevent such abuse.

Possession and Risk of Loss

Unless agreed otherwise, the seller retains possession until the close of escrow. If property is destroyed or seriously damaged after a purchase contract is entered into, the **Uniform Vendor and Purchaser Risk Act** (Civil Code Section 1662) provides the following, unless otherwise agreed:

- If neither title or possession has passed to the purchaser and damage is without fault of the purchaser, then the purchaser is entitled to recover all monies paid.

- If either possession or title has been transferred to the purchaser and damage or destruction was without fault of the seller, then the purchaser is not relieved of contractual obligations. Any expenses incurred for the property are the seller's responsibility until the close of escrow. Rents and other income also accrue to the seller until the close of escrow. However, rents paid in advance normally are prorated at closing.

During the escrow period, the legal title remains with the seller, even though the escrow holder has the deed. The buyer has an equitable title when all monies and documents have been deposited into escrow.

The parties normally agree that title passes when the deed is recorded, or on a particular date. In the absence of such agreement, the title could pass when all conditions are met. The risk of loss, therefore, could be on a buyer before the buyer realizes title has transferred. The buyer's insurance usually will not take effect until the close of escrow, so a buyer who takes possession or title prior to the close of escrow will need to obtain earlier insurance coverage.

Termination of Escrow

Full performance, by completion of the escrow, terminates the escrow. Escrows also can be terminated by the mutual agreement of both the buyer and the seller. In addition, impossibility of performance will terminate an escrow.

If only one party has signed the escrow instructions, that party can terminate the escrow prior to the other party's signing and forming a bilateral agreement. However, the person terminating the escrow still could be liable under the purchase contract.

Because escrows customarily provide for time being "of the essence," failure to complete an escrow on time will terminate the escrow. The parties then will have to agree to amend the escrow instructions if they want it to continue.

In practice, however, the majority of escrow instructions provide that they will continue unless canceled by either party. Nevertheless, a person whose failure to perform was the reason for a delay cannot use the delay as the basis for terminating the escrow.

Court decisions have shown some inconsistency relating to "time is of the essence" clauses. Several courts have allowed a reasonable period beyond the date specified.

> **Case Study**
> In the case of *First National Bank of La Habra v. Caldwell* (1927) 84 C.A. 438, no time limit was placed on an escrow. The court held that, where no time is specified in an escrow, it must be performed within a reasonable period of time. A delay from June 7 to September 21 was considered an unreasonable delay and allowed the purchaser to rescind.

Unless the purchase contract is terminated along with an escrow, unilateral cancellation of escrow will not cancel the rights and obligations of the parties. Specific performance or damages still might be possible based on the purchase contract.

A breach of a material provision of an escrow by one party will allow the other party to cancel. A breach can be waived by the party it was intended to benefit.

If the escrow agent dies, the parties select a substitute agent. After escrow instructions have been signed, escrow will not be terminated by the death of either the buyer or the seller. The escrow, unless agreed otherwise, will be binding on the estate of the deceased principal.

Buyer's Deposit.   When an escrow is terminated, the escrow agent ordinarily requests that the parties sign a termination or cancellation agreement that specifies how to dispose of funds being held. Returning funds to the buyer, or paying funds to the seller as liquidated damages, could subject the escrow holder to liability should the court later determine the action to have been improper.

For an escrow involving one to four residential units where the buyer indicated an intention to occupy a unit, Civil Code Section 1057.3 provides for a penalty for the wrongful refusal of a party to execute documents required by the escrow holder to release funds. The aggrieved party is entitled to

- the amount of the funds deposited in escrow,
- treble the amount of escrow funds (but not less than $100 or more than $1,000), and
- reasonable attorney fees.

When the buyer of one to four residential units indicates an intention to occupy a unit and then defaults, the liquidated damages cannot exceed 3 percent of the sales price.

If both buyer and seller claim a deposit when an escrow has terminated, the escrow agent should file an **interpleader action** asking the courts to determine who has valid claim to the funds held.

Money deposited by the buyer into escrow is given conditionally because it is to be paid to the seller only when title is transferred. The deposit ordinarily remains the property of the buyer until the closing, even though the buyer has given up control of the deposit.

The buyer generally assumes the risk of loss of the deposit through embezzlement by the escrow or bank failure. If, however, the loss results from a delay in closing caused by the seller's act or negligence, the seller bears the risk of loss.

If a buyer's deposit is a personal check rather than cash, a cashier's check, or a certified check, the escrow agent should wait until the check clears before conveying title. The escrow agent could be liable if the buyer's check fails to clear the bank.

Escrow Charges and Prorating.   Who pays for the escrow services is determined by agreement of the parties to the escrow (buyers and sellers). Normally, escrow charges are split between the parties. Title insurance costs are paid by the buyer or the seller according to their agreement. Taxes, insurance, interest, rents, etc., are prorated, with the seller usually responsible up to and including the day of closing and the buyer usually responsible after the date of closing. Proration is based on a 360-day year and a 30-day month. Parties may, however, make other payment or prorating agreements.

If no provision is made for who is to pay for escrow charges, title insurance, etc., local custom and usage generally prevail. Custom and usage among the counties in California vary. For example, in most areas of Southern California, the seller pays for the standard policy of title insurance, while in a number of northern areas, the buyer pays.

Doctrine of Relation Back.   Title does not pass until escrow conditions have been performed. Prior to title being passed, the property could acquire liens. If a lien is acquired during this period by a party who had knowledge or notice of the escrow or of the rights of the grantee, the buyer's rights relate back to the delivery of the deed to the escrow, to defeat these intervening liens.

If the grantor dies after the deed is given to escrow, the delivery date of the deed relates back to the date it was given to escrow. Because that date preceded the grantor's death, there is no need for probate court approval. If the deed were not delivered to escrow, the grantee could bring an action for specific performance against the seller's heirs.

Because the **relation-back doctrine** is equitable, it does not apply to third parties who obtain interest without the knowledge of the escrow agent or of the grantee's interest.

Mobilehome Escrows.   When money is deposited into an escrow account involving the sale or lease of a mobile home and the escrow receives written notice from a party of a dispute, the escrow must inform the parties of their right to submit a written request that the escrow hold the funds pending resolution of the problem.

■ TITLE INSURANCE

An **abstract of title** is a history of title showing every recorded document. Lawyers give opinions of the marketability of titles based on the abstracts. This method is still used in many states.

The problem with **opinions of title** based on abstracts is that abstracts do not show hidden items, such as the contractual capacity of a grantor, a forged or altered document in the chain of title, an unknown spousal interest, failure of delivery, or unrecorded documents. The abstractor is liable only for negligence in failing to report a recorded document, and the attorney is liable only for failing to discover problems that were evident in the abstract.

The need for greater protection led to title insurance. In California, title insurance is used to prove marketable title. For a single premium, title insurance companies insure a purchaser as to the marketability of title. **Title insurance** is a contract to indemnify the insured against loss through defects in the title or against liens and encumbrances that may affect the title at the time the policy is issued.

Case Study
In the case of *Southwest Title Ins. Co. v. Northland Bldg. Corp.* (1976) 542 S.W.2d 436, the title policy failed to indicate that a first trust deed included a dragnet clause. (A dragnet clause allows for later advances that take priority as of the date the original trust deed was recorded.) A lender gave a second trust deed based on the seller's equity revealed by the title policy. Subsequent advances on the first trust deed took precedence over the second trust deed. The title insurance company was held liable for the loss suffered. The court held that the policy should have revealed not only the prior liens but also the existence of dragnet clauses.

While title insurance also covers the executor, administrator, and heirs of the insured, it does not directly cover other successors in interest. A new buyer must obtain his or her own insurance protection.

> **Case Study**
>
> In the case of *Harrison v. Commonwealth Land Title Ins. Co.* (1979) 97 C.A.3d 973, at a sheriff's sale, the sheriff read from a title policy that had been issued to an attorney for the judgment creditor. The purchaser at the sheriff's sale discovered that the title policy failed to indicate a trust deed. The court held that the insurance company had no liability to the purchaser. The report was not issued to the purchaser as an insured, and the purchaser was held not justified in relying on it.

> **Case Study**
>
> In the case of *Kwok v. Transnation Title Insurance Co.* (2009) 170 C.A. 4th 1562, Patrick and Maria Kwok had formed the Mary Bell LLC to develop real estate. They built a single-family home. Because of a lengthy dispute with a neighbor about an easement, they decided to move into the house. They transferred title from the LLC to the Kwok Revocable Trust. Their title insurer refused to provide coverage for the easement problem, claiming the trust was not covered by the policy. The trial court held that the voluntary act of deeding property from the LLC to the trust terminated the coverage of the title policy.
>
> The Court of Appeal affirmed, noting they could not rewrite the policy. The insured LLC no longer had an interest in the property.
>
> *Note:* Changing the form of ownership could be costly.

Title insurance could, however, indirectly cover subsequent purchasers who successfully sue an insured grantor because of a title defect included in the grantor's coverage.

Title insurance offers indemnification against loss up to the amount of coverage purchased. Some policies have an inflation endorsement that provides increases in coverage. The title insurance company is obligated to defend the title in legal action, cure the defects, or pay for the loss up to the policy limits.

Prior to issuing a title insurance policy, the title company will search the records to determine if it will write a policy. Title insurance companies use a **title plant** that is a microfilm or computer system showing every document that has been recorded within the county.

The title insurer has no actual duty to ascertain if the title is good. Any records search it performs is for its own protection in deciding if it wants to take the risk of insuring title.

The California insurance commissioner regulates California title insurance companies.

For escrows in which no policy of title insurance is to be issued to the buyer, the following statement must be signed and acknowledged by all parties to the escrow:

Important: In a purchase or exchange of real property, it may be advisable to obtain title insurance in connection with the close of escrow since there may be prior recorded liens and encumbrances, which affect your interest in the property being acquired. A new policy of title insurance should be obtained in order to ensure your interest in the property that you are acquiring.

Preliminary Title Report

After deciding that it will issue title insurance, the title company issues a **preliminary title report**, which indicates exceptions to its coverage. The preliminary title report is not insurance. A separate fee is charged for the title insurance policy, which is usually issued at close of escrow.

> ### Case Study
> The case of *Soifer v. Chicago Title* (2010) 187 C.A. 4th 365 involved a foreclosure buyer who customarily contacted Chicago Title before bidding to determine the priority of loans being foreclosed. The title company contacted the plaintiff via an e-mail that a loan being foreclosed was a first trust deed when in fact it was a second trust deed. The plaintiff purchased the property based on the false information. The plaintiff suffered a loss of $1 million.
>
> The court held that a title insurer was not liable for the mistaken free information given to the plaintiff. He did not pay anything for it. There is no liability in the absence of a title policy.
>
> *Note:* Had the priority of the loan been set forth in a preliminary title report and had Soifer purchased the title policy, he would have been protected.

According to Section 12340.11 of the Insurance Code, preliminary title reports are offers to issue a title policy subject to stated conditions. The reports are not abstracts, nor are there any rights, duties, or responsibilities applicable to the issuance of the preliminary report. The report will not be construed as, or constitute a representation of, the condition of title, but will constitute a statement of the terms and conditions on which the issuer is willing to issue its title policy, if such offer is accepted.

> ### Case Study
> *Southland Title Corporation v. Superior Court* (1991) 231 C.A.3d 530 involved a preliminary title report that did not mention a flood control easement. The court held that the title insurer is not liable for its negligence in preparing the preliminary title report. It held that the report was merely an offer to issue a title policy. The home purchasers were able to collect only up to the limits of their title insurance policy. (They had sought to collect beyond their policy limits based on the negligence of the insurance carrier.)

Homeowner Standard Policy Coverage (California Land Title Association—CLTA)

The homeowner **standard policy of title insurance** covers matters of record not specifically excluded from coverage, as well as matters not of record, such as

- forgery,
- lack of capacity of a grantor,
- undisclosed spousal interest (a grantor who claimed to have been single could have a spouse with community property interests),
- failure of delivery of a prior deed,
- federal estate tax liens,
- deeds of a corporation whose charter has expired, and
- deeds of an agent whose capacity has terminated.

Standard Policy Exclusions.   Not covered by a homeowner standard policy of title insurance are

- defects known by the insured and not disclosed to the title insurer;
- zoning (a special endorsement is available stating that property currently is zoned properly, or that a current use is authorized by the zoning);
- mining claims (these are filed in mining districts, and legal descriptions are not required);
- taxes and assessments that are not yet liens;
- easements and liens not a matter of public record (such as mechanic's lien rights);
- rights of parties in possession (unrecorded deeds, options, leases, etc.) and matters that would be disclosed by making inquiry of persons on the property;
- matters not of record that would be disclosed by checking the property (such as encroachment);
- matters that would be revealed by a correct survey;
- water rights; and
- reservations in government patents.

Homeowner Extended-Coverage Policies

Both the California Land Title Association (CLTA) and the American Land Title Association (ALTA) now offer extended coverage title policies for homeowners. Most California title insurers now issue extended policies to homebuyers unless the purchaser requests the CLTA standard policy, which offers less coverage at a slightly lower premium. In addition to the standard coverage, these policies offer coverage, with limitations, for

- building permit violations,
- restrictive covenant violations,
- postpolicy forgery,

- postpolicy adverse possession,

- access,

- postpolicy encroachment,

- postpolicy prescriptive rights,

- map inconsistencies,

- living trust coverage (homeowner deeds to living trust), and

- structure damage from mineral extraction by others.

Lender Extended-Coverage Policy

Because many lenders are from other areas, the physical inspection necessary to protect their interests under a standard policy has not been feasible. Therefore, the **American Land Title Association (ALTA)** policy was developed to meet lender needs. Besides offering greater protection to the lenders, the **extended-coverage policy of title insurance** allowed assignment because loans frequently are transferred between lenders. The lender's policy provides coverage only until the loan is paid. It actually offers decreasing coverage each year.

> ### Case Study
> *Lick Mill Creek Apartments v. Chicago Title Co.* (1991) 231 C.A.3d 1654 involved a case where land with hazardous waste was purchased. The buyer sought reimbursement of removal costs from the title insurer. The court held that, while an ALTA title policy offers more complete off-record coverage than a CLTA policy, it does not cover physical defects, such as contamination. The court noted that encumbrances are defined (Civil Code Section 1114) as "taxes, assessments, and all liens upon real property." An order to clean up property is not a lien unless recorded. (Marketability of title and market value are not the same thing.)

> ### Case Study
> In the case of *Walters v. Marler* (1978) 83 C.A.3d 1, a house was constructed on the wrong lot. While the lender had an extended-coverage policy of title insurance, the owner had only a standard policy. The court held that, while the lender was insured for the risk, the owner was not. The owner cannot benefit from the extended-coverage policy without having paid the additional premium.

In addition to the coverage offered by the standard policy, an ALTA extended-coverage policy of title insurance includes

- unrecorded liens;

- off-record easements;

- rights of parties in physical possession, including tenants and buyers under unrecorded instruments;

- rights and claims that a correct survey or physical inspection of the land would show;

- mining claims;

- reservations in patents;

- water rights; and

- lack of access.

Lender Extended-Coverage Exclusions

Extended-coverage policies do not cover

- matters known by the insured but not conveyed to the insurer,

- government regulations such as zoning,

- liens placed by the insured,

- eminent domain,

- violations of the map act, or

- the physical condition of the property.

Table 14.1 shows what is covered by title insurance.

TABLE 14.1
Owner's Title
Insurance Policy

Standard Coverage	Lender Extended Coverage	Not Covered by Either Policy
1. Defects found in public records	Standard coverage plus defects discoverable through	1. Defects and liens listed in policy
2. Forged documents		2. Defects known to buyer
3. Incompetent grantors	1. property inspection, including unrecorded rights of persons in possession	3. Changes in land use brought about by zoning ordinances
4. Incorrect marital statements		
5. Improperly delivered deeds	2. examination of survey	
	3. unrecorded liens not known of by policyholder	

Special Policies

A number of special policies are available, including construction lender policies (with endorsements protecting against prior mechanics' liens), vendee policies for purchasers under real property sales contracts, leasehold loan policies, leasehold owners' policies, and oil and gas interest policies.

Endorsements can be obtained for special additional coverage, or exclusion from coverage.

Policy Interpretation

Title policies should be interpreted in accordance with the reasonable expectations of the insured. Any questions about ambiguities in a policy normally will be resolved against the insurer.

Title Insurance Companies

Every title insurance company in California must have at least $500,000 paid-in capital and must deposit with the insurance commissioner a guarantee fund of $100,000 in cash or approved securities.

Title insurance companies must set apart annually, as a title insurance surplus fund, a sum equal to 10 percent of premiums collected during the year until this fund equals the lesser of 25 percent of the paid-in capital of the company, or $1 million. This fund offers further security to the holders and beneficiaries of title insurance policies.

Rebate Law.   Title insurance companies in California must charge for services and make a sincere effort to collect such charges.

The **rebate law** extends the anticommission provisions of the Insurance Code to prohibit direct or indirect payments by a title insurer to principals in a transaction as a consideration for business. The rebate prohibition extends to any title business, including escrows.

It is a criminal offense for an employee of a title company or controlled escrow company to pay a commission (directly or indirectly) to a real estate licensee as an inducement for placement or referral of title business. The criminal penalties apply to both giving and receiving the kickback. The penalty is up to one year in jail and a fine up to $10,000 for each offense (Penal Code 641.4).

The title insurance company may, however, furnish the names of owners of record and the legal description of parcels of real estate without charge.

The California Department of Insurance has indicated that providing a broker with a "Comparative Market Analysis" is a prohibited inducement.

■ SUMMARY

Escrows are neutral depositories that handle the functions of real estate closings. The escrow is not effective until both the buyer and the seller sign identical or conforming escrow instructions. The escrow agent represents the buyer and seller and must obey their instructions.

Generally, escrow instructions that are signed after the purchase agreement will prevail if an ambiguity between the two develops.

Escrow instructions would include the names of the parties, how title is to be taken, special terms, contingencies, and transfer instructions, as well as the payment of costs and charges.

The escrow agent handles all of the paperwork of closing, such as drafting documents, obtaining signatures, paying off existing liens, dispersing funds, and issuing closing statements.

Escrows must be licensed by the commissioner of corporations, with the exception of banks and savings associations, title insurance companies, attorneys, and real estate brokers. Real estate brokers can serve as escrows on transactions in which they represented either the buyer or the seller, or were a principal. A real estate broker cannot delegate other than ministerial functions to others and cannot use the word "escrow" in the broker's fictitious or corporate name.

An escrow will be terminated by

- full performance,
- mutual agreement of the parties,
- failure to fulfill a condition necessary for closing, or
- a breach of a material provision by one party (which allows the other party to cancel).

Title insurance protects purchasers and/or lenders by insuring the marketability of title. A title insurance company agrees to indemnify against losses that are not excluded, up to the amount of coverage purchased. Title insurance protects only the named insured and the insured's estate or heirs.

A title insurer will issue a preliminary title report, which indicates that the insurer will insure with named exceptions. The preliminary title report provides no insurance protection if a policy of insurance is not issued.

A standard policy of title insurance (California Land Title Association—CLTA) covers matters of record, as well as matters not of record, including

- forgery,
- lack of capacity of a grantor,
- undisclosed spousal interest,
- failure of delivery of a prior deed,
- federal estate tax liens,
- deeds of a corporation whose charter has expired, and
- deeds of an agent whose capacity has terminated.

The need for greater protection for lenders who were not in an area led to the development of the American Land Title Association (ALTA) policy, which offers extended coverage to lenders. The same protection also can be obtained by buyers.

Extended coverage includes

- unrecorded liens,
- off-record easements,
- rights of parties in possession,
- rights and claims a correct survey would have revealed,
- reservations in patents,
- water rights, and
- lack of access.

Special title insurance policies are available for construction lenders, purchasers on real property sales contracts, lessees, leasehold lenders, oil and gas interests, etc.

Ambiguities in title policies generally are resolved against the insurance carrier.

Title insurers and escrows are prohibited from providing rebates to brokers for referral of business. This prohibition extends to special rates and not making a sincere effort to collect for services.

■ DISCUSSION CASES

1. An escrow delivered title to a buyer before the conditions of the escrow were met. **What are the rights of the parties?**

    Kish v. Bay Counties Title Guaranty Co. (1967) 254 C.A.2d 725

2. The sellers signed escrow instructions directing that the broker's commission be paid out of the sale proceeds. The sales agreement authorizing the commission was not deposited into escrow. On the day prior to closing, the seller instructed the escrow holder not to pay the commission. **In not paying the broker, was the escrow liable for the broker's loss?**

    Contemporary Invs., Inc. v. Safeco Title Ins. Co. (1983) 145 C.A.3d 999

3. An escrow received a check unaccompanied by any instructions. (The purchaser had not signed the escrow instructions.) The check was for $880 more than was required as an increased deposit in a transaction. The title company put the undeposited check in the file. The purchaser subsequently notified the seller that the transaction would not be completed. The seller's attorney demanded that the $5,000 be turned over to the seller. The purchaser had emptied the account, so the check could not be cashed. **Was the escrow liable to the seller?**

    Riando v. San Benito Title Guarantee Co. (1950) 35 C.2d 170

4. It was alleged that the escrow knew that the plaintiffs were being defrauded by others. **Does the escrow have a duty to warn the purchaser?**

    Lee v. Title Insurance & Trust Co. (1968) 264 C.A.2d 160

5. An amendment to escrow instructions called for security to be a fourth trust deed rather than a second trust deed as originally called for. A prior lienholder subsequently foreclosed on the property. The plaintiff claimed that the escrow was negligent and breached a fiduciary duty in that it failed to call the substituted consideration specifically to the attention of the plaintiff. **Was the plaintiff's claim valid?**

    Axley v. Transamerica Title Ins. Co. (1978) 88 C.A.3d 1

6. The plaintiff was to loan a property owner enough money to pay off an existing first trust deed and was to take back a new first trust deed as security. The plaintiff paid off the existing first trust deed outside of escrow. The escrow, contrary to oral instructions, recorded the deed of reconveyance. This allowed the owner to place another first trust deed on the property. **Is the escrow liable?**

Zang v. Northwestern Title Co. (1982) 135 C.A.3d 159

7. Warrington agreed to assume the mortgages of record. A preliminary title report issued to the seller in a different transaction failed to disclose a second mortgage. **Is the insurance company liable for its negligence?**

Warrington v. Transamerica Title Ins. Co. (1979) 546 P.2d 627

8. An insurance company failed to defend an attack on a title because it believed that the claim was not covered. **If the claim actually was covered by the policy, what would be the limits of the insurer's liability?**

Samson v. Transamerica Ins. Co. (1981) 30 C.3d 220

9. The buyers, the sellers, and the buyers' agent went to an escrow agent to draw up instructions on the sale of a chicken ranch. The escrow instructions included a bill of sale for all of the equipment that turned all of the fixtures into personal property and a trust deed for the ranch. The purchaser promptly removed all of the equipment and defaulted on the purchase price. Because it was a purchase-money trust deed, a deficiency judgment was not possible. **Was the escrow agent negligent?**

Cunningham v. Security Title Ins. Co. (1966) 241 C.A.2d 626

10. An escrow agent agreed to withhold funds to cover a debt due the plaintiff for material. The escrow agent failed to withhold the funds as agreed. The plaintiff was not a party to the escrow. **Is the escrow agent liable to the plaintiff?**

Warrington Lumber Co. v. Fullerton Mtg. & Escrow Co. (1963) 222 C.A.2d 706

11. A title insurer's policy had an exclusion for "water rights, claims, or title to water." The title insurance failed to discover a recorded easement given by the previous owner to a water company for drilling and running a pipeline. **Is the insurer liable?**

White v. Western Title Ins. Co. (1985) 40 C.3d 870

12. The buyer's deposit into escrow was a check that remained uncashed. The seller did not know that the check was not deposited. The buyer defaulted. **What, if anything, is the escrow agent's liability to the seller?**

Wade v. Lake County Title Co. (1970) 6 C.A.3d 824

■ CHAPTER QUIZ

1. After escrow instructions have been signed, the escrow agent may

   a. fill in blanks left by the parties.

   b. return the deposit to the buyer if the escrow fails to close on time.

   c. refuse to obey instructions received from the broker.

   d. do none of the above.

2. If escrow instructions fail to provide for the date of possession, possession will be given

   a. within 30 days of close of escrow.

   b. within a reasonable time.

   c. at close of escrow.

   d. prior to close of escrow.

3. An amendment to the escrow instructions requires the agreement of

   a. the buyer and the escrow.

   b. the agent and the escrow.

   c. the buyer, seller, agent, and escrow.

   d. none of the above.

4. When the signed escrow instructions differ from the purchase agreement,

   a. the escrow takes precedence.

   b. the purchase agreement takes precedence.

   c. the contract becomes void for lack of certainty.

   d. the escrow is required to commence an interpleader action.

5. Duties of an escrow do *NOT* include

   a. ordering preliminary title reports.

   b. mediating buyer-seller disputes.

   c. drafting deeds.

   d. issuing closing statements.

6. Exempt from the licensing requirements are escrows conducted by

a. a real estate broker in transactions in which the broker represents either the buyer or seller.

b. title insurance companies.

c. banks.

d. all of the parties above.

7. A real estate broker, not licensed as an escrow, can conduct an escrow when the broker is

a. a representative of the seller.

b. a representative of the buyer.

c. a principal to the transaction.

d. any of the above.

8. Which actions of an escrow would be improper?

a. Accepting fees from both buyer and seller

b. Refusing to pay a commission for referral to the escrow

c. Refusing to handle an escrow

d. Accepting escrow instructions with blanks to be filled in by the escrow after the instructions are signed

9. Which behavior is proper for a broker who, while not licensed as an escrow, conducts escrows on the broker's sales?

a. Delegating the escrow function to another

b. Using the name "Jones Realty and Escrow Company"

c. Charging for the escrow services

d. None of the above

10. A buyer given possession by the seller one week prior to close of escrow should be MOST concerned about

a. the impound account.

b. risk of loss.

c. extended title coverage.

d. designation of the escrow holder.

11.   Which statement is *TRUE* of the rights and obligations during escrow?

   a.   The seller retains risk of property loss.

   b.   Rents belong to the seller.

   c.   Property expenses are the responsibility of the seller.

   d.   All of the above are true.

12.   Which would *NOT* terminate an escrow?

   a.   Full performance of escrow duties

   b.   Mutual agreement of the parties

   c.   The broker's order to terminate

   d.   Impossibility of performance

13.   When both buyer and seller make demands on escrow for the buyer's deposit after the escrow failed to close, the escrow holder should

   a.   deduct its fees and return the deposit to the person who made it.

   b.   deduct its fees and return the deposit to the seller.

   c.   file an interpleader action.

   d.   give the deposit to the first party making a claim to it.

14.   Which *BEST* describes an abstract of title?

   a.   The complete legal description

   b.   An abbreviated description, such as a street address

   c.   A recorded history of title

   d.   An opinion of title

15.   Which is *TRUE* regarding title insurance?

   a.   Executors and heirs are protected by the title insurance of the deceased insured.

   b.   A buyer obtains greater title protection if the lender is issued an extended-coverage policy.

   c.   Both a and b are true.

   d.   Neither a nor b is true.

16. A title insurer will *NOT* be liable for a loss if

    a. its negligence was not the cause of the loss.

    b. the person suffering the loss was not the insured or the insured's estate or heirs.

    c. either a or b occurred.

    d. neither a nor b occurred.

17. To issue a standard title policy, the insurer must

    a. provide a survey.

    b. determine whether title is good.

    c. provide an abstract.

    d. do none of the above.

18. Which is *TRUE* of the preliminary title report?

    a. It provides interim coverage.

    b. It shows the condition of title.

    c. It provides no insurance.

    d. Both b and c are true.

19. A standard policy of title insurance protects against

    a. rights of parties in possession.

    b. unrecorded easements.

    c. zoning restrictions.

    d. forgery in the chain of title.

20. A standard policy of title insurance does *NOT* cover

    a. unknown spousal interests.

    b. rights of parties in possession.

    c. forgery.

    d. lack of capacity of the grantor.

21. A standard policy of title insurance covers

    a. unrecorded mechanics' liens.

    b. instruments outside the chain of title.

    c. easements that are not a matter of public record.

    d. none of the above.

22. After buying a home and receiving a standard policy of title insurance, you determine that the "tenant" claims to be an owner under an unrecorded grant deed. Which statement is *TRUE*?

    a. You are protected by your insurance.

    b. If you record first, you will be protected.

    c. You are not insured for this loss.

    d. An abstract would have given you greater protection.

23. Extended-coverage homeowners' title insurance adds which element to the coverage of the standard policy?

    a. Forgery   b. Unknown spousal interests

    c. Lack of capacity   d. Building permit violations

24. Extended-coverage policies of title insurance do *NOT* generally cover

    a. claims of a party in possession.

    b. building and zoning regulations.

    c. prescriptive easements.

    d. water rights.

25. The rebate law prohibits

    a. escrows from giving rebates to brokers.

    b. title companies from giving rebates to brokers.

    c. brokers from rebating commissions to buyers.

    d. both a and b.

CHAPTER FIFTEEN

LANDLORD-TENANT LAW

■ KEY TERMS

assignment	lease	surrender
constructive eviction	nondisturbance clause	tenancy at sufferance
Costa-Hawkins Rental Housing Act	periodic tenancy	tenancy at will
demise	quiet enjoyment	tenancy for years
exculpatory clauses	rent control	30-day notice
habitability	retaliatory evictions	three-day notice
implied warranty	security deposit	unlawful detainer action
	sublease	writ of possession

■ TYPES OF TENANCIES

A leasehold interest (also known as a **demise**) is a nonfreehold estate in real property.

Tenancy for Years

A **tenancy for years**, or estate for years, is a leasehold interest with a definite termination date. The tenancy does not renew itself, and no notice is required to end it. A tenancy for years could be a rental of a summer cabin for a weekend or a multiyear lease.

Agricultural land in California cannot be leased for more than 51 years. Other property leases and mineral leases cannot exceed 99 years. (Mineral leases differ from mineral rights, which are grants or reservations of a fee interest and can go on forever.) Leases that provide for renewal options that could exceed these statutory limits are unenforceable.

Periodic Tenancy

A **periodic tenancy** renews itself automatically from period to period unless notice of termination is given. Customarily, the period would be the rent-paying period, and the most common periodic tenancy is a month-to-month tenancy.

Either the lessor (landlord) or the lessee (tenant) can give notice to terminate. Notice of up to the length of the rent-paying period is generally required to terminate, but for month-to-month tenancies, it is usually 30 or 60 days. The parties to a periodic tenancy can agree to a notice period of less than 30 days, but notice always must be given at least 7 days before termination. If the tenant has lived in the property at least 12 months, then the landlord must give a 60-day notice to terminate. If a tenant is under a rental agreement with a government agency, such as Section 8 Housing, then a 90-day notice is required.

In California, the notice to terminate does not have to coincide with the rent-paying period. For example, on a month-to-month tenancy that ends on the first of the month, notice could be given to end the tenancy on the tenth of a month if the notice were given at least 30 days prior to the termination (**30-day notice**).

Rent increases and changes in the terms of a periodic tenancy also require notice for the length of the rent-paying period, but generally, notice need not be given more than 30 days in advance. However, if a rent increase is greater than a 10 percent increase over rent charged within the prior 12 months, then a 60-day notice of the rent increase is required.

In the absence of any agreement, housing units and nonresidential properties are presumed to be rented on a month-to-month basis when no local custom to the contrary exists. However, agricultural rentals are presumed to be for one year unless another period was indicated.

Tenancy at Will

A **tenancy at will** is held at the pleasure of the lessor for an unspecified period of time. Under a tenancy at will, there is possession without an agreement on the rent payment. If rent was paid or rent was agreed on, the tenancy would convert to a periodic tenancy. An example of a tenancy at-will might be a tenant given possession while a lease was still being negotiated, before any agreement on rent has been reached. Under common law, no notice was required to terminate a tenancy at will, and it could be terminated by the lessor or lessee. Because California requires a notice by statute, California does not have a true tenancy at will.

Tenancy at Sufferance

In a **tenancy at sufferance** the lessee is a holdover tenant. For example, one who retains possession beyond the expiration of a tenancy for years, or a homeseller who fails to vacate by the agreed move-out date, is a holdover tenant.

California regards a tenant at sufferance as a trespasser rather than a tenant and considers an ejectment action or an unlawful detainer action (discussed later in this chapter) to oust the trespasser a proper remedy.

When a lessor consents to the holdover or accepts rent from the tenant at sufferance, a periodic tenancy, which would require statutory notice to terminate, results.

■ THE LEASE

A **lease** is an agreement that transfers a right of exclusive possession for a stated term from a landlord (lessor) to a tenant (lessee). The lessor under the lease subordinates his or her rights of occupancy to the rights of the tenant. The lessor retains a reversionary interest; the lessor is entitled to possession when the tenancy has ended.

Leasehold interests are considered personal property (chattels real) rather than real property. The laws of personal property, therefore, apply.

Because a lease is a contract, all the requirements of a valid contract are required for a valid lease.

Leases can be oral or written agreements. However, an oral lease is enforceable only if it can be fully performed within one year of being agreed on. For example, a one-year oral lease beginning on the date of agreement is enforceable, but a one-year lease starting one month after the agreement must be in writing to be enforceable.

Leases may be recorded, but recordation is not necessary between the parties. Recording does give constructive notice of a tenant's interest, and this could be important in defining priority of interests when there is a subsequent trust deed or purchaser. A subsequent purchaser is not required to honor a lease for more than one year unless a memorandum of the lease is recorded, or the purchaser has constructive notice. Possession is deemed constructive notice, so a tenant's rights could be challenged by a subsequent purchaser only if the tenant had vacated or had not yet occupied the premises at the time of transfer and also had failed to record the lease.

To be recorded, a lease must be acknowledged by the lessor.

Form and Provisions of a Lease

No particular language is required to create a tenancy as long as the intent is clear. However, the language must include the names of the parties and clearly describe the premises, the amount of rent, and the term of the lease.

Commercial leases can be complex documents of dozens of pages, while residential leases are normally simpler contracts, as is the lease in Chapter 6.

If the lease is in writing, the lessor must sign the lease. A tenant who moves in or pays rent after receiving a copy of the lease will be viewed as having accepted the lease even when the tenant has not signed it.

If jointly owned property is leased by a husband and wife for more than one year, both spouses must sign the lease.

Unless use is restricted by the lease, the tenant can use the premises for any lawful purpose.

In the absence of any agreement or practice to the contrary, for leases of one year or less, rent is due at the end of each rent-paying period. The parties to a lease generally agree, however, that rent will be paid in advance.

Lease provisions that call for forfeiture of the premises upon some default must be stated clearly. The courts generally will construe agreements to avoid forfeiture if the result will be inequitable. For forfeiture, a demand must be made for performance unless such demand would be futile. Failure to pay rent does not justify forfeiture.

If a tenant breaches a provision of the lease that calls for forfeiture and the landlord accepts rent knowing of the breach, the landlord could be said to have waived his or her right to declare forfeiture. This would not be the case if the lease specifies that acceptance of rent will not waive the landlord's rights to declare a forfeiture in the event of a continuing or subsequent breach.

Civil Code Section 1670.5, which prohibits the enforcement of unconscionable contracts, also applies to leases. Clauses that are so harsh as to be considered unconscionable will not be enforced by the courts. For example, courts will not enforce acceleration clauses in leases where the entire rent for the term of the lease becomes due if the lessee fails to make a payment by a specified date.

Leases often provide that they are renewed automatically if either party fails to give notice. An automatic renewal under such a lease would be voidable by the lessee if the lessee did not prepare the lease, or if the automatic renewal clause was not printed in at least eight-point type and a reference to the automatic renewal was not placed in at least eight-point type just above where the lessee signs.

Notices and Management

The owner or agent of every multiunit dwelling of more than two units must disclose and keep current the name and address of each person authorized to manage the premises and to receive notices and demands on behalf of the owner.

Every residential property containing 16 or more units must have a resident manager.

Fair Housing

All the federal and state fair housing acts apply to discrimination in rentals. For a detailed discussion of these rights, see Chapter 4.

Fixtures

The lease may provide the tenant with rights to remove improvements. In the absence of such an agreement, fixtures stay with the property.

Because forfeiture is a harsh penalty, courts often will find tenant improvements to be personal property when they clearly would be justified in declaring the items fixtures. When there is doubt about whether an improvement can be defined as a fixture, courts generally will find in favor of the tenant.

As mentioned in Chapter 7, a tenant has the right to remove the annual crops that are the fruit of his or her labor, even after the tenancy has ended.

Trade Fixtures.   Trade fixtures, also discussed in Chapter 7, generally must be removed prior to the expiration of the lease. In the case of a month-to-month lease, the courts usually allow a reasonable period for removal of the fixtures; this period could extend beyond the termination date.

As discussed in Chapter 11, the lessor should record and file a notice of nonresponsibility to be protected from mechanics' liens when a tenant makes improvements or repairs. If the lease obligates the tenant to make alterations, improvements, or repairs, a lien could be placed against the property even when the notice of nonresponsibility was filed. The tenant may become an agent of the owner in authorizing the work required by the lessor.

Options

Leases frequently contain options to purchase or options to renew. Part of the rent is generally regarded as consideration for the option. Ordinarily, time is considered to be of the essence for options; that is, they must be exercised within the period provided.

Exculpatory Clauses

Leases frequently contain **exculpatory clauses**, which purport to relieve the landlord of all liability for injury to the tenant and others as well as damage to the tenant's property. Despite the language of these clauses, a lease cannot excuse the landlord for acts, fraud, or violations of the law that are either willful or negligent. The tenant cannot waive the landlord's duty. Civil Code Section 1953 declares that exculpatory clauses in residential leases executed after January 1, 1976, are invalid.

Case Study

The case of *Burnett v. Chimney Sweep, LLC* (2004) 123 C.A.4th 1057 involved a commercial lease that included an exculpatory clause, which stated, "Notwithstanding lessor's negligence or breach of this lease, lessor shall under no circumstance be liable for injury to lessee's business or for any loss of income or profit therefrom."

The complaint alleged excessive moisture and the growth of mildew and mold on the leased premises. The defendant was notified of the problems and allegedly refused to remediate them. The tenant was unable to conduct business on the premises and sued for damages. The Santa Barbara Superior Court granted judgment to the landlord on the pleadings (a demurrer) based on the exculpatory clause, and awarded $101,600 attorney fees to the owner and $38,020 attorney fees to the property management firm.

The Court of Appeal reversed, ruling that the exculpatory clause only shielded the landlord from passive negligence, not from active negligence. Chimney Sweep was allegedly actively negligent in refusing to remediate the problem caused by excessive moisture and mold infestation.

Note: This decision shows the disdain courts hold for exculpatory clauses in which landlords attempt to avoid all liability for causes that are under their control.

Security Deposits

A **security deposit** is any payment, fee, deposit, or charge (not limited to the advance payment of rent) required by the lessor to secure the performance of a rental agreement. The maximum allowable security deposit for unfurnished units is two months' rent. For furnished units, it cannot exceed three months' rent [Civil Code Section 1950.5(c)].

The lessor may appropriate necessary amounts from the deposit to remedy rent default, to repair damage done by the tenant, or to clean the premises upon termination of the tenancy if the deposit was made for those purposes [Civil Code Section 1950.5(e)].

The landlord must notify a tenant in writing of the tenant's right to request and be present at a pre-vacancy inspection of the tenant's rental unit. The purpose is to allow the tenant to correct any deficiencies so that the landlord does not deduct the correction costs from the tenant's security deposit. The tenant's right to a pre-vacancy inspection does not apply where the tenant is evicted for failure to pay rent or for violating conditions of the lease.

Security deposits do not apply to normal wear and tear. They apply to negligence and failure to maintain the premises in a reasonable manner.

No later than three weeks (21 days) after the tenant has vacated the premises, the landlord must furnish the tenant with an itemized written statement of the basis for, and the amount of, any security deposit retained, as well as the disposition of such security, and must return any remaining portion of such security [Civil Code Section 1950.5(e)]. If documentation is not provided as to actual costs incurred by the landlord to repair or clean the rental unit, the landlord may not retain any portion of the deposit. The landlord need not provide this documentation if the deductions are $125 or less.

When the landlord transfers the property, the security deposit must be either transferred to the new owner with notice given to the tenant, or returned to the tenant. In either case, the landlord can deduct sums due for rent, repairs, or cleaning. If the security deposits are not transferred to the new owner, the new owner and the former owner are jointly liable for the repayment of security deposits to the tenants [Civil Code Section 1950.5(i)].

An amendment to Civil Code Section 1950.5 makes the landlord liable for interest on unreturned security deposits at 2 percent per month. Any successor in interest of the landlord also will be liable.

The bad-faith retention by the landlord (or transferee in interest) of any portion of the deposit may subject the landlord to twice the amount of the security deposit plus actual damages to $600 in damages in addition to actual damages [Civil Code Section 1950.5(j)].

The tenant's right to the return of the security deposit is a priority claim above those of any creditor of the landlord other than a trustee in bankruptcy.

In the absence of any agreement to pay interest or a local statute requiring interest, a landlord need not pay interest on security deposits. (Berkeley and San Francisco had ordinances requiring such interest.)

Case Study

The case of *Korens v. Zukin Corp.* (1989) 212 C.A.3d 1054 was a $1.5 million class-action suit for interest on security deposits. In dismissing the lawsuit, the court pointed out there was no state law requiring landlords to pay interest on security deposits. "Any requirement that interest be paid should be enacted explicitly by the legislature, not developed through doctrinal manipulation by the courts."

If a lessor takes a security deposit in the form of the last month's rent, it is taxable to the lessor as regular income in the year received. If, however, the deposit is intended strictly to secure the payment of rent, cleaning, and possible damages, the deposit will be taxable only if and when it is forfeited.

Case Study

In the case of *People v. Parkmerced Co.* (1988) 198 C.A.3d 683, the district attorney sued the owner and management company of a 3,400-unit apartment complex. Tenants were charged $65 more for the first month's rent on a one-year lease than for the other 11 months and were also charged a $50 transfer fee if they wished to change apartments.

The Court of Appeal affirmed the trial court's decision that these fees were security deposits within the meaning of Civil Code Section 1950.5. Because the fees were not intended to cover repairs or tenant defaults, the defendants were not allowed to keep them. Defendants were ordered to reimburse past tenants for fees charged, notify current tenants of their right to receive a refund, and pay $222,000 in civil penalties and $40,000 in attorney fees.

A landlord can require a nonrefundable applicant screening fee for tenants (up to $49.50). Upon request, the landlord must supply the rental applicant a copy of a credit report paid for by the applicant (Civil Code 1950.6).

Civil Code Section 1950.7 sets forth rights and obligations as to security deposits for commercial tenancies.

■ ASSIGNMENTS AND SUBLEASES

An **assignment** of a lease transfers the entire leasehold interest. The assignee becomes the tenant of the original lessor. The assignee is primarily liable on the lease, while the assignor retains secondary liability. (The assignor remains as a surety on the lease.)

Instead of assigning, the lessee would be better off surrendering the premises to the lessor and letting the assignee become a tenant on a new lease. If the lessor agrees to this, the original lessee will be free from any liability on the lease.

In a **sublease**, the lessee becomes a lessor (sublessor), and the sublessee is the tenant of the original lessee, not the tenant of the original lessor.

Figure 15.1 illustrates the differences between an assignment and a sublease.

FIGURE 15.1

Assignment versus Subletting

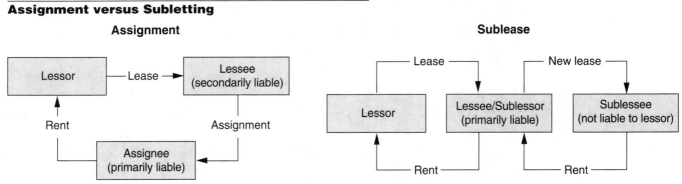

Under a sublease, the lessee remains primarily liable on the lease. A sublease can be for the same term or less than the term of the original lease, and can be for all or part of the leased premises.

No privity of contract between the sublessee and the lessor exists. If the original lessee is evicted or the lease otherwise terminates, the rights of the sublessee also terminate.

The sublessee cannot have any greater rights than the original lessee had, because the sublessee's rights were granted by the sublessor.

Besides the ability to sublet only part of the premises, an important advantage of subleasing is that a rent differential is possible.

An option to purchase in a lease would go with an assignment, or it even can be separated from the lease unless the transfer of the option is prohibited by its terms. An option to purchase does not go with a sublease.

If a lease fails to restrict assignment or subleases, the lessee can freely transfer the lease interest. A lease may prohibit transfer of a tenant's rights (Civil Code Section 1995.230), but if transfer is allowed with the lessor's consent, consent cannot be refused unreasonably. The lease can require that the landlord share in some or all of the profits from an assignment or sublease (Civil Code Sections 1995.240 and 1995.250).

See *Kendall v. Ernest Pestana Inc.* (1985) 40 C.3d 488 and *Pay 'N' Pak Stores v. Superior Court* (1989) 210 C.A.3d 1404.

An assignment or sublease made when prohibited by the lease may be voidable, but is not void. A lessor who accepts rent after having knowledge of the assignment or sublease, however, has consented to it.

■ TERMINATION OF LEASES

A lease can be terminated by or for the following reasons:

- Destruction of the premises—some leases, however, provide that the rent is merely tolled (temporarily suspended) and the landlord has a stated period of time to rebuild.

- Action of a public body (eminent domain)—the tenant is released if the entire property is taken, but in cases of partial condemnation, where the portion remaining continues to meet the needs of the lessee, the lessee could be required to continue to pay rent (or a reduced rent). For example, the taking of several feet to widen a road probably would not allow the tenant to terminate the lease. A tenant could have a claim of loss against the public body for condemnation. In some cases, commercial tenants have received as much compensation in condemnation cases as the owners of the structures.

- Commercial frustration—this applies to unforeseen events, the non-occurrence of which was a condition precedent of the contract (see Chapter 5).

- Merger—where the same party acquires the lessee's and the lessor's interests, the lesser interest is lost by merger. For example, when a tenant under a long-term lease purchases the premises from a landlord and later sells the property, the former tenant will have lost the rights under the lease. When the tenant purchased the property, the tenant became the owner and no longer was a tenant.

- Bankruptcy of the tenant—the bankruptcy court could, however, determine that the lease was an asset of the bankrupt and assign it to another.

- Expiration or notice—estates for years terminate automatically by their terms. Notice ends a periodic tenancy.

- Foreclosure—the foreclosure of a trust deed recorded prior to the lease terminates the lease. (The cancellation is not automatic, as the new owner can elect to accept the existing lease.) A tenant who is entering a lease that requires a great expenditure of labor and/or capital on the premises should consider obtaining the agreement of any prior trust deed beneficiary to recognize the lease in the event of foreclosure (**nondisturbance clause**).

- Failure to pay rent.

- Failure to give possession.

■ Violation of any material condition of the lease.

■ Use of the premises for an illegal or unauthorized purpose.

■ Abandonment of the premises by the lessee.

■ Surrender of the premises by the lessee (accepted by the lessor).

■ The landlord's violation of the implied warranties of quiet enjoyment and habitability.

■ The landlord's failure to make needed or agreed-on repairs.

■ Domestic violence, sexual assault, or stalking.

In the absence of an agreement to the contrary, the death of neither the lessor nor the lessee will terminate a lease.

■ RIGHTS AND RESPONSIBILITIES OF LANDLORDS

Right of Entry

In the absence of any agreement, the landlord can enter leased premises only when

■ an emergency requires entry;

■ the tenant consents to an entry;

■ the entry is during normal business hours after reasonable notice (24 hours is considered reasonable) to make necessary or agreed repairs, alterations, or improvements, or to show the premises to prospective or actual purchasers, mortgagees, tenants, workers, or contractors, and the notice must specify date and approximate time as well as purpose of entry (Civil Code Section 1954);

■ the tenant has abandoned or surrendered the premises; or

■ the landlord has obtained a court order to enter.

The tenant cannot waive or modify his or her rights to privacy (Civil Code Section 1953).

Habitability

A residential lease has an **implied warranty** of **habitability**. The landlord must put a building intended for human habitation in a condition fit for occupancy and repair subsequent dilapidation. The landlord does not have this duty when the problem relates to a tenant's cleanliness, willful damage, or use in a manner other than intended. Under English common law, the landlord had no responsibility for any repairs, and the tenant had a duty to make only minor repairs.

The landlord must ensure at least that

■ the plumbing is in proper working order;

■ hot and cold water supply will be maintained;

■ the heat, lights, and wiring work and are safe;

■ the floors, stairways, and railings are in good condition;

- when rented, the premises are clean, with no pests;
- areas under lessor control will be maintained;
- the roof does not leak and no doors or windows are broken; and
- adequate garbage receptacles must be supplied.

Effective in 2014, all pre-1994 residential and commercial property, as a condition for building permits or certificate of completion for alterations or improvements, must replace noncompliance plumbing fixtures with water conservancy fixtures.

The landlord is required to notify residential tenants in advance of pest control treatment, including repeat treatment.

A tenant cannot waive his or her rights under the landlord's implied warranty of habitability; however, the landlord and tenant can agree that the tenant will make the required repairs based on a rent reduction.

A landlord who demands or collects rent for an untenable dwelling as defined in Civil Code Section 1942.4 is liable for actual damages sustained by the tenant and special damages of not less than $100 or more than $5,000. The special damages also apply to landlords who raise rent or issue a three-day notice to quit or pay rent when the premises are untenable.

Landlords of substandard uninhabitable properties can be required to pay relocation costs for displaced tenants.

Civil Code Section 1174.2 provides that where a tenant prevails in an unlawful detainer action due to the landlord's breach of the warranty of habitability, the court will set the rent. The tenant must pay the rent set by the court within five days. The Code of Civil Procedure Section 1174.21 provides that a landlord shall be liable for tenant costs and attorney fees when the landlord initiated an unlawful detainer action for nonpayment of rent when the premises are not tenantable.

Case Study

In the case of *Hyatt v. Tedesco* (2002) 96 C.A.4th Supp. 62, a tenant raised the affirmative defense of habitability to an unlawful detainer action. The superior court appellate division in reversing the trial court held that the trial court is required to determine if a substantial breach has occurred. (Substantial breach is a failure of the landlord to comply with applicable building and housing standards that materially affect health and safety.) If so, the trial court should reduce the rent to reflect the breach, give the tenant right to possession conditioned upon paying the reduced rent, order the rent reduced until repairs are made, and award costs and attorney fees to the tenant. The landlord can also be ordered to make the repairs.

Case Study

In the case of *Espinoza v. Calva* (2008) 169 C.A. 4th 1393, a tenant defended an unlawful detainer action, claiming inhabitability and the fact that the rental was an illegal unit.

The court held that the landlord could not collect for the back rent. The landlord failed to obtain a certificate of occupancy for the unit. Therefore, the lease was an illegal contract and unenforceable. The landlord could, however, obtain possession.

Case Study

The case of *City and County of San Francisco v. Sainez* (2000) 77 C.A.4th 1302 involved landlords who failed to maintain their premises. Building inspection found no or inadequate heat; deterioration of walls, ceilings, and windows; lack of fire extinguishers; hazardous wiring; hazardous plumbing; lack of smoke detectors, etc. The superior court imposed fines of $767,000.

The Court of Appeal ruled the fines were proper but reduced them to $663,000 because of a miscalculation. The Court of Appeal ruled that fines were not excessive because the landlords own at least 12 properties with net equity of $2,300,000. While the landlords had the ability to do so, they had refused to bring the building up to a safe standard.

Note: This case shows court frustration with landlords who refuse to correct serious health and safety problems.

Municipalities are prohibited from requiring landlords to disclose, report, or take eviction action based on a tenant's (or prospective tenant's) citizenship status.

Liability for Injuries

If a landlord is negligent and that negligence results in injury to another, the landlord is liable for those resulting injuries. If defects at the time of leasing could have been discovered by a reasonable inspection, then the failure to cure the defect would be negligence. If a dangerous condition occurs after leasing and the landlord has a duty to repair, then failure to repair after notice of the problem could subject the landlord to liability for injury.

For a period of time, California courts were following a rule of strict liability, holding landlords liable for injuries to others, even when there was no negligence by the owner. The following case illustrates the present view as to landlord liability; now proof of negligence is required.

Case Study

The case of *Peterson v. Superior Court* (1995) 10 C.4th 1185 involved a hotel that was sued by a guest for an injury caused by a slippery bathtub. The court pointed out that because the innkeeper did not build the structure or its components, strict liability should not be imposed without proof of negligence. The court decided it was in error when it previously held landlords strictly liable in tort for personal injuries caused by defective components. The court pointed out that landlords still are liable under general tort principles for injuries caused by defects in their premises if the landlord is negligent.

Case Study

The case of *Penner v. Falk* (1984) 153 C.A.3d 858 indicated that punitive damages would be proper if the landlord knew of an existing dangerous condition and failed to correct it.

Commercial leases customarily require that tenants carry liability insurance coverage, which also protects the landlords from claims resulting from the condition of the premises.

A landlord who knows of a dangerous situation has, at the very least, a duty to warn a tenant.

See *Lundy v. California Realty* (1985) 170 C.A.3d 813.

Case Study

A child was bitten by a pit bull owned by a tenant in a neighboring property not owned by the plaintiff's landlord. In *Wylie v. Gresch* (1987) 191 C.A.3d 412, the parents sued the landlord because they had not been warned of the dog's dangerous propensities. The court held the landlord was not liable because the duty of disclosure applied to the landlord's own property but should not extend to the neighborhood.

A landlord, in some instances, could be liable for injuries occurring off the premises.

Case Study

The case of *Barnes v. Black* (1999) 71 C.A.4th 1473 involved a child who died from injuries received when his Big Wheel veered off the sidewalk to the play area, down a steep driveway into a busy street where he was hit by an automobile. The parents sued the apartment owners for negligence, premises liability, and negligent and intentional infliction of emotional distress. Several residents had complained to the apartment manager, who informed the owner of dangers to children passing the steep driveway.

Because the injury occurred in the street, not on the premises, the superior court granted summary judgment for the landlord.

The Court of Appeal pointed out that the fact that the injury was on a public street was not controlling.

The scope of the landlord's duty of care is related to the foreseeability of harm and the closeness of connection between the defendant's conduct and the injury. The Court of Appeal reversed.

Case Study

The case of *Tan v. Annel Management Co.* (2008) 162 C.A. 4th 621 involved a tenant who upon returning to his apartment around midnight could only find a parking space in the ungated leasing office parking lot (the tenant parking lot was gated). As he was parking, the tenant was attacked and shot in the neck, and his car was stolen. The tenant was rendered a quadriplegic. In a lawsuit against the apartment owners and property manager, it was alleged that there was failure to protect the tenant against foreseeable criminal acts of third parties. In the two years before the attack, three violent attacks occurred in the ungated areas of the project. The trial judge dismissed the action because the shooting was not foreseeable. There had been no prior carjackings involving a gun.

The Court of Appeal reversed and sent the case back for a jury trial, reasoning that the three prior criminal attacks put the parties on notice of foreseeable future criminal acts. The court noted that the cost of a security gates was minimal, about $14,000 for the 620-apartment project. The duty to act is determined by balancing foreseeability against the burden of security measures.

Case Study

The case of *Madhani v. Cooper* (2003) 106 C.A.4th 412 involved a plaintiff who complained to the landlord about an aggressive and verbally abusive new tenant. Continued problems were met by continued assertions by the building manager that they would take care of the problem. The problem tenant caused further problems. He allegedly shoved the plaintiff's mother. There were at least six complaints to the manager. The abusive tenant then allegedly followed the plaintiff into her apartment, pulled her out, hit her, and threw her down the stairs. Plaintiff suffered numerous injuries. When plaintiff sued the landlord for negligence, the superior court granted summary judgment for the landlord.

The Court of Appeal reversed stating, "It is difficult to imagine a case in which the foreseeability of harm could be more clear." The court held that there was a close connection in landlord's failure to react to at least six reports of the violent and threatening behavior of the tenant and the harm suffered by Madhani.

This case basically held that a landlord who knows of a dangerous situation under the landlord's control has a duty to prevent harm to a tenant.

Case Study

The case of *McDaniel v. Sunset Manor Co.* (1990) 220 C.A.3d 1 indicates any landlord who undertakes to protect a tenant can be liable if he or she does so negligently. The plaintiffs resided in a large, federally subsidized complex having approximately 300 children. The defendant had constructed a wood fence 857 feet on one side and 400 feet on the other. Evidence was given that holes in the fence would develop, and sometimes a week would pass before a hole was repaired. The plaintiff's two-year-old child was found floating in the creek on the other side of the fence. She suffered brain damage and quadriplegia, having apparently crawled through a large hole in the fence. The Court of Appeal noted that simply because the injuries occurred on adjacent property did not automatically bar recovery. In constructing the fence, Sunset Manor Company affirmatively assumed a duty.

Note: This case sends a message to landlords that they shouldn't build a fence because if they do so and the fence is not kept in good repair, they could be liable for injuries on adjacent property.

Case Study

In the case of *Barber v. Chang* (2007) 151 C.A. 4th 1456, the owner of an apartment building, Chang, was notified by certified letter by a tenant that Daniel, another tenant, had threatened her and aimed a shotgun at her. About three weeks later, Barber, a former tenant, visited the property and Daniel accused him of stalking his family. He produced a shotgun and shot Barber in the leg; he then kicked out one of Barber's teeth and again shot Barber in the leg. Barber sued Chang for negligence alleging he owed Barber a duty of reasonable care.

Chang moved for summary judgment on the grounds that he owed no duty of care to a visitor and it would be unreasonable to expect him to hire security guards.

The Court of Appeal reversed ruling the assault was foreseeable. There was a matter of fact for the jury as to whether Chang reasonably responded to the notice by not evicting Daniel. Forseeability is a crucial factor in determining not only the existence of the landlord's legal duty, but its scope. The case was remanded for trial.

Case Study

The case of *Davis v. Gomez* (1989) 207 C.A.3d 1401 involved Ms. Townsend, a tenant in the defendant's building who began to "deteriorate." Besides being observed talking to herself, she allegedly attempted to cast spells on other tenants. Other tenants alleged they had seen a gun in her apartment. Tenants complained to the manager about her behavior. Subsequently, she shot and killed another tenant. The parents of the victim sued the landlord for damages.

The court held that the landlord had no duty to check Townsend's background before renting. The landlord was also not qualified to judge whether she was psychotic. If the landlord had evicted Townsend, the landlord might have been subject to liability. While her conduct was bizarre, it had not been violent. Townsend was more of a nuisance than a danger. A landlord's failure to eliminate a nuisance is not the same as a failure to prevent a serious criminal act. In this case, it was not foreseeable that she would shoot another tenant.

Case Study

In the case of *Castaneda v. Olsher* (2007) 41 C. 4th 1205, Castaneda was shot by a stray bullet during a gang fight in the mobile home park where he lived. Castaneda sued the park owners alleging they breached a duty not to rent to known gang members or to evict them when they harassed other tenants. Vitoria, who lived across the street in Space 23, had fired the shots. Several months prior to the shooting, a complaint was made about the occupants of Space 23 to the manager. The manager notified the owner about gang-related problems and was told, "Their money is as good as yours."

At trial, testimony was given that persons dressed like gang members congregated at Space 23. Castaneda's attorney argued that the park should not have rented to gang members, should have evicted the gang members after the complaint, should have hired security guards, and should have repaired shot-out street lights. The Superior Court granted a nonsuit because plaintiff failed to show prior similar incidents such that a shooting was highly foreseeable.

The Court of Appeals reversed and remanded for trial stating plaintiff presented evidence that the park was aware they were renting to gang members and that there was a duty to undertake security measures to protect residents.

On appeal, the California Supreme Court reversed the decision stating a landlord owes a tenant a duty, arising out of their special relationship, to take reasonable measures to secure areas under the landlords control against foreseeable criminal acts of third parties. The court then explained a landlord does not have a duty to refuse to rent to or evict gang members without evidence of forseeability of harm to other tenants or guests. The court noted that the mobile home residency laws limit park owners to only two grounds for refusing to approve a tenant. 1. Lack of ability to pay park rent and charges; 2. a reasonable determination based on prior tenancies that the tenant will not comply with park rules and regulations.

The court also stated that, because of lack of forseeability, the owner had no duty to hire security guards or install brighter lighting. A shootout between two rival gangs was not highly foreseeable.

Note: A refusal to rent to a suspected gang member could be discriminatory based on race or ethnicity, dress, appearance, or reputation, which could subject a landlord to liability.

Case Study

The case of *Myrick v. Mastagni* (2010) 185 C.A. 4th 1082 involved two women who were killed when a building collapsed in an earthquake. The trial court found the owners negligent for failing to perform seismic retrofitting and awarded $1.9 million damages.

On appeal, the defendants contended they had no duty to retrofit. A city ordinance did not require retrofitting until 2018. The Court of Appeal indicated that compliance with an ordinance is not a defense as to negligence. The ordinance set the minimum standard of conduct. The owners must use ordinary care that a reasonable person would use in view of the probability of injury. The trail judgment was upheld.

Security

A landlord who represents a building to be secure or indicates it is protected by a security service or device and then fails to maintain security could subject the landlord to liability.

Failure of a landlord to take reasonable measures to correct a security problem after the landlord has become aware of the problem also could subject the landlord to liability. Civil Code 1941.3 requires that landlords install and maintain security devices in residential structures, which include deadbolt door locks, security or locking devices on windows and sliding doors, and specified locks on doors to common areas.

■ RIGHTS AND RESPONSIBILITIES OF TENANTS

Quiet Enjoyment

There is an implied warranty in a lease that the landlord will not interfere with the tenant's **quiet enjoyment** of the premises. Civil Code Section 1927 requires that the lessor secure quiet enjoyment of the lessee against all persons lawfully claiming the premises. A landlord who harasses a tenant by making unnecessary repairs, or encourages other tenants to disturb the tenant, has breached the tenant's right to quiet enjoyment.

Tenant Repairs

If, after a reasonable period of receiving written or oral notice, the landlord fails to make needed repairs, the tenant can make the repairs necessary to make the premises habitable, spending up to one month's rent. The tenant then can deduct the expenditures from rent payments. The tenant can use this remedy no more than twice during any 12-month period (Civil Code Section 1942). As an alternative, the tenant may consider the landlord's failure to make the premises habitable a breach of the lease and vacate the premises, relieved of all further lease obligations.

A tenant who acts to make repairs after the 30th day following a notice to repair is presumed to have acted after a reasonable notice. California courts have allowed another remedy: they will allow a tenant to remain in possession and pay a reduced rent, based on the reduction of usefulness of the premises, when the landlord fails to maintain a habitable dwelling [Hinson v. Delis (1972) 26 C.A.3d 62].

Case Study

In the case of *Schulman v. Vera* (1980) 108 C.A.3d 552, a commercial tenant raised as a defense in an unlawful detainer action that the owner had breached a covenant to repair. The court held that the tenant could not remain without paying rent. The court refused to extend the breach of an implied warranty of habitability as a defense available to commercial tenants.

Duties of Tenants

The tenant's duties include

- paying rents and other charges as agreed;

- the landlord may not require that rent be paid in cash unless the tenant had previously failed to pay the rent;

- keeping the premises under control in a clean and sanitary manner and disposing of garbage and trash properly (unless the lessor by agreement has taken this responsibility);

- exercising reasonable care in the use of plumbing, electrical and gas fixtures, and appliances.

- not permitting others to damage or deface the premises and not doing so himself or herself;

- using the premises for the purpose for which they were intended to be used; and

- using the leased premises for a lawful purpose.

Case Study

The case of *Sachs v. Exxon Co., U.S.A.* (1992) 9 C.A.4th 1491 involved refusal by the tenants to allow the landlord to conduct soil-contamination tests.

The landlord contended that leakage from tanks could damage the soil for which the landlord could be liable under state and federal laws. The trial court determined in favor of the lessee, but the decision was reversed by the Court of Appeal.

The lease required the tenants to comply with all laws and ordinances. The court pointed out that there is an implied covenant of good faith and fair dealing in the lease that provides a reasonable means for the landlord to get assurance of protection as to environmental hazards.

> ### Case Study
>
> The case of *Brown v. Green* (1994) 8 C.4th 812 involved a dispute between a landlord and a tenant as to responsibility for compliance with an order for asbestos abatement in a commercial building.
>
> The trial court determined that the language of the lease required the tenant to remove and clean up the asbestos and the superior court affirmed. The 15-year lease was a net lease for an entire warehouse building. The tenants were sophisticated business partners with substantial experience in leasing commercial property. Prior to the execution of the lease, they were on written notice of a potential for asbestos contamination; however, they failed to conduct any investigation. The court pointed out that the cost of the asbestos removal only amounted to 5 percent of the total rent due on the lease.
>
> *Note*: The court's consideration of the term of the lease, cost of repair, and sophistication of the tenant leaves the impression that if the tenant were less sophisticated, the lease were for a shorter term, and the cost to comply was great, then a different decision might have been made.

■ THE EVICTION PROCESS

"Self-help" evictions, such as removing doors, changing locks, seizing tenants' property, and engaging in extreme harassment could subject the landlord to damages, as well as require the landlord to return the premises to the tenant (Code of Civil Procedure Section 1174).

Evictions usually start with a **three-day notice** to quit, to quit or cure, or to quit or pay rent.

Notice to quit must be served in the following manner:

1. A copy of the notice must be delivered to the tenant personally.

2. If the tenant is absent, a copy must be left with a resident over the age of 18, and a copy must be sent through the mail to the tenant's place of residence.

> ### Case Study
>
> The case of *Camacho v. Shaefer* (1987) 193 C.A.3d 718 involved a self-help eviction action. The tenant had withheld rent because only one electrical outlet functioned, there were holes in the bathroom ceiling, there was no hot water or gas, and the apartment was infested with roaches and rats. The owner came to the apartment and removed the sofa, beds, table, and chairs. The tenant then obtained a restraining order against the landlord, but the landlord returned, forced the door open, breaking the chain, and removed the refrigerator. The Court of Appeal upheld compensation and punitive damages as well as attorney fees totaling $32,600 for the defendant's failure to follow unlawful detainer procedures.

3. If the tenant's place of residence or business cannot be found, or if a person of suitable age or discretion cannot be found, a copy of the notice may be affixed in a conspicuous place on the property; a copy should be given to a person residing on the property, if applicable; and a copy must be mailed to the property address by first-class mail. This process is informally called "nail and mail."

If the tenant does not quit, cure, or pay rent, the lessor may initiate an **unlawful detainer action** to evict the lessee. An unlawful detainer action can be used not only against a tenant who fails to pay rent or to perform conditions or covenants of the lease, but also against a tenant at sufferance.

For an unlawful detainer action, the landlord must allege that

■ proper three-day notice was given and the tenant is still in possession, and

■ rent is due or a condition of the lease has been breached.

The summons issued requires that the defendant (tenant) appear and answer the charges within five days after service.

If the tenant fails to respond within five days, a default hearing is set, and the court can issue a **writ of possession**. After service of the writ on the tenant, the tenant has five days to vacate, or the tenant can be evicted physically by the sheriff.

A tenant who does respond can appear and claim a defense, such as a denial, or that the landlord breached a condition or covenant, that the landlord failed to keep the premises in a habitable condition, that the landlord failed to cure lead defects, that the rent has been paid as agreed, that the tenant made an appropriate deduction from the rent, and so forth. The court then will decide on the facts and enter either a judgment for the landlord, entitling the landlord to a writ of possession, or a finding for the tenant, in which case the eviction will fail.

If the tenant delivers possession prior to trial or before judgment, the unlawful detainer action can be allowed to continue as a civil claim for damages.

Because of drug-related crime in Los Angeles County, the legislature authorized a pilot program allowing several city attorney and prosecutor offices to bring unlawful detainer actions to abate drug-related nuisances if the landlord did not act. The landlord was charged fees and costs.

Because the landlord is an unsecured creditor of the tenant, the landlord has no lien against the personal property of the tenant for rent.

Inventory of property left on the premises must be taken and verified by an enforcing officer. A tenant's personal property remaining on the premises after they are restored must be stored by the owner for 30 days and may be reclaimed by the tenant during that period upon payment of reasonable storage costs.

Any property not redeemed by the tenant within 30 days may be sold at a public sale, and the proceeds may be used by the owner to pay the costs of storage and sale. Any balance remaining after payment must be returned to the tenant.

A landlord can sue on each rent installment as it becomes due. Usually, however, the landlord retakes possession through eviction proceedings and sues the tenant at the end of the term for damages in the amount of the difference between the lease rental and any lesser amount obtained by reletting.

A landlord has a duty to mitigate damages after retaking possession. The landlord must use reasonable efforts to rerent to keep the damages as low as possible.

Protecting Tenants at Foreclosure Act

Under this federal act, tenants in foreclosed property have the right to remain in possession until their lease expires unless the owner will be occupying the property as a principal residence. If so, the tenant is entitled to a 90-day notice to vacate. If the tenant is on a month-to-month tenancy, there must be a 90-day notice to terminate tenancy after foreclosure.

Unlawful Detainer Assistants

A number of persons have gone into business offering assistance to persons being evicted. They would help tenants file questionable counterclaims and come up with, in some cases, defenses based on other than facts. Because of these abuses, Business and Professions Code 6400 et seq. requires that such assistants be registered and post a $25,000 bond. The advertisements of these assistants require disclosures, and if landlords or managers are awarded damages for acts of a registered assistant, they can recover their damages from the bond.

Retaliatory Eviction

A landlord cannot decrease services, increase rent, or evict within 180 days after a tenant exercises a protected right, including

- complaining to the landlord about the habitability of the premises,
- complaining to a public agency about defects, and
- lawfully organizing a tenant association.

A tenant cannot waive his or her rights of defending against such **retaliatory evictions.** If a landlord can be shown to have acted maliciously, the tenant will be entitled to receive from $100 to $1,000 in punitive damages.

Case Study

The case of *Vargas v. Municipal Court* (1978) 22 C.3d 902 concerned farm workers who received free housing as part of their compensation. The workers were fired for organizing a union and given notice to vacate their premises. The tenants raised the defense that their employment had been wrongfully terminated. The California Supreme Court held that, even though the employees had redress through labor legislation, wrongful discharge was a valid defense against eviction. The employees were not deprived of the defense of retaliatory eviction.

Menace

While a landlord may properly offer a tenant an inducement, such as cash, to vacate, it is unlawful for a landlord to attempt to influence a tenant to vacate a rental unit by force, threat, extortion, other menacing acts, or by interfering with a tenant's quiet enjoyment of the premises. A tenant may recover up to $2,000 from the landlord for each unlawful act.

Constructive Eviction

An act of the lessor that is inconsistent with the quiet enjoyment of the lessee or the implied covenant of habitability can be treated by the lessee as being **constructive eviction**, that is, equivalent to eviction. The tenant may vacate and will be released of all further obligations under the lease. If a tenant fails to vacate within a reasonable period after a noncontinuous act by the lessor, the tenant may waive his or her rights to declare the act to be constructive eviction.

Examples of acts, or failure to act, that could constitute constructive eviction include

- failing to make required repairs,
- failing to maintain the premises in a habitable condition,
- making needless or unnecessary repairs that interfere with the tenant's peaceful possession,
- interfering with the tenant's access to the premises,
- harassing the tenant,
- leasing the premises to another party,
- wrongfully entering the premises by the landlord, and
- cutting off utilities to the tenant.

A landlord who cuts off utilities, removes doors, removes tenant property, or prevents access to the premises will be subject to a penalty of $100 per day, but, in no event, less than $250 for each cause of action (Civil Code Section 789.3).

Case Study
The case of *Segalas v. Moriarty* (1989) 211 C.A.3d 1583 involved a landlord who sued for unpaid rent. The tenant cross-complained, alleging constructive eviction because remodeling in another part of the building had produced disruptive noise and inconvenience. The court held that a tenant who fails to vacate within a reasonable time after the breach waives the right to claim constructive eviction, with the exception of a tenant who commits to leasing other space before the breach is cured. In this case, Moriarty did not commit for other space until three months after the remodeling was finished, so the court held that he had no valid claim for constructive eviction.

Surrender

A **surrender** terminates all further obligations under the lease. Surrender is the turning over of possession by the tenant with the understanding that all future obligations are canceled. A new lease is considered a surrender of the obligations of the old lease.

When a tenant moves out and the landlord retakes possession, the landlord should inform the tenant that the tenant is still liable under the lease, that the landlord will attempt to rerent the premises to mitigate damages, and that taking possession is not an agreement to surrender of the premises.

■ MOBILE HOME TENANCIES

While the sale or lease of five or more lots in a mobile home park falls under the jurisdiction of the real estate commissioner under the Subdivided Lands Law, the rental of two or more lots in a mobile home park falls under the jurisdiction of the state Department of Housing and Community Development.

Mobile homes are not really mobile. Double-wide and triple-wide units generally are not intended to be moved after they are set in place. The addition of awnings, porches, and even permanent foundations makes removal extremely costly. Because of the special nature of mobile homes, the rights of landlords and tenants differ from those in other tenancy situations.

Tenants in mobile home parks are entitled to a 60-day notice to terminate. This 60-day notice also applies to rental increases and tenants who wish to terminate their leases.

Tenants in a mobile home park are entitled to a 12-month lease upon request at the prevailing month-to-month charge. A copy of the Mobile Home Residency Law must be attached to all rental agreements.

Park management must provide a written disclosure form that discloses any park defects in common facilities or utilities to lessees at least three days prior to signing the park's rental agreement. A signed copy of the rental agreement must be given to the tenant within 15 days.

Leases entered into after January 1, 2001, cannot prohibit a homeowner from keeping at least one pet subject to reasonable park rules.

A mobile home park can require that a single-wide mobile home 17 years old or older be removed from the park when sold. Other mobile homes must be 25 years old or older to require removal upon sale. (Mobile home park management is limited in requirements as to exterior repairs upon a sale or transfer of a mobile home.)

Park rental agreements may not include a right of first refusal for the park management to buy the mobile home unless there is a separate agreement with separate consideration paid.

Eviction

Tenants can be evicted from mobile home parks only under the following circumstances:

■ A tenant who fails to comply with a local or state law within a reasonable time after being notified of his or her violation can be evicted.

- A tenant who fails to comply with reasonable park rules and regulations that were either in the rental agreement or agreed to later by the tenant can be evicted. If, however, the rules were established without tenant permission, the tenant is entitled to a six-month notice to terminate. To change park rules, other than for recreational facilities, the park owner first must give six months' notice. Any rule violation must be spelled out, and the tenant must be given seven days to comply prior to notice to terminate tenancy.

- When the tenant's use interferes with the quiet enjoyment of (causes substantial annoyance to) other tenants, the tenant can be evicted.

- A tenant who fails to pay rent or other reasonable charges can be evicted.

- A park owner can evict the tenant from a mobile home park with a 60-day notice if the tenant has received more than three 3-day notices within a 12-month period for nonpayment of rent, utility charges, or reasonable incidental expenses. However, the legal owner, as well as junior lienholders, have a 30-day window to cure (this applies to individual lienholders, not financial institutions or mobile home dealers).

- A tenant convicted of prostitution, assault with a firearm, possession of illegal firearms or munitions, battery resulting in serious bodily harm, or of a felony-controlled substance offense, if the offense was committed on the mobile home park premises, can be evicted.

- If the park is condemned, its tenants can be evicted.

- When the use of the park is changed by the owner, tenants can be evicted. For changes in park use, the tenant is, however, entitled to 15 days' notice for appearances before local governing boards, and 6 months' notice of termination after approval of the changes. If no local approvals are needed, the park owner must give tenants 12 months' notice.

Other Rules

The lessor cannot terminate a tenancy to accommodate other mobile homes sold by the park owners.

Mobile home parks cannot require a cleaning deposit or liability insurance from tenants for use of the clubhouse or recreational facilities for meetings of residents and invited guests.

If a tenant in a mobile home park has made timely payments of rent, utilities, and other charges for a period of 12 months, the security deposit must be returned to the tenant within 60 days of request.

Mobile home parks cannot unreasonably refuse to approve a new purchaser for lease assignment or a new lease. The park may reject a new purchaser who has financial ability only on the basis of prior tenancy problems or failure to obey park rules.

Parks may not charge a fee for the sale or transfer of a mobile home if no services are performed.

Mobile home parks cannot charge a move-in fee unless a service is rendered for the fee (Civil Code Section 798.72).

Mobile home parks cannot require that sale listings be given to the park management or prohibit outside agents from listing for sale a mobile home in a park (Civil Code Section 798.71).

Parks cannot charge any fee for a lessee's guests who stay for 14 days or less (annually, not consecutively).

Mobile home parks cannot require submission of an applicant's income tax returns; however, an applicant can be required to document gross monthly income (Civil Code Section 798.74).

Parks cannot charge extra for larger families or discriminate based on family size.

Tenants in mobile home parks cannot waive any of their rights under the law. Any tenant in a mobile home park is entitled to a 12-month lease on request. The park cannot charge more for the lease than is charged for a month-to-month tenancy.

Park owners cannot enter mobile homes without the written permission of the owner, except in emergency situations.

A park owner who enters into a listing agreement to sell the park must provide written notice to the residents' association not less than 30 days or more than one year before entering into the agreement or making an offer to sell.

Homeowners' groups must be permitted to hold meetings in recreation halls during reasonable hours.

■ CONDOMINIUM CONVERSIONS

For conversion of existing residential units to a condominium project, a community apartment project, or a stock cooperative, certain actions are required of the subdivider:

- At least 60 days prior to the filing of a tentative map, written notification of this intention must be provided to the tenants.

- Tenants also must receive at least ten days' notice of application for a public report.

- Each tenant must be notified within ten days of approval of the final map for the proposed conversion.

- Each tenant must be given 180 days' written notice of intent to convert prior to termination of tenancy.

■ Each of the tenants must be given at least 90 days' notice from the date of issuance of the public report of an exclusive right to purchase the unit the tenant occupies, on the same terms and conditions under which the unit initially will be offered to the public.

A subdivider who wishes to convert a mobile home park to another use must file a report about the impact of the conversion on the displaced residents of the mobile home park. The report must address the availability of adequate replacement space in mobile home parks. The subdivider must make a copy of the report available to each resident of the park at least 15 days prior to the hearing on the map by the advisory agency (planning commission).

■ RENT CONTROL

Rent control has been held to be a legitimate government purpose. The argument that rent control violates an owner's due process rights because tenants are in the majority and always will vote in favor of rent control was rejected by the court in *Birkenfield v. City of Berkeley* (1976) 17 C.3d 129. In the same case, a prohibition on evicting a tenant in good standing at the end of the lease unless the property is withdrawn from the rental market, or the tenant refuses a new lease, was considered a reasonable means to enforce rent control.

The Ellis Act, Government Code Section 7060.7, allows a landlord to go out of business and withdraw property from the rental market.

> ### Case Study
> The case of *Channing Properties v. City of Berkeley* (1993) 11 C.A.4th 88 involved a landlord who wanted to remove 33 apartments from the rental market. Berkeley's Municipal Code requires that (1) tenants be given 180-day notice to move, (2) the landlord pay $4,500 per unit for relocation costs, and (3) the city be notified at least 60 days prior to terminating the rentals. Section 7060 of the Government Code (the Ellis Act) requires only 60-day advance notice to tenants and requires relocation payments only to low-income hotel residents. The Court of Appeal held that the Ellis Act preempts local action with respect to landlords who wish to withdraw accommodations from the rental market. The court noted that the Berkeley ordinance would create insurmountable obstacles for removal of rental units, and that was contrary to the intent of the Ellis Act, which allows rental removal regardless of local laws.

Because of fixed rents, landlords under rent control often reduce maintenance and defer repairs. In the case of *Sterling v. Santa Monica Rent Control Board* (1984) 162 C.A.3d 1021, the court held that the rent control board could reduce rents for Health and Safety Code violations.

The **Costa-Hawkins Rental Housing Act** (Civil Code Section 1954.53) provides that landlords who are subject to rent control are free to establish new base rents for new tenants, as well as for subleasees and assignees, where the landlord's consent is necessary for the sublease or assignment.

> ### Case Study
>
> The case of *Guggenheim v. City of Goleta* (2010) 638 F. 3d 1111 involved the rent control ordinance of the City of Goleta that allowed purchasers of mobile homes to assume the lease of the seller at the rent-controlled amount. The effect of the ordinance was that existing owners of units were able to sell their mobile homes for $100,000 more than they were worth, based on the ability to take over the unit at the existing rental rate. The park owners brought this action in federal court, claiming a taking of their park without compensation, a violation of their Fifth Amendment rights.
>
> The trial court ruled against the park owners, but the Court of Appeal reversed. The court pointed out that the rent control ordinance resulted in a transfer of 90 percent of the value from the park owners to the tenants. Because the park rent was below market, buyers had to pay a premium price, which went to the tenant who sold the unit.
>
> *Note:* The purpose of rent control was to protect the tenant and provide reasonable-cost housing, not to provide windfall profits to tenants. (The Costa-Hawkins Rental Housing Act [Civil Code Section1954.50 et seq.] is not applicable to mobile home parks, so a new base rent could not be established with a new tenant.)
>
> *Note:* The Supreme Court declined to review this decision.

Rent control can result in tenants getting the advantage of appreciation in value at the expense of the property owner.

Rent control regulations do not apply to mobile homes when the mobile home is not the owner's principal residence.

> ### Case Study
>
> In *Gross v. Superior Court* (1985) 171 C.A.3d 265, a purchaser of a San Francisco condominium rented the units and subsequently defaulted on his trust deed. The beneficiary foreclosed and then filed an unlawful detainer action against the tenant. While the court conceded that a foreclosure wipes out junior liens, this is subject to modification by legislative action under police power. The court compared rent control to zoning. While the trust deed was given before rent control, the parties could not agree that future rent control would not apply. Nor could they agree that future zoning would not apply. The fact that the value of the premises for resale was diminished by having a tenant does not make the ordinance unconstitutional. The court held that a foreclosure purchaser should be regarded as a successor in interest.

> ### Case Study
>
> The case of *Bisno v. Santa Monica Rent Control Board* (2005) 130 C.A. 4th 816 involved the Costa-Hawkins Rental Housing Act (Civil Code 1954.50 -1954.545), which allows for market-rate rent increases when a rent controlled unit becomes vacant. Santa Monica adopted Regulation 3304, which permits a landlord to petition to increase rent to the market-rate vacancy rates when the unit is not the principal residence of the tenant.
>
> The Bisnos rented their apartment in 1996, prior to Regulation 3304. After passage of the regulation, their landlord petitioned for a rental increase because the unit was not the principal residences of the tenants. A rental increase was granted from $1,111 per month to $4,295 per month, which was later reduced to $4,045 per month.
>
> Bisno sued the Rent Control Board alleging that the Costa-Hawkins Act did not provide for rent increases based on principal residence criteria. The Los Angeles Superior Court ruled that Regulation 3304 was valid and the Court of Appeal affirmed, ruling that allowing rent increases for nonprincipal residences was consistent with the purposes of local rent control law and was, therefore, valid.
>
> *Note:* The purpose of rent control was not to allow bargain rents for weekend retreats (the unit was at The Shores), but to protect renters from being forced out of their homes.

■ SUMMARY

Leasehold interests include

- ■ tenancies for years (leases for a definite period of time),
- ■ periodic tenancies (leases that automatically renew themselves unless a notice to terminate is given),
- ■ tenancies at will (tenancies at the pleasure of the lessor), and
- ■ tenancies at sufferance (tenancies in which the lessee holds over, which also are not true tenancies in California because the lessor can treat the holdover tenant as a trespasser).

Leases are personal property (chattels real). Leases for one year or less need not be in writing. For written leases, the lessor must sign to be bound. The lessee can be bound without signing by moving in or paying rent after receiving a copy of the lease.

When a lease contains an option, part of the rent will be considered consideration for the option.

Nonrefundable security deposits are not allowed. The total security deposit cannot exceed three months' rent for furnished rentals or two months' for unfurnished units.

An assignment of a lease is a transfer of all interests by the lessee to a third party, who becomes a tenant of the original lessor. The assignee becomes primarily liable under the lease, while the assignor (original lessee) remains secondarily liable.

Under a sublease, the original lessee becomes a sublessor and leases the premises to a sublessee. The sublessee is the tenant of the sublessor (original lessee) and not the tenant of the original lessor (owner).

A lease can be terminated by or for destruction of premises, eminent domain, commercial frustration, merger, bankruptcy of tenant, expiration of term, notice, foreclosure of a prior encumbrance, failure to pay rent, failure to give possession, violation of a material lease provision, illegal use of the premises, abandonment, surrender, violation of implied warranty, or failure to make needed or agreed-on repairs.

The landlord has the right of entry in an emergency, when the tenant consents, after reasonable notice to make repairs or show the premises, when the tenant has abandoned or surrendered the premises, and under court order.

A residential lease has an implied warranty of quiet enjoyment and habitability. As a minimum, the landlord must ensure that

- plumbing is in proper working order;
- heat, lights, and wiring work and are safe;
- floors, stairways, and railings are in good condition;
- the premises are clean and free of pests when rented;
- areas under lessor control will be maintained; and
- the roof will not leak, and no doors or windows are broken.

Landlords are liable for injury to others because of the landlords' negligence. Landlords also have been held liable for injuries to the tenant because of the condition of the premises, even when the lessor was unaware of the problem. Exculpatory clauses in residential leases do not protect the landlord.

Tenant duties include

- paying rent and other charges as agreed,
- keeping the premises in a clean and sanitary condition,
- exercising reasonable care in the use,
- not permitting others to damage or deface the premises, and
- using the premises for the purpose intended.

If a tenant fails to pay rent or violates a lease condition, the lessor can give a three-day notice to quit, quit or cure, or quit or pay rent. If the tenant does not vacate, cure, or pay rent, the lessor serves an unlawful detainer action on the tenant. The tenant must appear and answer the charges within five days or the court will issue a writ of possession that, after service, gives the tenant five days to vacate.

An eviction within 180 days of the tenant's complaining about habitability of the premises to the landlord or a public agency or lawfully organizing a tenant organization will be considered a retaliatory eviction. The tenant can defend against an eviction action by claiming that it is retaliatory.

An act of the lessor that is inconsistent with the quiet enjoyment of the lessee or the implied covenant of habitability can be treated by the tenant as being equivalent to eviction (constructive eviction).

Because of the immobility of mobile homes, tenants can be evicted only for limited reasons. Special notices of any change in the use of the park must be provided to tenants. Tenants are entitled to a 12-month lease upon request. Mobile home parks cannot unreasonably refuse to approve a new purchaser for lease assignment or a new lease.

Tenants in apartments being converted to condominiums must be given statutory notices. They also must be given a 90-day exclusive right to buy their units at the price, terms, and conditions at which they initially will be offered to the public.

Rent control has been held by the courts to be a legitimate government purpose. Rent control also can control the right to evict or to change property use.

■ DISCUSSION CASES

1. A tenant complained to the police that the landlord had molested her minor daughter. The landlord later pleaded guilty to the charge. After the complaint was made, the landlord started eviction proceedings. The landlord claimed that the charge made it impossible to live together peacefully. **Was the landlord's action a retaliatory eviction?**

    Barela v. Superior Court (1981) 30 C.3d 244

2. An exculpatory clause in a miniwarehouse lease stated that the warehouse operators would be free from all liability for damage to the property stored and that it was the customer's obligation to obtain insurance coverage. **Does this clause protect the lessor from damage caused by the lessor's negligence?**

    Cregg v. Ministor Ventures (1983) 148 C.A.3d 110

3. A tenant defended an unlawful detainer action by claiming that the lessor breached the implied warranty of habitability. **Is this a valid defense? What is habitability?**

Green v. Superior Court (1974) 10 C.3d 616

4. The plaintiff was raped in her apartment. It was alleged that the owners and manager of the apartment complex (the defendants) knew of three previous rapes in the complex. The defendants had been given a composite drawing as well as a description of the suspect by the police.

   The defendants did not disclose the information about the assaults to the plaintiff. It was alleged that the premises were represented as being safe and patrolled at all times by professional guards. The plaintiff alleged she was intentionally misled by the defendants to advance their own interests by renting the apartment. If the plaintiff's allegations are correct, are the defendants liable? **If they are liable, what is their liability?**

O'Hara v. Western Seven Trees Corp. (1977) 75 C.A.3d 798

5. An owner had not raised rents on some units for 15 to 20 years. After she finally raised rents, a rent control ordinance rolled back the rents to a time when she was charging below-market rents. The owner filed for a rent increase and was denied. The owner filed for a writ of mandate challenging the base-year rent. **Is the owner subject to the base-year rent?**

Vega v. City of West Hollywood (1990) 223 C.A.3d 1343

6. A lease provided for a renewal option at fair market rental value. The property was used as a movie theater. Appraisals indicated that at the highest and best use (retail stores), the property would have its highest rental value. **For renewal purposes, what should be the basis of the rent?**

Wu v. Interstate Consol. Indus. (1991) 226 C.A.3d 1511

7. In leasing her condominium, an owner told the tenant that the premises were safe and security precautions for tenants had been taken. The condominium association also represented the safety of the complex. After being assaulted, the tenant sued, claiming that security precautions had not been taken. **If the tenant was correct, are the owner and condominium association liable?**

Olar v. Schroit (1984) 155 C.A.3d 861

8.   A tenant leased garage space for the purpose of replacing a truck engine. While the defendant made a down payment on the rent and was given possession, the defendant failed to pay the balance. The owner went into the garage and found auto parts strewn about the garage. The owner contacted law enforcement authorities to ascertain whether illegal activity was taking place. A government investigator found stolen truck parts. The garage was placed under surveillance, and the defendant was arrested when he returned several days later. **Did the landlord act properly?**

People v. Roman (1991) 227 C.A.3d 674

9.   In checking a building prior to purchase, a buyer found several rooms were locked. After purchase, the buyer discovered these rooms were held by a lodge under an unrecorded ten-year lease that the purchaser had not been informed of. **Is the lease valid?**

Scheerer v. Cuddy (1890) 85 C. 270

10.   A party injured in an auto accident claimed that a property owner was negligent in maintaining shrubs that obscured the view of motorists. The property had been rented for several years, and the lease required the tenant to maintain the landscaping. **If the tenant was negligent in failing to trim the shrubs, is the owner liable?**

Swanberg v. O'Mectin (1984) 157 C.A.3d 325

11.   Prior to the Santa Monica rent control ordinance, which also limited removal of units from the rental market, a developer expended $1,700 for condominium conversion approval, and the final subdivision map was approved. **Is the developer subject to the rent control ordinance?**

Santa Monica Pines Ltd. v. Rent Control Board (1984) 35 C.3d 858

12.   The defendants owned six cabins rented to 16 persons. The defendants deliberately failed to pay the gas bill, knowing the gas would be cut off and the renters would be forced to leave.

The trial court awarded the plaintiffs compensatory damages of $7,901 plus $6,000 per cabin ($100 per day for 60 days), or a total of $36,000 in penalties. **Was the trial court's action proper?**

Kinney v. Vaccari (1980) 27 C.3d 348

13.   The City of Berkeley passed a tax relief ordinance that required a one-year reduction on commercial leases of 80 percent of the property tax savings resulting from the passage of Proposition 13. A landlord alleged the ordinance was unconstitutional because it violated the contract clauses of the state and federal constitutions. **Was the ordinance proper?**

Rue-Ell Enterprises Inc. v. City of Berkeley (1983) 147 C.A.3d 81

14. A tenant parked on the street because she was afraid to use her poorly lighted garage space. She was robbed and shot on the street outside her apartment. She sued the landlord alleging negligence for failure to install adequate garage lighting. **Should the landlord be held liable?**

Rosenbaum v. Security Pacific Corp. (1996) 43 C.A.4th 1084

15. A housing-authority lease had a zero-tolerance drug clause. During a lawful search, a tenant's son, who lived on the premises, was found to have four packets of narcotics on the premises. Even though the parents required their son to move out, the parents were evicted. **Was the eviction justified?**

City of South San Francisco Housing Authority v. Guillory (1996) 41 C.A.4th 13

16. Islay Investments managed many apartment complexes. Instead of charging new tenants a security deposit, Islay charged a higher rent for the first month than for the following months. **Did Islay charge an illegal nonrefundable security deposit?**

Granberry v. Islay Investments (1993) 18 C.A.4th 885

17. A commercial lessor conditioned consent to a lease assignment upon a $30,000 payment plus 75 percent of the profit from the sale of a business. **Was the requirement enforceable?**

Ilkhchooyi v. Best (1995) 37 C.A.4th 395

18. A mobile home park imposed a new rule requiring occupancy of the registered owner of the mobile home. **Is this rule enforceable?**

Rancho Santa Paula Mobile Home Park Ltd. v. Evans (1994) 26 C.A.4th 1139

19. A two-year-old child was injured after falling through a hall window in an apartment building. The window was 28 inches above the floor. While it had a screen, tenants would remove the screen to throw garbage into a Dumpster. The lease stated, "Children are not allowed to play in hallways, stairways, or other common areas in the project." **Did the landlord have a duty to ensure that a child would not fall through the window?**

Amos v. Alpha Property Management (1999) 73 C.A.4th 895

20. Tenants were 12 months behind in rent. A fire broke out in the garage, and the tenants' personal property was destroyed. **If the fire was the result of the landlord's breach of warranty of habitability, should the landlord be responsible for the tenants' loss?**

Fairchild v. Park (2001) 90 C.A.4th 919

21. A tenant persisted in annoying another tenant in a mobile home park despite many calls to park management. **If the park fails to take action, can the park be liable in damages for emotional distress?**

Andrews v. Mobile Aire Estates (2004) 125 C.A.4th 578

22. Landlords challenged a San Francisco ordinance requiring landlords to pay 5 percent interest on tenant security deposit. The landlords alleged that for 16 months, the highest interest paid on money market accounts was 2.2 percent. **Do the landlords have to pay 5 percent on the deposits?**

Small Property Owners of San Francisco v. City and County of San Francisco (2006) 141 C.A.4th 1388

23. California National Bank's lease had a provision for a lease extension at the prevailing rate but no more than the rent paid for space by another bank. The other bank failed, and the space was broken up and leased for offices and retail use. **Is there a cap on the rent for a lease extension?**

California National Bank v. Woodridge Plaza L.L.C. (2208) 164 C.A. 4th 137

■ CHAPTER QUIZ

1. Which estate is of definite duration?

    a. An estate at will   b. An estate for years

    c. A freehold interest   d. A periodic tenancy

2. A tenancy for years *MUST* be created by

    a. express agreement.   b. adverse possession.

    c. written agreement.   d. none of the above.

3. What is the maximum term for which a home in a rural area may be leased?

    a. 51 years   b. 99 years

    c. 100 years   d. None of the above

4. A tenant who remains in possession after giving notice that she would vacate the premises becomes

    a. a tenant at will.   b. a tenant at sufferance.

    c. an indefeasible tenant.   d. none of the above.

5. To be enforceable, a written lease must

    a. describe the premises.   b. be signed by the lessor.

    c. be both a and b.   d. be neither a nor b.

6. For a furnished apartment, the total security deposit cannot exceed

    a. one-half month's rent.   b. one month's rent.

    c. two months' rent.   d. three months' rent.

7. The landlord *MUST* return the security deposit to the residential tenant within what time frame after regaining possession if there is no damage other than normal wear and tear?

    a. 7 days   b. 3 weeks

    c. 30 days   d. None of the above

8. Which statement is *TRUE* regarding the assignment of a lease?

    a. The original lessee is the sole party liable for the payment of rent.

    b. It is the same as a sublease.

    c. The original lessee would retain a right to use the property for a limited time.

    d. The entire leasehold is transferred.

9. A tenant on a long-term lease at $500 per month wishes to go out of business. The premises are currently worth $1,000 per month. You would likely advise the tenant to consider

   a. surrendering the premises.
   b. subleasing.
   c. assigning the lease.
   d. doing none of the above.

10. An assignee of a lessee has a relationship to the lessor of

    a. sublessee.
    b. tenant.
    c. grantor.
    d. none of the above.

11. A tenant on a long-term lease purchased the premises from the lessor. Later, to raise cash, he sold the property to an investor, who gave the tenant a 30-day notice to vacate. What are the rights of the parties?

    a. The lease preceded the sale; therefore, the tenant prevails.
    b. Occupancy was constructive notice to the investor of the lease.
    c. The purchase by the tenant ended the lease.
    d. Tenant rights were lost by accord and satisfaction.

12. In the absence of a lease provision, when would a landlord have the right of entry?

    a. During normal business hours after reasonable notice to show to a prospective buyer
    b. In the event of an emergency
    c. Either a or b
    d. Neither a nor b

13. A landlord must ensure all of the following *EXCEPT* that the

    a. premises are air-conditioned.
    b. premises are clean and clear of pests at the time of rental.
    c. plumbing is in proper working order.
    d. roof does not leak and windows are not broken.

14. Under a residential rental, the tenant must do all *EXCEPT*

    a. use the premises for a lawful purpose.
    b. keep the plumbing in proper working order.
    c. pay rent as agreed.
    d. keep the portion of the premises under the tenant's control clean and sanitary.

15. Which statement accurately describes the liability of the landlord of a residential building?

    a. The landlord is liable for injury only if he or she knows of a dangerous situation and fails to act.

    b. The landlord is not liable for any injury to a tenant if the lease has an exculpatory clause.

    c. The landlord is liable only for risks that could be foreseen.

    d. The landlord is liable for injury caused by a dangerous condition if the landlord was negligent in acting or failed to act.

16. The landlord was notified by the residential tenant that the water heater was inoperative and the roof had a bad leak. After reasonable notice, the tenant could

    a. treat the landlord's failure to act as constructive eviction.

    b. spend up to one month's rent and make the repairs.

    c. do either a or b.

    d. do neither a or b.

17. When one residential tenant attacks another tenant, is the landlord liable?

    a. Yes, the landlord is strictly liable for the injury.

    b. Yes, if a check on the tenant's background would have shown aggressive behavior.

    c. Probably, if the attack was foreseeable.

    d. Yes, if the premises were represented as being safe.

18. A three-day notice to quit or pay rent could be used against a tenant who

    a. violated a lease provision.

    b. was delinquent in rent.

    c. used the premises for an illegal purpose.

    d. did all of the above.

19. After a landlord has served an unlawful detainer action, the tenant

    a. is given 3 days to quit or pay rent.

    b. has 5 days to answer the charges.

    c. must vacate within 5 days.

    d. must vacate within 30 days.

20. When a tenant abandons the premises with three years remaining on the lease, the landlord CANNOT

   a. sue for the balance due on the lease.

   b. consider the abandonment a surrender.

   c. rerent the premises.

   d. sue for the rent as it becomes due.

21. Which of the following would constitute constructive eviction?

   a. Expiration of a tenancy for years

   b. A notice to quit

   c. An unlawful detainer action

   d. The lessor's leasing the premises to a third party

22. A landlord cut off a tenant's electricity because the tenant was delinquent in rent. What would be the likely result of this action?

   a. The landlord could be subject to a $100-per-day penalty.

   b. The landlord could be subject to a $1,000 penalty.

   c. No penalty will be assessed if a proper three-day notice was served.

   d. There will be no penalty if there was a 24-hour notice of service cutoff.

23. When a lessor and lessee agree to terminate a lease three years prior to its termination, the lessee's turning over possession to the lessor is known as

   a. accord and satisfaction.   b. surrender.

   c. reformation.   d. novation.

24. A tenant of a mobile home park CANNOT be evicted because of

   a. failure to comply with a reasonable park rule.

   b. use that interferes with the quiet enjoyment of other tenants.

   c. forming a tenant organization.

   d. failure to comply with local or state laws.

25. In a condominium conversion of an apartment building, the residents MUST be given an option to purchase their units for

   a. 90 days from issuance of the final public report.

   b. 30 days from the sale announcement.

   c. 180 days from public hearing.

   d. none of the above.

DISCUSSION CASE ANALYSES

■ CHAPTER 1: SOURCES OF LAW AND THE JUDICIAL SYSTEM

Discussion Topics Analysis

For a detailed explanation of the maxims of jurisprudence, you might wish to check West's Annotated California Codes, *starting with Section 3509 of the Civil Code.*

CC3510 — When the purpose or reason for a requirement is no longer present, the failure to meet the requirement should not be punished.

CC3511 — Decisions of the same court or higher court should govern in order to maintain harmony and stabilization of the law. (Stare Decisis.)

In *Childers v. Childers* (1946) 74 C.A.2d 56, the court indicated that they would not rely on precedent if it persists in any absurdity or perpetuates a manifest error.

CC3512 — If a person waived rights, that person should not be allowed to later assert those rights to the detriment of another.

In *Noyes v. Schlegel* (1908) 9 C.A. 516, a vendor stated at the time of contract, as well as subsequently, that he did not care how payments were made as long as payment was within the time specified. The court held that the vendor could not declare a forfeiture for delay in making installments.

CC3513 — While people may not waive protection afforded to another party, they can waive requirements that benefit themselves. As an example, a seller can waive a provision that prohibits the buyer from assigning a contract. A person cannot waive rights that are against public policy. As an example, a buyer cannot generally waive statutory rights to redemption in the event of foreclosure.

CC3514 — A person cannot infringe on others by nuisance use of that person's own property. The use of real property is qualified by rights of others to the lawful enjoyment of their property. The maxim implies that one may use one's property in any legal way so long as it doesn't injure others.

In *People v. Gold Run Ditch & Mining Co.* (1884) 66 C. 138, the court held that accompanying ownership of property is a corresponding duty to use it so that it shall not abuse the rights of other recognized owners.

The rule also applies to water rights. A person may not unreasonably use water in a manner so that it deprives other water rights holders of reasonable use.

CC3515 — A person cannot claim to have been wronged by an act to which that person agreed.

In *Churchill v. Baumann* (1842) 95 C.541, the court found that the plaintiff consented to diverting water and actually aided in the building and maintenance of a dam. The plaintiff's consent to the diversion of water was held to be a complete defense as to the plaintiff's claim for damages caused by the diversion.

CC3516 – If parties, by their conduct, place an interpretation on an agreement that is not what they had actually agreed to, their acquiescence waives their right to later object.

CC3517 – For example, a convicted murderer cannot inherit from the deceased and a convicted arsonist cannot collect on the insurance. A broker who made a secret profit on a transaction would not prevail in a suit to recover commission. This is really a "clean hands doctrine."

CC3518 — Fraudulent transfers may be set aside.

CC3519 — A person who accepts benefits through an act of another has created an agency by ratification of the unauthorized act.

CC3520 — The innocent party should not be the one to suffer. This rule is applicable to tort law as well as the failure of a government official to perform an official duty.

CC3521 — An acceptance of the benefits of a transaction is consent to the obligations under it (assignment of rights also assigns obligations).

In *Walmsley v. Holcomb* (1943) 61 C.A.2d 217, the court held that a sublessee in possession in an action for rent could not raise the defense that there was no written assignment of the lease (Statute of Frauds).

CC3522 — Grantor of land landlocked by other land of grantor gives an implied easement.

In *Smith v. Corbit* (1897) 116 C. 587, the court held that transfer of part of the land, when the grantor had used water from a stream for the land, must be presumed to also grant that water necessary for reasonable enjoyment of the part granted.

CC3523—Where there is a legal wrong, the courts must grant an appropriate remedy. It does not apply to rights lost by Statute of Limitations. Courts will withhold relief for equitable reasons such as estoppel, laches, and waiver.

CC3524 — If both parties violate the law and are equally at fault (pari delicto), the court will not provide remedy. (Because the parties went outside the law to make the agreement, the law cannot be used to enforce it. Parties aren't held equally in the wrong as to usurious contracts).

CC3525 — We see this in our recording statutes. Also consider the doctrine of prior appropriation of water.

CC3526 — A person is not responsible in tort for an act of God. Acts of God are those which are independent of human agency.

CC3527 — Laches is an unreasonable delay in asserting a right that prejudices another party, making the granting of relief inequitable. *Long v. Long* (1948) 76 C.A.2d 716.

In *Goodfellow v. Barritt* (1933) 130 C.A. 548, the court held that reformation to a deed was barred by delaying an action until almost 2 1/2 years after knowledge of the defect of the deed.

Equitable Estoppel — A person can be stopped from raising a defense when, by words or actions, that person permitted or encouraged a course of action. A later enforcement of rights would not be equitable.

CC3528 — The substance of words is more important than form. A technicality should not be allowed to defeat justice. The court will place great emphasis on intent of the parties.

In *Weintraub v. Weingart* (1929) 98 C.A. 690, the court indicated that whether an instrument is an assignment of a lease should be determined by the instrument's legal effect and not the form of the instrument.

CC3529 — Unless otherwise proven, performance is presumed to be proper.

In *Beckwith v. Sheldon* (1914) 168 C. 742, a party agreed to give a mortgage for consideration received but failed to do so. The court held that equity required that there be an enforceable lien on the property.

CC3530 — A right required to be recorded that is not recorded, and that a good faith purchaser for value has no knowledge of, does not exist.

CC3531 — A contract that cannot possibly be performed is void. A contract calling for repair or maintenance would end with the destruction of the subject property.

CC3532 — A demand for performance need not be made when it would be futile. As an example, if an owner has incapacitated himself from making a conveyance by conveying to another, making demand for the conveyance would be a useless act.

CC3533 — Leaving out a nonessential element in a document does not invalidate the document.

Courts have set aside foreclosure for trifling sums. In *Mietzsch v. Berkhart* (1893) 35 P321, a lot sold for $2.50 for street improvements. Court allowed redemption by paying $3.90. Doctrine of Substantial Performance applies where the contractor has substantially performed. The right to compensation should not be defeated because of trivial defects. (Compensation is equivalent to contract price less the cost to correct.)

CC3534 — In case of an ambiguity between general and specific provisions of a contract, the specific should govern (*Scudder v. Perce* (1911) 159 C. 429).

CC3535 — Words should be given their meaning at the time of use. Actions at the time best indicate intent. In determining the meaning of statutes, courts will consider what was said by legislatures at the time of enactment.

CC3536 — A lesser penalty can be imposed than allowed by statute or contract. Therefore, the power to discharge an employee would include the right of suspension.

A court can award less damages than asked for. The power of an administrative agency to revoke a license carries with it the power to suspend.

CC3537 — Superfluous or unnecessary wording does not destroy or make void an agreement.

CC3538 — If parol evidence can make an agreement certain (to clarify an ambiguity), it can be admitted. If the contract is capable of being clarified, it should stand. If, from a description, property can be found and identified, then the description is sufficient.

CC3539 — This would apply to a forged deed or agreement otherwise void. However, adverse possession could give purchaser rights.

CC3540 — There cannot be an assignment of mortgage lien without assigning the debt.

Easements pass with real property. Incidental rights pass with the premises. A lien against the land would also be a lien against the improvements that go with the land.

CC3541 — Contracts that can be interpreted as being lawful or unlawful should be given the lawful interpretation. The law will avoid declaring a contract void if it is feasible to construe a valid agreement consistent with the intent of the parties.

In *Blume v. MacGregor* (1944) 64 C.A.2d 244, the court held that the interpretation given to a deed should be the one to make it effective rather than to defeat it.

CC3542 — Courts are bound to place a reasonable and workable interpretation on statutes and contracts.

In *Mitchell v. Whitford* (1920) 49 C.A. 46, the court held that the entire deed must determine whether a description in a deed is uncertain, and the construction put on it must be reasonable.

In *Cilibrasi v. Reiter* (1951) 103 C.A.2d 39, the court held that when a statute is susceptible to two interpretations, a court must give it such interpretation to avoid confusion and absurdity and that is consistent with sound reason and good morals.

CC3543 — We can see this in our recording statutes. If a prior grantee fails to record or take possession, that party should suffer for the party's negligence rather than a subsequent good faith purchaser for value who has no notice of the prior conveyance and records first. The first assignee who notifies obligor of the assignment prevails over other assignees, even if prior. A person whose negligence allowed a note to be raised should be the one to suffer rather than a later holder.

CC3545 — Courts will presume laws have been obeyed unless shown otherwise. Fraud and other wrongful acts will not be presumed but must be proven. There is a presumption by executing a conveyance that the person signing understands the act.

CC3546 — In the absence of proof to the contrary, the presumption is that ordinary care was used.

There is a presumption that every deceased person has heirs. There is a presumption that every person has parentage. There is a presumption of sanity unless shown otherwise. There is a presumption of accidental death or suicide.

CC3547 — An offer remains open for a reasonable period of time. A license to use continues as long as is usual. Once something is shown to exist, it is presumed to continue. When it is shown that property belongs to a particular person, the law presumes ownership continues unless shown to the contrary (*Moore v. California — Michigan Land & Water Co.* (1921) 55 C.A.2d 184). Where a principal and agent relationship has existed for an indefinite length of time, there is a presumption in favor of the continuance of the relationship. (*Walter v. Libby* (1946) 72 C.A.2d 138.)

CC3548 — We presume transactions to be fair, regular, and legal.

■ CHAPTER 1 SOURCES OF LAW AND THE JUDICIAL SYSTEM

**Discussion Case
Analysis**

1. **While the trial court granted a preliminary injunction, the Court of Appeals reversed.** The defendants were protected by First Amendment rights of freedom of speech. Procel was protected in spreading truthful information but was barred from entering or blocking the sales office.

2. **The Court of Appeals affirmed that the denial of the right to distribute leaflets in the parking lot was proper, as the ban on leaflets was reasonable because of litter and traffic problems.** However, the court pointed out that Savage could use his free speech rights in a reasonable time, place, and manner, such as by handing leaflets to patrons passing by on the sidewalk in the shopping center. The court pointed out that the free speech in *Robins v. Pruneyard Shopping Center*, involving political activity, also applied to religious activity.

3. **The trial court granted the injunction that was affirmed by the Court of Appeals.** The court held that the right to exclude others from your property is a fundamental aspect of property ownership. Note: If the medical center had been within a large shopping center, a different decision would seem to be indicated, based on the *Robins v. Pruneyard Shopping Center* case.

4. **The Court of Appeal reversed, ruling that an apartment complex is not a public forum so the owners can prohibit distribution of unsolicited literature.** The court noted that *Robins v. Pruneyard Shopping Center* involved a forum open to the public but an apartment complex is private for tenants and invited guests. The Court of Appeal found no violation of free speech rights by denying the association the right to distribute unsolicited literature. **The California Supreme Court upheld the Court of Appeal decision.**

5. **The District Court and Court of Appeals found the ordinance unconstitutional, which was affirmed by a unanimous decision of the U.S.** Supreme Court, which held that the city had "almost completely foreclosed a venerable means of communication that is both unique and important." The court stated that such signs may be the only alternative for people of modest means. While the

city can regulate signs to prevent cluttering neighborhoods, they cannot entirely prohibit them. Note: Size restrictions could be a proper regulation if reasonable.

6. **The Court of Appeals determined that the Superior Court cannot correct an arbitrator's award if the arbitrator did not exceed authority.** The courts are limited in their review in order to fulfill the expectations of the parties that the award will be binding and final. Note: Parties can be stuck with an arbitrator's error, even when it is obviously wrong.

7. **The Superior Court granted summary judgment to the landlord enjoining enforcement of the city ordinance.** The Court of Appeal affirmed that the ordinance violated procedural due process and is unconstitutional for violation of the 14th Amendment. Note: If this ordinance had been upheld, the landlord would have to evict all residents of the residence without any standards or appeal. The ordinance would require eviction of persons who had not been convicted of any crime or even maintaining a nuisance.

8. **The court held that listing a property for sale is an invitation to the public to view the interior of the home; therefore, what is observable to the public is observable to a police officer.** Police officers can pose as buyers and not violate Fourth Amendment rights.

9. **The California Supreme Court held that the right of free speech protected the picketers, even though the picketing may have hurt the mall's business.**

■ CHAPTER 2   LAW OF AGENCY

1. **Breach of fiduciary duty for either a seller's agent or dual agent in indicating that property could be obtained at less than listed price.** This action was contrary to the best financial interests of the owner. If the agent had given details of the first sale, then it would be a breach of loyalty as well. The agent cannot divulge, without permission, details of a previous offer; confidentiality of the agency must be maintained. A buyer's agent should properly inform the buyer what the buyer's agent knows.

2. **The Court of Appeals directed the trial court to direct a verdict against the broker as to both duty and breach.** In *White Allen v. Daily* (1928) 92 C.A. 308, the court held that under a net listing the agent may, without violating any trust relationship, purchase the property on the agent's own account or act as the agent of others.

   This previous ruling does not apply to this case because the agent helped set the price. For the *White Allen v. Daily* ruling to apply, the court held that the price would have had to have been set independently and uninfluenced by the broker. The broker, in this case, had a duty of full disclosure of the relationship of the buyers. Because the agent helped set the price, the agent had a duty of honesty and diligence to make certain it was fair. The Court of Appeals directed the trial court to direct a verdict against the broker as to both duty and breach.

3. **Broker had a duty to disclose to the principal any knowledge that he or she possessed that might have influenced the owner of the property.** The court determined in this case that the broker's right to the commission does not apply because **the broker had not acted in the utmost good faith toward his principal.**

4. **Broker breached the duty of honest dealing by making the false declaration.** In this case, the borrowers did not have knowledge of the defendant's dual agency, so the broker had made a secret profit. **The mortgage broker had a duty of full disclosure.** (In California, all parties would have to agree to the compensation.)

   The court determined the broker should forfeit the broker's commission to the borrower. In similar cases, courts have required that secret profits be turned over to the principal.

5. **The court held that the entire transaction was tainted by a breach of duties.** The buyer overpaid $15,000 so that the brokers could get their commissions. **The court held that the entire $15,000 could be recovered as secret profit from those brokers who jointly received it.**

6. **A failure to indicate relationship with the purported purchaser. A failure to indicate that he, in fact, was to be the purchaser. Failure to act in good faith is a violation of duties of full disclosure and honest dealings, as well as fiduciary duties.** It was apparent

from broker's dealings that he believed property was worth considerably more than price listed. Possible duty to disclose true value of property. There also was attempted fraud on the state.

7. **The court held that a broker has the highest duty of good faith toward the broker's principal. This precludes a broker from assuming a position adverse to that of the principal unless the broker has disclosed all of the facts in the matter and the principal consents.** The fact that the broker paid a fair price or that the property could not be sold for more money is not material to the agent's liability. **A broker who breaches duty of good faith is not only precluded from recovering compensation for the broker's services, but may be liable for damages.** (Owner also had a right to decide if the owner wanted the forfeited deposit or a sale, with the broker paying the balance of the deposit.)

8. **The court held that the failure to disclose the buyer's intent and that the defendant would profit from relisting the property could have affected the plaintiffs' accepting a lower price.** The plaintiffs made a prima facie case of breach of fiduciary duty. **The court also held that there was a basis for determining that the broker had negligently set the selling price too low.** The broker had not researched neighborhood values. (Setting a value unsupported by fact could subject an agent to liability.)

9. **The broker was guilty of negligent misrepresentation in advising the plaintiff that Fullmer appeared reliable (no facts to support this) and advising the plaintiff that the security was adequate without making an independent effort to ascertain the actual value of the property.** (The broker relied on statements of the buyer.) The broker also should have explained that Fullmer had no obligations under a purchase money deed of trust (no deficiency judgment). The broker was held liable by the broker's negligence for the broker's principal's loss.

10. **The court held that a real estate agent is authorized to consent to the entry only of persons the agent believes to be potential purchasers.** This would plainly exclude the police. The search was improper, as the police could not have reasonably believed that the agent had authority to consent to a search.

11. **The court held that Clark's negligence caused Foggy to make the loan, and Foggy was entitled to recover all damages proximately caused by Clark's action.** Note: The appraisal was made for the purpose of establishing value for a loan and the appraiser could expect it to be relied upon.

12. **While the Superior Court granted the broker's motion for summary judgment, the Court of Appeals reversed ruling that the salesperson appeared to be acting as the broker's loan agent and the broker was liable under the "respondeat superior" doctrine.** While the defendant may not have known of the alleged fraudulent conduct, the broker was vicariously liable for such conduct if the salesperson committed the fraud while holding himself out as a loan representative of the broker. Note: There might have been a case against the appraiser for fraud ($800,000 appraisal and $480,000 value).

13. **The court held that there was no duty of disclosure. The developer never believed or rationally could have believed that the agent represented the developer.**

■ CHAPTER 3 DUTIES AND RESPONSIBILITIES OF LICENSEES

1. **For his failure to disclose adverse facts known to him, the jury awarded the buyers $1,800 in actual damages as well as $20,000 in punitive damages,** which were upheld upon appeal.

2. **While the Superior Court ruled that Marcos had a cause of action for negligence, nuisance, and intentional infliction of emotional distress, the Court of Appeal reversed.** The court explained that in order to have a tort there must be a duty to the injured person. There was no duty to Marcos because Marcos was not a party to the sale. Note: The buyer would be the party who would have the cause of action for broker negligence, not her son.

3. **The court held that the board's action unlawfully restrained trade.** The board's action affected the public's ability to negotiate for alternative type listings. (The result has been that some brokers will put homeowners' open type listings into the multiple listing service for a fee. In these cases, there is no real listing broker. The

homeowner will pay whoever sells the homeowner's property in accordance with an agreement the homeowner works out with the agent.)

4. **The court indicated that failure to recommend a title search might constitute negligence because the agent knew the lessors intended to buy and expend funds on the ranch.** (Such a recommendation would seem to be proper.) **The statements as to the trust deed were misrepresentations of fact. The agent failed to exercise the skill expected of an agent and should be liable for negligence.**

5. **The California Supreme Court held that the broker made a secret profit and was liable to the purchaser for that profit.** (The broker's false representations were to the purchaser, not the seller.) The broker was also held for exemplary damages (punitive damages). The broker was held not to be entitled to have the damages reduced by commission the broker paid to others or for the broker's two escrow costs.

6. **While the trial court granted summary judgment in favor of the Sutherlands, the Court of Appeals reversed the decision, ruling that the Sutherlands had both a common law and statutory duty to disclose the disturbances if they amounted to a nuisance.** The court pointed out that an action for deceit does not require contractual privity. (It is clear that the Sutherlands expected the misrepresentations to be repeated by the relocation company.)

7. **By determining the kind of instrument to be executed the court held that it was the unauthorized practice of law.** The court held that if the Broker had only filled in blanks in a form, the action would have only been clerical and not the practice of law. (Apparently, a broker can follow the principal's instructions as to which instrument to use, but recommending another creates the problem of practicing law.)

8. **The court held that when brokers and salespersons affirmatively decide to show property, there is a duty of care to warn prospective tenants of concealed dangers.** The broker had a duty to warn the tenant of the hidden danger known to both the broker and the saleswoman. (Broker is liable for negligence of the salesperson.)

9. **The court held that the mortgage loan broker is retained by the borrower as borrower's agent. There was a duty of full and accurate disclosure of material facts that would affect the borrower's decision.** The court further held that there was a duty to call to plaintiff's attention the unfavorable provisions in the loan papers. Evidence was admitted showing misleading television commercials that did not call attention to unfavorable provisions. The court held that the loan broker lured plaintiff into the office by bait and switch advertising. The California Supreme Court held that $25,000 in compensatory damages and $200,000 in punitive damages was not excessive. (Alleged that the plaintiff's late charges brought in millions over the years.) The purpose of punitive damages is to punish wrongdoers to deter them in the future.

10. **The court determined there was no antitrust violation and the Plaintiff had no legal right to use the services of the Board of Realtors®.** While the court agreed that refusal of access to licensed brokers violates the antitrust laws (*Marin County Board v. Polsson*), no trade was infringed upon here because the plaintiff was not in the real estate business. He simply wanted to deal without an agent but have access to the tools of the industry.

11. **Carter breached his duty of disclosure.** The fact that the buyer is related to the agent is a material fact. The court held that it made no difference that the price paid may have been fair. (A resale for a higher price or evidence that the price was set too low would indicate fraud.)

12. **In an action for declaratory relief, the court held that Bernstein had failed to show any anticompetitive effect of the board's rule.** A voluntary organization may impose reasonable rules for members' inclusion in the organization.

13. **The broker purchaser was held liable because of fraud. The purchaser was not acting as a pure principal. Because he shared in the commission, he had a fiduciary duty to disclose a higher offer.** This case involved the liability of the Real Estate Recovery Fund. While the fund would not have been liable had a commission not been accepted, the fund was held liable as the purchaser was acting as an agent.

14. **A jury awarded Ballou $138,000 based on splitting all commissions equally between Ballou and Traweek. Ballou was also awarded $2 million in punitive damages.** The Court of Appeals upheld the awards because of the material nature of the misrepresentations. The court held that the guaranty to the limited partners could have been taken out of Traweek's share, rather than Ballou's.

15. **The court held that a seller has a duty to disclose to potential buyers that a neighborhood nuisance existed that diminished the value of adjoining residences.** "Failure to disclose a negative fact when it can reasonably be said to have a foreseeable depressing effect on the value of property is tortious." (This decision tends to clarify disclosure requirements of CC 1102.6.)

16. **The court held that it was not the obligation of the seller to research local land use ordinances and explain to a buyer the effect of such ordinances on realty.**

17. **The verbal disclosure was not sufficient and the court ruled for the plaintiff.** The court rules that the defendant knew of the existence of potential lead based paint and that written disclosure was required.

18. **The Superior Court granted summary judgment for CAL Fed, FSR, and Grasso. The Court of Appeal affirmed** ruling (1) as a foreclosing seller, Cal Fed had no Civil Code 1102.2 duty to provide a seller's disclosure statement to the buyer (as required for most other sellers of California one-to-four residential units), (2) Cal Fed properly disclosed the recently settled lawsuit for construction defects, and (3) realty broker FSR correctly conducted a visual inspection of the condo which satisfied the agent's Civil Code 2079 and 2079.3 disclosure duty by reporting the prior construction defect lawsuit which had been settled. The appellate court commented when the seller and/or agent knows of facts materially affecting the value or desirability of the property, and the buyer does not know those facts, they must be disclosed to the buyer. "The seller or his or her agent must have actual knowledge in order to be liable for failing to disclose a material fact."

The appellate court noted, "We conclude that the fiduciary duty of Sands and Grasso as a dual agent, representing both the buyer and seller, were fulfilled when the buyer was informed that a construction defect lawsuit had been filed and settled. At that point, the buyer should have investigated further and, if necessary, should have hired an attorney for advice on the legal aspects of the lawsuit and settlement. Neither Sands nor Grasso was required to read and analyze the legal documents located in the court file."

■ CHAPTER 4   REGULATION OF LICENSEES

1. **The court held that the broker was entitled to compensation if he was licensed at the time the services were performed.** The original agreement did not contemplate any further services. If the subsequent lease was in substantial compliance with the broker's contract for commission, the broker would be entitled to commission.

2. **The court held that the revocation of Katz's license was not excessive.** An "as is" clause and an express disclaimer of warranty did not protect Katz. The court held that these applied only to observable conditions. The court held that a seller is not protected from passive concealment. Katz's offer to rescind without paying for repairs would have been unjust enrichment to Katz.

3. **The court held the fund is only liable for an act for which a real estate license is required.** It is not required for a co-venture. The court also held the trust involved was not because of an agency trust, where one relies on a broker's representation; the trust in this case was a marital trust of a wife trusting a husband.

4. **The court held that recovery is limited to the actual loss suffered, and using the tax benefits as an offset restores the parties to their original condition.** (This decision seems to allow the Commissioner to readjudicate the judgment amount, as the court determines what the loss is.) The decision of *Acebo v. Real Estate Education and Recovery Fund* (1984) 155 C.A.3d 907 held that the fund need only pay compensatory damages and not punitive damages. The court allowed the fund to look into the nature of the judgment.

5. **The court held that Business and Professions Code 10242 prevented loan costs more than actual costs.** Pacific Plan's action resulted in some borrowers paying excess costs. The court said that individual accounting was required. The court also stated that using average costs would not be allowed by statute.

6. **The court held that the test did not violate the Unruh Act.** The court approved economic discrimination where applied evenly to all rental applicants. It affirms right of landlord to apply reasonable income-to-rental requirements. Note: Fannie Mae and Freddie Mac use a 28 percent of gross income test for maximum housing payments.

7. **The court held that the real estate Commissioner had failed to make a finding that the conviction was substantially related to the qualifications, functions, or duties of a real estate salesman.** Section 475(a) of the Business and Professions Code allows the denial of a license if "the crime is substantially related to the qualifications, functions, or duties of the business or profession for which application is made." Section 10177(b) of the Business and Professions Code is, therefore, limited by Business and Professions Code 475(a).

8. **The court held that the extent of participation must be considered. Attempting to smuggle a large quantity of marijuana involves moral turpitude and demonstrates the lack of honesty and integrity required to be a real estate broker.**

9. **The court ordered the reversal of the Commissioner's action in denying the broker's license.** Section 480 of the Business and Professions Code allows denial of a license for a conviction related to the qualifications of a profession. The court held that no relationship was shown between the conviction and the qualifications to be a broker. (This case takes a very narrow interpretation of the morality required to be a broker.)

10. **The court held the policy was discriminatory because it discriminated between children in contemplation over children in existence.** The court ruled that it violated a Los Angeles Municipal Code regarding discrimination. (It probably also violates the

Unruh and Rumford Acts, as well as the 1988 Amendment to the Civil Rights Act of 1968.)

11. **The fund was held liable.** The court held that because Kennedy claimed to be acting as a broker, Vinci was within the class of individuals the legislature intended to protect. (If Kennedy was not licensed as a salesperson, the results would likely have been different.)

12. **The fund is not liable because the discharge in bankruptcy voided the judgment, and without a judgment there can be no basis for recovery from the fund.** (This is not a very equitable decision and seems at odds with the purpose of the fund.)

13. **The court ruled that the town's refusal to rezone to allow multiple family units outside the urban area had a discriminatory effect because the area to be rezoned was 98% white.** The decision directed Huntington to remove its restriction of multiple family units to urban areas and ordered the town to rezone to allow multifamily construction. The court rejected the rationale for the zoning that restricting multi-family units to urban areas would encourage developers to invest in deteriorated and needy sections of the town. This case is important, as it is likely to be cited wherever a developer wants to rezone for higher density if the developer can show the discriminatory impact of single-family zoning.

14. **The court pointed out that landlords must make reasonable accommodations in rules to afford people with disabilities the equal opportunity to use and enjoy a dwelling.** The Ninth Circuit reversed a trial court that had dismissed the case and remanded it for trial.

15. **The court held that the automatic license suspension contained in Business and Professions Code 10475 did not violate due process because the licensee received ample notice and opportunity to challenge the claim that resulted in a judgment.** The court pointed out that a formal hearing would not have added significantly to the integrity of the administrative process.

16. **The claim was denied in U.S. District Court and the Court of Appeal affirmed ruling that Stewart was not an "aggrieved person" eligible to recover.** Stewart Title Guaranty Company was not

the defrauded party, the lenders and the borrowers were. By paying off their claims, Stewart did not take over their rights by subrogation. The fund is a limited fund of last resort to protect members of the public who would otherwise have no recourse against unscrupulous real estate professionals. Title insurers were not intended to be "aggrieved parties" as used in Business and Professions Code 10471(a).

17. **The District Court granted summary judgment for Fox, holding that the studio was not a place of public accommodation so was not covered by ADA. The Court of Appeals affirmed, as the lot was not open to the public.** Note: A disabled employee might have a claim as to an ADA violation.

18. **The U.S. District Court ruled that the Center's action violated the Americans With Disabilities Act as well as the California Unruh Act and Disabled Person's Act. The U.S. Court of Appeals affirmed** ruling that the Center must give persons with disabilities the "broadest feasible access" including service animals. The Center as well as employees was held liable for $7,000 in total awards to Lentini.

19. **The U.S. District Court granted the preliminary injunction.** Preliminary inunctions can be granted where the plaintiff has a strong likelihood of succeeding on the claims. Note: Apparently, the landlord wished to attract Korean tenants because of a perceived economic advantage. The owner, Donald Sterling, is also the owner of the Los Angeles Clippers.

20. **A declaratory judgment ruled that FSBO did not need a real estate license.** Commissioner regulation was unconstitutional as to free speech in requiring license for Internet listing, but not for newspapers (disparity of treatment). Commissioner was unable to show any compelling reason for a license requirement.

21. **The Court of Appeal affirmed the revocation,** holding there was a relationship between a misdemeanor conviction and qualification, functions and duties of a real estate broker. Note: Property managers of substandard housing, property where funds are not available for corrective action as well as property in foreclosure or

bank owned should be aware of this decision. If violations are not corrected, the broker's license could be in jeopardy.

22. **The Court of Appeal reversed the trial court and ordered the DRE to set aside the suspension.** While Civil Code 10177.5 allows the DRE to discipline a broker when there is a civil judgment based on fraud, misrepresentation or deceit, the court determined that the DRE application of the statute violated the California Constitution.

    When a party obtains a professional license, it is a protected property right. It cannot be taken away without clear and convincing evidence of disqualification. The jury did not find clear and convincing evidence of fraud.

■ CHAPTER 5   LAW OF CONTRACTS

1. **The statement satisfies the Statute of Frauds.** Either party could bring action to enforce the agreement because both have signed it. The maker signed the check on its face, and the payee signed as an endorsement. The property is sufficiently identified, as is the price. The court would imply that cash was to be paid at closing, that closing would be within a reasonable time period, and the seller would be giving marketable title.

2. **The court held that the mistake of a scrivener or draftsman in reducing the intent of the parties to writing is grounds for reformation.** The court held that the right of reformation went to subsequent holders.

3. **The court held that the telegram was not a sufficient writing to establish an agency.** There were no ambiguities to allow oral testimony. Plaintiff was a licensed real estate broker and was presumed to know that contracts for real estate commission are invalid and unenforceable unless they are in writing. The telegram did not satisfy the Statute of Frauds.

4. **The court held that the promise not to sell to one particular person is not an unreasonable restraint on alienation.** They also held that $20,000 was reasonable for liquidated damages (and not

a penalty), based upon the emotional distress caused by the breach of the specific promise made by the purchaser.

5. **Because the right to purchase was for $10,000 and the property was sold for $22,000, the court awarded $12,000 in compensatory damages plus interest.** A preemptive right is a right of first refusal. In this case, it was at an agreed price rather than meeting the price of a future offeror. A right of first refusal really becomes an option when the owner decides to sell. The court held the purchase of the first property was consideration for the preemptive right, so the right holder was entitled to damages when the holder's rights were breached.

6. **The court held this was a case of mutual mistake of fact and ordered the return of all monies paid under the lease.** Both parties assumed the premises could be used for the purpose rented. Even though "as is" was used, it was not contemplated that this applied to the structural ability of a building to support an activity. (In several cases, the courts have held that "as is" applies to patent or obvious defects, not to latent defects known to the seller or lessor.)

7. **The Orange County Superior Court denied Ultimo's motion to compel Arbitration and the Court of Appeal affirmed.** The contract was unconscionable in that the customer has no right to be fully compensated for a loss.

8. **The court held that a listing for real property must satisfy the Statute of Frauds.** While the Statute of Frauds does not require the signature to be at the bottom, it must be somewhere in the document. There was no evidence that the defendant intended to appropriate their letterhead as their signature. While the court determined that the broker was not entitled to a commission for sale of real property, they determined the personal property could be severed from the real property. Because the Statute of Frauds does not apply to personal property, they awarded the plaintiff $30,150 for arranging the sale of the personal property. It was obvious from the decision that the court did not like the result of the application of the Statute of Frauds and went out of their way to benefit the plaintiff. (The dissenting opinion was that the majority of the court was sanctioning fraud.)

9. **The court held that under California Civil Code, a minor under the age of 18 cannot directly or indirectly encumber the minor's property. Therefore, there could be no valid mechanic's lien against the property.** (Failure to act would indirectly encumber the property.)

10. **The court held that this was simply an agreement to agree in the future and that there is no remedy for the breach of such an agreement.** A contract requires a complete agreement. In this case, the essential term was left open. The court also held that parol evidence was not admissible to supply the missing agreement. (There wasn't an ambiguity.)

11. **The 9th Circuit Court affirmed an $18.5 million verdict in favor of the plaintiffs.** An oral agreement to lend money to purchase property does not come within the *Statute of Frauds* (Civil Code 1624), although the Statute of Frauds does apply to an oral promise to grant a lien against real property.

12. **While the trial court held that the parents had a legal duty to read the trust deed they signed, the Court of Appeals held that like the famous Peerless case** (*Raffles v. Wickelhaus* (1624) 159 Eng. Rep 375), **the parties had made a fundamental mutual mistake, so no agreement was made. Rescission was therefore proper.** Note: the lender lost the security for the loan.

13. **The court held that while the buyer offered the clause, the seller did not accept it.** All parties must agree to the clause for it to be effective. Note: The acceptance really was a counteroffer, since it was not in accordance with the offer.

14. **The court pointed out that there is a marital duty to support (Civil Code 5100 and 5132). The agreement of the wife to support the husband did not constitute any new consideration to support an alleged indebtedness.**

15. **The Court of Appeal reversed the award for lost profits because the evidence at trial was speculative.** The court held that lost profits could be compensable, but there must be reasonable certainty of the profits.

■ CHAPTER 6   REAL ESTATE CONTRACTS

1. **The listing was held to be properly cancelled for cause.** For an exclusive listing that is irrevocable for a stated period, consideration is required. The consideration is the promise to make diligent effort to find a buyer. The court held that the acceptance of an offer to pay for services to be performed would obligate the agent to due diligence even if it were not expressly stated. In this case, the broker indicated that they advertised the property with other property. The court felt it was a token effort. The right to rescind was based upon the partial failure of consideration. (For broker protection, files should indicate all efforts made under a listing in order to prove wrongful revocation. If a listing is wrongfully revoked, the agent would be entitled to a commission.)

2. **The court held that the broker was not entitled to a commission.** She did not produce a buyer, as she never put the owner in a position where he could have made a contract had he so desired. The letter was not an offer; it only informed the owner of an offer. If the broker had delivered a proper offer to turn into a contract by acceptance, then the broker would have performed. The court also held in this case that the duty of an agent to communicate an offer to the principal is the same whether the offer is written or oral.

3. **Rose was entitled to a commission.** In the absence of an exclusive right to sell listing (this was an open listing), a broker must be the procuring cause to be entitled to a commission.

   "Procuring cause is the cause originating a series of events that, without break in their continuity, result in the accomplishment of the prime object of employment. Procure does not necessarily imply the formal consummation of an agreement; the word in its broadest sense means to prevail upon, induce or persuade a person to do something."

   Ordinarily the price at which a broker is authorized to sell property is considered merely an asking price to guide negotiations. If the broker "procures a purchaser willing to pay a lower price, the owner cannot deprive the broker of his commission by conducting the final negotiations himself and selling at a lower price to the purchaser procured by the broker." "If the broker is in fact the procuring cause of a sale, it is unnecessary for him to prove that he was the first one to bring the purchaser's attention to the fact that the property in question was for sale."

4. **The court held that while agreements with owners must be in writing, the legislature did not intend to extend this requirement to others.** The court noted that agreements between brokers and brokers and salespersons need not be in writing. (A finder's fee agreement does not involve real estate, it involves people. All the finder is providing is an introduction.)

5. **The broker was held to be entitled to a commission.** While there is no estoppel from the Statute of Frauds for a mere oral promise to pay a commission or a promise to sign a listing, this is not the case here. The seller's agent (attorney) indicated that a listing was actually in existence. The court held that the broker reasonably relied on the representation of the seller's attorney. The seller was held to be estopped from raising the defense of the Statute of Frauds.

6. **The court held that the broker's right to the commission was not affected by the failure of either party to carry out the sale.** In this case, the court awarded the plaintiff the entire $8,250 commission. The court held that the broker's right to compensation was not dependent upon escrow instructions where broker did not consent to them. The court also held that the deposit receipt was a binding contract. (The defendant had chosen to sue for damages on the breach of contract rather than declare a forfeiture of the deposit.)

7. **The court held that the trial court was justified in determining the broker had produced a buyer ready, willing, and financially able.** The court held that the trial court was justified in determining that the buyer was able to purchase within the terms set forth in the listing agreement. The court cited *California Land Security Company v. Ritchie* 40 C.A. 246. This case held that if any of the terms are unsatisfactory to the vendor, the vendor should object to them on those grounds and not absolutely refuse to sell. Where he refuses to accept the purchaser, he should be held liable for the commission.

8. **The court held that the broker was entitled to a commission.** The court held that the fact that no offers were received did not require

a finding that the broker had failed to use diligence that would have been cause for withdrawal. The defense was raised that the commission was a penalty for withdrawal and unenforceable. The court held that a claim for compensation under the withdrawal clause is not a claim for damages, but indebtedness under the contractual agreement. The minority opinion felt the court had sidestepped the issue of whether the commission for withdrawal was damages or liquidated damages. The minority opinion indicated the court could not justify the full commission (on list price) as liquidated damages because damages must be assessed reasonably. (This could be an interesting issue in the future.)

9. **The court held that a finder who only brings parties together need not be licensed.** The court found for the plaintiff. The defendant claimed that Section 10131(d) of the Business and Professions Code requires anyone who solicits lenders for a loan secured by real estate to be licensed. While the statute seems to require licensing for soliciting lenders, the court held that this was not the legislative intent. Licensing requires knowledge of arithmetic and law. Such knowledge is not needed for a finder. The plaintiff did not participate in the loan negotiations.

10. **Section 2076 of the Code of Civil Procedures holds that one who does not object to a tender waives one's right to object. Therefore, the broker was not entitled to any further consideration.** This case is important in that it allows oral modification of written listings. (The court could have applied the doctrine of estoppel. The owners were not obligated to clear the title, but they acted to their detriment based on the verbal promise of the broker.)

11. **The court held that using "as is" in the escrow contract did not relieve the broker from his prior fraudulent representation. The court held the seller liable also as the seller gave the broker the power he misused.** The seller is liable even though innocent of any wrong when he accepts and retains the benefits of the transaction.

12. **The court held that a deposit belongs to the principal and cannot be returned without the principal's consent.** The broker breached an agency duty. The court also held that satisfaction to one party ordinarily means satisfaction to a reasonable person. Satisfaction

as to commercial value or quality, fitness, etc., cannot be denied arbitrarily or unreasonably.

13. **The builder was not required to pay the commission.** The requirement that a commission be paid was an illegal tie-in arrangement that violated both state and federal antitrust laws. The builder was not required to pay.

14. **The court held that the broker did not need a second writing to support the claim for commission.** Since the original sale agreement was replaced by a new agreement between the same parties, with the broker's help, the original commission agreement should be applicable to the final sale.

15. **The broker was entitled to a commission.** The court held in this Arkansas appellate case that title transfer to the builder, then to the buyer, was simply an attempt to avoid a commission. The former owner was really selling to the buyers, who were located by the agent during the term of the listing.

16. **The court awarded the broker the commission he would have received had the sale been completed ($100,000 minus seller's agent's share).** The court pointed out that although it is generally the seller's responsibility to pay the commission, in certain circumstances the broker can recover from a buyer. If the broker is retained by the buyer, locates property for the buyer, and the buyer agrees to buy at the price offered, the buyer promises to complete the transaction so the broker can recover his commission. If the buyer defaults, the broker can recover the full commission from the buyer based upon the breach of the implied promise. (The broker was a third party beneficiary of the purchase agreement.) Note: This case points out the advantage of being a buyer's agent, as a buyer's agent is apparently not limited to a share of the liquidated damages when buyer defaults.

■ CHAPTER 7 PROPERTY, ESTATES, AND RECORDING

1. **Adaptability and intent make the Queen Mary real property.** The fact that it can be moved doesn't change its nature. The vessel housed a museum, hotel, shops, and restaurants. It was developed

as a permanent tourist attraction. While it was capable of being moved, it was connected by service lines and permanent gangways. Its movement was minimal. In addition, great expense was involved in the removal of equipment, indicating the intended permanence.

2. **The court held that an inadvertent error cannot alter an intended relationship, so the trust deed recorded second was given priority.** The Supreme Court, in making its decision, emphasized the holders of the trust deed intended to be second and had actual knowledge of the other trust deed, which was to have been recorded first. The court pointed out that this party's position would not be hurt as they intended to have a second trust deed. (It is doubtful if the decision would be the same if the holders of the first recorded trust deed were assignees that, from the recording, assumed they were purchasing a first trust deed.)

3. **It was not constructive notice to the beverage firm.** Constructive notice of a mortgage recording only applies to subsequent purchasers and mortgages and not to others doing business with the corporation.

4. **The recording did not give constructive notice.** The party executing was required to be known by and acknowledge his or her signature or sign in the presence of the notary. In the absence of either, there was no constructive notice.

5. **The court held that the deed was a valid conveyance in granting a remainder interest.** The deed created a life estate in the grantor.

6. **The date discrepancy did not invalidate the acknowledgement.** This was a 9th Circuit Court case. The Court of Appeals held there was substantial compliance with the statutes as to acknowledgment. The mortgagees were still secured creditors.

■ CHAPTER 8   OWNERSHIP OF REAL PROPERTY

1. **A joint tenancy was created in the life estate.** The life tenants have survivorship rights with the last survivor having sole rights to

occupancy. Upon the death of the first life tenant, the remainder interest holder does not get the first life tenant's occupancy right.

2. **"Since each co-tenant has a right to occupy the whole of the property, the possession of one is deemed the possession of all and each may assume that another in exclusive possession is possessing for all and not adversely to the others . . ."** One co-tenant "does not gain title by adverse possession against the others unless notice is brought home to the others that such possession has become hostile."

3. **The parties are joint tenants and the former wife has survivorship rights.** A continued right of equal possession is not required to maintain a joint tenancy. The parties did not terminate the joint tenancy and right of survivorship. (In cases of marriage dissolution, joint tenancy interest in a single-family residence would be considered to be community property [CC5104]. This is a presumption only and can be overcome by evidence to the contrary. It is clear in this case by the life possession and prohibition against transfer that survivorship was intended. If the courts had treated the property as community property upon dissolution of the marriage, continued joint ownership would have been as tenants in common.)

4. **The U.S. District Court held that the United States was immune from liability because of the recreational user liability in Civil Code Section 846.** The landowner (United States) owes no duty to keep land safe for recreational users. The 9th Circuit asked the California Supreme Court to decide whether Section 846 exempts a landlord from liability for an employee's acts of vehicular negligence within the course and scope of employment. The California Supreme Court determined that Section 846 immunized landowners from liability as to recreational user as to the conditions of the property; however, the landowner is not immune from injuries from negligent active conduct.

5. **The action of the corporation was improper, and they could not assess the owners for costs.** The assessment was not for expenses incident to the enforcement of restrictions. No ambiguity existed as to the restrictions. The restrictions applied to the project and those covered by it, not to control nuisances elsewhere. Note: Since the corporation engaged in an ultra vires act (an act beyond

their authority), the individual directors who authorized the expenditures could be held liable. Many homeowner associations carry director liability insurance to protect the directors.

6. **The Sacramento Superior Court jury awarded the limited partners $165,527.73 actual compensatory damages plus $7 million in punitive damages.** The Court of Appeal affirmed the compensatory damages but reduced the 42-to-1 ratio of punitive damages to actual damages to 9-to-1 ratio based on a 2003 U.S. Supreme Court case, which held that punitive damages that exceed nine times compensatory damages are excessive (*State Farm Mutual Automobile Insurance Co. v. Campbell* (2003) 538 U.S. 408). The managing partner had been sued by his partners who alleged breach of judiciary duty, interference with economic advantage, misrepresentation, fraud, and breach of contract.

   Note: The court agreed with the trial jury that Oates's conduct breached his fiduciary duty to his limited partners. "The jury could find that the kickbacks, markups, and concealed commission(s) were part of a systematic pattern of Oates of bilking his partners." Nevertheless, the court was required to reduce the punitive damages to $1.5 million to reflect the 9-to-1 ratio, despite the fact that the sum is insignificant considering Oates's net worth of at least $600 million.

7. **While the trial court had ordered a sale, the Court of Appeal held that the trial court abused its discretion in ordering a property sale rather than a partition in kind.** The reason the plaintiff wanted a sale rather than a partition in kind was that he wanted the entire parcel. In order to have a sale, the plaintiff must show that either:

   1. physical division into equal value parcels is not possible; or

   2. a division of the land would substantially diminish its value. (The whole would be worth more than the sum of its parts.)

   The court held that neither reason was present, and they should not force a sale upon a co-tenant who does not want loss of use of property or the tax liability that would result from a sale. The court held the trial court abused its discretion in ordering a property sale rather than a partition in kind.

8. **The court held that an owner is not liable to a trespasser for injuries from dangerous conditions unknown.** They held that the owner had no duty to inspect the fence for holes, and even if he had known of the vats of acid, he would not be liable as they were not dangerous to persons behaving properly.

9. **While they took title in joint tenancy, the court held that they had actually taken title as tenants in common.** The court held title could not be in joint tenancy because joint tenancy requires equal ownership of every owner. (The woman owned one-half and the husband and wife owned the other one-half.) One joint tenant cannot have a greater interest than the others.

10. **The court held that all the husband had encumbered was his undivided interest. The purchaser at the foreclosure sale became a tenant in common with the wife.**

11. **The court held that a landlord not in possession or control of the premises was not liable for the injury.** It should be noted that in this case the fact that the landlord was in the process of evicting the tenant might have influenced the decision because the landlord could do nothing else to get the tenant out. If the landlord leased the premises for a use that could be anticipated as dangerous to others, then the fact that the landlord was not in control or possession would be unlikely to shield the landlord from liability.

12. **The court held that the school had no duty to light up public walks and streets so students could view dangers.** Without any duty, there is no negligence for failure to provide lighting.

13. **The court held that the evidence was such that a jury could conclude defendants' control over the vacant lot was sufficient to charge them with a duty of care.** This case differs from other offpremises injury cases in that the defendant had a right to use the off-premise site and had benefited by the use and had exercised control over it.

14. **The agreement to sell was null and void and the buyer had no relief against the community property.** There can be a sale or partition of community property only if both spouses consent to it. Any agreement made by one spouse can be entirely set aside by the other spouse.

15. **The court held the landlord was immune, citing CC846, which states that an owner of any estate in real estate has no duty of care to recreational users.** The court, however, did not see fit to extend this immunity to the other defendants. Being contractors, they had permission to enter the property to perform their work. The court indicated that they were not agents of the owner and were denied the protection of CC846.

16. **The subsequent mortgage payments, made with community property funds, created an after-acquired interest that was not transferred by the prior quitclaim deed, so the wife was entitled to her portion of this interest** (increase of value after the quitclaim deed). The wife had previously conveyed the entire community property interest by quitclaim deed. The deed was given for value without fraud.

17. **The California Supreme Court held that the grazing permit gave the defendant an interest in the land that is protected by Civil Code 846 regarding liability from injuries to recreational users.** Note: This case differs from *New v. Consolidated Rock Prods.* in that the court did not find that the defendant had acted willfully or in conscious disregard of a duty to warn the plaintiff.

18. **The court held that the landlord's duty as to the sidewalk created by municipal ordinance was to the city, not to the pedestrian.** The landlord was held not to be liable to the injured pedestrian.

19. **The court held that recreational immunity did not apply because the Curry Company made claims in its brochure stating that the trail was safe for cycling and its bikes were safe for cycling on the trail.**

20. **The court held that the landlord had no duty to protect the trespassers from their own activities** (a candle was used for illumination).

21. **The court held that while the wife was entitled to the $40,000 contribution to the community property, the $13,000 saved benefited the community property rather than just the wife.**

22. **The court held that there was no landlord negligence.** The only negligence concerned the tenant. (She was playing without adult supervision, and the bed was placed by the window.)

23. **The Superior Court ruled that the partnership was dissolved and found there was no constructive fraud.** The Court of Appeals affirmed ruling that while partners have a fiduciary duty to each other, there was no violation in this case. Partners could bid at a foreclosure sale to avoid losing their half of the property. Note: This couple that purchased at the trustee's sale had put up the down payment. The other couple was to have made the payments, but they defaulted.

24. **The court ruled that there was no duty of a homeowner to supervise a child in the vicinity of a residential swimming pool when the child's parent is present.** Padilla had claimed there was a joint parental duty of supervision. Note: It appears as this case was brought to reach the deep pockets of the homeowner's insurer.

25. **The trial court found the farm owner to be 35 percent negligent and awarded the plaintiff $1,637,226 damages.** The Court of Appeal reversed ruling that the farm owner had no duty to protect the injured worker from the negligence of the truck driver. The court noted that the greater the likelihood of injury, the greater the duty to protect members of the public. There was no reasonable foreseeability of harm as it could not be foreseen that members of the public would be driving on the private road at excessive speed.

■ CHAPTER 9 ACQUISITIONS AND CONVEYANCES

1. **If the life estate was based upon the life of a person other than the life tenant, then the life tenant's interest can be transferred by will.**

2. **Grantor retained title because inadequate description of the life estate interest rendered the deed void.**

3. **The court held that because grantor purported to convey a fee interest, the after-acquired interest passed to the grantee.**

4. **There was a present transfer so the deed was valid.** (Deed could have been recorded.)

5. **There was no transfer of title.** Court determined that it was clear that delivery was not intended.

6. Court held that the barges were peculiarly adapted to the condemnee's business and could be considered fixtures. Because prohibiting of commercial use of the lake was a taking, the barge owners were entitled to compensation.

7. Court held that the proper measure necessary under the Fifth Amendment is fair market value when that value can be ascertained (not replacement value). In this case, there were 11 recent camp sales for comparables.

8. **The loss was compensable.** If the business suffered a loss because it moved further away to a less expensive rental, the loss would be compensable as a loss in goodwill. (Code of Civil Procedure 1263.510.)

   By staying in the area, the corporation had to pay higher rent (the rent was not shown to be unreasonable). The court held that it would be arbitrary to award compensation in one case and not the other. (Keep in mind that a corporation is a separate legal entity.)

9. **An altered deed in escrow conveys no title because an unauthorized alteration makes it a forged deed.** Because no title passed, the plaintiffs are entitled to recover the property. Escrow, though at fault, isn't liable for property not intended to be conveyed, because it was not conveyed.

10. **The court held that compensation is not limited to real property and the owner was entitled to just compensation for taking of her property as a constitutional right.** Compensable losses in eminent domain do not ordinarily include compensation for personal property, as personal property can be moved. This was not the case here. (There were about 400 cars, which if relocated would be worth approximately $300,000, but were worth only $50,000 as they sat.)

11. **While the conveyance was not void, it only transferred one-half of the property.** It severed the joint tenancy; however, the forged signature transferred nothing.

12. **The court held that a resulting trust arises when title is taken by one person but consideration is paid by another.** The son tried to defend, claiming any agreement to purchase for his parents would have been an illegal contract and, therefore, void and unenforce-

able. The court held he was primarily at fault and to apply the pari delicto rule would unjustly enrich him. (Parties who are equally at fault may not recover under an illegal contract.)

13. **Court ruled the sale did not cause ademption (revocation or failure of a specific legacy in a will by disposal of the asset before death). Because the decedent owned the asset at the time of death, the specific legacy would stand.** If the sale had been closed before death, the proceeds would likely go to the residual beneficiary, which in this case was a charity.

14. **The court held that to comply with the restrictions in the deed by which the property was dedicated to the city, a proposed use must directly contribute to library purposes.** In this case, the use would actually destroy part of the existing library and might have a negative effect on the use as a library.

15. **While the San Diego Superior Court ruled that the taking was not for public use and dismissed the lawsuit, the Court of Appeal reversed.** They held the taking was for a public purpose even though they intended to sell the parcel to B.F. Goodrich. The redevelopment plan was a public purpose, and the agency could use eminent domain to accomplish that purpose even though private persons may benefit form the action.

    Note: This case comes to similar conclusion as *Kelo v. City of New London* 125 S. Ct. 2655, which is covered in Chapter 1. Proposition 99 was passed to prevent the use of eminent domain to gain property for private use.

■ CHAPTER 10 REAL PROPERTY SECURITY DEVICES

1. **While the mortgagee can obtain a deficiency judgment against the husband, the mortgagee has lost all rights in the property.** (In this case, the mortgagee apparently bid less than the value of the property to try for a greater deficiency amount and was hoisted on his own petard.) The grant deed from the husband after the foreclosure sale transferred only the husband's right of redemption. The redemption by the wife was free of the creditors' deficiency claim because the redemption was by a person other than the judgment

creditor. A mortgagee who underbids does so at the mortgagee's own peril. In this case, the property was the separate property of the husband.

2. **When the grantor of the trust deed gave the trust deed, she warranted that she had title. She cannot now claim defense of a first trust deed foreclosure that would be a denial of her title.** Court held that she was estopped from raising the foreclosure as a defense. The lien that was wiped out by a prior lien foreclosure was revitalized by a subsequent purchase. The Civil Code provides subsequently acquired property inures to the mortgagee (beneficiary). The court held that the code applied.

3. **The court held that the assignment to the mortgagor of the mortgagor's note and mortgage extinguished the mortgage by merger. A subsequent assignment could not revive a mortgage that no longer was in existence, so it could not be foreclosed.** The results allow the mortgagor to profit by the improper assignment. Perhaps the plaintiff should have brought action in equity for the return of the consideration or in reformation to get the proper mortgage and note for which he had bargained.

4. **Foreclosure on the purchase money trust deed eliminated the lien as to the second trust deed, as well as the subsequent loan by the first trust deed beneficiary.** (The additional loan was not a purchase money loan, so the trustor could be held personally obligated for the advance.)

5. **In this case, Miller and several strawmen were convicted of defrauding federally insured lenders.** The strawmen represented that they were purchasing the property for a high price, had paid a down payment, and intended to live on the property. While this was a federal case, the defendant could likely have been held liable under state law because he apparently took unconscionable advantage of owners in default.

6. **The court held that a late charge percentage that is a percentage of the unpaid balance is punitive and invalid and is not liquidated damages.** Late charges are customarily liquidated damages amounts agreed to in advance as to be the reasonable damages for paying late. In this case, the defendant failed to make a reasonable

endeavor to estimate fair compensation. The court indicated that a late charge calculated as a percentage of a delinquent installment might be treated differently.

7. **The court will not allow the remedy of specific performance where consideration is not just and reasonable.** The contract for sale was not just and reasonable because the subordination clause gave the sellers no security other than the purchaser's good faith.

8. **The estate, not the mortgagee, is entitled to the proceeds from crops.** If the mortgage does not provide that the mortgagee has rights in rent or crops, then the mortgagee has no rights prior to foreclosure (no assignment of rights to rents or crops in the event of foreclosure).

9. **Calling a loan a sale with an option to repurchase does not protect the transaction from the usury laws.**

10. **Court held that the usury exemption did not apply, as the loan to the broker was not "made or arranged by a broker" in the conventional sense.**

11. **The court determined that since statutory procedures were followed, the sale is presumed to be valid and there were no grounds for attacking the validity of the sale.** (Value was estimated at four times the sale price.)

12. **The defendant was not liable.** The court held that this unilateral mistake by Cal Fed did not result in unjust enrichment. The borrowers had no knowledge of Cal Fed's mistake. If Cal Fed had not agreed to waive the prepayment penalty, the refinancing would not have taken place. The court held that recovery by Cal Fed would not be equitable.

13. **While the San Diego County Superior Court ruled that California's anti-deficiency judgment statute barred a deficiency judgment, as it was a purchase money loan, the Court of Appeal reversed holding that CCP580b does not apply as this was not a purchase-money mortgage** (this was a lien on a property owned for three years prior to giving the lien).

14. **The trial court awarded the bank $358,000 property taxes and $8,333,333.33 in punitive damages. The Court of Appeal**

affirmed the award. They held that the borrower's failure to pay real estate taxes constituted bad faith waste justifying the punitive damages. The court noted that the owners had received $1.7 million from the property while the taxes remained delinquent. They pointed out that failure to pay taxes on a nonrecourse loan is a form of "milking" the property.

15. **The court ruled a clerical error setting the minimum bid is not grounds to set a sale aside.** A properly conducted sale is a final adjudication of rights of the borrower and lender. Inadequacy is not sufficient to set aside a sale. Note: The loan servicer would be liable for $90,000 in negligence damages.

16. The lender intended to return the check to the insurer; however, the buyer at the sheriff's sale claimed entitlement to the insurance proceeds to cover the property damage. **The trial court ruled that the insurance proceeds should be returned to the insurer, saying there was no privity of contract between the buyer and the insurer and so the buyer had no claim as to insurance proceeds. The Court of Appeal affirmed,** pointing out that a fire insurance policy does not run with the property. Note: By delaying paying a claim on a property in foreclosure, the insurer could be relieved of obligation of the sale proceeds payoff.

■ CHAPTER 11   INVOLUNTARY LIENS AND HOMESTEADS

1. **The building corporation hoped to assert its mechanics' liens against the property to defeat junior encumbrances** (they had given trust deeds to a lender who was now foreclosing). **The court held that a person who otherwise would have a mechanic's lien would lose it if it were against its alter ego.** Because the lumber company and building corporation were the same entity, they could have no lien against themselves and could not foreclose.

2. **The property was protected against mechanics' liens by the notice of nonresponsibility.** If an owner compels a tenant to make improvements to enhance the value of the premises, the lessor is considered a participant in lessee's contracts, and mechanics' liens would attach to the property even if the lessor filed a notice of

nonresponsibility. In this case, alterations were not contemplated at the time the lease was signed, and the owner specifically declined to participate in the expenses.

3. **Broker is entitled to foreclose on his mechanic's lien.** There is no requirement the provider of equipment be the owner of that equipment.

4. **Action to foreclose a mechanics' lien should not depend upon the amount of money secured by that lien.** In this case, the action was to foreclose a $97.50 mechanics' lien. The court found that the true amount due was $60, and the defendant had made a proper tender to pay $60. Court also held that an unintentional excessive claim did not invalidate the mechanic's lien. Note: Refusal of proper tender would, however, cause the lien to be lost.

5. **Yes, in order to be protected against a lien, a notice of nonresponsibility must have been filed.**

6. **The attachment did not give the creditor priority over the declaration of homestead.** The statute (Civil Code 1241) provides that homesteads do not take priority over prior recorded encumbrances. The previous statute had used the word "mortgages." The court held that the word "encumbrances" as used meant mortgages and trust deeds.

7. **The contractor had no right to a lien unless he had either completed the contract or the completion had been waived or excused.** Courts in later cases have held that minor irregularities do not defeat lien rights; they could, however, affect the amount of the claim.

8. **The court allowed the trustee in bankruptcy to set aside the conveyance as a fraud on the creditors.** If the bankrupt owner had not conveyed the property, she would have been protected up to the amount of her homestead exemption. In this case, the court held that her conveyance to her daughter was an abandonment of her homestead rights, and her homestead was lost.(This California case was tried in federal court because it involved the trustee in bankruptcy.)

9. **Court held that absence from the state tolled the Statute of Limitations. Execution of the judgment was allowed.** The court also held that a court could allow execution of a judgment after 10 years if the creditor exercised due care to collect within the 10-year period and was reasonable in concluding that execution was wasteful.

10. **No, the court held that placing markers and stakes were devises to assist the engineering company in preparing its plans, and it was not the start of site improvements.**

11. **The Court of Appeal affirmed.** While it results in an unfair result, the court felt that public policy demands that unlicensed contractors not be paid for material or services.

■ CHAPTER 12 ADJACENT PROPERTY RIGHTS

1. **The servient tenement may designate a suitable route.** Where the servient tenement fails to do so, the owner of the dominant tenement may designate it. (If the parties cannot agree on the location of an easement, a court of equity will, in an appropriate action, locate the easement.)

2. **The Court of Appeals held that if the lease did not authorize the disposal of hazardous waste on the property, a trespass action was proper. A nuisance can be a direct injury to the plaintiff's land as well as injury caused to adjacent land.** The defendant could be held liable even though he was no longer in possession. As to trespass, the lease did not give the tenant unrestricted possession of the property. Because both the trespass and nuisance were of a continuing nature, they were not barred by the statute of limitations.

3. **The court held that a reasonable use of land is not an infringement on rights of others.** (This changed the common law rule of strict liability.) The court held that reasonableness of a person's actions must be weighed against foreseeability of resulting harm. The question is: does the utility of land use outweigh the gravity of the resulting harm? The case was remanded back to the trial court with instructions to decide based upon the views of reasonableness.

4. **The statement in the easement was held not to be an agreement to rebuild.**

5. **Trees that sit on the boundary line and form the boundary are owned by the owners as tenants in common. Neither owner is at liberty to cut them down.** Cutting the trees for firewood is not a legitimate enjoyment by a tenant in common.

6. **In the absence of a statute or ordinance, an owner owes no duty to the neighbors to prevent seeds from naturally growing weeds on the owner's land from maturing and being blown by wind onto the neighbor's land.**

7. **The court held that a possessor is liable for ordinary care in managing her property and must act on both dangerous, artificial, and natural conditions.** (Ownership of hillside property can now carry with it extensive financial liability.) The defendant claimed no liability under the common law rule that a landowner is not liable for injuries caused by the natural conditions of the property. The trial court agreed. The California Supreme Court changed the common law rule and held that a landowner is no longer immune from losses suffered because of the natural conditions of the property.

8. **The court held that an upper landowner who collects surface water and discharges the water into a natural watercourse is not liable to the lower landowner for damages resulting from increased volume.** (This decision seems to agree with reasonable use doctrine of *Keys v. Romley*.)

9. **The court held that the use for the period of time without landowner interference is presumptive evidence of an easement by prescription.** In this case, Bel Air formerly owned the land, and it was a case of a grantor getting prescriptive easement rights against a grantee.

10. **The court determined, in this case, the plaintiff had a prescriptive easement.** While definite routes must be established to create an easement by prescription, slight deviations are permitted.

11. **Treating the ditch with gunite was held to be beyond the easement holder's right to repair. It enlarged the easement by altering**

the easement use. The servient owner was entitled to the benefits running with the easement including the vegetation that flourished from the easement use. Court held that the scope of the easement is fixed by the location, character, and use in existence at the time the land became subject to the easement.

12. **The English doctrine of "Ancient Lights" does not apply to this country.** A property owner does not have the right to prevent his neighbor from building as sees fit on own land, provided it is not a nuisance.

13. **The court held that this was a permanent nuisance/trespass, and the statute of limitations began at the time of original entry and had expired [CCP 338(b)].**

14. **The Court of Appeals dismissed the case on the grounds of insufficient personal injury in the absence of proof that electrical and magnetic fields cause harm.** The Supreme Court pointed out that the Public Utilities Commission (PUC) has exclusive jurisdiction, so homeowners cannot bring private nuisance or negligent actions against utilities. Note: The homeowner is apparently without recourse if high capacity transmission lines are placed on existing easements adjacent to the homeowner's property even though it would negatively affect value and possibly pose a threat to health.

15. **The wall may remain.** The court indicated that even though the oral agreement lacked the requirements of an easement, it was at least a license. When a party has made substantial expenditures in reliance on the license, the license acts as an easement, and the grantor and the grantor's successors are estopped from revoking it.

16. **The Court of Appeal upheld Quinone's right to remove the cacti but held that Quinone must pay the plaintiff's costs that were precipitated by the trespass.** Tremper had sued for quiet title, trespass, nuisance, and destruction of trees, declaratory relief, and a preliminary and permanent injunction. Quinone cross-complained for quiet title based on the doctrine of agreed boundaries and for relief as a good faith improver. The Superior Court denied relief under agreed boundaries (the true boundary was ascertainable) but found that Quinone was a good-faith improver of his neighbor's land and had the legal right to remove the cacti.

17. The court expanded the easement right to use the land of another to the taking of water by prescriptive use.

■ CHAPTER 13 LAND-USE CONTROLS

1. **The owner was entitled to compensation for taking of his property.** The court held that rezoning was the improper use of police power. It was the substitution of police power when eminent domain should have been used. (The action might have been proper if the rezoning was warranted under police power. In this case, the court determined that the purpose of rezoning was to gain public use without compensation.)

2. **Court held that downzoning is neither invalid nor is it inverse condemnation.** It is a proper regulation of land use. Court also pointed out that an aggrieved party must exhaust the administrative remedies provided before the party can resort to the courts.

3. **For the court to set aside the zoning, it must clearly be arbitrary, which was not the case in this instance.** The validity of zoning is not whether a judge would have made a different decision if the judge had the power to decide on the policies. Court held that aesthetics are relevant to zoning.

4. **Adaptability and suitability of property for business use is not the controlling factor in determining the validity of a zoning ordinance.** The fact that prior zoning granted exceptions in similar cases does not give an owner a vested right to an exception. A city placing a time limit commensurate with the investment involved, its character, age, and other relevant factors for removal, is not a taking of property. Damages suffered by loss in value by exercise of police power is merely one of the prices individuals must pay as members of society.

5. **This is a case of changed conditions. The court held it would be oppressive and inequitable to give effect to the covenant.** Enforcement would not have an effect other than to injure or harass the owners without affecting the purpose for which it was intended.

6. **Court held that a plan to contain an operation looking forward to the entire elimination of a nonconforming use was a recognized zoning objective.** (Nonconforming use does not have a vested right to expand scope of operations.)

7. **Requiring dedication for development is a reasonable exercise of police power.** A general plan showing street extension was not a taking of property.

8. **While the trial court held that zoning was arbitrary and the city was also estopped from rezoning, the Court of Appeal, however, held that because the city had a basis for rezoning, it was not arbitrary. They held that the public good was greater than an individual injustice.** The court also stated that the city had never promised how long they would keep the zoning. (While this case upholds the power of zoning, in its application it arrives at a result that does not appear equitable.)

9. **Because Krater's plan provided for continued housing for the special classes of tenants until relocation was possible, the city was not justified in refusing the conversion.** The ordinance did not justify rejection of a condominium conversion because of a low vacancy factor.

10. **If an ordinance completely barred adult bookstores it might not be upheld, but this was simply a reasonable regulation.** Court held that the burden of establishing unreasonableness was on the plaintiff. The court rejected an argument of the plaintiff that the zoning was an invalid restraint on speech.

11. **The zoning was held to be invalid.** The California Supreme Court held that people have the right of privacy, which includes the right to live with whomever they choose. They held that this statute violates that right of privacy. The court noted that the size of related families was not limited, but the limitation only applies to unrelated families.

12. **The court held that the residential care facility was not inconsistent with residential use and must be allowed by law.** (Six or fewer clients would be consistent with single-family use.)

13. **Yes, the California Supreme Court held that the growth control ordinance did not violate Pardee's vested right to complete the development; it only affected the timing.**

14. **The Court of Appeal affirmed a trial court decision that the restriction was unenforceable because it was unreasonable.** The court pointed out that the truck was not aesthetically unpleasant to a reasonable person, and pickup trucks are the convertibles of today and are socially acceptable.

15. **The court held that injuries to the plaintiff were foreseeable and actions of the association may have been a breach of duty to the plaintiff.** The court also held that a director may be personally liable for an organization's tort if the director authorized or participated in the tort. In this case, the facts were such to sufficiently allege the director's participation in tortious conduct.

    Because of the danger of director's liability, CC1365.7 was enacted, which places monetary limits on the liability of volunteer directors and officers of common interest developments. By carrying liability insurance up to these amounts, they are now protected unless they failed to act in good faith or were willfully or grossly negligent.

16. **The court held that in this case that restrictions were reasonable and that condominium owners can subject themselves to reasonable restrictions for the good of all.** The Court of Appeal held that CC&Rs are equitable servitudes that are enforceable unless they are unreasonable restraints on alienation (Civil Code 711).

17. **The Court of Appeal held that the use ordinance was valid under the police power for public welfare.** It did not infringe on owner's constitutional right of due process and was not vague. Note: This was the first California decision upholding a residential rental limitation.

18. **The Superior Court, which was affirmed by the Court of Appeal, ruled that the ordinance violated the equal-protection clause of the California Constitution.** Over- occupancy can also apply to homeowners, and the city can only validly address population density by an ordinance applying to all residents, not just renters.

19. **The U.S. District Court held that a permanent injunction against enforcement of the ordinance was proper because the conversion ordinance was a taking.** Even though the ordinance did not deny owners of all productive use, it interfered with an owner's basic right to use.

20. **An injunction should not be granted.** The court pointed out that while Health and Safety Code treats a residential facility for six or fewer persons as a residential use, the statute was clear that it did could not be used to allow the use in this case. However, the California Fair Employment and Housing Act makes it illegal to discriminate against persons with disabilities. A disability is an impairment that limits one or more life activities. The court also pointed out that the federal government also prohibits the use of restrictive covenants to discriminate against people with disabilities in group homes.

21. **The Court of Appeal held that the city must refund the $399,000 to the owner plus pay $1,199,237 for lost income and profits.** The unreasonable delay in issuing the building permit was a temporary taking, and the owner was entitled to compensation for the period of time that the use of the land was taken. The court cited the U.S. Supreme Court decision of *First English Evangelical Church v. County of Los Angeles*. Note: Under the Ellis Act (Chapter 15), the owner has the right to go out of business.

22. **The Superior Court ruled, "The restoration ordinance is a valid exercise of the city's police power . . ." The Court of Appeal affirmed that it was not a taking since the ordinance requires the applicant to pay.** Note: This was the second Appellate Court decision to uphold view protection ordinances.

23. **Design review cannot be used to exclude chain stores.** The Friends of Davis sought to compel the city to rescind development approval for a Borders Bookstore and force the city to use its design approval ordinance to keep out chain stores. The Appellate Court denied relief, noting local police power relates to health, safety, morals, and general welfare, not selection of specific tenants. (The Friends of Davis had sought to keep out competition for local bookstores.)

24. **The Superior Court jury ruled that the unrecorded fence regulation was enforceable and granted the injunction plus $318,293 in attorney fees. The Court of Appeal affirmed, noting that the enforcement procedure was fair, in good faith, and applied uniformly.**

■ CHAPTER 14   ESCROWS AND TITLE INSURANCE

1. **Seller can get quiet title, in which case buyer can recover the purchase money paid to the seller.** Of course, escrow would be liable for losses and costs caused by their negligence. [See *Hildebrand v. Beck* (1925) 196 C. 14. Escrow made unauthorized delivery of deed. The deed was held to be void and convey nothing.]

2. **Court held that the escrow had no duty to real estate broker.** There would only have been a duty if there had been an assignment of the money. Without a notice of assignment, escrow must obey its principals. If escrow had failed to follow the direction of the seller, then escrow could have been liable for any resulting loss.

   In this case, there was no evidence that the escrow knew of the contract, and even if they had known, the contract did not require payment out of escrow. Payment could still have been made outside of escrow.

3. **Without signed instructions, failure to deposit a check in excess of the instructions was not considered negligence.**

4. **Court held that no liability attaches to escrow holder for failure to do something not required by terms of the escrow, or for loss incurred while obediently following escrow instructions.** (Agency of an escrow is limited to specified duties.)

5. **Court held that the defendant was not liable as the defendant had not acted negligently or failed to obey instructions.** (Neutral escrows do not always offer advantages over formal closing where both parties are represented by attorneys.)

6. **While the lender was negligent in paying off the trust deed outside escrow, the escrow was liable for the loss.** Their affirmative act in recording Deed of Reconveyance violated the instructions and allowed the fraud to be perpetrated. In this case, instructions were verbal. Escrow instructions do not always have to be written to bind escrow.

7. **Because there was no contract between plaintiff and insurer, plaintiff has no rights based on breach of contract.** (Also, a pre-

liminary title report does not create any liability if insurance is not obtained.) Warrington was a stranger to the transaction in which the report was prepared and, therefore, was outside the scope of the insurer's liability.

8. **When an insurance company fails to defend the title, even though in good faith the company believes the title is not covered, it does so at its peril. If a court determines the claim was covered, the insurance company is liable to the full claim, even if it is in excess of its policy limits.** (The claim could probably have been settled within policy limits if the insurance company had acted in insured's best interests.)

9. **No negligence was found as the court held the escrow had no duty to warn the seller or give the seller information that equipment should remain fixtures under the trust deed or should be secured by a separate lien.** In this case, the agent represented the buyer. There could be agent liability in failing to disclose dangers in the arrangement.

10. **Where an agent intentionally made itself party to the agreement, the agent is liable for breach of contract.** After the agent agreed to withhold funds, the agent could not unilaterally fail to do so.

11. **Insurer was held liable for the decrease in value.** Court held that the exclusion should be construed as referring to the normal unrecorded water rights (riparian, prescriptive, or prior appropriation.) Court held that an ambiguity about coverage should be construed against the insurer in favor of the weaker party.

12. **Escrow was negligent to hold an undeposited check without notifying seller. The court held that escrow had the same liability as if they had been holding cash.** By giving a check that was not to be deposited, the buyer was able to tie up the property without cash. (If the seller was entitled to the deposit, escrow would have to turn over the cash.)

■ CHAPTER 15 LANDLORD/TENANT LAW

1. **Civil Code 1942.5 should not be literally construed as to retaliatory eviction. The court held that, even though not specifically**

covered by statute, common law rights to protect against retaliatory eviction still exist in California, and this eviction was retaliatory. While CC1942.5 does not cover a situation such as this, the reasons given for retaliatory eviction are concerned with the tenant asserting rights to the property, not attacks on persons. The state's interests in encouraging reporting of crime, particularly sexual assaults on children, outweigh the state's interests in preserving the summary nature of unlawful detainer action.

2. **While CC1668 holds that exculpatory clauses exempting people from their own negligence are against public policy, the court held that this does not really apply to this case.** There is no public policy that prohibits a lessee from assuming a risk from the lessor.

3. **The California Supreme Court held that a breach of implied warranty of habitability was a proper defense.** The common law rule that a landlord has no duty to maintain the premises no longer exists.

    The duty to pay rent is mutually dependent upon fulfillment of implied warranty of habitability. Habitability does not mean the premises must be perfect; it means bare living requirements must be maintained. Substantial compliance with building and housing code standards materially affecting health and safety would, in most cases, suffice to meet the landlord's obligation.

4. **There are no questions as to the defendants being liable for compensatory damages.** They knew of a danger and intentionally concealed it. **To collect punitive damages, the plaintiff must prove the defendant acted with conspicuous disregard to the plaintiff's safety.** The facts alleged were sufficient to support a claim for punitive damages as well as compensatory damages.

5. **The Court of Appeal ruled for the landlord and held that the base rent should have been adjusted to prevailing rents for comparable units.** (The court did not want to penalize a landlord for having charged below-market rents.)

6. **The court ruled that the renewal rent should be based on the particular purpose for which the premises had been leased and not the rental value of another use.**

7. **Once representations were made as to security, there was a duty to maintain security. If the tenant and owners' association mis-**

represented the security, it could be held liable. Some property owners' groups advise their members not to advertise security as it could be a warranty and expose them to liability.

8. **While the police may have believed the owner had authority to authorize a warrantless search, the court pointed out that a landlord lacks authority to consent to police entry absent any evidence of abandonment or eviction.** In this case, the tenancy had not expired, and the owner believed the tenant to still be in possession.

9. **The locked doors should have put the purchaser on inquiry as to claim of the lessee.** The burden of inquiry was on the purchaser. Whether the purchaser knew of the possession by the lodge is immaterial. It was the purchaser's duty to find out who was in possession and ascertain their interests. Because the purchaser had constructive notice of the tenant's interest, the purchaser is bound by the lease. (Modern courts would likely provide a buyer a remedy against the seller in a case such as this because of the failure to disclose the lease.)

10. **The court held that agreement to maintain the landscaping does not release the owner from liability.** The duty of care of an owner in possession is to inspect the property's condition. The same principle applies to owners not in possession.

11. **Approval of the final map was not held to be an exemption from the ordinance,** even though approval was prior to the ordinance because at the time of the ordinance the structure was still rental housing.

12. **The Court of Appeal, while agreeing that the plaintiff's act was without conscience, held that the automatic assessment for the entire 60-day period was constitutionally excessive. The Supreme Court, however, held that the evidence supported the court award.** They pointed out the rent received in the month the gas bill was not paid was over twice the gas bill. Utilities were cut off during cold weather, and seven of the tenants forced to live without heat were children. The court indicated the statutory $100 per day applies per unit, not per tenant. (This was also the trial court's interpretation.)

13. **The court held that while Proposition 13 did not include relief for renters, such relief was consistent with the initiative.** The court further held that the one-year reduction was not a substantial impairment of contract.

14. **The Superior Court held that there was no causal nexus between the plaintiff's injury and failure to light the garage. The Court of Appeals affirmed and held that a landlord is not liable for criminal acts of third persons off the premises.** Note: The landlord might be liable if the plaintiff had been robbed and shot next to her garage, but since she avoided the danger, the landlord escapes liability.

15. **The eviction was held to be proper because the parents were responsible for illegal conduct on the premises even though they did not know of the drugs.** Note: Use of such a clause gives landlords a powerful tool that can also serve as a deterrent to drug use.

16. **The trial court found that the excess was in fact a security deposit.** The trial court also refused to allow Islay to offset damages for return of deposits because Islay failed to make an accounting, and the court awarded attorney fees of 25 percent of the aggregate amount. The Court of Appeals affirmed all issues except offsets. (Penalties and interest were not awarded since the court had not found that Islay acted in bad faith.) The aggregate of claims in this class action exceeded $1,000,000. This case was an attempt to get around the *Baumann v. Islay* (1973) 30 C.A. 3d 752 decision, but it backfired.

17. **The court held that the condition for lease approval was unconscionable.** Civil Code 1995.240 allows only reasonable consideration for a lease assignment. Note: The lease could have set forth a sharing of excess rent agreement.

18. **The court ruled that the ban on subleasing was unreasonable and therefore unenforceable.** While park rules can be changed without homeowner consent upon a six-month written notice, unreasonable restrictions will not be enforced.

19. **The Court of Appeal reversed the Los Angeles Superior Court, ruling that the trial court erred in ruling that defendants had no duty to assure that a minor child would not fall out of a low, open**

window (window was kept open). **The court held that a landlord must exercise due care for residents' safety in areas under the landlord's control.** The defendants had moved for summary judgment arguing they had no duty to assure a child did not fall out of a window. The Los Angeles County Superior Court granted summary judgment for the owners and managers.

The Court of Appeal ruled that summary judgment was not proper and there was a triable issue as to whether the defendants breached their duty of care by maintaining a low, open, unprotected hallway window knowing that young children were likely to play there.

20. **The court awarded the tenants $89,000 for personal property plus $12,432 in court costs.** The court held that the landlord's duty to provide habitable premises is independent of the tenant's duty to pay rent.

21. **The park was held liable.** The court noted that Civil Code Sections 798.55 and 798.56 authorized the mobile home park owners to obtain an injunction or terminate a tenancy for a resident that constitutes a substantial annoyance to other homeowners or residents. The court stated, "The perpetrator of the interference with the tenants' quiet enjoyment need not be the landlord personally. There may be an actionable breach where the interference is caused by a neighbor or tenant claiming under the landlord." This case seems to require a reasonable response by a landlord to tenant complaints. In this case, it was approximately 50 calls to management of splashing mud on newly washed vehicles, aiming a video camera into a living room, racial epithets, other verbal abuse, forcing a vehicle off the road, and finally battery.

22. **There was no unconstitutional taking of property.** The landlords did not have to place their security deposits into special accounts. They could use the deposits as working capital or other investments. Note: This case was brought by property owners who were not subject to the trust fund requirements of the real estate law. If it had been brought by a property management firm, then the reasoning of the court would not hold up.

23. **The court ruled that there was no successor to the Bank of Irvine lease, so the clause could not be enforced. The court set the fair rent.**

GLOSSARY

For a more comprehensive explanation of legal terms, you may want to use *The Language of Real Estate* by John W. Riley (Dearborn Publishing).

abatement An action to remove a nuisance.

abstract of judgment A statement from the court of the judgment. When recorded, it becomes a general lien on all of the debtor's property in the county where recorded.

abstract of title A copy of all recorded documents dealing with a property. Attorneys give title opinions based on abstracts.

acceleration upon default All payments become due upon default of any payment. For trust deeds and mortgages in California, the debtor still can cure the default prior to foreclosure or sale by getting payments caught up and paying the costs.

accord and satisfaction An agreement to accept a lesser consideration than bargained for based on disagreement over performance.

accretion The gradual buildup of land by natural causes (generally by action of water).

acknowledgment A statement made before a notary or court officer that the signing of a document was the signer's own free act.

actual notice Notice that has been expressly given and is known to a party.

ademption The revocation of a specific property grant in a will by disposing of said property prior to death.

administrative agency A government agency that makes rules and regulations to carry out the law.

Administrative Procedure Act A procedural act that must be complied with prior to revocation, suspension, or denial of a real estate license.

administrator A person appointed by the court to administer the estate of a deceased person.

ad valorem taxes Taxes based on value, such as property taxes.

advance costs Advance payments made to an agent to cover expected cash outlays in carrying out the agency.

advance fee A fee for rental information accepted in advance, or a promotional fee for a sale listing.

advance fee addendum An agreement specifying activities for which the agent is to be compensated. It would include a provision for an advance payment of fees.

adverse possession A method to acquire title. It requires five-year, open, notorious, uninterrupted use under some claim of right and the payment of taxes.

aesthetic zoning Zoning for beauty. (Aesthetic zoning can require architectural styles and colors and regulate signs, etc.)

affirmation A formal declaration of the truthfulness of a statement, given in lieu of a verification.

affirmative covenant A covenant under which an owner is required to do something, such as build within a stated period of time.

affirmative easement Easement that gives the dominant tenement owner the right to use the servient tenement.

after-acquired title Title or interest acquired by the grantor after property has been conveyed.

agency Legal relationship under which an agent represents another (a principal) in dealings with third parties.

agency by estoppel An agency created when a principal's conduct led another to believe in the existence of the agency and thereby to act to his or her detriment.

agency by ratification An agency created by a principal's approving an unauthorized act of another.

agency coupled with an interest Agency in which an agent has a financial interest in the subject matter of the agency.

agent One who represents another in an agency relationship.

Alquist-Priolo Special Studies Zone Act Provides for project approval in close proximity to earthquake faults, as well as disclosures to buyers.

alteration A change made to a note or contract by one of the parties without the consent of the other.

amendments to the escrow instructions Changes in the escrow instructions, which require the agreement of both the buyer and the seller.

American Land Title Association (ALTA) The association that developed an extended-coverage policy of title insurance for lenders (same coverage available to buyers).

Americans with Disabilities Act Prohibits discrimination in a place of public accommodation based on an individual's physical or mental disabilities.

amortized note A note that will liquidate itself over its term in equal installments.

annual percentage yield (APY) Annual yield on investments considering the compounding of interest earned.

antimerger clause A clause in a mortgage or trust deed that the senior lienholder will retain lien priority in the event of a merger (title given to the senior lienholder).

anticipatory breach Act of a party that can be treated as a breach of contract because it makes performance by that party impossible.

appurtenance Something that belongs to and goes with property (examples are a structure and easement rights).

arbitration Nonjudicial process for resolution of disputes either by agreement or mandated by law.

Article 5 Part of the Business and Professions Code governing transactions in trust deeds and real property sales contracts.

Article 7 Part of the Business and Professions Code covering loan costs, commissions, and payment requirements relating to loan brokerage activity.

"as is" A phrase used in sale contracts by sellers as an attempt to limit liability for the condition of the premises (not generally valid when applied to latent defects known by the seller but not disclosed to the buyer).

assignment Transfer of all interest in a contract or lease.

assignment of contract Transfer of all rights under a contract to a third party. Assignor remains secondarily liability.

assignment of lease The transfer of all rights under a lease by a lessee to a third party, who becomes a tenant of the lessor. The assignee is primarily liable under the lease, while the assignor has secondary liability.

assignment of rent Owner assigns right to collect rent to another. Usually given to a lienholder when owner is delinquent in loan payments.

assumable loan A loan that can be taken over (assumed) by a purchaser. Such a loan would not have a due-on-sale clause.

assuming a loan The buyer's agreeing to be primarily liable on the loan while the seller has secondary liability.

attachment A prejudgment lien that can be obtained to ensure the availability of property for execution after a judgment is obtained.

attorney-in-fact A person appointed as an agent under a power of attorney.

attractive nuisance doctrine An owner has a duty to reasonably protect children from injury when the premises are likely to attract children.

avulsion The sudden removal of land by action of water, such as a river changing its course.

bait and switch Illegal practice of advertising where a seller will not sell an item at a price advertised or does not have the item to sell in order to bring in buyers for other items.

balloon payment A final payment that is more than twice the amount of the lowest payment.

bankruptcy Federal proceedings to declare a debtor bankrupt. The debtor is relieved of unsecured obligations (secured obligations when security is given up).

beneficiary Lender (or seller) in a trust deed loan situation.

beneficiary statement Statement by beneficiary as to balance due on loan.

bequest Personal property transferred by will.

bilateral contract A mutual exchange of promises; a promise given for a promise.

blanket encumbrance A mortgage or trust deed covering more than one property.

blind ad An advertisement that fails to reveal that the advertiser is an agent and not a principal.

blockbusting Inducing panic selling based on fear of the entry of persons of another race, color, religion, or ancestry into the area.

breach of contract Failure to comply with a material term or provision of a contract.

broker Licensed real estate agent who can deal directly with principals and employ licensed real estate salespersons.

broker's loan statement A disclosure statement given to borrowers by mortgage loan brokers that provides information on all costs, fees, and loan terms.

Bulk Sales Act An act that requires recording and publication of a sale not in the normal course of business.

bulk zoning Zoning for density with open-space requirements as well as setback, parking, and height restrictions.

bundle of rights All beneficial rights that go with ownership of real property.

burden of proof The party required to prove a fact when an issue is in dispute.

business opportunity A business including fixtures, stock in trade, and goodwill.

buyer listing An agreement whereby a buyer agrees to pay a commission if the broker locates a property the buyer purchases.

California Environmental Quality Act Law that allows local government to require environmental impact reports and allows private citizens to challenge a project if they feel proper procedures were not taken or a report is not complete.

California Fair Employment and Housing Opportunity Act California's fair housing act known as the Rumford Act.

California Housing Financial Discrimination Act of 1977 (Holden Act) California act prohibiting lender discrimination for any reason unrelated to the credit of the loan applicant.

carryback financing Financing where the seller is financing the buyer.

Cartwright Act California's antitrust act.

caveat emptor (let the buyer beware) Former rule of law that the buyer was responsible for determining condition of item purchased. It has been superseded by disclosure requirements and anti-fraud legislation.

CERCLA Federal Comprehensive Environmental Response, Compensation and Liability Act dealing with liability of owners, prior owners and polluters of property for clean up costs.

certificate of sale Certificate issued to purchaser at sheriff's sale. (The sheriff's deed is given at the expiration of the redemption period.)

cessation of work A period of 60 days without any work being conducted.

chattels Items of personal property

chattels real A personal property interest in real property, such as a leasehold interest, trust deed, or mortgage.

chose in action A right to demand money or personal property through legal action such as a promissory note.

civil law System of law codified by statutes.

Civil Rights Act of 1866 An act providing that every citizen shall have the same rights as white citizens to inherit, purchase, lease, sell, or hold real and personal property.

Civil Rights Act of 1968 Title VIII of this act is known as the federal Fair Housing Act. The act prohibits discrimination in housing with few exceptions.

clean hands doctrine A person in violation of an agreement will not be able to enforce compliance on another (applies to covenants, conditions, and restrictions).

closing The final performance of a real estate transaction where title is transferred and consideration is given.

Coastal Zone Conservation Act Law that requires permit or exemption to develop land within a coastal zone.

codicil An amendment to a will requiring the same formalities of the will.

color of title An appearance of having title without necessarily having any legal interest.

commercial frustration Performance that is not impossible but is impractical because of an unforeseen occurrence. The nonoccurrence of the act or event was considered an implied condition for the contract, which allows relief from the contractual obligations.

commingling Failure to properly separate property of the agent from property of the principal.

common elements Jointly owned areas in a common interest development for use of all owners.

common interest subdivision Subdivision where areas are owned in common with other owners for mutual use.

common law Law that has evolved based on precedent rather than statutes.

community apartment project An apartment building owned by the tenants in tenancy in common, with each owner having the right to occupy a unit.

community property Property acquired during marriage that is considered, as a matter of law, to be owned equally by the spouses.

community property with right of survivorship Community property where neither spouse can separately will their portion of the community property to another.

compensatory damages Monetary damages to reimburse an injured party for a sustained loss.

competent parties Parties having the legal and mental capacity to contract.

comprehensive zoning A broad plan of zoning over a large area.

concurrent estates More than one estate interest in a property at the same time (such as a leasehold estate in a fee simple ownership).

conditional public report An interim report that allows a subdivider to enter a binding contract prior to issuance of a public report.

conditional-use permit A change in the zoning granted for the best interest of the community, where the zoning contemplated the use based on approval.

condition precedent A condition that must take place before an estate is granted. Provisions in a title that, if breached, could result in forfeiture of interest.

condition subsequent A condition that, if it occurs, results in the reversion of an estate to another.

condominium Separate ownership of the airspace of a unit and common ownership of land and common areas.

condominium conversion The conversion of a property (generally an apartment building) to condominiums.

consideration Value that is given for the promise of another.

constitutional law Law set forth in federal and state constitutions.

constructive eviction An act of the landlord that would be inconsistent with the quiet enjoyment of the tenant or the implied covenant of habitability. The tenant can treat the action of the landlord as being equivalent to eviction and may vacate the premises and be relieved of all future obligations.

constructive notice Notice imputed by law although not necessarily actually known (recording, as well as possession by another provides constructive notice to a purchaser of other interests).

contingent remainder A remainder interest that is not certain but requires something to happen.

continuation statement A statement that when filed continues a financing statement for an additional five years.

contract An enforceable agreement.

contract of adhesion A "take it or leave it" contract that takes unreasonable advantage of the party who did not prepare the instrument.

controlled business arrangement Businesses that are owned or controlled by real estate brokers that the broker refers buyers and sellers to (RESPA requires disclosure).

cooperating broker fee agreement Agreements between brokers as to the commission split should the cooperating broker sell a property listed by the listing broker.

corporation A separate legal entity established under state law. An artificial person.

corporation license Real estate license held by a broker in a corporate capacity as an officer of the corporation.

Costa-Hawkins Rental Housing Act Act that allows a new base rent for rent control property upon change of tenants.

Court of Appeal (California) Primarily appellate jurisdiction from superior court.

Court of Appeals (federal) Appellate jurisdiction from the district courts.

covenants Promises, the breach of which could entitle another party to damages.

covenants, conditions, and restrictions (CC&Rs) Private restrictions created by grantors that run with the land.

Covered Loan Act California act setting forth prohibited predatory lending practices for specified FNMA-conforming loans.

cumulative zoning Zoning that allows more restrictive uses. For example, a lot zoned for a duplex would allow a single-family residence if the zoning were cumulative.

customary authority Authority implied by virtue of an agent's position.

declaration of homestead When recorded, this declaration provides the homeowner a statutory exemption from execution by unsecured creditors.

declaration of restrictions Declaration recorded by a subdivider and incorporated by reference in every deed.

declaratory relief action An action to have a court determine the rights of parties.

dedication The transfer of real property to a public entity without consideration.

deed The transfer instrument for real property.

deed in lieu of foreclosure A deed given by the debtor to his or her creditor to avoid foreclosure.

deed of reconveyance The deed from the trustee to the trustor that is given when the note is paid in full. It returns the title to the trustor.

defeasance clause A clause that cancels the lien on payment of the note.

defeasible estate An estate that can be defeated by some future happening (condition subsequent).

deficiency judgment A judgment given to a creditor when a foreclosure sale is for less than the amount owed (judgment is for deficiency amount).

delivery The actual transfer of an interest. Delivery requires the intent to make an irrevocable transfer.

demise A transfer of a leasehold interest.

demurrer An answer to a complaint stating that even if the alleged facts are as stated, there is no cause of action.

Department of Real Estate Administers the California real estate law (part of the Business, Transportation, and Housing Agency).

devise The transfer of real property by will.

district court Federal court of original jurisdiction.

divisible contract A contract consisting of separate agreements that are not dependent on each other.

division fence A fence on a boundary line.

doctrine of agreed boundaries Parties can agree to boundaries. They are binding on successors after being accepted by the parties for five years.

domestic corporation A corporation organized in California under California law.

dominant tenement The estate having an easement right over land of another.

double taxation Corporate taxation whereby first corporate profits and then stockholders' dividends are taxed.

downzoning A change in zoning to a more restrictive use.

dragnet clause Clause in a trust deed that allows future advance to take precedence over intervening liens.

dual agency An agency situation in which the agent represents more than one party to the transaction.

due care Reasonable (nonnegligent) care.

due diligence A proper good faith effort to perform or investigate.

due-on-encumbrance clause A clause that makes the loan balance all due and payable should the owner put another encumbrance on the property.

due-on-sale clause (alienation clause) A clause that makes the entire loan balance due when the property is sold. A loan having a due-on-sale clause cannot be assumed.

duress Force or confinement that makes a contract voidable.

easement A right the owner of one property has to the land of another.

easement by eminent domain An easement that is taken for a public purpose under the power of eminent domain.

easement by estoppel An easement created when a person's words or actions led another to believe in the existence of the easement. If, in relying on those words or actions, the easement user acts to his or her detriment, the party will be estopped from denying the existence of the easement.

easement by necessity An easement that may be granted by the court when no other access to property exists and the easement is necessary for reasonable use of the property.

easement by prescription An easement obtained through five years' continuous, open, notorious, and hostile use of the property of another under a claim of right.

easement in gross An easement that is not appurtenant to land. It is personal in nature, and there is no dominant tenement.

Education, Research, and Recovery Allocation A fund maintained by 20 percent of license fees; 12 percent of the fund goes into a Recovery Account, and 8 percent goes into the Education and Research Account.

elder abuse law Requires that realty agents and escrow holders report elder financial abuse, or undue influence.

emancipated minor A minor who is allowed to contract (in military service, declared emancipated by a court, married, or formerly married).

emblements The right of a tenant to harvest the annual crops that were the fruit of his or her labor. This right extends beyond the expiration of a lease.

eminent domain The power of the government to take private property for the public good. Consideration must be given for the property taken.

employee One who works under the direction and supervision of an employer.

enabling legislation Legislation that gives cities and counties the right to enact zoning.

encroachment An intrusion into, over, or under the land of another.

endangered species Federal legislation limiting development when it will have a negative effect on an endangered species.

Endangered Species Act (ESA) Federal act that can limit or prohibit development when a development adversely effects a species designated as endangered.

environmental impact report (EIR) A report that can be required under the California Environmental Quality Act when projects may have a significant effect on the environment.

environmental impact statement A statement required under the National Environmental Policy Act when a federal project will affect the environment significantly.

Equal Credit Opportunity Act A federal act prohibiting credit discrimination because of sex, marital status, age, race, religion, or national origin, or because the credit applicant is receiving welfare.

equal dignities rule If an agency act must be in writing, the agency authority to perform the act also must be in writing.

Equal Housing Opportunity Poster Failure of a broker to post this HUD notice shifts the burden of proof to the broker as to a discrimination complaint.

escheat A reversion of property to the state when a person dies without a will or heirs.

escrows Neutral depositories to carry out the closing function of a real estate transaction.

escrow instructions The instructions given to the escrow agent by the buyer and seller.

estate Any interest in property.

estoppel The legal doctrine that a person cannot raise a right or defense after their words or actions to the contrary led another party to act to their detriment.

ethics Morals. The golden rule is considered to be the test of whether an act is ethical.

eviction Removal of a tenant by action of law.

exception in a deed An exclusion of part of the property from a grant.

exclusionary zoning Zoning that excludes stated uses, such as adult entertainment.

exclusive-agency listing A listing whereby the owner can sell the property personally without paying a commission, but if it is sold by any agent, the listing agent is entitled to a commission.

exclusive authorization and right-to-sell listing A listing whereby the agent is entitled to a commission no matter who sells the property, including the owner.

exculpatory clauses Clauses in an agreement that purport to relieve a party of all obligation for his or her acts, or failure to act.

executed contract A contract that has been fully performed.

execution The signing of an instrument.

executor Party appointed by testator to administer their estate.

executory contract A contract that has yet to be performed fully.

exemplary damages (punitive damages) Monetary damages to punish or make an example of a wrongdoer for willful, wrongful conduct.

express agency An agency agreement that is stated either verbally or in writing.

express authority The stated authority of an agent (written or verbal).

express contract A contract in which the terms have been stated either verbally or in writing.

extended-coverage policy of title insurance A policy that includes coverage for rights of parties in possession and claims that a survey would have revealed, as well as other risks.

Fair Credit Reporting Act Provides consumer rights as to knowledge of, and correction to, credit reports.

Fair Housing Amendment Act of 1988 Extends the Civil Rights Act of 1968 to include disability and familial status.

fee simple The highest possible degree of ownership in real property.

Federal Personal Responsibility and Work Opportunity Act Act that denies government benefits to illegal immigrants.

fictitious name A name that does not include the surname of every principal in an enterprise.

fictitious name statute Provides procedure for filing and advertising a fictitious name. When the statute is complied with, the firm can sue and defend a suit under the fictitious name.

fictitious trust deed A trust deed that is recorded for the sole purpose of being referenced in other trust deeds to incorporate its terms.

fiduciary duty The duty of trust and confidence.

final map Under the Subdivision Map Act, the final map is recorded when local approval has been obtained.

financing statement A statement that when filed with the secretary of state becomes a lien on personal property for five years.

finder's fee A fee paid to a nonlicensee for introducing a party.

fixtures Items of personal property that have become so attached to realty as to become real property.

foreclosure Procedure to bar all rights of a debtor in property.

foreign corporation A corporation organized in a state other than California.

forfeiture Loss of a right as punishment for an act or nonperformance of an act.

four-by-fouring The illegal attempt to avoid the Subdivided Lands Law by breaking a parcel into four parcels and having the grantees again break each parcel into four parcels.

franchise The right to engage in a business under a common marketing plan.

Franchise Investment Law A disclosure law administered by the corporation commissioner to protect prospective purchasers of franchises.

fraud An act or omission for the purpose of deceiving another.

freehold estates Fee simple or life estates.

fructus industriales Crops produced by labor and industry.

fructus naturales Products of the land produced by nature alone.

Garn Act Allowed lenders to enforce due-on-sale clauses.

general agent An agent with broad powers for the purpose of conducting a business.

general lien A lien against all of the property of the debtor rather than specific property.

general partner A partner with management responsibility and unlimited liability.

general plan Every city and county is required to develop a general plan of comprehensive zoning for the area.

gift deed A deed given for love and affection.

good faith Conscientious and honest behavior.

good faith estimate Realistic estimate of closing costs by lender. Required by RESPA.

good-faith improver An improver acting honestly under a mistake of fact or law who makes improvements to the land of another.

grandfather clause A provision that exempts present users from a requirement, such as zoning, and allows existing nonconforming uses.

grant deed Most common deed used in California to convey title. The grant deed warrants that the seller has not conveyed title previously and the grantor knows of nothing against the property that has not been disclosed.

granting clause The words of conveyance in a deed.

grantor-grantee index The index of a county recorder that is kept by grantor and grantee names alphabetically.

group boycott An agreement not to do business with a particular party or group (Sherman Act violation).

habitability Reasonably fit for human habitation.

historical designations Buildings that have federal or state historical designations; could be limited as to alterations and/or removal.

hold harmless clauses Clauses that purport to relieve a person of liability for his or her actions.

holder Person having legal possession of a negotiable instrument.

holder in due course A purchaser of a negotiable instrument for value before its due date when the instrument appears proper on its face and the purchaser has no notice of any prior dishonor, defenses of the maker, or defects in title of the transferor.

holdover tenant A tenant who remains in possession after the end of a tenancy for years or after having given notice to vacate.

holographic will A will that is handwritten and signed by the testator.

Homeowner Association (HOA) Governing association of owners required for common interest subdivision.

homestead The residential property for which an owner has recorded a declaration of homestead.

homestead exemption The amount of homestead protection from unsecured creditors. It is $50,000 for single persons, $75,000 for family units, and $150,000 for persons over 65 years of age and persons with physical or mental disabilities unable to work.

hypothecate To use property as security for a loan without giving up possession.

illusory contract Apparent contract that is no contract at all because parties have not agreed to be bound.

implied agency An agency created by the conduct of the parties rather than express agreement.

implied authority Understood (not express) authority that is reasonably necessary to carry out the agency.

implied contract A contract not expressly agreed to but understood by the parties.

implied dedication An implied donation of the property to the government that could result from allowing open government use of private property for five years.

implied easement An easement intended but not expressly provided for.

implied warranty Warranty understood but not stated. For residential leases, the implied warranties are of quiet possession and habitability.

impossibility of performance When required performance is impossible, the contract will be considered void.

impound account An account kept by a lender for taxes and insurance (included in borrower's payments).

incentive zoning Zoning that offers an incentive to developers, such as allowing retail stores on the street level in an area zoned for offices.

inclusionary zoning Zoning that requires developer to include some element, such as a percentage of units for low income housing.

independent contractor A contractor employed for the completion of a task who is not under the supervision or control of his or her employer.

injunction A court order to desist from some activity.

installment note A note that is paid off according to an installment payment schedule.

interim occupancy agreement An agreement that allows the buyer to take possession as a tenant prior to the close of escrow.

intermediate theory (mortgage) Mortgage in which title remains with the mortgagor but automatically transfers to mortgagee in the event the mortgagor defaults.

interpleader action An action brought by a third party (escrow or broker) when two or more parties claim property or money held by the third party. The action forces the parties to litigate their rights.

Interstate Land Sales Full Disclosure Act A disclosure act for subdivisions of 25 or more unimproved residential lots offered for sale in interstate commerce.

intestate succession The succession of property to the heirs when the deceased died without a will.

inverse condemnation An owner's forcing a governmental unit to take property by eminent domain when the government's actions resulted in the owner's inability to use the property.

involuntary liens Liens placed against property by creditors, such as judgments, as opposed to those voluntarily placed against the property by owners.

joint tenancy Undivided ownership by two or more persons with the right of survivorship.

joint ventures Partnerships for particular ventures rather than continuing businesses.

judgment Order of a court as to amount due to plaintiff.

judgment lien A general lien against all property of the debtor in the county where the abstract of judgment is recorded.

junior lien A lien recorded later in time than another lien (senior lien).

jurisdiction The authority of a court to adjudicate a type of lawsuit.

laches Loss of rights because the delay in enforcing them now makes enforcement inequitable.

late charge A lender charge for a late payment.

latent defects Defects that are not apparent by visually checking the property.

lateral support Right of a property owner to have his or her property supported by the adjacent properties.

law Enforceable rules that govern conduct.

lease A tenancy agreement between a landlord (lessor) and a tenant (lessee).

leasehold A lease estate in realty.

lease option A lease whereby the lessee has an option to purchase (or extend the lease).

legacy Money that is transferred by will.

legal capacity Being of legal age.

license A revocable privilege to use the land of another.

lien An encumbrance against real property that can be foreclosed.

lien theory (mortgage) Theory in California that a mortgage conveys lien rights and not title to the mortgagee.

life estates Estates conveyed for the life spans of particular persons.

limited common elements Common areas in a common interest development that are designated for exclusive use of particular owners.

limited liability Liability limited to the extent of a person's investment.

limited liability company A company of one or more principals without personal liability for company actions.

limited partnerships Partnerships having partners who are not active and whose liability is limited to the extent of their investment (limited partners).

Limited Partnership Act That part of the corporation code that provides for limited partnerships.

liquidated damages Damages agreed to, prior to a contractual breach, as the remedy in the event of a default.

lis pendens A notice of a pending lawsuit in which an interest in real property is involved.

littoral rights Rights of a landowner to reasonable use of water from lakes, seas, or oceans (nonflowing water) bordering his or her property.

livery of seisin Early English ceremony of transfer of title by delivery of a symbol of title, such as a key or clod of earth.

loan broker (mortgage loan broker) A broker who solicits borrowers and investors for loans secured by real estate.

loan broker listing A loan broker's contract with a buyer to obtain a loan.

lockbox authorization An owner's authorization that allows the broker to install a lockbox. It includes a warning of danger and recommends that valuables be removed and insurance coverage be considered.

lock-in clause A loan prohibiting prepayment so that the borrower is locked in to all of the interest should he or she wish to repay.

marketable title A defensible title that a reasonably prudent purchaser would accept.

master lease The original lease between the lessor and lessee when the lessee subleases the premises.

maxims of jurisprudence Rules of common law that have been codified into the California Civil Code.

mechanics' liens Statutory liens by improvers of property for labor, material, and equipment.

mediation A nonjudicial process for resolving disputes in which the third-party mediator works with the parties to reach an agreement.

Megan's Law A law requiring public availability of location of sex offenders.

menace Threat of confinement of a person, detention of property, or injury to a person or property. Menace makes a contract voidable at the option of the injured party.

mental capacity Being of sound mind.

merger The joining of a lesser right with a greater right so that the lesser right is lost. When a dominant tenement owner purchases the servient tenement, the easement is lost by merger. An owner would not have an easement over his or her own land.

mineral lease Lease of the right to extract minerals for the lease period (also oil and gas leases).

mineral, oil, and gas (MOG) broker A broker authorized to engage in transactions involving mineral, oil, and gas rights; options; leases; exchanges; and properties.

mineral, oil, and gas (MOG) permit A permit formerly issued to a broker who did not have a mineral, oil, and gas license to engage in a mineral, oil, and gas transaction.

misrepresentation A false statement to induce another to act. Unlike fraud, misrepresentation does not require intent. It makes a contract voidable at the option of the injured party.

mobile home A factory-built housing unit that is transported on its own chassis.

MOG See mineral, oil, and gas broker; mineral, oil, and gas permit.

mortgage A two-party instrument that creates a lien on real estate. The mortgagor (the borrower) gives a lien to the mortgagee (the lender).

mortgagee The lender under a mortgage.

Mortgage Forgiveness Debt Relief Act of 2007 Provides that debt forgiveness will not be taxed as a gain to debtor for principal residence of debtor.

Mortgage Loan Disclosure Statement California disclosure of loan terms by mortgage loan brokers.

mortgage loan originator (MLO) Someone who, for compensation or gain, takes a residential mortgage loan application or offers or negotiates terms of a residential mortgage loan (Title V of P.L. 110-289).

mortgagor The borrower under a mortgage. The mortgagor gives the lien to the mortgagee.

mutual consent The meeting of the minds required for a binding contract.

mutual mistake A mistake by both parties to an agreement. A mutual mistake as to fact allows a mistaken party to void the contract.

National Environmental Policy Act This act requires an environmental impact statement on federal projects that could significantly affect the environment.

Nationwide Mortgage Licensing System and Registry A uniform system for license applications and reporting requirements for all loan originators established by the Conference of State Bank Supervisors and the American Association of Residential Mortgage Regulators.

Natural Hazards Disclosure Statement Indicates if a property is in a special flood hazard area, an area of potential flooding, a very high fire hazard severity zone, a wildlife area that may contain substantial fire risks and hazards, an earthquake fault zone, or a seismic hazard zone.

Natural monument A point or boundary in a metes-and-bounds description that is natural, such as a rock, tree, or river, as opposed to an artificial monument, such as a road, iron stake, wall, etc.

navigable Waters capable of being used for commerce.

negative covenants Promises not to do something, such as a prohibition against any detached garages or sheds.

negative declaration Declaration by developer that a project will not have an adverse effect on the environment.

negative easement An easement that prohibits the servient tenement owner from a use. An example would be a building height restriction so the dominant tenement owner retains a view.

negotiable instruments Written, signed, unconditional promises or orders to pay to bearer or a payee a sum certain in money now or at a definite time in the future.

net listing A listing whereby the agent receives all money received over a net price as his or her commission.

no deal–no commission A listing requiring that escrow actually be closed and title transferred before the agent is entitled to a commission.

nominal damages Damages awarded in a token dollar amount for a wrongful act where no actual loss occurred.

nonconforming uses Existing uses that are not in conformance with the zoning.

noncumulative zoning Zoning that allows only the stated use and not more restrictive uses, as well.

nondisturbance clause An agreement where the mortgagee agrees to honor the tenant's lease in the event that the prior mortgage (trust deed) is foreclosed.

nonfreehold estates Less-than-freehold interests; leasehold estates.

nonresident licensee A licensee who is a resident of a state other than California.

notice of cessation A notice that, when recorded, gives subcontractors 30 days to file their liens and the prime contractor 60 days.

notice of completion A notice that, when recorded, gives subcontractors 30 days to file their liens and the prime contractor 60 days.

notice of default Notice given to interested parties of the default of the trustor.

notice of delinquency Notice requested by junior creditor of delinquency of a priority lien.

notice of nonresponsibility A notice by an owner, or a vendor under a real property sales contract, that the owner will not be liable for work on the property authorized by a tenant or vendee under a real property sales contract. The notice must be recorded and posted in a timely manner to protect the property from mechanics' liens.

novation A substitution of a party to a contract or the substitution of one agreement for another.

nuisance An act that disturbs the use or enjoyment of the property of another.

obligatory advances Advances that the lender is obligated to make to the borrower; e.g., progress payments on a construction loan.

Omnibus Nondiscrimination Act California act that makes every California nondiscrimination act consistent with the California Fair Employment and Housing Act regarding protected groups.

open listings Nonexclusive-right-to-sell listings.

opinions of title Opinions of the marketability of a title given by an attorney based on the abstract of title.

option An irrevocable right given to one party to bind another party to an agreement if the party wishes to do so.

optional advances Advances on a loan that the lender is not obligated to make.

option listing A listing combined with an option of the agent to purchase the property.

order paper A negotiable instrument payable to the order of a named party.

or more clause A clause that allows debtor to increase payments without prepayment penalties.

ostensible agency An agency created by implication when the principal intentionally, or by want of ordinary care, causes a third person to believe another person is the agent of the principal, although no actual agency exists.

parol evidence rule The general rule that verbal evidence cannot be used to modify a clearly written contract.

partial zoning Zoning that does not take into consideration its effect on other areas.

partially amortized loan A loan in which payments fail to liquidate loan by due date, resulting in a final balloon payment.

partition action A legal action to break up a joint ownership.

partnership Two or more persons associated to carry on a business and to share in the profits.

party wall A wall established by agreement for the common benefit of adjacent owners.

patents Original conveyances of land from the government.

patent defects Defects that would be obvious from a reasonable inspection of the property.

per stirpes Inheritance by right of representation. Children share equally in the share their deceased parent would have taken.

periodic tenancy A leasehold interest from period to period that automatically renews itself unless a notice to terminate is given.

permanent trespass A continuing trespass, such as an encroachment.

personal defenses Defenses the maker of an instrument would have against the payee.

personal property Chattels.

planned unit development (PUD) Ownership of the individual unit and land under it by the unit owner, plus common areas owned in common with others.

police power The power of the government to regulate use for health, safety, morals, and general welfare.

power of attorney A written agency agreement whereby a principal appoints an attorney-in-fact as an agent.

predatory lending Unfair and costly lending practices that strip homeowners of their equity and often result in foreclosures.

Preemption Act A federal act that gave purchase preference to occupants of land.

preliminary notice A notice must be given by a lien claimant that the work is subject to a mechanic's lien if a lien is to be obtained. The notice covers work subsequent to the notice and up to 20 days prior to the notice.

preliminary public report Under the Subdivided Lands Law, the preliminary public report can be issued prior to the public report. The preliminary public report allows the subdivider to take reservations but not to sell parcels.

preliminary title report A report of the condition of title given by a title insurer prior to issuance of a title policy. The preliminary title report does not provide any insurance of title.

prepayment penalty Payment penalty for paying an obligation before it is due.

presumption A legal inference, which can be overcome by evidence to the contrary.

principal The employer of an agent for whom the agent acts.

private easement An easement given to specific property or persons.

private nuisance A nuisance that is limited in scope. A private nuisance does not affect the entire community or neighborhood.

privity of contract The relationship between contracting parties.

probate The legal procedure to carry out the wishes of the deceased and pay his or her debts.

procuring cause That cause that initiated an uninterrupted chain of events that led to a sale.

promissory note A two-party instrument whereby a maker unconditionally promises to pay a payee a certain sum of money now or at a definite time in the future.

promotional note A subordinate promissory note on real estate for a term of three years or less issued to finance improvements prior to the first sale (subdivision).

Proposition 99 (Homeowner and Private Property Protection Act) prohibits the taking of private property by eminent domain when the intention is to turn the property over to a private party rather than take it for public use.

publication period The 20-day period prior to a trustee's sale during which the notice of the sale is published.

public easement An easement given to the general public.

public nuisance A use that disturbs the use and enjoyment of an entire neighborhood or community.

public report A disclosure statement required under the Subdivided Lands Law. A purchaser is not obligated until he or she has read the report and signed a receipt.

puffing Statements of opinion (not fact) made to induce a party to contract.

punitive damages See exemplary damages.

pur autre vie A life estate given for the life of someone other than the life tenant.

qualified endorsement An endorsement on a note "without recourse." The endorser will not be liable if the maker dishonors the note.

quasi contract A contract implied by law, as a matter of equity, when no actual contractual agreement took place.

quiet enjoyment An implied warranty that the landlord will not interfere with the tenant's reasonable use and enjoyment of the premises.

quiet title Legal action to determine ownership or rights in real property.

quitclaim deed A deed that conveys whatever interest the grantor has without claiming any specific interest.

race of the diligent Recording priority based on date and time of recording.

ratification Approval of an agreement to which the approving party was not legally bound. By ratification, the party agrees to be bound by the agreement.

real defenses Defenses that could be raised against a holder in due course.

Real Estate Advisory Commission An advisory group consisting of six brokers and four public members that advises the real estate commissioner.

real estate commissioner Executive officer of the Department of Real Estate, who is appointed by the governor.

real estate investment trust (REIT) A trust organized under federal law having at least 100 investors. Ownership interest is in the form of certificates or shares that are freely transferable.

Real Estate Settlement Procedures Act (RESPA) A federal loan disclosure act applicable to federally related first mortgages and trust deeds.

real property Land and those appurtenances that go with the land.

real property sales contract (land contract) Contract whereby seller retains title and the buyer is given possession.

real property securities Securities with guaranteed yields, promotional notes, and designated by Article 6 of the real estate law to be real property securities. (Repealed)

real property securities dealer A broker whose license has been endorsed to sell real property securities.

real property securities dealer statement A disclosure statement issued to purchasers of real property securities.

Realtist A member of the National Association of Real Estate Brokers (NAREB).

Realtor® A member of the National Association of Realtors® (NAR).

rebate law Law that prohibits escrows and title insurers from giving rebates or favorable treatment as consideration for the referral of business.

recording Making an interest public knowledge by recording the interest with a county recorder. Recording provides constructive notice of the interest.

recreational user immunity Immunity of owners for liability to injury to others who enter property for recreational use. It does not apply to failure to warn as to dangerous conditions.

redlining Refusal to loan (or insure) within an area.

reformation A court action to reform a contract to read as it was intended to read.

regulatory law The rules and regulations enacted by government agencies.

relation-back doctrine The doctrine that a buyer's rights relate back to the delivery of the deed into escrow regarding intervening liens of a party who had knowledge or notice of the escrow.

reliction Rights of property owners bordering on lakes or seas to the land increase when the water recedes.

remainder interest An interest that goes to other than the original grantor upon some event, generally the death of a life tenant.

rent control Ordinances that limit the rent a lessor can charge for premises, as well as other lessor rights.

rent skimming Collecting rent and not using it to make mortgage payments or collecting rent on property not owned or controlled by the renter.

request for notification of default A recorded request by a junior lienholder to be informed if the trustor is given a notice of default.

rescission Setting a contract aside and returning the consideration given.

reservation in a deed The retention of a right, such as an easement, in the grantor.

respondeat superior The doctrine that the master is liable for the acts of his or her servants (applies to agency and employment relationships).

restraint against alienation A restriction on the power to convey property.

restricted license Probationary real estate license granted after a license was revoked, suspended, or denied.

retaliatory evictions Evictions because of a tenant's complaints to landlord or a public agency about defects or for lawfully organizing a tenant association. Landlord cannot decrease services, increase rent, or evict within 180 days of tenant's exercising any of these rights.

reversionary interest An interest that returns to the grantor, or his or her heirs upon some event, such as the death of a life tenant.

rezoning A change in the zoning.

right of correlative use The right of a landowner to the reasonable use of the underground percolating water.

right of first refusal Right given to a party to meet the price and terms of a third party if the owner decides to sell.

right of prior appropriation A concept in California and other states that the first user of riparian water obtains priority over later users.

right of redemption The redemption right of the mortgagor after a foreclosure sale.

riparian rights Right of a landowner to water flowing through, under, or adjacent to his or her property.

rule against perpetuities The rule that an estate must vest in an owner within the life of a person in being plus 21 years and a gestation period.

Rumford Act California's fair housing law.

SAFE Act The Secure and Fair Enforcement for Mortgage Licensing Act. Requires a licensing system for mortgage originators.

safety clause A clause in a listing that provides that should the seller sell to a person the agent negotiated with within a set period of time after the listing expires, and whose name the agent submitted to the owner in writing prior to expiration, the broker shall be entitled to the sale commission.

salesperson A real estate licensee who must be employed by a licensed broker.

satisfaction of mortgage Instrument given by the mortgagee to the mortgagor that releases the mortgage lien when recorded.

S corporation A small corporation whose earnings are taxed as a partnership rather than as a corporation.

secret agent—undisclosed agent The third party can hold agent or undisclosed principal liable.

secret profit A profit of the agent that was not fully disclosed to the principal.

security agreement An instrument that creates a security interest in personal property.

security deposit A deposit for the last month's rent or to secure against tenant damage that must be refundable.

seal A mark or impression to attest to authenticity of a signature. Not required in California.

self-help eviction A nonlegal act by the lessor to force the tenant to vacate.

send-out slip An agreement that if a property is disclosed, the prospective buyer will negotiate for it only through the broker who made the disclosure.

separate property Property owned by a spouse in severalty rather than jointly with the other spouse.

servient tenement The land being used by another under an easement.

severalty Ownership in severalty is ownership by one individual or corporation alone.

severance damage Damage to the remainder of the property resulting from the taking of a portion by eminent domain.

sexual harassment Offensive sexually, related actions or language that could constitute a tort and/or discriminatory act.

sheriff's deed A deed given after a sheriff's sale.

simultaneous death When parties die in the same accident and it is unclear which one died first, they are presumed to have died at the same time. Each estate will be probated as if that person had survived the other.

small claims court (California) A division of the superior court. Jurisdiction is limited to $5,000 or less.

Solar Shade Act An act providing an easement of light after a person has installed a solar collector.

Soldiers and Sailors Civil Relief Act An act that prohibits foreclosures while a person is in military service and within three months thereafter except by court order.

special agent An agent whose authority is limited to specified duties.

special assessments Tax assessments for improvements, such as streets and sewers. Liens for special assessments are priority liens.

special endorsement An endorsement on a negotiable instrument to a named party.

special-use permit See conditional-use permit.

specific lien A lien against particular property only, such as a trust deed, mechanic's lien, or tax lien.

specific performance Requiring a person to perform as he or she agreed to perform.

spite fence A fence over ten feet in height maliciously erected or maintained to annoy a neighbor; a spite fence is considered a nuisance.

spot zoning Zoning of parcels not in conformance with the general area zoning.

standard policy of title insurance A policy of title insurance that covers matters of record not specifically excluded, as well as forgery, lack of capacity of a grantor, undisclosed spousal interests, failure of delivery, federal estate tax liens, corporation deeds when a charter has expired, and deeds of agents whose capacity has ended.

standard subdivision Subdivision that does not contain any common areas.

stare decisis Principle that previous decisions should be used to determine present rights and obligations.

statute of frauds The requirement that certain agreements must be in writing to be enforceable (adopted from the common law).

statute of limitations The period in which legal action must be started or the right to bring action is lost.

statutory law Law that is based on enacted statutes rather than precedent; civil law.

steering Directing prospective buyers to areas based on race, religion, national origin, etc.

stock cooperative Corporate ownership of real property with each shareholder entitled to occupancy of a unit under a lease.

stop notice A notice to a lender that a mechanic has not been paid. Unless a bond is posted, the lender must withhold monies due to the prime contractor.

straight note A note whereby interest only is paid and the entire balance is due on the due date.

strict foreclosure Common law foreclosure whereby the mortgagee receives the property without a sale upon the mortgagor's default.

strict liability Liable for injury occurring without regard to negligence or fault.

subagent Agent appointed by an agent. Subagents have agency duties to the principal.

Subdivided Lands Law A disclosure law to protect purchasers of subdivided parcels. A public report is required for subdivisions of five or more parcels.

Subdivision Map Act An act providing local control of the physical aspects of land divisions.

subjacent support Support from below that an excavator must provide.

subject to Purchasing a property without agreeing to pay encumbrances. If there is a default, no deficiency judgment is possible.

sublease A lease given by the original lessee (sublessor) to a sublessee. The sublessee is the tenant of the sublessor and not the original lessor.

subordination clauses Clauses that make a mortgage or trust deed secondary to a later recorded mortgage or trust deed.

subrogation Substitution of one person's rights for another's. When an insurer pays a claim of the insured, the insurer can sue the party who caused the damage. The insurer has the insured's rights by subrogation.

substantial performance Inadvertent, minor variance from the required performance.

successive estates Estates established to succeed other estates, such as a remainder estate to follow a life estate.

successor liability Liability of business purchaser for unpaid sales tax of prior owner.

superior court (California) Court of original jurisdiction for matters over $25,000, as well as appellate jurisdiction from the municipal court.

supreme court (California) Appellate jurisdiction over all California courts.

Supreme Court (U.S.) Discretionary appellate jurisdiction from federal courts, as well as state courts if a federal issue is involved.

surrender The giving up of leasehold rights by a tenant in exchange for being released from future obligations under the lease.

survivorship Right of the surviving joint tenant(s) to interests of another joint tenant on the latter's death.

syndicate A limited partnership.

table funding Mortgage made in name of mortgage broker and then transferred at closing to lender who advanced funds.

tacking on Allowing successors in interest to add on their adverse use in obtaining the five years necessary for an easement by prescription or title by adverse possession.

tax deed A deed given at a tax sale.

tax liens Liens for property taxes are specific priority liens against the property assessed. Liens for state and federal income tax are general liens against the property of the taxpayer.

tenancy at sufferance The tenancy of a holdover tenant. The lessor can treat such a tenant as a trespasser.

tenancy at will A tenancy at the pleasure of the lessor.

tenancy by the entirety Not used in California, it is a joint tenancy between spouses where neither spouse can separately convey his or her interest.

tenancy for years A tenancy for a definite period of time. The tenancy does not renew automatically, and the tenant must give up possession at the end of the lease unless an extension to the lease or a new lease is agreed on.

tenancy in common Undivided interest in property without the right of survivorship.

tender An offer of money or full performance of an agreement without any conditions.

tentative map Initial map filed by a subdivider under the Subdivision Map Act. When all approvals and changes are made, the final map is recorded.

termination statement A statement that, when filed, releases the lien of the financing statement.

testator A person who died having a will.

third-party beneficiary A person, not a party to a contract, who was the intended beneficiary of the contract and therefore has a standing to sue if the contract is breached.

30-day notice A notice to vacate under a periodic tenancy. Notice must be for the length of the rent-paying period, but need not be for more than 30 days.

three-day notice A notice to quit, quit or pay rent, or quit or cure that must be given prior to an unlawful detainer action.

tidelands Land between ordinary high and low tides.

tie-in agreement Requirement that a party agree to another nonrelated transaction as a condition of purchase or sale (Sherman Act violation).

"time is of the essence" A statement in a contract that requires performance within the stated time period if the other party is to be bound by the agreement.

time-share Fractionalized ownership whereby each owner has exclusive right of occupancy for an agreed-on period of time.

title insurance A policy that insures the marketability of title. The insurance contract indemnifies the insured against losses not excluded by the policy, up to the policy amount.

title plant The title records of a title insurer to determine marketability of title.

title theory (mortgage) The theory in some states that a mortgage transfers title to the mortgagee as security for the loan.

tort A civil wrong or violation of a duty.

trade fixtures Fixtures installed by a tenant for the purpose of conducting a business or trade. The trade fixture remains personal property and can be removed by the tenant.

Transfer Disclosure Statement Requires seller disclosures for residential sales.

Treaty of Guadalupe Hidalgo Treaty ending the Mexican-American War whereby the United States agreed to honor property rights of Mexican citizens, which included the community property concept.

trespass Unlawful entry of, or injury to, the property of another.

trust deed A three-party security transaction in which the trustor (borrower) gives a note to the beneficiary (lender) and a title (trust deed) to a trustee as security for the note.

trustee The third party holding naked legal title for security purposes under a trust deed.

trustee sale Sale by the trustee when the trustor defaults. A trustee's deed is given to the purchaser.

trustee's deed Deed given by trustee to purchaser after trustee's sale.

trustor The buyer or borrower under a trust deed.

Truth-in-Lending Act A disclosure law that informs borrowers of credit costs. It provides a right of rescission when credit is secured by a borrower's residence.

Truth in Savings Act Requires lender disclosure of costs and annual percentage yield.

undivided interest subdivision A development where the entire subdivision is owned in common for use of all owners with no separate exclusive use rights.

undue influence Improper influence so that a person really is not acting under his or her own free will. Such influence makes a contract voidable.

Uniform Electronic Transactions Act (UETA) Sets forth rules for entering into an enforceable contract using electronic means.

uniform laws Laws drafted by the National Conference of Commissioners on Uniform State Laws to provide uniformity for commercial purposes.

uniformed settlement statement RESPA required settlement statement for federally related loans.

Uniform Vendor and Purchaser Risk Act Sets forth who bears risk of loss in purchase situations.

unilateral contract An offer that is accepted through performance rather than a mutual promise.

unilateral mistake A mistake by only one party to a contract. It does not void the agreement.

unincorporated association Nonprofit association.

unlawful detainer action A legal eviction action. The tenant must appear and answer charges within five days of service.

Unruh Civil Rights Act The act that prohibits businesses from discriminating.

upzoning Change in zoning allowing less-restrictive development, such as more units or more intensive use.

usury An illegally high rate of interest.

valid Good and enforceable.

variance A special exception to the zoning generally granted to avoid hardship.

vendee Buyer on a real property purchase contract.

vendor Seller on a real property purchase contract.

venue The proper place for a lawsuit to be filed.

verification Swearing under oath as to the truthfulness of a statement.

vested remainder A certain interest after a life tenant dies.

vicarious liability Liability of an individual for acts of one acting in his behalf.

voidable contract A contract whereby one party only can declare the contract void.

void contract A contract that has no effect.

waiver Voluntary relinquishment of a right. A person can waive rights that are for his or her sole benefit. Failure to insist on proper performance could be a waiver of the right to the required performance.

warranty deed A deed in which the grantor warrants good title.

waste Unreasonable and destructive use of property.

wild document A recorded instrument outside the chain of title that fails to give constructive notice.

will A testamentary instrument.

wraparound loan A loan written for the amount of an existing loan, as well as an additional amount, usually used by sellers to take advantage of a low-interest existing loan.

wraparound trust deed (all-inclusive deed of trust) A trust deed written for the amount of the existing encumbrances plus the seller's equity.

writ of execution A court writ directing the sheriff to seize and sell property of a debtor to satisfy the claim of the judgment creditor.

writ of possession A court order for the tenant to vacate.

zoning Public control of land use enacted under police power for the health, safety, morals, and general welfare of the community.

INDEX OF CASES*

*Cross-Indexed Plaintiff-Defendant

564 acres of land. *See* U.S. v. 564 acres of land

967.905 acres of land. *See* U.S. v. 967.905 acres of land

1333 N CA. Blvd. *See* Nippon Credit Bank v. 1333 N. CA Blvd.

A

Aas v. Superior Court (2000) 24 C.4th 627,   442

Ach v. Finkelstein (1968) 264 C.A.2d 667, 47

Adamson Cos. *See* Sprecker v. Adamson Cos.

Adamson. *See* City of Santa Barbara v. Adamson

Aerojet General Corp. *See* Mangini v. Aerojet General Corp.

Alamo School District v. Jones (1960) 182 C.A.2d 180,   242

Alatriste v. Cesar's Exterior Designs (2010) 183 C.A. 4th 656,   388

Aldridge. *See* No GWEN Alliance v. Aldridge

Alexander v. McKnight (1992) 7 C.A.4th 973,   88

Allen. *See* Smith v. Allen

Ali v. City of Los Angeles (1999) 77 C.A.4th 246,   447–448

Allred v. Harris (1993) 14 C.A.4th 1386, 22

Allstate Ins. Co. v. County of Los Angeles and Security Nat'l Bank v. County of Los Angeles (1984) 161 C.A.3d 877,   239

Alpha Property Management. *See* Amos v. Alpha Property Management

Altus Bank v. State Farm Fire and Gas Co. (1991) 758 F. Supp. 567,   339

Alvarado. *See* Emeric v. Alvarado

American Mortgage Company. *See* Phelps v. American Mortgage Company

American Savings. *See* Gibbs v. American Savings

Amos v. Alpha Property Management (1999) 73 C.A.4th 895,   512

Anderson v. Reynolds (1984) 588 F.Supp. 814,   305

Andrade Development Co. V. Martin (1982) 188 C.A.3d 330,   290

Andrews v. Mobile Aire Estates (2004) 125 C.A.4th 578,   513

Annel Management Co. *See* Tan v. Annel Management Co.

Annicelli v. Town of South Kingston, R.I. (1983) 463 A.2d 133,   444

Anthony v. Enzler (1976) 61 C.A.3d 872,   196

Appellate Dept. *See* Randone v. Appellate Dept.

Araj. *See* Asdourian v. Araj

Armenta v. Edmonds (1988) 201 C.A.3d 464,   136

Armitage v. Decker (1990) 218 C.A.3d 887,   394

Arrospide. *See* Carboni v. Arrospide

ARYA Group, Inc. v. Cher (2000) 77 C.A.4th 610,   171

Assilzadeh v. California Federal Bank (2000) 82 C.A.4th 399,   89

Autopsy/post services Inc. v. City of Los Angeles (2005) 129 C.A. 4th 521, 425

Asuncion. *See* People v. Asuncion

Auburn Woods 1 Homeowners Association v. Fair Employment and Housing Council (2004) 121 C.A.4th 1578, 121

AVCO Community Developers, Inc. v. South Coast Regional Commission (1976)17 C.3d 785,   438

AVNER v. Longridge Estates (1982) 272 C.A.2d 607,   441

Axley v. Transamerica Title Ins. Co. (1978) 88 C.A.3d 1,   471

Ayres. *See* Fair Housing Council of Orange County, Inc. v. Ayres

B

B D Inns v. Pooley (1990) 218 C.A.3d 289,   167

Baker v. Hubbard (1980) 101 C.A.3d 226,   387

Baldwin Park Redev. Agency v. Irving (1984) 156 C.A.3d 428, 321

Balistreri v. Nevada Livestock Prod. Credit Association (1989) 214 C.A.3d 635,   178

Ballou v. Masters Props. No 6 (1987) 189 C.A.3d 65,   88

Baltimore County. *See* Greater Baltimore Board of REALTORS® v. Baltimore County

Bank of America v. Daily (1984) 152 C.A.3d 767,   345

Bank of America. *See* Montgomery v. Bank of America

Bank of America. *See* Wellenkamp v. Bank of America

Bank of Stockton v. Church of Soldiers of the Cross of Christ (1996) 44 C.A.4th 1623,   5

Banville v. Schmidt (1974) 37 C.A.3d 92,   52

Barber v. Chang (2007) 151 C.A. 4th 1456,   494

Barberi v. Rothchild (1939) 7 C.2d 537, 362

Bardis v. Oates (2004) 119 C.A.4th, 289

Barela v. Superior Court (1981) 30 C.3d 244,   509

Barham. *See* Beverly Way Associates v. Barham

Barnes v. Black (1999) 71 C.A.4th 1473, 492

Barry. *See* Ingwersen v. Barry

Barry v. Raskov (1991) 232 C.A.3d 447, 61

Bate v. Marsteler (1959) 175 C.A.2d 573,   52

Bay Counties Title Guaranty Co. *See* Kish v. Bay Counties Title Guaranty Co.

Beach "N" Bay Realty, Inc. *See* Jorgensen v. Beach "N" Bay Realty, Inc.

Becker v. Lindsay (1976) 16 C.3d 188, 387

Beckwith. *See* Otay Water District v. Beckwith

Behniwal v. Mix (2005) 133 C.A. 4th 1027, 33

Bel Air Country Club. *See* McDonald Properties, Inc. v. Bel Air Country Club

Beliveau v. Caras (1995) 873 F. Supp. 1393, 130

Berghold. *See* Vankiompenberg v. Berghold

Bernardo Vilas Mgmt Corp. v. Black (1987) 190 C.A.3d 153, 446

Berns. *See* Orlando v. Berns

Bernstein. *See* United Multiple Listing Service v. Bernstein

Best. *See* Ilkhchooyi v. Best

Beverly Way Associates v. Barham (1990) 226 C.A.3d 49, 212

Big Boy Restaurants of America. *See* Ursino v. Big Boy Restaurants of America

Bihr. *See* Fry v. Bihr

Birkenfield v. City of Berkeley (1976) 17 C. 3d 129, 505

Bisetti v. United Refrigeration Corp. (1985) 174 C.A.3d 643, 289

Bisno v. Santa Monica Rent Control Board (2005) 130 C.A. 4th 816, 507

Black. *See* Barnes v. Black

Black. *See* Bernardo Vilas Mgmt Corp. v. Black

Black v. Black (1949) 91 C.A.2d 328, 260

Blank v. Borden (1974) 11 C.A.3d 963, 228

Blickman Turkus L.P. v. MF Downtown Sunnyvale, LLC (2008) 162 C.A. 4th 858, 53

Boarts v. Imperial Irrigation District (1947) 80 C.A.2d 574, 411

Boething Treeland Farms. *See* Shipman v. Boething Treeland Farms

Booska v. Patel (1994) 24 C.A.4th 1786, 395

Borelli v. Brusseau (1993) 12 C.A.4th 647, 178

Borden. *See* Blank v. Borden

Borough of Metuchen. *See* United Advertising Corp. v. Borough of Metuchen

Botosan v. Paul McNally Realty (2000) 216 F.3d 827, 131

Boustred. *See* Melton v. Boustred

Branco. *See* In re Marriage of Branco

Brandt v. Fox (1979) 90 C.A.3d 737, 135

Brenlar. *See* Strebel v. Brenlar

Brewer v. Murphy (2008) 161 C.A. 4th 928, 413

Broadmoor San Clemente Homeowners Assn. v. Nelson (1994) 25 C.A.4th 1, 447

Broderick. *See* Marriage of Broderick

Brown. *See* Hubbard v. Brown

Brown v. FSR Brokerage, Inc. (1998) 62 C.A.4th 766, 34

Brown v. Gordon (1966) 240 C.A.2d 659, 95

Brown. *See* Green v. Brown

Brown v. Green (1994) 8 C.4th 812, 498

Brown. *See* Hubbard v. Brown

Brown. *See* Robinett v. Brown

Brown v. Sweet (1928) 95 C.A. 117, 299

Brunnelle v. Signore (1989) 215 C.A.3d 122, 283

Brusseau. *See* Borelli v. Brusseau

BT-1 v. Equitable Life Assurance Society (1999) 75 C.A.4th 1406, 274

Buck. *See* Merrill v. Buck

Burgess v. Rodom (1953) 121 C.A.2d 71, 177

Burnand v. Irigoyen (1947) 30 C.2d 861, 177

Burnett v. Chimney Sweep, LLC (2004) 123 C.A.4th 1057, 483

Butte Creek Island Ranch v. Crim (1982) 136 C.A.3d 360, 289

Byers. *See* People v. Byers

C

Caldwell. *See* First National Bank of La Habra v. Caldwell

Calif. Dept. of Real Estate. *See* Donaldson v. Calif. Dept. of Real Estate

Calif. Dept. of Real Estate. *See* Rodriguez v. Calif. Dept. of Real Estate

California Center for the Arts, Escondido. *See* Lentini v. California Center for the Arts, Escondido

California Coastal Commission. *See* Feduniak v. California Coastal Commission

California Coastal Commission. *See* Grupe v. California Coastal Commission

California Coastal Commission. *See* Nollan v. California Coastal Commission

California Federal Bank. *See* Assilzadeh v. California Federal Bank

California Federal Bank v. Matreyek (1992) 8 C.A.4th 125, 363

California Mobile Home Park Management Co. *See* U. S. v. California Mobile Home Park Management Co.

California National Bank v. Woodridge Plaza LLC (2008) 164 C.A. 4th 137, 513

California Realty. *See* Lundy v. California Realty

California Western School of Law. *See* Donnell v. California Western School of Law

Calva. *See* Espinoza v. Calva

Calvo. *See* Kurtz v. Calvo

Camacho v. Shaefer (1987) 193 C.A.3d 718, 498

Capital Growth Investors XIV. *See* Harris v. Capital Growth Investors XIV

Caras. *See* Beliveau v. Caras

Carboni v. Arrospide (1991) 2 C.A.4th 76, 98, 109

Carleton v. Tortosa (1993) 14 C.A.4th 745, 65

Carter. *See* Sierra Pacific Industries v. Carter

Carty v. Ojai (1978) 77 C.A.3d 329, 445

Casper. *See* Raab v. Casper

Castaneda v. Olsher (2007) 41 C. 4th 1205, 495

Castner v. City of Oakland (1982) 129 C.A.3d 94, 446

Causby. *See* U.S. v. Causby

Century 21 Klowden-Forness Realty. *See* Field v. Century 21 Klowden-Forness Realty

Cerda. *See* Sanders Construction Co. v. Cerda

Cesar's Exterior Designs. *See* Alatriste v. Cesar's Exterior Designs

Chambers. *See* Riley v. Chambers

Chan v. Tsang (1991) 1 C.A.4th 1578, 228

Chang. *See* Barber v. Chang

Channing Properties v. City of Berkeley (1993) 11 C.A.4th 88, 505

Cher. *See* ARYA Group, Inc. v. Cher

Chevron U.S.A., Inc. *See* Ellis v. Chevron U.S.A., Inc.

Chevron U.S.A. Inc. *See* Lingle v. Chevron U.S.A. Inc.

Chicago Metallic Ceilings, Inc. *See* Warsaw v. Chicago Metallic Ceilings, Inc.

Chicago Title Co. *See* Lick Mill Creek Apartments v. Chicago Title Co.

Chicago Title. *See* Soifer v. Chicago Title

Chimney Sweep, LLC. *See* Burnett v. Chimney Sweep, LLC

Christenson v. Commonwealth Land Title Insurance Company (1983) 666 P.2d 302, 459

Church of Soldiers of the Cross of Christ. *See* Bank of Stockton v. Church of Soldiers of the Cross of Christ

Citizens Sav. & Loan Assn. *See* South Bay Engineering Corp. v. Citizens Sav. & Loan Assn.

City and County of San Francisco v. Sainez (2000) 77 C.A.4th 1302, 490

City and County of San Francisco. *See* Small Property Owners of San Francisco v. City and County of San Francisco

City Council. *See* Save the Welwood Murray Memorial Library Comm. v. City Council

City of Berkeley. *See* Birkenfeld v. City of Berkeley

City of Berkeley. *See* Channing Properties v. City of Berkeley

City of Berkeley. *See* Rue-Ell Enterprises v. City of Berkeley

City of Buena Park. *See* Cook v. City of Buena Park

City of Camarillo. *See* Pardee Construction Co. v. City of Camarillo

City of Carmel-by-the-Sea. *See* Ewing v. City of Carmel-by-the-Sea

City of Cleburne v. Cleburne Living Centers, Inc. (1985) 473 U.S. 432, 423

City of Corona. *See* Ebel v. City of Corona

City of Goleta. *See* Guggenheim v. City of Goleta

City of Hanford. *See* Hernandez v. City of Hanford

City of Ladue v. Gilleo (1994) 114 S. Ct. 2038, 22

City of Los Angeles. *See* Ali v. City of Los Angeles

City of Los Angeles. *See* Autopsy Post Services v. City of Los Angeles

City of Los Angeles. *See* Consolidated Rock Products v. City of Los Angeles

City of Los Angeles. *See* Jones v. City of Los Angeles

City of Los Angeles. *See* Krater v. City of Los Angeles

City of Los Angeles v. Gage (1954) 127 C.A.2d 442, 444

City of New London. *See* Kelo v. City of New London

City of Oakland. *See* Castner v. City of Oakland

City of Oceanside v. McKenna (1989) 215 C.A.3d 1420, 447

City of Oxnard. *See* Griffin Dev. Co. v. City of Oxnard

City of Rancho Palos Verdes. *See* Echevar-rieta v. City of Rancho Palos Verdes

City of San Buenaventura. *See* Selby Realty v. City of San Buenaventura

City of San Diego. *See* College Area Renters and Landlord Association v. City of San Diego

City of San Diego v. Sobke (1998) 65 C.A.4th 379, 309

City of Santa Barbara v. Adamson (1980) 27 C.3d 123, 446

City of Santa Cruz. *See* Gion v. City of Santa Cruz

City of South Lake Tahoe. *See* Springmeyer v. City of South Lake Tahoe

City of South San Francisco Housing Authority v. Guillory (1996) 41 C.A.4th 13, 512

City of Stanton v. Cox (1989) 207 C.A.3d 1557, 426

City of Tigard. *See* Dolan v. City of Tigard

City of Turlock v. Paul M. Zagaris, Inc. (1989) 209 C.A.3d 189, 185

City of West Hollywood. *See* Vega v. City of West Hollywood

City of Yorba Linda. *See* Ross v. City of Yorba Linda

Classen v. Weller (1983) 145 C.A.3d 27, 228

Cleburne Living Centers, Inc. *See* City of Cleburne v. Cleburne Living Center, Inc.

Clements v. Snider (1969) 409 F.2d 549, 253

Cline v. Yamaga (1979) 97 C.A.3d 239, 134

Cloud. *See* U.S. v. Cloud

Coast Resorts, Inc. *See* Long v. Coast Resorts, Inc.

Coast & Southern Federal Savings & Loan Ass'n. *See* Garrett v. Coast & Southern Federal Savings & Loan Ass'n

Cobblestone Village Community Rentals L.P. *See* Coronado v. Cobblestone Village Community Rentals L.P.

Coldwell Banker and Co. v. Pepper Tree Office Center Assocs. (1980) 106 C.A.3d 272, 193

Coldwell Banker Real Estate Services. *See* Smith v. Coldwell Banker Real Estate Services

Coldwell Banker Residential Brokerage Co., Inc. v. Superior Court (2004) 117 C.A.4th 158, 86

Cole v. Cole (1956) 139 C.A.2d 691, 288

Coleman v. Mora (1968) 263 C.A.2d 137, 226

College Area Renters and Landlord Association v. City of San Diego (1994) 43 C.A.4th 677, 447

Collier v. Oelke (1962) 202 C.A.2d 843, 411

Commonwealth Land Title Ins. Co. *See* Harrison v. Commonwealth Land Title Ins. Co.

Commonwealth Land Title Insurance Company. *See* Christenson v. Commonwealth Land Title Insurance Company

Community Bank. *See* Little v. Community Bank

Connolly v. McDermott (1984) 162 C.A.3d 973, 405

Consolidated Rock Prods. *See* New v. Consolidated Rock Prods.

Consolidated Rock Products v. City of Los Angeles (1962) 57 C.2d 515, 445

Contemporary Invs., Inc. v. Safeco Title Ins. Co. (1983) 145 C.A.3d 999, 471

Continental Lawyers Title Co. *See* Summit Financial Holdings Ltd. v. Continental Lawyers Title Co.

Contractors Dump Truck Service, Inc. v. Gregg Construction Co. (1965) 237 C.A.2d 1, 387

Cook v. City of Buena Park (2005) 126 C.A. 4th 1, 22

Cooke v. Ramponi (1952) 38 C.2d 282, 409

Cooper. *See* Madhani v. Cooper

Cordano v. Wright (1911) 159 C. 610, 300

Cornelison v. Kornbluth (1975) 15 C.3d 590, 346

Coronado v. Cobblestone Village Community Rentals L.P. (2008) 163 C.A. 4th 831, 128

County of Alameda. *See* Seatrain Terminal of California, Inc. v. County of Alameda

County of DuPage. *See* Hope v. County of DuPage

County of Los Angeles and Security Nat'l Bank. *See* Allstate Ins. Co. v. County of Los Angeles and Security Nat'l Bank

County of Los Angeles. *See* Specialty Restaurants Corp. v. County of Los Angeles

County of Riverside. *See* Deckert v. County of Riverside

Cournale. *See* Ford v. Cournale

Cowert. *See* Larkin v. Cowert

Cox. *See* City of Stanton v. Cox

Crawford v. Nastos (1960) 182 C.A.2d 659, 228

Creative Capital Leasing Group LLC. *See* Schaffter v. Creative Capital Leasing Group LLC

Cregg v. Ministor Ventures (1983) 148 C.A.3d 100, 509

Crigler. *See* Walker v. Crigler

Crim. *See* Butte Creek Island Ranch v. Crim

Crogan v. Metz (1956) 47 C.2d 398, 51

C. R. Oosterbaan et al. *See* Storage Services v. C. R. Oosterbaan et.al

CTC Real Estate Services v. Lepe (2006) 140 C.A. 4th 856, 344

Cuddy. *See* Scheerer v. Cuddy

Cunningham v. Security Title Ins. Co. (1966) 241 C.A.2d 626, 472

Cunningham v. Superior Court (1998) 67 C.A.4th 743, 429

D

D & I Investments, Inc. *See* Melendrez v. D & I Investments Inc.

Daily. *See* Bank of America v. Daily

Daily. *See* Stone v. Daily

Davi. *See* Robbins v. Davi

Davis v. Gomez (1989) 207 C.A.3d 1401, 494

Decker. *See* Armitage v. Decker

Deckert v. County of Riverside (1981) 115 C.A.3d 885, 411

De La Mater. *See* O'Meara v. De La Mater

de la Quesla. *See* Fidelity Federal Savings & Loan v. de la Quesla

Del Monte Beverage Co. *See* Nesbitt Fruit Products, Inc. v. Del Monte Beverage Co.

DeMarrais. *See* Huijers v. DeMarrais

Del Taco, Inc. *See* Madden v. Del Taco, Inc.

Department of Real Estate. *See* Grubb v. Department of Real Estate

Department of Real Estate. *See* Madrid v. Department of Real Estate

Department of Real Estate. *See* Katz v. Department of Real Estate

Derish v. San Mateo-Burlingame Board (1982) 136 C.A.3d 534, 87

Dieterich International Truck Sales v. J. S. & J. Services, Inc. (1992) 3 C.A.4th 1601, 404

Dimmick v. Dimmick (1962) 58 C.2d 417, 288

Dina v. People ex. rel. Dept. of Transp. (2007) 151 C.A. 4th 1029, 311

Direnfield v. Stabile (1988) 198 C.A.3d 126, 106

Dolan v. City of Tigard (1994) 114 S. Ct. 2309, 306

Dolan-King. *See* Rancho Santa Fe v. Dolan-King

Donaldson v. California Department of Real Estate (2006) 134 C.A. 4th 948, 11

Donald Sterling Corp. *See* Housing Rights Center v. Donald Sterling Corp.

Donnell v. California Western School of Law (1988) 200 C.A.3d 715, 289

Dover Village Assn. v. Jennison (2010) 191 C.A. 4th 123, 279

Dubin v. Robert Newhall Chesebrough Trust (2001) 96 C.A.4th 465, 406

Duin v. Security First National Bank (1955) 132 C.A.2d 904, 226

E

Easton v. Strassburger (1984) 152 C.A.3d 90, 68–74

Ebel v. City of Corona (1985) 767 F.2d 635, 426

Echevarrieta v. City of Rancho Palos Verdes (2001) 86 C.A.4th 472, 448

Edmonds of Fresno v. McDonald Group Ltd. (1985) 171 C.A.3d 598, 428

Edmonds. *See* Armenta v. Edmonds

Edmonds. *See* Sheetz v. Edmonds

Edmonds. *See* Vinci v. Edmonds

Ellis v. Chevron U.S.A., Inc. (1988) 201 C.A.3d 132, 160

Emeric v. Alvarado (1891) 90 C. 444, 320

Enea v. Superior Court (2005) 132 C.A. 4th 1559, 272

Ennabe. *See* Pineda v. Ennabe

Enzler. *See* Anthony v. Enzler

Equitable Life Assurance Society. *See* BT-1 v. Equitable Life Assurance Society

Erickson. *See* Muzio v. Erickson

Erlich v. Menezes (1999) 21 C.4th 543, 165

Ernest Pestana, Inc. *See* Kendall v. Ernest Pestana, Inc.

Ersa Grae Corp. v. Fluor Corp. (1991) 1 C.A.4th 613, 152

Escrow Consultants, Inc. *See* Lee v. Escrow Consultants, Inc.

Espinoza v. Calva (2008) 169 C.A. 4th 1393, 490

Estate of Leslie (1984) 37 C.3d 186, 267

Estate of Lopez (1992) 8 C.A.4th 317, 311

Estate of Vargas (1974) 36 C.A.3d 714, 267

Estate of Worthy (1988) 205 C.A. 3d 760, 321

ETCO Corporation v. Hauer (1984) 161 C.A.3d 1154, 151

E*TRADE Mortgage Corporation. *See* Jones v. E*TRADE Mortgage Corporation

Evans. *See* Rancho Santa Paula Mobile Home Park Ltd. v. Evans

Ewing v. City of Carmel-by-the-Sea (1991) 234 C.A.3d 1579, 447

Exxon Co. U.S.A. *See* Sachs v. Exxon Co. U.S.A.

F

Fairchild v. Park (2001) 90 C.A.4th 919, 512

Fair Employment & Housing Commission. *See* Smith v. Fair Employment & Housing Commission

Fair Employment and Housing Council. *See* Auburn Woods 1 Homeowners Association v. Fair Employment and Housing Council

Fair Housing Council of Orange County, Inc. v. Ayres (1994) 855 F. Supp 315, 126

Falcon Television. *See* Salvaty v. Falcon Television

Falk. *See* Penner v. Falk

Fasano. *See* Sabo v. Fasano

Fashion Valley Mall L.L.C. v. National Labor Relations Board (2007) 42 C.A. 4th 850, 23

Feduniak v. California Coastal Commission (2007) 148 C.A. 4th 1346, 440

Fidelity Federal Savings & Loan v. de la Quesla (1982) 458 U.S. 141, 330

Fidler v. Schiller (1963) 212 C.A.2d 569, 228

Field v. Century 21 Klowden-Forness Realty (1998) 63 C.A.4th 18, 45

Filante v. Kikendall (1955) 134 C.A.2d 695, 194

Finkelstein. *See* Ach v. Finkelstein

First Bank of San Luis Obispo. *See* Moore v. First Bank of San Luis Obispo

First Commercial Mortgage Co. v. Reece (2001) 89 C.A.4th 731, 339

First National Bank of Fresno. *See* Nystrom v. First National Bank of Fresno

First National Bank of La Habra v. Caldwell (1927) 84 C.A. 438, 461

First National Bank. *See* Duin v. Security First National Bank

Flores v. Transamerica Home First Inc. (2001) 93 C.A.4th 846, 163

Fluor Corp. *See* Ersa Grae Corp. v. Fluor Corp.

Foggy v. Ralph F. Clark & Assoc., Inc. (1987) 192 C.A.3d 1204, 53

Ford v. Cournale (1974) 36 C.A.3d 172, 80

Forsalebyowner.com Corporation v. Zimmeran (2005) 347 Fed Supp. 2nd 868, 137

Formosa Corp. v. Rogers (1952) 108 C.A.2d 397, 264

Foulks. *See* Seck v. Foulks

Foundation for Ocean Research. *See* Owens v. Foundation for Ocean Research

Fox. *See* Brandt v. Fox

Fox. *See* Froid v. Fox

Fox. *See* Golde v. Fox

Fox. *See* Gray v. Fox

Fox. *See* Pieri v. Fox

Fox. *See* Powers v. Fox

Francis T. v. Village Green Owner's Ass'n. (1986) 42 C.3d 490, 447

Franklin v. Hansen (1963) 59 C.2d 570, 176

Freeman. *See* Los Banos Gravel Company v. Freeman

Friends of Davis v. City of Davis (2000) 83 C.A.4th 1004, 448

Froid v. Fox (1982) 132 C.A.3d 832, 135

Fry v. Bihr (1970) 6 C.A.3d 248, 362

Fry v. George Elkins Company (1958) 162 C.A.2d 256, 211

FSR Brokerage, Inc. *See* Brown v. FSR Brokerage, Inc.

Fullerton Mtg. & Escrow Co. *See* Warrington Lumber Co. v. Fullerton Mtg. & Escrow Co.

Furla v. Jon Douglas Co. (1998) 65 C.A.4th 1069, 44

G

Gage. *See* City of Los Angeles v. Gage

Gagnard. *See* Realmute v. Gagnard

Garcia v. Paramount Citrus Assn. (2008) 161 C.A. 4th 321, 291

Garcia v. World Savings (2010) 183 C.A. 4th 1031, 349

Gardner v. Johnson (1952) 195 F.2d 717, 388

Garland. *See* McKay and Company v. Garland

Garrett v. Coast & Southern Federal Savings & Loan Ass'n (1973) 9 C.3d 731, 362

Gates Rubber Co. v. Ulman (1989) 214 C.A.3d 356, 248

Geernaent v. Mitchell (1995) 31 C.A.4th 601, 75

Gentile. *See* Wilson v. Gentile

George Elkins Company. *See* Fry v. George Elkins Company

Geothermal Kinetics, Inc. v. Union Oil Co. (1977) 77 C.A.3d 56, 238

Giannoni. *See* Lyon v. Giannoni

Gibbs v. American Savings (1990) 217 C.A.3d 1372, 150

Giebler v. M&B Associates a Limited Partnership (2003) 343 F.3d 1143, 121

Gilbert v. Mercer (1960) 179 C.A.2d 29, 148, 167

Gilbert v. State (1990) 218 C.A.3d 234, 311

Gilleo. *See* City of Ladue v. Gilleo

Gilligan v. Jamco Development Corporation (1997) 108 F.3d 246, 126

Godfrey v. Steinpress (1982) 128 C.A.3d 154, 86

Golden Gate Hotel v. San Francisco City and County (1993) 836 F. Supp. 707, 447

Golden Gateway Center v. Golden Gateway Tenants Association (1999) 73 C.A.4th 908, 22

Golde v. Fox (1979) 98 C.A.3d 167, 135

Goldman. *See* Preston v. Goldman

Gomez. *See* Davis v. Gomez

Goodyear Rubber Corporation v. Munoz (1985) 170 C.A.3d 919, 153

Gordon. *See* Brown v. Gordon

Gordon. *See* Handy v. Gordon

Goswick. *See* Welsch v. Goswick

Gould. *See* Mitchell v. Gould

Granberry v. Islay Investments (1993) 18 C.A.4th 885, 512

Grant. *See* Jackson v. Grant

Grant v. Marinell (1980) 112 C.A.3d 617, 227

Gray v. Fox (1984) 151 C.A.3d 482, 88

Greater Baltimore Board of REALTORS® v. Baltimore County (1990) 752 F. Supp. 193, 4

Green v. Brown (1951) 37 C.2d 391, 235, 288

Green v. Superior Court (1974) 10 C.3d 616, 510

Green. *See* Brown v. Green

Greenwich S.F. LLC v. Wong (2010) 190 C.A.4th 739, 178

Gregg Construction Co. *See* Contractors Dump Truck Service, Inc. v. Gregg Construction Co.

Gresch. *See* Wylie v. Gresch

Griffin Dev. Co. v. City of Oxnard (1985) 39 C.3d 256, 425

Gross v. Superior Court (1985) 171 C.A.3d 265, 506

Grubb & Ellis Company v. Spengler (1983) 143 C.A.3d 890, 61

Grupe v. California Coastal Commission (1985) 166 C.A.3d 148, 438

Guggenheim v. City of Goleta (2010) 638 F. 3d 1111, 506

Guillory. *See* City of South San Francisco Housing Authority v. Guillory

Gutzie Assoc. v. Switer (1989) 215 C.A.3d 1636, 161

H

Hall. *See* Skinner v. Hall

Handley. *See* Wilson v. Handley

Handy v. Gordon (1967) 65 C.2d 578, 363

Handy v. Shiells (1987) 190 C.A.3d 512, 321

Hansen. *See* Franklin v. Hansen

Harmon. *See* Riddle v. Harmon

Harper v. Ultimo (2004) 113 C.A.4th 1402, 177

Harris v. Capital Growth Investors XIV (1991) 52 C.3d 1142, 135

Harris. *See* Allred v. Harris

Harris. *See* Stickel v. Harris

Harrison v. Commonwealth Land Title Ins. Co. (1979) 97 C.A.3d 973, 464

Harrison v. Heinzroth Mortgage Co. (1977) 430 F. Supp. 893, 122

Hartell. *See* Petersen v. Hartell

Hartzheim v. Valley Land & Cattle Co. (2007) 153 C.A. 4th 383, 160

Hauer. *See* ETCO Corporation v. Hauer

Hawley. *See* King v. Hawley

Hawn. *See* Spraltin v. Hawn

Hayes. *See* Marchant v. Hayes

Heinzroth Mortgage Co. *See* Harrison v. Heinzroth Mortgage Co.

Herman. *See* Adams v. Herman

Hernandez v. City of Hanford (2007) 41 C. 4th 279, 423

Higashi. *See* Yokohama Specie Bank Ltd. v. Higashi

Higgins v. Superior Court (Disney/ABC) (2006) 140 C.A. 4th 1238, 162

Hirshfield v. Schwartz (2001) 91 C.A.4th 749, 396

Hisey. *See* Wilson v. Hisey

Hitzel. *See* Simons Brick Company v. Hitzel

Hochstein v. Romero (1990) 219 C.A.3d 447, 250

Hock Investment Co. *See* Marcus Millichap Real Estate Investment Brokerage Co. v. Hock Investment Co.

Hofer v. Young (1995) 38 C.A.4th 52, 149

Hollister. *See* Sweat v. Hollister

Hope v. County of DuPage (1983) 717 F.2d 1061, 420

Horning v. Shilberg (2005) 13 C.A. 4th 197, 67

Housing Rights Center v. Donald Sterling Corp. (2003) 274 F. Supp. 2d 1129, 137

Howell. *See* In re Howell

Hubbard. *See* Baker v. Hubbard

Hubbard v. Brown (1990) 50 C.3d 189, 290

Hu. *See* Shapiro v. Hu

Hubert v. Williams (1982) 133 C.A.3d Supp. 1, 131

Hughes v. Morrison (1984) 160 C.A.3d 103, 228

Huijers v. DeMarrais (1993) 11 C.A.4th 676, 34

Huntley Financial. *See* Kane v. Huntley Financial

Hunter. *See* Rose v. Hunter

Huntington Branch NAACP. *See* Town of Huntington v. Huntington Branch NAACP

Huth v. Katz (1947) 30 C.2d 605, 320

Hyatt v. Tedesco (2002) 96 C.A.4th Supp. 62, 489

Hydrotech Systems v. Oasis Waterpark (1991) 52 C.3d 988, 377

I

Ilkhchooyi v. Best (1995) 37 C.A.4th 395, 512

Imperial Irr. Dist. *See* Salton Bay Marina v. Imperial Irr. Dist.

Imperial Irrigation District. *See* Boarts v. Imperial Irrigation District

Ingwersen v. Barry (1897) 118 C. 342, 412

Inland Investments, Inc. *See* Webber v. Inland Investments, Inc.

In re Estate of De Harte (1961) 196 C.A.2d 452, 67

In re Howell (1980) 638 F.2d 81, 384

In re Marriage of Branco (1996) 47 C.A.4th 1621, 266

In re Marriage of Campbell (1999) 74 C.A.4th 1058, 269

In re Marriage of Cloney (2001) 91 C.A.4th 429, 460

In re Marriage of Stitt (1983) 147 C.A.3d 579, 267

In re Marriage of Tallman (1994) 22 C.A.4th 1697, 291

In re Patterson's Estate (1939) 34 C.A.2d 305, 9

In re Rabin (2006) 336 B. R. 459, 384

In re Wallace Reed Phelps (2001) 93 C.A.4th 451, 349

Interland. *See* Salazar v. Interland

Inter Mountain Mortgage, Inc. v. Salimen (2000) 78 C.A.4th 1434, 53

Interstate Consol. Indus. *See* Wu v. Interstate Consol. Indus.

Irigoyen. *See* Burnand v. Irigoyen

Irving. *See* Baldwin Park Redev. Agency v. Irving

Islay Investments. *See* Granberry v. Islay Investments

J

J. S. & J. Services., Inc. *See* Dieterich International Truck Sales v. J. S. & J. Services, Inc.

Jackson v. Grant (1989) 876 F.2d 764, 357

Jacoby. *See* Washington Mutual Bank v. Jacoby

James Daniel Good. *See* U.S. v. James Daniel Good

Jamco Development Corporation. *See* Gilligan v. Jamco Development Corporation

Jankey v. Twentieth Century Fox Film Corporation (2000) 212 F.3d 1159, 137

Jaoudi Industrial & Trading Corporation. *See* L. Byron Culver & Assoc. v. Jaoudi Industrial & Trading Corporation

Jaquez. *See* People v. Jaquez

Jaramillo v. JH Real Estate Partners, Inc. (2003) 3 Cal. Rptr. 3d 525, 163

Jennison. *See* Dover Village Assn. v. Jennison

Jensen v. Kenneth Mullen Co. (1989) 211 C.A.3d 653, 290

Jensen. *See.* Lo v. Jensen

Johansen. *See* Lipton v. Johansen

Johnson. *See* Gardner v. Johnson

Johnson v. Johnson (1987) 192 C.A.3d 551, 321

Jon Douglas Co. *See* Furla v. Jon Douglas Co.

Jones. *See* Alamo School District v. Jones

Jones v. City of Los Angeles (1930) 211 C. 304, 426

Jones v. E*TRADE Mortgage Corporation (2005) 397 F. 3d 810, 358

Jones v. Mayer (1968) 392 U.S. 409, 119

Jones v. Turnage (1989) 699 F. Supp. 795, 338

Jones v. Wagner (2001) 90 C.A.4th 466, 291

Jorgensen v. Beach "N" Bay Realty, Inc. (1981) 125 C.A.3d 155, 52

Jue v. Smiser (1994) 23 C.A.4th 312, 78

K

Kamp. *See* Lehman v. Kamp

Kane v. Huntley Financial (1983) 146 C.A.3d 1092, 289

Katz. *See* Huth v. Katz

Katz v. Department of Real Estate (1979) 96 C.A.3d 895, 135

Kelley. *See* Tyrone v. Kelley

Kelo v. City of New London (2005) 125 S. Ct. 2655, 7

Kemptor. *See* Maldonado v. Kemptor

Kendall v. Ernest Pestana, Inc. (1985) 40 C.3d 488, 486

Kenneth Mullen Co. *See* Jensen v. Kenneth Mullen Co.

Kentwood Home Guardians. *See* Spitzer v. Kentwood Home Guardians

Kikendall. *See* Filante v. Kikendall

Kinder. *See* Pacific Plan of California v. Kinder

King v. Hawley (1952) 113 C.A.2d 534, 244

King. *See* Reed v. King

Kinney v. Vaccari (1980) 27 C.3d 348, 511

Kish v. Bay Counties Title Guaranty Co. (1967) 254 C.A.2d 725, 471

Klein v. United States of America (2010) 50 C. 4th 68, 288

Klunker. *See* Locke v. Klunker

Kohn. *See* National Land and Investment Co. v. Kohn

Korens v. Zukin Corp. (1989) 212 C.A.3d 1054, 485

Kornbluth. *See* Cornelison v. Kornbluth

Kraemer. *See* Shelley v. Kraemer

Krater v. City of Los Angeles (1982) 130 C.A.3d 839, 445

Krieger v. Pacific Gas & Electric Co. (1981) 119 C.A.3d 137, 412

Kuish v. Smith (2010) 181 C.A. 4th 1419, 166

Kurtz v. Calvo (1999) 75 C.A.4th 191, 363

Kwok v. Transnation Title Insurance Co. (2009) 170 C.A. 4th 1562, 464

L

La Jolla Village Homeowners' Ass' n., Inc. v. Superior Court (1989) 212 C.A.3d 1131, 442

Lake County Title Co. *See* Wade v. Lake County Title Co.

Lake Nacimiento Ranch v. San Luis Obispo County (1987) 830 F.2d 977, 421

LaMarche. *See* Mason v. LaMarche

L & B Real Estate v. Housing Authority (2007) 149 C.A. 4th 950, 303

L. Byron Culver & Assoc. v. Jaoudi Industrial & Trading Corporation (1991) 1 C.A.4th 300, 38

Landes Constr. Co. v. Royal Bank (1987) 833 F.2d 1365, 178

Larkin v. Cowert (1968) 263 C.A.2d 27, 238

Leakes v. Shamoun (1986) 187 C.A.3d 772, 289

Lee v. Escrow Consultants, Inc. (1989) 210 C.A.3d 915, 459

Lee v. Lee (2009) 175 C.A. 4th 1553, 304

Lee v. Title Insurance & Trust Co. (1968) 264 C.A.2d 160, 471

Leff v. Gunter (1983) 33 C.3d 508, 272

Lehman v. Kamp (1969) 273 C.A.2d 701, 320

Lemmens. *See* Mercer v. Lemmens

Lentini v. California Center for the Arts, Escondido (2004) 370 F. 3d 837, 137

Lepe. *See* CTC Real Estate Services v. Lepe

Leslie. *See* Estate of Leslie

Levy v. Wolff (1956) 46 C.2d 367, 154

Lew v. Superior Court (1993) 20 C.A.4th 866, 398

Lick Mill Creek Apartments v. Chicago Title Co. (1991) 231 C.A.3d 1654, 467

Liebermensch. *See* Patel v. Liebermensch

Liebler v. Point Loma Tennis Club (1995) 40 C.A.4th 1600, 431

Lien. *See* Moller v. Lien

Lindsay. *See* Becker v. Lindsay

Lingle v. Chevron U.S.A. Inc. (2005) 544 US 528, 421

Lipton v. Johansen (1951) 105 C.A.2d 363, 227

Little v. Community Bank (1992) 234 C.A.3d 355, 371

Lo v. Jensen (2001) 88 C.A.4th 1093, 344

Locke v. Klunker (1898) 123 C. 231, 363

Lomanto. *See* Roberts v. Lomanto

Lonberg v. Sanborn Theatres Inc. (2001) 259 F.3d 1029, 128

Long v. Coast Resorts Inc. (2002) 267 F.3d 918, 128

Longridge Estates. *See* AVNER v. Longridge Estates

Lopez. *See* Estate of Lopez

Los Angeles Federal Savings and Loan et al. *See* Rubin v. Los Angeles Federal Savings and Loan et al.

Los Banos Gravel Company v. Freeman (1976) 58 C.A.3d 785, 379

Los Feliz Towers. *See* Southern California Housing Rights Center v. Los Feliz Towers

Loviet v. Seyforth (1972) 22 C.A.3d 841, 387

Lowe v. Ruhlman (1945) 67 C.A.2d 828, 253

Lozo. *See* Pacific Shore Funding v. Lozo

Lucas v. Pollock (1992) 7 C.A.4th 668, 291

Lucas v. South Carolina Coastal Council (1992) 112 S. Ct. 2886, 422

Lundy v. California Realty (1985) 170 C.A.3d 813, 491

Lyon v. Giannoni (1959) 168 C.A.2d 336, 229

M

M&B Associates a Limited Partnership. *See* Giebler v. M&B Associates a Limited Partnership

Mabry v. Superior Court (2010) 165 C.A. 4th 208, 342

MacDonald Properties, Inc. v. Bel Air Country Club (1977) 72 C.A.3d 693, 412

MacFadden v. Walker (1971) 5 C.3d 809, 347

Madden v. Del Taco, Inc. (2007) 150 C.A. 4th 294, 127

Madhani v. Cooper (2003) 106 C.A.4th 412, 493

Madison. *See* Marbury v. Madison

Madrid v. Department of Real Estate (1984) 152 C.A.3d 454, 104

MF Downtown Sunnyvale LLC. *See* Blickman Turkus LP v. MF Downtown Sunnyvale, LLC

Mains v. City Title Insurance Company (1949) 34 C.2d 580, 455

Maldonado v. Kemptor (2006) 422 Fed Supp 2nd 1169, 5

Malson. *See* Roth v. Malson

Manderville v. PCG & S Group, Inc. (2007) 146 C.A. 4th 1486, 81

Mangini v. Aerojet General Corp. (1991) 230 C.A.3d 1125, 411

Marbury v. Madison (1803) 1 Cranch 137, 13

Marchant v. Hayes (1897) 117 C. 669, 388

Marcus Millichap Real Estate Investment Brokerage Co. v. Hock Investment Co. (1998) 68 C.A.4th 83, 178

Marler. *See* Walters v. Marler

Marin County Board v. Polsson (1976) 16 C.3d 920, 83

Marina Point Ltd. v. Wolfson (1982) 30 C.3d 721, 131

Marinell. *See* Grant v. Marinell

Marks v. Walter G. McCarty Corp. (1949) 33 C.2d 814, 177

Marriage of Broderick (1989) 209 C.A.3d 489, 290

Marriage of Rico (1992) 10 C.A.4th 706, 266

Marriott Hotels, Inc. *See* Pacific Landmark Hotel, Ltd. v. Marriott Hotels, Inc.

Marsteler. *See* Bate v. Marsteler

Martin. *See* Andrade Development Co.

Martin. *See* Salinas v. Martin

Martin v. Bridgeport Community Association (2009) 173 C.A. 4th 1024, 427

Marvin v. Marvin (1976) 18 C.3d 660, 268

Maryland Bank & Trust. *See* United States of America v. Maryland Bank & Trust

Masin v. LaMarche (1982) 136 C.A.3d 687, 406

Mastagni. *See* Myrick v. Mastagni

Masters Props. No. 6. *See* Ballou v. Masters Props. No. 6

Matreyek. *See* California Federal Bank v. Matreyek

Mayer. *See* Jones v. Mayer

Mayo. *See* Bucella v. Mayo

McCarthy v. Security Trust & Savings Bank (1922) 188 C. 229, 320

McDaniel v. Sunset Manor Co. (1990) 220 C.A.3d 1, 493

McDonald Group Ltd. *See* Edmonds of Fresno v. McDonald Group Ltd.

McKay and Company v. Garland (1986) 701 S.W.2d 392, 228

McKenna. *See* City of Oceanside v. McKenna

McKnight. *See* Alexander v. McKnight

McPhetridge v. Smith (1929) 101 C.A. 122, 35

Melendrez v. D & I Investments, Inc. (2005) 127 C.A. 4th 1238, 343

Melton v. Boustred (2010) 183 C.A. 4th 521, 282

Menezes. *See* Erlich v. Menezes

Mercer v. Lemmens (1964) 230 C.A.2d 167, 176

Mercer. *See* Gilbert v. Mercer

Merrill. *See* Warren v. Merrill

Merrill v. Buck (1962) 58 C.2d 552, 87

Merzoian v. Papazian (1921) 53 C.A., 227

Metz. *See* Crogan v. Metz

Michel v. Moore & Associates (2007) 156 C.A. 4th 756, 71

Miller v. Weitzen (2005) 133 C.A. 4th 732, 284

Miller. *See* United States v. Miller

Mills. *See* Roberts v. Mills

Ministor Ventures. *See* Cregg v. Ministor Ventures

Mitchell v. Gould (1928) 90 C.A. 647, 40

Mitchell. *See* Geernaent v. Mitchell

Mix. *See* Behniwal v. Mix

Mobile Aire Estates. *See* Andrews v. Mobile Aire Estates

Moller v. Lien (1994) 25 C.A.4th 822, 363

Montgomery v. Bank of America (1948) 85 C.A.2d 559, 321

Moore v. First Bank of San Luis Obispo (1998) 68 C.A.4th 768, 22

Moore v. Turner (1952) 137 WV 299, 71 S.E.2d 342, 51

Moore & Associates. *See* Michel v. Moore & Associates

Mora. *See* Coleman v. Mora

Moriarty. *See* Segalas v. Moriarty

Morrison. *See* Hughes v. Morrison

Muller. *See* People ex rel. Dept. of Transportation v. Muller

Municipal Court. *See* Vargas v. Municipal Court

Munoz. *See* Goodyear Rubber Corporation v. Munoz

Murphy. *See* Brewer v. Murphy

Muzio v. Erickson (1919) 41 C.A. 413, 411

MW Erectors, Inc. v. Niederhauser Ornamental and Metal Works, Inc. (2005) 36 C.A. 4th 412, 376

Myrick v. Mastagni (2010) 185 C.A. 4th 1082, 496

N

Nash v. Superior Court (1978) 86 C.A.3d 690, 150

Nastos. *See* Crawford v. Nastos

National Association of REALTORS®. *See* People v. National Association of REALTORS®.

National Labor Relations Board. *See* Valley Fashion Mall LLC v. National Labor Relations Board

National Land and Investment Co. v. Kohn (1965) 215 A.2d 597, 420

Nelson. *See* Broadmoor San Clemente Homeowners Assn. v. Nelson

Nelson. *See* Shupe v. Nelson

Nesbitt Fruit Products, Inc. v. Del Monte Beverage Co. (1966) 177 C.A.2d 353, 253

New v. Consolidated Rock Prods. (1985) 171 C.A.3d 681, 284

Niederhauser Ornamental and Metal Works, Inc. *See* MW Erectors, Inc. v. Niederhauser Ornamental and Metal Works, Inc.

Nippon Credit Bank v. 1333 N CA Blvd. (2001) 86 C.A.4th 486, 364

NL Industries, Inc. *See* Wiegman & Rose International Corp. v. NL Industries, Inc.

No GWEN Alliance v. Aldridge (1988) 855 F.2d 1380, 437

Nollan v. California Coastal Commission (1987) 107 S. Ct. 3141, 438

Noronha v. Stewart (1988) 199 C.A.3d 485, 413

Norris v. Williams (1947) 54 A.2d 331, 445

Northland Bldg. Corp. *See* Southwest Title Ins. Co. v. Northland Bldg. Corp.

Northwestern Title Co. *See* Zang v. Northwestern Title Co.

Nussbaum v. Weeks (1989) 214 C.A.3d 1589, 84

Nutt v. Nutt (1966) 247 C.A.2d 166, 388

Nystrom v. First National Bank of Fresno (1978) 81 C.A.3d 759, 191

O

O'Hara v. Western Seven Trees Corp. (1977) 75 C.A.3d 798, 510

O'Meara v. De La Mater (1942) 52 C.A.2d 665, 362

O'Mectin. *See* Swanberg v. O'Mectin

Oasis Waterpark. *See* Hydrotech Systems v. Oasis Waterpark

Ocean Harbor House Homeowners Association v. California Coastal Commission (2008) 163 C.A. 4th 215, 438

Oates. *See* Bardis v. Oates

Oelke. *See* Collier v. Oelke

Ojai. *See* Carty v. Ojai

Olar v. Schroit (1984) 155 C.A.3d 861, 510

Olsher. *See* Castaneda v. Olsher

Ong. *See* Pintor v. Ong

Opp v. St. Paul Fire & Marine Ins. Co. (2007) 154 C.A. 4th 71, 375

Orlando v. Berns (1957) 154 C.A.2d 753, 363

Ornelas v. Randolph (1993) 4 C.4th 1095, 283

Osborne v. Osborne (1954) 42 C.2d 358, 245

Otay Water District v. Beckwith (1991) 1 C.A.4th 1041, 405

Owens v. Foundation for Ocean Research (1980) 107 C.A.3d 179, 227

P

Pacific Bell. *See* Spar v. Pacific Bell

Pacific Landmark Hotel. Ltd. v. Marriott Hotels., Inc. (1993) 19 C.A.4th 615, 49

Pacific Plan of California v. Kinder (1978) 84 C.A.3d 215, 135

Pacific Shore Funding v. Lozo (2006) 138 C.A. 4th 1342, 358

Padilla v. Rodas (2008) 160 C.A. 4th 742, 291

PAL Investments, Inc. *See* Wells Fargo Bank v. PAL Investments, Inc.

Palmer v. Zaklama (2003) 109 C.A.4th 1367, 383

Pan Pacific Properties, Inc. v. Santa Cruz (1978) 81 C.A.3d 244, 444

Papazian. *See* Merzoian v. Papazian

Paradise Hills Associates v. Procel (1991) 235 C.A.3d 1528, 21

Paramount Citrus Assn. *See* Garcia v. Paramount Citrus Assn.

Pardee Construction Co. v. City of Camarillo (1984) 37 C.3d 465, 446

Park. *See* Stewart Title Guaranty Co. v. Park

Park. *See* Fairchild v. Park

Parkmerced Co. *See* People v. Parkmerced Co.

Paul v. Schoellkopf (2005) 128 C.A.4th 147, 210

Patel. *See* Booska v. Patel

Patel v. Liebermensch (2008) 45 C. 4th 344, 199

Paul McNally Realty. *See* Botosan v. Paul McNally Realty

Paul M. Zagaris, Inc. *See* City of Turlock v. Paul M. Zagaris, Inc.

Pau v. Yosemite Park (1991) 928 F.2d 880, 290

Payne v. White House Properties, Inc. (1980) 112 C.A.3d 465, 61

PCG & S Group, Inc. *See* Manderville v. PCG & S Group, Inc.

Penner v. Falk (1984) 153 C.A.3d 858, 491

People ex rel. Caltrans v. Woodson (2002) 93 C.A.4th 954, 309

People ex rel. Department of Transportation v. Muller (1984) 36 C.3d 263, 320

People v. Asuncion (1984) 152 C.A.3d 422, 334

People v. Byers (1979) 90 C.A.3d 140, 434

People v. Jaquez (1984) 163 C.A.3d 918, 53

People v. Lucatero (2008) 166 C.A. 4th 1110, 22

People v. National Association of Realtors® (1981) 120 C.A.3d 459, 86

People v. Parkmerced Co. (1988) 198 C.A.3d 683, 485

People v. Roman (1991) 227 C.A.3d 674, 511

People v. Sanders (1998) 67 C.A.4th 1403, 298

People v. Sipper (1943) 61 C.A.2d 844, 87

Pepitone v. Russo (1997) 64 C.A.3d 685, 76

Pepper Tree Office Center Assocs. *See* Coldwell Banker and Co. v. Pepper Tree Office Center Assocs.

Petersen v. Hartell (1985) 40 C.3d 102, 348

Peterson. *See* U.S. v. Peterson

Peterson v. Superior Court (1995) 10 C.4th 1185, 491

Pfaff v. U.S. Department of Housing and Urban Development (1996) 88 F.3d 739, 123

Phelps v. American Mortgage Company (1936) 6 C.2d 604, 253

Phillippe v. Shapell Indus., Inc. (1987) 43 C.3d 1247, 172

Pieri v. Fox (1979) 96 C.A.3d 802, 136

Pike v. Tuttle (1971) 18 C.A.3d 746, 362

Pineda v. Ennabe (1998) 61 C.A.4th 1403, 291

Pintor v. Ong (1989) 211 C.A.3d 837, 341

Point Loma Tennis Club. *See* Liebler v. Point Loma Tennis Club

Pollock. *See* Lucas v. Pollock

Polsson. *See* Marin County Board v. Polsson

Pooley. *See* B D Inns v. Pooley

Powers v. Fox (1979) 96 C.A.3d 440, 135

Preciado v. Wilde (2006) 139 C.A. 4th 321, 308

Preston v. Goldman (1986) 42 C.3d 108, 283

Price. *See* Sui v. Price

Privette v. Superior Court (1993) 5 C.4th 689, 282

Procel. *See* Paradise Hills Associates v. Procel

Pruneyard Shopping Center v. Robins (1980) 447 U.S. 74, 4

Puccinelli. *See* William v. Puccinelli

Q

Quinones. *See* Tremper v. Quinones

R

Raab v. Casper (1975) 51 C.A.3d 866, 396

Rados Bros. *See* Redevelopment Agency of The City of Chula Vista v. Rados Bros.

Ralph F. Clark & Assoc., Inc. *See* Foggy v. Ralph F. Clark & Assoc., Inc.

Ramponi. *See* Cook v. Ramponi

Rancho Santa Barbara. *See* Taylor v. Rancho Santa Barbara

Rancho Santa Fe Association v. Dolan-King (2004) 115 C.A.4th 28, 448

Rancho Santa Paula Mobile Home Park Ltd. v. Evans (1994) 26 C.A.4th 1139, 512

Randolph. *See* Ornelas v. Randolph

Randone v. Appellate Dept. (1971) 5 C.3d 536, 372

Raskov. *See* Barry v. Raskov

Rattray v. Scudder (1946) 28 C.2d 214, 199

Realmuto v. Gagnard (2003) 110 C.A.4th 193, 70

Realty Projects, Inc. v. Smith (1973) 32 C.A.3d 204, 104

Redevelopment Agency of the City of Chula Vista v. Rados Bros. (2002) 95 C.A.4th 309, 321

Reece. *See* First Commercial Mortgage Co. v. Reece

Reed v. King (1983) 145 C.A.3d 261, 76

Reese v. Wong (2001) 93 C.A.4th 51, 104

Regency Outdoor Advertising, Inc. v. City of Los Angeles (2006) 39 C.A. 4th 507, 310

Rent Control Board. *See* Santa Monica Pines Ltd. v. Rent Control Board

Reynolds. *See* Anderson v. Reynolds

Riando v. San Benito Title Guarantee Co. (1950) 35 C.2d 170, 471

Rickard. *See* Smith v. Rickard

Rico. *See* Marriage of Rico

Riddle v. Harmon (1980) 102 C.A.3d 524, 264

Riley v. Chambers (1919) 181 C. 589, 11

Ring Bros. Management Corp. *See* Smith v. Ring Bros. Management Corp.

R. J. Kuhl Corp. v. Sullivan (1993) 13 C.A.4th 1589, 186

Robert Newhall Chesebrough Trust. *See* Dubin v. Robert Newhall Chesebrough Trust

Roberts. *See* Winet v. Roberts

Roberts v. Lomanto (2003) 112 C.A.4th 1553, 42

Roberts v. Mills (1922) 56 C.A. 556, 240

Robinett v. Brown (1914) 167 C. 735, 387

Robbins v. Davi (2009) 175 C.A. 4th 118, 138

Robins. *See* Pruneyard Shopping Center v. Robins

Rodas. *See* Padilla v. Rodas

Rodom. *See* Burgess v. Rodom

Rodriguez v. Calif. Dept. of Real Estate (1997) 51 C.A.4th 1289, 136

Rogers. *See* Formosa Corp.

Roman. *See* People v. Roman

Romero. *See* Hochstein v. Romero

Romike Properties. *See* Schoenberg v. Romike Properties

Rosenbaum v. Security Pacific Corp. (1996) 43 C.A.4th 1084, 512

Rose v. Hunter (1957) 155 C.A.2d 319, 226–227

Ross v. City of Yorba Linda (1991) 1 C.A.4th 954, 424

Rothchild. *See* Barberi v. Rothchild

Roth v. Malson (1998) 67 C.A.4th 552, 151

Royal Bank. *See* Landes Constr. Co. v. Royal Bank

Rubin v. Los Angeles Federal Savings and Loan et al. (1984) 159 C.A.3d 292, 331

Rudolph. *See* Wall v. Rudolph

Rue-Ell Enterprises v. City of Berkeley (1983) 147 C.A.3d 81, 511

Ruhlman. *See* Lowe v. Ruhlman

Russo. *See* Pepitone v. Russo

S

6 Angels, Inc. v. Stuart-Wright Mortgage, Inc. (2001) 85 C.A.4th 1279, 364

Sabo v. Fasano (1984) 154 C.A.3d 502, 214

Sachs v. Exxon Co. U.S.A. (1992) 9 C.A.4th 1491, 497

Safeco Title Ins. Co. *See* Contemporary Invs., Inc. v. Safeco Title Ins. Co.

Sainez. *See* City and County of San Francisco v. Sainez

St. Paul Fire & Marine Ins. Co. *See* Opp v. St. Paul Fire & Marine Ins. Co.

Salahutin v. Valley of Calif., Inc. (1994) 24 C.A.4th 555, 78

Salazar v. Interland (2007) 152 C.A. 4th 1031, 116

Salimen. *See* Inter Mountain Mortgage, Inc. v. Salimen

Salinas v. Martin (2008) 166 C.A. 4th 1098b, 281

Salton Bay Marina v. Imperial Irr. Dist. (1985) 172 C.A.3d 914, 166

Salvaty v. Falcon Television (1985) 165 C.A.3d 798, 402

Samson v. Transamerica Ins. Co. (1981) 30 C.3d 220, 472

San Benito Title Guarantee Co. *See* Riando v. San Benito Title Guarantee Co.

Sanborn Theatres Inc. *See* Lonberg v. Sanborn Theatres Inc.

Sanders. *See* People v. Sanders

Sanders Construction Co. v. Cerda (2009) 175 C. A. 4th 430, 377

San Diego Gas and Electric Co. v. Superior Court (1996) 13 C.4th 893, 412

San Francisco City and County. *See* Golden Gate Hotel v. San Francisco City and County

San Luis Obispo County. *See* Lake Nacimiento Ranch v. San Luis Obispo County

San Mateo-Burlingame Board. *See* Derish v. San Mateo-Burlingame Board

Santa Cruz. *See* Pan Pacific Properties, Inc. v. Santa Cruz

Santa Monica Pines Ltd. v. Rent Control Board (1984) 35 C.3d 858, 511

Santa Monica Rent Control Board. *See* Bisno v. Santa Monica Rent Control Board

Savage v. Trammell Crow Co., Inc. (1990) 223 C.A.3d 1562, 22

Save the Welwood Murray Memorial Library Comm. v. City Council (1989) 215 C.A.3d 1003, 321

Sawyer. *See* Yeoman v. Sawyer

Scarborough v. Woodill (1907) 7 C.A. 39, 411

Schaffter v. Creative Capital Leasing Group LLC (2008) 166 C.A. 4th 745, 194

Scheerer v. Cuddy (1890) 85 C. 270, 511

Schiller. *See* Fidler v. Schiller

Schmidt. *See* Banville v. Schmidt

Schoellkopf. *See* Paul v. Schoellkopf

Schoenberg v. Romike Properties (1967) 251 C.A.2d 154, 63

Schroit. *See* Olar v. Schroit

Schulman v. Vera (1980) 108 C.A.3d 552, 497

Schwartz. *See* Hirshfield v. Schwartz

Scudder. *See* Rattray v. Scudder

Seatrain Terminal of California, Inc. v. County of Alameda (1978) 83 C.A.3d 69, 239

Seck v. Foulks (1972) 25 C.A.3d 556, 170

Security Pacific Corp. *See* Rosenbaum v. Security Pacific Corp.

Security Title Ins. Co. *See* Cunningham v. Security Title Ins. Co.

Security Trust & Savings Bank. *See* McCarthy v. Security Trust & Savings Bank

Segalas v. Moriarty (1989) 211 C.A.3d 1583, 501

Selby Realty v. City of San Buena ventura (1973) 10 C.3d 100, 445

Selger v. Steven Bros., Inc. (1990) 222 C.A.3d 1585, 290

Seyforth. *See* Loviet v. Seyforth

Shaefer. *See* Camacho v. Shaefer

Shamoun. *See* Leakes v. Shamoun

Shapiro v. Hu (1986) 188 C.A.3d 324, 214

Shapiro v. Sutherland (1998) 60 C.A.4th 666, 87

Shapell Indus., Inc. *See* Phillippe v. Shapell Indus., Inc.

Sheetz v. Edmonds (1988) 201 C.A.3d 1432, 99

Shelley v. Kraemer (1948) 344 U.S. 1, 430

Shiells. *See* Handy v. Shiells

Shilberg. *See* Horning v. Shilberg

Shipman v. Boething Treeland Farms, Inc. (2000) 77 C.A.4th 1424, 284

Shupe v. Nelson (1967) 254 C.A.2d 693, 176

Sierra Pacific Industries v. Carter (1980) 104 C.A.3d 579, 51, 87

Signore. *See* Brunnelle v. Signore

Simons Brick Company v. Hitzel (1925) 72 C.A. 1, 381

Sipper. *See* People v. Sipper

Skinner v. Hall (1886) 69 C. 195, 385

Small Property Owners of San Francisco v. City and County of San Francisco (2006) 141 C.A. 4th 1388, 513

Smiser. *See* Jue v. Smiser

Smith. *See* Realty Projects, Inc. v. Smith

Smith v. Allen (1968) 68 C.2d 93, 347

Smith v. Coldwell Banker Real Estate Services (2000) 122 F. Supp. 2d 267, 88

Smith. *See* Kuish v. Smith

Smith v. Fair Employment & Housing Commission (1996) 12 C.4th 1143, 132

Smith v. Rickard (1989) 205 C.A.3d 1354, 69

Smith v. Ring Bros. Management Corp. (1986) 183 C.A.3d 649, 136

Smith v. Zak 1971 20 C.A.3d 785, 52

Smith. *See* McPhetridge v. Smith

Snider. *See* Clements v. Snider

Sobke. *See* City of San Diego v. Sobke

Soifer v. Chicago Title (2010) 187 C.A. 4th 365, 465

South Bay Engineering Corp. v. Citizens Sav. & Loan Assn. (1975) 51 C.A.3d 453, 388

South Carolina Coastal Council. *See* Lucas v. South Carolina Coastal Council

South Coast Regional Commission. *See* AVCO Community Developers, Inc. v. South Coast Regional Commission

Southern Burlington County NAACP v. Township of Mount Laurel (1975) 336A2d 713, 421

Southern California Housing Rights Center v. Los Feliz Towers (2006) 426 C.A. 2d 1061, 127

Southland Corp. v. Superior Court (1988) 203 C.A.3d 656, 290

Southland Title Corporation v. Superior Court (1991) 231 C.A.3d 530, 465

Southwest Title Ins. Co. v. Northland Bldg. Corp. (1976) 542 S.W.2d 436, 463

Spar v. Pacific Bell (1991) 235 C.A.3d 1480, 412

Specialty Restaurants Corp. v. County of Los Angeles (1977) 67 C.A.3d 924, 252

Speck. *See* Thomas v. Speck

Sprecher v. Adamson Cos. (1981) 30 C.3d 358, 411

Spengler. *See* Grubb & Ellis Company v. Spengler

Spitzer v. Kentwood Home Guardians (1972) 24 C.A.3d 215, 288

Spraltin v. Hawn (1967) 156 S.E.2d 402, 57

Springmeyer v. City of South Lake Tahoe (1982) 132 C.A.3d 375, 242

Stabile. *See* Direnfield v. Stabile

State Farm Fire and Gas Co. *See* Altus Bank v. State Farm Fire and Gas Co.

State. *See* Gilbert v. State

Steele. *See* Wilson v. Steele

Steiner v. Thexton (2010) 48 C. 4th 411, 159

Steinpress. *See* Godfrey v. Steinpress

Sterling v. Santa Monica Rent Control Board (1984) 162 C.A.3d 1021, 505

Sterling v. Taylor (2007) 40 C.A. 4th 757, 153

Stewart. *See* Noronha v. Stewart

Stewart Title Guaranty Co. v. Park (2001) 250 F.3d 1249, 137

Stickel v. Harris (1987) 196 C.A.3d 575, 333

Stitt. *See* In re Marriage of Stitt

Stone v. Daily (1919) 181 C. 571, 299

Storage Services v. C. R. Oosterbaan et al. (1989) 214 C.A.3d 498, 165

Strassburger. *See* Easton v. Strassburger

Strebel v. Brenlar (2006) 135 C.A. 4th 740, 43

Sui v. Price (2011) 196 C.A. 4th 933, 279

Sullivan. *See* R. J. Kuhl Corp. v. Sullivan

Summit Financial Holdings Ltd. v. Continental Lawyers Title Co. (2002) 27 C.4th 705, 459

Sunset Manor Co. *See* McDaniel v. Sunset Manor Co.

Superior Court. *See* Aas v. Superior Court

Superior Court. *See* Barella v. Superior Court

Superior Court. *See* Coldwell Banker Residential Brokerage Co. Inc. v. Superior Court

Superior Court. *See* Cunningham v. Superior Court

Superior Court. *See* Green v. Superior Court

Superior Court. *See* Gross v. Superior Court

Superior Court. *See* Higgins v. Superior Court (Disney/ABC)

Superior Court. *See* La Jolla Village Homeowners' Ass'n., Inc. v. Superior Court

Superior Court. *See* Lew v. Superior Court

Superior Court. *See* Mabry v. Superior Court

Superior Court. *See* Nash v. Superior Court

Superior Court. *See* Peterson v. Superior Court

Superior Court. *See* Privette v. Superior Court

Superior Court. *See* San Diego Gas and Electric Co. v. Superior Court

Superior Court. *See* Southland Corp. v. Superior Court

Superior Court. *See* Southland Title Corporation v. Superior Court

Superior Lumber Co. v. Sutro (1979) 92 C.A.3d 954, 387

Superscope, Inc. *See* Tenzer v. Superscope, Inc.

Sutherland. *See* Shapiro v. Sutherland

Southern California Housing Rights Center v. Los Feliz Towers (2006) 426 C.A. 2d 1061, 127

Sutro. *See* Superior Lumber Co. v. Sutro

Swanberg v. O'Mectin (1984) 157 C.A.3d 325, 511

Sweat v. Hollister (1995) 37 C.A.4th 603, 88

Sweet. *See* Brown v. Sweet

Switer. *See* Gutzie Assocs. v. Switer

T

Taggart. *See* Ward v. Taggart

Tallman. *See* In re Marriage of Tallman

Tan v. Annel Management Co. (2008) 162 C.A. 4th 621, 492

Target Corp. *See* Van v. Target Corp

Taylor v. Rancho Santa Barbara (2000) 206 F.3d 932, 120

Taylor. *See* Sterling v. Taylor

Tedesco. *See* Hyatt v. Tedesco

Tenzer v. Superscope, Inc. (1985) 39 C.3d 18, 84

The Grubb Co. Inc. v. Department of Real Estate (2011) 194 C.A. 4th 1494, 138

Thexton. *See* Steiner v. Thexton

Thomas v. Speck (1941) 47 C.A.2d 512, 253

Title Insurance & Trust Co. *See* Lee v. Title Insurance & Trust Co.

Tortosa. *See* Carleton v. Tortosa

Town of Huntington v. Huntington Branch, NAACP (1989) 488 U.S. 15, 136

Town of South Kingston, R.I. *See* Annicelli v. Town of South Kingston, R.I.

Township of Mount Laurel. *See* Southern Burlington County NAACP v. Township of Mount Laurel

Trammell Crow Co., Inc. *See* Savage v. Trammell Crow Co., Inc.

Transamerica Home First Inc. *See* Flores v. Transamerica Home First Inc.

Transamerica Ins. Co. *See* Samson v. Transamerica Ins. Co.

Transamerica Title Ins. Co. *See* Axley v. Transamerica Title Ins. Co.

Transamerica Title Ins. Co. *See* Warrington v. Transamerica Title Ins. Co.

Transnation Title Insurance Co. *See* Kwok v. Transnation Title Insurance Co.

Tremper v. Quinones (2004) 115 C.A.4th 944, 413

Tsang. *See* Chan v. Tsang

Tucker. *See* Zlotoff v. Tucker

Tucker v. Lassen Savings and Loan Association (1974) 12 C.3d 629, 347

Turner. *See* Moore v. Turner

Tuttle. *See* Pike v. Tuttle

Twentieth Century Fox Film Corporation. *See* Jankey v. Twentieth Century Fox Film Corporation

Tyrone v. Kelley (1973) 9 C.A.3d 1, 228

U

U.S. v. 3814 N.W. Thurman St. (1999) 164 F.3d 1191, 312

U.S. v. 564 acres of land (1979) 99 S. Ct. 1854, 320

U.S. v. 967.905 acres of land (1969) 305 F. Supp. 83, 320

U.S. Department of Housing and Urban Development. *See* Pfaff v. U.S. Department of Housing and Urban Development

U.S. v. California Mobile Home Park Management Co. (1994) 29 F.3d 1413, 136

U.S. v. Causby (1946) 328 U.S. 256, 237

U.S. v. Cloud (1989) 872 F.2d 846, 158

U.S. v. James Daniel Good (1993) 114 S.C. 492, 313

U.S. v. Peterson (2008) 538 F. 3d 1064, 79

Ultimo. *See* Harper v. Ultimo

Union Mortgage Company. *See* Wyatt v. Union Mortgage Company

Union Oil Co. *See* Geothermal Kinetics, Inc. v. Union Oil Co.

United Advertising Corp. v. Borough of Metuchen (1964) 198 A.2d 447, 444

United Multiple Listing Service v. Bernstein (1982) 134 C.A.3d 486, 87

United Refrigeration Corp. *See* Bisetti v. United Refrigeration Corp.

United States of America. *See* Klein v. United States of America

United States of America v. Maryland Bank & Trust (1986) 632 F. Supp. 573, 286

United States v. Miller (1982) 676 F.2d 359, 362

Ursino v. Big Boy Restaurants of America (1987) 192 C.A.3d 394, 283

V

Vanklompenberg v. Berghold (2005) 126 C.A. 4th 345, 401

Van v. Target Corp (2007) 155 C.A. 4th 1375, 6

Vaccari. *See* Kinney v. Vaccari

Valley Land & Cattle Co. *See* Hartzheim v.Valley & Cattle Co.

Valley of Calif., Inc. *See* Salahutin v. Valley of Calif., Inc.

Vargas v. Municipal Court (1978) 22 C.3d 902, 500

Vargas. *See* Estate of Vargas

Vega v. City of West Hollywood (1990) 223 C.A.3d 1343, 510

Vera. *See* Schulman v. Vera

Village Green Owner's Ass'n. *See* Francis T. v. Village Green Owner's Ass'n.

Vinci v. Edmonds (1986) 185 C.A.3d 1251, 136

W

Wade v. Lake County Title Co. (1970) 6 C.A.3d 824, 473

Wagner. *See* Jones v. Wagner

Walker. *See* MacFadden v. Walker

Walker v. Crigler (1992) 976 F.2d 900, 47

Wall v. Rudolph (1961) 198 C.A.2d 684, 411

Walter G. McCarty Corp. *See* Marks v. Walter G. McCarty Corp.

Walters v. Marler (1978) 83 C.A.3d 1, 467

Ward v. Taggart (1959) 51 C.2d 736, 86

Warren v. Merill (2006) 143 C.A. 4th 96, 41

Warrington Lumber Co. v. Fullerton Mtg. & Escrow Co. (1963) 222 C.A.2d 706, 472

Warrington v. Transamerica Title Ins. Co. (1979) 546 P.2d 627, 472

Warsaw v. Chicago Metallic Ceilings, Inc. (1984) 35 C.3d 564, 412

Washington Mutual Bank v. Jacoby (2009) 120 C.A. 4th 639, 364

Webber v. Inland Investments, Inc. (1999) 74 C.A.4th 884, 336

Weeks. *See* Nussbaum v. Weeks

Wellenkamp v. Bank of America (1978) 21 C.3d 943, 330

Weller. *See* Classen v. Weller

Wells Fargo Bank v. PAL Investments, Inc. (1979) 96 C.A.3d 431, 370

Welsch v. Goswick (1982) 130 C.A.3d 398, 446

Western Seven Trees Corp. *See* O'Hara v. Western Seven Trees Corp.

Western Title Ins. Co. *See* White v. Western Title Ins. Co.

White v. Cridlebaugh (2009) 175 C.A. 4th 1535, 378

White House Properties, Inc. *See* Payne v. White House Properties, Inc.

White v. Western Title Ins. Co. (1985) 40 C.3d 870, 472

Wiegmann & Rose International Corp. v. NL Industries, Inc. (1990) 735 F. Supp. 957, 285

Williams. *See* Hubert v. Williams

Williams. *See* Norris v. Williams

William v. Puccinelli (1965) 236 C.A.2d 512, 176

Wilson v. Gentile (1992) 8 C.A.4th 759, 161

Wilson v. Handley (2002) 97 C.A.4th 1301, 395

Wilson v. Hisey (1957) 147 C.A.2d 433, 86

Wilson v. Steele (1989) 211 C.A.3d 1053, 329

Winet v. Roberts (1986) 179 C.A.3d
    909,   363
Wolff. *See* Levy v. Wolff
Wolfson. *See* Marina Point Ltd. v.
    Wolfson
Wong. *See* Greenwich S.F. LLC v. Wong
Woodill. *See* Scarborough v. Woodill
Woodson. *See* People ex rel Caltrans v.
    Woodson
World Savings. *See* Garcia v. World
    Savings
Wu v. Interstate Consol. Indus. (1991)
    226 C.A.3d 1511,   510

Wyatt v. Union Mortgage Company
    (1979) 24 C.3d 773,   87
Wylie v. Gresch (1987) 191 C.A.3d 412,
    491

Y

Yamaga. *See* Cline v. Yamaga
Yeoman v. Sawyer (1950) 99 C.A.2d 43,
    289
Yokohama Specie Bank Ltd. v. Higashi
    (1943) 56 C.A.2d 709,   240
Yosemite Park. *See* Pau v. Yosemite Park
Young. *See* Hofer v. Young

Z

Zak. *See* Smith v. Zak
Zaklama. *See* Palmer v. Zaklama
Zang v. Northwestern Title Co. (1982)
    135 C.A.3d 159,   472
Zimmerman. *See* For Sale By Owner.com
    v. Zimmerman
Zlotoff v. Tucker (1984) 154 C.A.3d 988,
    176
Zukin Corp. *See* Korens v. Zukin Corp.

SUBJECT INDEX OF CASES

A

Acceptance (of offer)

Gibbs v. American Savings (1990) 217 C.A.3d 1372, 150

Roth v. Malson (1998) 67 C.A.4th 552, 151

Acceptance (by fax)

Hofer v. Young (1995) 38 C.A.4th 52, 149

Acknowledgment

Clements v. Snider (1969) 409 F.2d 549, 253

Cordana v. Wright (1911) 159 C. 610, 300

Administrative Agency Power

Riley v. Chambers (1919) 181 C. 589, 11

After Acquired Title

Emeric v. Alvarado (1891) 90 C. 444, 320

Adverse Possession

Preciado v. Wilde (2006) 139 C.A. 4th 321, 308

Agency

Agent as Buyer

Gray v. Fox (1984) 151 C.A.3d 482, 88

Horning v. Shilberg (2005) 13 C.A. 4th 197, 67

In re Estate of DeHarte (1961) 196 C.A.2d 452, 67

Roberts v. Lomanto (2003) 112 C.A 4th 1553, 42

Smith v. Zak (1971) 20 C.A.3d 785, 52

Coupled with an Interest

Pacific Landmark Hotel, Ltd v. Marriott Hotels, Inc. (1993) 19 C.A.4th 615, 49

Disclosure

Blickman Turkus L.P. v. MF Downtown Sunnyvale, LLC (2008) 162 C.A. 4th 858, 53

Brown v. FSR Brokerage, Inc. (1998) 62 C.A.4th 766, 34

Huijers v. DeMarrais (1993) 11 C.A.4th 676, 34

L. Byron Culver & Assoc. v. Jaoudi Industrial & Trading Corporation (1991) 1 C.A.4th 300, 38

Disclosure (to buyer)

Easton v. Strassburger (1984) 152 C.A.3d 90, 68–74

Geernaent v. Mitchell (1995) 31 C.A.4th 601, 75

Jue v. Smiser (1994) 23 C.A.4th 312, 78

Pepitone v. Russo (1997) 64 C.A.3d 685, 76

Reed v. King (1983) 145 C.A.3d 261, 76

Smith v. Rickard (1989) 205 C.A.3d 1354, 69

Strebel v. Brenlar (2006) 135 C.A. 4th 740, 43

Duty to Buyer

Crogan v. Metz (1956) 47 C.2d 398, 51

Field v. Century 21 Klowden-Forness Realty (1998) 63 C.A.4th 18, 45

Ford v. Cournale (1974) 36 C.A.3d 172, 80

Furla v. Jon Douglas Co. (1998) 65 C.A.4th 1069, 44

Godfrey v. Steinpress (1982) 128 C.A.3d 154, 86

Merrill v. Buck (1962) 58 C.2d 552, 87

Mitchell v. Gould (1928) 90 C.A. 647, 40

People v. Sipper (1943) 61 C.A.2d 844, 87

Wilson v. Hisey (1957) 147 C.A.2d 433, 86

Duty to Principal

Banville v. Schmidt (1974) 37 C.A.3d 92, 52

Bate v. Marsteler (1959) 175 C.A.2d 573, 52

Carleton v. Tortosa (1993) 14 C.A.4th 745, 65

Foggy v. Ralph F. Clark & Assoc., Inc. (1987) 192 C.A.3d 1204, 53

Inter Mountain Mortgage, Inc. v. Salimen (2000) 78 C.A.4th 1434, 53

Mitchell v. Gould (1928) 90 C.A. 647, 40

Moore v. Turner (1952) 137 WV 299 71 S.E.2d 342, 51

Schoenberg v. Romike Properties (1967) 251 C.A.2d 154, 63

Sierra Pacific Industries v. Carter (1980) 104 C.A.3d 579, 51, 87

Spraltin v. Hawn (1967) 156 S. E.2d 402, 51

Wyatt v. Union Mortgage Company (1979) 24 C.3d 773, 87

Duty to Third Parties

Coldwell Banker Residential Brokerage Co. Inc. v. Superior Court (2004) 117 C.A.4th 158, 86

People v. Jaquez (1984) 163 C.A.3d 918, 53

Fraud of Agent

Ach v. Finkelstein (1968) 264 C.A.2d 667, 47

Jorgensen v. Beach "N" Bay Realty, Inc. (1981) 125 C.A.3d 155, 52

Smith v. Zak 1971 20 C.A.3d 785, 52

Gratuitous

McPhetridge v. Smith (1929) 101 C.A. 122, 35

Independent Contractor

Barry v. Raskov (1991) 232 C.A.3d 447, 61

Liability of Principal

Walker v. Crigler (1992) 976 F.2d 900, 47

Ratification

Behniwal v. Mix (2005) 133 C.A. 4th 1027, 33

Salesperson's Status

Grubb & Ellis Company v. Spengler (1983) 143 C.A.3d 890, 61

Payne v. White House Properties (1980) 112 C.A.3d 465, 61

Americans with Disabilities Act

Botosan v. Paul McNally Realty (2000) 216 F.3d 827, 132

Coronado v. Cobblestone Village Community Rentals L.P. (2008) 163 C.A. 4th 831, 128

Jankey v. Twentieth Century Fox Film Corporation (2000) 212 F.3d 1159, 137

Lentini v. California Center for the Arts, Escondido (2004) 370 F. 3d 837, 137

Lonberg v. Sanborn Theatres, Inc. (2001) 259 F.3d 1029, 128

Long v. Coast Resorts, Inc. (2002) 267 F.3d 918, 128

Madden v. Del Taco, Inc. (2007) 150 C.A. 4th 294, 127

Southern California Housing Rights Center v. Los Feliz Towers (2006) 426 C.A. 2nd 1061, 127

U.S. v. Causby (1946) 328 U.S. 256, 237

Arbitration

Moore v. First Bank of San Luis Obispo (1998) 68 C.A.4th 768, 22

Harper v. Ultimo (2004) 113 C.A.4th 1402, 177

As Is

Assilzadeh v. California Federal Bank (2000) 82 C.A.4th 399, 89

Katz v. Department of Real Estate (1979) 96 C.A.3d 895, 135

Assignment and Sublease

Ilkhchooyi v. Best (1995) 37 C.A.4th 395, 512

Kendall v. Ernest Pestana, Inc. (1985) 40 C.3d 488, 486

Attachment

Becker v. Lindsay (1976) 16 C.3d 188, 387

Randone v. Appellate Dept. (1971) 5 C.3d 536, 372

Attorney Fees

Paul v. Schoellkopf (2005) 128 C.A.4th 147, 210

B

Boundaries

Armitage v. Decker (1990) 218 C.A.3d 887, 394

Booska v. Patel (1994) 24 C.A.4th 1786, 395

Noronha v. Stewart (1988) 199 C.A.3d 485, 413

Scarborough v. Woodill (1907) 7 C.A.39 411

Tremper v. Quinones (2004) 115 C.A.4th 994, 413

Wilson v. Handley (2002) 97 C.A.4th 1301, 395

Broker's Duty to Other Brokers

Ballou v. Masters Props. No 6 (1987) 189 C.A.3d 65, 88

Building Permit

Ali v. City of Los Angeles (1999) 77 C.A.4th 246, 447–448

Buyer's Duty

Gray v. Fox (1984) 151 C.A.3d 482, 88

Nussbaum v. Weeks (1989) 214 C.A.3d 1589, 84

C

Civil Rights Act of 1866

Jones v. Mayer (1968) 392 U.S. 409, 119

Coastal Zone Conservation Act

AVCO Community Developers, Inc. v. South Coast Regional Commission (1976)17 C.3d 785, 439

Feduniak v. California Coastal Commission (2007) 148 C.A. 4th 1346, 440

Grupe v. California Coastal Commission (1985) 166 C.A.3d 148, 438

Nollan v. California Coastal Commission (1987) 107 S. Ct. 3141, 438

Ocean Harbor House Homeowners Association v. California Coastal Commission (2008) 163 C.A. 4th 215, 438

Commission

Cline v. Yamaga (1979) 97 C.A.3d 239, 134

Common Law

In re Patterson's Estate 34 C.A.2d 305, 9

Community Property

Andrade Development Co. v. Martin (1982) 188 C.A.3d 330, 290

Estate of Leslie (1984) 37 C.3d 186, 267

Estate of Vargas (1974) 36 C.A.3d 714, 267

In re Marriage of Branco (1996) 47 C.A.4th 1621, 266

In re Marriage of Campbell (1999) 74 C.A.4th 1621, 269

In re Marriage of Stitt (1983) 147 C.A.3d 579, 267

In re Marriage of Tallman (1994) 22 C.A.4th 1697, 291

Marriage of Broderick (1989) 209 C.A.3d 489, 290

Marriage of Rico (1992) 10 C.A.4th 706, 266

Marvin v. Marvin (1976) 18 C.3d 660, 268

Conditional Use Permit

City of Cleburne v. Cleburne Living Centers, Inc. (1985) 473 U.S. 432, 423

Griffin Dev. Co. v. City of Oxnard (1985) 39 C.3d 256, 425

Condition Subsequent

Alamo School District v. Jones (1960) 182 C.A.2d 180, 242

Springmeyer v. City of South Lake Tahoe (1982) 132 C.A.3d 375, 242

Condominium Conversion

Griffin Dev. Co. v. City of Oxnard (1985) 39 C.3d 256, 425

Krater v. City of Los Angeles (1982) 130 C.A.3d 839, 445

Constitution

Marbury v. Madison (1803) 1 Cranch 137, 13

Constructive Eviction

Kinney v. Vaccari (1980) 27 C.3d 348, 511

Constructive Notice

Gates Rubber Co. v. Ulman (1989) 214 C.A.3d 356, 248

Nesbitt Fruit Products, Inc. v. Del Monte Beverage Co. (1966) 177 C.A.2d 353, 253

Thomas v. Speck (1941) 47 C.A.2d 512, 253

Contracts

Acceptance

Marcus Millichap Real Estate Investment Brokerage Co. v. Hock Investment Co. (1998) 68 C.A.4th 83, 178

Nash v. Superior Court (1978) 86 C.A. 3d 690, 150

Capacity

Burnand v. Irigoyen (1947) 30 C.2d 861, 177

Consideration

Borelli v. Brusseau (1993) 12 C.A.4th 647, 178

Steiner v. Thexton (2010) 48 C. 4th 411, 159

Contract of Adhesion

Higgins v. Superior Court (Disney/ ABC) (2006) 140 C.A. 4th 1238, 162

Jaramillo v. JH Real Estate Partners, Inc. (2003) 3 Cal. Rptr. 3d 525, 163

Counteroffer

Roth v. Malson (1998) 67 C.A.4th 552, 151

Damages

Erlich v. Menezes (1999) 21 C.4th 543, 165

Greenwich SF LLC v. Wong (2010) 190 C.A. 4th 739, 178

Kuish v. Smith (2010) 181 C.A. 4th 1419, 166

Storage Services v. C. R. Oosterbaan et al. (1989) 214 C.A.3d 498, 165

Zlotoff v. Tucker (1984) 154 C.A.3d 988, 176

Interpretation

Gutzie Assoc. v. Switer (1989) 215 C.A.3d 1636, 161

Wilson v. Gentile (1992) 8 C.A.4th 759, 161

Mutual Agreement

Burgess v. Rodom (1953) 121 C.A.2d 71, 177

Sterling v. Taylor (2007) 40 C.A. 4th 757, 153

Mutual Mistake

Balistreri v. Nevada Live stock Prod Credit Ass'n. (1989) 214 C.A.3d 635, 178

Levy v. Wolff (1956) 46 C.2d 367, 154

William v. Puccinelli (1965) 236 C.A.2d 512, 176

Reformation

Shupe v. Nelson (1967) 254 C.A.2d 693, 176

Restraint on Alienation

Zlotoff v. Tucker (1984) 154 C.A.3d 988, 176

Revocation

Ersa Grae Corp. v. Flour Corp. (1991) 1 C.A.4th 613, 151

Specific Performance

B D Inns v. Pooley (1990) 218 C.A.3d 289, 167

Gilbert v. Mercer (1960) 179 C.A.2d 29, 167

Statute of Frauds

ARYA Group, Inc. v. Cher (2000) 77 C.A.4th 610, 171

Franklin v. Hansen (1963) 59 C.2d 570, 176

Landes Constr. Co. v. Royal Bank (1987) 833 F.2d 1365, 178

Marks v. Walter G. McCarty Corp. (1949) 33 C.2d 814, 177

Phillippe v. Shapell Indus., Inc. (1987) 43 C.3d 1247, 172

Seck v. Foulks (1972) 25 C.A.3d 556, 170, 171

Unconscionable

Flores v. Transamerica Home First Inc. (2001) 93 C.A.4th 846, 163

Jaramillo v. JH Real Estate Partners, Inc. (2003) 3 Cal. Rptr. 3d 525, 163

Salton Bay Marina v. Imperial Irr. Dist. (1985) 172 C.A.3d 914, 166

Covenants, Conditions, and Restrictions

Bernardo Vilas Mgmt Corp. v. Black (1987) 190 C.A.3d 153, 446

Broadmoor San Clemente Homeowners Assn. v. Nelson (1994) 25 C.A.4th 1, 447

City of Oceanside v. McKenna (1989) 215 C.A.3d 1420, 447

Cunningham v. Superior Court (1998) 67 C.A.4th 743, 429

Edmonds of Fresno v. McDonald Group Ltd. (1985) 171 C.A.3d 598, 428

Francis T. v. Village Green Owner's Ass'n (1986) 42 C.3d 490, 447

Liebler v. Point Loma Tennis Club (1995) 40 C.A.4th 1600, 431

Martin v. Bridgeport Community Association (2009) 173 C.A. 4th 1024, 427

Norris v. Williams (1947) 54 A.2d 331, 445

Shelley v. Kraemer (1948) 334 U.S. 1, 430

Spitzer v. Kentwood Home Guardians (1972) 24 C.A.3d 215, 288

Welsch v. Goswick (1982) 130 C.A.3d 398, 446

D

Dedication

Dolan v. City of Tigard (1994) 114 S. Ct. 2309, 306

Selby Realty v. City of San Buenaventura (1973) 10 C.3d 100, 445

Deed (delivery)

Brown v. Sweet (1928) 95 C.A. 117, 299

Huth v. Katz (1947) 30 C.2d 605, 320

Stone v. Daily (1919) 181 C. 571, 299

Deed (description)

Lehman v. Kamp (1969) 273 C.A.2d 701, 320

Deed (forgery)

Handy v. Shiells (1987) 190 C.A.3d 512, 321

Lee v. Lee (2009) 175 C. A. 4th 1553, 304

Montgomery v. Bank of America
(1948) 85 C.A.2d 559, 321

People v. Sanders (1998) 67 C.A.4th
1403, 298

Deed (fraud)

Anderson v. Reynolds (1984) 588 F.
Supp. 814, 305

Johnson v. Johnson (1987) 192
C.A.3d 551, 321

Deed (not to be recorded)

McCarthy v. Security Trust & Savings
Bank (1922) 188 C. 229, 320

Deed of Reconveyance

Pintor v. Ong (1989) 211 C.A.3d
837, 341

Deficiency Judgment

Altus Bank v. State Farm Fire and
Cas Co. (1991) 758 F. Supp. 567,
339

Cornelison v. Kornbluth (1975) 15
C.3d 590, 346

First Commercial Mortgage Co. v.
Reece (2001) 89 C.A.4th 731,
339

Kurtz v. Calvo (1999) 75 C.A.4th
191, 363

Locke v. Klunker (1898) 123 C. 231,
363

Definiteness (of agreement)

ETCO Corporation v. Hauer (1984)
161 C.A.3d 1154, 153

Goodyear Rubber Corporation v.
Munoz (1985) 170 C.A.3d 919,
153

Demolition Permit

Ali v. City of Los Angeles (1999) 77
C.A.4th 246, 447–448

Department of Real Estate

Brown v. Gordon (1966) 240 C.A.2d
659, 95

Developer Liability

Aas v. Superior Court (2000) 24
C.4th 627, 442

AVNER v. Longridge Estates (1982)
272 C.A.2d 607, 441

La Jolla Village Homeowners' Ass'n.,
Inc. v. Superior Court (1989) 212
C.A.3d 1131, 442

Development Agreement

Pardee Construction Co. v. City of
Camarillo (1984) 37 C.3d 465,
446

Due-on-Sale Clause

Fidelity Federal Savings & Loan v. de
la Quesla (1982) 458 U.S. 141,
330

Pepitone v. Russo (1997) 64 C.A.3d
685, 76

Rubin v. Los Angeles Federal Savings and Loan et al. (1984) 159
C.A.3d 292, 331

Wellenkamp v. Bank of America
(1978) 21 C.3d 943, 330

Due Process

Cook v. City of Buena Park (2005)
126 C.A. 4th 1, 22

E

Easements

Brewer v. Murphy (2008) 161 C.A.
4th 928, 413

Collier v. Oelke (1962 202 C.A.2d
843, 411

Connolly v. McDermott (1984) 162
C.A.3d 973, 405

Dieterich International Truck Sales v.
J. S. & J. Services, Inc. (1992) 3
C.A.4th 1601, 404

Dubin v. Robert Newhall Chesebrough Trust (2001) 96 C.A.4th
465, 406

Echevarrieta v. City of Rancho Palos
Verdes (2001) 86 C.A.4th 472,
448

Ingwersen v. Barry (1897) 118 C.
342, 412

Krieger v. Pacific Gas & Electric Co.
(1981) 119 C.A.3d 137, 412

Masin v. LaMarche (1982) 136
C.A.3d 687, 406

McDonald Properties, Inc. v. Bel Air
Country Club (1977) 72 C.A.3d
693, 412

Muzio v. Erickson (1919) 41 C.A.
413, 411

Otay Water District v. Beckwith
(1991) 1 C.A.4th 1041, 405

Salvaty v. Falcon Television (1985)
165 C.A.3d 798, 402

San Diego Gas and Electric Co. v.
Superior Court (1996) 13 C.4th
893, 412

Spar v. Pacific Bell (1991) 235
C.A.3d 1480, 412

Vanklompenberg v. Berghold (2005)
126 C.A. 4th 345, 401

Wall v. Rudolph (1961) 198 C.A.2d
684, 411

Warsaw v. Chicago Metallic Ceilings,
Inc. (1984) 35 C.3d 564, 412

Eminent Domain

Baldwin Park Redev. Agency v. Irving
(1984) 156 C.A.3d 428, 321

Fidelity Federal Savings & Loan v. de
la Questa (1982) 458 U.S. 141,
330

City of San Diego v. Sobke (1998) 65
C.A.4th 379, 309

People ex rel. Caltrans v. Woodson
(2002) 93 C.A.4th 954, 309

People ex rel. Dept. of Transportation v. Muller (1984) 36 C.3d
263, 320

Redevelopment Agency of the City of
Chula Vista v. Rados Bros. (2002)
95 C.A.4th 309, 321

U.S. v. 564 acres of land (1979) 99 S.
Ct. 1854, 320

U.S. v. 967.905 acres of land (1969)
305 F. Supp. 83, 320

Encroachment

Booska v. Patel (1994) 24 C.A.4th
1786, 395

Hirshfield v. Schwartz (2001) 91
C.A.4th 749, 396

Raab v. Casper (1975) 51 C.A.3d
866, 396

Tremper v. Quinones (2004) 115
C.A.4th 944, 413

Environmental Impact Statement

No GWEN Alliance v. Aldridge
(1988) 855 F.2d 1380, 437

Escrow (duties)

Axley v. Transamerica Title Ins. Co.
(1978) 88 C.A.3d 1, 471

Christenson v. Commonwealth Land
Title Insurance Company (1983)
666 P.2d 302, 459

Contemporary Invs., Inc. v. Safeco
Title Ins. Co. (1983) 145 C.A.3d
999, 471

Cunningham v. Security Title Ins.
Co. (1966) 241 C.A.2d 626, 472

First National Bank of La Habra v.
Caldwell (1927) 84 C.A. 438,
461

In re Marriage of Cloney (2001) 91 C.A.4th 429, 460

Kish v. Bay Counties Title Guaranty Co. (1967) 254 C.A.2d 725, 471

Lee v. Escrow Consultants, Inc. (1989) 210 C.A.3d 915, 459

Lee v. Title Insurance & Trust Co. (1968) 264 C.A.2d 160, 471

Riando v. San Benito Title Guarantee Co. (1950) 35 C.2d 170, 471

Summit Financial Holdings Ltd. v. Continental Lawyers Title Co. (2002) 27 C.4th 705, 459

Wade v. Lake County Title Co. (1970) 6 C.A.3d 824, 473

Warrington Lumber Co. v. Fullerton Mtg. & Escrow Co. (1963) 222 C.A.2d 706, 472

Warrington v. Transamerica Title Ins. Co. (1979) 546 P.2d 627, 472

Zang v. Northwestern Title Co. (1982) 135 C.A.3d 159, 472

Estate Sale

Estate of Lopez (1992) 8 C.A.4th 317, 311

Eviction

Barela v. Superior Court (1981) 30 C.3d 244, 509

City of South San Francisco Housing Authority v. Guillory (1996) 41 C.A.4th 13, 512

Camacho v. Shaefer (1987) 193 C.A.3d 718, 498

Green v. Superior Court (1974) 10 C.3d 616, 510

Hyatt v. Tedesco (2002) 96 C.A.4th Supp. 62, 489

Schulman v. Vera (1980) 108 C.A.3d 552, 497

Segalas v. Moriarty (1989) 211 C.A.3d 1583, 501

Vargas v. Municipal Court (1978) 22 C.3d 902, 500

Exculpatory Clause

Burnett v. Chimney Sweep, LLC (2004) 123 C.A.4th 1057, 483

F

Fair Housing

Auburn Woods 1 Homeowners Association v. Fair Employment and Housing Council (2004) 121 C.A.4th 1578, 121

Fair Housing Council of Orange County, Inc. v. Ayres (1994) 855 F. Supp. 315 126

Giebler v. M&B Association a Limited Partnership (2003) 343 F.3d 1143, 121

Gilligan v. Jamco Development Corporation (1997) 108 F.3d 246, 126

Harrison v. Commonwealth Land Title Ins. Co. (1979) 97 C.A.3d 973, 464

Housing Rights Center v. Donald Sterling Corp. (2003) 274 F. Supp. 2d 1129, 137

Hubert v. Williams (1982) 133 C.A.3d Supp. 1, 131

Jones v. Mayer (1968) 392 U.S. 409, 119

Lentini v. California Center for the Arts, Escondido (2004) 370 F.3d 837, 137

Pfaff v. U.S. Department of Housing and Urban Development (1996) 88 F.3d 739, 123

Taylor v. Rancho Santa Barbara (2000) 206 F. 3d 932, 120

Town of Huntington v. Huntington Branch, NAACP (1989) 488 U.S. 15, 136

U.S. v. California Mobile Home Park Management Co. (1994) 29 F.3d 1413, 136

Familial Status

Smith v. Fair Employment & Housing Commission (1996) 12 C.4th 1143, 132

Smith v. Ring Bros. Management Corp. (1986) 183 C.A.3d 649, 136

Taylor v. Rancho Santa Barbara (2000) 206 F.3d 932, 120

Finder's Fee

Grant v. Marinell (1980) 112 C.A.3d 617, 227

Salazar v. Interland (2007) 152 C.A. 4th 1031, 116

Tenzer v. Superscope, Inc. (1985) 39 C.3d 18, 84

Tyrone v. Kelley (1973) 9 C.A.3d 1, 228

First Amendment

Allred v. Harris (1993) 14 C.A.4th 1386, 22

Bank of Stockton v. Church of Soldiers of the Cross of Christ (1996) 44 C.A.4th 1623, 5

City of Ladue v. Gilleo (1994) 114 S. Ct. 2038, 22

Golden Gateway Center v. Golden Gateway Tenants Association (1999) 73 C.A.4th 908, 22

Greater Baltimore Board of Realtors® v. Baltimore County (1990) 752 F. Supp. 193, 4

Maldonado v. Kemptor (2006) 422 F. Supp. 1169, 5

Paradise Hills Associates v. Procel (1991) 235 C.A.3d 1528, 21

Pruneyard Shopping Center v. Robbins (1980) 447 U.S. 74, 4

Savage v. Trammell Crow Co., Inc. (1990) 223 C.A.3d 1562, 22

Van v. Target Corp. (2007) 155 C.A. 4th 1375, 6

Fifth Amendment

Kelo v. City of New London (2005) 125 S. Ct. 2655, 7

Fixtures

Allstate Ins. Co. v. County of Los Angeles and Security Nat'l Bank v. County of Los Angeles (1984) 161 C.A.3d 877, 239

Larkin v. Cowert (1968) 263 C.A.2d 27, 238

Seatrain Terminal of California, Inc. v. County of Alameda (1978) 83 C.A.3d 69, 239

Foreclosure

6 Angels, Inc. v. Stuart-Wright Mortgage, Inc. (2001) 85 C.A.4th 1279, 364

Bank of America v. Daily (1984) 152 C.A.3d 767, 345

Barberi v. Rothchild (1939) 7 C.2d 537, 362

CTC Real Estate Services v. Lepe (2006) 140 C.A. 4th 856, 344

Garcia v. World Savings (2010) 183 C.A. 4th 1031, 349

Lo v. Jensen (2001) 88 C.A.4th 1093, 344

Mabry v. Superior Court (2010) 165 C.A. 4th 208, 342

Melendrez v. D & I Investments Inc. (2005) 127 C.A. 4th 1238, 343

Moller v. Lien (1994) 25 C.A.4th 822, 363

Nippon Credit Bank v. 1333 N. California Blvd. (2001) 86 C.A.4th 486, 364

O'Meara v. De La Mater (1942) 52 C.A.2d 665, 362

Pike v. Tuttle (1971) 18 C.A.3d 746, 362

Washington Mutual Bank v. Jacoby (2009) 120 C.A. 4th 639, 364

Webber v. Inland Investments, Inc. (1999) 74 C.A.4th 884, 336

Foreclosure Consultants

In re Wallace Reed Phelps (2001) 93 C.A.4th 451, 349

United States v. Miller (1982) 676 F.2d 359, 362

Foreclosure of Lien

Superior Lumber Co. v. Sutro (1979) 92 C.A.3d 954, 387

Foreclosure (one form of action)

Bank of America v. Daily (1984) 152 C.A.3d 767, 345

Fourteenth Amendment

Cook v. City of Buena Park (2005) 126 C.A. 4th 1, 22

Fourth Amendment

People v. Lucatero (2008) 166 C.A. 4th 1110, 22

Fraud

Manderville v. PCG & S Group, Inc. (2007) 146 C.A. 4th 1486, 81

Salahutin v. Valley of Calif., Inc. (1994) 24 C.A.4th 555, 78

U.S. v. Cloud (1989) 872 F.2d 846, 158

U.S. v. Peterson (2008) 538 F. 3d 1064, 79

Ward v. Taggart (1959) 51 C.2d 736, 86

G

Government Seizure

U.S. v. 3814 N.W. Thurman St. (1999) 164 F.3d 1191, 312

U.S. v. James Daniel Good (1993) 114 S. Ct. 492, 313

H

Habitability

City and County of San Francisco v. Sainez (2000) 77 C.A. 4th 1302, 490

Espinoza v. Calva (2008) 169 C.A. 4th 1393, 490

Hyatt v. Tedesco (2002) 96 C.A.4th Supp. 62, 489

Hazardous Waste

United States of America v. Maryland Bank & Trust (1986) 632 F. Supp. 573, 286

Wiegman & Rose International Corp. v. NL Industries, Inc. (1990) 735 F. Supp. 957, 285

Holder in Due Course

Wilson v. Steele (1989) 211 C.A.3d 1053, 329

Homestead

Becker v. Lindsay (1976) 16 C. 3d 188, 387

Gardner v. Johnson (1952) 195 F.2d 717, 388

In re Howell (1980) 638 F.2d 81, 384

In re Rabin (2006) 336 B. R. 459, 384

Little v. Community Bank (1992) 234 C.A.3d 355, 371

Skinner v. Hall (1886) 69 C. 195, 385

Homeowners' Association

Dover Village Assn. v. Jennison (2010) 191 C.A. 4th 123, 279

Rancho Santa Fe Association v. Dolan-King (2004) 115 C.A. 4th 28, 448

Spitzer v. Kentwood Home Guardians (1972) 24 C.A.3d 215, 288

Sui v. Price (2011) 196 C.A. 4th 933, 279

I

Inverse Condemnation

Dina v. People ex. rel. Dept. of Transp. (2007) 151 C.A. 4th 1029, 311

Gilbert v. State (1990) 218 C.A.3d 234, 311

Regency Outdoor Advertising, Inc. v. City of Los Angeles (2006) 39 C.A. 4th 507, 310

U.S. v. 967.905 acres of land (1969) 305 F. Supp. 83, 320

J

Joint Tenancy

Dimmick v. Dimmick (1962) 58 C.2d 417, 288

Kane v. Huntley Financial (1983) 146 C.A.3d 1092, 289

Marriage of Rico (1992) 10 C.A.4th 706, 266

Riddle v. Harmon (1980) 102 C.A.3d 524, 264

Yeoman v. Sawyer (1950) 99 C.A.2d 43, 289

Judgment (execution)

Nutt v. Nutt (1966) 247 C.A.2d 166, 388

L

Landlord Duties

City and County of San Francisco v. Sainez (2000) 77 C.A.4th 1302, 490

Kinney v. Vaccari (1980) 27 C.3d 348, 511

People v. Roman (1991) 227 C.A. 3d 674, 511

Schulman v. Vera (1980) 108 C.A.3d 552, 497

Landlord Liability

Amos v. Alpha Property Management (1999) 73 C.A.4th 895, 512

Andrews v. Mobile Aire Estates (2004) 125 C.A.4th 578, 513

Barber v. Chang (2007) 151 C.A. 4th 1456, 494

Barnes v. Black (1999) 71 C.A.4th 1473, 492

Castaneda v. Olsher (2007) 41 C. 4th 1205, 495

Cregg v. Ministor Ventures (1983) 148 C.A.3d 110, 509

Davis v. Gomez (1989) 207 C.A.3d 1401, 494

Fairchild v. Park (2001) 90 C.A.4th 919, 512

Lundy v. California Realty (1985) 170 C.A.3d 813, 491

Madhani v. Cooper (2003) 106 C.A.4th 412, 493

McDaniel v. Sunset Manor Co. (1990) 220 C.A.3d 1, 493

Myrick v. Mastagni (2010) 185 C.A. 4th 1082, 496

O'Hara v. Western Seven Trees Corp. (1977) 75 C.A.3d 798, 510

Olar v. Schroit (1984) 155 C.A.3d 861, 510

Penner v. Falk (1984) 153 C.A.3d 858, 491

Peterson v. Superior Court (1995) 10 C.4th 1185, 491

Preston v. Goldman (1986) 42 C.3d 108, 283

Rosenbaum v. Security Pacific Corp. (1996) 43 C.A.4th 1084, 512

Swanberg v. O'Mectin (1984) 157 C.A.3d 325, 511

Tan v. Annel Management Co. (2008) 162 C.A. 4th 621, 492

Wylie v. Gresch (1987) 191 C.A.3d 412, 491

Landslide

Sprecher v. Adamson Cos. (1981) 30 C.3d 358, 411

Late Charge

Garrett v. Coast & Southern Federal Savings & Loan Ass'n. (1973) 9 C.3d 731, 362

Lead Paint Disclosure

Smith v. Coldwell Banker Real Estate Services (2000) 122 F. Supp. 2d 267, 88

Lease (validity)

Scheerer v. Cuddy (1890) 85 C. 270, 511

License

Cook v. Ramponi (1952) 38 C.2d 282, 409

Forsalebyowner.com Corporation v. Zimmeran (2005) 347 Fed Supp. 2nd 868, 137

License Denial

Brandt v. Fox (1979) 90 C.A.3d 737, 135

Donaldson v. California Department of Real Estate (2006) 134 C.A. 4th 948, 11

Pieri v. Fox (1979) 96 C.A.3d 802, 136

License Revocation

Golde v. Fox (1979) 98 C.A.3d 167, 135

Katz v. Department of Real Estate (1979) 96 C.A.3d 895, 135

Madrid v. Department of Real Estate (1984) 152 C.A.3d 454, 104

Realty Projects, Inc. v. Smith (1973) 32 C.A.3d 204, 104

Robbins v. Davi (2009) 175 C.A. 4th 118, 138

The Grubb Co. Inc. v. Department of Real Estate (2011) 194 C.A. 4th 1494, 138

Life Estates

Cole v. Cole (1956) 139 C.A.2d 691, 288

Green v. Brown (1951) 37 C.2d 391, 235, 288

King v. Hawley (1952) 113 C.A.2d 534, 244

Lowe v. Ruhlman (1945) 67 C.A.2d 828, 253

Osborne v. Osborne (1954) 42 C.2d 358, 245

Lis Pendens

Palmer v. Zaklama (2003) 109 C.A.4th 1367, 383

Listings

Buyer Agent (buyer default)

Chan v. Tsang (1991) 1 C.A.4th 1578, 229

Schaffter v. Creative Capital Leasing Group LLC 166 C.A. 4th 745, 194

Contingency Commission

City of Turlock v. Paul M. Zagaris, Inc. (1989) 209 C.A.3d 189, 185

Hughes v. Morrison (1984) 160 C.A.3d, 229

Exclusive Agency

Coldwell Banker and Co. v. Pepper Tree Office Center Assocs. (1980) 106 C.A.3d 272, 193

Listing/Option

Rattray v. Scudder (1946) 28 C.2d 214, 199

No Deal-No Commission

Lipton v. Johansen (1951) 105 C.A.2d 363, 227

R. J. Kuhl Corp. v. Sullivan (1993) 13 C.A.4th 1589, 186

Option to Avoid Commission

Anthony v. Enzler (1976) 61 C.A.3d 872, 196

Revocation of

Coleman v. Mora (1968) 263 C.A.2d 137, 226

Safety Cause

McKay and Company v. Garland (1986) 701 S. W.2d 392, 229

Sale after Expiration

Rose v. Hunter (1957) 155 C.A.2d 319, 226–227

Submitted

Duin v. Security First National Bank (1955) 132 C.A.2d 904, 226

Termination

Blank v. Borden (1974) 11 C.A.3d 963, 228

Merzoian v. Papazian (1921) 53 C.A. 112, 227

Termination Date

Nystrom v. First National Bank of Fresno (1978) 81 C.A.3d 759, 191

Verbal

Filante v. Kikendall (1955) 134 C.A.2d 695, 194

Grant v. Marinell (1980) 112 C.A.3d 617, 227

Owens v. Foundation for Ocean Research (1980) 107 C.A.3d 179, 227

Verbal Modification

Fidler v. Schiller (1963) 212 C.A.2d 569, 228

M

Mechanic's Lien (priority)

South Bay Engineering Corp. v. Citizens Sav. & Loan Assn. (1975) 51 C.A.3d 453, 388

Mechanics' Liens

Alatriste v. Cesar's Exterior Designs (2010) 183 C.A. 4th 656, 388

Contractors Dump Truck Service, Inc. v. Gregg Construction Co. (1965) 237 C.A.2d 1, 387

Hydrotech Systems v. Oasis Waterpark (1991) 52 C.3d 988, 377

Loviet v. Seyforth (1972) 22 C.A.3d 841, 387

Marchant v. Hayes (1897) 117 C. 669, 388

MW Erectors Inc. v. Niederhauser Ornamental and Metal Works Inc. (2005) 36 C.A. 4th 412, 376

Opp v. St. Paul Fire & Marine Ins. Co. (2007) 154 C.A. 4th 71, 375

Robinett v. Brown (1914) 167 C. 735, 387

Sanders Construction Co. v. Cerda (2009) 175 C.A. 4th 430, 377

Simons Brick Company v. Hitzel (1925) 72 C.A. 1, 381

South Bay Engineering Corp. v. Citizens Sav. & Loan Assn. (1975) 51 C.A.3d 453, 388

Superior Lumber Co. v. Sutro (1979) 92 C.A.3d 954, 387

White v. Cridlebaugh (2009) 175 C.A. 4th 1535, 378

Mineral, Oil, and Gas Rights

Geothermal Kinetics, Inc. v. Union Oil Co. (1977) 77 C. A.3d 56, 238

Mobile Home Park (rules)

Rancho Santa Paula Mobile Home Park Ltd. v. Evans (1994) 26 C.A.4th 1139, 512

Mortgage Loan Broker

Pacific Plan of California v. Kinder (1978) 84 C.A.3d 215, 135

Mortgage Redemption

Fry v. Bihr (1970) 6 C.A.3d 248, 362

Multiple Listing Service

Derish v. San Mateo-Burlingame Board (1982) 136 C.A.3d 534, 87

Marin County Board v. Polsson (1976) 16 C.3d 920, 83

People v. National Association of Realtors® (1981) 120 C.A.3d 459, 86

United Multiple Listing Service v. Bernstein (1982) 134 C.A.3d 486, 87

Mutual Mistake (contracts)

Levy v. Wolff (1956) 46 C.2d 367, 154

N

Net Listing

Sierra Pacific Industries v. Carter (1980) 104 C.A.3d 579, 51, 87

Nonconforming Use

City of Los Angeles v. Gage (1954) 127 C.A.2d 442, 444

City of Stanton v. Cox (1989) 207 C.A.3d 1557, 426

Ebel v. City of Corona (1985) 767 F.2d 635, 426

Jones v. City of Los Angeles (1930) 211 C. 304, 426

Notice of Nonresponsibility

Baker v. Hubbard (1980) 101 C.A.3d 226, 352, 387

Los Banos Gravel Company v. Freeman (1976) 58 C.A.3d 785, 379

Nuisance

Boarts v. Imperial Irrigation District (1947) 80 C.A.2d 574, 411

Lew v. Superior Court (1993) 20 C.A.4th 866, 398

Mangini v. Aerojet General Corp. (1991) 230 C. A.3d 1125, 411

Wilson v. Handley (2002) 97 C.A.4th 1301, 395

O

Option

Patel v. Liebermensch (2008) 45 C. 4th 344, 199

Owner Liability

Bisetti v. United Refrigeration Corp. (1985) 174 C.A.3d 643, 289

Brunelle v. Signore (1989) 215 C.A.3d 122, 283

Donnell v. California Western School of Law (1988) 200 C.A.3d 715, 289

Garcia v. Paramount Citrus Assn. (2008) 161 C.A. 4th 321, 291

Hubbard v. Brown (1990) 50 C.3d 189, 290

Leakes v. Shamoun (1986) 187 C.A.3d 772, 289

Lucas v. Pollock (1992) 7 C.A.4th 668, 291

Melton v. Boustred (2010) 183 C.A. 4th 521, 282

Padilla v. Rodas (2008) 160 C.A. 4th 742, 291

Pineda v. Ennabe (1998) 61 C.A.4th 1403, 291

Preston v. Goldman (1986) 42 C.3d 108, 283

Privitte v. Superior Court (1993) 5 C.4th 689, 282

Salinas v. Martin (2008) 168 C.A. 4th 1098b, 281

Selger v. Steven Bros., Inc. (1990) 222 C.A.3d 1585, 290

Southland Corp. v. Superior Court (1988) 203 C.A.3d 656, 290

Wiegman & Rose International Corp. v. NL Industries, Inc. (1990) 735 F. Supp. 957, 285

P

Partition Action

Butte Creek Island Ranch v. Crim (1982) 136 C.A.3d 360, 289

Formosa Corp. v. Rogers (1952) 108 C.A.2d 397, 264

Partnership

Bardis v. Oates (2004) 119 C.A.4th 1, 289

BT-1 v. Equitable Life Assurance Society (1999) 75 C.A.4th 1406, 274

Enea v. Superior Court (2005) 132 C.A. 4th 1559, 272

Jones v. Wagner (2001) 90 C.A.4th 466, 291

Power of Attorney

Sheetz v. Edmonds (1988) 201 C.A.3d 1432, 99

Prepayment Penalty

California Federal Bank v. Matreyek (1992) 8 C.A.4th 125, 363

Priority of Liens

Wells Fargo Bank v. PAL Investments, Inc. (1979) 96 C.A.3d 431, 370

Probate Sale

Estate of Lopez (1992) 8 C.A.4th 317, 317

R

Real Estate Purchase Contracts

As Is Provision

Crawford v. Nastos (1960) 182 C.A.2d 659, 228

Shapiro v. Hu (1986) 188 C.A.3d 324, 214

Contingency Rejection

Beverly Way Associates v. Barham (1990) 226 C.A.3d 49, 212

Lyon v. Giannoni (1959) 168 C.A.2d 336, 229

Financing Contingency

Fry v. George Elkins Company (1958) 162 C.A.2d 256, 211

Late Acceptance

Sabo v. Fasano (1984) 154 C.A.3d 502, 214

Tie-in Sale

Classen v. Weller (1983) 145 C.A.3d 27, 229

Real Property

Specialty Restaurants Corp. v. County of Los Angeles (1977) 67 C.A.3d 924, 252

U.S. v. Causby (1946) 328 U.S. 256, 237

Real Property Sales Contracts

Handy v. Gordon (1967) 65 C.2d 578, 363

MacFadden v. Walker (1971) 5 C.3d 809, 347

Petersen v. Hartell (1985) 40 C.3d 102, 348

Smith v. Allen (1968) 68 C.2d 93, 347

Recording

Hochstein v. Romero (1990) 219 C.A.3d 447, 250

Phelps v. American Mortgage Company (1936) 6 C.2d 604, 253

Recovery Fund

Armenta v. Edmonds (1988) 201 C.A.3d 464, 136

Direnfield v. Stabile (1988) 198 C.A.3d 126, 106

Froid v. Fox (1982) 132 C.A.3d 832, 135

Powers v. Fox (1979) 96 C.A.3d 440, 135

Rodriguez v. Calif. Dept. of Real Estate (1997) 51 C.A.4th 1289, 136

Stewart Title Guaranty Co. v. Park (2001) 250 F.3d 1249, 137

Vinci v. Edmonds (1986) 185 C.A.3d 1251, 136

Recreational User Immunity

Hubbard v. Brown (1990) 50 C.3d 189, 290

Jensen v. Kenneth Mullen Co. (1989) 211 C.A.3d 653, 290

Klein v. United States of America (2010) 50 C. 4th 68, 288

Miller v. Weitzen (2005) 133 C.A. 4th 732, 284

New v. Consolidated Rock Prods. (1985) 171 C.A.3d 681, 284

Ornelas v. Randolph (1993) 4 C.4th 1095, 283

Pau v. Yosemite Park (1991) 928 F.2d 880, 290

Shipman v. Boething Treeland Farms, Inc. (2000) 77 C.A.4th 1424, 284

Redlining

Harrison v. Heinzroth Mortgage Co. (1977) 430 F. Supp. 893, 122

Rent Control

Birkenfield v. City of Berkeley (1976) 17 C.3d 129, 505

Bisno v. Santa Monica Rent Control Board (2005) 130 C.A. 4th 816, 507

Channing Properties v. City of Berkeley (1993) 11 C.A.4th 88, 505

Gross v. Superior Court (1985) 171 C.A.3d 265, 506

Guggenheim v. City of Goleta (2010) 638 F. 3d 1111, 509

Santa Monica Pines Ltd. v. Rent Control Board (1984) 35 C.3d 858, 511

Sterling v. Santa Monica Rent Control Board (1984) 162 C.A.3d 1021, 505

Vega v. City of West Hollywood (1990) 223 C.A.3d 1343, 510

Rent Formula

California National Bank v. Woodridge Plaza LLC (2008) 164 C.A. 4th 137, 513

Wu v. Interstate Consol. Indus. (1991) 226 C.A.3d 1511, 510

Revocation (of offer)

Ersa Grae Corp. v. Fluor Corp. (1991) 1 C.A.4th 613, 146

Right of First Refusal

Ellis v. Chevron U.S.A., Inc. (1988) 201 C.A.3d 132, 153

Hartzheim v. Valley Land & Cattle Co. (2007) 153 C.A. 4th 383, 160

Mercer v. Lemmens (1964) 230 C.A.2d 167, 176

S

Salesperson's Status

Grubb & Ellis Company v. Spengler (1983) 143 C.A.3d 890, 61

Payne v. White House Properties, Inc. (1980) 112 C.A.3d 465, 61

Security Deposits (leases)

Granberry v. Islay Investments (1993) 18 C.A.4th 885, 512

Korens v. Zukin Corp. (1989) 212 C.A.3d 1054, 485

Small Property Owners of San Francisco v. City and County of San Francisco (2006) 141 C.A. 4th 1388, 513

People v. Parkmerced Co. (1988) 198 C.A.3d 683, 485

Seller's Duty to Buyer

Alexander v. McKnight (1992) 7 C.A.4th 973, 88

Jue v. Smiser (1994) 23 C.A.4th 312, 78

Sweat v. Hollister (1995) 37 C.A.4th 603, 88

Sexual Harassment

Beliveau v. Caras (1995) 873 F. Supp. 1393, 130

Subdivided Lands Law

People v. Byers (1979) 90 C.A.3d 140, 434

T

Tax Deed

L & B Real Estate v. Housing Authority (2007) 149 C.A. 4th 950, 303

Tenant Duties

Brown v. Green (1994) 8 C.4th 812, 498

People v. Roman (1991) 227 C.A.3d 674, 511

Sachs v. Exxon Co. U.S.A. (1992) 9 C.A.4th 1491, 497

Schulman v. Vera (1980) 108 C.A.3d 552, 497

Tenant in Common

Black v. Black (1949) 91 C.A.2d 328, 260

Tenant Tax Relief Credit

Rue-Ell Enterprises v. City of Berkeley (1983) 147 C.A.3d 81, 511

Title Insurance

Kwok v. Transnation Title Insurance Co. (2009) 170 C.A. 4th 1562, 464

Soifer v. Chicago Title (2010) 187 C.A. 4th 365, 465

Southwest Title Ins. Co. v. Northland Bldg. Corp. (1976) 542 S.W.2d 436, 463

White v. Western Title Ins. Co. (1985) 40 C.3d 870, 472

Title Insurance (duty to defend)

Samson v. Transamerica Ins. Co. (1981) 30 C.3d 220, 472

Title Insurance (extended coverage policy)

Lick Mill Creek Apartments v. Chicago Title Co. (1991) 231 C.A.3d 1654, 467

Walters v. Marler (1978) 83 C.A.3d 1, 467

Title Insurance (liability to third parties)

Harrison v. Commonwealth Land Title Ins. Co. (1979) 97 C.A.3d 973, 464

Title Insurance (preliminary title report)

Southland Title Corporation v. Superior Court (1991) 231 C.A.3d 530, 465

Trade Fixtures

Roberts v. Mills (1922) 56 C.A. 556, 240

Yokohama Specie Bank Ltd. v. Higashi (1943) 56 C.A.2d 709, 240

Transfer Disclosure Statement

Alexander v. McKnight (1992) 7 C.A. 4th 603, 88

Michel v. Moore & Associates 156 C.A. 4th 756, 71

Realmuto v. Gagnard (2003) 110 C.A.4th 193, 70

Shapiro v. Sutherland (1998) 60 C.A.4th 666, 87

Sweat v. Hollister (1995) 37 C.A.4th 603, 88

Trespass

Spar v. Pacific Bell (1991) 235 C.A.3d 1480, 412

Truth-in-Lending

Jackson v. Grant (1989) 876 F.2d 764, 357

Jones v. E*TRADE Mortgage Corporation (2005) 397 F. 3d 810, 358

Pacific Shore Funding v. Lozo (2006) 138 C.A. 4th 1342, 358

U

Unruh Act

Harris v. Capital Growth Investors XIV (1991) 52 C.3d 1142, 135

Hubert v. Williams (1982) 133 C.A.3d Supp. 1, 131

Marina Point Ltd. v. Wolfson (1982) 30 C.3d 721, 131

Usury

Carboni v. Arrospide (1991) 2 C.A.4th 76, 109

Orlando v. Berns (1957) 154 C.A.2d 753, 363

People v. Asuncion (1984) 152 C.A.3d 422, 334

Stickel v. Harris (1987) 196 C.A.3d 575, 333

Winet v. Roberts (1986) 179 C.A.3d 909, 363

View

Echevarrieta v. City of Rancho Palos Verdes (2001) 86 C.A.4th 472, 448

W

Water Runoff

Deckert v. County of Riverside (1981) 115 C.A.3d 885, 411

Z

Zoning

Annicelli v. Town of South Kingston R.I. (1983) 463 A.2d 133, 444

Autopsy/post services Inc. v. City of Los Angeles (2005) 129 C.A. 4th 521, 425

Carty v. Ojai (1978) 77 C.A.3d 329, 445

Castner v. City of Oakland (1982) 129 C.A.3d 94, 446

City of Cleburne v. Cleburne Living Centers, Inc. (1985) 473 U.S. 432, 423

City of Santa Barbara v. Adamson (1980) 27 C.3d 123, 446

College Area Renters and Landlord Association v. City of San Diego (1994) 43 C.A.4th 677, 447

Consolidated Rock Products v. City of Los Angeles (1962) 57 C.2d 515, 445

Ewing v. City of Carmel-by-the-Sea (1991) 234 C.A.3d 1579, 447

Friends of Davis v. City of Davis (2000) 83 C.A.4th 1004, 448

Golden Gate Hotel v. San Francisco City and County (1993) 836 F. Supp. 707, 447

Hernandez v. City of Hanford (2007) 41 C. 4rh 279, 423

Hope v. County of DuPage (1983) 717 F.2d 1061, 420

Lake Nacimiento Ranch v. San Luis Obispo County (1987) 830 F.2d 977, 421

Lingle v. Chevron U.S.A. Inc. (2005) 544 U.S. 528, 421

Lucas v. South Carolina Coastal Council (1992) 112 S. Ct. 2886, 422

National Land and Investment Co. v. Kohn (1965) 215 A.2d 597, 420

Pan Pacific Properties, Inc. v. Santa Cruz (1978) 81 C.A.3d 244, 444

Ross v. City of Yorba Linda (1991) 1 C.A.4th 954, 424

Southern Burlington County NAACP v. Township of Mount Laurel (1975) 336 A.2d 713, 421

United Advertising Corp. v. Borough of Metuchen (1964) 198 A.2d 447, 444

INDEX

A

abatement 398
abstract of judgment 369–370
abstract of title 463
acceleration upon default 331
acceptance 149–151
accord and satisfaction 163
accretion 400
accusation 97
acknowledgment 246–247
action in personam 17
action in rem 17
actual notice 248
ademption 314
administrative agencies 8, 10, 12
Administrative Procedures Act 10
administrator 315
ad valorem taxes 373
advance fee rental agents 114
adverse possession 306–307
advertising 107, 108, 129–130, 357
aesthetic zoning 424
affirmation 380
affirmative easement 403
after-acquired title 250, 301
agency 29–52
    accounting 44
    authority of 38–39
    breach of 48–49
    by estoppel 32
    by ratification 32
    coupled with an interest 49
    creation 31–34
    customary authority 39
    definition 29–30
    delegation of authority 39–40
    designated 35
    disclosure 36–37, 40, 43–44, 66–77, 110
    dual 33–37
    due care 43–44
    duties as a buyer 66–67
    duties to buyers 67–77
    duties to other brokers 81–82
    duties to principal 62–67
    duties to third persons 45–46
    election 35–38
    express 31
    express authority 38
    fees to nonlicensees 83–84
    fiduciary duty 40–45
    general agent 30
    gratuitous 35
    honest 44
    implied 31
    implied authority 39
    integrity 44–45
    liability of agents 46
    liability of principals 47–48
    loyalty 44
    obedience 45
    ostensible agent 31
    power of attorney 30
    proof of 38
    ratification 32
    secret profit 64
    special agent 30
    termination of 48
AIDS 76
alienation clause 330–331
Alquist-Priolo Special Studies Zone Act 437
alternative dispute resolution 18–19
Americans with Disabilities Act 126–128
amortized note 328
antimerger clause 340
appraiser licensing 118
appurtenance 236
arbitration 18
Article 5 106
Article 7 108–110
as is 71, 214
assignment (lease) 485–487
assumption of loan 354
attachment 372
attorney fees 210, 335
attorney-in-fact 30
attractive nuisance 283
avulsion 400

B

bait and switch 357
balloon payments 330
bankruptcy 355
beneficiary statement 456
bilateral contract 146
bilateral mistake 154
blanket encumbrances 354
blind ad 79
blockbusting 122
boundary disputes 393–395
breach of agency 48
broker-salesperson agreement 216
broker's license 100–101
builder liability 441
Bulk Sales Act 116–117
bulk zoning 424
bundle of rights 241
burden of proof 185
business opportunity brokers 115–118
buyer's duty 67

C

California 14–15
California Association of REALTORS® xv
California Constitution 9
California courts 14
California Environmental Quality Act 437
California Fair Employment and Housing Act 131–134
California Housing Financial Discrimination Act of 1977 356
California statutes 9
Cartwright Act 83
Caveat Emptor 67
CERCLA 285–286
certificate of sale 337
cessation of work 380
change of ownership notice 251
chattels 237
chattels real 237
civil law 2
Civil Rights Act of 1866 119
Civil Rights Act of 1968 119, 122
civil wrong 18
clearance receipt 115
Coastal Zone Conservation Act 437–439
codicil 313

commercial frustration 161
commission 185
common elements 278
common interest subdivision 278
common law 2
community apartment project 280
community property 265–270
Community Property with Right of Survivorship 270
compensatory damages 16, 164
competent parties 147–148
comprehensive zoning 424
concurrent estates 245
conditional public report 436
conditional-use permit 425
condition precedent 242
condition subsequent 242–243
condominium 278–279
condominium conversions 504
consideration 156–157
constitutional law 3–7
construction loans 350
constructive eviction 501–502
constructive notice 247–249
consumer protection acts 355–359
contingencies 211–212
contingent remainder 243
contract
    voidable 157–158
contracts 145–173, 183–216
    adhesion 162–163
    anticipatory breach 163–164
    assignment, of 169
    bilateral 146
    breach of 162–163
    commercial frustration 161
    competent parties 147–148
    consideration 156–157
    counteroffer 151–152
    definitiveness 152–154
    delegation of duties 169
    delivery 299
    discharge 161
    divisible 155
    exception 305
    executed 147
    executory 147
    express 145
    foreign language 170
    granting clause 299
    illusory 153–154

implied 146
impossibility of performance 161
legal purposes 155–156
mistakes 154–155
mutual consent 149–156
not required 300–301
offer and acceptance 149–152
quasi 146
rememdies 164–167
rescission 168
revocation 151–152
tender 164
unconscionable 162–163
unilateral 146–147
valid 147–157
void 157–158
controlled business arrangement 356
cooperating broker agreements 200
cooperatives 279
corporation licenses 101
corporations 276–277
Costa-Hawkins Rental Housing Act 505
counteroffer 215
court of appeal 13
    California supreme court 14
    district courts 13
    federal 12
    small claims courts 14
    special courts 14
    superior courts 14
courts 12–15
covenants, conditions, and restrictions 427–431
    creation of 428–429
    ending restrictions 431–432
    unenforceable restrictions 429–430
criminal wrong 18, 104
cumulative zoning 422
customary authority 39

D

death on the premises 75
declaration of homestead 382–386
Declaration of restrictions 427
declaratory relief action 18, 168
dedication 305, 305–306
deed in lieu of foreclosure 340
deeds 297–305
    acceptance 299
    acknowledgment 300
    competent parties 300

consideration 300–301
recording 300
requirements of 298–300
reservation 305
types 301–304
void 304–305
voidable 304–305
defeasance clause 335
defeasible estate 241–242
deficiency judgments 338–339
delegation of duties 169
demises 479
Department of Real Estate 10
designated agency 35
developer liability 441
devise 313
disability 126, 129
disciplinary action 97, 102–104
divisible contracts 155
division fence 394–395
doctrine of agreed boundaries 393
domestic partnerships 266
dominant tenement 401
downzoning 424
dragnet clause 350
dual agency 33
due-on-encumbrance clause 331
due-on-sale clause 330–331
duress 158

E

easement 401–409
    affirmative 403
    by eminent domain 407
    by estoppel 408
    by grant 403
    by implication 406–408
    by necessity 407
    by prescription 404–406
    by reservation 404
    dominant tenement 402
    in gross 402–403
    maintenance of 402
    negative 403
    servient tenement 401
    termination of 408
education, research, and recovery allocation 105
ejectment 480
elder abuse law 460
Ellis Act 505

emancipated minor 148
emblements 237
eminent domain 308
employee 60–61
encroachment 395–397
endangered species 440
environmental impact report 437
environmental impact statement 437
environmental law 436–439
Equal Credit Opportunity Act 356
equal dignities rule 38
equitable remedies 17–18, 167–168
escheat 315
escrow agent 111
escrows 453–463
    charges and prorating 462
    deposits 461–462
    designating escrow 456
    disclosures 458–460
    doctrine of relation back 462
    duties 456
    escrow agents 111, 456
    escrow amendments 455
    escrow instructions 454–455
    exemptions 456
    licensing 456
    mobile home 463
    prohibitions 457–458
    risk of loss 460
    termination 460–461
estimated buyer's costs 215
estoppel 32, 170
ethics 59–60
eviction 498–503
exception in a deed 305
exclusionary zoning 422
exculpatory clause 483
executed contract 147
execution sale 371–372
executor 315
executory contract 147
exemplary damages 16, 165
express agency 31
express authority 38–39
express contract 145

F
facilitator 35–36
Fair Credit Reporting Act 356
fair housing 118–132, 482
Fair Housing Poster 124–125

familial status 119, 129
federal administrative agencies 8
federal courts 12
Federal Personal Responsibility and Work
    Opportunity Act 100
federal statutes 8
fee simple 241–242
fictitious name 273–274
fictitious trust deed 346
fiduciary duty 40–45
Fifth Amendment 6
financing statement 354
finder's fee 199
FIRREA 312
First Amendment 4
fixtures 238–240, 482–483
foreclosure 17, 336–345
foreign corporations 276
forged deed 304
Fourteenth Amendment 7
Fourth Amendment 6
franchisees 62
franchise sales 117–118
fraud 63, 79, 157
freehold estates 245
fructus industriales 237
fructus naturales 237

G
Garn Act 347
general lien 374
general partner 270, 272
general plan 420
gift deed 304
good faith 185
good-faith estimate 355
government seizure 312–313
grandfather clause 426
grant deed 301
group boycotting 83

H
habitability 488–489
hazardous substance disclosure 285–286
historical designations 440
history (California land) 235–236
Holden Act 356
holder in due course 329
hold harmless clauses 184
holographic will 314
homeowners' association 278–280, 373

homestead declaration 382–386, 383–384
hypothecate 335

I
illusory contract 153–154
implied agency 31
implied authority 39
implied contract 145–146
impossibility of performance 161
impound accounts 334–335
incentive zoning 424
inclusionary zoning 424
Independent Administration of Estates Act
    317
independent contractor 60–62
injunction 17, 167–168
installment note 328
interim occupancy agreement 214–215
Internet resources x
interpleader action 462
interpretation 160–161
interpretation of contracts 160–161
Interstate Land Sales Full Disclosure Act
    436–437
intestate succession 314–315
inverse condemnation 310
involuntary liens 369–381
involuntary transfers 306–312

J
joint tenancy 261–264
    creation of 262–263
    termination 263–265
    unities 263
joint ventures 273
judgment liens 369–372
judgments 173–174
judicial remedies 16–17, 164–165
junior lienholders 345
jurisdiction 15

L
laches 173
landlord rights and responsibilities 488
    entry 488
    habitability 488
    security 496–497
late charges 109, 331
latent defects 71
lateral support 400–401
law, definition 1, 59

lawsuit procedure 15–16
lead paint disclosure 200
lease options 351, 483
Leases 216, 219–224, 481–488
    assignments and subleases 485–487
    exculpatory clause 483
    fixtures 482–483
    forms and provisions 481–482
    notices and management 482
    options 483
    security deposits 484–485
    termination of 487–488
Legal citations viii–ix
Legal purpose 155–156
liability for injuries 490–494
Liability of agents 46
Liability of principals 46–47
License 409
License renewals 101–102
Licensing 96–102
Liens (placed by nonowners) 345
Life estates 243–245
Limited common elements 278
Limited liability companies 277
Limited partnerships 274–275
Liquidated damages 16, 165
Lis pendens 382
Listings 183–195
    advance costs 195
    advance fee addendum 195
    arbitration 191
    burden of proof 185
    buyer listings 194–206
    commission 185
    copies 186
    exclusive-agency listing 192
    exclusive authorization and right-to-sell 191
    exclusive listings 186–190
    hold harmless clause 184
    keybox 191
    loan broker listings 196–197
    modification 196
    net listings 65, 194–195
    no deal-no commission 185
    open listing 192–193
    option listings 65–66
    oral listings 194
    procuring cause 193
    safety clause 191
    signed 186

    subagents 184
    termination date 186
Littoral rights 399
Livery of seisin 297
Living trust 317–318
Lock-in clause 332

M
Marital agreements 267
Marketable title 307
Market allocation 83
Maxims of jurisprudence 19–21
Mechanics' liens 374–381
    cessation of work 380
    enforcing 381
    notice of completion 379–380
    notice of nonresponsibility 378–379
    preliminary notice 379
    priority of 381
    recording 380–381
    stop notice 382
    termination of 381–382
Mediation 19–20
Megan's Law 76
Mello-Roos notice 200
Menace 158, 501
Merger 408, 487
Mineral, oil, and gas brokers 110–111
Mineral, oil, and gas rights 237–238
Minor 147–148
Misrepresentation 80, 158
Mistaken improver 240
mitigation of damages 165
Mobile home disclosures 75
Mobile home evictions 502–503
Mobile home park rules 503–504
Mobile homes 240–241
Mobile home sales 112–113
Mobile home tenancies 502–503
Monetary damages 164
Mortgage brokers 105–106
Mortgage Forgiveness Debt Relief Act of 2007 340
Mortgage Loan Disclosure Statement 110, 215–216
Mortgages 335–340
    deficiency judgment 338–340
    foreclosure 336–337
    right of redemption 337–338
Multiple-listing service 210
Mutual consent 149–156

N
National Environmental Policy Act 436
Natural Hazards Disclosure Statement 75
Negative declaration 437
Negative easement 403
Negotiable instruments 328–329
Net listing 65, 194–195
Nominal damages 16–17, 165
Nonconforming use 426
Noncumulative zoning 422
Nondisturbance clause 487
Nonfreehold estates 245, 252
Nonjudicial remedies 18–19
Nonresident licensees 101
Notice of cessation 380
Notice of completion 379
Notice of default 342–343, 345
Notice of delinquency 345
Notice of nonresponsibility 378–379
Notice of sale (trust deed) 342
Novation 164
Nuisance 397–399
Nuncupative will 314

O
Obligatory advances 350
Omnibus Housing Nondiscrimination Act 133
Open listing 192–193
Opinion of title 463
option listing 65–66
Options 158–159, 196–198
Ordinances 11–12
Or more clause 332
Ostensible agency 31
Owner liability 281–285
Ownership 241–246, 260–285
Ownership in severalty 260–261

P
Parol evidence rule 170
Partial zoning 424
Partition action 264
Partnership license 101
Partnerships taxation 273
Party walls 394–395
Patent defects 71
patents 236
periodic tenancy 480
Personal property 237–240

Personal Responsibility and Work Opportunity Act 100
Place of public accommodation 126
Planned developments 280
Police power 308
Power of attorney 30
Predatory lending 358–359
Preliminary notice 379
Preliminary public report 436
Preliminary title report 465
Premarital agreements 267
Prepayment penalties 109, 332
Price-fixing 83
Principal 29–30
Priority of recording 248–249
Privity of contract 184
Probate 315–317
procuring cause 193
promissory notes 328–333
property 236–241
Property taxes 373–374
Proposition 13 251, 373
Public Report 434–436
Puffing 80
punitive damages 165
pur autre vie 243

Q

quasi contract 146
quiet enjoyment 496
Quiet title 18
Quitclaim deed 303

R

ratification 32
real estate investment trusts 275
real estate purchase contract 200–216
   contingencies 201, 211
   disclosures 200, 217–218
Real Estate Settlement Procedures Act (RESPA) 334–335, 355–356
Real property 236–237
real property sales contract 346–347
real property transfer disclosure statement 70–74
Rebate law 469
recording 246–251, 380–381
recovery fund 105
Recreational Use Immunity 283–284
Redemption rights (execution sale) 372
redlining 122, 356

Referral fees 81
Reformation 17, 167
release clause 354
Release of contract: 226
Reliction 400
remainder interest 243
rent control 505–506
rent skimming 63
Repossession of mobile homes 346–347
Request for notice of default 345
Rescission 17, 168
Reservation in a deed 305
Residential lease 219–224
respondeat superior 46
Restraints against alienation 242
Restricted licenses 104
retaliatory eviction 500
Retention of records 216
reversionary interest 241, 243
Revocation of offer 151–152
Rezoning 424
right of correlative user 399
right of first refusal 159–160
right of prior appropriation 400
Riparian rights 399
Rule against perpetuities 245
Rumford Act 131, 132
Runoff damage 399–400

S

SAFE Act 111
safety clause 191
Sales in foreclosure 348
Salesperson's license 100
salesperson status 60–62
S corporations 276–277
seals 173, 301
secret profit 64
Security agreements (personal property) 353–354
security deposits 484–485
Security (premises) 496–497
Seller financing 350–352
Seller financing disclosure statement 215, 351–353
Seller's net 196
send-out slip 102
servient tenement 401
Severance damage 311
Sheriff's deed 303
Sherman Antitrust Act 83–84

Silence to offer 150
simultaneous death 314
Solar Shade Act 407
special assessments 373–374
specific liens 373
Specific performance 17, 167–170
Spite fence 395
Spot zoning 424
Standard subdivision 278
stare decisis 2
statute of frauds 169–170
Statute of limitations 104, 172–173, 354
statutory law 3
steering 122
Stock cooperatives 279
Stop notice 382
Straight note 328
subagents 82
Subdivided Lands Law 278, 433
   conditional public report 436
   preliminary public report 436
   public report 434–436
Subdivision Map Act 431
   exceptions 432
   final map 433–434
   tentative map 432–433
Subdivisions 278–280
Subjacent support 401
subject to a loan 354
subleases 485–487
Subordination clause 63, 353
Substantial performance 164
Successive estates 245
successor liability 115
surrender 501
Survivorship 260
syndicates 110, 274–275

T

table funding 111
Tax deed 303
Taxes (real property) 373–374
tax liens 373
Tenancies
   joint tenancy 261–265
   periodic tenancy 480
   tenancy at sufferance 480
   tenancy at will 480
   tenancy by the entirety 265
   tenancy for years 479
   tenancy in common 260–261

tenancy in partnership 270–272
Tenant rights and responsibilities 496–497
  duties 497–498
  quiet enjoyment 496
  repairs 496
tender 164
Tenth Amendment 7
termination of agency 48–49
Termination of partnerships 273
Testate succession 313
testator 314
third-party beneficiary 163
Thirteenth Amendment 7
thirty-day notice 480
three-day notice 498
Three-month notification of default
  342–343
Tie-in agreements 83
time is of the essence 150
time-shares 280
title insurance 463–467
  exclusions 466
  extended-coverage policy 466–467
  lender policies 467–468
  policy interpretation 468
  preliminary title report 465
  rebate law 469
  special policies 468
  standard policy 466, 468
  title insurance companies 468
Trade fixtures 240, 483
transaction broker 35–36
Transfer disclosure statement 70–74
treaties 8
Treaty of Guadalupe Hidalgo 3

Trees (boundary) 395
trespass 397
Trust deeds 304, 340–345
Trustee's deed 304
Trustee's Sale 343–345
Trusts 275
Truth-in-lending 357–358
Truth in Savings Act 356

U
Undivided interest subdivision 278
Undue influence 158
Uniform codes 9
Uniform Electronic Transactions Act 149
Uniform Partnership Act 270
Uniform Settlement Statement 355
Uniform Simultaneous Death Act 262
unilateral contract 146–147
unilateral mistake 154
unincorporated associations 277
unlawful detainer 499–500
Unlawful detainer assistants 500–501
Unruh Civil Rights Act 130–132
unsophisticated buyers 77–78
upzoning 424
usury 110, 333–334

V
valid contract 147–157
Variance 424
venue 15
vested remainder 243
vicarious liability 46
voidable contract 157–158
voidable deed 304

void contract 157–158
void deed 304

W
Waiver 166, 168
Warranty deed 303
waste 244
water rights 399–400
wild document 250
will 313
Wraparound Trust Deed 350–351
Writ of execution 370–371
writ of possession 499

Z
zoning 419–427
  aesthetic 424
  bulk 424
  Comprehensive 424
  conditional-use permit 425
  cumulative 422
  downzoning 424
  exclusionary 422
  incentive 424
  inclusionary 424
  nonconforming use 426
  noncumulative 422
  partial 424
  rezoning 424
  spot 424
  upzoning 424
  variance 424

Notes

Notes

Notes

Notes

Notes